AN ARCHAEOLOGICAL PERSPECTIVE

STUDIES IN ARCHEOLOGY

Consulting Editor: Stuart Struever

Department of Anthropology
Northwestern University
Evanston, Illinois

Charles R. McGimsey III. **Public Archeology**

Lewis R. Binford. **An Archaeological Perspective**

Muriel Porter Weaver. **The Aztecs, Maya, and Their Predecessors: Archaeology of Mesoamerica**

Joseph W. Michels. **Dating Methods in Archaeology**

C. Garth Sampson. **The Stone Age Archaeology of Southern Africa**

Fred T. Plog. **The Study of Prehistoric Change**

Patty Jo Watson (Ed.). **Archeology of the Mammoth Cave Area**

George C. Frison (Ed.). **The Casper Site: A Hell Gap Bison Kill on the High Plains**

W. Raymond Wood and R. Bruce McMillan (Eds.). **Prehistoric Man and His Environments: A Case Study in the Ozark Highland**

Kent V. Flannery (Ed.). **The Early Mesoamerican Village**

Charles E. Cleland (Ed.). **Cultural Change and Continuity: Essays in Honor of James Bennett Griffin**

Michael B. Schiffer. **Behavioral Archeology**

Fred Wendorf and Romuald Schild. **Prehistory of the Nile Valley**

Michael A. Jochim. **Hunter-Gatherer Subsistence and Settlement: A Predictive Model**

in preparation

Stanley South. **Method and Theory in Historical Archeology**

Timothy Earle and Jonathan Ericson (Eds.). **Exchange Systems in Prehistory**

Lewis R. Binford. **Background Studies for Theory Building in Archaeology: Faunal, Remains, Aquatic Resources, Spatial Analysis, Systemic Modeling**

AN ARCHAEOLOGICAL PERSPECTIVE

LEWIS R. BINFORD

University of New Mexico
Albuquerque, New Mexico

with a contribution by

George I. Quimby
University of Washington
Seattle, Washington

SEMINAR PRESS New York San Francisco London
A Subsidiary of Harcourt Brace Jovanovich, Publishers

SEMINAR PRESS, INC.
111 Fifth Avenue, New York, New York 10003

United Kingdom Edition published by
SEMINAR PRESS LIMITED
24/28 Oval Road, London NW1

LIBRARY OF CONGRESS CATALOG CARD NUMBER: 76-182629

PRINTED IN THE UNITED STATES OF AMERICA

This book is dedicated to

JAMES BENNETT GRIFFIN

Director of the Museum of Anthropology
University of Michigan, Ann Arbor, Michigan

Contents

PART I

METHOD AND ARCHAEOLOGICAL REASONING

Archaeology as Anthropology

Smudge Pits and Hide Smoking:
The Use of Analogy in Archaeological Reasoning

Archaeological Reasoning and Smudge Pits—Revisited

Methodological Considerations of the Archaeological Use of Ethnographic Data

Reply to K. C. Chang's "Major Aspects of the Interrelationship of Archaeology and Ethnology"

Review of K. C. Chang's "Rethinking Archaeology"

Archaeological Perspectives

Comments on Evolution

Some Comments on Historical Versus Processual Archaeology

A Consideration of Archaeological Research Design

Hatchery West: Site Definition—Surface Distribution of Cultural Items

"Red Ochre" Caches from the Michigan Area:
A Possible Case of Cultural Drift

Directionality in Archaeological Sequences

PART IV

ANALYSIS

A New Method of Calculating Dates from Kaolin Pipe Stem Samples

Indian Sites and Chipped Stone Materials in the
Northern Lake Michigan Area

Lewis R. Binford and George I. Quimby

An Analysis of Cremations from Three Michigan Sites

Analysis of a Cremated Burial from the Riverside Cemetery, Menominee County, Michigan

Galley Pond Mound

Post-Pleistocene Adaptations

Retrospect and Prospect

Introduction

All of the articles collected here were written during the last ten years. So much has changed in this time that it may be difficult for the younger reader to appreciate the character of the field and my views at the time some of the articles were originally published. For this reason I have decided to present in very brief form something of a personal history of the field of archaeology, as I experienced it over the last twenty years. This is not to be considered a historical account as such, rather a personal statement as to how I perceived archaeology through my exposure to certain influential members of the field.

I came into the field of archaeology from two previous academic experiences. I initially did undergraduate work in the field of forestry and wildlife conservation. After a period of military service during which I was exposed to many experiences of anthropological relevance, I decided to go into the field of anthropology upon my return to the United States.

In 1954 I reentered academic life at the University of North Carolina, intent upon becoming an ethnographer. My first class, called Anthropology 41, was given by an instructor with a brand new Ph.D.—his first teaching assignment. We were exposed to a straight Boasian argument as to the evils of evolution, the unique features of cultural behavior, and the need to understand the great variety of human culture in a historical frame of reference, tracing the lines of diffusion for different culture traits from one place to another. I remember the instructor reading with an almost religious reverence a passage from Ralph Linton in which all the traits of the typical middle class act of eating breakfast were related back to their sources of origin. Truly culture was a "thing of shreds and patches." Everything we had for breakfast came from somewhere other than North Carolina! I left this class and went into a very small room labeled Laboratory of Anthropology. In reality this was the office and small adjacent work room of Dr. Joffre Coe. I walked into his office saying with a knowing look that an assigned reading he had given us was "really very evolutionary." Coe looked up at me with a shy smile and asked, "What other classes are you taking?" I replied that I was taking Anthropology 41, etc. Coe sat quietly for a

moment and asked if I was really serious about anthropology, to which I replied
that I was. He said, "Are you willing to do some outside reading?" That night, I
learned for the first time the name Leslie White.

Throughout my several years at North Carolina I found myself hanging
around Coe's office. At first I continued to maintain my commitment to be an
ethnographer. Gradually, however, I began to come to the realization that if
anthropology was going to cope scientifically with the problems of why cultures
changed, the anthropologist had to have data with time depth. I began going on
regular weekend field trips, and archaeology became my commitment. Joffre
Coe taught me all I was to ever learn in formal training sessions about practical
field work.

From Coe I learned three other names besides Leslie White: Walter Taylor,
Albert C. Spaulding, and James B. Griffin. Taylor's (1948) original publication
was out of print at that time, and I found in a used-book store a bound copy
which still sits on my book shelf—full of stratified marginal notes, reflecting
something of the changes in my thinking since 1955. I met Albert C. Spaulding
briefly in the summer of 1956 while he was visiting Coe. My meeting with
Griffin came first in the fall of 1956. On Coe's suggestion I transferred to the
University of Michigan for further graduate work with Griffin, Spaulding, and
White.

Michigan was an interesting place during the middle fifties. I was one of the
first of the "second generation" postwar students. The first generation were
largely men who had worked as archaeologists during prewar WPA days. Those
who returned after the war in many cases went to Michigan to get their degrees.
Griffin had maintained a rather unique position in Eastern archaeology during
WPA days, and this gave him something of a priority as the stimulator to
synthesis for Eastern archaeology.

Prior to the large body of work done under WPA sponsorship, most
archaeology in eastern North America had been museum sponsored, and the
interests were clearly in museum collections. Little that could be considered
"systematic" data collection had been characteristic. Dr. Fay-Cooper Cole of the
University of Chicago had started a program in archaeology beginning in the late
1920's. Cole is sometimes credited with the "invention" of the five foot square,
a concern with accurate field description, and an attempt to put the variety of
archaeological materials into some realistic temporal perspective. Many of the
men who served as leaders for the large WPA crews had been students of Cole or
had worked on his excavations. Griffin had been among Cole's students, as had
Joffre Coe and many others.

Griffin, after completion of his masters degree at the University of Chicago,
left Cole and began a very interesting phase of his career. He was subsidized by
Eli Lilly, owner of the Lilly pharmaceutical company, to travel from one WPA
excavation to another in order to gain some comparative perspective of the

wealth of material being excavated. I have heard Griffin say that he must have travelled over a million miles during those days. Griffin came to two major positions as a result of his comparative travels. The older arguments presented by his senior generation of archaeologists were generally wrong in that they almost always sought to "explain" changed or different features of the archaeological record by postulating migrations from distant sources. Griffin began to strongly argue that many of the cultural developments in eastern North America were the result of in-place changes occurring among essentially stable populations. Waves of migrants and violent replacements of population were not always the explanations for culture change. Griffin loved the word "influence"; if something looked as if it were from another area it was clear evidence of a cultural influence from that area. Diffusion-and-the-plotting-of-cultural-influences-from-one-region-to-another became the name of the game.

The other clear commitment of Griffin was to the generation of a concise taxonomy for the archaeological materials in eastern North America. He had embraced the Midwestern taxonomic system of McKern (Griffin, 1943). This is not surprising since the wealth of raw data exposed by the WPA excavations had provided the need for some systematic evaluation of differences and similarities, a must even for intelligent discussion. The trait list became the instrument for measurement. Griffin had also become interested in the potential of detailed ceramic analysis as an aid to chronological ordering as well as taxonomic ordering. In fact, ironically enough, Griffin's report on the ceramics from the Norris basin (1938) was reviewed as being a masterful demonstration of the use of statistics, and Griffin was hailed as the "master of the statistical technique." This meant that Griffin had counted something.

Of all the anthropologists I met during my student years, Griffin was the least self-conscious about being antitheoretical. To Griffin, theory was to be equated with speculation, and one only did that when there were no data. If data were available, it was quite clear what one did: One summarized the data, and the "self-evident" units of meaning were historically synthesized. In Griffin's mind there was no question about what data meant or what they were telling us about the past.

My first class with Griffin was held in his office, where there were two wooden desks, one in the center of the large room and a smaller one to the side. Griffin always wore a white lab coat. I arrived to the first meeting of the class a little late. There was Griffin sitting behind the center desk in a large swivel chair. Senior graduate students were seated on a couch facing the front of his desk. Junior students like myself were seated cross-legged on the floor around the desk. I went in and settled myself near the end of the couch. Griffin got up, pulling his lab coat together, and walked to the hall door with a smile. As he approached the door he yelled at the top his voice, "Spaulding!" This gentle reminder to Dr. A. C. Spaulding that class was about to begin resulted a few moments later in Spaulding's appearance. Spaulding entered, also in a white lab coat, and seated himself at the small desk to the side of the room. Spaulding was not smiling. He sat pensively in his chair, politely apologizing to a student for having brushed his shoulder as he entered the room.

As I experienced this first class with Griffin, two scenes flashed through my mind. The first was a mental picture that had stayed with me from my days in philosophy classes at North Carolina. There the teacher had described the school of the great teacher Socrates: The toga-clad teacher had sat on a raised marble stoop, outside an imposing Greek building, with his students seated at his feet on the ground below. This mental picture was shattered as Griffin screamed for Spaulding, bringing to mind another picture: As a child my first conscious act of rebellion had been directed toward my grandmother. She was always telling me that picking my nose was not nice. One hot summer day she had continuously called for me to do one thing or another, while I wanted to be outside with my dog. Late in the evening I was sitting on the back porch steps when my grandmother called in a loud voice, "Come here. What are you doing?" My face flushed and eyes squinted as I replied, "I'm picking my nose." I imagined that Spaulding was feeling some of the same emotions.

Class consisted of each student's taking an area of eastern North America, steeping himself in the literature, and presenting a descriptive synthesis of the archaeological materials. During student presentations Griffin would get up from his chair, quietly moving around to an imposing set of files or book shelves while the student continued his presentation. Griffin would return to his desk, lean over and place a photograph on the cluttered desk top, relax back in his chair with a smile, and point to the photograph, interrupting the student. "What do you think of that?" The student would look at the blown-up photo of a pottery sherd, turn it around, and if he were lucky answer that it looked like "Hopewell rim" or "Marksville incised." Griffin would not answer but only ask, "Where do you think it came from?" Spaulding would shift in his chair, lean over and glance at the photograph, then resettle in his chair. The student gave an answer; if it was correct Griffin smiled and said, "Well, what does that do to your argument?" We looked worried, not knowing what we should be seeing. It finally came out: That sherd proved "Hopewell influence!" We took notes and wondered after class how "Hopewell influence" could have anything to do with the evidence for agriculture or the appearance of palisaded villages. We must be pretty dull since it was obviously clear to our teacher in the white lab coat.

Our chances to gain some insight came at 10:30 each weekday morning. Griffin arrived promptly and seated himself in a chair in the middle of a long bank of cabinets in which his reprints were stored. He crossed his legs, moving sideways up against the back of the chair in a posture which seemed to give him more height. The students assembled, and if one was late Griffin turned and asked, "Where is Papworth?" We all assured him that he would certainly be along in a moment. Students generally stood or they sat on the long table top at the end of the room. Spaulding arrived and sat opposite Griffin; other staff appeared and coffee break began. Griffin rarely directed his comments to students, mostly to other staff members. Conversation generally took the form of some smiling, leg slapping, and sarcastic remarks about a recent publication by an archaeologist Griffin did not consider to be in the fold. If the staff did not enter willingly into the character destruction, Griffin turned to the students. We laughed, smiled, and tried to make some knowing remarks to reassure Griffin that we indeed concurred in his opinion and understood the deep intellectual basis for it, rooted, of course, in the files of empirical data stored in his office.

To become an archaeologist one had to position himself so as to gain access to all the empirical data which spoke so forcefully the truth of Eastern prehistory. These critical empirical data were stored in Griffin's office— thousands of pictures of pot sherds, unpublished. These data spoke to Griffin, and if you were lucky you too could have access to the data which screamed forth self-evident truths from the past. Of course all the data were not in Griffin's office. Some minor things were in other places such as the Illinois State Museum (enemy territory) or in Rochester, New York, at Bill Ritchie's lab (also enemy territory). Some might be in Indiana at Glen Black's place (also enemy territory). If the student was chosen to become an archaeologist, he got to travel to these places on weekends or in conjunction with meetings when the entire "Michigan crew" traveled together, Griffin driving over 70 miles per hour all the way. We got a chance to see the sherd or projectile point or broken gorget that spoke so clearly to Griffin. We could only stand in awe wishing that some day we might also be so intimate with the data, know all the secret places where it was hidden, and be able to see the big picture like our lab-coated teacher.

I was chosen. I got to travel and became familiar with the data in most of the great museums of the country. I was even allowed into the photo files in Griffin's office. In my enthusiasm to learn, to know, to pass that magic threshold where the sherds would talk, I sneaked into Griffin's office when he was out and went through his files. I knew every small drawer where the type collections were kept and the "typical" sherds, so important to the development of a good dialogue between the archaeologist and other sherds. These became a part of me. Yet I was a failure: The sherds never spoke to me with the ring of truth which Griffin confidently translated to his students.

Spaulding, walking down the hall with his hands in his lab coat pockets, chin and head thrust forward, a forbidding look on his face, answering Griffin's screaming summons, became a different man in his class room. His eyes flashed, his wit was sophisticated, and his mind at work was explicit, beautiful, and unrelentingly logical. What a contrast! In Griffin's class one had the impression of witnessing a mystical experience; conclusions were drawn from photographs whose meaning was far from clear. Spaulding demanded that each proposition, each argument, be defended with explicit statements as to how meaning was being derived from observations and what relevance the data had to the conclusions. It was a different world.

Few students had the guts to take Spaulding's methods course; he required that you learn some statistics. The chosen ones, advanced Griffin students, knew that the important thing was to get on intimate terms with the data. Spaulding demanded that you use the data. How could you count Griffin's pictures or the whispered reports of a "checked stamped pot" in the private collection of some farmer in central Ohio. You didn't need to. They spoke for themselves. Analysis was unnecessary. Some of us began to wonder if maybe the pot sherds could speak in two languages! Those of us who couldn't learn Griffin's secret language could possibly establish the needed contact through Spaulding's tongue; certainly it was less mysterious, in spite of its obvious demands on our time.

Spaulding seemed to try to scare students out of his class. He announced that he gave A's only to those students who knew as much as he did. To the chosen ones, Griffin's students, this generally resulted in a drop slip on the second day. After all, what Spaulding knew was not really archaeology. He didn't even show slides of artifacts! Seven of us stayed. We worked on problems, and we learned of a site called Jebel-Moya where analysis had produced a different kind of data. You couldn't take a picture of it; it was a series of demonstrated relationships between things, not the things themselves. Walter Taylor's book came off my shelf; the second level of marginal notes were accumulated.

I don't think I have ever worked as hard in a class. At the end of the course I experienced one of the proudest days of my student life. I had already turned in Spaulding's final exam and had dropped into his office to get the results. Spaulding was sitting behind the desk in his newly remodeled office. I sat down. He scowled and said that my paper was practically unreadable. I had misspelled eight words, left out three periods, and had several nonstop sentences—one of which was not even a sentence! (I never could write, and would jump at the chance to do anything orally. English was a mystery to me, almost like Griffin's communications with the pot sherds.) I didn't say much at first, but then got up the courage to ask Spaulding if in spite of the poor writing the content of the paper was worthwhile. He swung around in his chair, leaned back, scowled, and said that he didn't want to do it because he really didn't think that I knew as much as he did, but that I had earned an A.

There was a way to learn about the past: I could speak Spaulding's tongue. The archaeological record was not a mine, which yielded up an inventory of contents; it was a static, dead organization. Our job was to expose that organization and explain it. If our explanations could be defended, then we had learned something about the past.

Leslie White—the dragon slayer of Boasianism, the terror in debate, the irascible "deviant" who insisted that science was not a popularity pole—was my teacher. Every student had to take his History of Anthropology. I had pictured a large man with a strong voice, stern face, and cold, forbidding exterior. I walked into class, seating myself in the third chair from the front, directly in front of the teacher's desk. All the students were in their places before class began. A gentle conversation was heard coming from the hall. A small man with a shy smile and an arm full of papers came into the room. He placed the papers on the desk, shuffled them, and looked up, quietly saying, "My name is Leslie White."

He looked more like a postmaster in a small Midwestern town than the dragon slayer I had pictured. He took out his note cards and began lecturing. His mind worked like Spaulding's: sharp, sophisticated wit and a devastating sarcasm, all presented in a gentle voice. Yet his cards seemed to bear some analogy to Griffin's pictures. He would offer an empirical generalization regarding some position or bias alleged to have characterized Boas and proceed to read fifteen quotes documenting the validity of his generalization. It was, however, a very different approach to data. White gave you the generalization or meaning first and then proceeded to document its validity by an appeal to empirical data. His logic was made explicit, his interpretations were put out for criticism, and he supplied you with the criteria and rules for criticism. To argue with White, you had to know the data. You had to have read everything the authors being discussed had ever written. In a way it was like a game, searching the hidden corners of the library for obscure materials. It was like Griffin's game of hide-and-seek with the empirical materials, yet it was different. White used the data. It wasn't something which conveyed self-evident messages.

Early in the course I became annoyed with White's seemingly devastating treatment of Boas. After all, Boas had been my first exposure to anthropology back in Chapel Hill. I played White's game—searched the literature, gathered the empirical data, came to class with a stack of file cards with typed quotes. White came to class with his selection of quotes and began another assault. I raised my hand, was acknowledged, and began reading quotes which I believed disproved White's generalizations about the "father" of modern anthropology. White listened, at first attentively; then gradually his face flushed. The little vein running up his forehead began to protrude and he stiffened, saying in a raised voice, "That's irrelevant, Mr. Binford. See me in my office. Class dismissed."

I was crushed. I had thought I was going to get a chance to see that mind at work in argument. Frightened, I left the class, fully expecting to find the aroused dragon in his office. His office was a small cubicle in Angel Hall, nothing like Griffin's expansive room. White sat quitely behind a standard university plastic-topped desk. "Sit down," he said. I thanked him and nervously searched for something to say to explain myself. He said, Mr. Binford, do you know the meaning of relevance? Boas is like the *Bible,* you can find anything you want to in his writings. He was not a scientist. Scientists make their assumptions explicit and are ready to defend their arguments within an explicit logical framework.

Boas was muddle-headed. Better to read clerical literature, at least the priests know why they hold their opinions! "I suggest that you read some philosophy of science." I did.

I never again tried to argue with White. I listened; I outlined in logical paradigms the arguments presented in the assigned readings. I tried to isolate in the writings of anthropologists the writers' assumptions, hidden for the most part. Theory became a meaningful word. White's arguments became clear, logical vignettes. Culture was not some ethereal force, it was a material system of interrelated parts understandable as an organization that could be recovered from the past, given the language to be learned from Spaulding. We were searching for laws. Laws are timeless and spaceless; they must be equally valid for the ethnographic data as well as the archaeological data. Ethnology and archaeology are not separated by a wide, unbridgeable gap.

I returned to the Museum excited by White and in my enthusiasm asked Griffin what kind of social system he thought the Hopewell peoples had. He laughed and said that he had never seen anyone dig up a kinship system. Sometimes he commented that the people in Angel Hall really wasted the time of archaeology students with all their social nonsense. Archaeology should be separated from anthropology and allied with geology, where we could learn something worthwhile.

Spaulding surprised me; he rarely talked about archaeology in Griffin's sense, as "What caused the Hopewell decline?" Similarly, he rarely talked about anthropological theory. He much preferred to talk about a new statistical technique or a new property of the latest desk calculator. The teachers in the Department of Anthropology considered archaeology synonomous with Griffin, and archaeology students were therefore atheoretical diggers and pot sherd hunters tolerating their classes in ethnology and theory because there were required. Discussion about archaeology's role in anthropology was restricted to underground student discussion.

Walter Taylor came off the bookshelf again, destined for another stratum of marginal notes. When he discussed culture it was a mental phenomenon, not a material-based organization of behavior. It was something to be inferred from material remains, not something to be understood organizationally. Although Taylor wanted us to consider the relationships between things, these were simply new traits to be added to the trait list. He wanted behavioral reconstructions, he wanted the past to live, but this was to be done through interpretation. His examples of the "conjunctive approach" seemed to lack rigor and to demand some of Griffin's magic rather than the theoretical sophistication of White and the rigorous methods of Spaulding. Taylor had the aims but not the tools. As White might paraphrase Morgan, the "germs of thought" were all there, but the theory was underdeveloped and the suggested methods were crude. It was in methods and theory that the advances had to be made. Archaeologists were all little Linnaean beings classifying things for the sake of classification. There were two Darwins, White and Spaulding, who together could provide some meaning for the endless taxonomic schemes of the archaeologists. White essentially refused to take archaeology seriously, and Spaulding appeared disinterested in theory. I was going to be the Huxley, the mouthpiece.

This role really didn't come to me until after some two years of work exploring the techniques of Spaulding. Endless hours were spent at the desk calculator trying to specify the character of relationships between things and attributes of things. I met with some success, although today many of the things I hailed as great successes appear trivial. Some of these products are reprinted here: "A New Method of Calculating Dates from Kaoline Pipe Stem Samples," "The Pomranky Site: A Late Archaic Burial Station" (Binford, 1963b), and "An Analysis of Cremations from Three Michigan Sites."

My greatest frustration came in my studies of projectile points. I was convinced that attribute analysis was the key to typology. I developed a long and cumbersome attribute list ambitiously conceived as adequate for characterizing the full range of variability in projectile points over eastern North America (Binford, 1963a). The initial test of this attribute list was on the comparative study of Lamoka points from New York and morphologically similar forms from the western Great Lakes. Working with edge punch cards and a desk calculator I tried to isolate attribute clusters for the purpose of determining projectile point types. The trouble was that I was able to isolate many different clusters varying independent of one another. In addition the statistical problems of simultaneously handling discrete nominal data and continuous metrical data were never solved. I am still working on this problem, as are some of my students. The Lamoka study was never finished.

I went to the University of Chicago after teaching at the University of Michigan for one year. Chicago, the home of Fay-Cooper Cole, was the hearth of modern archaeology in the eastern United States. This was my big chance; archaeology's Huxley was on the move. My first general seminar before faculty and students was a disaster. The topic was "Evolutionary Anthropology." (A much revised version is published here: "Comments On Evol.") There was practically a riot. I was defending Leslie White; I was seriously considering the role of technology in culture change. I was questioning Julian Steward. I was informed that only a "fool" could follow such dogma since, surely I must realize, it is man's ideas put into practice that results in technological innovations. This could be clearly observed any day at Argonne National Laboratory! I was not allowed to finish my presentation.

In those days Chicago students were assigned Kroeber's answer to Leslie White, but White was not assigned. I was getting my feet wet; I was surprised at every turn. Archaeologists at national meetings did not want to hear about new approaches; they wanted the latest Carbon-14 date on some taxonomic creation of their own. Anthropologists did not want to hear about archaeology's potential contribution to the field of anthropology; clearly it could make none. It was one of those academic burdens which anthropologists had to bear because for some obscure reason it had historically been considered part of anthropology. I can remember one eminent member of the Chicago anthropology faculty passing through Walker Museum and pausing at an open office door. He got a funny expression on his face and asked a student, "How can a bright girl like you be seriously interested in those rocks?"

Frustrated, sitting in my office in Walker Museum late at night, I decided I would fight. I took out a sheet of paper, placed it in the typewriter, and wrote "Archaeology as Anthropology". Before dawn it was finished. The next day I passed it among some of the students' who offered the inevitable suggestions of translating my writing into English and encouraged me to publish it. That afternoon it was typed in final draft and mailed to *American Antiquity*.

I was encouraged. My students at Chicago were enthusiastic; some of my ideas were going to be published, and an awful lot of work was being done. It was exciting: Computers were available; whole new worlds through analysis could be opened up. We went to work. Stuart Struever, Bill Longacre, Robert Whallon, James Hill, Leslie Freeman, James Brown, for a time Richard Gould, Kent Flannery, and Sally Schanfield (later Sally Binford) were among those that were continually in Walker Museum: things were humming. I started a field project in the Carlyle reservoir in collaboration with Mike Fowler. Stuart Struever started his excavations at the Apple Creek site in the Lower Illinois valley. Jim Hill and Bill Longacre, encouraged by Paul S. Martin, began trying new field techniques in the Southwest. Freeman went off as the field foreman for Clark Howell's now famous excavations at Torralba. Things were beginning to happen at every turn. We were trying new ideas, building models, trying new methods of analysis, and we were getting results. It was time to display our wares.

The Society for American Archaeology meetings were to be held in Boulder, Colorado, in 1963. I wrote for and received time for a symposium. Struever, Longacre, Freeman, and Brown, together with myself and Howard Winters, held forth on our recent accomplishments. I delivered a paper, later published, entitled, "A Consideration of Archaeological Research Design" (see this volume pp. 135–161). Howard Winters presented his ideas, revolutionary for the time, regarding the nature of settlement systems. Trait list differences may not simply be measures of "cultural" affinity; they can be expected to vary with the nature of seasonally regulated activities occurring at different locations through a yearly round of settlement. Our presentation was poorly attended, and I recall that near the end, after Longacre's paper, a hand went up in the audience and an archaeologist said, "If I may be permitted to ask an old-fashioned question, what is the date on your Carter Ranch material?" I could have bellowed. They had missed the point. Longacre in his polished manner fielded the question unemotionally.

We went back home and back to work—a second field season in Carlyle and the stimulating results of excavations at Hatchery West. In the winter I prepared a National Science Foundation application for a joint research project with Howard Winters in southern Illinois for the following summer. I submitted it to the Department Chairman for his signature before sending it to the Dean. The chairman, David Schneider, refused to sign, telling me that although my contract had been renewed for the 1964–1965 academic year, there was no assurance that I would be given tenure. In view of that prospect, the Department could not serve as sponsor for a two-year research grant. I had known there were problems; I had not received the Ph.D. from Michigan. Griffin had eventually come to the position that I would get a degree only "over his dead body." Encouraged by Clark Howell and the students, I called James Spuhler, then Chairman at Michigan, and asked if something could be done so that I could be examined for the degree. Spuhler went to Griffin's office and behind closed doors accomplished something that I had thought would never happen; Griffin resigned from my committee. Spuhler asked Richard Beardsley to serve and he accepted. In the spring of 1964 I was examined at Ann Arbor and the degree was awarded at the end of the summer session. Meanwhile my friend Clark Howell was leading a fight for me to be given tenure. I was informed that the "senior archaeologist" had the say over the fate of archaeologists. Clark Howell, after all, was a physical anthropologist! Braidwood's letter arrived stating politely that I was "incompetent."

The previous year Braidwood and I had given our normal "team-taught" course for beginning graduate students. Braidwood was to present the Old World material and I was to present the New World data up to the appearance of civilization, at which time Bob Adams would take over. Struever was the teaching assistant. The students were told that they could write papers either for Professor Braidwood or for Professor Binford. Struever had the job of delivering forty-one papers to my office and two to Braidwood's.

Braidwood is a tall, handsome man. He presents an impressive professorial image, the Sir Mortimer Wheeler of Rolling Prairie, Indiana. His coats are always tweed, he wears woven single-colored ties, and his shirts are lumberjack plaid. He speaks in a melodious, deep, condescending tone of voice. Above all, Braidwood is a gentleman: He sips Cherry Heering, rides the commuter train, and entertains under the spreading trees of his country home. Archaeology is like a detective story, full of mystery and romance. It reveals the upward struggle of man toward civilization. Only a gentleman at the end of such a progressive line could understand the character of the struggle and recognize when man and "culture" were ready for that first great step away from our crude forebears—the appearance of agriculture.

In our classes together I had taken somewhat different views. My arguments had been a novelty; my emphasis on changes to the exploitation of aquatic resources near the end of the Pleistocene had interested Braidwood at first. After all, he had found snails at Jarmo. Braidwood seemed to think at first that I was salvageable. The rough edges would wear off, exposure to the great man would bring me around. Teaching with Braidwood had the opposite effect. I learned the data of his field. I studied hard so that I could make meaningful comparisons between the New and Old Worlds. I argued evolution, a materialist's philosophy of history; I taught Leslie White, Albert Spaulding, and my own thoughts. I was incompetent.

My reactions were quite mixed, unscientific to be sure; I was angry, hurt, and intolerably arrogant. I wrote with my former wife, Sally, "The Predatory Revolution: A Consideration of the Evidence for a New Subsistence Level" (Binford and Binford, 1966). This was done over a weekend. We searched the writings of Braidwood for every silly statement; we paraphrased them and wove them into a plausible sounding argument. That article was worth three months on a psychiatrist's couch. At first we did this as a joke, to be passed for approval among the students, but then we decided how great it would be if it were published as a "straight" article. We submitted it to *American Anthropologist*; the editor recognized it as a put-on but accepted it anyway. He joined in the fun and sent it to the reviewers. I don't know who they were, but the editor returned their anonymous statements; they had taken the article seriously! Some even commented about the originality of the ideas! Great Gods! that proved what a state archaeology was in.

I was floundering around, and as a kind of psychic boot-straps measure I decided to organize a full day's symposium to be presented before the American Anthropological Association at its annual meeting in Denver in 1966. It was arranged. The day came, and we were scheduled for the largest room at the meetings. I was certain that only a few people would be seated in the front rows of that cavernous room. I arrived early, fussing like a mother hen to be sure that the PA system worked, and I could not believe my eyes. Something had happened in the field. The room was filling up, and they were not just my students and a few rebel fellow travelers from other schools. I looked around; some of the best known faces in American anthropology were arriving early for a morning presentation. Impossible. Things went well, papers were received with enthusiasm. I had been boiling under the "incompetent" label—anyone who got an A from Al Spaulding was not incompetent—and had written a paper designed to settle that point; it was called "Post Pleistocene Adaptations." Jim Sackett commented as I was leaving my seat to go to the podium, "My God, Lew, they're standing up in the rear." It was a polished paper and I began reading it. I can't stand papers read to an audience; I talk to people. Gradually I took off from my written presentation and talked to the audience. I had a message, I wanted them to hear it, and I relaxed with a subject I knew like the back of my hand. I don't recall whether I made all the points in the paper, but at least the ones I made were presented with feeling. I don't remember finishing. The first thing that I knew there was applause, and people began rising to their feet clapping their hands. It continued until I was back in my seat. I was choked up and wondered if Huxley had ever cried.

We had fun that night. All my students from Chicago were there—the old ones and some of the "second tier," Chris Peebles, Jerry Eck, John Fritz, Mel Thurman, Henry Wright, and my old friend Arthur Saxe. People from other places who were doing innovative things were at the party—Jim Sackett, Howard Winters, of course, and Jim Deetz. We laughed, we sang, we joked, and above all, we, all of us, were proud; we were doing something, we were making a dent in the field. Change could occur. The younger students began to refer to us as the "Mafia." The next day people I had never seen would stop me in the halls: "Dr. Binford, Dr. Binford, I'm _____ from _____ and I wonder if it would be possible for me to get into Santa Barbara?", where I was then teaching. "Dr. Binford, Dr. Binford, I'm working on _____ and I wonder if you have any suggestions as to how I might analyze that kind of data." We decided to try and publish the entire symposium, and after much trouble finding a publisher it appeared in 1968 as *New Perspectives in Archeology.*

Since then I have not tried to organize another big symposium. The following year I participated in a symposium on mortuary practices organized by James Brown. It is finally scheduled for publication this year as a Memoir of the Society for American Archaeology. The original "Mafia" have all now received their degrees and are off teaching at universities all over the country. The "New Archaeology" is taken seriously and the field is changing.

References

Binford, Lewis R. (1963a). A proposed attribute list for the description and classification of projectile points. In *Miscellaneous Studies in Typology and Classification,* Anthropological Papers, No. 19, pp. 193–221. Museum of Anthropology, University of Michigan.

Binford, Lewis R. (1963b). The Pomranky Site: A late archaic burial station. In *Miscellaneous Studies in Typology and Classification,* Anthropological Papers, No. 19, pp. 149–192. Museum of Anthropology, University of Michigan.

Binford, Lewis R., and Sally R. Binford. (1966). The predatory revolution: A consideration of the evidence for a new subsistence level. *American Anthropologist* 68, 508–512.

Binford, Sally R., and Lewis R. Binford, eds. (1968). *New Perspectives in Archeology.* Aldine Publ. Co., Chicago, Illinois.

Griffin, James B. (1938). The ceramic remains from Norris Basin, Tennessee. *Bureau American Ethnology, Bulletin* 188, 253–359.

Griffin, James, B. (1943). *The Fort Ancient Aspect.* Univ. of Michigan Press, Ann Arbor.
Taylor, Walter W. (1948). A study of archeology. *American Anthropologist* **50,** Mem. No.
       69.

Part I

METHOD AND ARCHAEOLOGICAL REASONING

Most of the papers printed in this section have appeared previously, with the single exception of "Archaeological Reasoning and Smudge Pits–Revisited." Most of the articles were written during my days at Chicago, with the exceptions of "Archaeological Perspectives" and the previously unpublished paper mentioned above, as well as the review of Chang. As something of a record of the development of thought one could do a seriation on these articles. The earliest, "Archaeology as Anthropology," has several basic ideas: (1) The archaeological record is an organization. (2) The archaeologists' job is to explicate the relationships extant in the record. (3) We can expect that once explicated the relationships will refer to the operation of many variables, most of which will not be directly observable in the archaeological record, or for that matter directly observable if one could witness the dynamics of the living system as it was in the past. (4) Explanation of the relationships observed will refer to the character of the organized properties of the living cultural system as it existed in the past. These were essentially the ideas stimulated by White and Spaulding. Although White had told me to study the philosophy of science, the "relevance" of my readings had not quite yet registered.

At the time I wrote "Archaeology as Anthropology" I had not explored the implications of the epistemological problems associated with the task of explanation. At that time explanation was intuitively conceived as building models for the functioning of material items in past systems. Already model building was considered important. The Pomranky site (Binford, 1963) and the cremation analysis printed in later sections of this book were attempted applications of my ideas at the level of development represented by the "Archaeology as Anthropology" article. Rereading the article today, I feel some empathy for the many critics who poked fun at the terms *technomic, sociotechnic,* and *idiotechnic.* I pulled them out of White's thoughts late at night while writing this article in a state of frustration. My point, I think, was valid; all material items did not function in a single material subsystem of the extinct culture. It was, however, a bit naive. I elaborated on this point in the "Archaeological Systematics" paper included in Part III of this volume. I can recall the Chicago students and myself trying to operationalize means for isolating items into taxonomic units which would be isomorphic with these three broad categories of primary function. We discussed at great length the morphological characteristics of items or patterns of variability which might serve as discriminant attributes for "technomic" versus "sociotechnic" artifacts. This seems somewhat silly in looking back on it; we of course never satisfactorily accomplished our goal. We came to realize that any artifact may exhibit properties relating in a broad sense to all three subsystems; no artifact as such exhibited only attributes relative to its primary functional context. This conclusion was stated in "Archaeological Systematics."

Once one adopted a strategy of "model building"—attempting to specify the properties of an extinct organization which would accommodate all the observed relationships between the attributes of the archaeological record in any given location—one was immediately forced to cope with the philosophical problem of how do we build models, where do we get the ideas, and how do we *know* we are accurate. It was in the context of facing these problems that I began to take White's advice to heart. I began doing extensive reading in the philosophy of science.

The obvious place to start was with the problem of ethnographic analogy. We clearly recognized that most of our ideas about the kinds of organization which might have existed in the past came from our knowledge of the range of variability in organized human life as documented ethnographically. Educationally speaking, I started something of a crusade which I continue today: Archaeologists must be trained comparative ethnographers. I must admit this position resulted in many raised eyebrows and puzzled looks from my ethnographic colleagues on the staff at Chicago. I began teaching such courses which I continue to teach today. "Smudge Pits and Hide Smoking: The Use of Analogy in Archaeological Reasoning" followed by "Methodological Considerations of the Archaeological Use of Ethnographic Data" and "Archaeological Reasoning and Smudge Pits—Revisited" are three articles directly concerned with this problem.

Analogy was not the only problem associated with model building. The epistemological problems of verification loom large. After surveying most of the argumentative debate in the literature on the philosophy of science, I concluded that from a practical-science point of view, the arguments of Karl Hempel (see particularly Hempel, 1965) were the most useful. Many of the ideas of White were presented in explicit analytical form by Hempel. I can recall a comment by White stating that "Julian Steward doesn't know the difference between a universal fact and a law." At the time I really didn't understand what White was saying. Were not law statements universally true? The difference of course is the role of theory. An empirical "law" and a "covering" law are very different. One implies lots of looking; the other implies lots of thinking. Here was the real difference between Griffin on the one hand and Spaulding and White on the other. I certainly understood there was a difference, but in my student days I had reacted emotionally, and didn't know what it was that bothered me so much. I began to mellow in my ambivalent feelings toward Griffin; I began to feel sorry for him. He was a dedicated man; he really wanted to know about the past. He certainly worked hard, but he was committed to an inductive strategy, which, in fact, most archaeologists were.

I began to include in other articles comments on explanation. The theme became more important in my writings as time went on. It appears in my comments on Chang's book, strongly in "Archaeological Perspectives," and quite explicitly in "Some Comments on Historical Versus Processual Archaeology." It was the final recognition of the significance of White's comment on Steward which prompted the revisions in my original Chicago lecture, published here as "Comments on Evolution."

References

Binford, Lewis R. (1963). The Pomranky Site. A late archaic burial station. In *Miscellaneous Studies in Typology and Classification,* Anthropological Papers, No. 19, pp. 149–192. Museum of Anthropology, University of Michigan.

Hempel, Carl G. (1965). *Aspects of Scientific Explanation and Other Essays in the Philosophy of Science.* Free Press, Glencoe, Illinois.

Archaeology as Anthropology *

Abstract

It is argued that archaeology has made few contributions to the general field of anthropology with regard to explaining cultural similarities and differences. One major factor contributing to this lack is asserted to be the tendency to treat artifacts as equal and comparable traits which can be explained within a single model of culture change and modification. It is suggested that "material culture" can and does represent the structure of the total cultural system, and that explanations of differences and similarities between certain classes of material culture are inappropriate and inadequate as explanations for such observations within other classes of items. Similarly, change in the total cultural system must be viewed in an adaptive context both social and environmental, not whimsically viewed as the result of "influences," "stimuli," or even "migrations" between and among geographically defined units.

Three major functional subclasses of material culture are discussed: technomic, sociotechnic, and ideotechnic, as well as stylistic formal properties which cross-cut these categories. In general terms these recognized classes of materials are discussed with regard to the processes of change within each class.

Using the above distinctions in what is termed a systemic approach, the problem of the appearance and changing utilization of native copper in eastern North America is discussed. Hypotheses resulting from the application of the systemic approach are: (1) the initial appearance of native copper implements is in the context of the production of sociotechnic items; (2) the increased production of sociotechnic items in the late Archaic period is related to an increase in population following the shift to the exploitation of aquatic resources roughly coincident with the Nipissing high water stage of the ancestral Great Lakes; (3) this correlation is explicable in the increased selective pressures favoring material means of status communication once populations had increased to the point that personal recognition was no longer a workable basis for differential role behavior; (4) the general shift in later periods from formally "utilitarian" items to the manufacture of formally "nonutilitarian" items of copper is explicable in the postulated shift from purely egalitarian to increasingly nonegalitarian means of status attainment.

It has been aptly stated that "American archaeology is anthropology or it is nothing" (Willey and Phillips, 1958, p. 2). The purpose of this discussion is to evaluate the role which the archaeological discipline is playing in furthering the

* Originally published in *American Antiquity* **28**, No. 2, 217–225 (1962).

aims of anthropology and to offer certain suggestions as to how we, as archaeologists, may profitably shoulder more responsibility for furthering the aims of our field.

Initially, it must be asked, "What are the aims of anthropology?" Most will agree that the integrated field is striving to *explicate* and *explain* the total range of physical and cultural similarities and differences characteristic of the entire spatial–temporal span of man's existence (for discussion, see Kroeber, 1953). Archaeology has certainly made major contributions as far as *explication* is concerned. Our current knowledge of the diversity which characterizes the range of extinct cultural systems is far superior to the limited knowledge available fifty years ago. Although this contribution is "admirable" and necessary, it has been noted that archaeology has made essentially no contribution in the realm of explanation: "So little work has been done in American archaeology on the explanatory level that it is difficult to find a name for it" (Willey and Phillips, 1958, p. 5).

Before carrying this criticism further, some statement about what is meant by explanation must be offered. The meaning which explanation has within a scientific frame of reference is simply the *demonstration* of a constant articulation of variables within a system and the measurement of the concomitant variability among the variables within the system. Processual change in one variable can then be shown to relate in a predictable and quantifiable way to changes in other variables, the latter changing in turn relative to changes in the structure of the system as a whole. This approach to explanation presupposes concern with process, or the operation and structural modification of systems. It is suggested that archaeologists have not made major explanatory contributions to the field of anthropology because they do not conceive of archaeological data in a systemic frame of reference. Archaeological data are viewed particularistically and "explanation" is offered in terms of specific events rather than in terms of process (see Buettner-Janusch, 1957, for discussion of particularism).

Archaeologists tacitly assume that artifacts, regardless of their functional context, can be treated as equal and comparable "traits." Once differences and similarities are "defined" in terms of these equal and comparable "traits," interpretation proceeds within something of a theoretical vacuum that conceives of differences and similarities as the result of "blending," "directional influences," and "stimulation" between and among "historical traditions" defined largely on the basis of postulated local or regional continuity in the human populations.

I suggest that this undifferentiated and unstructured view is inadequate, that artifacts having their primary functional context in different operational subsystems of the total cultural system will exhibit differences and similarities differentially, in terms of the structure of the cultural system of which they were a part. Further, that the temporal and spatial spans within and between

broad functional categories will vary with the structure of the systematic
relationships between sociocultural systems. Study of these differential
distributions can potentially yield valuable information concerning the nature of
social organization within, and changing relationships between, sociocultural
systems. In short, the explanation of differences and similarities between
archaeological complexes must be offered in terms of our current knowledge of
the structural and functional characteristics of cultural systems.

Specific "historical" explanations, if they can be demonstrated, simply
explicate mechanisms of cultural process. They add nothing to the explanation
of the processes of cultural change and evolution. If migrations can be shown to
have taken place, then this explication presents an explanatory problem; what
adaptive circumstances, evolutionary processes, induced the migration
(Thompson, 1958, p. 1)? We must seek explanation in systemic terms for classes
of historical events such as migrations, establishment of "contact" between areas
previously isolated, etc. Only then will we make major contributions in the area
of explanation and provide a basis for the further advancement of
anthropological theory.

As an exercise in explication of the methodological questions raised here, I
will present a general discussion of a particular systemic approach in the
evaluation of archaeological assemblages and utilize these distinctions in an
attempted *explanation* of a particular set of archaeological observations.

Culture is viewed as the extrasomatic means of adaptation for the human
organism (White, 1959, p. 8). I am concerned with all those subsystems within
the broader cultural system which are: (a) extrasomatic, or not dependent upon
biological process for modification or structural definition (this is not to say that
the form and process cannot be viewed as rooted in biological process, only that
diversity and processes of diversification are not explicable in terms of biological
process), and which (b) function to adapt the human organism, conceived
generically, to its total environment both physical and social.

Within this framework it is consistent to view technology, those tools and
social relationships which articulate the organism with the physical environment,
as closely related to the nature of the environment. For example, we would not
expect to find large quantities of fishhooks among the recent archaeological
remains from the Kalahari desert! However, this view must not be thought of as
"environmental determinism" for we assume a systematic relationship between
the human organism and his environment in which culture is the intervening
variable. In short, we are speaking of the ecological system (Steward, 1955,
p. 36). We can observe certain constant adaptive requirements on the part of the
organism and similarly certain adaptive limitations, given specific kinds of
environment. However, limitations as well as the potential of the environment
must be viewed always in terms of the intervening variable in the human
ecological system, that is, culture.

With such an approach we should not be surprised to note similarities in technology among groups of similar levels of social complexity inhabiting the boreal forest (Spaulding, 1946) or any other broad environmental zone. The comparative study of cultural systems with variable technologies in a similar environmental range or similar technologies in differing environments is a major methodology of what Steward (1955, pp. 36–42) has called "cultural ecology," and certainly is a valuable means of increasing our understanding of cultural processes. Such a methodology is also useful in elucidating the structural relationships between major cultural subsystems such as the social and ideological subsystems. Prior to the initiation of such studies by archaeologists we must be able to distinguish those relevant artifactual elements within the total artifact assemblage which have the primary functional context in the social, technological, and ideological subsystems of the total cultural system. We should not equate "material culture" with technology. Similarly we should not seek explanations for observed differences and similarities in "material culture" within a single interpretative frame of reference. It has often been suggested that we cannot dig up a social system or ideology. Granted we cannot excavate a kinship terminology or a philosophy, but we can and do excavate the material items which functioned together with these more behavioral elements within the appropriate cultural subsystems. The formal structure of artifact assemblages together with the between element contextual relationships should and do present a systematic and understandable picture of *the total extinct* cultural system. It is no more justifiable for archaeologists to attempt explanation of certain formal, temporal, and spatial similarities and differences within a single frame of reference than it would be for an ethnographer to attempt explanation of differences in cousin terminology, levels of sociocultural integration, styles of dress, and modes of transportation all with the same variables or within the same frame of reference. These classes or items are articulated differently within an integrated cultural system, hence the pertinent variables with which each is articulated, and exhibit concomitant variation are different. This fact obviates the single explanatory frame of reference. The processes of change pertinent to each are different because of the different ways in which they function in contributing to the total adaptive system.

Consistent with this line of reasoning is the assertion that we as archaeologists must face the problem of identifying *technomic* artifacts from other artifactual forms. Technomic signifies those artifacts having their primary functional context in coping directly with the physical environment. Variability in the technomic components of archaeological assemblages is seen as primarily explicable in the ecological frame of reference. Here, we must concern ourselves with such phenomena as extractive efficiency, efficiency in performing biocompensatory tasks such as heat retention, the nature of available resources, their distribution, density, and loci of availability, etc. In this area of research and explanation, the archaeologist is in a position to make a direct contribution to the field of anthropology. We can directly correlate technomic items with environmental variables since we can know the distribution of fossil flora and fauna from independent data—giving us the nature of extinct environments.

Another major class of artifacts which the archaeologists recover can be termed *sociotechnic*. These artifacts were the material elements having their primary functional context in the social subsystems of the total cultural system. This subsystem functions as the extrasomatic means of articulating individuals one with another into cohesive groups capable of efficiently maintaining themselves and of manipulating the technology. Artifacts such as a king's crown, a warrior's coup stick, a copper from the Northwest coast, etc., fall into this category. Changes in the relative complexity of the sociotechnic component of an archaeological assemblage can be related to changes in the structure of the social system which they represent. Certainly the evolutionary processes, while correlated and related, are not the same for explaining structural changes in technological and social phenomena. Factors such as demography, presence or absence of between-group competition, etc., as well as the basic factors which affect technological change, must be considered when attempting to explain social change. Not only are the relevant variables different, there is a further difference when speaking of sociotechnic artifacts. The explanation of the basic form and structure of the sociotechnic component of an artifactual assemblage lies in the nature and structure of the social system which it represents. Observable differences and changes in the sociotechnic components of archaeological assemblages must be explained with reference to structural changes in the social system and in terms of processes of social change and evolution.

Thus, archaeologists can initially only indirectly contribute to the investigation of social evolution. I would consider the study and establishment of correlations between types of social structure classified on the basis of behavioral attributes and structural types of material elements as one of the major areas of anthropological research yet to be developed. Once such correlations are established, archaeologists can attack the problems of evolutionary change in social systems. It is my opinion that only when we have the entire temporal span of cultural evolution as our "laboratory" can we make substantial gains in the critical area of social anthropological research.

The third major class of items which archaeologists frequently recover can be termed *ideotechnic artifacts*. Items of this class have their primary functional context in the ideological component of the social system. These are the items which signify and symbolize the ideological rationalizations for the social system and further provide the symbolic milieu in which individuals are enculturated, a necessity if they are to take their place as functional participants in the social system. Such items as figures of deities, clan symbols, symbols of natural agencies, etc., fall into this general category. Formal diversity in the structural complexity and in functional classes of this category of items must generally be related to changes in the structure of the society, hence explanations must be sought in the local adaptive situation rather than in the area of "historical explanations." As was the case with sociotechnic items, we must seek to establish correlations between generic classes of the ideological system and the structure of the material symbolism. Only after such correlations have been established can archaeologists study in a systematic way this component of the social subsystem.

Cross-cutting all of these general classes of artifacts are formal characteristics which can be termed stylistic, formal qualities that are not directly explicable in terms of the nature of the raw materials, technology of production, or variability in the structure of the technological and social subsystems of the total cultural system. These formal qualities are believed to have their primary functional context in providing a symbolically diverse yet pervasive artifactual environment promoting group solidarity and serving as a basis for group awareness and identity. This pansystemic set of symbols is the milieu of enculturation and a basis for the recognition of social distinctiveness. "One of the main functions of the arts as communication is to reinforce belief, custom, and values" (Beals and Hoijer, 1953, p. 548). The distribution of style types and traditions is believed to be largely correlated with areas of commonality in level of cultural complexity and in mode of adapatation. Changes in the temporal–spatial distribution of style types are believed to be related to changes in the structure of sociocultural systems either brought about through processes of *in situ* evolution, or by changes in the cultural environment to which local sociocultural systems are adapted, thereby initiating evolutionary change. It is believed that stylistic attributes are most fruitfully studied when questions of ethnic origin, migration, and interaction between groups is the subject of explication. However, when explanations are sought, the total adaptive context of the sociocultural system in question must be investigated. In this field of research archaeologists are in an excellent position to make major contributions to the general field of anthropology, for we can work directly in terms of correlations of the structure of artifact assemblages with rates of style change, directions of style-spread, and stability of style-continuity.

Having recognized three general functional classes of artifacts: technomic, sociotechnic, and ideotechnic, as well as a category of formal stylistic attributes, each characterized by differing functions within the total cultural system and correspondingly different processes of change, it is suggested that our current theoretical orientation is insufficient and inadequate for attempting explanation. It is argued that explanations of differences and similarities between archaeological assemblages as a whole must first consider the nature of differences in each of these major categories and only after such evaluation can adequate explanatory hypotheses be offered.

Given this brief and oversimplified introduction, I will turn to a specific case, the Old Copper complex (Wittry and Ritzenthaler, 1956). It has long been observed and frequently cited as a case of technological "devolution" that during the Archaic period fine and superior copper utilitarian tools were manufactured, whereas, during Early and Middle Woodland times copper was used primarily for the production of nonutilitarian items (Griffin, 1952, p. 356). I will explore this interesting situation in terms of: (1) the frame of reference presented here, (2) generalizations which have previously been made concerning the nature of culture change, and (3) a set of hypotheses concerning the relationships between certain forms of sociotechnic artifacts and the structure of the social systems that they represent.

The normal assumption when thinking about the copper artifacts typical of the Old Copper complex is that they are primarily technomic (manufactured for use in directly coping with the physical environment). It is generally assumed that these tools were superior to their functional equivalents in both stone and bone because of their durability and presumed superiority in accomplishing cutting and piercing tasks. It is a common generalization that within the realm of technology more efficient forms tend to replace less efficient forms. The Old Copper case seems to be an exception.

Absolute efficiency in performance is only one side of the coin when viewed in an adaptive context. Adaptive efficiency must also be viewed in terms of *economy*, that is, energy expenditure versus energy conservation (White, 1959, p. 54). For one tool to be adaptively more efficient than another there must be either a lowering of energy expenditure per unit of energy conservation in task performance, or an increase in energy conservation per unit of performance over a constant energy expenditure in tool production. Viewed this way, we may question the position that copper tools were technologically more efficient. The production of copper tools utilizing the techniques employed in the manufacture of Old Copper specimens certainly required tremendous expenditures of both time and labor. The sources of copper are not in the areas of most dense Old Copper implements (Wittry, 1951), hence travel to the sources, or at least the establishment of logistics networks based on kin ties extending over large areas, was a prerequisite for the procurement of the raw material. Extraction of the copper, using the primitive mining techniques exemplified by the aboriginal mining pits on Isle Royale and the Keewenaw Peninsula (Holmes, 1901), required further expenditure of time and labor. Raw materials for the production of the functional equivalents of the copper tools was normally available locally or at least available at some point within the bounds of the normal exploitative cycle. Extraction was essentially a gathering process requiring no specialized techniques, and could be accomplished incidental to the performance of other tasks. Certainly in terms of expenditures of time and energy, as regards the distribution of sources of raw materials and techniques of extraction, copper required a tremendous expenditure as opposed to raw materials of stone and bone.

The processing phase of tool production appears to present an equally puzzling ratio with regard to expenditure of energy. The processing of copper into a finished artifact normally requires the separation of crystalline impurities from the copper. Following this processing phase, normal procedure seems to have been to pound and partially flatten small bits of copper which were then pounded together to "build" an artifact (Cushing, 1894). Once the essential shape had been achieved, further hammering, grinding, and polishing were required. I suggest that this process is more time consuming than shaping and finishing an artifact by chipping flint, or even the pecking and grinding technique employed in the production of ground stone tools. It follows that there was a much greater expenditure of time and energy in the production of copper tools than in the production of their functional equivalents in either bone or stone.

Turning now to the problem of energy conservation in task performance, we may ask what differentials existed. It seems fairly certain that copper was probably more durable and could have been utilized for a longer period of time. As far as what differentials existed between copper and stone, as regards cutting and piercing functions, only experiments can determine. Considering all of the evidence, the quality of durability appears to have been the only possible realm which could compensate for the differentials in expenditure of energy between stone and bone as opposed to copper in the area of procurement and processing of the raw material. What evidence exists that would suggest that durability was in fact the compensatory quality which made copper tools technologically more efficient?

All the available evidence suggests the contrary interpretation. First, we do not have evidence that the raw material was reused to any great extent once an artifact was broken or "worn out." If this had been the case, we would expect to have a general lack of battered and "worn out" pieces and some examples of reworked pieces, whereas evidence of use is a common characteristic of recovered specimens, and to my knowledge reworked pieces are uncommon if not unknown.

Second, when found in a primary archaeological context, copper tools are almost invariably part of burial goods. If durability was the compensatory factor in the efficiency equation, certainly some social mechanism for retaining the copper tools as functioning parts of the technology would have been established. This does not appear to have been the case. Since durability can be ruled out as the compensatory factor, we must conclude that copper tools were not technologically more efficient than their functional equivalents in both stone and bone. Having reached this "conclusion," it remains to explore the problem of the initial appearance of copper tools and to examine the observation that there was a shift from the use of copper for the production of utilitarian tools to nonutilitarian items.

It is proposed that the observed shift and the initial appearance of copper tools can best be explained under the hypothesis that they did not function primarily as *technomic items.* I suggest that in both the Old Copper and later cultural systems to the south, copper was utilized primarily for the production of *sociotechnic items.*

Fried (1960) discusses certain pertinent distinctions between societies with regard to systems of status grading. Societies on a low general level of cultural complexity, measured in terms of functional specialization and structural differentiation, normally have an "egalitarian" system of status grading. The term "egalitarian" signifies that status positions are open to all persons within the limits of certain sex and age classes, who through their individual physical and mental characteristics are capable of greater achievement in coping with the environment. Among societies of greater complexity, status grading may be less egalitarian. Where ranking is the primary mechanism of status grading, status positions are closed. There are qualifications for attainment that are not simply a function of one's personal physical and mental capabilities.

A classic example of ranking is found among societies with a ramage form of social organization (Sahlins, 1958, pp. 139–180). In such societies status is determined by one's proximity in descent from a common ancestor. High status is accorded those in the direct line of descent, calculated in terms of primogeniture, while cadet lines of descent occupy positions of lower status depending on their proximity to the direct line.

Another form of internally ranked system is one in which attainment of a particular status position is closed to all except those members of a particular kin group who may occupy a differentiated status position, but open to all members of that kin group on an egalitarian basis.

Other forms of status grading are recognized, but for the purposes of this discussion the major distinction between egalitarian and ranked systems is sufficient. I propose that there is a direct relationship between the nature of the system of status grading within a society and the quantity, form, and structure of sociotechnic components of its archaeological assemblage.

It is proposed that among egalitarian societies status symbols are symbolic of the technological activities for which outstanding performance is rewarded by increased status. In many cases they will be formally technomic items manufactured of "exotic" material or elaborately decorated and/or pains-takingly manufactured. I do not imply that the items could not or were not used technomically, simply that their presence in the assemblage is explicable only in reference to the social system.

Within such a system the structure of the sociotechnic components as regards "contextual" relationships should be simple. Various status symbols will be possessed by nearly all individuals within the limits of age and sex classes, differentiation within such a class being largely quantitative and qualitative rather than by formal exclusion of particular forms to particular status grades. The degree to which sociotechnic symbols of status will be utilized within an egalitarian group should largely be a function of group size and the intensity and constancy of personal acquaintance among all individuals composing the society. Where small group size and general lack of interaction with nearby groups is the normal pattern, then the abundance of status symbols should be low. Where group size is large and/or where between-group interactions are widespread, lowering the intimacy and familiarity between interacting individuals, then there should be a greater and more general use of material means of status communication.

Another characteristic of the manipulation of status symbols among societies with essentially egalitarian systems of status grading would be the destruction at death of an individual's symbols of status. Status attainment being egalitarian, status symbols would be personalities and could not be inherited as such. Inclusion as grave accompaniments or outright destruction would be the suggested mode of disposal for status items among such groups.

Among societies where status grading tends to be of a nonegalitarian type, the status symbols should be more esoteric in form. Their form would normally be dictated by the ideological symbolism which rationalizes and emphasizes the particular internal ranking system or the means of partitioning the society. The structure of the sociotechnic component of the assemblage should be more complex, with the complexity increasing directly as the complexity of the internal ranking system. Possession of certain forms may become exclusively restricted to certain status positions. As the degree of complexity in ranking increases there should be a similar increase in the differentiation of contextual associations in the form of differential treatment at death, differential access to goods and services evidenced in the formal and spatial differentiation in habitations and storage areas, etc. We would also expect to observe differentiation among the class of status symbols themselves as regards those which were utilized on a custodial basis as opposed to those that were personalities. Similarly, we would expect to see status symbols more frequently inherited at death as inheritance increases as the mechanism of status ascription.

Certainly these are suggestions which must be phrased as hypotheses and tested against ethnographic data. Nevertheless it is hoped that this discussion is sufficient to serve as a background against which an explanatory hypothesis concerning the Old Copper materials can be offered as an example of the potential utility of this type of *systemic* approach to archaeological data.

I suggest that the Old Copper copper tools had their primary functional context as symbols of achieved status in cultural systems with an egalitarian system of status grading. The settlement patterns and general level of cultural development suggested by the archaeological remains is commensurate with a band level of sociocultural integration (Martin *et al.*, 1947, p. 299), that level within which egalitarian systems of status grading are dominant (Fried, 1960). The technomic form, apparent lack of technomic efficiency, relative scarcity, and frequent occurrence in burials of copper artifacts all suggest that their primary function was as sociotechnic items. Having reached this "conclusion," we are then in a position to ask, in systemic terms, questions concerning their period of appearance, disappearance, and the shift to nonutilitarian forms of copper items among later prehistoric sociocultural systems of eastern North America.

I propose that the initial appearance of formally "utilitarian" copper tools in the Great Lakes region is explicable in terms of a major population expansion in the region following the Nipissing stage of the ancestral Great Lakes. The increase in population density was the result of increases in gross productivity following an exploitative shift to aquatic resources during the Nipissing stage. The increased populations are generally demonstrable in terms of the increased number of archaeological sites ascribable to the post-Nipissing period. The shift to aquatic resources is demonstrable in the initial appearance of quantities of fish remains in the sites of this period and in the sites of election for occupation, adjacent to prominent loci of availability for exploiting aquatic resources. It is proposed that with the increasing population density, the selective pressures fostering the symbolic communication of status, as opposed to the dependence on personal recognition as the bases for differential role behavior, were sufficient to result in the initial appearance of a new class of sociotechnic items, formally technomic status symbols.

The failure to perpetuate the practice of the manufacture of copper tools on any extensive basis in the Great Lakes region should be explicable in terms of the changing structure of the social systems in that area during Woodland times. The exact type of social structure characteristic of Early Woodland period is at present poorly understood. I would suggest that there was a major structural change between the Late Archaic and Early Woodland periods, probably in the direction of a simple clan and moiety basis for social integration with a corresponding shift in the systems of status grading and the obsolescence of the older material means of status communication.

The presence of copper tools of essentially nonutilitarian form within such complexes as Adena, Hopewell, and Mississippian are most certainly explicable in terms of their sociotechnic functions within much more complex social systems. Within the latter societies status grading was not purely on an egalitarian basis, and the nonutilitarian copper forms of status symbols would be formally commensurate with the ideological rationalizations for the various ascriptive status systems.

This explanatory "theory" has the advantage of "explaining": (1) the period of appearance of copper and probably other "exotic" materials in the Late Archaic period; (2) the form of the copper items; (3) their frequently noted contextual relations, for example, placement in burials; (4) their disappearance, which would be an "enigma" if they functioned primarily as technomic items; and (5) the use of copper for the almost exclusive production of "nonutilitarian" items in later and certainly more complex cultures of the eastern United States. This explanatory theory is advanced on the basis of currently available information, and regardless of whether or not it can stand as the correct explanation of the "Old Copper Problem" when more data are available, I suggest that only within a systemic frame of reference could such an inclusive explanation be offered. Here lies the advantage of the systemic approach.

Archaeology must accept a greater responsibility in the furtherance of the aims of anthropology. Until the tremendous quantities of data which the archaeologist controls are used in the solution of problems dealing with cultural evolution or systemic change, we are not only failing to contribute to the furtherance of the aims of anthropology but retarding the accomplishment of these aims. We as archaeologists have available a wide range of variability and a large sample of cultural systems. Ethnographers are restricted to the small and formally limited extant cultural systems.

Archaeologists should be among the best qualified to study and directly test hypotheses concerning the process of evolutionary change, particularly processes of change that are relatively slow, or hypotheses that postulate temporal-processual priorities as regards total cultural systems. The lack of theoretical concern and rather naïve attempts at explanation which archaeologists currently advance must be modified.

I have suggested certain ways that could be a beginning in this necessary transition to a systemic view of culture, and have set forth a specific argument which hopefully demonstrates the utility of such an approach. The explanatory potential which even this limited and highly specific interpretative approach holds should be clear when problems such as "the spread of an Early Woodland burial cult in the Northeast" (Ritchie, 1955), the appearance of the "Buzzard cult" (Waring and Holder, 1945) in the Southeast, or the "Hopewell decline" (Griffin, 1960) are recalled. It is my opinion that until we as archaeologists begin thinking of our data in terms of total cultural systems, many such prehistoric "enigmas" will remain unexplained. As archaeologists, with the entire span of culture history as our "laboratory," we cannot afford to keep our theoretical heads buried in the sand. We must shoulder our full share of responsibility within anthropology. Such a change could go far in advancing the field of archaeology specifically, and would certainly advance the general field of anthropology.

References

Beals, Ralph L., and Harry Hoijer. (1953). *An Introduction to Anthropology*. Macmillan, New York.

Buettner-Janusch, John. (1957). Boas and Mason: Particularism versus generalization. *American Anthropologist* 59, 318–324.

Cushing, F. H. (1894). Primitive copper working: An experimental study. *American Anthropologist* 7, 99–117.

Fried, Morton H. (1960). On the evolution of social stratification and the state. In *Culture in History: Essays in Honor of Paul Radin* (S. Diamond, ed.), pp. 713–731. Columbia Univ. Press, New York.

Griffin, James B. (1952). Culture periods in eastern United States archaeology. In *Archaeology of Eastern United States* (J. B. Griffin, ed.), pp. 352–364. Univ. of Chicago Press, Chicago.

Griffin, James B. (1960). Climatic change: A contributory cause of the growth and decline of northern Hopewellian culture. *Wisconsin Archeologist* 41, 21–33.

Holmes, William H. (1901). Aboriginal copper mines of Isle Royale, Lake Superior. *American Anthropologist* 3, 684–696.

Kroeber, A. L. (1953). Introduction. In *Anthropology Today* (A. L. Kroeber, ed.), pp. xiii–xv. Univ. of Chicago Press, Chicago.

Martin, Paul S., George I. Quimby, and Donald Collier. (1947). *Indians Before Columbus.* Univ. of Chicago Press, Chicago.

Ritchie, William A. (1955). Recent suggestions suggesting an early woodland burial cult in the northeast. *New York State Museum and Science Service, Circ.* No. 40.

Sahlins, Marshall D. (1958). *Social Stratification in Polynesia.* Univ. of Washington Press, Seattle.

Spaulding, Albert C. (1946). Northeastern archaeology and general trends in the northern forest zone. In *Man in Northeastern North America* (Frederick Johnson, ed.), Vol. 3, pp. 143–167. Phillips Academy, Andover, Massachusetts.

Steward, Julian H. (1955). *Theory of Culture Change*. Univ. of Illinois Press, Urbana.

Thompson, Raymond H. (1958). Preface. In *Migrations in New World Culture History* (R. H. Thompson, ed.), pp. v–vii. Univ. of Arizona, Tucson.

Waring, Antonio J., and Preston Holder. (1945). A prehistoric ceremonial complex in the southeastern United States. *American Anthropologist* 47, 1–34.

White, Leslie A. (1959). *The Evolution of Culture*. McGraw-Hill, New York.

Willey, Gordon R., and Philip Phillips. (1958). *Method and Theory in Archaeology*. Univ. of Chicago Press, Chicago.

Wittry, Warren L. (1951). A preliminary study of the old copper complex. *Wisconsin Archeologist* 32, 1–18.

Wittry, Warren L., and Robert E. Ritzenthaler. (1956). The old copper complex: An archaic manifestation in Wisconsin. *American Antiquity* 21, 244–254.

Smudge Pits and Hide Smoking:
The Use of Analogy in Archaeological Reasoning*†

Abstract

It is argued that as a scientist one does not justifiably employ analogies to ethnographic observations for the "interpretation" of archaeological data. Instead, analogies should be documented and used as the basis for offering a postulate as to the relationship between archaeological forms and their behavioral context in the past. Such a postulate should then serve as the foundation of a series of deductively drawn hypotheses which, on testing, can refute or tend to confirm the postulate offered. Analogy should serve to provoke new questions about order in the archaeological record and should serve to prompt more searching investigations rather than being viewed as a means for offering "interpretations" which then serve as the "data" for synthesis. This argument is made demonstratively through the presentation of formal data on a class of archaeological features, "smudge pits," and the documentation of their positive analogy with pits as facilities used in smoking hides.

The purpose of this paper is twofold: (1) to present a discussion of analogy and provide an example of the use of analogy in archaeological reasoning, and (2) to present a functional argument regarding a particular formal class of archaeological feature. The justification for this type of presentation is a conviction that (a) archaeologists have generally employed analogy to ethnographic data as a means of "interpreting" archaeologically observed phenomena, rather than as a means for provoking new types of investigation into the order observable in archaeological data. It is the latter role for analogy which is hopefully exemplified; (b) archaeologists have neglected the formal analysis and investigation of relationships between classes of archaeological features. That this situation should be corrected can best be defended by the demonstration of provocative results obtained through the analysis of features.

* Originally published in *American Antiquity* **32**, No. 1, 1–12 (1967).

† This paper was presented at the 31st Annual Meeting of the Society for American Archaeology, Reno, Nevada, 1966.

Analogy is the term used to designate a particular type of inferential argument. Thus, in discussing analogy we may profitably consider the criteria employed in judging the relative strength of such an argument regardless of subject matter. Having explored the general characteristics of such arguments, we may turn to a consideration of *anthropological* arguments from analogy, attempting to isolate more general characteristics. Finally, using the conclusions from these two kinds of discussions, we shall offer certain programmatic suggestions which we believe could be profitably followed.

The term *analogy* is defined in Webster's Unabridged Dictionary with the following discussion:

> A relation of likeness, between two things or of one thing to or with another, consisting in the resemblance not of the things themselves, but of two or more attributes, circumstances or effects . . .
>
> Analogy is frequently used to denote similarity or essential resemblance but its specific meaning is a similarity of relations and in this consists the difference between the argument from example and that from analogy. In the former we argue from the mere similarity of two things, in the latter we argue from the similarity of their relations . . .
>
> Biology—correspondence in function between organs of parts of different structures with different origins—distinguishing from homology . . .
>
> Logic—form of inference in which it is reasoned that if two or more things agree with one another in one or more respects they will probably agree in yet other respects. The degree of probability will depend upon the number and importance of their known agreements (Neilson, 1956, p. 94).

The crucial or distinctive characteristic common to all the definitions is that an analogy is not strictly a demonstration of formal similarities between entities; rather it is an inferential argument based on implied relationships between demonstrably similar entities. All those arguments which exhibit this form can be studied, and we can ask what characteristics are shared by those arguments which on investigation were verified. Three such characteristics have often been found to characterize successful arguments by analogy (these are paraphrased from Stebbing, 1961, pp. 243–256):

1. *If the initial resemblances are such that the inferred property would account for the resemblances, then the conclusion is more likely to be true.* A good example might be the following argument: (1) A distinctive pattern of wear is observable on the unmodified end of an end scraper recovered from a Magdalenian site in western Europe. (2) The same pattern of wear is observable on the unmodified end of an end scraper hafted in a wooden haft collected from the Plains Indians of North America. (3) One infers the presence of a functionally similar haft during the period when the archaeologically recovered (Magdalenian) end scraper was in use. The inferred property, the haft, would account for the resemblances in wear observed on both end scrapers. In this case, where it can be said that the inferred relationship or property accounts for the

known positive analogy, the positive analogy is said to consist of "important" properties. The term "important" refers to properties which, on the basis of other knowledge or conviction (in this case knowledge regarding the properties resulting from mechanical friction under certain conditions), the posited relationship is said to be justified.

The obvious corollary of the above generalization is that *if the initial resemblances are not such that the inferred property would account for the resemblances, then the conclusion is more likely to be false.* For example, almost any case of attempting to infer specific meaning from an abstract design on an artifact by analogy to a design of known context when there is no demonstrable continuity between the symbolic contexts of the two designs in question would be more likely to be false.

2. *The more comprehensive the positive analogy and the less comprehensive the inferred properties, the more likely the conclusion is true.* This criterion simply recognizes a major distinction between an argument from example and one from simple enumeration, where a large number of cases sharing limited numbers of attributes are cited, as opposed to an argument from analogy in which a large number of common attributes are cited and the number of cases may be quite small. The more numerous the similarities between analogs, the greater the probability that inferred properties are similar. The corollary of this is: *The more comprehensive the inferred properties, the less likely is the conclusion to be true.* This guide to judging the strength of an argument from analogy rests with the common-sense notion that the more detailed the inference, the more specific must be one's ability to cite the determinants of the positive analogy.

These criteria are derived as arguments from example since they can be viewed as generalizations from a large sample of arguments by analogy. The incidences of confirmation, as opposed to the incidences of disproof, are tabulated and studied for common properties. In short, these "criteria" are simply a statement of probable outcome generalized from a large sample of cases of reasoning by analogy. They are believed to be independent of the content of particular arguments.

In the examination of anthropological arguments from analogy, we are not concerned with the criteria which will allow us to judge the *form* of a particular argument from analogy as in the previous discussion. Instead, we are concerned with the *content* of the argument. The only guide which I can discover for aiding in this evaluation rests with our previous mention of the citation in an argument of "important" properties. We mean by this properties which, on the basis of other knowledge or conviction, are posited as relevant to the relationship argued. A common situation in which argument from analogy is offered by archaeologists is that in which similarities in form of artifacts are cited between archaeologically and ethnographically observed data, with the proposition that behavior observed in the ethnographic situation (unobserved in the archaeological situation) was also present in the past when the artifacts were in use.

Several persons have addressed themselves to a consideration of the problem of citing "important" properties in argument from analogy and have offered the following suggestions for establishing the conditions of relevance for archaeological arguments from analogy.

1. Relevance can be established by demonstrating, or accepting as demonstrated, that there is a historical continuity between the archaeologically observed unit and the ethnographically cited society or social unit.

2. In the absence of the above demonstrated justification, relevance could be justified by seeking analogies in cultures which manipulate similar environments in similar ways (Ascher, 1961).

While certainly not subject to question as such, one wonders at the utility of attempting to specify in the form of suggestions for the "new analogy" all those conditions under which one would expect to find functional linkages between cultural elements. For only with such an exhaustive listing of contemporary anthropological theory and knowledge could one hope to enumerate all of the conditions of relevance which might arise in various anthropological arguments from analogy. Stating this point another way, the only means open to anthropologists attempting to evaluate by inspection any given argument by analogy is in terms of the degree to which the inferred property could be expected to vary concomitantly with the cited features in the positive analogy. Such an evaluation must therefore be made on the basis of our current understanding of the form, structure, and functioning of cultural systems. It is my hope that contemporary understanding goes far beyond the "canon for the selection of analogs" recently advanced (Ascher, 1961).

We now turn to the crucial question of the function of arguments from analogy in the broader field of archaeological reasoning. I have chosen to offer one example of such an argument and to attempt an analysis of its form and structural position in a broader logical system of analytical method. Hopefully by such a procedure the formal, functional, and structural characteristics of arguments from analogy in archaeological analytical method will be made explicit.

Previous archaeological reports have occasionally cited the occurrence of small "caches" of carbonized corncobs (Cole *et al.,* 1951, pp. 34 and 40); yet the specific functions of these small pits have not been previously considered analytically nor has there been any formal analysis of the characteristics common to a number of samples of these "corncob caches." Recent archaeological investigations in the Carlyle Reservoir of south-central Illinois resulted in the excavation of a number of these caches (Binford *et al.,* 1964). The recognized formal homogeneity of these features prompted their analysis and systematic description and justification as a distinctive class of feature which, in all probability, had a single function in the activities of the extinct societies represented.

Our procedure here will be: (1) provide a summary of the formal characteristics of this class of cultural feature; (2) document and evaluate the analogy which is demonstrable between this class of feature and certain facilities described ethnographically; (3) offer a postulate as to the function of the archaeological features; (4) develop certain deductively drawn hypotheses that could be investigated to test the probability of the postulates; and (5) cite the procedure employed as an example of a role for analogy in archaeological reasoning which is not believed to be commonly employed among practicing archaeologists.

Form of the Features

The particular cultural features under discussion are best known from the Toothsome site, Clinton County, Illinois, where a total of 15 such features were excavated and detailed observations were made (Binford *et al.,* 1964). Since this sample constitutes the best available data, I will duplicate here the original description of this sample of 15 features.

The features exhibited so little internal formal variability that there is little doubt that they represent a single type of feature and a single activity. The contents of the pit are always primary and are unaltered by subsequent cultural activity. In addition, the size, shape, and contents of each feature are almost identical to all others included in this category.

Size

These pits are slightly oval, having a mean length of 30.27 cm and a mean width of 27.40 cm. They extend below the present surface to a mean depth of 33.53 cm.

Shape

All are slightly oval and are generally straight-sided, with essentially flat bottoms.

Elements of the Feature

   (a) Grayish loam soil
   (b) Charred and carbonized corncobs

(c) Charred and carbonized twigs (possibly corn stalks)
(d) Charred and carbonized bark of an as yet unidentified tree
(e) Charred vegetable material, possibly from other as yet unidentified plants
(f) Occasionally a minor oxidation of soil near the mouth of the pit

Distribution of the Elements

The very bottom of the pit is filled with the charred material for a variable depth of from 7 cm to within 8 cm of the mouth of the feature. The charred twigs are generally curled around in the bottom of the pit with the cobs nested in the center. The upper part may be partially filled with the grayish loam soil which was the characteristic soil on the surface of the site. The latter would have *no* included charred material.

General Observations

The invariable presence of the grayish loam soil in the upper fill demonstrates intentional covering of the pit contents, rather than an accumulative filling with midden and surface debris.

DISTRIBUTION OF THESE FEATURES ON THE SITE

The pits are distributed peripherally around a small Mississippian farmstead composed of two house structures and one storage structure. In addition to these buildings, the site is internally differentiated into several activity areas, which include outdoor cooking areas and a dump. There is no obvious tendency for these features to cluster; they appear rather well dispersed in a peripheral fashion around the boundary of the site.

DISCUSSION

In the original report on these features it was suggested that they were probably small "smudge pits," since the conditions of combustion which would have resulted in the carbonization of the recovered plant materials would certainly have produced vast quantities of smoke. It was further speculated whether these obvious sources of smoke might have been employed in the control of mosquitoes, which in the experience of the excavators, had constituted a real pest during the summer months.

POSSIBLE OCCURRENCE AT OTHER LOCATIONS

In addition to the occurrence of these features at the Toothsome site, pits of identical form were observed at a slightly earlier Mississippian farmstead site at the Sandy Tip site in the Carlyle Reservoir (Binford, 1964). Later investigations at the Texas #1 site, also in the Carlyle Reservoir, exposed nine additional features of this type (Morrell, 1965). The small size of the feature led the investigator to interpret eight of them as postmolds.

Features 22, 23, 26, and 27; small pits or postmolds filled with charred corncobs. Average diameter 0.21 m. A total of nine cob concentrations were located within Unit No. 3, eight of which appear to have been postmolds. The cobs are arranged generally in a crescent on the outer edges of the molds, possibly indicating the use of cobs for post tamping and support (Morrell, 1965, pp. 24–27).

Cutler (1963) suggests that the cobs were broken before they were deposited and probably before they were carbonized. Cutler further suggests that the cobs do not represent a cache of cobs discarded after shelling. Radiocarbon dates were obtained from Features 22 and 23; these are A.D. 1030 ± 85 (GX-0364) and A.D. 1090 ± 100 (GX-0365), respectively (Morrell, 1965, pp. 24–27).

Small features characterized by the clustering of carbonized corncobs were recently reported from the Lloyd Village site in the American Bottoms near East Saint Louis, Illinois (Hall and Vogel, 1963, pp. 25–26), and similar features were noted on the nearby Cahokia site (Cutler, 1963, p. 16).

The Kincaid site on the Ohio River in southern Illinois, extensively investigated during the 1930's, yielded features which appear to be identical to those described from the Toothsome site. It is interesting that although they were observed at three different locations on the site (Mx^{v}1D Section I and East Section; Mx^{v}1c), all were in the village area, while none was reported from the mounds so intensively investigated on the site (Cole *et al.*, 1951, pp. 34, 40, and 53, Fig. 3).

Quimby (1957, p. 105) noted the occurrence of "a deposit of fragmentary corncobs that had been burned" in the village deposits under Mounds 1 and 2 at the Bayou Goula site, which is interpreted by Quimby as the remains of a historically known group, closely related to the Natchez, occupying the location between 1700 and 1739.

The archaeological feature of this type believed to be the earliest thus far known is reported from the Williams site, Gordon County, Georgia. This find is described as follows:

The most important find . . . was Feature 7. This was a group of 30 to 40 burnt corn cobs in an area about eight inches in diameter and four inches in depth . . . . Also included mixed in with the cobs was ash, wood, cane and one half of a shelled acorn. No pit was discernible since the group was in the dark brown sand. The cobs were oriented in every conceivable direction and it appears as if the whole unit was thrown into a pit . . . . At 9-Wd-L . . . a group of cobs were found which exhibited evidence of being deposited during a corn-planting ceremony. These differed from the Williams Site specimens in being placed in four orderly rows in a specially prepared pit . . . . The Williams Site cache does not give evidence for or against a corn ceremony. However, the cobs were not badly broken up and some sort of a ceremony would be expected, whether at planting, harvesting, or in between, in a culture concerned with the success of a corn crop. There are many instances of corn ceremonialism in the eastern United States, but they are mainly found in a Mississippian or historical context (Morse and Morse, 1960, p. 88).

The Williams site find has been radiocarbon dated at A.D. 470 ± 75 (M-1107, Crane and Griffin, 1963, p. 239).

Carbonized corncobs were recovered in two general contexts at the George C. Davis site, Cherokee County, Texas (Newell and Krieger, 1949, pp. 248–249). Five cases of recovered corncobs are reported from "postmolds" of Structures 31, 8, and 6, respectively, all of which are buildings not constructed on mounds. Three finds were of "caches" of quantities of carbonized cobs similar to those features described from the Toothsome site. Recent radiocarbon dating suggests that these features date at A.D. 1307 ± 150 (M-1186), a period somewhat later than originally proposed (Griffin and Yarnell, 1963).

Summarizing our findings, one point is strikingly clear: the geographical distribution of these features is spotty. On sites from the same general geographical provinces, where they are documented and where one would expect them to have been reported had they been present, there is no suggestion that they were observed. For example, they are absent from sites in the Chickamauga Lake section of the Tennessee River (Lewis and Kneberg, 1946); similarly they are unreported from the Norris Basin and the Pickwick Basins of the Tennessee drainage (Webb and DeJarnette, 1942; Webb, 1938). Moreover, they are not present at the Bessemer site in north-central Alabama (DeJarnette and Wimberly, 1941), nor at the Rood's Landing site in Stewart County, Georgia (Caldwell, 1955), nor at the Macon Group (Kelly, 1938) at Macon Georgia. The Gordon site also appears to lack these features (Myre, 1928). This list of eastern sites apparently lacking the "corncob" features could be greatly expanded. On the other hand, a search of the literature for the Upper Illinois valley and prairie fringe areas as well as for the Great Plains, the Eastern coastal region, the Upper Ohio valley, and the Great Lakes regions failed to yield a single incidence of the "corncob pit." This latter finding is based on my investigation of the context of all the reported incidences of corn which were recently inventoried by Yarnell (1964). In all cases where the context of finds of corn could be determined, it was generally as charred kernels, and when cobs were reported, they were generally single or in small numbers occurring in the midden fill of recognizable cooking or storage pits.

These investigations suggest that the smudge pits are a feature characteristic of the societies of the Middle and Lower Mississippi River area, with extensions into the Georgia-Creek area to the east and the Texas-Caddo area to the west. The spotty distribution and the lack of data from numbers of sites in this area, however, further suggest that this feature is probably restricted in use to certain limited kinds of activities. This inference is further supported by the documented cases' being limited to associations with village house-remains and never with public buildings. Although the functional specificity of the feature may be a major contributor to the spotty distribution of documented examples, my search of the literature made it painfully obvious that archaeologists have neglected the analysis and systematic description of cultural features, which makes it impossible to assess the degree to which the spotty distribution is a function of events in the past or of the data-collecting techniques and analytical methods employed by archaeologists.

The earliest documented example is from the Williams site in northwest Georgia, A.D. 470 ± 75 (M-1107) where such an early date stands as a unique case. All of the other known examples (if one accepts the revised dating of the George C. Davis site corn) are relatively late, postdating A.D. 1000. These data suggest that we could reasonably expect the activity in the context of which these features were used to have been practiced by the historically documented groups in the "agricultural east."

There is a variety of functional interpretation offered by investigators who observed these features. At Kincaid they were interpreted as "caches" (Cole *et al.*, 1951, p. 156) in spite of the fact that none of the corncobs had kernels attached. Morse and Morse (1960, p. 88) entertain the probability of a "ceremonial" function for the feature. At both the George C. Davis site (Newell and Krieger, 1949, pp. 248–249) and the Texas site (Morrell, 1965) they were interpreted as postmolds, presumably because of their small size. The author (Binford, *et al.*, 1964) offered the interpretation of a smudge pit, but at that time he could only suggest that the smudge was produced as a means of controlling mosquitoes!

In summary, smudge pits are a class of archaeological features sharing (a) small size, (b) contents composed diagnostically of carbonized corncobs, lacking kernels, and (c) contents exhibiting a primary depositional context. These features are documented from a number of Mississippian sites in the southern Illinois area as well as from sites in the lower reaches of the Mississippi Valley, northern Georgia, and eastern Texas. The context in which the features occur at these sites is invariably that of house areas, as opposed to areas of public buildings, and, in the case of the known farmstead, they are distributed peripherally around the centers of activity within the site. These features are dated as early as A.D. 470; however, the majority are referable to a post-A.D.-1000 time period.

Previous attempts at "interpretation" have shown considerable originality, but all must be considered as conjecture.

Relevant Ethnographic Observations

The distinctive form of these features, together with their necessarily limited possible range of uses (all of which must have involved the production of quantities of smoke), made an optimistic search for relevant ethnographic descriptions and references realistic and potentially profitable. The following descriptions from ethnographic accounts were located.

I. Descriptions of the Process of Smoking Hides as Observed among the Southeastern Indians

A. The Natchez, 1700–1750

According to Swanton (1911, p. 64), Dumont in 1753 said:

They first dig a hole in the earth about 2 feet deep, with a diameter of six inches at the top and a little less toward the bottom. They fill this hole with cow dung, rotted wood, and maize ears and place it over two rods in the shape of a cross, the four ends of which are slanted in the earth so as to form a kind of cradle on which they stretch the skin they wish to tan. They then set fire to the combustible substance in the hole and fasten the skin down all around by means of many little pegs driven into the ground. Then they cover it with earth over and along the edges, so as to keep in the smoke. The materials in the hole becoming consumed without throwing out the flame, the thick smoke that comes out of it, especially owing to the lack of any exit . . . fastens itself to the skin which it smoke-dries and dyes a yellow color.

B. The Creek, 1900–1950

. . . next, they scooped a hole in the ground, built a fire in it, and put corncobs upon this so that a thick smoke was produced with little flame. The hide was fastened down over this pit with the other surface down and left until it was smoked yellow (Swanton, 1946, p. 445).

C. The Choctaw, 1900–1950

If the skins are to be smoked, a process that renders them more durable, a hole a foot or more in depth is dug in which a fire is kept until a bed of hot ashes accumulates. On this are put pieces of rotten oak, no other wood being used for this purpose, these are not permitted to blaze, as the more smoke that arises the better is it for the skins. These, already tanned soft and white and perfectly dry, are stretched over the hole and allowed to remain in the smoke an hour or more (Bushnell, 1909, pp. 11–12).

D. The Seminole, 1900–1950

Usually, however, the leather is finished by smoking. The skin is sewed up in a bag-like form and suspended, bottom up, from an inclined stick. The edges are pegged down about a small hole in which a smouldering fire burns. The smoke and fumes are allowed to impregnate the hide thoroughly, and then the tanning is completed . . . . (Skinner, 1913, pp. 72–73).

II. Description of the Process of Smoking Hides as Observed among the Plains Tribes

A. The Omaha, 1850–1900

Skins to be used in making moccasins were browned by smoke (Fletcher and La Flesche, 1911, p. 345).

B. The Dacotah (Sioux), 1800–1850

If after all this working, the skin is hairy or stiff, it is drawn over a cord as large as a finger, for some time, as hard as they can pull, which softens it much: sometimes this is the last process, except smoking. This is done by digging a hole in the ground about a foot deep, putting in a little fire and some rotten wood, when the skin is sewed into a bag and hung over the smoke: in 10 minutes the skin is ready for use (Schoolcraft, 1856, p. 61).

C. The Blackfoot, 1850–1900

The color and finish were imparted by smoking. The skins were spread over a frame similar to that of a sweat house, a hole was dug underneath and a smouldering fire maintained with sage or rotten wood (Wissler, 1910, p. 65).

D. The Crow, 1800–1850

The greater part of these skins, however, go through still another operation afterwards, which gives them a greater value and renders them much more serviceable—that is, the process of smoking. For this, a small hole is dug in the ground and a fire is built in it with rotten wood, which will produce a great quantity of smoke without much blaze; and several small poles of the proper length stuck in the ground around it and drawn and fastened together at the top, around which the skin is wrapped in form of a tent, and generally sewed together at the edges to secure the smoke within it, within this the skins to be smoked are placed, and in this condition the tent will stand a day or so, enclosing the heated smoke (Catlin, 1880, p. 52).

E. The Arapaho, 1900–1939

. . . After it was as soft as she wanted it she dug a hole, about 20 inches deep and about 15 inches in diameter, and built a smudge in it, using either fine chips of wood or bark of cottonwood. She then sewed up the hide to make a sack of it with one end open. She placed this sack over a tipi-shaped framework made of saplings and set this over the smudge. She watched the smudge carefully so there would be no blaze, but only smoke. At the closed end of the sack she had sewed a strip of buckskin with which she tied the sack to the top of the saplings. This held the hide in place. When one side of the hide was sufficiently smoked, the sack was turned inside out and again smoked, thus giving both sides a tan (Hilger, 1952, p. 184).

III. Descriptions of the Process of Smoking Hides as Observed among the Indians of the Great Lakes Region

A. Iroquois–General, 1850–1860

. . . a smoke is made, and the skin placed over it in such a manner as to inclose it entirely. Each side is smoked in this manner until the pores are closed, and the skin has become thoroughly toughened with its color changed from white to a kind of brown (Morgan, 1901, p. 13).

B. Iroquois–Specifically the Sececa, 1800–1890

A hole 18 inches in diameter was then made in the ground and the skin suspended above it on upright sticks and smoked until the desired color is produced, by turning rotten wood beneath. The skin was then ready for use (Mason, 1891, p. 573).

C. Ojibwa, 1930–1940

After the hide was dry the informant removed it from the stretcher, laid it on the ground folding it on head-to-tail line, turned both edges together, and beginning with head end fastened them together by means of clothespins. This made a nearly airtight compartment. In former days edges were sewed together tightly with basswood fiber. The head end of the hide was next fastened to the branch of a tree; the tail end placed so it encircled the rim of a pail of smudge. Two granddaughters . . . prepared the smudge by placing bits of birchbark on burning embers fetched from the kitchen stove and packing the remainder of the pail with white pine and Norway cones. Punk was sometimes used in place of cones since it was less inflammable. Jack pine cones were not used. They give an unsatisfactory color.

The worker swung the pail back and forth several times to enhance the smudge and then placed it under the hide, holding it there carefully as to permit the hide to fill with smoke . . . . When it was sufficiently tanned, she loosened the clothespins, turned and folded the edges and again pinned them, she then tanned the reverse side. Smoking not only gave color to hides but preserved them from moths (Hilger, 1951, pp. 131–132).

D. Menomini, 1900–1920

A hole about a foot wide and six inches deep is dug in the earth in a locality sheltered from the wind, and a slow glowing, smoky fire is made in the bottom of the pit with dead branches, punk, or even dry corn cobs. Over this the inverted bag is suspended and pegged down about the base (Skinner, 1921, p. 228).

It is readily observable that two of the documented incidences of the use of corncobs as fuel for smoking hides fall within the distribution as known archaeologically for corncob-filled smudge pits. The single exception, the Menominee, are described as making use of corncobs in the 1920's. It seems reasonable to suggest this might be a relatively recent practice, related to the reservation period rather than to the period of aboriginal adjustment to the northwestern Great Lakes region. This suggestion is further credited by the fact that in all the cases of ethnographic documentation which fall outside of the area of archaeologically known smudge pit distribution, with a single exception, the Choctaw, fuels other than corncobs are cited as being used. This supports the archaeological observations of the absence of corncob-filled smudge pits in the Plains, Great Lake, and northern Ohio valley. In short, the ethnographic and archaeological distributions of the use of corncobs as fuel in smudge pits are strikingly similar, in spite of obvious lacks in the coverage from both sources.

The correspondence in *form* of smudge pits as known archaeologically and of hide-smoking smudge pits as described ethnographically is essentially perfect.

Table I presents in summary the comparative information regarding the form of the facilities as known from archaeological and ethnographic sources.

On the basis of (a) the convincing correspondence between the formal attributes of smudge pits as known archaeologically and smudge pits used in smoking hides as known ethnographically, (b) the strong positive analogy between the distribution of smudge pits in which corncobs were used as fuel and the use of corncobs as fuel for smoking hides as documented ethnographically, and (c) the relatively late archaeological documentation for the use of smudge pits, which would make continuity between the archaeological and ethnographic periods reasonable, we postulate that the archaeologically known features described were in fact facilities employed in the task of smoking hides by the former occupants of the archaeological sites on which they were found.

TABLE I   *Smudge Pit Attributes*

Class of attributes and archaeologically observed attributes	Ethnographically described attributes
1. Size Relatively small, shallow excavations in the ground when the facility is a pit *Mean ·* *Range* Length, 30.27 cm 23.0–42.0 cm Width, 27.40 cm 20.2–31.0 cm Depth, 33.53 cm 25.0–37.1 cm	The cited sizes range from 15.24–30.48 cm (6 in.–12 in.) in diameter and 15.24–60.96 cm in depth
2. Contents Soft, porous, poorly combustible organic materials. Corncobs, bark, twigs, and possibly cornstalks	Corncobs, bark, twigs, (dead branches), rotten wood, dung, pine cones, and sage
3. Treatment of contents Contents burned in a reducing atmosphere resulting in the carbonization of the fuels	Contents burned in a reducing atmosphere resulting in the production of quantities of smoke
4. Final condition of the facility The facility was abandoned with no disturbance of the carbonized fuels; nothing was removed from the pit, showing that it did not contain the fuels and the items being processed as in the case of roasting pits, fire pits, etc. The archaeological remains of the pit exhibit a primary fill, and secondary fill if present is superimposed	All the descriptions cite the suspension of the hides over the smudge pit. The items being processed are not contained in the facility with the fuels. Completion of the smoking process and the removal of the hides for use does not result in a disturbance of the contents of the smudge pit

The procedure which should be followed in refuting or increasing the probability of the validity of the proposition would be as follows:

1. Determine if there are any spatial correlates of the activity of smoking hides; in other words, determine if the activity was regularly conducted in any particular location. If so, determine whether or not the smudge pits exhibit such a distinction.

2. Determine if there are any temporal correlates of the activity of smoking hides; was the activity regularly conducted at any particular period of the annual cycle? If so, determine whether or not the smudge pits exhibit such an association with respect to relevant seasonally variable phenomena.

3. Determine if there are any formal correlates of the activity with respect to other implements or facilities which were employed as parts of a set which also included hide-smoking pits. Was hide smoking normally conducted at the same place and at approximately the same time as the manufacture of clothing from the hides? If so, then there should be demonstrable concomitant variation between the incidence of smudge pits and implements used in clothing manufacture, such as needles.

4. Determine if there are any other activities which employed facilities which shared the same formal attributes as observed in hide-smoking pits. If so, then the specific postulate could be refuted, but a more general one could be stated which could then be tested along the dimensions of time, space, and form.

The following observations are made in the hope that they are pertinent to the formulation of sytematic hypotheses:

a. In all the ethnographic cases cited the smoking of hides was women's work; therefore, we would expect stylistic variation in smudge pits to vary directly with stylistic variation in other female-produced items such as ceramics.

b. In all the ethnographic cases cited, when temporal data were given, hide smoking was a spring and summer activity conducted in the "base camp" after the major hunting season was concluded and before the winter hunts were begun. We therefore offer the following hypothesis: Smudge pits should occur almost exclusively in "base camps" occupied during the period of the year when hunting activity was at a minimum.

c. In many cases there were indications in the ethnographic literature that hide smoking and the related manufacture of clothing from smoked hides were activities which would be more frequently performed by individuals possessing recognized skills in these tasks. Therefore, the incidence of smudge pits might be expected to vary independently of the number of persons occupying the appropriate site for any given unit of time. In short, they would be expected to vary independently of such direct measures of the number and duration of occupants as cooking fires and sleeping facilities.

Aside from these interesting and potentially informative avenues for future research, I think it is necessary to point out another and as yet unmentioned potential source of additional understanding; namely, that the survey of ethnographic literature demonstrated that the practice of smoking hides, particularly deer hides, for use in the manufacture of moccasins, shirts, and leggings, was a practice common to most, if not all, of North America. The major characteristic which appeared to vary from region to region was the fuel used in the smudge pits, as well as the idiosyncrasies of construction for suspension of hides over the smudge pit. Our investigations have been limited to the citation of archaeological remains in which corncobs were the fuel. An acquaintance with the general range of size of the feature and with the depth of it can be extremely beneficial. The size appears to be limited by the circumference of a deer skin when sewn into a "bag"; the depth seems to be limited by two general considerations: (a) deep enough to provide an oxygen-starved environment; (b) shallow enough to contain only a limited amount of fuel. This knowledge, along with an acquaintance with the generic class of fuel and the probability that the contents would not be disturbed (resulting in the archaeological recovery of fairly complete carbonized fragments of soft spongy fuels), enables the recall of numerous examples of features observed on sites from the east coast, the Great Lakes, and the pre-Mississippian occupations in central Illinois which were almost certainly smudge pits in which fuels other than corncobs had been burned.

Our investigations have resulted in the recognition of a generic class of facility which can be expected to vary regionally with respect to the specifics of its contents. This recognition could aid in the documentation of seasonally variable activities in the areas of less aboriginal sedentism, such as the Great Lakes.

The final consideration to be taken up is the degree to which this study can be cited as an example of the use of analogy in archaeological argument and its pertinence to general statements regarding the role of analogy in archaeological reasoning.

The logical steps followed in this argument were as follows:

A. THE ANALOGY

1. The recognition and demonstration of a positive formal analogy between a class of archaeologically observed phenomena and a class of ethnographically observed phenomena.

2. A consideration of the positive analogy between the spatial distribution of the facility as documented archaeologically and ethnographically, and the observation that, although poorly documented, the known distributions show a strong positive analogy.

3. A consideration of the degree to which it would be reasonable to expect a

continuity between the archaeologically and ethnographically known cases; for example, the dating of the archaeologically known materials as reasonably viewed as cases of historical priority to the ethnographic data.

B. THE POSTULATE

1. The behavioral context of the use of the archaeologically known features was the same as that described ethnographically for the analogous facilities.

C. THE DEVELOPMENT OF TESTABLE HYPOTHESES IN A DEDUCTIVE FRAMEWORK GIVEN THE POSTULATE OFFERED

1. An examination of the ethnographic "context" of the activity for correlated formal characteristics which could be directly observed or studied archaeologically.

2. Given the postulate set forth in B (1) above and the knowledge of the formal, spatial, and temporal correlates of the activity designated in the postulate, the specification of a number of hypotheses as to the predicted mode of variation expected between the archaeologically observed analog and other archaeologically observable phenomena as specified by the studies of C (1) above.

3. The testing of the stated hypotheses and the refutation, refinement, or verification in probabilistic terms of the truth of the stated postulate.

D. EXPLORATION OF THE ARCHAEOLOGICAL RECORD FOR NEW RELATIONSHIPS

Finally this particular procedure should lead the investigator into the recognition of previously unrecognized relationships as suggested above in C, 1: the explanation of previously unexplained variation in archaeological data as the outcome of C and, as in the case of this particular example, the recognition of a generic class of phenomena definable by certain general formal characteristics where previously only a restricted class was recognized, isolated by the common occurrence of specific formal similarities (for example, charred corncobs).

Conclusions

The procedure discussed here is appropriate in the context of a positivistic philosophy of anthropology and archaeology. It denies categorically the assertion of antipositivists that the final judgment of archaeological reconstruction must be based on an appraisal of the professional competence of the archaeologist (Thompson, 1956, p. 331). The final judgment of the archaeological reconstruction presented here must rest with testing through subsidiary hypotheses drawn deductively. Questions were also raised concerning the argument made by Robert Ascher (1961) that by following certain of his suggestions for "placing analogy on a firmer foundation" we could in any way directly increase our knowledge of archaeologically documented societies. The arguments presented by Ascher (1961), if followed, could at best serve to increase our understanding of archaeological observations in terms of ethnographically described situations. The archaeologist would be performing a role analogous to that of a historical critic who attempts to translate data of the past into the context of relatively contemporary or culturally prescribed experience. It is maintained here that as anthropologists we have a task quite different; we seek to explain cultural differences and similarities. We approach our task by developing methods and procedures that will permit us to demonstrate order in our data. It is assumed that the demonstration of order implies a set of systematic relationships among cultural phenomena that existed in the past. The understanding of the operation of systems rests in the measurement of concomitant variation between various classes of ordered phenomena and the eventual statement of general laws of cultural variability.

The role of analogy in this process has hopefully been demonstrated in this particular example. Analogy serves to provoke certain types of questions which can, on investigation, lead to the recognition of more comprehensive ranges of order in the archaeological data. In short, we ask questions about the relationships between types of archaeologically observable phenomena that had possibly not been placed in juxtaposition or viewed as orderly. In doing so we can develop a common "explanation" for observed variability in a number of formally independent classes of archaeological data, and thereby we can approach more closely the isolation of systematic variables which operated in the past. It should be pointed out that these gains may obtain regardless of whether the original analogy led to a correct postulate. In short, I do not view interpretations, or syntheses of interpretations as an end product of our investigations; on the contrary, we should be seeking generalizations regarding the operation of cultural systems and their evolution—something which has not been described ethnographically nor thus far achieved through the observation and analysis of contemporary events.

References

Ascher, Robert. (1961). Analogy in archaeological interpretation. *Southwestern Journal of Anthropology* 17, 317–325.
Binford, Lewis R. (1964). The Sandy Tip Site; Carlyle Reservoir. Manuscript at University of California, Los Angeles.

Binford, Lewis R., James Schoenwetter, and M. L. Fowler. (1964). Archaeological investigations in the Carlyle Reservoir. *Southern Illinois University Museum, Archaeological Salvage Report* No. 17, pp. 1–117.

Bushnell, David I., Jr. (1909). The Choctaw of Bayou Lacomb, St. Tammany Parish, Louisiana. *Bureau of American Ethnology, Bulletin* 48.

Caldwell, Joseph R. (1955). Investigations at Rood's Landing, Stewart Co., Georgia. *Early Georgia* 2, 22–49.

Catlin, George. (1880). *North American Indians,* Vol. 1, p. 52. Egyptian Hall, Piccadilly, London.

Cole, Fay-Cooper, and others. (1951). *Kincaid, A Prehistoric Illinois Metropolis.* Univ. of Chicago Press, Chicago.

Crane, H. R., and J. B. Griffin. (1963). University of Michigan radiocarbon dates. VIII. *Radiocarbon* 5, 228–253.

Cutler, Hugh C. (1963). Identification of plant remains. In *Second Annual Report: American Bottoms Archaeology* (M. L. Fowler, ed.), pp. 16–18. Illinois Archaeological Survey. Univ. of Illinois Press, Urbana, Illinois.

DeJarnette, David L., and Steve B. Wimberly. (1941). The Bessemer Site. Excavation of three mounds and surrounding village areas near Bessemer, Alabama. *Geological Survey of Alabama, Museum Paper* 17.

Fletcher, Alice C., and Francis La Flesche. (1911). The Omaha tribe. *27th Annual Report of the Bureau of American Ethnology* pp. 15–655.

Griffin, James B., and Richard A. Yarnell. (1963). A new radiocarbon date on corn from the Davis Site, Cherokee County, Texas. *American Antiquity* 28, 396–397.

Hall, Robert L., and Joseph O. Vogel. (1963). Illinois State museum projects. In *Second Annual Report: American Bottoms Archaeology* (M. L. Fowler, ed.), pp. 24–31. Illinois Archaeological Survey. Univ. of Illinois Press, Urbana, Illinois.

Hilger, Sister M. Inez. (1951). Chippewa child life and its cultural background. *Bureau of American Ethnology, Bulletin* 146.

Hilger, Sister M. Inez. (1952). Arapaho child life and its cultural background. *Bureau of American Ethnology, Bulletin* 148.

Kelly, A. R. (1938). A preliminary report on archaeological explorations at Macon, Georgia. *Bureau of American Ethnology, Bulletin* 119, 1–68.

Lewis, Thomas M. N., and Madeline Kneberg. (1946). *Hiwassee Island, an Archaeological Account of Four Tennessee Indian Peoples.* Univ. of Tennessee Press, Knoxville.

Mason, Otis T. (1891). *Aboriginal Skin Dressing; A Study Based on Material in the U.S. National Museum,* Report of the National Museum, 1888–1889, pp. 553–589. Smithsonian Institution, Washington, D.C.

Morgan, Lewis H. (1901). *League of the Ho-De-No-Sau-Nee or Iroquois,* Vol. 2, p. 13. Dodd, Mead and Company, New York.

Morrell, L. Ross. (1965). The Texas Site, Carlyle Reservoir. *Southern Illinois University Museum, Archaeological Salvage Report* No. 23.

Morse, Dan, and Phyllis Morse. (1960). A preliminary report on 9-Go-507: The Williams Site, Gordon County, Georgia. *Florida Anthropologist* 8, 81–91.

Myre, William Edward. (1928). Two prehistoric villages in Middle Tennessee. *41st Annual Report of the Bureau of American Ethnology* pp. 485–626.

Neilson, W. A., ed. (1956). *Websters New International Dictionary of the English Language,* 2nd ed., unabridged. G. C. Merriam Co., Springfield, Illinois.

Newell, H. Perry, and Alex D. Krieger. (1949). The George C. Davis site, Cherokee County, Texas. *Memoirs of the Society for American Archaeology* No. 5.

Quimby, George I. (1957). The Bayou Goula site, Iberville Parish, Louisiana. *Fieldiana: Anthropology* 47, 91–170.

Schoolcraft, H. R. (1856). *Indian Tribes of the United States,* Part IV, p. 61. Lippincott, Philadelphia, Pennsylvania.

Skinner, Alanson. (1913). Notes on the Florida Seminole. *American Anthropologist* [N.S.] **15,** 66–77.

Skinner, Alanson. (1921). Material culture of the Menomini. In *Indian Notes and Monographs,* No. 28 (F. W. Hodge, ed.), Misc., No. 20, p. 228. Museum of the American Indian, Heye Foundation, New York.

Stebbing, L. Susan. (1961). *A Modern Introduction to Logic,* Harper Torchbooks ed. Harper, New York.

Swanton, John R. (1911). Indian tribes of the Lower Mississippi Valley and adjacent coast of the Gulf of Mexico. *Bureau of American Ethnology, Bulletin* 20,

Swanton, John R. (1946). The Indians of the Southeastern United States. *Bureau of American Ethnology, Bulletin* 137.

Thompson, Raymond H. (1956). The subjective element in archaeological inference. *Southwestern Journal of Anthropology* **12,** 327–332.

Webb, William. (1938). An archaeological survey of the Norris Basin in Eastern Tennessee. *Bureau of American Ethnology, Bulletin* **118.**

Webb, William, and David DeJarnette. (1942). An archaeological survey of Pickwick Basin in the adjacent portions of the states of Alabama, Mississippi and Tennessee. *Bureau of American Ethnology, Bulletin* **129.**

Wissler, Clark. (1910). Material culture of the Blackfoot Indians. *Anthropological Papers of the American Museum of Natural History* **5,** Part 1.

Yarnell, Richard Asa. (1964). Aboriginal relationships between culture and plant life in the Upper Great Lakes region. *Anthropological Papers, Museum of Anthropology* No. 23.

Archaeological Reasoning and Smudge Pits—Revisited*

LEWIS R. BINFORD

Abstract

In a recent article Patrick J. Munsen (1969) has offered an alternative functional interpretation of archaeologically known "corn cob caches" from the eastern United States. The entire argument as organized by Munsen is designed to meet certain limited conditions which I previously outlined for evaluating a proposition advanced through an argument from analogy (Binford, 1967, p. 8). In so doing, Munsen has provided me with the opportunity for reevaluating some of my previous arguments. He has presented a particular argument, the consideration of which makes possible some further clarification in the logic of the use of analogy in archaeological argument.

V. G. Childe once wrote, "Ethnographic parallels in fact afford only clues in what direction to look for an explanation in the archaeological record itself" (Childe, 1956, p. 49). This point was the central argument of my earlier paper on analogy to which Munsen refers (Binford, 1967), namely that the truth value of an argument offered as to the significance of archaeologically observed phenomena to past conditions and events must be determined by the testing of relevant hypotheses against the archaeological record. Munsen did not address himself to this argument; instead he considered another which I did not develop nor in fact give any critical thought. He concerned himself with the situation to which two or more valid and independent propositions might be advanced with respect to the significance of an observed archaeological situation. I use the term valid here in counterdistinction to *accurate* in recognition of the fact that an argument may be logically valid but at the same time false or untrue with regard to particular situations. I had argued that on the basis of a strong positive analogy between archaeologically observed small pits containing charred corn cobs, or other "punk"-like material, and ethnographically described smudge pits utilized in the smoking of hides, the significance of the archaeologically observed features to past behavior was that they were probably hide smoking pits. Munsen argues that there is an equally strong analogy between the archaeologically observed features and ethnographically described smudge pits utilized in the smudging of ceramics. Here we have a case where there is seemingly equal support for two independent propositions as to the significance of archaeologically observed features. I had previously suggested that when one could demonstrate two or more equally reasonable propositions, the strength of one or both is diminished (I actually used the term *refuted* with respect to the initial proposition) and "a more general proposition could be stated which could then be tested [against the

* Not previously published.

archaeological record] along the dimensions of time, space, and form" (Binford, 1967, p. 8). Prompted by Munsen's argument I have been led to reevaluate my earlier statement. As far as the truth value of any given proposition is concerned, the presence of equally defensable alternative propositions does not in any way diminish the potential truth value of any of the alternatives. The only method available for testing the truth value of equally valid propositions is to test them against relevant materials from the archaeological record. The possibility that there were two contexts in which small "smudge pits" were used in North America does not in any way provide us with sufficient information for determining in any concrete situation whether an observed smudge pit was used for hide smoking, ceramic smudging, or some other task for which we currently lack ethnographic description. The only method for determining the truth value of a proposition, and hence refuting it, is to devise deductively reasoned hypotheses regarding expected relationships between phenomena in question and other classes of archaeological remains. Munsen, by offering the alternative that the small pits in question were used in smudging pottery, does not refute the proposition that they were used in smoking hides since neither proposition has been tested.

The second point of this discussion is an evaluation of the specifics of Munsen's argument. I have previously argued that in probabilistic terms "the more numerous the similarities between analogs, the greater the probability that inferred properties are similar" (Binford, 1967, p. 2). The suggestion here is that prior to testing one might be able to make some evaluation of the relative merit of different arguments from analogy on the basis of the internal logic and strength of competing arguments. Munsen has claimed that "the correspondence of the formal characteristics of these ethnographical features [pottery smudging pits] and the characteristics of the corncob caches of the archaeological literature as summarized by Binford is essentially perfect" (Munsen, 1969, p. 83). I will evaluate this conclusion and will seek to demonstrate that there are probabilistic criteria which may be applied in evaluating the relative strength of alternative propositions. The following ethnographic descriptions of pottery smudging are offered in the development of this argument.

1. *Description of Pottery Manufacture by Catawba Women Living with the Cherokee ca. 1890*

Oak bark was used for firing; Sally Wahuhu stated that poplar bark gave a superior color and finish. Bark was preferred to wood because it was more easily broken up and was more convenient. A heap of bark was laid on a bed of living coals; the vessel was filled with broken bark and inverted over the pile of ignited bark and then completely covered with the same fuel. The exterior bark was fired and the supply renewed for an hour, when the red-hot vessel was taken out. It was kept away from drafts during the burning and the first part of the cooling to prevent cracking. It was allowed to cool near the fire until the red heat had disappeared, when it was removed to the open air. On examination it was found that the inside had been colored a deep, glistening black by the burning, but the exterior, save in spots where the bark had been dense and the fire much smothered, was of grayish and reddish tints (Holmes, 1903, pp. 54–55).

2. *Description of Eastern Cherokee Pottery Manufacture ca. 1908*

"In order to be good for cooking, these pots should be smoked," she said. "If this is not done the water will soak through." So she dropped a handful of bran in each one while they were still almost red-hot, stirred it with her stick, tipped the pots this way and that, and finally, turning out the now blazing bran from each in turn, inverted the vessels upon it. In this way the inside was smoked black and rendered impervious and this without leaving any odor of smoke in the vessels when they became cold. Generally, Iwi told me, corncobs were employed for this purpose, but she always used bran when cobs were not available (Harrington, 1909, p. 226).

3. *Description of Eastern Cherokee Pottery Manufacture, ca. 1890*

When . . . [the firing] process was completed the vessel was taken outside the house and inverted over a small hole in the ground, which was filled with burning corncobs. This fuel was renewed a number of times, and at the end of half an hour the interior of the vessel had acquired a black and glistening surface. Sometimes the same result is obtained by burning small quantities of wheat or cob bran in the vessel, which is covered over during the burning to prevent the escape of the smoke (Holmes, 1903, p. 56).

4. *Description of Pottery Manufacture by the Pawnee, ca. 1840*

When the material was sufficiently dry, they lifted it from the mold and burned it in the fire, and while it was baking, put corn in the pot and stirred it about, and this made it hard as iron (Holmes, 1903, p. 59).

5. *Description of Pottery Manufacture by the Cherokee, ca. 1925*

The modern Cherokee produce a black [on the interior of their vessels] . . . by burning ground corncobs in a small excavation in the soil, over which the vessel to be blackened is inverted (Myer, 1928, p. 522).

In these descriptions we note that interior smudging was produced by (1) filling the interior of the vessel with bark and firing it at the same time the vessel was fired, no functionally specific smudging pit being employed; (2) burning wheat or corncob bran inside the vessel after the initial firing of the vessel, no functionally specific smudging pit being employed; (3) inverting the fired vessel over a small excavation in which ground corncob bran was smouldering (no ground corncobs were described for the "corncob caches" described by me); and (4) inverting the newly fired vessel over a small hole in the ground which was filled with burning corncobs. This case is the only one exhibiting any analogy to the archaeological features described by me. The variability documented above clearly demonstrates that there is no necessary relationship between the use of a functionally specific pit facility and interior smudging of pottery. Smudging is described in the majority of cases as being produced by either using the pottery vessel itself as the facility for the smudge or accomplishing the smudging in the kiln, a facility which could hardly be confused with the smudge pits described by me. One case is given in the ethnographic literature which is descriptive of a functionally specific facility for smudging pottery. The particular context in which this facility was used is provocative and potentially relevant. The pottery being described was manufactured specifically at the request of the ethnographer and was fired inside a European-style dwelling. The use of a functionally specific smudge pit in this case may well be directly related to (a) the manufacture of pottery at the request of the ethnographer under conditions which in no way could be considered similar to the precontact firing conditions and (b) the simple desire of the potter to avoid the presence of dense smoke inside his house where he had fired the pottery.

Two points of contrast are of importance here: First, the techniques employed in smudging the interior of pottery vessels were sufficiently variable to preclude the possibility of inferring the technique used from the presence of smudged pottery; in short, there is no necessary relationship between the use of a functionally specific smudge pit and interiorly smudged pottery. In contrast all of the ethnographic descriptions of sufficient detail cited by me describe the use of a functionally specific smudge pit in the smoking of hides. In addition a survey of over 127 different social units from western United States studied with regard to variations in skin dressing techniques (King, 1947) showed that in all cases the smoking of hides was accomplished by the use of a functionally specific smudging fire. Variations were noted in the types of fuels used, but all were different types of "punk": "Four main stipulations of form of fuel were made: rotten wood, bark, cones, and wood chips" (King, 1947, p. 99). Given the above state of knowledge concerning the two alternative propositions, we may reach a probabilistic conclusion that in any given instance of archaeological observation of a small pit facility filled with fuels such as corncobs, bark, twigs, rotten wood, dung, pine cones, and sage fired in a reducing atmosphere and not disturbed after firing, the probability is greater of its having been employed in the smoking of hides than used for smudging pottery. The latter can be demonstrably accomplished by many other means while the former context of use always includes the use of such a facility.

The second point of contrast has to do with the relevance of the alternative propositions to archaeological remains of precontact age in North America. As previously pointed out, the ethnographic case cited by Munsen in support of his argument that archaeologically observed smudge pits filled with corncob fuel were used in smudging the interior of pottery vessels was an extraordinary case of expediently firing pottery inside of an European style house, and smudging it outside the house, presumably to prevent the house from being filled with smoke. These conditions are not analogous to conditions of firing pottery as known for aboriginal North America. In contrast, the descriptions of smoking hides cited by me as well as those summarized by other workers (King, 1947) are statements of activities conducted under conditions generally unmodified by European contact. Thus using probabilistic criteria, namely "the more numerous the similarities between analogs, the greater the probability that inferred properties are similar" (Binford, 1967, p. 2), we may reach a probabilistic conclusion in favor of hide smoking as the most likely context of use for archaeologically observed smudge pits.

I have demonstrated that Munsen's proposition of functional significance is weaker in probabilistic terms than my original argument. I have not disproven the validity of his analogy nor provided anything other than a basis for making a probabilistic judgment of accuracy in any given concrete situation of archaeological observation. The accuracy of a proposition can only be determined by the testing of deductively drawn hypotheses against independent data, something which has not been done thus far for either proposition.

Finally, I would like to address myself to Munsen's distributional discussions since they provide us with other interesting situations bearing on the problem of archaeological reasoning. Specifically Munsen alludes to the possibility that there may be some relationship between exteriorly blackened ceramics and corncob-filled smudge pits. Munsen notes in speaking of the Mississippi valley:

> There is a high correspondence in the distribution of smudge pits and exteriorly blackened ceramics; for example Fatherland Incised in the lower Valley and Powell Plain in the Cahokia region. The obvious analogy between these two classes of phenomena is tempting, but, although we are not certain how the shiny black exterior surface of such ceramics was achieved, it appears that, at least in the Cahokia area, the process involved something more than simple smudging (Munsen, 1969, p. 84).

The implication in Munsen's statement is that if simple smudging could be shown to be characteristic of exteriorly blackened ceramics he would suggest a functional relationship between corncob-filled smudge pits and such pottery. This would clearly be an argument of *possibilism* since it would be based on the assumption that the methods of exteriorly smudging pottery were identical with the methods of interiorly smudging pottery. The latter is the only context for which ethnographic data has been advanced that links the smudging of pottery and corncob-filled smudge pits. Regarding the ethnographically documented methods of exterior smudging of pottery, I have located the following in a cursory survey of the literature:

1. *Catawba Indians, ca. 1906*

I was informed that when uniform shiny black color is desired [on the exterior], they are, after the preliminary heating, imbedded in bits of bark in a larger vessel of clay or iron, which is then inverted upon the glowing coals and covered with bark. After one or two hours the firing is complete and the vessels have acquired a brilliant black color (Harrington, 1908, p. 405).

2. *Catawba Indians, ca. 1884*

When the potter desires they produce a black shining surface by covering the articles with some inverted receptacle during the baking process (Holmes, 1903, p. 55).

3. *San Ildefonso Pueblo, ca. 1930*

Such an effect [smudged surface] is secured today by San Ildefonso potters who fire a vessel once, take it from the fire, and cover it with smouldering manure (Hawley, 1931, p. 40).

In all of the above cases the mechanics and techniques of producing exteriorly smudged pottery are different from those employed in the smudging of the interior of pottery. There is no indication that a feature such as a corncob-filled smudge pit would be of any utility in smudging the exterior of pots. These data seem sufficient to demonstrate that Munsen's potential argument of possibilism based on an assumption of identity in techniques for exterior and interior smudged pottery would be completely unfounded. Clearly, arguments of possibilism based on observed coincident distributions and assumed analogs are logically quite distinct from analogical arguments per se. Ethnographic data may frequently be utilized in testing the validity of assumptions used in such arguments. This particular situation demonstrates the necessity of examining the validity of arguments presented before considering them seriously and proceeding to the testing of their accuracy. Invalid arguments may be dismissed; valid arguments must be tested to determine their accuracy.

I have discussed the differences between logically valid arguments and the accuracy of arguments as established through hypothesis testing. I have also discussed the problem of evaluating the strength and relevance in probabilistic terms of alternative propositions offered as to the significance of archaeologically observed phenomena based on ethnographic analogies. I am grateful to Pat Munsen for giving me the opportunity to rethink some of my earlier statements. For instance, according to my own criteria and wording, Munsen's assertion that "Binford's specific postulate, i.e., that the archaeological 'corncob caches' of the eastern United States were functionally hide-smoking features, has been refuted" was a justified statement. I had stated that one should "determine if there are any other activities which employed facilities which shared the same formal attributes as observed in hide-smoking pits. If so then the specific postulate could be refuted" (Binford, 1967, p. 8). This is exactly what Munsen did and therefore claimed to have refuted my original argument. The argument presented here is that the presence of a valid alternative. proposition based on ethnographic analogy is not sufficient to refute an equally valid but different proposition. A valid proposition can only be refuted through hypothesis testing. However, when faced with valid alternatives, one can evaluate in probabilistic terms the relative strength of alternatives and make decisions as to how to invest research time in hypothesis testing.

In cases where hypothesis testing of alternative propositions such as hide smoking versus pottery smudging proves inconclusive, one may then be forced, as I previously suggested (Binford, 1967, p. 8), to offer a more general and inclusive proposition. In this case the more general inclusive proposition would be that the observed archaeological features were smudge pits as distinct from lighting fires, roasting pits, etc.

References

Binford, Lewis R. (1967). Smudge pits and hide smoking: The use of analogy in archaeological reasoning. *American Antiquity* **32,** 1–12.

Childe, V. Gordon. (1956). *Piecing Together the Past.* Praeger, New York.

Harrington, M. R. (1908). Catawba potters and their work. *American Anthropologist* [N.S.] **10,** 399–407.

Harrington, M. R. (1909). The last of the Iroquois potters. *New York State Museum Bulletin* **133,** 222–237.

Hawley, Florence M. (1931). Chemistry in prehistoric American arts. *Journal of Chemical Education* **8,** 35–42.

Holmes, W. H. (1903). Aboriginal pottery of the Eastern United States. *20th Annual Report of the Bureau of American Ethnology* pp. 1–237.

King, Arden R. (1947). *Aboriginal Skin Dressing in Western North America.* Unpublished Ph.D. Dissertation, Department of Anthropology, University of California, Berkeley.

Munsen, Patrick J. (1969). Comments on Binford's "Smudge pits and hide smoking: The use of analogy in archaeological reasoning." *American Antiquity* **34,** 83–85.

Myer, William E. (1928). Two prehistoric villages in middle Tennessee. *41st Annual Report of the Bureau of American Ethnology* pp. 485–614.

Methodological Considerations of the Archaeological Use of Ethnographic Data*

Any consideration of the implications for archaeological interpretation of new ethnographic data on hunter–gatherers requires an examination of the general relationship between ethnographic observations and archaeological reasoning. Only then can the particulars of any new ethnographic data be placed in proper perspective.

It is frequently stated that one of the main tasks of the archaeologist is the interpretation of the past and that the primary means available is reconstruction based on analogies to living peoples. Such a view presupposes that our knowledge of the past is only as good as our knowledge of the present and that our reconstructions are valid only insofar as we are justified in projecting knowledge of living peoples into the past. I would like to take exception to the above-stated position and set as the task of the archaeologist and the anthropologist the explanation and explication of cultural differences and similarities. Ethnologists may, by virtue of their particular field of observation, explicate certain cultural forms not directly observable in the archaeological record. The archaeologist, on the other hand, may explicate forms of cultural phenomena not generally discussed by the ethnologist, although these phenomena may be available to the ethnologist for observation. However, some phenomena, particularly those of a processual nature covering considerable periods of time, may be unavailable for direct observation by the ethnologist.

Adequate explanations are in no way dependent upon the data having been collected within any particular frame of reference; ethnologists can and do use archaeological data, and vice versa. Cultural systems function within an ecological field whose structural changes are most frequently not synchronously phased with the life span of an individual. It follows that even if an individual

* Originally published in *Man the Hunter* (R. B. Lee and I. DeVore, eds.), pp. 268–273. Aldine Publ. Co., Chicago, Illinois, 1968.

were to devote his life exclusively to observation, he could not be expected to give an accurate or replicable account of the operation of cultural evolutionary processes. We would expect that some explanations for phenomena explicated through ethnographic observation to be found in archaeological data, and vice versa. Further, archaeological research might be expected to yield explanations for some observations of cultural phenomena made exclusively through archaeological data.

If we define a hypothesis as the statement of a relationship between two or more variables, and if both variables are observable in the archaeological record, then the hypothesis formulated is testable. It is only through the testing of hypotheses logically related to a series of theoretical propositions that we can increase or decrease the explanatory value of our propositions. The same procedure is the only means available to the ethnologist for generating adequate explanations. Methodologically, then, the archaeologist is in no way dependent upon the ethnologist. Archaeologists are dependent for building models upon the knowledge currently available on the range of variability in form, structure, and functioning of cultural systems. Much of this information has, of course, been provided by ethnographic investigation. It is this background information which serves the archaeologist in offering explanatory propositions for some of the differences and similarities observed in the archaeological record, many of which may not necessarily reveal differences or similarities between distinct cultural systems.

For example, some observed differences and similarities may be explained by differences in preservation; others may reveal differences in function between sites occupied by the same social unit; others may document different occupation histories by social units at separate locations. Many adequate and accurate explanations may refer to functional relationships between locations, material items, and classes of human activities, etc. However, as I have argued elsewhere (Binford, 1967) the "interpretation" of the archaeological record by the citation of analogies between archaeologically observed phenomena and phenomena from a known behavioral context simply allows one to offer his *postulate* that the behavioral context was the same in both cases. In order to increase the probability that the postulate is accurate, a number of testable hypotheses must be formulated and tested.

Archaeologists are not limited to analogies to ethnographic data as the sole basis for offering explanatory postulates; models can be formulated in a theoretical calculus some of which may deal with forms without ethnographic analogs. Archaeologists are certainly indebted to ethnographers for providing sources which can be used as inspirations for model building. The crucial point, however, is that our understanding of the past is not simply a matter of interpreting the archaeological record by analogy to living societies, as has been commonly asserted (cf. Thompson, 1956, p. 329). Our knowledge is sound to the degree that we can verify our postulates scientifically, regardless of the source of their inspiration. Scientific verification for archaeologists is the same as for other scientists; it involves testing hypotheses systematically.

If archaeologists and ethnologists are to overcome the limitations of their observational fields and contribute to the general field of anthropology, they must develop methods which will allow explanatory propositions regarding the operation of cultural systems to be tested by both archaeological and ethnographic data. The archaeologist, independent of the ethnologist, must search for order in the data available to him. After the recognition of classes of order in the record, the archaeologist must then develop models that will allow him to relate the archaeologically observed phenomena to variables which, although observable in different form among living peoples, are thought to have explanatory value. The only other alternative is to advertise his findings as indicating a new explanatory variable previously not isolated which might still be operative in the cultural systems of living peoples.

For example, archaeologists and ethnologists may observe different phenomena to gain knowledge of a common variable. Ethnologists may interview informants and determine verbally the jural rules regarding postmarital residence. In addition they may take a census to determine the degree of conformity between the stated jural rule and actual decisions. These data may then be descriptively summarized and later treated as a case in testing various hypotheses regarding the conditions determining form of postmarital residence.

For many years it would have been argued that knowledge of postmarital residence rules of prehistoric communities was unobtainable by archaeologists since it was not "material culture." A Soviet archaeologist, Tretyakov, was the first to my knowledge to suggest that there was evidence for the forms of postmarital residence preserved in the archaeological record (Tretyakov, 1934, p. 141). His work was summarized and commented upon favorably by Childe (1943, p. 6). Tretyakov's argument was fairly straightforward: The form of fingerprints on the inside of vessels indicated that it was females who manufactured pottery. In societies where matrilocal residence was the rule, there would be less formal variability expected in the execution of ceramic designs within any single community than under conditions where patrilocality was the rule, since patrilocality brings about a mixed population of female potters. Quimby (1956) suggested a similar argument to account for observed differences in variability between samples of pottery from Huron and Chippewan historic sites in the Great Lakes. The development and refinement of this particular argument and the perfection of reliable analytical methods have been accomplished by several recent workers (Deetz, 1965; Freeman and Brown, 1964; Hill, 1965; Longacre, 1964a, b; McPherron, 1965; Whallon, 1965). As a result of this work, we can today state within definable confidence limits the postmarital residence patterns of prehistoric communities. Given the discussions at this conference over the nature of the determinants of residence rules and the degree to which patrilocality characterizes "pristine" hunter–gatherers, we may find that some of the answers will be found in archaeological data.

This case provides a good example of a study in which different forms of information were relevant in the elucidation of a single variable. It also exemplifies another important point—the interpretive model for the archaeological data was not based on simple analogy to ethnographically known societies. The model was drawn deductively from several assumptions and propositions:

1. Females were the potters.

2. Homogeneity of cultural expression within a group varies directly with the homogeneity of the group's composition.

3. Many formal characteristics of pottery are stylistic and tend to vary with tradition rather than utilitarian or mechanical factors.

The model developed from these propositions states the nature of the expected relationship between two variables: formal variability in items produced at a given location by females and variability in premarital residence of these females. While the points of premarital residence of females of an archaeologically known community are not directly observable, this proposition remains a postulate. However, among contemporary groups, or groups whose residence patterns are known through documents, the proposition may be stated as a testable hypothesis. This illustrates one of the functions of ethnographic data in archaeological reasoning. These data may be used for testing hypotheses for which information on one or more of the relevant variables is not obtainable through archaeology. While models for the interpretation of archaeological data may be tested and verified on other than ethnographic sources, it may often be more impressive or scientifically more efficient in obtaining high levels of confidence to make such tests with ethnographic data.

This latter kind of investigation was strongly advocated by Kleindienst and Watson (1956) in urging a kind of inquiry they termed "action archaeology." Watson actually did carry out a study of a living community from the perspective of an archaeologist while she was a member of the staff of Braidwood's 1959–1960 Iranian project. Since then there have been increasing numbers of workers studying archaeologically relevant data among living peoples. Ascher (1962) studied the Seri; Leshnik (1964) lived with village agriculturalists in India; Richard Gould of the American Museum of Natural History is currently engaged in research among the Australian aborigines. Margaret Hardin, a graduate student at the University of Chicago, is currently studying functional variability in ceramic styles among Mexican potters. Longacre and Ayres recently reported their analysis of an abandoned Apache wickiup (1966).

From the preceding discussion, we see that ethnographic data can play two basic roles in archaeological investigation: first, they serve as resources for testing hypotheses which seek to relate material and behavioral cultural phenomena; second, they may often (but need not always) serve as the basis for models of particular social relations which are postulated to have been the context for an observed archaeological structure. In the former case, "action archaeology" studies are relevant; in the latter, model building and testing can be related to ethnographic facts, but verification of propositions would remain a problem to be solved by the formulation of hypotheses testable by archaeological data.

Given this relationship between ethnographic data and archaeological inquiry, how can cooperation between the two specialists be maximized for the solution of common problems? In the first place, if archaeologists and ethnologists are to work with common problems, their observations must be geared toward gathering data on the same variables, despite the obvious differences in their fields of observation. Second, they must work in terms of comparable sociocultural units. Finally, there must be a free exchange of information between archaeologists and ethnologists to achieve the first two aims.

The kind of profitable feedback that can occur through such interdisciplinary exchange is nicely illustrated by this conference. Archaeologists have worked too long without the benefits of the understandings of ethnology as to the operation of sociocultural systems. Further, some of the work discussed at this conference was directly relevant to the perfecting of techniques for gaining information on identical variables. I am referring to the "action archaeology" studies of Richard Lee among the Bushmen and Bob Williams among the Birhor. These two studies add tremendously to our knowledge and are two of the most comprehensive in seeking to document the relationships between behavior and the spatial structure of artifacts which would be observable in the archaeological record. Such information will be very useful in testing some of the propositions of Cook and Treganza (1950), Cook and Heizer (1965), and Naroll (1962) as to the relationships between population size and site size as well as population size and amount of enclosed space required. The site maps and structural details illustrating the internal spatial-formal structure of settlements, documented by Lee and Williams, will be valuable in testing a number of propositions regarding spatial disposition and correlates of social status. With the data now available it would be possible to measure the degree to which proximity between living areas in a settlement is correlated with social distance as measured in kinship affiliations. Exceptions to such correlations and the kinds of contingencies which intervene can be more easily spotted with data like Lee's and Williams' available.

On a slightly more critical note, and writing from only a superficial knowledge of the data gathered by Lee, some of the observations made and some of the emphases stressed at this conference bear witness to the need for freer communication between ethnographers and archaeologists. For example, Lee's site maps are informative, yet he uses them to illustrate how little of the physical remains of a living people are left for the archaeologist to observe. However, it should be noted that Lee made only surface observations and did no excavation. In the discussion of the relative importance of meat versus plant food, Lee's exact measurements of intake of the !Kung Bushmen is good to have, but it does duplicate many of the points raised and resolved fourteen years ago and reported in *An Appraisal of Anthropology Today* (Tax, 1953). In this work Linton discussed many of the points raised here and stated:

There are very few places in the world where people live entirely by hunting . . . . You may remember that the occupation layers of Peking Man at Choukoutien have hackberry seeds (Linton, 1953, p. 238).

I suspect that an archaeologist actively engaged in research might have made many different observations than those made by Lee. In his site maps Lee does plot hearths and fire areas but treats them all as the same. Detailed descriptive data on the formal differences in discrete and metrical attributes of hearths used in lighting, heating, and cooking of various kinds of food might have contributed greatly to our understanding of the functional variables which must be considered in dealing with archaeologically observed hearths. This kind of information might help to prevent the simplistic kind of archaeological interpretation recently made by Movius in which the size of the hearth is taken as an index of the size of the social unit occupying the site (Movius, 1966, p. 321).

This critical note is not meant to discourage "action archaeology" studies, but it is to be hoped that ethnologists in making such observations might do well to put their observations in the framework of archaeological question-asking.

The emphasis by the participants in this symposium on questioning certain propositions which have generally been accepted as truisms has far-reaching implications for archaeological research. To my knowledge all archaeological theorists who have considered the role of subsistence technology in evolutionary change have used a rather simplistic Malthusian model for population dynamics. The traditional view, superbly dealt with here by Sahlins, has been termed by Boulding (1955, p. 197) the Dismal Theorem. It holds that the ultimate check on population is misery; population will grow until the nutritional level falls and disease brings about population equilibrium. The fresh and challenging viewpoint put forth by Sahlins, and less playfully by Birdsell and Williams certainly brings into question many anthropological cliches about the origins of agriculture and animal domestication.

One of the most encouraging aspects of this conference is that archaeologists and ethnologists are moving in the direction of dealing with comparable units. For example, archaeologists assume that the size, composition, and spatial structure of an assemblage are jointly determined by, first, the size and composition of the social unit responsible and, second, the form of differential task performance carried out by individuals and segments of the occupying social unit. Such assumptions allow us to analyze in structural terms the contents of sites and permit the definition of the different tasks represented (see Binford and Binford, 1966). In all his work the archaeologist has available information on the behavior of persons making up either task-specific work groups or local residential groups. Any social unit larger than these are known archaeologically only through comparative analysis of differences and similarities in form, composition, and distribution in a generally unbounded universe of sites yielding archaeological data. Local groups and task forces are the social units about which archaeologists can get information without having to work their data through a fairly elaborate body of culture theory.

In view of this, it is very heartening to hear at this conference considerable discussion on form and cyclically varying composition of local groups. The work of Helm and Watanabe is especially useful in this regard and will undoubtedly serve archaeologists as a basis for model building.

But perhaps the major contribution of this conference for me is the stimulation it has provided; the specific data as they were presented were literally food for thought. At the risk of presenting some of these ideas before—to continue the metaphor—they have been properly digested, I would like to offer an argument which is the direct result of on-the-spot linkages made between data presented here and archaeological problems. The following observations are drawn largely from archaeological data:

1. Judging from the scanty information on settlements and from the inferred functions of recovered tools, man's adaptations during the Pleistocene were accomplished almost exclusively through the use of *implements*. Implements have been defined by Wagner (1960) as tools which serve to translate or enhance energy exchanges; examples would be spears, knives, digging sticks, atlatls, etc.

2. Near the close of the Pleistocene and during the immediately post-Pleistocene period there was increased elaboration in the use of *facilities* (this is Wagner's term also). Facilities are objects which serve to prevent motion and/or energy transfers—that is, fish weirs, nets, pottery.

Let us add to these observations some points made at this meeting. Hunters and gatherers whose subsistence is largely obtained through the use of implements (Bushmen, Hadza, forest Pygmies, and during the winter the Central Eskimo) are said to be somewhat casual about death and nonchalant in their treatment of the dead or dying. An exception was the Birhor discussed by Williams who hunt with facilities—nets.

Let us now add one more archaeological observation: Systematic burial of the dead and elaborate mortuary ritual are greatly increased on a worldwide basis at the close of the Pleistocene. True cemeteries appear first in the Mesolithic in the Old World and the Archaic in the New World; the Archaic and the Mesolithic are further characterized by a heavy dependence on facilities in their subsistence activities.

It is tempting to make functional linkages between the structure of technological adjustment, nature of status definition, and hence of attitudinal involvement with persons occupying these statuses as expressed in mortuary ritual. Facilities to be efficient require precise placement in space; their effectiveness is dependent upon energy flow and they must be placed so as to maximize the interruption of this flow. Fish weirs are an excellent example. Facilities further require cooperative labor for their construction and maintenance.

All of this implies that the responsibility for coordination of effort will be assumed and, more important, that stewardships involving maintenance will be established. There would also be a necessary development of rules governing access to the facility and the distribution of its yields. Many other elements of role content would become part of newly defined status positions arising out of the use of facilities at the close of the Pleistocene. It is also suggested that emotional involvements would thus have been linked to interstatus dependencies of an order unknown in societies in which implements dominated the technology. In this new kind of facility-dependent society the death of an individual occupying a structured status position would necessitate the reallocation of his position to others, the retirement of "debts" to his descendants, and many other kinds of socially defined obligations which may well have been effected through mortuary rites.

If some of the ideas briefly outlined above should prove upon testing to have explanatory value, the coincident appearance of cemeteries in the New and Old Worlds at the close of the Pleistocene (as well as some of the "aberrant" features of the Birhor) might be elucidated simultaneously. The development and refinement of ideas stimulated by this conference will be one of the chief profits of having been in attendance.

References

Ascher, Robert. (1962). Ethnography for archaeology: A case from the Seri Indians. *Ethnology* **1**, 360–369.
Binford, Lewis R. (1967). Smudge pits and hide smoking; the use of analogy in archaeological reasoning. *American Antiquity* **32**, 1–12.
Binford, Lewis R., and Sally R. Binford. (1966). A preliminary analysis of functional variability in the Mousterian of Levallois facies. *American Anthropologist* **68**, No. 2, pt. 2, 238–295.

Boulding, Kenneth E. (1955). The Malthusian model as a general system. *Social and Economic Studies (Kingston, Jamaica)* **4**, 195–205.

Childe, V. Gordon. (1943). Archaeology in the U.S.S.R.; the forest zone. *Man* **43**, 4–9.

Cook, Sherburne F., and Robert F. Heizer. (1965). *The Quantitative Approach to the Relation Between Population and Settlement Size,* Report of the University of California Archaeology Survey, p. 64. Univ. of California Press, Berkeley.

Cook, Sherburne F., and A. E. Treganza. (1950). The quantitative investigation of Indian mounds. *University of California, Berkeley, Publications in American Archaeology and Ethnology* **40**, 223–261.

Deetz, James J. F. (1965). *The Dynamics of Stylistic Change in Arikara Ceramics,* Illinois Studies in Anthropology, No. 4. Univ. of Illinois Press, Urbana.

Freeman, Leslie G., and James A. Brown. (1964). Statistical analysis of Carter Ranch pottery. *Fieldiana Anthropology* **55**, 126–154.

Hill, James N. (1965). *Broken K: A Prehistoric Community in Eastern Arizona.* Unpublished Ph.D. Dissertation, University of Chicago.

Kleindienst, Maxine R., and Patty Jo Watson. (1956). Action archaeology; the archaeological inventory of a living community. *Anthropology Tomorrow* **5**, 75–78.

Leshik, Lorenz S. (1964). *Sociological Interpretation in Archaeology; Some Examples from a Village Study in Central India.* Unpublished Ph.D. Dissertation, University of Chicago.

Linton, Ralph. (1953). *In* "An Appraisal of Anthropology Today" (Sol. Tax, ed.), p. 238. Univ. of Chicago Press, Chicago, Illinois.

Longacre, William A. (1964a). Archaeology as anthropology, a case study. *Science* **144**, 1454–1455.

Longacre, William A. (1964b). Sociological implications of the ceramic analysis. *Fieldiana Anthropology* **55**, 155–170.

Longacre, William A., and James E. Ayres. (1966). Archaeological theory; some lessons from an Apache wickiup. Paper presented at 31st Annual Meeting of the Society for American Archaeology, Reno, Nevada.

McPherron, Alan. (1965). Pottery style clustering, marital residence, and cultural adaptations at an Iroquoian/Algonkian border. Paper delivered at the New York Academy of Sciences.

Movius, Hallam L., Jr. (1966). The hearths of the Upper Perigordian and Aurignacian horizons at the Abri Pataud, Les Eyzies (Dordogne) and their possible significance. *American Anthropologist* **68**, 296–325.

Naroll, Raoul S. (1962). Floor area and settlement population. *American Antiquity* **27**, 587–589.

Quimby, George I. (1956). Remarks made in conversation with graduate students.

Tax, Sol, ed. (1953). *An Appraisal of Anthropology Today.* Univ. of Chicago Press, Chicago.

Thompson, Raymond H. (1956). The subjective emement in archaeological inference. *Southwestern Journal of Anthropology* **12**, 327–332.

Tretyakov, P. N. (1934). I Istorii doklassovogo obsh'chestva verkhnego Povolzhya (On the history of pre-class society in the area of the Upper Volga). *Gosudarstavannaia Akademiia Istorii Material'noi Kul'tury (Moscow)* **106**, 97–180.

Wagner, Philip L. (1960). *The Human Use of the Earth.* Free Press, Glencoe, Illinois.

Whallon, Robert. (1965). *The Owasco Period: A Reanalysis.* Unpublished Ph.D. Dissertation, University of Chicago.

Reply to K. C. Chang's "Major Aspects
of the Interrelationship of Archaeology and Ethnology" *

In short comment like this, it is impossible to analyze in detail the arguments set forth by Chang. Since I am in basic disagreement with the propositions on which his discussion is predicated, I shall address myself to these.

Chang states that the taxonomies with which we work should agree in their formal characteristics with the cognitive systems of the producers of the cultural elements under study. His argument can be summarized as follows: (1) Classification "*must* single out modes" (italics mine), the latter being "any standard, concept, or custom which governs the behavior of the artisans of a community." The role of taxonomy in archaeology is seen as the expression of identified "modes," or norms and values, held by extinct people. (2) Modes, or norms and values, can be abstracted from the patterned and repetitive occurrence of attributes in a population of artifacts. Chang's argument is in line with Herskovits' view of culture (1955, p. 354): "The very definition of what is normal or abnormal is relative to the cultural frame of reference." Therefore, Chang appears to be arguing that our taxonomies should be compatible with the cognitive frame of reference of the people under study; then and only then are our taxa meaningful. (3) A typology is judged successful if it works. How do we know it works? It works if with it we are able to identify modes. How do we identify modes? In the recognition of patterning in the archaeological record. Therefore, all workable classifications are "cognitively meaningful," although their workability is always relative.

Chang's position is an archaeological version of extreme cultural relativism, which, if carried to its logical conclusion, would deny to archaeology the possibility of becoming an objective, comparative science. As Bidney has pointed out (1953, p. 425): "the fact of cultural variations in historic cultures does not

* Both article and review were published in *Current Anthropology* 8, No. 3, pp. 234-235 (1967).

imply the absolute value of cultural differences and the obligation to respect them."

I maintain that given the theoretical tools available to us we may: (1) ask certain questions about the past or about the operation of cultural systems generally; (2) develop classifactory criteria which inform on variables believed relevant to the questions being asked; (3) investigate the archaeological record in terms of these criteria and draw valid conclusions, irrespective of the degree of conformity between our criteria and the cognitive systems of the manufacturers of the artifacts we study. It is, in fact, quite unlikely that the cognitive systems of extinct peoples would be in any way adequate to, or relevant for, modern scientific investigation of the processes responsible for observed differences and similarities between cultural systems.

I further question the utility of the general normative frame of reference in which Chang's arguments are cast [see Aberle (1960) and L. R. Binford (1965) for general criticisms of normative theory]. If we were to attempt to work within the frame of questions Chang seeks to answer, we would be forced to explain cultural differences and similarities in the archaeological record in terms of different modes (norms) held by extinct peoples. The value of Chang's position would lie in explanation of the past in psychological terms. In this case, we would be palaeopsychologists, and our training equips us poorly for this role. If explanation is sought in cultural or ecological terms, direct linkages can be made between the relevant variables without translating them into ideational terms. Ideas are cultural and should therefore vary in functional congruence with other cultural elements. Since they are cultural elements, they can never be cited as the independent variables bringing about change in a system of which they are a part, unless one is willing to say that basic biological differences determine variability in ideas independently of their cultural setting. This position was rejected long ago when considering the archaeological remains of anatomically modern man.

I disagree with Chang's view of the aims of archaeology:

Is it possible and fruitful to reconstruct culture and history by classifying artifacts (p. 227)?

The more such elements are available [material referents in ethnographic description] the greater number of unobservables can be restored, and the more specific and realistic characterizations . . . can be given (p. 229).

Indeed . . . archaeological reconstruction is analogy (p. 231).

The importance of . . . the reconstruction of the sociocultural system cannot be overstated (p. 230).

I propose a methodological procedure to identify and characterize the social groups of archaeological cultures (p. 231).

It [archaeology] is a method of reconstructing . . . the ethnology of a people now gone (p. 233).

If the reconstruction of the past were the major aim of archaeological investigation, then archaeology would be doomed to be a particularistic, nongeneralizing field. Our taxonomies would be as numerous as the different historical entities identified, and our analytical tools would be geared to the explication of those aspects of prehistoric life which our current values and biases deemed meaningful to contemporary audiences. This is not to say that reconstruction and characterization of the past do not have their role in the general education of the public; they may also serve to make significant contributions to the intellectual climate of today, as suggested recently by Clark (1966, p. 99). I maintain, however, that they are not the ultimate aims of archaeology. I have elsewhere stated (L. R. Binford, 1962, p. 217) what I believe these aims are: the explication and explanation of cultural differences and similarities. Chang is asking for explication of the past; I would claim that archaeology is capable of more—explanation. Spaulding (1968, p. 4) has argued that the reconstruction of past events does not constitute explanation, that there "is no such thing as 'historical' explanation, only the explanation of historical events." We must demand of ourselves concepts and methods which go beyond the mere reconstruction of the past.

I also disagree with Chang on the roles of analogy and of ethnographic data in archaeology. On analogy, he says:

> Analogy is the principal theoretical apparatus by which an archaeologist benefits from ethnological knowledge (p. 229).
> In short, "archaeology is the ethnography and culture history of past peoples" (Kluckhohn, 1957, p. 46) and its cornerstone is analogy (p. 230).
> Since each archaeological object and situation is unique, every archaeological reconstruction is analogy based upon a number of ... presumptions and assumptions (p. 230).

In his discussion Chang makes no distinction between theory, generalizations of abstract qualities, arguments by enumeration, and arguments from analogy. This is one of the old confusions of anthropology (see Buettner-Janusch, 1957, pp. 320–321, on Boas). Even if we were to admit that archaeological arguments always include an analogical component (and I am not convinced of this), this does not make these arguments analogies (L. R. Binford, 1967). The basic form of archaeological argument, or of any argument which seeks to formulate general propositions, should be logicodeductive. From a set of premises, we can frame testable hypotheses whose confirmation will lend support to the postulates and assumptions (premises) on which the hypotheses are based. It is in the testing of hypotheses as to the relationship between two or more variables that we can raise our hypotheses to the level of general laws of culture.

With regard to the role of ethnographic data in archaeological investigation, Chang writes:

The ethnological recourse does not make analogy possible; it only renders its results probable or even scientifically true (p. 228).

Can information additional to what is already available in living societies be thus obtained when the model of archaeological social grouping necessarily depends on knowledge provided by existing societies? The answer must perhaps be negative until archaeological techniques are better and more self-contained (p. 232).

A behavioral correlate for an archaeological fact may be postulated on the basis of ethnographically known conditions; but recourse to ethnography could never render such an argument probable or true, except in the form of an argument by enumeration. [This is not the same as an argument by analogy; see Stebbing (1950, pp. 243–256) for a full statement of this distinction.] In discussing analogy Childe writes (1956, p. 49):

> Ethnographic parallels in fact afford only clues in what direction to look for an explanation in the archaeological record itself.

I have argued elsewhere (L. R. Binford, 1967) that analogical arguments are more probable or true only when subsidiary hypotheses, drawn from the postulate made possible by the analogy, have been tested against other archaeological data.

There have been several recent statements on the role of ethnographic data in archaeological reasoning (Freeman, 1968; S. R. Binford, 1968; L. R. Binford, 1968); in all of these, arguments are given against the proposition that our knowledge of the past is limited by our knowledge of the present. We have available today both the techniques and sufficient self-containment to formulate testable hypotheses to explain archaeological observations.

The limitations imposed by Chang's approach are further exemplified by his discussion of "activity systems." Chang endorses the suggestion that these should be the basic units with which archaeologists deal. He goes so far as to suggest that "archaeologists . . . structure their types around a series of activity systems such as subsistence, domestic, technological, and other behavioral categories" (p. 230). He further suggests that we might classify our materials according to an activity paradigm such as that provided by Murdock's *Outline of Cultural Materials*. The crucial question to be asked here is: What new information could possibly be gained about variations in the activity systems of the past by simply fitting archaeological remains into types which are ordered in terms of our preconceptions of what those activites were? Our task as archaeologists is to devise analytical means of *discovering* what past activities were, not to fit artifacts into activity classifications arrived at arbitrarily. If all of this has a familiar ring, it is, I fear, because it is just another facet of the old argument about arbitrary versus discovered types (Ford, 1954a, b versus Spaulding, 1953, 1954). Techniques for discovering activities in the past are available and have already been fruitfully employed (Hill, 1965; L. R. Binford and Binford, 1966).

If we take an analytical, rather than a descriptive, approach to the past, the limits on our generalizations are set only by the analytical techniques available, not by our substantive knowledge of the present. The issues raised by Chang have been debated for more than 20 years and are important ones. Chang's views are shared by many of our colleagues. In stating this I am not accusing Chang of being a traditionalist; the originality and usefulness of his work argues against this. I have expressed my views here in the belief that discussion of our basic ideas is essential to progress.

References

Aberle, D. R. (1960). The influence of linguistics on early personality and culture theory. In *Essays in the Science of Culture* (G. Dole and R. L. Carneiro, eds.), pp. 1–29. Crowell-Collier, New York.

Bidney, D. (1953). *Theoretical Anthropology*. Columbia Univ. Press, New York.

Binford, Lewis R. (1962). Archaeology as anthropology. *American Antiquity* 28, 217–225.

Binford, Lewis R. (1965). Archaeological systematics and the study of culture process. *American Antiquity* 31, 203–210.

Binford, Lewis R. (1967). Smudge pits and hide smoking: The use of analogy in archaeological reasoning. *American Antiquity* 32, 1–12.

Binford, Lewis R. (1968). Methodological considerations in the archaeological use of ethnographic data. In *Man the Hunter* (R. B. Lee and I. DeVore, eds.), pp. 268–273. Aldine Publ. Co., Chicago, Illinois.

Binford, Lewis R., and Sally R. Binford. (1966). A preliminary analysis of functional variability in the Mousterian of Levallois facies. *American Anthropologist* 68, No. 2, pt. 2, 238–295.

Binford, Sally R. (1968). Ethnographic data and understanding the Pleistocene. In *Man the Hunter* (R. B. Lee and I. DeVore, eds.), pp. 274–275. Aldine Publ. Co., Chicago, Illinois.

Buettner-Janusch, J. (1957). Boas and Mason; particularism versus generalization. *American Anthropologist* 59, 318–324.

Childe, V. Gordon. (1956). *Piecing Together the Past: The Interpretation of Archaeological Data*. Praeger, New York.

Clark, Grahame. (1966). Prehistory and human behavior. *Proceedings of the American Philosophical Society* 110, 91–99.

Ford, James A. (1954a). Comment on A. C. Spaulding's 'Statistical techniques for the discovery of artifact types.' *American Antiquity* 19, 390–391.

Ford, James A. (1954b). The type concept revisited. *American Anthropologist* 56, 42–54.

Freeman, L. G. (1968). A theoretical framework for interpreting archaeological materials. In *Man the Hunter* (R. B. Lee and I. Devore, eds.), pp. 262–267. Aldine Publ. Co., Chicago, Illinois.

Herskovits, M. J. (1955). *Cultural Anthropology*. Knopf, New York.

Hill, J. N. (1965). *Borken K: A Prehistoric Society in Eastern Arizona*. Unpublished Ph.D. Dissertation, University of Chicago.

Spaulding, A. C. (1953). Review of: Measurement of some prehistoric design developments in the Southeastern States, by J. A. Ford. *American Anthropologist* **55,** 588–591.

Spaulding, A. C. (1954). Reply to Ford. *American Antiquity* **19,** 391–393.

Spaulding, A. C. (1968). Explanation in archaeology. In *New Perspectives in Archaeology* (S. R. Binford and L. R. Binford, eds.), pp. 33–39. Aldine Publ. Co., Chicago, Illinois.

Review of K. C. Chang's "Rethinking Archaeology"[*][†]

This book presents Chang's opinions on the basic issues in Archaeological theory. In criticizing such a work, both the identification of basic issues and the views offered could equally occupy the critic. I shall restrict my comments to Chang's presentation of views since my disagreements also serve to question his identification of basic issues.

Two issues are discussed by Chang which provide the foundation for much of his subsequent presentation. His argument regarding "the primary archaeological unit that regulates the conceptualization as well as the operation of ... archaeological method" (p. 13) is crucial. He asserts that archaeologists have traditionally accepted the artifact as the basic unit of archaeological research: He states:

> Artifacts are end-products or bi-products of human behavior; a study of human behavior and human history, therefore, cannot operate by using typologies designed on the basis of artifacts themselves. The category selected for such study must be a unit that is both meaningful in terms of socio-cultural behavior and practical for archaeological application (p. 14).

Chang proposes that we shift from the artifact as the basic unit to the settlement.

> The reason we shift from the artifact to settlement as the primary unit for conceptualization and operation is that we are primarily interested in past peoples living in social groups having common cultural traditions (p. 39).

The second basic issue identified by Chang is classification:

> If I were permitted to focus upon just a single issue and treat it as the focal point of the

[*] *Random House Studies in Anthropology*. Random House, New York, 1967.
[†] Originally published in *Ethnohistory* **15**, 422–426 (1968).

complex and tricky business of archaeological theory and its development, I should single out the concept and operation of classification (p. 4).

He argues further that by shifting the basic unit of archaeological research from the artifact to the settlement there must be an accommodation to this shift in classificatory concepts. Thus in Chang's analysis these basic issues are tied together closely.

His discussion of settlement is central to an evaluation of his argument. A site (a spatial clustering of artifacts) may not be equated directly with a settlement; sites may be multicomponent, i.e., they may represent the archaeological record of a number of settlements. Thus the archaeologist who takes Chang's advice is initially faced with the problem of identifying the elements in the archaeological record which were components in the life of one community versus another. Chang provides us with the following formula for the identification and isolation of a settlement:

The basic data . . . for recognition and delineation consist [of] (1) artifacts, (2) other evidence of human occupations and (3) their depositional context (p. 41).

The recognition of a settlement involves the recognition of the prior existence of a stable structure; such a structure can be identified when

[the archaeological data] represent either a single cultural tradition or a strong coherence of different cultural strains; that they complete an actual or presumable self-sufficient sphere of day-in–day-out activities, that they exhibit contrast with other such spheres in other areas, nearby or distant, and that they contrast with other such spheres in another micro-time, immediately or remotely preceeding or following (p. 42).

It is evident that using Chang's criteria, the identification of a settlement depends upon prior analysis of artifacts (using some classification) which allows us to measure the homogeneity of cultural tradition and the nature of activities represented and also which provides the facts for comparative study. How can we reconcile the fact that definition of a settlement is dependent upon artifact analysis with the proposed shift from the artifact to the settlement as the basic unit of research and Chang's statement that "settlement is empirical, but anything beyond that is model building" (p. 109)? This problem in Chang's argument stems from his failure to distinguish between units of observation and units of relevance for synthesis. The basic units of observation are artifacts (and minimally, their attributes); these observational units may be variously limited by their availability in the archaeological record. On the other hand, the organizational features of the archaeological record derive from the structure of the extinct sociocultural system whose operation produced the archaeological record. Analysis of the observational units should be directed toward the identification of organizational components of past systems; the settlement is only one such organizational unit. Chang's urging archaeologists to isolate the remains of settlements is fine, but this does not constitute a shift in the "basic unit of archaeological research." At best it is a shift in emphasis regarding aims of synthesis.

Chang's insistence on the settlement as a basic organizational unit reflects further confusion. Other organizational components or properties of past systems might be more relevant, depending upon the problems which the archaeologist is attempting to solve through analysis: units of political integration, sodalities, economic or trade systems, kinship units, etc. The data necessary for the study of such units would not be available if our analytical tools were geared exclusively toward the isolation of and formal comparison among settlements.

Additional problems arise from Chang's discussion of classification and typology. Chang begins by asking:

> Can culturally meaningful classifications be made according to physically observable differences? (p. 77).

I can only point out that physically observable differences are all we have to classify! Chang answers his own question in the following way:

> The "right" categories are those that reflect or approximate the natives' own thinking about how their physical world is to be classified . . . within which framework they accordingly act (p. 78).

This statement shows that for Chang our classificatory units should coincide with the emic categories in the cognitive systems of past peoples. However, typology is the analytical procedure for generating scales for measurement; classification is the application of the scale to a body of data. The value of a classification is directly proportional to its utility for measuring a stated variable or set of variables. There are many sets of variables which we must measure if we are to succeed in studying extinct sociocultural systems. Many of these may be of scientific interest to us but cannot be expected to have had relevance in the cognitive systems of past peoples. Why should we handicap our analytical abilities for studying cultural processes by restricting our classifications to emic categories cognatively meaningful to past peoples? The analysis of cultural process is an activity which can scarcely be expected to have occupied many of the peoples we study. Why should we expect their cognative schemes to be useful as scales for measuring processual variables?

In evaluating a classification Chang argues that the demonstration of "historical significance" or "cultural meaningfulness" for the derived categories is necessary. He states further that such demonstration must be at the level of intersite comparison.

For this demonstration we must leave the single settlement and enter a larger sphere of research, not forgetting, however, that the settlement is the context for objects under study (pp. 81–82).

Once again I take exception. We are concerned with measuring more than intersettlement variability. The utility of a classification can be judged by the degree to which different values for the variables being measured can be discriminated among the units in the investigator's frame of analysis. Why must this frame be one of multiple settlements? Can't we study stylistic variability in craft items among arbitrary and/or natural units within a settlement (for example: 10-ft squares, houses, pits, cooking areas, etc.)? It seems reasonable that a classification which discriminates at this level of analysis might not be the most useful one for measuring variations among settlement units. Chang fails to accommodate his considerations of classification to his advocated shift to the settlement as a basic unit of relevance for synthesis. His discussion of classification is also inconsistent with his discussion of levels of analysis (see p. 108).

Chang's section on microenvironments (pp. 57–70) involves a confusion of terms. "Microenvironment" is a concept borrowed from Michael Coe and Kent Flannery; in their paper this term clearly refers to the components of an ecosystem or more specifically to the ecological subsystems in the habitat of a social unit. Chang uses the term in a way which equates microenvironment to the immediate environment of a settlement. The conventional term *habitat* would be more accurate. This terminological problem is one of many in Chang's discussion of ecology. For example, he ignores the meaning of the word *ecology* and uses it as a synonym for *environment* (example; "local ecological resources," p. 59). He prefers to use the term *ecological niches* to refer to the constituent components of the habitat, ignoring completely the functional meaning which *niche* connotes. These usages are wildly inaccurate, and tend to perpetuate confusion in the literature.

Let us turn now to the more valuable sections of Chang's book. His discussion of intra–inter site analysis is both innovative and more carefully thought out than analogous discussions by many authors. Chang recognizes that similarities and differences in the archaeological record may reflect different and possibly independent types of sociocultural phenomena. This is a welcome break from traditional views which treat culture traits as additive and as measures of one nebulous "variable"–cultural relationships.

Chang is evidently unhappy with the approaches and achievements of traditional archaeology. His efforts for change are necessary and welcome. However, his "rethinking" has missed the mark.

Archaeological Perspectives[*]

A book whose title proclaims something new immediately challenges the reader to verify the claim to novelty or innovation. The purpose of this paper is to justify this book's title by making explicit what is new and, also, how familiar ideas and arguments gain a new significance when viewed in the perspective being developed.

This paper does not attempt an exhaustive historical analysis of the field of archaeology but is rather the selective treatment of several general areas of archaeological concern put into historical perspective. It is hoped that this background will offer the reader a greater depth of field against which to view the substantive papers which follow.

The Aims of Archaeology

The most profitable inquiry [of archaeology] is the search for the origin of epoch-making ideas in order to comprehend the history of civilization (Mason, 1893, p. 403).

Archaeology, by etymology the study of beginnings, has historical reconstruction for its objective (Kroeber, 1937, p. 163).

These early statements summarize the generally accepted view on the aims of archaeology. Taylor (1948, pp. 26 and 207) has thoroughly documented the fact that reconstruction of culture history was widely accepted as the end of archaeological research. Since Taylor's publication, this aim has been reiterated frequently and continues to be stated in very recent publications (Rouse, 1965, p. 2; Meggers *et al.,* 1965, p. 5; Willey, 1966, pp. 2–3; Deetz, 1967, p. 3).

If seeking origins and tracing the history of culture was one task of archaeology, some researchers considered a further aim to be the reconstruction of the lifeways of the peoples responsible for the archaeological remains. Such

* Originally published in *New Perspectives in Archaeology* (S. R. Binford and L. R. Binford, eds.), pp. 5–32. Aldine Publ. Co., Chicago, Illinois, 1968.

an aim appears early in the literature—for example, in H. I. Smith (1910) and Sollas (1924). Concern with the reconstruction of lifeways of extinct peoples has been expressed by many, but probably the most influential advocate for more attention toward this end has been Taylor:

The conjunctive approach ... has as its primary goal the elucidation of cultural conjunctives, the associations and relationships, the "affinities," within the manifestation under investigation. It aims at drawing the completest possible picture of past human life in terms of its human and geographic environment (1948, pp. 95–96).

Most archaeologists would agree that we should not lose sight of "the Indian behind the artifact" (Braidwood, 1959, p. 79) and would accept as a major aim of archaeology the reconstruction of lifeways.

While these aims of reconstructing culture history and lifeways cannot be said to have been satisfactorily achieved, a few archaeologists during the 1930's began to suggest aims reaching far beyond these:

Some day world culture history will be known as far as archaeological materials and human intelligence permit. Every possible element of culture will have been placed in time and space. The invention, diffusion, mutation and association of elements will have been determined. When taxonomy and history are thus complete, shall we cease our labors and hope that the future Darwin of Anthropology will interpret the great historical scheme that will have been erected? ... Candor would seem to compel the admission that archaeology could be made much more pertinent to general cultural studies if we paused to take stock of its possibilities. Surely we can shed some light not only on the chronological and spatial arrangements and associations of elements, but on conditions underlying their origin, development, diffusion, acceptance and interaction with one another. These are problems of cultural process ... (Steward and Setzler, 1938, pp. 5–7).

One year earlier a Scandinavian archaeologist also urged that his colleagues take stock of where they have been and where they were going:

It appears that archaeology, in spite of its remarkable achievements, has got into a cul-de-sac .... The whole subject consists merely of a comparison of forms and systematization .... Brilliant systematization, regarded as exact, has not led to and does not lead to an elucidation of the organic structure of the whole life of the period studied, to an understanding of social systems, of economic and social history .... Forms and types ... have been regarded as much more real and alive than the society which created them and whole needs determined these manifestations of life .... Have we reached a crisis where the procedure and aim of our science must be revised? (Tallgren, 1937, pp. 154–155).

Statements urging archaeologists to concern themselves with problems of process appeared with increasing frequency in the literature of the next twenty years (Steward, 1942, p. 139; Bennett, 1943, p. 208; Childe, 1946, p. 248; G. Clark, 1953a, b; Barth, 1950; and especially Caldwell, 1958). As recently as 1958 this concern with process was still being defined and distinguished from other aims of archaeology:

So little work has been done in American archaeology on the explanatory level that it is
difficult to find a name for it . . . . In the context of archaeology, processual interpretation
is the study of the nature of what is vaguely referred to as the culture-historical process.
Practically speaking, it implies an attempt to discover regularities in the relationships given
by the methods of culture-historical integration . . . . On this explanatory level of
organization . . . we are no longer asking merely what but also how and even why (Willey
and Phillips, 1958, pp. 5–6).

Willey and Phillips' statement about so little work having been done on the
explanatory level was made despite such efforts as Steward's (1937)
investigation of settlement patterns which were later elaborated on in the Viru
Valley project. Willey himself had expressed great optimism about the
possibilities for "processual interpretation" as well as for the reconstruction of
cultural institutions (Willey, 1953, p. 1). Some of the other efforts made
between the late 1930's and the late 1950's toward gaining an understanding of
cultural process were White's arguments on the role of energy in the evolution of
culture (White, 1943, pp. 335–356), Steward's "Cultural Causality and Law . . ."
(1949), and Steward and Wittfogel's study of irrigation (Steward *et al.,* 1955).

In his 1962 Presidential Address to the American Anthropological
Association, Willey again commented on the lack of progress in gaining a
processual understanding of culture history:

Certainly the answers to the . . .. causal questions as to why the ancient American
civilizations began and flourished as they did and when they did still elude us, and what I
can offer . . . will do little more . . . than describe and compare certain situations and series
of events (Willey, 1962, p. 1).

There began to appear in the literature a general dampening of enthusiasm of
those who some twenty years earlier had called for the archaeologist to turn his
attention to processual investigations. There was a similar pessimism expressed in
the writing of British scholars despite the work of such authors as Childe (1936),
Crawford (1953), and G. Clark (1951, 1953a):

We have lost the confidence of the nineteenth century, and are children of an age of
doubt . . . . We must recognize that in archaeology . . . there are no facts other than those
which are . . . "observational data." . . . What we have at our disposal, as prehistorians, is the
accidentally surviving durable remnants of material culture, which we interpret as best we
may and inevitably the peculiar quality of this evidence dictates the sort of information we
can obtain from it (Piggott, 1965b, pp. 4–5).

The linking together of the limits of archaeological interpretation with the
fragmentary nature of the archaeological record is a phenomenon we examine in
some detail later (see pp. 91–96), but the points to be made here are: (1) There
was general acceptance of the three aims of archaeology—reconstruction of

culture history, reconstruction of lifeways, and the delineation of cultural process; and (2) there has been increasing despair over the feasibility of achieving the third aim.

The Methods of Archaeology—Traditional Approaches

This section examines the methods traditionally used in attempts to achieve the aims of archaeology. We shall deal with each of the aims separately, attempt to describe the methods employed, and analyze some of the problems underlying the application of method to problem.

Reconstructing Culture History

Reconstructing culture history consists of arranging cultural units in a way which accurately reveals their generic affinities. Archaeologists have generally operated on the basis of the following two assumptions:

1. The degree of genealogical affinity between two cultural units varies directly with the similarities they exhibit in generically related characteristics (for example, whole culture traits or complexes, design elements on artifacts, etc.).
2. The degree of genealogical affinity between two cultural units can be measured by the ratio of shared generically related characteristics to the number of such traits not shared.

It is evident that each culture trait tabulated in obtaining the ratio which measures degree of genealogical affinity must be evaluated *to determine whether the similarity between traits arose as a function of lineal transmission, diffusion between cultural units, or independent development within each cultural unit.* It is here that a basic, unsolved problem lies: *How can archaeologists distinguish between homologous and analogous cultural similarities?*

As early as 1896 E. B. Tylor concerned himself with this problem and suggested a procedure for analyzing observed similarities by

. . . division into constituent elements showing so little connection with one another that they may be reasonably treated as independent. The more numerous such elements, the more improbable the recurrence of the combination (1896, p. 66).

In other words, Tylor suggests that one might calculate the probabilities of independent occurrences of identical combinations among a set of independently varying characteristics.

Other workers worrying over the same problem offered similar suggestions. For example, Graebner (1911) cites two criteria for evaluating cultural similarities: the criterion of form and that of quantitative coincidence. For Graebner the criterion of form consisted of the degree to which there was a coincidence of characteristics which did not necessarily stem from "the nature of the objects compared"; the criterion of coincidence lay in determining whether or not the trait or item under study occurred as an isolated similarity or as an element of a greater cultural complex. On the basis of the criterion of form, this greater cultural complex could not reasonably be viewed as having arisen independently.

Robert Lowie pointed out some of the shortcomings of Graebner's reasoning: "The comparison of form can never do more than establish the identity of forms; that such identity is to be explained by genetic relationship is an hypothesis" (1912, p. 28). He also noted that Graebner's quantitative criterion was not probabalistic as was Tylor's but was simply the criterion of form raised to a higher level of abstraction and was therefore not an independent criterion for judgment (1912, p. 27).

A recent evaluation of the applications of Tylor's probability method notes that probability calculations of concrete cases have seldom been performed accurately, and in many instances the apparent accuracy of probability reasoning has been a semantic rather than a methodological addition to the anthropological literature (Erasmus, 1950, pp. 374–375). A more basic flaw in Tylor's procedure is the assumption of a worker's *ability to recognize constituent elements which are in fact independent variables.* This problem has been discussed (Erasmus, 1950, pp. 375–387; Rands and Riley, 1958; and indirectly by Sackett, 1966), but no methods have been advanced for the solution of the problem other than the intensive analysis of the distribution and patterns of covariation demonstrable among selected characteristics. Such studies have rarely been conducted by archaeologists and certainly have never been a routine analytical component of the works of archaeologists proposing historical reconstructions. This particular problem has been the almost exclusive concern of ethnographers and is one of which archaeologists involved in reconstructions of culture history have seemed deliciously unaware.

Lowie (1912, pp. 24–27) pointed out another problem in method—that while some workers have attempted to identify similarities which arose from generic connections between cultural units, no one had considered the means for evaluating the alternative of independent development, except by lack of ability to demonstrate historical connections. Without first gaining some understanding of laws of cultural development, such independent means for evaluating particular cases will continue to be lacking.

Despite these unsolved problems of method and our consequent inability to distinguish accurately analogies and homologies, archaeologists have continued to formulate reconstructions using the procedures set forth by Tylor and Graebner on a common sense level, often adding distributional criteria. The principles of interpretation which have guided archaeologists' reconstructions of culture history can be summarized as follows:

1. The probability of diffusion having taken place increases directly with the degree of formal resemblance between items and traits (Jennings, 1957, p. 265; Linton, 1936, p. 372) and with the degree of componential complexity of the traits compared (Linton, 1936, p. 372).

2. The probability of diffusion having taken place decreases with the amount of temporal and spatial separation between the traits being compared (Linton, 1936, p. 370; for relevant discussions, see Wallis, 1928; Meggers *et al.*, 1965, pp.157–178; Rowe, 1966, pp. 334–337).

Such guides to interpretation ignore the inherent unsolved problems of method and epistemology, and most taxonomic schemes proposed as aids to historical reconstruction also fail to cope with them. For example, McKern in his discussion of the Midwestern Taxonomic System made it quite clear that classifications are to be made with respect to a list of culture traits undifferentiated as to the likelihood of their representing analogies or homologies:

All the traits characteristic of a given culture manifestation comprise the culture complex for that manifestation . . . . In any comparison of this manifestation with another, made for purposes of classification, certain traits may be demonstrated as present in both complexes, and these linked traits [serve] to show cultural similarity between the two culture variants (1939, p. 205).

Numerous cases of the application of the Midwestern Taxonomic System (B. L. Smith, 1940; Cole and Deuel, 1937, pp. 207–219; Griffin, 1943; Morse, 1963) demonstrate that there was no attempt made to distinguish between analogous and homologous traits. (It should be pointed out, however, that the McKern system is internally consistent and logical; most of the problems with it have arisen from those who have misused it.) Other schemes have also employed summations of observations whose relevance to discussions of cultural phylogeny and contact might well be questioned (Gladwin, 1934; Colton, 1939). Rouse (1955) recognized the difference between classification based on gross measures of similarity and "genetic correlations"; he went on to suggest that for the purpose of historical reconstruction

. . . it would seem advisable first to eliminate all those resemblances which do not appear to have been accompanied by contact. Next, one must decide which of the remaining resemblances are due to genetic connection rather than to some other factor such as adaptation to a similar environment or attainment of the same level of cultural development. Only then will it be safe to choose from among two various possible forms of genetic connection (1955, p. 719).

However, Rouse offers no guidelines for deciding which traits are generically related and which ones might exhibit similarity from other causes. In short, Rouse's statement shows an awareness of many of the shortcomings of taxonomic schemes but offers no solution to one of the major underlying methodological problems.

It is argued here that the accomplishment of the reconstruction of culture history is predicated upon an overhaul of method and theory, that traditional methodology and analytical procedures are inadequate for the successful achievement of the stated aims of the field. Given our current sophistication in dating techniques, we can fairly accurately place archaeological remains in their proper chronological relationships to one another. We can inventory the remains and discuss additions, deletions, and "hybridizations" in the inventories of sites through time. We can also formulate classifications of assemblages on the basis of summary measures of formal similarities between recovered items (see Ford, 1954); we can also measure likenesses by comparing the total composition of the sample of recovered materials (see Bordes, 1953). Arguments can then be formulated about the probability of one such taxon being the cultural ancestor, descendant, or collateral relative of another taxon (see Hodson *et al.,* 1966; Doran and Hodson, 1966), or whether another unit might be more appropriately considered (see Warren, 1967, pp. 168–185; Sanger, 1967, pp. 186–197; Aikens, 1967, pp. 198–209; Schlesier, 1967, pp. 210–222).

These procedures, however, do not help to achieve the stated aims of archaeology. An accurate and meaningful history is more than a generalized narrative of the changes in composition of the archaeological record through time (see, for example, Griffin, 1967); it is also more than a reconstruction from that record using interpretive principles such as those discussed above which can be shown to have inherent flaws. If we hope to achieve the aim of reconstructing culture history, we must develop means for using archaeological remains as a record of the past and as a source of data for testing propositions which we set forth regarding past events, rather than as a record we can read according to a set of *a priori* rules or interpretive principles whose application allow the skilled interpreter to "reconstruct" the past. We know much too little about both archaeological data and processes of cultural development to make "reading the archaeological record" anything but a shallow and suspicious pastime. What we seek to investigate is cultural process, and only with an understanding of such processes can we construct the events which form the context in which the archaeological record was produced.

RECONSTRUCTING PAST LIFEWAYS

The reconstruction of the lifeways of extinct peoples is the second aim of archaeology which we will examine in order to evaluate traditional methods. The standard operating procedure for achieving this aim is set forth in the following quotation:

> Everyone is aware of the fact that it is impossible to explain and to give absolute meaning to all the discoveries which are made while digging ancient villages. All we can do is to interpret what we find in the light of our knowledge of modern ... [peoples] .... In this way, it is possible to moderate our conjectures, and piece them together by means of reasonable imagination. Thus, the cold, unrelated and often dull archaeological facts are vivified and the reader may have some sort of reconstruction in his mind's eye of what [past peoples] ... were like and how they lived (Martin and Rinaldo, 1939, p. 457). [This statement is one of the first in the literature of American archaeology that deals with the reconstruction of lifeways. Paul Martin was in the avant-garde of archaeological thought in the 1930's, and he still is today. This quotation should in no way be considered a statement of his current views, which have grown and changed remarkably in thirty years—Eds.].

Most archaeologists would agree with this statement (see Willey, 1966, p. 3; Chang, 1967a, p. 109; Ascher, 1961). Analogy to living peoples has been the traditional answer to the question of how one goes about reconstructing lifeways (see Randall-MacIver, 1932, pp. 6–7; Hawkes, 1954, pp. 157–158; Vogt, 1956, p. 175; Piggott, 1965b, p. 12; Rouse, 1965, p. 10; Willey, 1966, pp. 3–4). The major controversy has concerned the appropriateness of a given ethnographically known group or set of conditions as a model for the lifeways of the groups under archaeological study (see Lowie, 1940, pp. 369–370; Slotkin, 1952; S. R. Binford, 1968).

Given the method of analogy to living peoples, appeals have been made by archaeologists to explore the record in search of units which can be meaningfully compared in analogies to living peoples. One obvious plea has been for archaeologists to excavate the remains of entire communities, to concern themselves with the comparative study of settlement, as well as with the internal organization of sites. Taylor (1948), in appealing for archaeologists to study in detail the contextual relationships among the archaeological remains, asked for a search for order demonstrable among the elements in an archaeological deposit. Willey (1953, 1956), Chang (1958, 1967a), and Trigger (1967), among others, have stressed the desirability of the investigation of settlement patterns, since these are observable among living peoples and are said to be informative about social organization.

Pleistocene archaeologists also are increasingly viewing sites as the remains of activities conducted by social units; this kind of data collection is stressed in the search for living floors and in attempts at fairly complete excavation of sites.

The living places of Pleistocene peoples are capable of yielding the same kind of evidence as to the behavior and ecology as do those of much later times when the appropriate techniques of exposure and excavation are applied to their recovery . . . . Such field studies . . . of . . . Paleolithic sites [are] infinitely more rewarding and significant, as can be . . . appreciated from papers . . . relating to living floor excavation (J. D. Clark and Howell, 1966, pp. v–vi).

Another aspect of data collection which has been dealt with in recent years is the problem of sampling. There has been frequent discussion of the use of sampling techniques which are designed to increase the probability that archaeological samples taken are in fact representative of what remains from the past (see L. R. Binford, 1964; Rootenburg, 1964).

Along with these refinements in data collection, there has been a growing interest in the study of living peoples by archaeologists (Crawford, 1953; Kleindienst and Watson, 1956; Thompson, 1958; Ascher, 1962; Watson, 1966). Such studies have as their aim the delineation of behavioral correlates for material items (Chang, 1958; Robbins, 1966), and the purpose of archaeologists undertaking such research has been to maximize their interpretive powers by increasing their knowledge of living peoples—that is, to make more secure the analogies they draw between lifeways of peoples known archaeologically and those known ethnographically.

While we applaud all attempts to increase the reliability of data collected archaeologically and while we certainly favor a firmer basis for determining the behavioral correlates of material culture, both refinements in data collection and increased ethnographic knowledge cannot by themselves increase our knowledge of the past. Facts do not speak for themselves, and even if we had complete living floors from the beginning of the Pleistocene through the rise of urban centers, such data would tell us nothing about cultural process or past lifeways unless we asked the appropriate questions. We can infinitely expand our knowledge of the lifeways of living peoples, yet we cannot reconstruct the lifeways of extinct peoples unless we employ a more sophisticated methodology. Fitting archaeological remains into ethnographically known patterns of life adds nothing to our knowledge of the past. In fact, such a procedure denies to archaeology the possibility of dealing with forms of cultural adaptation outside the range of variation known ethnographically (see S. R. Binford, 1968). In view of the high probability that cultural forms existed in the past for which we have no ethnographic examples, reconstruction of the lifeways of such sociocultural systems demands the rigorous testing of deductively drawn hypotheses against independent sets of data.

This perspective is in marked contrast to the epistemological basis of traditional method, whose implications can readily be seen in a recent statement:

As to analogy, archaeology as a whole is analogy, for to claim any knowledge other than the objects themselves is to assume knowledge of patterns in culture and history and to apply these patterns to the facts (Chang, 1967a, p. 109).

I have criticized this view elsewhere (L. R. Binford, 1967a, b, 1968) and would state here that so long as we insist that our knowledge of the past is limited by our knowledge of the present, we are painting ourselves into a methodological corner. The archaeologist must make use of his data as documents of past conditions, proceed to formulate propositions about the past, and devise means for testing them against archaeological remains. It is the testing of hypotheses that makes our knowledge of the past more certain, and this is admittedly a difficult business. Archaeology as part of anthropology and anthropology as a social science are often guilty of the charges made against them by the "harder" scientists:

The most important feature about a hypothesis is that it is a mere trial idea . . . [and] until it has been *tested,* it should not be confused with a *law* . . . . The difficulty of testing hypotheses in the social sciences has led to an abbreviation of the scientific method in which this step is simply omitted. Plausible hypotheses are merely set down as facts without further ado (Wilson, 1952, pp. 26–27).

Traditional archaeological methodology has not developed this final link in scientific procedure. For this reason, reconstruction of lifeways has remained an art which could be evaluated only by judging the competence and honesty of the person offering the reconstruction (Thompson, 1956).

THE STUDY OF CULTURAL PROCESS

Different authors have referred to different phenomena in their discussions of culture process. The phrase has been used to refer to the dynamic relationships (causes and effects) operative among sociocultural systems, to those processes responsible for changes observed in the organization and/or content of the systems, or to the integration of new formal components into the system. The term cultural process has been used by others to refer to patterns or configurations in the temporal or spatial distributions of the archaeological materials themselves (see Wauchope, 1966, pp. 19–38). The first set of meanings—that of dynamic relationships operative among cultural systems—is the one used by this author and by the other authors in this volume.

Let us examine the methods and procedures traditionally followed in seeking an understanding of culture process, regardless of the meaning given to the term. Most often, the procedure has been to equate process to a transformational sequence of forms, normally summarized in a stage classification. A second, or sometimes an alternative, procedure has been to pursue a comparative study of temporal and spatial changes of archaeologically known cultural forms, to note certain trends or regularities. These trends are then stated as empirical generalizations which, in turn, are taken as statements regarding culture process (see Steward, 1949; Braidwood, 1952, 1960; Braidwood and Reed, 1957; Willey and Phillips, 1958; Willey, 1960; Beardsley *et al.,* 1956). The criticism to be offered here is that any stage classification is simply an ordinal scale for measurement. The application of such a scale to innumerable empirical cases, or even the ultimate systematization of all archaeological materials, can never provide us with an understanding of the processes operative in the past which resulted in the stadial sequence. An empirical generalization of data—no matter how accurate it is—is never an explanation for the data. The ordering of forms of life, the end-products of evolution, by Linnaeus, did not describe or define the process of organic evolution.

Steward has suggested that the comparative study of distribution of cultural forms in space and through time will reveal certain trends, regularities, or patterns for which historical or generic interpretations are appropriate; he suggests further that these trends or patterns reflect cultural process (Steward, 1949, p. 3). This suggestion is, however, predicated on our ability to discriminate between cultural analogies and homologies. As pointed out above methods for such discrimination have yet to be developed. Even if we were capable of making this distinction, the demonstration of empirical "regularities" simply documents similarities which need to be explained; it is to be hoped that the explanations offered would deal with cultural or ecological processes operative in the past.

Rouse (1964, 1965) has offered archaeologists an "out," and his ideas undoubtedly have great appeal for those who would like to study cultural processes but lack the methods for doing so. He states that since we recognize a difference between the *process* of evolution and the *products* of evolution, that the study of the process should properly be the domain of ethnologists, "who are able to observe change as it is still going on" (Rouse, 1964, p. 465). He suggests further that the archaeologists might more appropriately study the products of evolution in systematic terms—by descriptive taxonomic and distributional schemes. In this view, processes of cause and effect cannot legitimately be studied by archaeologists since they are not part of the archaeological record, cannot be dug up, and are not available for direct observation.

Others, working within the traditional framework, have stated that archaeologists *can* gain understanding of cultural process and that the means for doing so is to interpret data from the past in the light of our understanding of the present. An example of this approach can be seen in what Willey and Phillips term "developmental interpretation"—a process which allows the archaeologist to "abstract . . . certain characteristics that seem to have significance from the point of view of the general development of . . . culture" (Willey and Phillips, 1958, p. 77).

However, the decisions as to which characteristics are significant in the general development of culture do not derive from the data themselves; they are given meaning by the ideas we hold about the processes of cultural development. If we simply employ these ideas for interpreting archaeological remains, then no new information can be gained from the archaeological record about processes which operated in the past. In short, traditional archaeological studies have often recognized the desirability of investigating process, but methods for successfully conducting such studies have not been developed. It is toward this end that much of the thought and work of the authors in this volume have been directed.

Archaeological Theory and Method—New Perspectives

We have offered a brief review of the methods commonly employed for achieving the stated aims of archaeology. In this section we hope to compare and contrast some aspects of traditional method and theory with very recent developments in the field which are substantively illustrated in this book. This discussion of theory and method will be conducted under several problem headings.

INDUCTION AND DEDUCTION

One striking feature of traditional archaeological method, regardless of the aims of the research, has been the lack of any rigorous means of testing, and thereby gaining confidence in, propositions about the past. Statements about the historical, functional, or processual significance of observed characteristics of the archaeological record have been evaluated by two criteria: (1) the degree to which our knowledge of contemporary peoples might justifiably be projected back to extinct sociocultural systems, and (2) the degree to which we might have confidence in the professional competence and intellectual honesty of the archaeologist advancing interpretations (see Thompson, 1956, p. 33). Traditional methodology almost universally espouses simple induction as the appropriate procedure, and the archaeological record is viewed as a body of phenomena from which one makes inductive inferences about the past. Such inferences are to be guided by our knowledge of contemporary peoples and also by certain principles, such as mechanical principles which govern the fracture of flint. The application of ethnographic knowledge and of guiding principles are the traditional means for increasing confidence in our inferential generalizations about the past.

Inference is the key or the methodological pivot of archaeology, for it is only through inference that inanimate objects are reassembled into the milieu of life. Inferences are drawn from analogies (Willey, 1966, p. 3).

At the inferential level, the archaeologist is at last providing the flesh for the bare bones of his data, and, if done with care and imagination, such a procedure makes possible the delineation and ultimate understanding of past cultures (Deetz, 1967, p. 11).

The changes in archaeology which are documented in this book are more than simply new methods and new theories; the changes consist of theories and methods developed in the context of a new epistemological perspective on such basic issues as the appropriate scientific procedures to be followed in investigating the past. In this perspective, a central point to be made concerns the role of induction in science:

There can be no general rules of induction; the demand for them rests on a confusion of logical and psychological issues . . . . What determines the soundness of a hypothesis is not the way it is arrived at (it may have been suggested by a dream or a hallucination), but the way it stands up when tested, i.e., when confronted with relevant observational data (Hempel, 1965, p. 6).

In stressing induction and the drawing of sound inferences, then, the stress falls on the psychological issue, as pointed out by Hempel, of how to make meaningful statements about archaeological remains and what they represent from the past. What is argued here is that the generation of inferences regarding the past should not be the end-product of the archaeologist's work. While an awareness of as great a range of variability in sociocultural phenomena as possible and the citation of analogy to living peoples are not belittled here, the main point of our argument is that independent means of testing propositions about the past must be developed. Such means must be considerably more rigorous than evaluating an author's propositions by judging his professional competence or intellectual honesty.

We assert that our knowledge of the past is more than a projection of our ethnographic understanding. The accuracy of our knowledge of the past can be measured; it is this assertion which most sharply differentiates the new perspective from more traditional approaches. The yardstick of measurement is the degree to which propositions about the past can be confirmed or refuted through hypothesis testing—not by passing judgment on the personal qualifications of the person putting forth the propositions. The role of ethnographic training for archaeologists, the use of analogy, and the use of imagination and conjecture are all fully acknowledged. However, once a proposition has been advanced—no matter by what means it was reached—the next task is to deduce a series of testable hypotheses which, if verified against independent empirical data, would tend to verify the proposition.

The shift to a consciously deductive philosophy, with the attendant emphasis on the verification of propositions through hypothesis testing, has far-reaching consequences for archaeology. As an example of such consequences I will discuss briefly two topics commonly treated in presentations on archaeological theory and method: the limitations of the archaeological record, and the appropriate units of archaeological observation.

LIMITATIONS OF THE ARCHAEOLOGICAL RECORD

The arguments on this topic generally begin by citing the fact that much of the material content of an ongoing sociocultural system is lost through decay or the action of other physical agents (such as fire) before the time the archaeologist can make his observations. It is then asserted that our knowledge of the past is limited to those classes of data which survive and that, depending on variations in past behavior, our knowledge of the operation of the sociocultural system in question may be enormously distorted (see, for example, Piggott, 1965a, p. 8). Such arguments also frequently take the form of asserting that since we can never know what is missing from the archaeological record, we can never correctly evaluate what *is* present. How can we know that an empirical generalization about archaeological data is accurate since there may be pertinent and noncomforming evidence that has been lost? (See M. A. Smith, 1955, p. 6; Heider, 1967, p. 62; Deetz, 1968a.)

An excellent example of reasoning of this kind is found in a recent discussion of the proper historical interpretation of distributions of African art styles:

> It is a curious fact that, with certain exceptions in Tanganyika, little rock art in the form of either painting or engraving, has been found north of the Zambezi . . . . It would appear that there is an almost complete break between the painting and engraving traditions of southern Africa and those of the Sahara. If this is so it makes the similarity between the two groups . . . appear as a striking example of parallel development. This would be a very hard case to prove . . . in view of the practice in many parts of the world of painting and engraving on such perishable substances as wood . . . . Indeed there is no reason to suppose that Late Stone Age man in East Africa and in the Congo did not paint or draw or engrave, simply because his work has not been preserved (Allchin, 1966, p. 41).

Allchin's dilemma arises directly and inevitably from the fact that she is offering an empirical generalization directly from the data and makes use of an *a priori* principle for interpreting the historical–cultural significance of the generalization. In this case the unstated principle would be that an interrupted distribution signifies a cultural boundary and independence for the two traditions represented. If one accepts the interpretive principle, the only possible way of invalidating the interpretation is to question the validity of the empirical generalization itself (namely, that there is a geographical break between the painting and engraving traditions of southern Africa and those of the Sahara). The validity of the generalization can be destroyed by citing an empirical case to the contrary (an instance of painting or engraving in the "empty zone"). The generalization can also be challenged, and this is what Allchin does, by suggesting the possibility of such an empirical case to the contrary.

The possibility of an undocumented case to the contrary normally takes the form used in Allchin's argument—speculation about conditions under which data might be destroyed, overlooked, or "hidden." The validity of all generalizations may be questioned if this procedure is followed, since the possibilities for speculation about "hidden data" are infinite. Further, the validity of the interpretive principle itself can never be independently tested since its accuracy is tested only by reference to the empirical generalization it is said to cover. Extension of the generalization to cover new cases simply provides more instances for which the principle might be relevant; it in no way tests the principle itself. Cases to the contrary of the generalization only show that the data generalized are inappropriate to the principle employed; they in no way serve to test the principle itself. This is one of the crucially weak points of a purely inductive methodology. Thus, Allchin's principle implicitly used for interpretation of her generalization cannot, with the methodology employed, be validated or refuted, and the generalization itself can always be questioned by the possibility of citing hidden data or the incompleteness of the archaeological record.

The procedure we would advocate as a way out of Allchin's dilemma would be as follows:

Observations

1. There is a geographical break in the archaeological distribution of rock paintings and engravings between southern Africa and the Sahara.
2. The style of paintings and engravings from the two areas are very similar.

Proposition

The geographic break is the result of there having been two independent cultural traditions in the respective areas.

Deduction

Therefore, the similarity in form of painting and engraving is the result of parallel development.

Prediction

We would expect a similar break in the distribution of stylistic attributes of other items—for example, bead forms, decoration on bone implements, projectile point forms, etc.

Bridging Arguments

Here we would attempt to establish the relevance of some classes of archaeological data to our deduction and prediction. We would try to establish that certain formal characteristics of artifacts, other than rock paintings and engravings, were stylistic and would therefore vary as a function of tradition.

Hypothesis

The distribution of the data whose relevance has been argued will exhibit interrupted distributions between southern Africa and the Sahara.

If the hypothesis were confirmed, then arguments about hidden data would be irrelevant since the existence of cultural boundaries would have been established by independent data. If the hypothesis were refuted, arguments of hidden data, while possibly relevant to the original generalization, would in no way place limits on our ability to gain knowledge of cultural boundaries from the archaeological record.

High-probability statements covering a broad range of phenomena are the aim of science, not empirical generalizations which can be destroyed by the citation of a single empirical case to the contrary. The endless search for data in harmony with empirical generalizations is a wasteful procedure at best, and the data can never serve to validate the generalization. Propositions can be evaluated by deducing hypotheses which must be tested against independent data. The argument of hidden data can always be made about generalizations, but it is significant only insofar as it prompts testing the validity of propositions made regarding the significance of the generalization. The citation of possible hidden data has no inherent value as a statement of limitation of our knowledge of the past, nor is it applicable to the truth or falsity of propositions. Confidence in any given proposition can be evaluated only with respect to the history of hypothesis formulation and with testing relevant to that proposition.

Another common argument on the limitations of the archaeological record asserts that the reliability of conclusions reached by an archaeologist varies directly with the degree to which the subject is removed from discussions of artifacts themselves (see MacWhite, 1956, pp. 4–6; Hawkes, 1954, p. 161; M. A. Smith, 1955, pp. 3–4; Piggott, 1965a, pp. 10–11).

Artifacts and the study of artifacts—including typologies—are placed at the lowest level, and historic interpretations based upon such studies are considered to be of the greatest reliability. Moving into the socio-cultural system is moving up the levels of abstraction with increased use of inferences, and moving down the ladder of reliability . . . . Those who want to make inferences and to step beyond the limitations of archaeological remains can do so and engage in the fancy game of socio-cultural reconstruction (Chang, 1967a, pp. 12–13).

A frequent way of stating this argument is to propose a formal ladder of reliability:

1. To infer from the archaeological phenomena to the techniques producing them I take to be relatively easy.

2. To infer to the subsistence-economies of the human groups concerned is fairly easy.

3. To infer to the socio/political institutions of the groups, however, is considerably harder.

4. To infer to the religious institutions and spiritual life . . . is the hardest inference of all (Hawkes, 1954, pp. 161–162).

These statements are predicated upon two major premises: first, that the archaeological record is incomplete, that many items of the material culture have been lost through decay, destruction, etc.; second, that the archaeological record is lacking in all the nonmaterial features of the sociocultural system under study. The conclusion is then drawn that the reliability of our interpretations will vary directly with the degree to which we can justify the acceptance of a partial record as representative of the total material culture, and also with the degree to which we can believe that the nonmaterial components of any sociocultural system are reflected in the imperfectly preserved material items.

This reasoning is functionally linked to a methodology that limits the archaeologist to generalizing about the "facts" he uncovers. Since preservation is always imperfect, inferences from the facts of material culture to statements about the nonmaterial culture move us away from the primary data and thus diminish the reliability of our statements.

There has been a wide range of opinion expressed on this latter point—the degree to which nonmaterial aspects of culture can be inferred from material facts; the ultraconservative range of this spectrum can be seen in the following statement:

Since historical events and essential social divisions of prehistoric peoples don't find an adequate expression in material remains, it cannot be right to try to arrive at a knowledge of them through archaeological interpretation (M. A. Smith, 1955, p. 7).

Most of the authors in this volume would take strong exception to this statement. In the first place, the argument that archaeologists must limit their knowledge to features of material culture is open to serious question; and second, the dichotomy between material and nonmaterial aspects of culture itself and the relevance of this dichotomy for a proposed hierarchy of reliability have also been the subject of critical discussion (Service, 1964; L. R. Binford, 1962, 1965). It is virtually impossible to imagine that any given cultural item functioned in a sociocultural system independently of the operation of "nonmaterial" variables. Every item has its history within a sociocultural system—its phases of procurement of raw material, manufacture, use, and final discarding (see Deetz, 1968b). There is every reason to expect that the empirical properties of artifacts and their arrangement in the archaeological record will exhibit attributes which can inform on different phases of the artifact's life history.

Many different determinants which were operative in the past might be cited as proper explanatory variables for archaeologically recovered items. For example, pottery vessels manufactured in two different communities for use in identical tasks may vary significantly in form, depending on local habits of ceramic manufacture and on local design and decorative concepts. On the other hand, different forms of vessels made for different uses (for example, cooking versus storage) might be produced with the same techniques and have similar decorative elements. In this latter case, the formal properties of the vessels relating to use would vary independently of formal properties relating to local ceramic techniques. It is conceivable that many other independently varying classes of attributes in combination might characterize the final form of any given class of item. Each kind of independently varying attribute might be relevant to a different set of determinants and would thus require independent explanation for their form and distribution in the archaeological record. Each such independent explanation would, upon verification, inform us about the operation of different variables in the cultural system under study. It is highly improbable that the multiple, independent variables which determined the form of any item or the distribution of items should be restricted to only one component of a cultural system. This means that data relevant to most, if not all, the components of past sociocultural system *are* preserved in the archaeological record (L. R. Binford, 1962, pp. 218–219).

Our task, then, is to devise means for extracting this information from our data, and this demands more than making summary generalizations about items of material culture. There is no reason to expect that our explanations of the archaeological record should necessarily refer to the same order of phenomena as that being explained. If this is so, it follows that we cannot be restricted to the knowledge of "material culture"; rather, to explain our observations from the archaeological record, we must deal with the full range of determinants which operate within any sociocultural system, extant or extinct.

There has been as yet no attempt to assess the limitations of the archaeological record for yielding different kinds of information; nor does there seem to be the means of accurately determining these limits short of total knowledge of all the systematic relationships which characterized past cultural systems. Thus, present discussions of limitations of reliability are inappropriate and are based on speculation. And it is speculation which the more conservative exponents of such arguments have sought to avoid!

The position being taken here is that different kinds of phenomena are never remote; they are either accessible or they are not. "Nonmaterial" aspects of culture are accessible in direct measure with the testability of propositions being advanced about them. Propositions concerning any realm of culture—technology, social organization, psychology, philosophy, etc.—for which arguments of relevance and empirically testable hypotheses can be offered are as sound as the history of hypothesis confirmation. The practical limitations on our knowledge of the past are not inherent in the nature of the archaeological record; the limitations lie in our methodological naiveté, in our lack of development for principles determining the relevance of archaeological remains to propositions regarding processes and events of the past.

UNITS OF OBSERVATION AND UNITS OF RELEVANCE: A BASIS FOR ANALYSIS

The shift to a rigorous hypotheticodeductive method with the goal of explanation implies changes also in our perception and use of the archaeological record. Archaeologists have normally accepted certain observational units—such as the item, the industry, or the assemblage—as the appropriate units for comparative investigation. Such investigation generally proceeds by breaking down archaeological remains into categories based on raw materials: bone, stone, ceramics, basketry, etc. Or, in other cases, the investigator may use functional classes, such as projectile points, knives, axes, etc. Whatever the breakdown used, such analysis serves only to clarify information already available; it cannot increase our knowledge. After his initial comparative analysis, the archaeologist may offer descriptive generalizations regarding his analytical categories; he may also offer some kind of synthetic statement, assigning categories to proposed events which presumably were the context in which the materials in question were produced. The end-product of this kind of analysis is normally comparison, either by verbal generalizations or summary statistics, among a series of sites in order to evaluate differences and similarities which are then used to reconstruct culture history or formulate statements about culture process.

One of the assumptions underlying such a procedure is that the analytical categories used are adequate and useful components of a nominal scale for measuring cultural differences and similarities. By definition the categories of a nominal scale are mutually exclusive and presumably part of an exhaustive scale which can accommodate all archaeological observations (see Siegel, 1956, pp. 21–30; Blalock, 1960, pp. 11–16, for a discussion of scales for measurement). One other linked assumption is that information tabulated by such a scale is additive (this is well documented in Thompson, 1956, pp. 42–45). Stated another way, the assumption is that culture consists of a single class of phenomena which can be accurately measured by our analytical units and about which accurate summary statements, based on those analytical units, can be made. When we compare the summary statements or statistics from a number of sites and observe differences or similarities, these are generally taken as indicators of degrees of cultural relationship.

We can criticize this kind of analysis on two grounds. First, it is highly questionable that the analytical categories used by archaeologists actually measure a single class of phenomena; we would argue that they are measuring along several dimensions simultaneously, that culture is neither simple nor additive. Second, intuitively established analytical units, whose significance is not specified, can at best be of limited utility in testing hypotheses. For in hypothesis testing we must always be able to justify our observations as relevant measures of the variables identified in the propositions we have formulated (see Nagel, 1967, p. 10).

With respect to the first criticism—that culture is not additive and consists of more than summed traits—we would argue further that culture is a system of interrelated components. The archaeological record must be viewed as the byproduct of the operation of such a system, and any single facet of that record can be referred back to multiple variables or components of that system. The determinants which operated to produce one part of the archaeological record need not be, and probably are not, the same determinants which produced another part of the archaeological record.

We may explain changes or differences in certain attributes of artifacts or features in terms of variations in prehistoric economy; such explanations may be largely irrelevant for explaining variations in motor habits as documented in the same artifacts. If we treat both these kinds of variation as undifferentiated measures of cultural difference, we are scarcely getting reliable information about past cultural systems. This same criticism is applicable to consideration of a single attribute and also to generalizations about summed attributes. A single characteristic observed in the archaeological record might well be the compounded byproduct of a number of codeterminant variables.

An example of the confusion produced by treating independent variables as though they were one compounded variable can be seen if we take the case of measuring attributes of people rather than of artifacts. Let us assume that what we wish to explain is variation in human size, and the attribute we select as informing most economically on size is that of volume. We might proceed to measure a large number of people and even work out a taxonomy based on variation as measured by volume. The next step would be to attempt to explain variability in size and the distribution of size among human groups. We might investigate the degree to which size as measured by volume tends to covary with other variables such as environment, diet, disease, etc. Any such attempt would necessarily be doomed to failure, since at least two independent variables—height and weight—were being observed compounded into a single variable—volume. Someone who is 6½ feet tall and very thin might yield an identical value for volume as someone who is 5 feet tall and exceedingly stout. In studying the archaeological record, there is no reason to expect that our units of observation are, in their form and distribution, referrable to the operation of a single variable in the past.

The crucial question for archaeology is the relationship of our observations to the operation of past cultural systems. What are we measuring when we apply various scales to the archaeological record: either nominal scales (typologies) or ordinal scales (stage classifications)? Do our stone tool typologies, for example, measure function or style, or do the attributes which define types involve two or more variables? At each juncture of explaining observations from the archaeological record, we must question anew to what variables operative in the past our observations refer. Any explanatory proposition must be reasoned in terms of relevance to the operation of the cultural system under study (see Spaulding, 1957, p. 87). These arguments of relevance frequently result in the modification of our analytical units and the generation of further analytical categories. This procedure insures the expansion of our knowledge of the past since it facilitates the testing of propositions. With the acceptance of a hypotheticodeductive method for archaeology and the use of a multiple-stage scientific procedure—observation and generalization, formulation of explanatory propositions, testing these against the archaeological data—it becomes evident that the analytical units employed in the initial stage may not be very useful during the final stages of testing. The sets of phenomena selected for observation, from the infinite number of possible observations, are not most profitably determined by the formal structure of the archaeological record itself. On the contrary, they are data which we must justify as relevant to the particular propositions advanced and as useful for hypothesis testing. A crucial role is thus given to the development of analytical techniques and to the generation of increasingly accurate analytical units for measuring cultural and environmental variables. During the past thirty years archaeologists have warned against the mixing of levels and inaccurate partitioning of archaeological deposits; the warning offered here is against the analytical mixing of variables and against the partitioning of our observational universe into irrelevant analytical units.

Relevance is established by reference to the propositions being advanced and by the theoretical context of those propositions. We can anticipate that progress toward achieving the goals of archaeology will be marked by continued refinement of the units of observation by which the archaeological record can be summarized and by the development of more accurate and less multivariate scales for measurement.

Conclusions

I have attempted to point out rather specifically what is new about the new perspectives. In doing so, I have made several points of contrast with more traditional approaches. I have noted that most archaeologists of whatever theoretical persuasion would agree on the triple aims of the discipline—

reconstruction of culture history, reconstruction of extinct lifeways, and the delineation of culture process. There are, however, major differences among archaeologists when it comes to theory and method, and it is argued that revamping traditional theory and method is essential for achieving any or all of the generally agreed-upon aims of the field.

The major methodological and theoretical points of contrast involve distinctions between cultural analogies and homologies, between culture viewed as a summation of traits and culture viewed as a system, between units of observation and units of analysis, between inductive and deductive approaches to the archaeological record. A basic underlying problem involves the use of scales of measurement. It was argued that traditional archaeological measures compound variables which probably operated independently in the past, and that a solution of the problem of measuring along several dimensions simultaneously must be reached in order to determine just what it is we *are* measuring. Despite remarkable advances in data collection techniques and in techniques of analysis, so long as the data from the past are considered within the framework of traditional theory, they can bring nothing new to bear on our knowledge of the past. It is a concern with the nature of knowledge, with the testing and verification of hypotheses, and with the relevance of questions asked that distinguishes much of the work in this book. We assume that the past is knowable; that with enough methodological ingenuity, propositions about the past are testable; and that there are valid scientific criteria for judging the probability of a statement about the past besides ad hominem arguments or "common sense."

The problems raised by the relationship of theory, method, and question-asking were elegantly dealt with fifteen years ago by Sherwood L. Washburn. Although Washburn was writing specifically about physical anthropology, his statement seems uncannily relevant for archaeology in the 1960's:

> The assumption seems to have been that description (whether morphological or metrical), if accurate enough and in sufficient quantity, could solve problems of process, pattern, and interpretation . . . . But all that can be done with the initial descriptive information is to gain a first understanding, a sense of problem, and a preliminary classification. To get further requires an elaboration of theory and method along different lines (Washburn, 1953, pp. 714–715).

The elaboration of theory and method which characterizes much of the recent work in archaeology consists minimally of two elements: First, the active search for understanding variability in the archaeological record—all of the variability and not just that judged *a priori* to be significant; second, an attempt to explain variability scientifically, rather than by conjecture or by "hunch." Some variability may be more apparent than real and may reflect sampling error, partial erosion, redeposition, etc. Only with the self-conscious use of sophisticated method can this "noise" be factored out. Many kinds of variation will be shown to be the result of the normal functioning of internally differentiated cultural systems; others may document evolutionary changes within cultural systems. Still other kinds of variation may reflect changes in content within an essentially stable cultural system. In our search for explanations of differences and similarities in the archaeological record, our ultimate goal is the formulation of laws of cultural dynamics.

Many of the authors in this volume would agree that advances in achieving the aims of archaeology necessitate the enforced obsolescence of much of traditional theory and method, and thus many of the papers in this book are radical in the original sense of the word. If we are successful, many traditional archaeological problems will prove to be irrelevant, and we will see an expansion of the scope of our question-asking which today would make us giddy to contemplate. Despite a recent statement that one should not speak of a "new archaeology" since this alienates it from the old (Chang, 1967a, p. 3), we feel that archaeology in the 1960's is at a major point of evolutionary change. Evolution always builds on what went before, but it always involves basic structural changes.

In a rather caustic analysis of the field of archaeology, Spaulding has stated that apparently

... truth is to be determined by some sort of polling of archaeologists, that productivity is doing what other archaeologists do, and that the only purpose of archaeology is to make archaeologists happy (Spaulding, 1953, p. 590).

We think that this statement was more appropriate in 1953 than it is today, and its inappropriateness today is a rough measure of the extent to which our field has advanced.

References

Aikens, C. Melvin. (1967). Plains relationships of the Fremont Culture: A hypothesis. *American Antiquity* **32**, 198–209.

Allchin, Bridget. (1966). *The Stone Tipped Arrow, Late Stone Age Hunters of the Tropical Old World*. Barnes & Noble, New York.

Ascher, Robert. (1961). Analogy in archaeological interpretation. *Southwestern Journal of Anthropology* **17**, 317–325.

Ascher, Robert. (1962). Ethnography for archeology: A case from the Seri Indians. *Ethnology* **1**, 360–369.

Barth, Frederik. (1950). Ecologic adaptation and cultural change in archaeology. *American Antiquity* **15**, 338–339.

Beardsley, R. K. *et al.* (1956). Functional and evolutionary implications of community patterning. *American Antiquity* **22**, No. 2, pt. 2, 129–157.

Bennett, John W. (1943). Recent developments in the functional interpretation of archaeological data. *American Antiquity* **8**, 208–219.

Binford, Lewis R. (1962). Archaeology as anthropology. *American Antiquity* **28**, 217–225.

Binford, Lewis R. (1964). A consideration of archaeological research design. *American Antiquity* **29**, 425–441.

Binford, Lewis R. (1965). Archaeological systematics and the study of culture process. *American Antiquity* **31**, 203–210.

Binford, Lewis R. (1967a). Smudge pits and hide smoking: The role of analogy in archaeological reasoning. *American Antiquity* **32**, 1–12.

Binford, Lewis R. (1967b). Comment on K. C. Chang's "Major aspects of the interrelationship of archaeology and ethnology." *Current Anthropology* **8**, 234–235.

Binford, Lewis R. (1968). Methodological considerations of the archeological use of ethnographic data. In *Man the Hunter* (R. B. Lee and I. DeVore, eds.), pp. 268–273. Aldine Publ. Co., Chicago, Illinois.

Binford, Sally R. (1968). Ethnographic data and understanding the Pleistocene. In *Man the Hunter* (R. B. Lee and I. DeVore, eds.), pp. 274–275. Aldine Publ. Co., Chicago, Illinois.

Blalock, Hubert M., Jr. (1960). *Social Statistics.* McGraw-Hill, New York.

Bordes, François. (1953). Essai de classification des industries "moustériennes." *Bulletin de la Société Préhistorique Française* **50**, 457–466.

Braidwood, Robert J. (1952). *The Near East and the Foundations for Civilization,* Condon Lectures. Univ. of Oregon, Eugene.

Braidwood, Robert J. (1959). Archeology and the evolutionary theory. In *Evolution and Anthropology: A Centennial Appraisal,* pp. 76–89. Anthropological Society of Washington, Washington, D.C.

Braidwood, Robert J. (1960). Levels in prehistory, a model for the consideration of the evidence. In *The Evolution of Man* (S. Tax, ed.), Vol. 2 of *Evolution after Darwin.* Univ. of Chicago Press, Chicago, Illinois.

Braidwood, Robert J., and Charles Reed. (1957). The achievement and early consequences of food production. *Cold Spring Harbor Symposia in Quantitative Biology* **22**, 19–31.

Caldwell, Joseph R. (1958). The new American archeology. *Science* **129**, 303–307.

Chang, K.-C. (1958). Study of the Neolithic social grouping: Examples from the New World. *American Anthropologist* **60**, 298–334.

Chang, K.-C. (1967a). *Rethinking Archaeology.* Random House, New York.

Chang, K.-C. (1967b). Major aspects of the interrelationship of archaeology and ethnology. *Current Anthropology* **8**, 227–234.

Childe, V. Gordon. (1936). *Man Makes Himself.* Watts & Co., London.

Childe, V. Gordon. (1946). Archaeology and anthropology. *Southwestern Journal of Anthropology* **2**, 243–251.

Clark, Grahame. (1951). *Star Carr.* Cambridge Univ. Press, London and New York.

Clark, Grahame. (1953a). The economic approach to prehistory. *Proceedings of the British Academy* **39**, 215–238.

Clark, Grahame. (1953b). Archaeological theories and interpretation: Old World. In *Anthropology Today* (A. L. Kroeber, ed.), pp. 343–385. Univ. of Chicago Press, Chicago, Illinois.

Clark, J. Desmond, and F. Clark Howell. (1966). Preface. *American Anthropologist* **68**, No. 2.

Cole, Fay-Cooper, and Thorne Deuel. (1937). *Rediscovering Illinois.* Univ. of Chicago Press, Chicago, Illinois.

Colton, Harold S. (1939). *Prehistoric Culture Units and their Relationships in Northern Arizona.* Bulletin 17. Museum of Northern Arizona, Flagstaff.

Crawford, O. G. S. (1953). *Archaeology in the Field.* Phoenix House, London.

Deetz, James. (1967). *Invitation to Archaeology.* American Museum Science Books, Natural History Press, Garden City, New York.

Deetz, James. (1968a). The archeological visibility of food-gatherers. In *Man the Hunter* (R. B. Lee and J. DeVore, eds.), pp. 281–287. Aldine Publ. Co., Chicago, Illinois.

Deetz, James. (1968b). "The inference of Residence and Descent Rules from Archaeological Data". In *New Perspectives in Archaeology* (S. R. and L. R. Binford, eds.) pp. 41–48. Aldine Publ. Co., Chicago, Illinois.

Doran, J. E., and F. R. Hodson. (1966). A digital computer analysis of Palaeolithic flint assemblages. *Nature (London)* **210**, 688–689.

Erasmus, Charles J. (1950). Patolli, parchisi, and the limitation of possibilities. *Southwestern Journal of Anthropology* **6**, 369–387.

Ford, J. A. (1954). The type concept revisited. *American Anthropologist* **56**, 42–54.

Gladwin, Harold S. (1934). *A Method for Designation of Cultures and their Variations.* Medallion Papers, No. 15. Gila Pueblo, Globe, Arizona.

Graebner, Fritz. (1911). *Methode der Ethnologie.* Universitätsbuchhandlung, Heidelberg.

Griffin, James B. (1943). *The Fort Ancient Aspect.* Univ. of Michigan Press, Ann Arbor.

Griffin, James B. (1967). Eastern North American archaeology: A summary. *Science* **156**, 175–191.

Hawkes, Christopher. (1954). Archeological theory and method: Some suggestions from the Old World. *American Anthropologist* **56**, 155–168.

Heider, Karl G. (1967). Archaeological assumptions and ethnographical facts: A cautionary tale from New Guinea. *Southwestern Journal of Anthropology* **23**, 52–64.

Hempel, Carl G. (1965). *Aspects of Scientific Explanation.* Free Press, New York.

Hodson, F. R., P. H. A. Sneath, and J. E. Doran. (1966). Some experiments in the numerical analysis of archaeological data. *Biometrika* **53**, 311–324.

Jennings, Jesse D. (1957). Danger Cave. *American Antiquity* **23**, No. 2, Part 2.

Kleindienst, Maxine R., and Patty Jo Watson. (1956). Action archeology: The archeological inventory of a living community. *Anthropology Tomorrow* **5**, 75–78.

Kroeber, A. L. (1937). Archaeology. *Encyclopedia of the Social Sciences* **2**, pp. 614–617.

Linton, Ralph. (1936). *The Study of Man* Appleton, New York.

Lowie, Robert H. (1912). The principle of convergence in ethnology. *Journal of American Folk-Lore* **25**, 24–42.

Lowie, Robert H. (1940). *An Introduction to Cultural Anthropology,* 2nd ed. Farrar & Rinehart, New York.

McKern, W. C. (1939). The Midwestern taxonomic method as an aid to archaeological culture study. *American Antiquity* **4**, 301–313.

MacWhite, Eoin. (1956). On the interpretation of archeological evidence in historical and sociocultural terms. *American Anthropologist* **58**, 3–25.

Martin, Paul S., and John Rinaldo. (1939). Modified basket maker sites Ackmen-Lowry area southwestern Colorado. *Anthropological Series, Field Museum of Natural History* **23**, Publ. 444, 307–444.

Mason, Otis T. (1893). *The Birth of Invention,* Annual Report of the National Museum, 1892. Smithsonian Institution, Washington, D.C.

Meggers, Betty J., Clifford Evans, and Emillio Estrada. (1965). Early formative period of coastal Ecuador: The Valdivia and Machalilla phases. *Smithsonian Contributions to Anthropology* **1**.

Morse, Dan F. (1963). The Steuben village and mounds: A multicomponent late Hopewell site in Illinois. *Anthropological Papers* No. 21.

Nagel, Ernest. (1967). The nature and aim of science. In *Philosophy of Science Today* (S. Morganbesser, ed.), pp. 3–13. Basic Books, New York.

Piggott, Stuart. (1965a). *Ancient Europe: From the Beginnings of Agriculture to Classical Antiquity.* Aldine Publ. Co., Chicago, Illinois.

Piggott, Stuart. (1965b). *Approach to Archaeology.* McGraw-Hill, New York, Illinois. (Paperbacks, Harvard Univ. Press, Cambridge, Massachusetts).

Randall-MacIver, David. (1932). Archaeology as a science. *Antiquity* 7, 5–20.

Rands, Robert L., and Carroll L. Riley. (1958). Diffusion and discontinuous distribution. *American Anthropologist* 60, 274–297.

Robbins, Michael C. (1966). House types and settlement patterns: An application of ethnology to archaeological interpretation. *Minnesota Archaeologist* 28, 3–35.

Rootenberg, S. (1964). Archaeological field sampling. *American Antiquity* 30, 111–188.

Rouse, Irving. (1955). On the correlation of phases of culture. *American Anthropologist* 57, 713–722.

Rouse, Irving. (1964). Archaeological approaches to cultural evolution. In *Explorations in Cultural Anthropology* (W. Goodenough, ed.), pp.455– 468. McGraw-Hill, New York.

Rouse, Irving. (1965). The place of "peoples" in prehistoric research. *Journal of the Royal Anthropological Institute* 95, 1–15.

Rowe, John Howland. (1966). Diffusionism and archaeology. *American Antiquity* 31, 334–337.

Sackett, James R. (1966). Quantitative analysis of Upper Paleolithic stone tools. *American Anthropologist* 68, 356–394.

Sanger, David. (1967). Prehistory of the Pacific northwest plateau as seen from the interior of British Columbia. *American Antiquity* 32, 186–197.

Schlesier, Karl H. (1967). Sedna Creek: Report on an archaeological survey of the arctic slope of the Brooks Range. *American Antiquity* 32, 210–224.

Service, Elman R. (1964). Archaeological theory and ethnological fact. In *Process and Pattern in Culture: Essays in Honor of Julian H. Steward* (R. A. Manners, ed.), pp. 364–375. Aldine Publ. Co., Chicago, Illinois.

Siegel, Sidney. (1956). *Nonparametric Statistics for the Behavioral Sciences.* McGraw-Hill, New York.

Slotkin, J. S. (1952). Some basic methodological problems in prehistory. *Southwestern Journal of Anthropology* 8, 442–443.

Smith, Benjamin L. (1940). The Midwestern taxonomic method and its application to an eastern Massachusetts group. *Bulletin of the Massachusetts Archaeological Society* 2, 1–13.

Smith, H. I. (1910). Prehistoric ethnology of a Kentucky site. *Anthropological Papers* 6, No. 2.

Smith, M. A. (1955). The limitations of inference in archaeology. *Archaeological Newsletter* 6, 3–7.

Sollas, W. J. (1924). *Ancient Hunters and their Modern Representatives,* 3rd rev. ed. Macmillan, New York.

Spaulding, A. C. (1953). Review of "Measurements of some prehistoric design developments in the southeastern states" by James A. Ford. *American Anthropologist* 55, 588–591.

Spaulding, A. C. (1957). Review of "Method and theory in American archaeology," by Gordon R. Willey and Philip Phillips. *American Antiquity* 23, 85–87.

Steward, Julian H. (1937). Ecological aspects of southwestern society. *Anthropos,* 32, 87–114.

Steward, Julian H. (1942). The direct historical approach to archaeology. *American Antiquity* 7, 337–343.

Steward, Julian H. (1949). Cultural causality and law: A trial formulation of the development of early civilizations. *American Anthropologist* **51**, 1–28.

Steward, Julian H. (1960). Evolutionary principles and social types. In *The Evolution of Man* (S. Tax, ed.), Vol. 2 of *Evolution after Darwin.* Univ. of Chicago Press, Chicago.

Steward, Julian H., and Frank M. Setzler. (1938). Function and configuration in archaeology. *American Antiquity* **4**, 4–10.

Steward, Julian H., *et al.* (1955). Irrigation civilizations: A comparative study. *Social Science Monographs* **1**.

Tallgren, A. M. (1937). The method of prehistoric archaeology. *Antiquity* **11**, 152–161.

Taylor, Walter W. (1948). A study of archeology. Memoir No. 69. *American Anthropologist* **50**, Part 2.

Thompson, Raymond H. (1956). The subjective element in archaeological inference. *Southwestern Journal of Anthropology* **12**, 327–332.

Thompson, Raymond H. (1958). Modern Yucatan Maya pottery making. Memoirs of the Society for American Archaeology, No. 15. *American Antiquity* **23**, Part 2.

Trigger, Bruce G. (1967). Settlement archaeology—its goals and promise. *American Antiquity* **32**, 149–159.

Tylor, E. B. (1896). On American lot-games as evidence of Asiatic intercourse before the time of Columbus. *Internationales Archiv für Ethnographie* **9**.

Vogt, Evon Z. (1956). An appraisal of "Prehistoric settlement patterns in the New World." In *Prehistoric Settlement Patterns in the New World* (G. R. Willey, ed.), Viking Fund Publications in Anthropology No. 23. Wenner-Gren Foundation for Anthropological Research, New York.

Wallis, Wilson D. (1928). Probability and the diffusion of culture traits. *American Anthropologist* **30**, 94–106.

Warren, Claude N. (1967). The San Dieguito complex: A review and hypothesis. *American Antiquity* **32**, 168–185.

Washburn, S. L. (1953). The strategy of physical anthropology. In *Anthropology Today* (A. L. Kroeber, ed.), pp. 714–727. Univ. of Chicago Press, Chicago.

Watson, Patty Jo. (1966). *Clues to Iranian Prehistory in Modern Village Life.* University Museum of the University of Pennsylvania, Philadelphia.

Wauchope, Robert. (1966). Archaeological survey of northern Georgia, with a test of some cultural hypotheses. *American Antiquity* **3**, Part 2, Mem. No. 21.

White, Leslie A. (1943). Energy and the evolution of culture. *American Anthropologist* **45**, 335–356.

Willey, Gordon R. (1953). Prehistoric settlement patterns in the Viru Valley, Peru. *Bureau of American Ethnology Bulletin* **155**.

Willey, Gordon R., ed. (1956). *Prehistoric Settlement Patterns in the New World,* Viking Fund Publications in Anthropology No. 23. Wenner-Gren Foundation for Anthropological Research, New York.

Willey, Gordon R. (1960). Historical patterns and evolution in native New World cultures. In *The Evolution of Man* (S. Tax, ed.), Vol. 2 of *Evolution after Darwin.* Univ. of Chicago Press, Chicago.

Willey, Gordon R. (1962). The early great styles and the rise of the Pre-Columbian civilizations. *American Anthropologist* **64**, 1–14.

Willey, Gordon R. (1966). *An Introduction to American Archaeology,* Vol. 1: *North and Middle America.* Prentice-Hall, Englewood Cliffs, New Jersey.

Willey, Gordon R., and Philip Phillips. (1958). *Method and Theory in American Archaeology.* Univ. of Chicago Press, Chicago.

Wilson, E. Bright, Jr. (1952). *An Introduction to Scientific Research.* McGraw-Hill, New York.

Originally published in *New Perspectives in Archaeology* (S. R. Binford and L. R. Binford, eds.), pp. 5–32. Aldine Publ. Co., Chicago, Illinois, 1968.

Comments on Evolution*

The purpose of this paper is to discuss the problem of evolutionary studies in anthropology from the perspective of general systems theory and ecology. Distinctions recently advanced by Sahlins and Service between general and specific evolution will be considered since they might contribute to the resolution of problems in evolutionary anthropology.

If we specify that we are interested in evolutionary change, does the qualification "evolutionary" suggest that there are other kinds of change and that evolutionary change is only one among several forms? The modifier *evolutionary* implies that we are dealing with change occurring within maximizing systems. Evolutionary theorists refer to "adaptation" (Simpson, 1952; Odom, 1959), to more efficient utilization of resources (Huxley, 1943, p. 387), to maximizing energy flux through the system (Lotka, 1922, p. 149), and reproductive advantage. These statements are all made in terms of a basic (although perhaps implicit) distinction between living and nonliving systems. The importance of this distinction has been dealt with extensively by White:

> The second Law of Thermodynamics tells us that the cosmos as a whole is breaking down structurally and running down dynamically; matter is becoming less organized and energy more uniformly diffused. But in a tiny sector of the cosmos, namely in living material systems, the direction of the cosmic process is reversed; matter becomes more highly organized and energy more concentrated. Life is a building up process. But in order to run counter to the cosmic current, biological organisms must draw upon free energy in non-living systems, capture it and put it to work in the maintenance of the vital process. All life is a struggle for free energy. Biological evolution is simply an expression of the thermodynamic process that moves in the direction opposite to that specified for the cosmos as a whole, by the Second Law. It is a movement toward greater organization,

* Originally published under the title "Conceptual Problems in Dealing with Units and Rates of Cultural Evolution," *Anthropology U.C.L.A.* **1**, 27–35 (1969). The material printed here has been revised considerably since published in 1969. The content of this paper is essentially my lecture before the University of Chicago faculty in 1960.

greater differentiation of structure, increased specialization of function, higher levels of integration, and greater degrees of energy concentration (White, 1949, p. 367).

Evolutionary processes might be defined minimally as those which operate between a living system and its environmental field. They may result in modification of the magnitude or complexity of the living system. The term "field" is used here in the same sense in which the term is used by physicists—that is, the totality of the subsystem, elements, or conditions external to the organization of the system under study that may impinge on it in a determinant manner. Living systems normally exist in a field which also includes other living systems, and the study of the interrelationships that one such system maintains with field variables is an ecological study; by this definition, evolutionary processes are one form of ecological dynamics. Since evolution is the dynamic process of interaction between a living system and its field, very different problems might be discussed under the ecological or evolutionary rubic, depending upon the criteria the scientist uses for isolating a system and specifying its field.

In anthropology the term evolution has frequently been used to designate sequences of "progressive" change, with no attention given to the organizational properties of the field (environment) which constitutes the context in which change occurred. For example, the term "evolution" has been employed to describe the sequence of changes in the history of writing, picture writing, rebus, to phonetic script. In White's terms these changes represent a "temporal–formal process" and therefore evolution. Similarly, many authors have written of the evolution of stone tools, the ax, the gun, or other artifactural or mechanical systems which, in their history of usage can be shown to progress from simple to complex forms of componental arrangement. [An excellent analysis of this type of evolution can be found in Wagner (1960, p. 103).] This type of change occurs *within* cultural systems; systems in which a logical, goal-oriented human being, or a group of humans, may initiate change of a maximizing type with regard to some incorporated component. This type of evolution is limited by the stability of the cultural environment of the actors and by the generality of function of the particular cultural element or complex being studied. In short we are always initially dealing with a *functional* problem rather than an evolutionary one. A nonliving component of a living cultural system such as a tool type, an ax, and forms of writing may exhibit change through time but cannot properly be said to evolve since they are not living systems.

I have thus far stressed the point that evolution is a process operative at the interface of a living system and its field. We may generalize that we can identify the operation of evolution at the living systems level when we can demonstrate structural change. We may do this by isolating certain components of a system and monitoring their patterns of variability with respect to the reference dimensions of time and space. If we are successful in demonstrating directionality in the patterning of variability, either temporally or spatially, we may suspect that this patterning is informing us about structural changes or differences occurring within or between cultural systems. It should be pointed out that such patterning may not always be informative with regard to evolutionary processes. Other processes (succession, see this volume, Part IV) and functional modifications with regard to the content of a system unrelated to structural change in the organizational properties of the system itself may result in patterns of directionality for forms viewed against the reference dimensions of time and/or space. We can also expect variability in and among components of a system to result from the action of homeostatic regulators within the cultural system serving to maintain equilibrium relationships between the system and its environment. Such variability would not be indicative of evolutionary change.

In short, formal change in parts of systems, while possibly indicative of evolutionary change in the systems of which they were components, cannot be properly referred to as evolutionary since the explanations for the observed patterning in a partative unit are primarily functional and only secondarily evolutionary. The unit of evolutionary relevance is the organizationally integrated living system as a whole, not its participant parts.

As a way of explicating this point consider for a moment the problem of rates of evolution. We must distinguish between rates with regard to the process of evolution and rates of change in designated classes of phenomena which were organizationally parts or components or characteristics of living systems. I would assert that we cannot yet begin to measure evolutionary processes operative per time unit. We can identify variations in the magnitude and duration of evolutionary episodes; we can also measure rates of change in some classes of phenomena. The latter we may accept as indicators of evolutionary process, but we are far from the level of theoretical or methodological sophistication needed to measure rates of the operation of evolutionary processes per se.

For example, if we wish to study the formal changes in spear points through the Pleistocene, on the assumption that this indicates something about the evolution of the cultural systems in which they were elements we can actually arrange stone points against a time scale for the Pleistocene and determine the rate of change per time unit. This measurement, however, tells us nothing of the selective pressures which operated on the systems to produce accommodative changes in its parts. What we measure is the rate of change of formal attributes of artifacts and certainly not "rates of evolution." (We add parenthetically that until anthropologists come to grips with the necessity of analyzing the environmental field of the system which they choose to study, they cannot even begin to identify the selective pressures producing change, let alone measure the intensity of such pressures and the response of the system to them.)

The problem of appropriate units for evolutionary study has been discussed in a number of contexts; however, recently it has arisen in the context of arguments regarding units appropriate to the study of different "aspects" of evolution. Sahlins and Service (1960) have proposed the distinction between "general" and "specific" evolution as different "aspects" of total evolution which should be appropriately studied with different units and hence different research strategies. White (1960) has stated that these proposals should "help to end the inane debate about unilinear (or universal) evolution versus multilinear evolution." The distinctions offered by Sahlins and Service were designed to handle problems arising from their recognition that evolution may result in different kinds of change—diversification as well as the appearance of progressive forms:

> Any given change in a form of life or culture can be viewed either in the perspective of adaptation or from the point of view of overall progress. However, the context is very important: a difference in taxonomy is required in examining these two aspects of evolution. Concerned with lines of descent the study of specific evolution employs phylogenetic classification. In general, evolutionary outlook emphasis shifts to the character of progress itself, and forms are classed in stages or levels of development without reference to phylogeny.

Elsewhere they state:

> In sum, specific evolution is the phylogenetic, adaptive, diversifying specializing, ramifying aspect of total evolution. It is in this respect that evolution is often equated with movement from homogeneity to heterogeneity. But general evolution is another aspect. It is the emergence of higher forms of life, regardless of particular lines of descent or historical sequences of adaptive modification. In the broader perspective of general evolution, organisms are taken out of their respective lineages and grouped into types which represent the successive levels of all around progress that evolution has brought forth.

According to these statements, "specific" evolution involves the study of change arising from the operation of evolutionary processes with respect to a concrete, temporally–spatially discrete system. The study of "general" evolution involves the comparison of systems scaled according to some acceptable measure of progress. The objectives of general evolutionary research are defined as the "determination and explanation of the successive transformations of culture through its several stages of overall progress" (Sahlins and Service, 1960, p. 29).

In short the general evolutionist attempts to explain certain ordered arrangements of the products of evolution; the specific evolutionist studies the organized relationships existing between a living system and its environmental field. As presented there, these research strategies would be complementary and certainly equally appropriate. Nevertheless, it is believed by this author that the above is an inappropriate summary of the differences between White and Steward. More than strategy preferences are involved.

We argue that the locus of evolutionary change is between a system and its environment, and the outcome of the operation of evolutionary process could be extinction, a decrease in complexity, reorganization of the system without any major increase or decrease in complexity, or the "emergence of higher forms." Explanations offered for any of these different "outcomes" must have reference to common sets of ecological conditions, in short must have reference to forms and kinds of selective pressures operative in concrete environments.

Methodologically speaking, Sahlins and Service cite a strategy for the study of the "general" aspect of "total evolution" which makes use of a formal scale for measurement, an instrument designed to order either intervally or ordinally sociocultural systems with respect to "progress" or complexity. This procedure takes "organisms are taken out of their respective lineages and grouped then into types" (Sahlins and Service, 1960, p. 16). Cannot we study the "adaptive, diversifying specializing ramifying aspect of total evolution" with a similar strategy? Of course we can. We can control for complexity differences by selecting all those societies tabulated as alike on our scale for measuring complexity and then devise nominal scales for tabulating them into "types" controling for "diversity." Similarly we may select a specific system for phylogenetic study and scale it at different times in its history for increases in complexity. If differences are noted, is the explanatory problem any different than if we had noted the difference in complexity between systems unrelated phylogenetically? I think not. The proposed strategies are not mutually exclusive in their appropriateness for studying problems of "progress" versus "diversity."

Taking a different approach let us examine the alternative strategies. If we are concerned with the problem of societies differing in complexity or degrees of "progress," we would need to develop a scale for measuring this variable. We may then tabulate a sample of societies with respect to this scale. At this juncture we may ask a series of empirical questions regarding characteristics not included in our original scale for measuring complexity necessarily shared among societies grouped as *alike* on that scale. We might also investigate differences notable among societies grouped as *different* on that scale and offer empirical generalizations regarding diversity not correlated with complexity. By following these approaches would we be doing general evolutionary studies? I think not. The crucial point would be when we turned our attention to the *explanation* of noted differences and similarities. At that point we would necessarily be involving ourselves in evolutionary studies.

If, on the other hand, we were investigating a specific concrete system "multilineally" describing its properties and formal patterning through time, we might equally approach this study in different ways. We might seek to explain any transformations noted in levels of complexity, or forms or organization, or we might seek to offer empirical generalizations regarding the observed patterning through time or to note parallels with other known sequences. In the latter situation, we would be observing the results of evolution, and until we asked the explanatory question we would not be engaged in an evolutionary study.

If our concern is with empirical generalization and descriptions of difference and similarities and we never ask explanatory questions or venture explanatory propositions, our study will never be evolutionary. This is true regardless of numerous demonstrations of directionality in complexity, transformational sequences of forms through time, etc. Concern with evolution is concern with the operative processes which explain temporal patterning in the products of evolution. Descriptive concern with the patterning, in the absence of explanatory concern, is not evolutionary research.

I would argue that the strategies outlined as general and specific: (in the former case using a dimension of form (complexity) as the reference dimension against which to view variability and in the latter using time and space as reference dimension against which to view an array of variability) do not distinguish between evolutionary or nonevolutionary studies nor do they distinguish between different aspects of evolution. The distinction simply differentiates between research strategies, and these strategies are not mutually exclusive in appropriateness for investigating problems of diversity versus progress.

How then does Sahlin's and Service's distinction help to end the debate between White (unilinear evolution) and Steward (multilinear evolution)? I suggest that it does not since a much more basic issue stands behind this debate in which the choice of strategies is only epiphenomenal.

The most outspoken advocate of unilinear evolution has been Leslie White. He has provided us with a set of propositions concerning the status of culture as a living system investigated from a materialistic perspective. He has argued that culture exhibits characteristics which demonstrate that its operation is not covered by the second law of thermodynamics and, therefore, that it can justifiably be considered a living system. White has laid the theoretical framework for a logicodeductive science of culture.

White's writings have consisted of arguments documenting the inadequacies of idealistic, vitalistic, and reductionist philosophies. The specifics of White's work—his demonstrations of the relevance of systems theory to culture—do not exhaust the potential of his theoretical propositions for increasing our understanding of culture as has been claimed by some authors (see Steward, 1955, p. 17). On the contrary, his work offers the theoretical framework for a science of culture.

The work of Julian Steward has often been placed in juxtaposition to White's work as an alternative approach. Steward advocates a "multilinear" approach to the study of cultural evolution:

Multilinear evolution is essentially a methodology based on the assumption that significant regularities in cultural change occur, and it is concerned with the determination of cultural laws. Its method is empirical rather than deductive. It is inevitably concerned also with historical reconstruction, but it does not expect that historical data can be classified in universal stages. It is interested in particular cultures, but instead of finding local variations and diversity, troublesome facts which force the frame of reference from the particular to the general, it deals only with those limited parallels of form, function, and sequence which have empirical validity . . . . It simply poses the question of whether any genuine or meaningful similarities between certain cultures exist and whether these lend themselves to formulation (Steward, 1955, pp. 18–19).

In summary, Steward's work is inductive, rather than deductive; it is concerned not with the formulation of *general* laws but rather with the formulation of empirical generalizations about similarities in configurations of change demonstrated by a selected number of cultural systems. The demonstration of differences and similarities is only the first step in any science; such demonstrations provide the raw material for questions, the answers to which must be given with respect to covering laws stated as hypotheses and tested against independent classes of data:

A hypothesis to be regarded as a natural law must be a general proposition which can be thought to explain its instances; if the reason for believing the general proposition is solely direct knowledge of the truth of its instances, it will be felt to be a poor sort of explanation of these instances. If, however, there is evidence for it which is independent of its instances, such as the indirect evidence provided by instances of a same-level general proposition subsumed along with it under the same higher-level hypothesis, then the general propositions will explain its instances in the sense that it will provide grounds for believing in their truth independently of any direct knowledge of such truth (Braithwaite, 1960, pp. 302–303).

Once explanatory hypotheses have been tested and confirmed, they gain the status of laws only when they are integrated into a body of theory. In his writings Steward has never addressed himself to the problem of the development of cultural evolutionary theory; his substantive work has consisted, by his own admission, of limited empirical generalizations. I would argue, therefore, that the distinction between specific and general evolution cannot and does not resolve the differences between White and Steward, these differences are based on differing understandings of scientific methods and the role of deduction and induction [see Hempel (1966) for relevant discussion]. The major gulf between White and Steward is not the scale of their studies, the units studied, or the strategies recommended, as one might be led to believe by Sahlins and Service; rather it is rooted in fundamental incompatible positions with regard to epistomology and the logic of science.

If the "general" and "specific" distinction has no utility for clearing up the points of conflict between White and Steward, does it contribute to evolutionary methodology or an understanding of evolutionary process. I would have to answer this in the negative. I have already shown how the alternative strategies might be equally appropriate to the consideration of problems of "progress" or "diversification." Explanation of results studied using either strategy would require testing, and testing would demand general validity for the explanatory proposition with respect to all qualifying cases "taken out of their respective lineages" and its integration into a body of theory.

If evolutionary laws are statements of relationships between environmental and systemic variables which can be observed (and predicted) to behave in regular ways among structurally diverse systems, what units are appropriate to observe and analyze? In the study of the evolution of culture, our units must be independent sociocultural systems. Any attempt to use units which are partitive or units which represent classes of cultural phenomena will necessitate the added investigation of intersystemic relationships (functional relationships) which condition internal, accommodative changes. These kinds of change must be distinguished from those which arise in response to extrasystemic selective pressures. In dealing with the components of a system, we cannot assume that formal variability in a class of phenomena arises as the result of the operation of a constant set of determinants. Numerous variables, acting multivariately, may determine change or variability in a single class of phenomena. Therefore, units appropriate for the study of evolution, cultural or otherwise, are those units for which we can make the assumption that all variability occurs either as a direct response to extrasystemic variables or as means of controlling internal pressures through accommodation.

With regard to rates of evolution, it was suggested above that strictly speaking there are only variations in the magnitude and duration of selective stress and/or the magnitude or intensity of such stress. In the absence of means adequate for measuring evolution in these terms, we seek to monitor evolutionary processes by studying rates of change in various classes of phenomena, change which results from the operation of evolutionary processes. Time is the conventional referent for evaluating a progression of systemic processes; to argue that time acts causally in activating systemic change or to cite change per unit of time as having determinant effects on a concrete system is inconceivable. Time and space are coordinants along which we monitor systemic processes. If we are studying rates of change in any given class of phenomena and we observe changing rates, interruptions in regular patterns of change through time or contrasts in rates of change between various classes of phenomena, our observations are simply descriptive. Such observations are scientifically relevant only in the context of hypotheses attempting to explain the dynamics of functioning among a number of variables. Observations on rates of change serve either as empirical data in need of explanation or as data relevant for testing hypotheses regarding expected configurations of variability per unit of time in a specified variable.

These comments are made from the point of view that anthropology should be a science and that scientific method proceeds in the context of complementary inductive–deductive methods executed in the context of theory. Units are relevant insofar as they can be justified as informative observational referents for measuring the behavior of certain specified variables. Rates are means of monitoring instances of the operation of evolutionary processes, given proper controls over the significance of variability in the units being observed.

The arguments presented by Sahlins and Service were introduced to point out that there are cross-cutting problems in anthropology related to philosophy of science and epistomology. These problems need to be treated in their own terms and are not to be confused with substantative problems of evolution and processes of change and variablity observable among cultural systems.

References

Braithwaite, R. B. (1960). *Scientific Explanation,* Harper Torchbooks ed. Harper, New York.

Hempel, Carl G. (1966). *Philosophy of Natural Science.* Prentice-Hall, Englewood Cliffs, New Jersey.

Huxley, Julian. (1943). *Evolution, the Modern Synthesis.* Harper, New York.

Lotka, Alfred J. (1922). Contribution to the energetics of evolution. *Proceedings of the National Academy of Sciences of the United States* 8, 147–151.

Odom, Eugene P. (1959). *Fundamentals of Ecology* Saunders, Philadelphia.

Sahlins, Marshall D., and Elman R. Service, eds. (1960). *Evolution and Culture.* Univ. of Michigan Press, Ann Arbor.

Simpson, George Gaylord. (1952). *The Meaning of Evolution: A Study of the History of Life and of its Significance for Man.* Yale Univ. Press, New Haven, Connecticut.

Steward, Julian H. (1955). *Theory of Culture Change.* Univ. of Illinois Press, Urbana.

Wagner, Philip. (1960). *The Human Use of the Earth.* Free Press, Glencoe, Illinois.

White, Leslie A. (1949). *The Science of Culture.* Grove Press, New York.

White, Leslie A. (1960). Forward. In *Evolution and Culture* (M. D. Sahlins and E. R. Service, eds.), pp. v–xii. Univ. of Michigan Press, Ann Arbor.

Some Comments on Historical Versus Processual Archaeology[*]

A recently published article by Sabloff and Willey (1967) discussed some aspects of historical versus processual approaches in archaeology. Those authors acknowledge the need for archaeologists to concern themselves with processual questions but argue that archaeologists must give research priority to the reconstruction of historical events:

> It is our feeling that, at least at the present state of . . . knowledge, an understanding of historical events can lead to placement of processual factors in proper perspective, rather than the reverse . . . Furthermore, we do not wish to imply in our statements that by switching the historical–processual priorities we have accepted a theoretical position which is essentially non-evolutionary (Sabloff and Willey, 1967, p. 313).

Sabloff and Willey add in a footnote that their view "would approach that of Steward's (1955) 'multilinear evolution' " (Sabloff and Willey, 1967, p. 313).

The purpose of this paper is to discuss their proposals with respect to two major points: first, the nature of explanation; and second, the feasibility of working according to the priorities set forth by Sabloff and Willey. It is disagreement over these two fundamental points, I feel, that creates the greatest difficulties between the more traditional archaeologists and the advocates of what has come to be known as the "new archaeology."

Sabloff and Willey are concerned with understanding the collapse of the Classic Lowland Maya cultural system about 900 A.D. The evidence they cite to document the collapse consists of widespread abandonment of sites, decline in frequency of construction, decline in ceramics, apparent population reduction, and so forth. The authors then propose a "new hypothetical solution":

[*] Originally published in *Southwestern Journal of Anthropology* **24**, 267–275 (1968).

In boldest form, the hypothesis states that the Southern Lowlands . . . were invaded by non-Classic Maya peoples. This invasion began in the 9th Century A.D., and it set in motion a train of events that destroyed the Classic Maya within 100 years (Sabloff and Willey, 1967, p. 312).

Does this hypothetical formulation of Sabloff and Willey constitute a valid explanation of the collapse of the Lowland Maya? A distinguished philosopher of science, Carl Hempel, in a discussion of explanation, states:

The explanation of the occurrence of an event of some specific kind . . . at a certain place and time consists . . . in indicating the causes or determining factors [of the event in question]. Now the assertion that a set of events . . . have caused the event to be explained, amounts to the statement that, according to certain general laws, a set of events of the kinds mentioned is regularly accompanied by an event of the kind [for which an explanation is sought] (Hempel, 1965, p. 232).

According to Hempel, an explanation consists of two parts: First, the events believed to be relevant which temporally precede the event to be explained are set forth; second, a set of general laws is formulated which connects the "causes" with their "effects" in such a way that if we know that the earlier events have taken place, we would be able to predict the event we wish to explain.

Sabloff and Willey hypothesize that there was an invasion of the Lowland Maya area by non-Classic Mayan peoples. This statement can be taken as a specification of the prior event that the authors consider relevant to the Maya collapse. But where are the general laws which allow us to connect the proposed cause and effect? Is the statement that the hypothesized invasion "set in motion a train of events that destroyed the Classic Maya" (Sabloff and Willey, 1967, p. 313) a general law? It can be reasonably argued that invasions have no necessary relevance to the general explanation of sociocultural collapse as such. For example, we might cite cases where invasions occurred that did not precipitate the collapse of the society invaded. Similarly, we might cite instances of sociocultural collapse—such as the 12th–13th century abandonment of major sites in the American Southwest—that do not appear to be explicable by reference to invasions. Such empirical cases to the contrary would cast doubt on the relevance of invasions to the explanation of sociocultural collapse.

Would we be any closer to understanding the collapse of the Classic Lowland Maya even if Sabloff and Willey had thoroughly documented the fact that an invasion had occurred? Since they offer no processual arguments regarding the characteristics of the invaders which might have been crucial in bringing about the collapse of the Classic Lowland Maya, we must answer negatively. Sabloff and Willey do not refer this event—the invasion—to any general propositions regarding cultural dynamics which are amenable to testing. Because of this lack, it is impossible to assess the relevance of the proposed invasion or to evaluate this particular case in terms of propositions made by others about general laws of cultural dynamics.

These same criticisms can be made every time an argument is offered which proposes a cause-and-effect relationship between events when the only justification for such a proposal is the sequential nature of the events cited. In actual practice this is rarely done; it is more common for the proponents of "historical" explanations to make assumptions about the "plausible" response of people to certain situations. These *"laws" of human behavior* remain implicit in their arguments. Given the methods of most historians, such connective propositions are rarely tested to determine their validity. This failure of historical explanation is alluded to in a statement which Spaulding (1968) cites from Brodbeck (1962, p. 254): "There is no such thing as 'historical' explanation, only the explanation of historical events."

Sabloff and Willey might well counter the criticism offered here by pointing out that they were not attempting to explain the Maya collapse. They state:

> It must be obvious, at this point . . . that our hypothesis does not really solve the whole "mystery" of the fall of Maya civilization in the Southern Lowlands, nor does it rigorously attempt to do so . . . . To repeat, one of the major purposes of this paper has been to show that the best way to get answers to the processual problems connected with the fall of the Maya is through the building of a proper historical framework (Sabloff and Willey, 1967, pp. 329–330).

If their efforts were not directed toward the explanation of cultural dynamics, how can we evaluate their suggestions on proper research procedures and priorities to be followed in seeking explanations? Their major point is stated several times in different ways. For example, they emphasize that *"by first gaining control of the historical variables we will then be in an excellent position to eventually gain control of the processual ones"* (Sabloff and Willey, 1967, p. 330). The problem of critical importance here is the criterion used for judging what constitutes a "proper historical framework" (Sabloff and Willey, 1967, p. 330). Sabloff and Willey appear to assume that the relevance of historical facts is self-evident and primary and that processual understanding is to be gained through the inductive study of these facts. Although this position is not explicitly stated, their agreement with Steward's multilinear approach seems to substantiate their adherence to this point of view. Steward explicitly states: "I wish to stress that my delimitation of problem and method precludes all efforts to achieve universal explanations or formulations of human behavior" (Steward, 1955, pp. 7–8). In another place he asserts that the method of multilinear evolution "is empirical rather than deductive" (Steward, 1955, p. 18). That Sabloff and Willey subscribe to an inductivist philosophy is further documented by their very argument that gaining an understanding of processual factors is secondary to gaining an understanding of historical events.

I think it can be argued, however, that a "proper historical perspective" cannot be gained without coping with processual problems. Process, as I understand it, refers to the dynamic relationships (causes and effects) operative among the components of a system or between systematic components and the environment. In order to deal with process we must seek explanations for observed phenomena, and it is only through explanations of our observations that we gain any knowledge of the past. *Explanation begins for the archaeologist when observations made on the archaeological record are linked through laws of cultural or behavioral functioning to past conditions or events.* Successful explanation and the understanding of process are synonymous, and both proceed dialectically—by the formulation of hypotheses (potential laws on the relationships between two or more variables) and the testing of their validity against empirical data. Hypotheses about cause and effect must be explicitly formulated and then tested. Only when this is done are we in a position to judge what facts might be relevant; only then can we objectively evaluate the implicit propositions which underly "plausible" historical interpretations of archaeological data.

Sabloff and Willey (1967, p. 313) refer to my concerted efforts to redirect the attention of archaeologists to problems of process. These urgings have been prompted not by a messianic vision but by a conviction that archaeologists must proceed by sound scientific method. We begin with observations on the archaeological record, then move to explain the differences and similarities we observe. This means setting forth processual hypotheses that permit us to link archaeological remains to events or conditions in the past which produced them. Once hypotheses are explicitly stated, we can determine what additional observations must be made or available data collected to test the validity of our hypotheses. If validated, such hypotheses would be raised to the status of laws regarding the role of archaeological remains in the functioning of extinct cultural systems. It was in the context of such functioning that the artifacts or features were produced, used, and discarded or abandoned; it was also in the context of a functioning cultural system that the characteristic associations and distributions were produced. This procedure—observation, hypothesis formulation and testing—is necessarily involved with problems of process and is what constitutes the scientific method.

If we omit any of these steps and appeal to unstated processual propositions in explaining observations, we can have little confidence in the historical reconstruction offered. The only recourse at this point is the one offered by Raymond Thompson (1956, p. 335) that we evaluate reconstructions or interpretations by evaluating the competence of the person who is proposing the reconstruction. This is scarcely sound scientific procedure, and I feel it is necessary for us to have objective means for judging the validity of statements in archaeology instead of relying upon faith or personal opinion.

If the propositions appealed to in explaining our observations of the archaeological record are correct, then we will have gained knowledge of the past. Otherwise, we will have achieved only knowledge of the archaeological record itself, which is, of course, a contemporary phenomenon. It might also be pointed out that most textbooks and syntheses in the contemporary archaeological literature are descriptive expositions of our knowledge of the archaeological record and not summaries of our knowledge of the past; nor do they present knowledge gained regarding the functioning or evolutionary dynamics of past cultural systems. (See, for instance, Griffin, 1967; Jennings, 1968.) If we can attain knowledge of the past and of the operation of past cultural systems through the explanation of observations made on the archaeological record, we can then proceed to the task of explaining past events and seek to formulate laws dealing with the dynamics of systemic functioning and the evolution of cultural systems.

As in any scientific situation, when one changes the context in which one considers things and events observable in the external world, different features or characteristics of those things or events become relevant. (For a good discussion of this point, see White, 1959.) Thus, as we shift our perspective from one of explaining archaeological observations in terms of processes and events in the past to an attempt to explain those past processes and events, the characteristics of the archaeological record sought as relevant for testing explanatory propositions will be quite different from those characteristics observed as relevant in the earlier phase of work. This means that there are minimally two contexts of relevance in terms of which we observe and conceptualize the archaeological record. In addition to ignoring the contextual differences between "facts" with respect to explanations of differences and similarities observed in the archaeological record and explanations for differences and similarities between cultural systems or past events, the inductive procedure assumes as self-evident a single context of relevance for facts as they relate to scientific method. The inductive procedure is to gather facts, study them inferentially, and interpret them in terms of assumed laws of culture and/or human behavior. This procedure organizes observational materials in terms of implicit assumptions about their interrelationships (interpretation) or as a means to the formulation of new propositions (Steward's recommendation), but it never allows for the testing of these assumptions or new propositions. A simple inductive method does not recognize that once empirical materials are employed in the context of testing, the context of relevance has changed and new or different facts may be needed. It is maintained here that we must continually work back and forth between the contexts of explaining the archaeological record and explaining the past; between the contexts of proposition formulation (induction) and proposition testing (deduction). This is necessary if we are to maximize the potential information contained in the archaeological record; our destruction of this record in search of facts relevant in a single context precludes the possibility of subsequent search for facts relevant in a different context.

I argue that Sabloff and Willey's suggestions regarding historical priorities are defensible only in the context of an inductivist philosophy and that such a philosophy is unacceptable scientific procedure. Even if we do not accuse them of advocating an inferential methodology, how can we understand their argument favoring priority for the construction of a "proper historical framework"? If they mean by this that archaeologists have not yet solved all the explanatory problems of the significance of archaeological remains for past conditions and events and that our first job should be the sound explanation of the archaeological record, I would be in full agreement with them. But in that case they would be urging archaeologists to give priority to processual studies, and they explicitly deny this.

The failure of their method and the inadequacies of their suggested priorities is demonstrated by their failure to deal directly with the problem of how they derived their proposed invasion of the Mayan Lowlands from the facts of the archaeological record. We are presented with the following archaeological facts:

1. At the site of Seibal during the 9th century, fine paste pottery is a common ware associated with both public and residential structures.

2. Fine paste pottery is a non-Classic trait, stylistically and technically most similar to analogous wares from the Gulf Coast area.

3. Stelae erected at Seibal between A.D. 850 and 890 exhibit non-Classic traits similar to those known from Yucatan and Central Mexico; these stelae also share more than twenty stylistic features with the fine paste wares.

4. A building constructed with a round plan, previously unknown in Classic Maya sites, has analogies to structures in Yucatan and Central Mexico.

5. Figurines at Seibal are similar in form to Gulf Coast specimens.

6. The location of "ceremonial activities" within the site of Seibal was shifted from Group D structures (a defensible area) to Group A structures (a nondefensible area).

7. The population of Seibal reached its peak during this period.

From these facts how do Sabloff and Willey arrive at the proposition that they signify an invasion by "non-Classic" peoples? As far as I can determine, this conclusion is reached by the traditional archaeological method of "plausible interpretation." The laws underlying such an interpretation are implicit and assumed to be true; therefore, the interpretation is plausible. This implicit law of archaeological interpretation appears to be that temporal continuity in the formal properties of artifacts varies directly with social continuity. There are, however, many cases to the contrary which demonstrate that this is not necessarily true.

It would seem likely, furthermore, that if there had been an invasion there should be some evidence of conflict. Is there archaeological evidence at Seibal for the "superior weapons"—darts and atlatls—which, it is suggested (Sabloff and Willey, 1967, p. 327), gave the invaders a military advantage? Is there evidence for the existence at Seibal of military compounds which one might expect if the invaders were militaristic and engaged in "raiding of the rest of the Peten" (Sabloff and Willey, 1967, p. 329)? Why should the population of Seibal have reached its peak after the proposed takeover by the invaders? How was food procured and distributed for the invaders? Should there not have been evidence of a major change in the economic and subsistence logistics of such a group?

Until empirical materials from the archaeological record can be shown to conform to expectations in terms of deduced consequences of the proposed invasion, and until the validity of the propositions which permit the arguments of relevance offered for relating archaeological facts to past events and conditions has been demonstrated, Sabloff and Willey's interpretation cannot be said to have provided us with a "proper historical framework." If future research should prove their interpretation correct, such proof would be dependent upon an understanding of processual relationships among various classes of material items in the dynamics of cultural systems. Only then would we be able to relate reliably our contemporary archaeological observations to past conditions and events.

In summary, I have argued that there is a necessary first step in archaeological research—the attempt to explain observations made on the archaeological record by hypothesis formulation and testing. It has been stressed that this step *necessarily* involves coping with problems of process. We attempt to explain similarities and differences in archaeological remains in terms of the functioning of material items in a cultural system and the processual features of the operation or evolution of the cultural systems responsible for the varied artifact forms, associations, and distributions observable in the ground. Sabloff and Willey are not unique in approaching this task intuitively and inferentially; this has been the accepted procedure in archaeology. Advocates of the so-called "new archaeology" are not, as Jennings would have us believe, simply reinterpreting old data and old ideas:

Some of the more impatient young scholars refer to the "new archaeology." This term seems to imply the utilization of new "theoretical" viewpoints (which are less theories than new hypotheses or restatements of old assumptions) and the assistance of the ancillary sciences along with the old data and old ideas (Jennings, 1968, p. 329).

Insofar as the ideas and theories of science are old, Jennings is right; however, in the field of archaeology these ideas are revolutionary. Most of my own efforts and those of my colleagues in the "new archaeology" have been directed toward the disproof of the old principles of interpretation which gave the ring of plausibility to traditional reconstructions and interpretations. We seek to replace these inadequate propositions by laws that are validated in the context of the epistemology of science, so that we may gain an accurate knowledge of the past. This paper is one more attempt to demonstrate that a change in methodology is needed so that archaeologists will begin to test the validity of explanatory principles currently in use and attempt to refine or replace them by verified hypotheses relating the significance of archaeological data to past conditions. Only after these procedures are followed will we be in a position to establish a "proper historical framework."

References

Brodbeck, May. (1962). Explanation, prediction, and "imperfect" knowledge. In *Scientific Explanation, Space and Time* (H. Feigl and G. Maxwell, eds.), pp. 231–272.

Griffin, James B. (1967). Eastern North American archaeology: A summary. *Science* **156**, 175–191.

Hempel, Carl G. (1965). The function of general laws in history. In *Aspects of Scientific Explanation and Other Essays in the Philosophy of Science,* pp. 231–243. Free Press, Glencoe, Illinois.

Jennings, Jesse D. (1968). *Prehistory of North America.* McGraw-Hill, New York.

Sabloff, Jeremy A., and Gordon R. Willey. (1967). The collapse of Maya civilization in the southern lowlands: A consideration of history and process. *Southwestern Journal of Anthropology* **23**, 311–336.

Spaulding, Albert C. (1958). Explanation in archeology. In *New Perspectives in Archeology* (S. R. Binford and L. R. Binford, eds.), pp. 33–40. Aldine Publ. Co., Chicago, Illinois.

Steward, Julian H. (1955). *Theory of Culture Change: The Methodology of Multilinear Evolution.* Univ. of Illinois Press, Urbana.

Thompson, Raymond H. (1956). The subjective element in archaeological inference. *Southwestern Journal of Anthropology* **12**, 327–332.

White, Leslie A. (1959). The concept of culture. *American Anthropologist* **61**, 227–251.

Part II

METHOD OF DATA COLLECTION

Beginning long before I left the University of Michigan, I became deeply concerned with the problems of data collection and method. It was quite clear that if we as archaeologists were going to successfully search the archaeological record for organized relationships between things and properties of things, we had to exercise rigorous data quality control.

I had gained every one of my field experiences largely from Joffre Coe who was a fine field man. He had stressed the importance of keeping records, of accurate recording of observations, and of meticulous care in the maintenance of the exposed surfaces during excavation. I can recall his smiling and saying, "Indians' holes are round and irregular; archaeologists' holes are square and straight." In spite of Coe's careful approach to field work we normally threw away fire-cracked rock. Flint chips were saved only because we might miss some artifacts, and features were excavated more with an eye to their contents than to an understanding of their internal structure. Burials and houses were the exception.

Mark Papworth and I had been contemporary students at Michigan. We had gone through Spaulding's class together and were selected by Griffin to initiate a long-range archaeological program in Michigan. Griffin had never really been involved in any intensive way in local archaeology, but he saw the need for a local student training program. He also expressed some intrinsic interest in the problems of Michigan archaeology. Mark and I had to learn what we could about work done earlier. We searched the Great Lakes Range for curated collections from sites previously excavated, and we traveled extensively to other museums as well as to houses of local amateur collectors. We tried to collect data that we could experiment with in the implementation of the statistical techniques learned from Spaulding. Old amateur collections were tabulated, and the hand-crank desk calculator turned endlessly. Mark and I worked long, hard hours, drove uncounted miles, drank hard, and knew we were going to do something different, but we didn't know what. In the "enemy territory" around other state museums, we became known as the Gold Dust Twins, full of energy and going in all directions at once.

Gradually several principles began to emerge as a result of all our expended energies. (1) In order to use statistics you had to have comparable observations. (2) The traditional units of comparison were the artifact, and the site. There was an intermediate unit of observation which archaeologists had not given systematic attention to, namely, the feature. (3) In order to compare artifacts you had to have representative populations. (4) In order to compare sites your data had to be collected in terms of comparable strategies.

In spite of our alleged job of developing a long-range program in Michigan archaeology, we were in fact sent out on assignments. In the summer of 1957 our assignment was to go to Alpena, Michigan, and dig a site where a local amateur had recovered many "Old Copper" artifacts. This was completely consistent with Griffin's approach—data are artifacts, so go where you can get the most in the least amount of time. I have faced impossible situations before and since, but never one quite like that one. It was a working sand dune. The only remnant of a stabilized land surface we could find was referrable to the period of tense lumbering operations in upper Michigan. Trees had been cut down and the debris had been burned along with broken double bladed axes and a lumber chain. We found some artifacts—flint chips, even a copper bead or two, each in a separate lens which extended only several feet in any direction. By God, we *would* understand that site. We started plotting profiles across the dune, projecting lines and digging in places predicted to have certain characteristics if our projected profiles were correct, trying to isolate some understandable superpositioning. Griffin arrived for inspection saying, "Well boys, let me see the artifacts." "Oh—Dr. Griffin, we haven't found very many, but look at our profiles. We think there is possibly an old land surface running at this angle . . ., etc., etc." That afternoon we packed up and moved to Saginaw where there was a site known to have yielded lots of artifacts.

Two days later we started the excavations at the Andrews site. It was located in the back yard of a man who kept a dog kennel. There were from ten to forty dogs in small pens who relieved their boredom by barking endlessly at the archaeologists. We lived at the YMCA and stayed at the site as long as possible each day. In our initial excavation we came down on one cremated burial and the spongy remains of an extended burial with a good assortment of artifacts. We cleaned back the areas around the features and worked meticulously to uncover each little detail of association. Griffin had told us if we hit anything to call him immediately. Instead we waited until we had the features fully exposed, each artifact *in situ,* clearly identifiable with respect to the things around it.

We made a mistake—we had not plotted everything on our record sheets before calling Griffin. We covered the site with old sheets, then called Griffin from a nearby service station. He said, "Don't move a thing; Spaulding and I will be up immediately." We sat around the site waiting and before long Griffin came screeching to a halt in front of the site. He and Spaulding walked up and Griffin asked "Where is the birdstone?" We uncovered the excavation and Griffin jumped down onto our clean troweled sand floor getting on his knees beside the extended burial. "Give me a trowel," he yelled. Mark tossed him a trowel; I held my head. "Mark, get the camera and take my picture as I remove the birdstone." I walked over to the dog kennels.

That afternoon, Griffin returned to Ann Arbor leaving us with a series of holes in our excavations. Mark had hurriedly made out slips of paper giving the feature number and the site number to be included with each artifact. The artifacts were carried back to Ann Arbor. Later we had to get permission to take them out of Griffin's office so they could be catalogued with the other artifacts recovered from the site. Mark and I both recalled with horror the small brown stains running lineally away from each notched projectile point—Griffin's knee had finished those. Mark and I got drunk that night.

Quite clearly, our long-range program for Michigan archaeology had to change. Some other criteria for site selection had to be developed. We had to insure that good records were kept for each exposed floor and for each feature. A demonstration of associational relationships depends upon associational observations.

Mark prepared an application for National Science Foundation support with Griffin as the principal investigator. Plans for the next summer were begun. Mark and I worked on developing a field manual and a series of data-recording forms. [These were later published (Papworth and Binford, 1962).] We held briefings and "underground" classes. We acted like knowledgeable dictators demanding that everything be saved and recorded.

We began the dangerous game of playing hide and seek with Griffin himself. We didn't really tell him what we were up to as we took students off and made decisions without consulting him. At first we saw this as a way of getting the kind of data we thought necessary. We had been unsuccessful in making him understand the importance of our strategies, so we thought that if we could first get the data, then he would understand when he saw the results.

Griffin surprised us many times: Mark and I had assumed that he wouldn't go along with spending the money for having record forms printed. We contacted the helpful amateurs in hopes of finding a way to get the printing done at no cost. Griffin found out and was hurt. "Take them out and get them printed," he said. Mark and I had been selling him short; he did understand. The next day he would surprise us again and scream out a command to stop some project which Mark and I had started.

Anyone should have recognized the importance of building screens! We would have to approach him again and convince him. Finally I built the first screens myself. Griffin then ordered the others built by the museum carpenter.

Sampling was a whispered notion. I had discussed it as a possible strategy to be followed, but the idea of digging to prove that nothing was there was as far as Griffin's understanding went at that time. The joking sarcasm in the coffee room was enough to make me soft peddle the sampling problem while at Michigan.

The practical problems far outweighed the methodological ones. Mark became disgusted and said, "Let's just get *some*thing going. I don't give a damn about the theory; we *have* to get some work started." I would argue, Mark and I would argue, and large quantities of beer would be consumed.

The first field season of the "New Archaeology" (1958) was a madhouse. We got many different kinds of data which were not generally collected. In fact, the hall outside Griffin's office was filled with fire-cracked rock; the newly opened lab was filled with fire-cracked rock. When Griffin saw all this rock the expression on his face (and lips) was one of total disbelief: "What in God's name are you going to do with all that fire-cracked rock?" I answered knowingly, "Why, count and weigh it, of course." What I could possibly do with such data, I didn't know, but it was part of the archaeological record, and there must be something you could learn.

Griffin was sometimes unbelievably tolerant: He supplied the assistants to count and weigh the rock. I don't think anyone ever did anything with that data. My justification for its collection was simple: If your are using statistics in analysis, the larger the sample the better. The most common item on the sites we were digging was fire-cracked rock. It follows therefore that it was the most important item, statistically speaking, that is. My logic was perfect.

I do recall being upset when Griffin refused to spend the time cataloguing the coke bottle tops and the nails recovered from the excavated plow zone. Looking back, if Griffin was impossible, then Mark and I must have been nothing short of intolerable.

All this confusion generated even greater confusion. To the poor students participating in that field season, the periodic visits of Papworth (concerned about the number of grease pencils being consumed), Griffin (wanting more artifacts and less fire-cracked rock), and me (interested in surveying the site and digging control squares to locate the bounds of the site) clearly represented incompatible demands: Fewer artifacts were found along the margins of the site, and the more provenience units excavated, the more grease pencils were needed!

The students solved the problem by choosing up sides. Some hated me, some hated Griffin, and some hated Papworth. Everyone hated someone, no one could let it out, all were insecure. The animosities among those students continue to this day. That was the first year of the implementation of the New Archaeology.

What came out of all this chaos? One thing is certain, when later critics wrote that the New Archaeology was really not new and "traditionalists" had been doing it all along, I had a series of experiences indelibly impressed on my mind. No amount of citing quotations, as I had done to White from the Boas literature, would do anything except strengthen my conviction that the traditionalist literature was like the Bible or the writings of Boas. You could find *any*thing you wanted in it; the critics didn't know what they were talking about.

What about data collection? I can't say for certain that anything really constructive came out of that first field season beyond the solidifications of the bias which I already had. Criteria had to be developed for selecting sites to be excavated beyond the obvious criteria of "dig where the goodies are." The archaeological record had information to yield beyond the recovery of "goodies." Comparable observations had to be made if meaningful comparisons were to be made. Features had to be studied for information they might yield above and beyond simply their contents.

The following season Griffin "strongly urged" me to go as the University of Michigan representative to a dig starting at the historic site of Fort Michilimackinac. Dr. Moreau Maxwell was to be in charge. It's hard to say what Griffin's motives were, but clearly had I been Griffin, I would have sent me anywhere in order to prevent a recurrence of the madness experienced the previous summer. I jumped at the opportunity to be away from Griffin and to have the chance of implementing some of my ideas. Surely Maxwell would recognize their value and let me do as I pleased!

Maxwell had been a student of Cole and had excavated at Kincaid where he ran WPA crews. He had logged an impressive number of hours in archaeological field work. He expected a graduate-student assistant to help him execute his excavation plans. After all, trained assistance was a necessity since our crew was to be made up of long-term prisoners from the state penitentiary at Marquette, Michigan.

I arrived with a very different notion. I had been suffering frustrations in the implementation of data collection strategies while developing our long-range plan for Michigan archaeology. By God! this was a chance to put them into practice without Griffin looking over my shoulder.

Maxwell and I arrived in Mackinaw City, Michigan, and visited the site together. We talked and we speculated about what we might find. I began to push, "We need screens, we need data forms, we need a survey, we need . . . ." Sometimes the expression on Maxwell's face reminded me of Griffin when he saw all that fire-cracked rock. Maxwell was polite, interested, and he even saw some merit in many of my suggestions. I built the screens the way I had learned from Joffre Coe, and I brought graph paper for recording, etc. We worked out an operational plan, where I took one-half of the crew and Maxwell took the other half to work in another place. I must have driven Maxwell to the limits of his patience. I wasn't content with that arrangement since after all, if meaningful comparisons were to be made, comparable data collection strategies had to be followed. Maxwell had to record things the way I was doing it.

The Fort's equivalent of fire-cracked rock was nails. There were thousands of nails. They were the most numerous item and had to be catalogued and saved. Maxwell let me save nails, but I could never convince him of their importance. I never let up; almost every day my suggestions must have led Maxwell near the point of strangling me, but he never did. He never really stopped me from doing anything.

I did have a chance to explore the nature of the archaeological record and try my wings. I learned an awful lot about the complexities of the structure of an archaeological site. I learned that if you are interested in an archaeological site as a preserved static organization of relationships between things, excavating random squares or test pits would never yield the necessary information. Large scale excavation of contiguous units was the only way. You might be able to get a representative sample of items by excavating random squares or a series of noncontiguous squares, but you cannot get a meaningful body of data regarding the character and distribution of features. I learned another fact: Large complicated archaeological sites are very difficult to understand. I generalized this observation into a field strategy which I later implemented, namely, dig the little, simple sites first. What you learn from them might permit you to intelligently dig the big, complicated ones. This was surely a different strategy from the traditionalist's one of digging where the greatest number of artifacts could be recovered. Griffin would never understand. The tolerance which Maxwell exhibited resulted in one of my most valuable experiences. I began to understand in a concrete way some of the problems inherent in the development of a data collection strategy for the New Archaeology.

If this experience was valuable to me, it was a potential disaster for the situation back at Ann Arbor. I returned from Mackinaw City not only convinced that we were on the right track, but also with some additional concrete suggestions toward accomplishing the long-range plan for Michigan archaeology. Although Maxwell had been unbelievably tolerant of me, it was decided that *he* would be in charge of the excavations the following summer (1960). I was to return to Fort Michilimackinac as director in 1961. This meant that I would be in Ann Arbor during the 1960 summer. I don't know if the two facts are related, but Griffin made plans to go to Europe during part of that summer. I was to stay in Ann Arbor to help Papworth with the field project and to finish writing my thesis, which was well under way.

It was funny, the way Mark and I felt about Griffin. Almost everything he stood for archaeologically we were trying to change, yet we both thought of him as a helpful, impossible, lovable father. For instance, we would have never gone to Spaulding with a personal problem, yet we would have gone to Griffin immediately. In an unrealistic way we wanted Griffin to approve of what we were doing, we wanted him to see its value, we wanted him to join us. We liked him in spite of what we considered his impossible approach to archaeology. When we laughed and called him names, it was with a generation-gap kind of warmth. We did things which must have appeared to Griffin as though he was surrounded by insane beings. In an off the wall kind of way we were announcing to him that he didn't understand what we were doing. We wanted to *provoke* his understanding.

I remember one day when one of the traditional Griffin students had returned from a field trip to the Upper Illinois valley. He had burst into the museum with the announcement that he had found a "unique" item, a negative-painted sherd from the _____ site. Griffin was obviously stimulated, and Papworth said, "Let me see." He took the sherd, looked at it and then threw it to the floor and ground it to pieces with the heel of his shoe. "That's what I think of your 'unique' sherd." Griffin was in total shock, the student was practically in tears with hate, and I was laughing inside. Things were complicated.

Both of us really lived through those days with the unconsidered assumption that no matter what we did, Griffin would ultimately back us up. It was the same kind of tenuous security that one feels with parents: They may raise the roof, punish you, and even hurt you and certainly don't understand you, but when the chips are down, they can always be counted on.

I telephoned Griffin at his office one Saturday afternoon in the spring of 1960 and asked if I could talk to him. He could tell I was upset and said he would come by my house and pick me up. He did, and we drove around, finally ending up in his office. My wife had just told me she wanted a separation; she was in love with Papworth. The Gold Dust Twins had melted.

I don't think Griffin could bring himself to believe that this was happening. He called my lawyer to tell him that I must be mistaken. He searched for any little piece of gossip which might indicate that his "sons" were not Cain and Abel. I saw all of Griffin's behavior as betrayal; Papworth saw it as Griffin supporting him at my expense. Mark and I were like fighting cocks over my wife and Griffin. Self-pity, depression, outrage—Mark, my best friend; my wife; Griffin—everyone had done me in. Those were wild days, impossible days, painful days, but Griffin begged both Mark and I to not let it break up the long-range plan for Michigan archaeology.

Somehow, during the summer of 1960 we put in the field the largest, best-trained crews ever fielded in Michigan. I drove many miles that summer, scheduling my visits to the sites so as to avoid seeing Papworth. Sometimes we did meet; both of us tried hard to pretend, to talk of the New Archaeology, to do anything but let our feelings out. Sometimes we were unsuccessful. Griffin left for Europe. That summer, we got results. The Feeley site was excavated, the Juntanen site was started, test pits were put in many sites later excavated in the Saginaw area, priorities not based on "goodie" return were established for site selection. Large areas were stripped and uncovered. Field notes were the finest I had seen up until that summer. We now had good data to use in the application of the techniques learned from Spaulding.

Spaulding had accepted the job as Program Director for Anthropology with the National Science Foundation, and I had been appointed as his replacement on the teaching staff. Physically, I moved into Spaulding's office. Psychologically, I moved into his shoes. I was to teach his methods course, the survey course in Old World Archaeology, and a seminar in African archaeology. My office was at one end of the hall, Griffin's was in the middle, and Papworth's was at the far end.

When Griffin had returned from Europe he had not directly faced either Mark or me. He had gotten every scrap of speculative, exaggerated gossip from the many persons who seemed to talk of nothing else. The hall seemed to be a tense, vibrating, supercharged no-man's land through which you had to cut your way. Students were clustered at my end doing analysis. Students were clustered at Papworth's end doing analysis. Griffin was alone.

Much work was done that year, I wrote the "Attribute List for Projectile Points," the Eastport-site report (Binford and Papworth, 1963), the Pomranky-site report (1963), the analysis of cremation, finished my thesis, and wrote the major part of the "culture drift" paper. All of these were to appear in published form much later. We established site-reporting standards based on the assumption of statistical analysis which still characterizes the contemporary archaeological reports from Michigan. In spite of the emotional horrors, it was an exciting year. Analysis was done at each small desk and half-hidden table. Alan McPherron, Henry Wright, David Taggert, and Charles Cleland were all hard at work making step-by-step progress in the New Archaeology.

I openly poked at Griffin, I bated the students in my class with his ideas. He had let me down; I didn't owe him anything. On the other hand I felt guilty for these aggressions. If it could only be the way it had been before. I missed the conversations in his office. After all he knew the data, and I had learned the data. There was no one else who could talk data like Griffin. I needed that. How strange to realize it only when it was no longer available.

It's not difficult to understand why my and Papworth's contracts were terminated at Michigan. We moved out to very different subsequent careers.

At Chicago I had a stimulating group of students. All that I had learned about the problems of data collection during those tense years at Michigan and during my periods of freedom at Fort Michilimackinac could be clarified and put into practice. Controlled surface collecting was urged on Struever at the beginning of his work at Apple Creek. Sampling was drilled into Longacre and Hill. Opening wide horizontal excavations was demanded of Freeman. Practice in taking comparable field notes and actual drill based on analysis of old field notes was a part of the field methods course. I contended that there is no better way of learning how critical is note taking than to analyze someone else's field notes. Paul S. Martin became convinced, and some of the best applications of new field strategies were implemented at his field school in Vernon, Arizona. Longacre and later Hill were the ramrods.

I started the field projects in the Carlyle Reservoir; this was a real chance to demonstrate some of the potential. I wrote "Considerations of Archaeological Research Design" after our first season in Carlyle. The reader will clearly recognize many of the points for which Papworth and I tried to fight as early as 1958. The emphasis was on the structural independence between features and items. Emphasis was on a site-selection strategy which would permit evaluation of the degree to which the data are representative. Emphasis was on an informed strategy for selecting places on a site to dig so as to get representative information. The reader of today will clearly recognize that all these suggestions follow logically from a change in orientation toward the search for *relationships* rather than things. If you are going to use statistical techniques to demonstrate relationships, you must be able to evaluate the degree that isolated relationships are referable to conditions in the past and not to the activities of the archaeologist. As long as the orientation was to things, clearly the things referred to the past.

The second paper reprinted in this section is an empirical demonstration of the partial independence between populations of features and populations of items. Much of the work done in Carlyle was in the nature of exploring the properties of the archaeological record itself to see what expectations the archaeologist might justifiably have when approaching an archaeological site and making strategy decisions. Hatchery West surprised even me, the doubter of traditional assumptions. Much more work needs to be done along these lines. I am sure, for instance, that there are certain features common to rock shelters which condition their patterns of occupation regardless of "culture" or time period. What are they? Are the limits of natural light a meaningful variable? Is the area adjacent to the wall versus the drip line systematically utilized differently? I suspect so. The needed research has not been done for the development of "informed" excavation strategies.

Many of my students have made significant advances in the development of more precise and useful sampling procedures. These are only the first steps, much more attention has to be given to the investigation of the structural properties of the archaeological record itself in its different manifestations.

The reader may well find some incompatibility in my insistence on deductively formulated research problems and my advocacy of an essentially inductive data collection procedure based on sampling theory. I, too, find some incompatibility. I look forward in the future to the increased use of computer simulation modeling of regions as a means of predicting from organizational or processual assumptions the character of the archaeological record. In such a strategy, excavation itself becomes hypothesis testing as to the validity of suspected relationships between variables. Clearly we cannot use inductive strategies, attempting to sample all the past. If we are to gain both greater confidence in our understanding of the past and data relevant to its understanding, we must begin to move into a deductively based data collection strategy.

There is a great deal of work to be accomplished in advancing scientific archaeology. Hopefully, few will have to live through the kinds of turmoil which Mark Papworth and I did when we initiated the first field season consciously conceived as the New Archaeology.

References

Binford, Lewis R. (1963). The Pomranky Site. A late archaic burial station. In *Miscellaneous Studies in Typology and Classification,* Anthropological Papers, No. 19, pp. 149–192. Museum of Anthropology, University of Michigan.

Binford, Lewis R., and Mark L. Papworth. (1963). The Eastport site, Antrim County, Michigan. In *Miscellaneous Studies in Typology and Classification,* Anthropological Papers, No. 19, pp. 71–123. Museum of Anthropology, University of Michigan.

Papworth, Mark L., and Lewis R. Binford. (1962). A guide to archaeological excavations. *Southwestern Lore* **28,** 1–24.

A Consideration of Archaeological Research Design*†

Abstract

It is argued that the methodology most appropriate for the task of isolating and studying processes of cultural change and evolution is one which is regional in scope and executed with the aid of research designs based on the principles of probability sampling. The various types of observational populations which archaeologists must study are discussed, together with an evaluation of the methodological differences attendant upon adequate and reliable investigation of each. Two basic sampling universes are discussed, the region and the site, together with their methodological and research-design peculiarities. These are used as a basis for discussion, and past and current research programs are evaluated in terms of what are believed to be major limitations in obtaining the "facts" pertinent to studies of cultural processes.

It seems fair to generalize that archaeologists are becoming more interested in the explanatory potential which studies of paleoecology, paleodemography, and evolution offer for increasing our understanding of formal and structural change in cultural systems. Several anthropologists have recognized a growing interest in questions dealing with the isolation of conditions and mechanisms by which cultural changes are brought about (Adams, 1960; Braidwood, 1959; Haag, 1959; Steward, 1960). In short, we seek answers to some "how and why" questions in addition to the "what, where, and when" questions so characteristically asked by archaeologists. This paper is concerned with presenting certain methodological suggestions, some of which must be adopted if we are to make progress in the study of processes and move archaeology into the "explanatory level" of development (Willey and Phillips, 1958, pp. 4–5).

In any general discussion of method and theory there is inevitably an argumentative bias on the part of the writer. It should be pointed out that I believe the isolation and study of cultural systems, rather than aggregates of culture traits, is the only meaningful approach to understanding cultural

* Originally published in *American Antiquity* **29,** 425–441 (1964).

† This paper was presented at the Annual Meeting of the Society for American Archaeology at the University of Colorado, Boulder, Colorado, May 1963.

processes (Steward, 1960, pp. 173–174). A cultural system is a set of constant or cyclically repetitive articulations between the social, technological, and ideological extrasomatic, adaptive means available to a human population (White, 1959, p. 8). The intimate systemic articulation of localities, facilities, and tools with specific tasks performed by social segments results in a structured set of spatial–formal relationships in the archaeological record. People do not cooperate in exactly the same way when performing different tasks. Similarly, different tasks are not uniformly carried on at the same locations. As tasks and cooperating groups vary, so do the implements and facilities (Wagner, 1960, pp. 88–117) of task performance. The loss, breakage, and abandonment of implements and facilities at different locations, where groups of variable structure performed different tasks, leaves a "fossil" record of the actual operation of an extinct society. This fossil record may be read in the quantitatively variable spatial clusterings of formal classes of artifacts. We may not always be able to state or determine what specific activities resulted in observed differential distributions, but we can recognize that activities were differentiated and determine the formal nature of the observable variability. I have argued elsewhere (Binford, 1962, p. 219) that we can recover, both from the nature of the populations of artifacts and from their spatial associations, the fossilized structure of the total cultural system. The archaeological structure of a culture should, and in my opinion does, reflect all other structures, for example, kinship, economic, and political. All are abstracted from the events which occur as part of the normal functioning of a cultural system. The archaeological structure results from these same events. The definition of this structure and the isolation of the archaeological remains of a cultural system are viewed as research objectives. Such an isolation can be made by the demonstration of consistent between-class correlations and mutual covariations among classes of artifacts and other phenomena. The isolation and definition of extinct cultural systems, both in terms of content and demonstrable patterns of mutual formal–spatial covariation, can be accomplished. Once accomplished, such an archaeological structure is amenable to analysis in terms of form and complexity; in short, we can speak of culture types. Methods for correlating archaeologically defined culture types with structural forms defined in terms of behavioral attributes can be developed. When this is accomplished, archaeologists and "social anthropologists" will be in the position to make joint contributions to the solution of common anthropological problems, a condition that hardly obtains today.

In addition to maintaining the position that we should strive to isolate the archaeological structure of extinct cultural systems, it is argued that changes in cultural systems must be investigated with regard to the adaptive or coping situations which are presented to human populations. If we are profitably to study process, we must be able to isolate cultural systems and study them in their adaptive milieu conceived in terms of physical, biological, and social dimensions. The physical and biological dimensions need little explanation because anthropologists are familiar 'with the problems of the nature and stability of natural environment and in the physical and demographic human basis of cultural systems. However, the social dimension is frequently excluded from considerations of adaptation. There is little need to belabor the point that as the density and complexity of separate sociocultural systems increase within a major geographic zone, the cultural means for articulating and "adjusting" one society with another become more complex. Certainly the coping situations and hence the adaptive stresses associated with a changing pattern of sociopolitical distribution within a major zone must be considered when attempting to understand changes in any given system (Gearing, 1962). As long as "cultures" are defined in terms of stylistic similarity, and the question of possible differences in the material inventory of functional classes and in the internal structure of the assemblage is unanswered, there is little possibility of dealing realistically with questions of process. It is a system that is the seat of process.

Because of these convictions I will frequently mention the "regional approach" or the detailed and systematic study of regions that can be expected to have supported cultural systems. The extent of such regions will vary because it is recognized that cultural systems differ greatly in the limits of their adaptive range and milieu. As cultural systems become more complex, they generally span greater ecological ranges and enter into more complex, widespread, extrasocietal interaction. The isolation and definition of the *content,* the *structure,* and the *range* of a cultural system, together with its ecological relationships, may be viewed as a research objective. Admittedly it is an objective which may or may not be successfully accomplished under any given research design. The research design should be aimed at the accomplishment of this isolation which, I believe, is most profitably prosecuted within a regional unit of investigation. Under current programs of salvage archaeology and increased foundation support for archaeological research, we are being given the opportunity to study major regions intensively. In spite of the opportunities currently available, it is my impression that very little thought has been given to research design. Methods and approaches utilized in such investigations seem to be little more than expanded or greatly enlarged field sessions of the type that has traditionally characterized American archaeological data collection. To be sure, the work may be neater, more attention may be given to stratigraphy, more classes of phenomena may be observed and collected than in the field work of years past; yet the general methods of data collection and observation remain unchanged. I wish to argue that current lack of concern with the development of planned research designs generally obviates the recovery of data pertinent to questions which derive from current theoretical interests. Investigatory tools must fit the job; current field procedures were developed to provide data relevant to a limited number of problems. Concern has been with problems of stylistic chronological placement and historical continuity between and among archaeologically defined units. The methodological tools developed for the investigation of such problems are inappropriate for supplying information relevant to our broadening research interests in cultural processes.

Methodological Problem Areas

Laymen frequently ask: "What are you digging for?" I think most of us will agree that we are digging to recover facts for the elucidation of past cultures. In the absence of explicit statements concerning the kinds of facts which archaeologists hope to obtain, we can only assume that we know how to recover the "pertinent" ones. Most of us will agree that this is not true. I not only have been unable to use other investigators' data, but I have also frequently found my own data lacking in many important "facts"—facts which could have been collected had I been aware of the questions to which the given observation was relevant. For instance, I recently wanted to demonstrate that most of the sites in a particular area were located adjacent to streams. This was impossible because I had no data as to where the archaeologist reporting on the area had concentrated his survey efforts. Was the failure to report sites in areas not adjacent to streams the result of sites being absent, or was it simply a lack of investigation in those area not adjacent to streams? In another instance, I wanted to compare the relative density of Middle Woodland sites in two major river basins in order to make statements about the relative occupational intensity in the two areas. This was impossible because I was unable to determine whether or not the reported differential densities were the result of differences in the intensity of survey, presence or absence of forest cover affecting the likelihood of sites being recognized, or differential aboriginal use of the valleys under consideration. Such uncertainties make it obvious that we are concerned with answering questions for which our research designs, field methods, and reporting procedures are not adequate to supply the "pertinent facts." Such a situation cannot be prevented entirely, but we can strive to devise techniques for gathering the facts which are pertinent to questions currently being asked of our data. As the general theoretical development within archaeology goes forward, more and more facts previously ignored will be recognized as important and pertinent. We can look forward to continued concern with keeping our investigatory tools sufficient to the task; in short, we will be increasingly involved in the development of new and improved research designs and methodologies by means of which they may be operationalized.

One clue to a "methodological problem area" in our current practices can be found in another question which laymen are apt to ask: "How do you know where to dig?" My answer to such a question is that we dig where there are surface indications of past occupations or cultural activity—a seemingly accurate answer, yet we do not excavate every location which yields surface indications. What are the means whereby we select certain sites for excavation and not others? A quick review of 37 regional reports spanning the period from 1954 to 1963 failed to reveal a single exposition by the authors as to the criteria they utilized in selecting sites for excavation. A typical statement may read as follows:

> During this time a total of 51 sites was located in survey work and 13 of the more important sites were excavated to some extent.

It is my impression that there is no single set of criteria for selecting "important" sites. Some archaeologists select sites because they represent a time period. Others are selected because they are large and productive. Certainly some have been excavated because they were accessible to modern roads. Despite the lack of systematic statement, it is repeatedly mentioned that sites are representative or that they are large and yield much material. Less frequently, economy is cited as a reason for selecting a particular site. Although it is not commonly expressed, we may generalize that *archaeologists want representative and reliable data within the bounds of their restricted time and monetary resources.* This is practically the definition of the aims of modern sampling procedures. Sampling, as used here, does not mean the mere substitution of a partial coverage for a total coverage. It is the science of controlling and measuring the reliability of information through the theory of probability (Deming, 1950, p. 2). Certainly we are all aware that we must substitute partial coverage for complete coverage in our investigation. Given this situation, there is only one currently known means for accomplishing coverage so that the results can be evaluated as to their reliability in representation of the population investigated. This is through the application of sampling theory in the development and execution of data-collecting programs.

Sampling

In this discussion of sampling we shall introduce certain terms that are used by writers on sampling and attendant statistical problems. A *universe* is the isolated field of study. In most cases archaeological field work is conducted within a universe of territory, a universe spatially defined. A *population* consists of an aggregate of analytical units within the universe so that, at least in principle, each unit may be assigned a definite location for a given unit of time. The population has a distribution in space consisting of the aggregate of individual locations (Duncan *et al.,* 1961, p. 21). In addition to a distribution, we can speak of the *spatial structure* of a population. Structure suggests a pattern of interrelationships among distinguishable parts of an organized whole (Duncan *et al.,* 1961, p. 2), and for our purposes the spatial structure of archaeological populations derives from the complex interrelationships between people, activities, and material items within a cultural system. In addition, we may speak of the *form of a population,* which is the nature and quantitatively variable constitution of subclasses and the relative frequency of analytical units.

The application of the method of probability sampling presupposes that a universe can be subdivided into distinct and identifiable units called *sample units.* These units may be natural units, such as sites or individual projectile points, or they may be arbitrary units, such as 6-in. levels in an excavation, or surface areas defined by a grid system. Regardless of the basis for definition, the application of the method of probability sampling presupposes the availability of a list of all the potential sample units within the universe. This list is called the *frame* and provides the basis for the actual selection of the sample units to be investigated. The frame varies with the nature of the archaeological population under investigation. When a population of sites is sampled, the frame is normally a list of sites within a stated universe, such as the alluvial bottoms of the Rock River between two specified points. When partial coverage of a population within a stated universe is attempted, the sample units are selected from the frame so that all units of the frame have an equal chance of being chosen for investigation; the selection is governed by the "laws of chance" alone, maximizing the reliability of the sample.

Before we approach the subject of different methods of probability sampling and their range of application in archaeological research, certain principles which underlie and guide the research design aimed at the proper and efficient execution of sampling techniques will be mentioned. This presentation is adapted from a section entitled "Types of Sampling" by Parten (1950).

(1) The population to be sampled and the units composing it must be clearly defined so that there will be no question as to what the sample represents.

(2) A universe partitioned by a frame composed of many small units is preferable to one composed of fewer but larger units. This is a safeguard against accidental inclusion of an unrepresentative amount of "heterogeneity" in any given sample.

(3) The units of the frame should be approximately equal in size. This eliminates bias which could result from a systematic relationship between the structure and the size of the population.

(4) All units should be independent of each other so that if one is drawn for sampling, it will in no way affect the choice of another.

(5) The same units should be used in sampling, tabulation, and analysis. A sample of mounds is of no use if generalizations about general site distributions are being attempted.

(6) The universe must be present or cataloged so that every unit in it is listed or can be given an identifying symbol to be used during the drawing of a sample. For instance, a grid

system is established with 12 ten-foot squares on a side, and 20 of the 144 squares are chosen for excavation by a random method. Later, it is decided to extend the grid system six more squares in one direction. The enlarged system does not have the random character of the sample drawn under the frame defined by the original grid system.

(7) The method of drawing the sample should be completely independent of the characteristics to be examined.

(8) In order for the sample to remain random, every unit drawn must be accessible. For instance, in the case where a site has been selected for sampling and the property owner refuses permission to dig, inaccessibility biases the sample. This is particularly true because refusal of permission may be related to ideas of the "value" of materials on his property relative to those on others' property.

With these principles serving as a background, we can turn to a discussion of types of sampling and their ranges of applicability to archaeological investigation. Although there are many types of sampling, only two will be discussed: simple random sampling and stratified sampling.

Simple Random Sampling

This is by far the simplest of the methods of probability sampling. It implies that an equal probability of selection is assigned to each unit of the frame at the time of sample selection. The term random refers to the method of selecting the sample units to be investigated rather than to the method of investigating any given unit. A practical procedure for selecting a random sample is by utilizing a table of random numbers (Arkin and Colton, 1957, p. 142). The procedure is to (1) determine the number of units in the frame, identifying them serially from 1 to *n*; (2) determine the desired size of the sample, that is, actual number of units to be investigated; (3) select the required series of numbers from the table of random numbers (the required series is the number determined sufficient to constitute a representative sample of the population); and (4) investigate those units in the frame that correspond to the numbers drawn from the table of random numbers. It cannot be overemphasized that this is a technique for selecting the units to be investigated and does not refer to the procedures used in gathering the data.

Stratified Sampling

It can be shown that the precision of a sample depends upon two factors: (1) the size of the sample and (2) the variability or heterogeneity of the population being sampled. If we desire to increase the precision, aside from increasing the sample size, we may devise means which will effectively reduce the heterogeneity of the population. One such procedure is known as the method of stratified sampling. The procedure is to partition the universe or divide it into classes, each of which is treated as an independent sampling universe from which simple random samples are drawn, following the methods outlined above. This procedure has a number of advantages. Classes may be established with regard to different variables that one wishes to control, which makes possible the reliable evaluation of variability in other phenomena with respect to the class-defining variables.

As has been suggested, the size of the sample is an important factor for consideration in striving for reliability in the sample as representative of the population. An optimum sample is one which is efficient, representative, reliable, and flexible. The sample size should be small enough to avoid unnecessary expense and large enough to avoid excessive error. To arrive at a sample size which is considered optimum in terms of the above criteria, there are a number of factors which must be considered, each largely integrated with the other rather than independent. Each will vary, in different sampling situations, as to their relative importance in influencing decisions about the appropriate sample size. Of particular importance to archaeologists is the realization that the size of the sample necessary to meet normal requirements of reliability and economy is greatly affected by the number of subclasses into which the recovered data will be divided. For instance, in the case of a sample of ceramics composed of 100 sherds, it is likely that if only two "types" are represented, the sample may be sufficient to give a fairly reliable estimate of the relative proportions of the two types in the population. On the other hand, if within the sample there are 15 "types," then the reliability of the sample as an estimate of the relative proportions of the recognized types in the parent population is very low. A further caution applies to samples drawn from multicomponent sites where there are clearly several recognizable populations of separate historical origin. In the latter case, some of the subclasses are independent of one another, and any given subclass may be representative of only one of the multiple historical populations. Also, in the latter case, sample size must be determined by the relative frequencies of the smallest independent subclass. In other words, sample size should be large enough to give reliable measures of the smallest important breakdowns made within the sample. If the population is relatively homogeneous, then sample size may be relatively small and still reliable. On the other hand, if the population is heterogeneous, more observations are needed to yield reliable data.

This discussion of sampling is very elementary, but enough has been presented to serve as a basis for evaluation of the types of observational populations which archaeologists investigate and their investigatory peculiarities as a basis for further discussion of research design.

Basic Units of Archaeological Observation

Albert Spaulding has provided us with a classic statement of what we as archaeologists are doing, thereby setting forth an operational definition of the field of archaeology. Spaulding's introductory statement is reproduced here as a point of departure for further discussion of archaeological data collection.

A science deals with some class of objects or events in terms of some specified dimensions of the objects or events. The simplest (and most elegant) of the sciences, mechanics, has all physical objects as its center of attention, and the dimensions of these objects as studied are length, mass, and time; i.e., roughly speaking mechanics has three kinds of measuring instruments: a yardstick, a set of scales, and a clock. The interrelationships and transformations of measurements with these scales is the business of mechanics. It is clear that prehistoric archaeology also has a class of objects, artifacts, as its center of attention. The concept "artifact" presupposes the idea of culture, which I will treat as a given. Thus we can define an artifact as any material result of cultural behavior. Since cultural behavior is our ultimate referent, it follows that we are interested in only those properties, characteristics, aspects, and attributes of artifacts which are the result of or have a significant relation to cultural behavior. What are the dimensions of artifacts whose interrelationships are the special business of archaeology? Plainly there are two in the strict sense of dimension: time and space. We want to know where and when artifacts were made, used, and deposited. Plainly there is another class of dimensions fundamental to archaeological study; the many dimensions which are sets of physio-chemical properties of the artifacts. We can group them for convenient reference under the label, formal properties, and collectively as the formal dimension. We are now in a position to define archaeology as the study of the interrelationships and transformations of artifacts with respect to the formal, temporal, and spatial dimensions. As a footnote, formal and spatial attributes can be observed directly, but temporal attributes are always inferred from formal and spatial attributes. Indeed strictly speaking artifacts are objects and do not have temporal attributes—they merely exist. But artifacts do imply events, and events do have the property of occurring at a definite time, so when we speak of the temporal attributes of an artifact, we really refer to an inference about some event or process implied by the formal and/or spatial attributes of the artifact. This leaves us with describing and ordering formal and spatial attributes as the primary task. These are the empirical data of archaeology and this describing and ordering are prerequisite to the chronological inferences (Spaulding, mimeographed version, revised 1960, pp. 437–439.

Artifacts as a class of phenomena represent a number of different types of populations which are definable in terms of their spatial, formal, or spatial and formal attributes taken in combination. Because of the different nature of artifactual populations, investigation of the several recognizable populations must differ as regards the appropriate means to provide the necessary information for their formal, spatial, and temporal analysis. The several classes of artifactual populations recognized here will be termed *types of observational populations* since it is argued that different sampling techniques, and hence research strategy, are necessary for the investigation of each.

Populations of Cultural Items

Cultural items are discrete entities, the formal characteristics of which are at least partially the result of cultural activity or events. A further qualification is that the formal characteristics of the item are not altered through removal from their matrix; they are transportable and may be formally analyzed without recourse to information about their provenience. This is not to say that such information is not crucial to interpretation of the formal properties, only that the formal properties themselves are independent of the matrix and provenience associations.

The form of the cultural item may vary in terms of the function of the item as an element in the cultural system, for example, technologically (manufacturing techniques and raw materials) or stylistically.

The sampling universe for the investigation of populations of cultural items is necessarily the site. The sampling and field-observation procedures utilized do not affect our ability to analyze items formally, but they greatly affect our ability to study the distribution, form, and structure of *a population of cultural items*. It will be remembered that a population necessarily has spatial attributes both in its distribution and its structure. Sampling control is therefore necessary to provide data for the description of populations of cultural items. We as anthropologists hope to be able to assess the range of formal variability in classes of cultural items and to study their distribution and population structure in terms of spatial clusters of quantitatively variant class associations. It is necessary to define accurately the range of formal variation within classes of cultural items as well as relative frequencies among recognized classes within the population. While excavating, we have no precise knowledge of the boundaries of the population of cultural items being investigated, and we generally sample in terms of areal units designed to cover the territory defined by the presence of artifacts. We are sampling "artifact space" as a means to both definition and segregation of populations of cultural items. We can only accomplish this through exercising tight spatial controls for gaining information necessary to the analytic determination of what cultural items are spatially and temporally clustered one with another and with other artifactual materials. Such insights are a clue to the "role played" by various items in the operation of extinct cultural systems. Similarly, the same control is necessary to the definition of the spatial structure and form of the population. We want to utilize techniques which will insure reliable and representative data regarding the range of formal variability within a given subclass of cultural items, the content of the population of cultural items defined by the relative frequencies of the recognized classes, and the structure of the population defined by the spatial structure of between-class associations of items and other classes of artifacts.

Error arising in the sampling of populations of cultural items normally results from (1) incomplete and nonrepresentative coverage of the universe; (2) failure to partition the universe so that a single undifferentiated collection is made, thereby excluding the possibility of investigating the homogeneity or heterogeneity of the population; or (3) samples are far too small to allow the adequate evaluation of the variability represented in a given class of cultural items or to yield a reliable estimate of the between-class relative frequencies.

Populations of Cultural Features

Cultural features are bounded and qualitatively isolated units that exhibit a structural association between two or more cultural items and types of nonrecoverable or composite matrices. The cultural feature cannot be formally analyzed or at least formally observed after its dissection in the field. Many of the formal observations must be made while the feature is being excavated. Features include such classes of remains as burials, mounds, structures, pits, and hearths. Formal variations among cultural features are dependent upon (1) their functions within the represented cultural system, (2) technology in terms of the raw materials utilized in their production, (3) alterations occurring as a result of the participation in other natural systems, for example, organic decay, (4) their cultural history (how often they were parts of successive cultural events, resulting in their repair, secondary modification, and destruction), and (5) stylistic variation. Unlike cultural items, the cultural feature cannot be formally defined without precise and detailed observation and "analysis" in the field. The field investigator must at least make decisions as to what attributes are culturally relevant and meaningful prior to beginning field observation and recording. This adds an additional field burden to the normal exercise of sampling control characteristic of the investigation of cultural items.

As in the case of cultural items, the sampling universe for populations of cultural features is the site. Similarly, our sampling procedures should insure reliable and representative data regarding (1) the variability within any class of features, (2) the formal content of the population of features, and (3) the structure of the population of cultural features.

Sources of error which frequently arise in sampling such populations are (1) incomplete and nonrepresentative coverage of the "artifact space" so that, while the number of recovered features may be large, there is no way of demonstrating or determining whether the between-class frequencies are representative of the population present; (2) samples are far too small to allow adequate evaluation of the variability represented in a given class of features or to yield reliable estimates of the between-class relative frequencies.

Populations of Cultural Activity Loci: Sites

The site is a spatial cluster of cultural features or items, or both. The formal characteristics of a site are defined by its formal content and the spatial and associational structure of the populations of cultural items and features present.

1. Sites vary in their depositional context. Sites exhibiting primary depositional context have not been altered in their formal properties except through the natural processes of the decay of organic material, or the physicochemical alteration of features and items since the period of occupancy. Sites exhibiting secondary depositional context are those whose formal characteristics, defined in terms of soils, features, and items, have been spatially altered through physical movement or deletion from the loci. Some or possibly all of the original associations between the various classes of artifacts have been changed. This disruption in the structure of the site may have occurred through the agency of erosion, geophysical changes, or through destruction as a result of later cultural activity. Sites with primary depositional context yield the most complete archaeological record. However, sites with secondary depositional context must frequently be studied in order to understand the regional distribution of activity loci.

2. Sites vary in their depositional history. The culturally dependent characteristics of a site may have been the result of a single short-term occupation, a single long-term occupation, multiple occupation over a rather limited temporal span, multiple occupations over an extended period of time, or combinations of all of these.

3. Sites vary in their culture history. Sites exhibiting a complex depositional history may or may not exhibit a complex cultural history. A site could be repeatedly occupied by representatives of the same stable sociocultural system for the same purposes, in which case there may be a complex depositional history with a simple cultural history. Similarly, a site with a simple depositional history may exhibit a complex cultural history, for example, an extended long-term occupation spanning a period of major structural changes in the cultural system. A single locus may be sequentially occupied by social units of different sociocultural or sociopolitical units, adding to the complexity of the cultural history of the site.

4. Sites and areas within sites vary functionally. Since sites are the result of cultural activities performed by social units within restricted spatial bounds, we would expect them to vary formally as a function of the activities of the social units represented. It is a known and demonstrable fact that sociocultural systems vary in the degree to which social segments perform specialized tasks, as well as in the cyclical pattern of task performance at any given location. These differences have spatial correlates with regard to the loci of task performance; hence we expect sites to vary formally and spatially with regard to the nature of the tasks performed at each, and the social composition of the units performing the tasks.

All possible combinations of the above-mentioned basic forms of variation may occur at sites which archaeologists investigate. Archaeologists must be prepared to make the pertinent observations needed to define the form and structure of the populations of artifacts and culturally relevant nonartifactual material present, and to isolate the form and structure of historically different archaeological assemblages represented. Unlike populations of cultural items or features where the normal universe is the site, the sampling universe for populations of sites is of necessity a region. Once the archaeologist has determined the relative homogeneity of the sampled site population as regards the historical and functional nature of the archaeological assemblage present, he is in a position to consider the nature of the site as a whole and to classify it within a typology of sites (based on the attributes of both the form of the artifactual elements present and the structure of their spatial and formal associations). Such an approach is the methodological aim of sampling a universe of sites regionally defined.

Two major sources of error arise in the investigation of site populations. The first source of error is incomplete and nonrepresentative coverage of the range of variation represented among sites within the universe. This arises inevitably as a result of the "selection" of sites for investigation on the basis of criteria other than those of the method of probability sampling. For instance, sites are frequently selected because of a high density of cultural items almost to the exclusion of sites with low density. The density of cultural items at a site is a formal attribute of the specific activity loci and is only relevant to the selection of sites for excavation as an attribute in a provisional site typology. A given universe may have very few sites with dense concentrations of cultural items, while the number of sites exhibiting less-dense concentrations may be quite high. In this case, the sample of sites for investigation must be composed of a proportionally higher number of sites exhibiting low densities of cultural items. The second source of error is failure to sample with sufficient intensity to yield a reliable measure of the variability present in the population. Inadequate sample size measured by the number of investigated sites is one of the major sources of error. Ideally, a sample of sites should be adequate to represent the formal range of variability in site form, the relative frequencies of recognized site types, and their spatial structuring within the universe.

Populations of Ecofacts

In addition to the investigation of cultural items, features, and activity loci, we must sample populations of ecofacts. Ecofact is the term applied to all culturally relevant nonartifactual data. Cultural systems are adaptive systems, and in order to understand their operation and the processes of their modification, we must be in a position to define their adaptive milieu. All those elements which represent or inform about the points of articulation between the cultural system and other natural systems must be sampled. This is an extremely important phase of archaeological data collection and is accompanied by many field complications in terms of methods of observation and sampling. The general class of ecofacts can be broken down into many subclasses representing different populations, such as pollen, soil, and animal bone, each with specific attendant sampling problems. However, for the purpose of this presentation, we will consider ecofacts as a single population which, in general, requires certain methodological considerations distinct from the problems associated with sampling artifact populations.

Basic Sampling Universes

Although we have recognized four major types of observational populations, each differing in the way it must be observed and sampled, there are only two basic sampling universes in excavation or field work: the region and the site. Populations of sites must be investigated within a universe defined in spatial terms, the region. Populations of cultural items and features must be investigated within a universe defined by the bounds of artifactual distribution at a given location, the site. Ecofactual populations may be sampled within both universes, depending on the types of information desired. If culture types are to be defined, it is essential that we isolate a reliable and representative sample of the population of sites characteristic of a given culture. For adequate definition of types of activity loci we need a reliable sample of populations of cultural items and features assignable to any given occupation. In order to obtain such information, we must have well-planned research designs rooted in the application of probability sampling procedures.

Limitations of Current Procedures

It is my impression that archaeologists have not consciously aimed at sampling populations of sites. They have concentrated on collecting "samples" of cultural items within regionally defined universes. The sites have been treated largely as "mines" for such items. In exceptional cases, where sites have been intensively investigated and populations of cultural features studied, there is little attempt to analyze the population of cultural items with regard to its spatial structure or form, while inordinate attention is frequently given to describing the "norms" of recognized formal subclasses within the population. When cultural features are investigated, they are usually reported cartographically, with little attempt to conduct a detailed formal analysis aimed at the description of types of features. One rarely finds a report in which correlations between the spatial structure of populations of cultural features and items have been attempted as a matter of "standard" procedure. For the most part, archaeologists have concerned themselves with vertical spatial analysis, and the search has been for stratified sites in which a limited "test pit" will yield a stylistic sequence that may be used to develop a regional chronology. This results in "cultures" being isolated on a regional basis and defined largely in terms of the stylistic characteristics of cultural items. The resulting information is insufficient for the structural definition of artifact assemblages and site typologies in precise terms. Cultural "taxonomy" remains almost exlusively in stylistic terms.

On the other hand, there has been inordinate interest in certain classes of cultural features, such as burial mounds and platform mounds. It was early recognized that such mounds were excellent "mines" for exotic and artistically pleasing objects and were therefore attractive to untrained investigators and relic hunters. Work in mounds, whether prompted through humanistic interests or through the "salvage motive," has contributed inordinately to our "sample" of artifactual data which serves as the taxonomic basis of many archaeologically defined cultures. This lack of representative data plus inadequate information on the form of the features is a real and limiting bias in the data currently available for study. Data have been gathered in terms of problems which concentrate investigations on populations of cultural items at the expense of and to the exclusion of cultural features. Investigation has also been concentrated on particular types of obvious features, such as mounds, and there has been very little awareness that the aim of archaeological investigation is the definition of the structure of an archaeological assemblage in addition to its content. These factors have contributed greatly to our current inability to deal systematically with archaeological data.

Current interests demand that we do not perpetuate these limitations in our methodology. We must approach our work with the methodological ideal of sampling a spatial universe, regardless of whether it is conducted under large-scale regional research programs or over an extended period of time through a series of small-scale investigations. Such sampling is aimed at obtaining a reliable and representative sample of the range of variation in formal–structural terms of sites within a given region. Selection of sites for excavation should be made on the basis of some method of probability sampling as the best means of insuring that the expenditure of time and money in excavation will yield the desired information. Sites selected for excavation must be investigated so that they can be formally defined from the standpoint of the nature of the populations of cultural items present, but equal attention must also be given to the population of cultural features. This is the only way to approach the necessary task of developing a site typology in functional and structural terms, an absolute necessity for the definition and isolation of the archaeological structure of extinct cultural systems. The latter is judged a necessary step toward the scientific investigation of cultural processes.

A Hypothetical Research Design

In an initial attempt to think through some of the practical problems associated with the design and execution of a research program which attempts to operationalize some of the suggestions advanced thus far, I will present a "hypothetical" research program. Hypothetical is placed in quotes because many of the ideas and problems discussed are the result of work currently being undertaken in the southern part of Illinois, specifically in the Carlyle Reservoir. Regardless of the projected implementation of many of the ideas set forth, the program remains hypothetical because the suggestions are untried and undemonstrated. It is hoped that by presenting these ideas in the form of a research "model," others may gain a clearer understanding of what is intended by the application of probability sampling approaches in field work. It is further hoped that this model can serve as a "whipping boy" for the improvement and further development of field methods and the execution of well-planned research designs.

Let us assume that we are given the task of investigating the prehistoric remains within a region. Our aim is to determine with the greatest degree of precision and reliability the nature of the extinct cultural systems represented for the entire range of human occupation. We must face the problem of isolating the variable cultural items, cultural features, and sites of activity for the cultural systems represented. In addition, we must gather ecofactual data as a basis for understanding the way in which the extinct cultural systems participated in the regional ecosystems of the past. We want to know the internal structure of the systems, the degree of structural differentiation and functional specialization of the social segments, as well as how these segments were articulated into a functional cultural system. We want to know the demographic basis and how it varies with respect to isolated structural changes in the cultural systems. In short, we want to know all we can about the structure and functioning of the extinct cultural systems and how they relate one to another as regards processes of change and evolution.

The initial problem is the location of the various loci of past cultural activity within the region. This phase of the work should be directed toward determining the density and distribution of activity loci with respect to classes of ecofactual phenomena, such as plant communities, physiographic features, and soil types. In order to accomplish this task, there is only one appropriate procedure short of complete coverage, a procedure rooted in some form of probability sampling. One suggested approach is to stratify the regional universe on the basis of ecofactual criteria judged desirable to control, such as soil types. If we assume for purposes of presentation that soil types have been decided upon for the areal stratification, in most cases the bounds of the various soils will be defined fairly accurately on a soil map, and we can simply determine the extent of each in square miles, acres, or other appropriate units. Having accomplished this, we can impose a *frame* within each sampling stratum (areas of common soil type). It will be remembered that a universe partitioned by many small sample units is preferable to one with fewer but larger units, and that the units of the frame should be approximately equal in size. Using these guides, we can impose a grid system over the areas of the various soil types. The actual size of a given unit in the frame would be determined by considerations of survey logistics and the need to have multiple but also practicable units for investigation. For purposes of presentation, it is assumed that the grid is composed of squares equaling $\frac{1}{2}$ mile^2. We would then count and enumerate each unit in the separate frames for each sampling stratum (soil type). The next methodological consideration is arriving at a "sample size." This can be quite complicated. For purposes of argument, it will be dismissed and we will assume that a 20% areal coverage within each sampling stratum has been judged sufficient. The next step is to draw the sample for each sampling stratum, and this may be accomplished by use of a table of random numbers. The sampling units within each frame will then be *completely* surveyed for purposes of locating sites.

What are the advantages of such a procedure? If executed under ideal conditions, it will permit the objective evaluation of site density in terms of ecofactual controls and also provide data relevant to summary statements about the intensity of past activities in the region as a whole within definable limits of error. The procedure will also permit the concentration of efforts on intensive study areas, making the logistical expenditure less than if the entire region were surveyed in a haphazard fashion. In addition to these advantages, it eliminates "hidden bias" in the form of differential attention paid to ecological situations which the investigator "feels" were preferred by prehistoric inhabitants. By following such a plan it is possible to demonstrate the ecological preferences of past occupants of the region.

On the other hand, there are certain problems which arise with any attempt to sample in this manner. Of primary importance are the conditions of the area itself in terms of the type of cover, presence or absence of modern communities, and distribution of agricultural land. Such factors could variously affect one's access to the land for site locational survey as well as the relative efficiency of observation. These complications are not new nor are they stumbling blocks to the suggested procedures. They are present no matter what type of research design we attempt to execute. The advantage of this particular approach is that it provides a methodological frame of reference for documenting and evaluating such bias. There are many ways to correct complicated sampling conditions. When approaching the problem of locating sites as outlined, it becomes imperative that the investigator concern himself with the control of bias resulting from differential survey conditions, something not generally considered under normal haphazard survey procedures.

Assuming that we have executed a research plan as outlined, the next step is to *define spatially* and sample initially the populations of cultural items present at each of the identified loci of cultural activity. This is prerequisite to the evaluation of the formal characteristics of the sites themselves; the ultimate aim is a classification of activity loci as to their degrees of similarity and difference. A working taxonomy of sites is a necessary prerequisite to the selection of sites for excavation and investigation of the populations of cultural items and features present. Limited data are obtainable through sampling populations of cultural items present on the surface of a site as well as through exercising spatial control over the "context" of the artifactual populations as regards ecofactual data. This information provides the classes of attributes utilized in classifying sites. There are three main attribute classes which can be normally controlled through the use of surface–sample data: the size and density of the cluster of cultural items, the formal constitution of the population of cultural items, and the degree of stylistic and functional homogeneity of the population.

The methods utilized to control the attributes of size and density will also allow us to partition the population of cultural items and speak of the relative densities and of its formal classes, that is, the spatial structure of the population. A further class of data, largely ecofactual, can and must be controlled. This is the topographic and physiographic nature of the location. Such information can be obtained at the same time that the spatial controls are established for sampling the population of cultural items.

In order to control the relevant variables and obtain the necessary data, we must have a number of sample units distributed over the area of the site and its immediate environs. These sample units must be rather evenly distributed within and beyond the suspected bounds of the site. In addition to establishing areal limits of the frame, we must determine the appropriate size of each sampling unit to insure the recovery of an adequate sample. A normal topographic survey of the site will provide a basis for the notation of ecofactual data as well as for the spatial control of the sampling frame and the location of sampling units.

Some method of "systematic sampling" is suggested as being the most appropriate to surface sampling. Only the first unit is selected at random and then others are selected in terms of a preestablished interval (Vescelius, 1960, p. 463). Systematic sampling ensures an equal dispersion of sample units, a desirable condition when densities and aggregational analysis are attempted. There is a further advantage in that spatial control on the placement of sampling units is easier to maintain with an equal spatial unit between them; thus, it is easier to lay out and identify the selected sampling units in the field.

A typical example of the execution of such a program is given below:

1. Impose a frame over the area of the site in the form of a grid system composed of sampling units of appropriate size.

2. Enumerate the sampling units in the frame from 1 to *n*. Determine the necessary sample size and then determine the appropriate sampling interval.

3. Consult a table of random numbers and draw the initial sample units. Then draw each sample unit separate from the initial one by the designated sampling interval.

4. Locate on the site the selected sampling units and collect all cultural items within the bounds of that unit.

This procedure can be speeded considerably in open or cultivated areas by use of a "dog-leash" technique. Each person who collects items has attached to his belt a cord of predetermined length to which is attached a stake. The stake is placed in the ground at the appropriate location, and the person collects all the cultural items within the radius of the circle defined by the "dog leash." The location of sampling units can be determined quickly by means of a tape and compass or with a transit. Such a method is considerably faster than setting up a grid and collecting items from a square unit, all four corners of which must be defined.

Regardless of the particular procedure followed, application of the principles of probability sampling to the collection of cultural items from the surface makes possible the objective definition of the site in terms of density clines. This permits objective comparison of sites in terms of site size and item density, in addition to the form, homogeneity, and structure of the population of cultural items present. On the basis of such comparisons, we can arrive at a provisional typology of the range of variability in the population of sites within the regional universe. Working hypotheses can be generated to account for the observable differences and similarities in form, density, and spatial structure, and these hypotheses can be tested by excavation.

A comparative study of information collected through the application of sampling techniques provides a basic set of data for the construction of a stratified sampling frame of provisional site types within which selection of sites for excavation can be made. This brings us to one of the major questions considered: How do we know where to dig? I think that the answer to this question logically rests with a methodology which attempts to test working hypotheses concerning the nature of variation that is observable in populations of surface-collected cultural items and with techniques of probability sampling. Are sites that exhibit similar size, density, and composition of cultural item populations similar with respect to populations of cultural features, depositional and cultural history, and general function within the cultural systems represented? If such a hypothesis were to be confirmed, we would be in a position to generalize far beyond the data derived from direct excavation and could make statements about settlement systems based largely on surface-collected data. This is not possible when sites are not treated within a sampling universe or when surface data are not used in the generation of structural hypotheses.

How do we actually go about the selection of sites for excavation? The following procedure is suggested:

1. Develop a taxonomy of sites based on formal attributes investigated during the surface survey.

2. Determine the relative frequencies and distributions of site types according to the original sampling strata, for example, soil types.

3. Stratify the population of sites into sampling strata based on the typology further stratified in terms of the original areal strata, that is, soil types.

4. Determine in terms of the time and funds available what proportion of the total number of each site type can be excavated to yield reliable information on their internal composition.

5. Enumerate each site in each sampling stratum from 1 to *n*.

6. Consult a table of random numbers and draw the appropriate sampling units designated by the random numbers.

7. Proceed to excavate all those sites whose unit-designator number was drawn from the table of random numbers.

The use of such a procedure can be justified in a number of ways. First, it will be remembered that the initial taxonomy based on surface-collected materials grouped sites judged to be similar or different. Within each taxonomic class, sites are excavated to test the reliability of this judgment and to further explicate the nature of the variability through more detailed investigation of populations of cultural items and features. Only by the use of such a procedure can we explicate the meaning of observed differences in the surface-collected material and thereby provide the necessary information for confirming the validity of generalizations based on such data. Secondly, the procedure insures an adequate and representative sample of the population of cultural activity loci within the defined universe. It is a complete and unbiased across-the-board investigation of the full range of formal variability within the population.

The next phase of research planning is to many the most important, and it is the phase that has received most attention under the rubric of "field methods." Initially, it must be recognized that in excavation we are not sampling activity loci; we are sampling populations of cultural items, cultural features, and ecofacts at an activity locus that may or may not have a complex cultural and depositional history. We want data which will allow us to understand the historical aspects of the various occupations, as well as the functions of the occupations in the total cultural system represented.

If we view excavation as having a particular role in the scheme of data collection, it is reasonable to think in terms of an excavational strategy. First, it must be kept in mind that all excavation is exploratory in addition to being a method for securing samples. Some phases of excavation may be parametric in the sense of it being possible to enumerate a sampling frame prior to data collection, while other phases are exploratory and sampling must be only provisionally parametric. Spatial control on a horizontal axis makes possible the parametric definition of a sampling frame in terms of spatial units. This type of frame is ideal for investigation of the homogeneity or heterogeneity of the population of cultural items, and it is appropriate for exploratory work that seeks the solution of problems of depositional and cultural history. However, it is with excavation that we hope to accomplish the maximum correlational control and thereby obtain the data that will allow reliable interpretation of the internal variation in the spatial structure of functional and stylistic classes of cultural items. Excavations will further provide well-documented and correlated samples of ecofacts, the basic data relevant to the nature of the local environment, and the way in which the represented social units were adapted to it. It is by correlating the distributions of cultural items with different functional classes of cultural features that insight into the "causes" of differential distributions is obtained, and hence understanding of the range, location, and nature of the various activities conducted at the site. Sampling frames designed solely to obtain cultural items and provide information concerning depositional and cultural history are generally inadequate as a sampling frame for cultural features. Ideally, we should have an X-ray machine which would allow us to locate and formally evaluate the range of variation manifest in cultural features. Given such information, we could construct a frame and excavate features within each recognized formal class in proportion to their relative frequency. Such a procedure would be analogous to excavating sites selected on the basis of a previously defined frame of site types. Unfortunately, no such X-ray machine exists, and we must attempt to obtain the desired sample by opening up areas of the site in such a way as to (1) allow the recognition of the presence of cultural features, (2) provide a representative spatial coverage of the universe in order to define the spatial distribution and structure of the features, and (3) provide the necessary contextual data for the formal analysis of the recognized features.

This discourse is not intended as a discussion of excavational techniques. However, a limited discussion of some widely utilized approaches as they relate to the general problems of research strategy seem to be in order.

Ideally, once a site is selected as a unit in a sampling frame of sites, it should be completely excavated. In such a case, there will be no question about one's ability to give parametric definition to a sampling frame for cultural items commensurate with the efficient investigation of cultural features. Complete excavation will insure complete recovery of the entire record of past activities at the given location.

In most cases it is impossible to undertake complete excavation of a site; only rarely are funds and personnel available for such an undertaking, particularly when sites are large. One method frequently resorted to when faced with a large site, or when the investigator is interested in obtaining information concerning the constitution of the population of cultural features, is to open up large "block" areas such as was done at Kincaid (Cole, 1951). A relatively large number of contiguous excavation units were opened, and this resulted in the complete excavation of a large "block" of the site area. This method insures recovery of the formal range of cultural features present in any given block but, as normally implemented, does not insure that the excavated block is representative of the range of features and activity loci present at the site. As normally practiced, the block or blocks selected for excavation are in the "core" area of the site and therefore bias the sample toward features and activity areas that were centrally located. As previously noted, our aim should be for adequate, reliable, and representative data. Block excavations as normally utilized do not supply this type of information.

Test pits and test trenches are appropriate units of excavation when one is investigating certain limited, formal properties of the site, but they are inappropriate to investigation of the site as a whole. Test pits are by definition small, noncontiguous units. Such units are useful in preliminary investigations of depositional problems and as a means of solving site cultural history problems. They can also be profitably employed in the collection of a dispersed number of samples of cultural items, but they do not normally expose areas large enough to define and sample populations of cultural features.

Test trenches are excellent means of investigating and defining problems of cultural and depositional history, but they have most of the limitations of test pits when sampling cultural features. However, they frequently provide more information on the differential distribution of feature types if they happen to be opened in sufficient density to "cross cut" major areas of the site. Data gathered from test trenches also have the advantage of being particularly useful for analysis of item densities on a linear axis. The limitations of test trenches are those of any technique which does not open up a large contiguous area, and does not cover, in a representative manner, the entire site.

As test pits and trenches are normally utilized, they do not provide adequate data regarding the population of cultural items because they are not normally distributed at random in sufficient numbers over the site. A greater limitation is the failure to expose large contiguous areas, a necessary condition for adequate sampling of cultural features.

Phase excavations seems to be the most appropriate term to apply to the procedures which will be suggested as a means of overcoming some of the difficulties inherent in sampling the different types of observational populations at a site. The term implies that the excavation of a site may involve several different excavational steps, each largely dependent upon the results of the earlier "phase" for the details necessary to the proper planning and execution of the succeeding phase. Each phase is designed to answer certain specific questions with the most economical and expedient means.

As an example, initial discussion will center around a relatively small, single-component site that lacks primary archaeological context below the plow zone (except, of course, cultural features). Initially, we want to know whether or not there are clusters of differential density in cultural items, a clue to the possible location of cultural features. In addition, we want a complete and unbiased sample of the population of cultural items in order to make judgments as to the "meaning" of demonstrable differential distributions of recognized stylistic and functional classes. Such a sample could be obtained by the excavation of a series of "test pits," the size and density of which would be determined by the estimated density of cultural items present. The distribution of the pits would be determined by some technique of probability sampling normally executed within a grid frame. The plow zone would be excavated and sifted for each of the selected excavation or sample units. This methodology could be further implemented by combining controlled surface collection from selected sample units. The data collected in this way should yield the desired information concerning population form, structure, and content. Once this is accomplished the next phase of excavation should be planned to yield the sufficient controlled data on the population of cultural features present. In this particular case, where there is no primary archaeological context below the plow zone, we can most efficiently accomplish our task by complete removal of the plow zone with the aid of power equipment. The result would be the exposure of cultural features which could be mapped and excavated, utilizing techniques designed to yield maximum correlational control.

The suggested excavation program would amount to a two-phase sequence. The first phase is designed to yield information about the population of cultural items present, whereas the second phase would yield the desired information concerning the population of cultural features.

In many field situations the sites are more complex, having multiple occupations with primary archaeological deposits below the disturbed plow zone. In such a case, a three-phase excavation program may be more appropriate. The initial phase would consist of opening up a series of test pits selected for excavation on the basis of a random or systematic sampling pattern within a grid frame. This procedure, as in the earlier case, should provide the data necessary for the reliable definition and isolation of different stylistic and functional areas within the total site area. Next is the problem of sampling populations of cultural features. Since the site has several components, tight correlational control must be exercised to ensure the possibility of correlating feature forms with forms of cultural items representative of discrete occupational episodes. An appropriate procedure is to employ block excavations as the second phase. Since the multicomponent nature of the site presumably would have been recognized during the early stages of the test-pitting phase, such a procedure also ensures that the initial exploratory exposures will yield information obtained under conditions of maximum correlational control. This hopefully makes possible the correlation of feature types with old soil surfaces, which in turn can be isolated and investigated in terms of cultural-item content. With this type of information we should, assuming that the block exposures have been successful, be able to develop a formal taxonomy of features which can be correlated with the variable populations of cultural items representative of the separate occupations. Once such correlations are established, the third phase of excavation can begin, the "stripping phase." This is removal, by means of power equipment or by hand, without attempting to recover cultural items, of the complete cultural deposit down to the level where cultural features can be observed intruding into the natural. Once this is accomplished, these features can be mapped and excavated, using techniques that will ensure maximum correlational control. The distributional data thus obtained will supplement that already collected and make possible the definition of activity areas and the general internal community structure representative of the separate occupations.

If we have been careful in planning and successful in the execution of the three phases of excavation, we should have the data necessary for the *demonstration* of differences and similarities between occupations in terms of the formal, spatial, and structural composition of the separate populations defined by both cultural items and features.

Enough has been said to suggest what is intended by phase excavations. As the complexity of a site is compounded in depositional and culture historical aspects, more and more attention must be given to maintaining maximum correlational control. The intensity of sampling or the sample size needed to ensure adequate data increases with the heterogeneity of the universe under investigation. This means that data necessary for justifying the step from one phase to another become expanded, and in general the nature of the appropriate phases changes with the complexity and form of the universe. The more complex the site, the more complex the excavational procedures, and the larger must be the recovered samples for any given phase of excavation.

This recognition provides the justification for what I call the planning of an excavational sequence. In areas where a number of sites have been selected for excavation, the temporal sequence of excavation can be very important in promoting the efficient use of resources in both labor and funds. The initial sites excavated should be the least complex, so that the chances of making false correlations are diminished and the maximum conditions obtain for observing the formal spatial structure of features and cultural items. Once an understanding is gained of the formal and structural characteristics which may be encountered, one is in a much better position to investigate a complex site where the nature of the variability may not be so clearly depicted. Informed excavation of a complex site can often greatly expedite its efficient investigation.

It is hoped that by following this "hypothetical" research program, the reader has gained a clearer understanding of what is intended by the argument that methods of probability sampling are applicable on all levels of field investigation. By pointing out some of the complications, I trust an appreciation can be gained as to the potential which the application of probability sampling methods holds for improving our data-collection methods. Such methods further provide a basis for a greatly expanded analysis of archaeological data directed toward the definition of archaeological assemblages in structural terms, ultimately with a view toward the isolation and definition of extinct cultural systems.

Of equal importance is the recognition that field work must not be conducted separately from analysis. Running analysis is a necessary part of feature description, and of even greater importance is the recognition that the results of running analysis largely serve as the basis for the planning and decision making regarding successive methodological steps taken in the execution of a field program. Much ink has been spilt on the argument that the archaeologist as such is a technician (Taylor, 1948, p. 43). Only in a very restricted sense can such a position be defended because the field archaeologist is forever making decisions as to what are pertinent and relevant "facts." Such decisions can only be made with knowledge and understanding of the questions being asked of the data. The field archaeologist must also be an anthropologist [in order] to make such decisions efficiently and effectively. As Brew (1946, p. 65) has argued that there is no single or even adequate taxonomy sufficient for "bringing out all the evidence," so I also argue that there is no sufficient set of field techniques. Field work must be conducted in terms of a running analysis and against a backdrop of the widest possible set of questions to which the data are potentially relevant. This is no technician's job. This is the job of an anthropologist specialized in the collection and analysis of data concerning extinct cultural systems. Only after the myth of simplicity which surrounds the training of field archaeologists is dispelled, and after more attention is given to recovering information concerning the operation of extinct cultural systems as opposed to the recovery of things, will archaeologists make significant advances in studies of cultural process.

Summary and Conclusions

It has been argued that as archaeologists we are faced with the methodological task of isolating extinct sociocultural systems as the most appropriate unit for the study of the evolutionary processes which result in cultural similarities and differences. If we view culture as man's extrasomatic means of adaptation, we must isolate and define the ecological setting of any given sociocultural system, not only with respect to the points of articulation with the physical and biological environment, but also with points of articulation with the sociocultural environment. It is suggested that changes in the ecological setting of any given system are the prime causative situations activating processes of cultural change.

It is argued that the methodology most appropriate to the study of cultural process is a regional approach in which we attempt to gain reliable and representative information concerning the internal structure and ecological setting of successive cultural systems. It is observed that under current programs of salvage archaeology and greater foundation support for archaeological research, archaeologists are actually being given the opportunity to study such regions. It is argued that, in spite of such opportunities, our current practices largely obviate the recovery of data necessary to the study of cultural process. The development of techniques for the recovery of data in structural terms is believed to be crucial, for it is the structure of archaeological remains that informs about the cultural system, and it is the cultural system which is the seat of process.

Probability sampling is suggested as a major methodological improvement which, if executed on all levels of data collection in full recognition of the inherent differences in the nature of observational populations which archaeologists investigate, can result in the production of adequate and representative data useful in the study of cultural process.

Observational populations of cultural items, features, and activity loci are recognized as having certain characteristics which demand different treatment in both field observation and sampling methodology. On the other hand, only two major sampling universes, regions and sites, are recognized as appropriate to field investigations. Many of the limitations of currently available data are believed to derive from the failure to sample populations of activity loci within a regional universe. Emphasis has been on sampling populations of cultural items within a regional rather than a site universe. This procedure has made impossible the structural definition of populations of cultural items or the study of activity loci from a structural point of view. Consequently, our current understanding of the prehistoric past is largely in terms of style distributions and cultures defined in terms of discrete traits and stylistic characteristics; this is certainly not a situation conducive to studies of cultural process.

The argument for planned and well-paced execution of research design has been presented in the form of a "hypothetical" research program, along with a limited discussion of the techniques and levels of applicability of probability sampling procedures. Problems attendant upon the recovery of structural information within both the regional and site universe have been made explicit in a number of examples of types of sampling problem and excavational situation. It is concluded that the design and execution of a research program is the job of an anthropologist, and only in a limited way can the field archaeologist be considered a "technician." Field work is an on-going process demanding methodological decisions based on a running analysis of the data recovered from prior field work. It is concluded that if we are to be successful in the collection of data relevant to studies of cultural process, field work must be conducted within the framework of a well-planned research design which provides for the application of probability sampling techniques at all levels of investigation. The field strategy executed within the framework of the research design must be directed by a well-trained anthropologist capable of making interpretations and decisions in terms of the widest possible factual and theoretical knowledge of general anthropology, and the types of questions must be drawn up which his data may be useful in solving. It is believed that modification of current practices along these lines is a necessary prerequisite for moving archaeology on to the level of development which Willey and Phillips (1958, pp. 4–5) have called the "explanatory level."

References

Adams, Robert M. (1960). The evolutionary process in early civilizations. In *The Evolution of Man: Mind, Culture, and Society* (S. Tax, ed.), pp. 153–168. Univ. of Chicago Press, Chicago.

Arkin, H., and Raymond Colton. (1957). *Tables for Statisticians.* Barnes & Noble, New York.

Binford, Lewis R. (1962). Archaeology as anthropology. *American Antiquity* **28,** 217–225.

Braidwood, Robert J. (1959). Archaeology and the evolutionary theory. In *Evolution and Anthropology: A Centennial Appraisal* (B. J. Meggers, ed.), pp. 76–89. Anthropological Society of Washington, Washington, D.C.

Brew, John Otis. (1946). Archaeology of Alkali Ridge, Southeastern Utah. *Papers of the Peabody Museum of American Archaeology and Ethnology, Harvard University* **21.**

Cole, Fay-Cooper. (1951). *Kincaid, A Prehistoric Illinois Metropolis.* Univ. of Chicago Press, Chicago.

Deming, William Edwards. (1950). *Some Theory of Sampling.* Wiley, New York.

Duncan, O. T., Ray P. Cuzzort, and Beverly Duncan. (1961). *Statistical Geography.* Free Press, Glencoe, Illinois.

Gearing, Fred. (1962). Priests and warriors. *Memoirs of the American Anthropological Association* No. 93.

Haag, William G. (1959). The status of evolutionary theory in American history. In *Evolution and Anthropology: A Centennial Appraisal* (B. J. Meggers, ed.), pp. 90–105. Anthropological Society of Washington, Washington, D.C.

Parten, Mildred. (1950). *Surveys, Polls and Samples: Practical Procedures.* Harper, New York.

Spaulding, Albert C. (1960). The dimensions of archaeology. In *Essays in the Science of Culture: In Honor of Leslie A. White* (G. E. Dole and R. L. Carneiro, eds.), pp. 437–456. Crowell-Collier, New York.
Steward, Julian H. (1960). Evolutionary principles and social types. In *The Evolution of Man: Mind, Culture and Society* (S. Tax, ed.), pp. 169–186. Univ. of Chicago Press, Chicago.
Taylor, Walter W. (1948). A study of archaeology. *Memoirs of the American Anthropological Association* No. 69.
Vescelius, G. S. (1960). Archaeological sampling: A problem of statistical inference. In *Essays in the Science of Culture: In Honor of Leslie A. White* (G. E. Dole and R. L. Carneiro, eds.), pp. 457–470. Crowell-Collier, New York.
Wagner, Philip. (1960). *The Human Use of the Earth*. Free Press, Glencoe, Illinois.
White, Leslie A. (1959). *The Evolution of Culture*. McGraw-Hill, New York.
Willey, Gordon R., and Philip Phillips. (1958). *Method and Theory in American Archaeology*. Univ. of Chicago Press, Chicago.

Hatchery West: Site Definition —
Surface Distribution of Cultural Items*

The initial problem in approaching an archaeological site as a structural entity
is to define the boundaries of the sampling universe within which the
investigator must work. In the case of Hatchery West, it was hoped that by
following the procedures mentioned earlier (having the fields especially plowed,
waiting until there had been sufficient rain to settle the newly plowed earth,
laying out a grid over the entire plowed area, and collecting all items exposed on
the surface and bagging them by grid square) the analysis of the resulting data
would permit definition of the boundaries, as well as something of the internal
structure of the site. Aside from the obvious advantages of defining the universe
in which we would work, we hoped to investigate the nature of the relationship
between the structure of the site as defined by the surface distribution of
cultural items and the structure of the site as defined by the spatial
configuration of subsurface cultural features. This kind of investigation was
prompted by an awareness that certain general principles of site selection as well
as guide lines to selecting the locations on a site for excavation have been
traditionally employed for many years. It seems fair to say that archaeologists
have tended to select for excavation sites with the greatest yield of cultural items
from surface collections and have tended to excavate areas on such sites selected
in terms of two general criteria: (1) where there are above-ground indications of
cultural features, e.g., such things as mounds, house depressions, walls, etc.; and
(2) where there is the greatest density of cultural items observed in the surface
reconnaissance. I have previously addressed myself to the problem of obtaining
an adequate and representative sample of both cultural items and cultural
features (Binford, 1964). The work reported here is an attempt to evaluate
objectively the assertion that traditional methods of selecting locations for

* These are sections abstracted from *Archaeology at Hatchery West* by Lewis R. Binford,
Sally R. Binford, Robert Whallon, and Margaret Ann Hardin, Memoir No. 24. *American
Antiquity* **35** (1970).

excavation could lead to inadequate and misrepresentative data about the site being investigated.

The plowed area of the West Field of Hatchery site consisted of 3.69 acres covered by 416 squares six meters on a side. Each of these squares was searched, all exposed items were recovered and bagged by square. After having been catalogued by provenience unit, overall inventories and distributional plots of gross categories of cultural items were made. Table I presents the inventory of recovered items tabulated by gross category as separated at the time of cataloguing.

Of immediate interest is the striking abundance of introduced cobbles, presumably primarily used in various indirect cooking or heating tasks (see Hough, 1926, for discussion of types of cooking). Second in frequency are unmodified by-products from knapping flint, indicative of tool manufacture as a major task conducted at the site. If one eliminates these items which are not manufactured artifacts (as well as other by-products such as daub), the inventory of normally tabulated items is very small, such things as stone artifacts and sherds numbering far less than a thousand. Bounded density of sherds was only 264.2/acre which is very low by midwestern "standards" as to what are "good" archaeological sites. In short, this site is unimpressive in its yield of cultural items in a very complete surface survey, and it is my opinion that under traditional approaches to field work would have been recorded as an "insignificant" site not worthy of investigation.

By plotting the varying frequency of occurrence of the different gross categories of cultural items by grid square on topographic maps of the field, we can gain some impression of the form of the site—its internal structure as defined by the differential distributions of cultural items.

Ceramics

Of the 325 sherds recovered in the surface collection, all but 40 are representative of a local variant of two types known from the Wabash River Valley designated recently as Embarrass Simple Stamped and Embarrass Cordmarked (see Winters, 1963, pp. 101–104). The identity of the ceramics from the Hatchery site as local examples of the Embarrass series has been verified by Howard Winters, who commented that there was some minor difference between the ceramics from the Hatchery site and the population serving as the type collections of the Embarrass series. However, these were very minor indeed and were primarily in the nature of the paste and relative frequency of varying modes of surface finish, e.g., lower percentages of simple stamped pottery on Hatchery than on the analogous sites in the Wabash. Analogy is certainly also evident between these ceramics and those of Southern

TABLE I   *Inventory of Cultural Items Recovered in the Surface Collection*

Class of item	Number recovered	Percentage of total
1. Bones	25	0.34
2. Shells	14	0.19
3. Hoe chips	11	0.15
4. Chipped stone artifacts	182	2.48
5. Chipped debris	2852	36.22
6. Ground and/or pecked stone	120	1.64
7. Daub	71	0.97
8. Pottery sherds	325	4.17
9. Introduced limestone	169	2.03
10. Introduced sandstone	136	1.70
11. Introduced unbroken cobbles	484	6.20
12. Introduced broken cobbles	3428	43.90
	7817	99.99

Illinois known as Raymond (Maxwell, 1951, p. 278) and Lewis (Cole *et al.,* 1951, pp. 178–183). In the latter comparisons, certain features, such as dowel impressions in the interior of the lip appear widely distributed in the midwest between A.D. 250 and A.D. 750 and taken together with thin vessel wall and generally undecorated fine cordmarked pottery are "stylistic" diagnostics of the Late Woodland period. Future detailed analysis of the ceramics from the Carlyle Reservoir and similar comparative study of extant collections from other areas will make possible the definition of a ceramic tradition in the Illinois–Indiana area of magnitude comparable to the increasingly well-defined Havana tradition but which is areally distributed over the area previously occupied by both the Crab Orchard and Havana traditions (see Struever, 1964, for a discussion of the areal distribution of these two traditions). The details of the form of the ceramics must await future analysis, and for the moment we will concern ourselves with the differential distribution of ceramics on Hatchery site.

A continuous distribution of ceramics was observed over 1.23 acres of the 3.69 acres investigated. Within this bounded distribution (as shown in Fig. 1, a and b) there were two minor areas of concentration.

The greatest concentration is located in area B (Fig. 1b) where a density of over 16 sherds/6-m^2 was observed. Some 35 m to the south of this cluster is a second minor cluster of sherds where a density of 7 sherds/6-m^2 is reached.

Our observations suggest that there were two major areas of ceramic usage and that the northern area was by far the locus of greatest activity. Judging from the relative homogeneity of the form of the ceramics recovered, these two areas could represent two discrete occupations but very closely spaced in time, or two major activity areas in which ceramics were in common use within a single community.

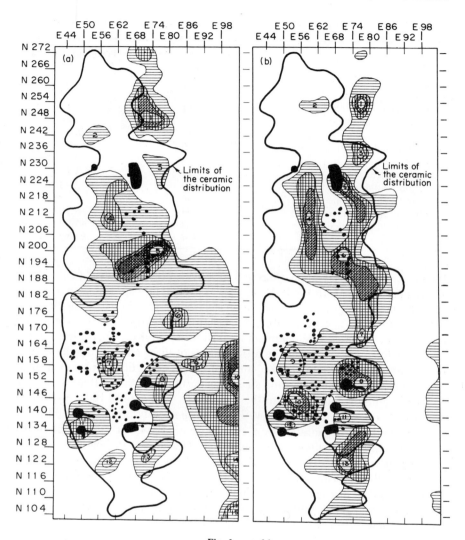

Fig. 1. a and b

Cracked Cobbles

Items included in this class were all fine-grained rock not identifiable as sandstone and/or limestone. By far the major type of rock represented was crystalline rock (quartzite), but gabbro and granite were also represented. These were introduced to the site since the deposits making up the site were of fine sedimentary origin, mainly fluvial silts overlain by loess. These were assumed to

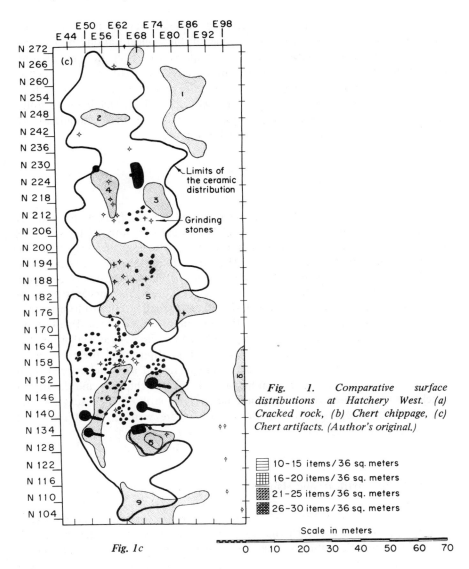

Fig. 1. Comparative surface distributions at Hatchery West. (a) Cracked rock, (b) Chert chippage, (c) Chert artifacts. (Author's original.)

E 50   E 62   E 74   E 86   E 98
E 44 | E 56 | E 68 | E 80 | E 92 |

(c)

Limits of
the ceramic
distribution

Grinding
stones

10-15 items / 36 sq. meters
16-20 items / 36 sq. meters
21-25 items / 36 sq. meters
26-30 items / 36 sq. meters

Scale in meters

0   10   20   30   40   50   60   70

Fig. 1c

have been primarily introduced to the site for use in various indirect cooking methods.

The observed distribution is very different from that seen for pottery. In the first place, cracked cobbles are distributed over a much larger area and have a continuous distribution over the entire 3.69 acres investigated. Concentrations of cracked cobbles are shown plotted against the observed ceramic distribution in Fig. 1a. Several points should be made about this distribution: (a) there are

15 observable concentrations of cracked cobbles versus two observable concentrations of ceramics; (b) only nine of the concentrations of cracked cobble are within the limits of the ceramic distribution; (c) there is only one coincidence between a ceramic concentration and a concentration of cracked cobbles, concentration 4, Fig. 1a. The above observations suggest that there were occupations of Hatchery West that were preceramic, and it seems quite likely that there were numerous occupations involved in the accumulation of cultural items distributed in the West Field of the site.

Chipping Debris

Items included in this class were all fractured pieces of chert that did not exhibit any obvious evidence of having been modified into tools; this class included cores, chips, flakes, and shatter, all by-products of flint knapping. The observed distribution of chipping debris (Fig. 1b) exhibits many more analogies to the distribution of cracked cobbles than it does to the distribution of ceramics, but there are analogies to both. There are 15 observable concentrations of chipping debris on the site of which 13 are numbered. Concentrations which show no observable analogy in either the ceramic or cracked rock distributions are number 5, located in the area of square N224 and E68-74, as well as number 11, located in the vicinity of square N134 E68. In general there is a good correspondence between areas of concentrated cracked rock and concentrated chippage; however, the correlation between density of chippage and density of cracked rock at these locations is not particularly striking. This suggests that many of them represent occupations where there were different ranges of activities being carried out.

Chipped Stone Artifacts and Manos

This is a very gross category in which there is no distinction made between projectile points, end-scrapers, flake knives, etc. Thus as a functional category it has little utility. Nevertheless, it should reflect intensity of activity and as such can be informatively compared with the distribution of ceramics, cracked cobbles and chipping debris. The distribution is shown in Fig. 1c. There are 10 localizations of chipped stone artifacts shown by the stippled areas. These simply represent areas where chipped stone artifacts were recorded and do not imply any relative density data. Again there is a strong analogy to the areas defined by the distribution of chipping debris as well as to that of the cracked cobbles. On the same distribution are plotted the locations of finds of manos and metates. There are four obvious concentrations, one coinciding with concentration 4 of cracked rock and chippage, which coincides with the area of greatest ceramic density. The second concentration is in the area of cracked rock concentration 5, while the third is in the area of cracked rock concentration 7 and chipping debris 9. There is also a minor concentration adjacent to cracked cobble concentration 14, far outside the area of ceramic concentration.

Structure of the Site Defined by Surface Distributions

The plotting and comparison of the densities of these five classes of items should be sufficient to demonstrate the following points: There are activity areas outside the bounds of the ceramic distribution which are believed to reveal the presence of preceramic occupations of the site, and there are strong analogies between the density plots of the cracked cobbles and chert debris, suggesting that we can recognize at least 15 different locations on the site which were the seats of spatially differentiated activity and in all probability represent numerous separate and discrete occupations of the site.

In order to assess the historical meaning of the areas of localized activity on the site, the inventories of the squares covering the areas of the recognized 14 localizations as shown in Fig. 2 were made and are given in Table II. In addition to the counts, the table provides the percentages and the cumulative percentages for each area of artifact concentration. The cumulative percentages are plotted graphically in Fig. 3, resulting in two different graphs. In one (Fig. 3a) there is a very low or negligible percentage of ceramics with correspondingly low frequencies of daub and limestone. The second type (Fig. 3b) exhibits appreciable quantities of pottery and higher incidences of hoe chips, daub, limestone, and ground-stone tools. Within these generic types of graph, groupings can be observed, leading to the question of whether the observed variability between the several samples contributing to the grouping of graphs might not reasonably be seen as simple sampling error. In order to test this possibility, chi-square calculations were made for the following groups of samples (spatial clusters): ceramic graphs for areas F, D, and K (X in Fig. 4) and nonceramic graphs for areas B, G, J, and N (Z in Fig. 4), as well as areas M and I (Y in Fig. 4). The results of the chi-square calculations are given in Table III. The chi-square results indicate that observed differences between the relative frequencies of the various classes of items recovered from the different areas grouped together as shown could have arisen simply as a result of sampling error. Therefore, we are justified in asserting that the separate samples in each of the three groups could have been drawn from a single population. Each group does, however, represent a very different population as do the samples from areas A, L, H, C, and E. Thus, we can recognize eight types of activity area of the 15 recognized localizations of cultural items. Summary information concerning these recognized types of "areas" on the site are given in Table IV and Fig. 4.

TABLE II Inventories for Crude Classes of Cultural Items Recovered in the 15 Recognized Areas of Activity Localization on Hatchery West

Class of item	A	B	C	D	E	F	G	H	I	J	K	L	M	N
							Number of items							
Chert	33	82	136	91	15	151	31	147	99	85	64	205	127	27
Shell	0	0	0	0	0	0	0	5	0	0	0	0	0	0
Bone	0	0	3	0	0	1	0	1	0	0	2	1	0	0
Hoe chips	0	0	2	0	0	0	1	3	0	0	2	0	0	0
Daub	4	1	2	1	2	3	0	7	0	5	2	9	0	0
Artifacts	3	3	12	6	1	11	2	9	6	5	3	10	6	1
Gr. artifacts	0	1	18	5	2	3	0	12	4	0	1	2	2	0
Pottery	1	2	90	14	4	36	0	29	5	0	10	13	6	0
Limestone	1	4	8	6	10	14	1	21	1	0	7	19	6	0
Sandstone	0	1	1	0	0	1	1	4	1	2	3	25	6	0
Crystalline	50	143	167	97	35	179	72	90	83	164	76	158	78	28
Pebbles	5	14	19	10	7	9	2	8	9	14	11	32	11	2
	97	251	458	230	76	408	110	336	208	275	181	474	242	58
							Cumulative percentages							
Chert	34.0	32.7	29.7	39.6	19.7	37.0	28.2	43.7	47.6	30.9	35.6	43.2	52.5	34.7
Shell	34.0	32.7	29.7	39.6	19.7	37.0	28.2	45.2	47.6	30.9	35.6	43.2	52.5	34.7
Bone	34.0	32.7	30.5	39.6	19.7	37.3	28.2	45.5	47.6	30.9	36.7	43.4	52.5	34.7
Hoe chips	34.0	32.7	30.8	39.6	19.7	37.3	29.1	46.4	47.6	30.9	37.8	43.4	52.5	34.7
Daub	38.1	33.1	31.2	40.0	22.4	38.0	29.1	48.5	47.6	32.7	38.9	45.3	52.5	34.7
Artifacts	41.2	34.2	33.8	42.6	23.7	40.7	30.9	51.2	50.5	34.5	40.6	47.4	55.0	36.7
Gr. artifacts	41.2	34.6	37.8	44.8	26.3	41.4	30.9	54.7	52.4	34.5	41.1	47.9	55.8	36.7
Pottery	42.3	35.4	57.5	50.9	31.6	50.3	30.9	63.7	54.8	34.5	46.9	50.6	58.3	36.7
Limestone	43.3	37.0	59.2	53.5	44.7	53.7	31.8	69.6	55.3	34.5	50.8	54.6	60.8	38.8
Sandstone	43.3	37.4	59.4	53.5	44.7	53.9	32.7	70.8	55.8	35.3	52.5	59.9	63.2	38.8
Crystalline	94.8	94.3	95.8	95.7	90.7	97.7	98.1	97.5	95.7	94.8	94.5	93.2	95.4	95.9
Pebbles	99.9	99.9	99.9	100.0	99.9	99.9	99.9	99.9	100.0	99.9	100.0	99.9	99.9	99.9

Percentages

Chert	34.0	32.7	29.7	39.6	19.7	37.0	28.2	43.7	47.6	30.9	35.6	43.2	52.5	34.7
Shell	0.0	0.0	0.0	0.0	0.0	0.0	0.0	1.5	0.0	0.0	0.0	0.0	0.0	0.0
Bone	0.0	0.0	0.7	0.0	0.0	0.3	0.0	0.3	0.0	0.0	1.1	0.2	0.0	0.0
Hoe chips	0.0	0.0	0.4	0.0	0.0	0.0	0.9	0.9	0.0	0.0	1.1	0.0	0.0	0.0
Daub	4.1	0.4	0.4	0.4	2.6	0.7	0.0	2.1	0.0	1.8	1.1	1.9	0.0	0.0
Artifacts	3.1	1.2	2.6	2.6	1.3	2.7	1.8	2.7	2.9	1.8	1.7	2.1	2.5	2.0
Gr. artifacts	0.0	0.4	4.0	2.2	2.6	0.7	0.0	3.6	1.9	0.0	0.6	0.4	0.8	0.0
Pottery	1.0	0.8	19.7	6.1	5.3	8.8	0.0	8.6	2.4	0.0	5.8	2.7	2.5	0.0
Limestone	1.0	1.6	1.7	2.6	13.2	3.4	0.9	6.3	0.5	0.0	3.9	4.0	2.5	0.0
Sandstone	0.0	0.4	0.2	0.0	0.0	0.3	0.9	1.2	0.5	0.7	1.7	5.3	2.5	0.0
Crystalline	51.5	56.9	36.4	42.2	46.0	43.8	65.4	26.7	39.9	59.6	42.0	33.3	32.2	57.1
Pebbles	5.2	5.6	4.2	4.4	9.2	2.2	1.8	2.4	4.3	5.1	6.1	6.8	4.6	4.1

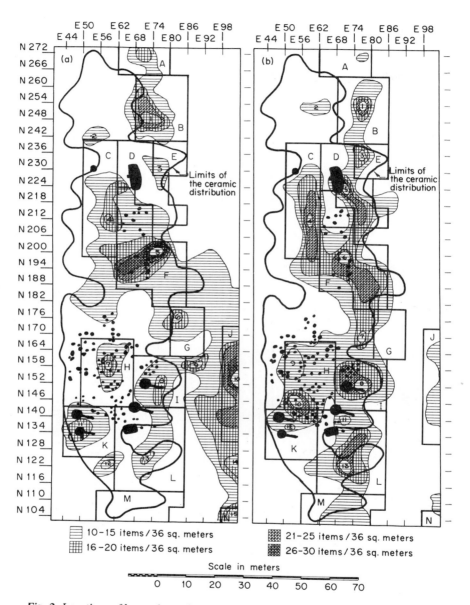

Fig. 2. Locations of lettered sample areas superimposed upon surface distributions. Scale in meters is the same as for Fig. 1. (Author's original.)

TABLE III   *Summary of Chi-Square Data Localization Comparisons*

Areas grouped	B,J,G,N	F,D,K	M,I
Degrees of freedom	27.0	18.0	7.0
Level of probability	0.05	0.05	0.05
Expected chi-square value	40.11	28.87	14.07
Observed chi-square value	30.90	24.11	9.21
Conclusion	Not different	Not different	Not different

TABLE IV   *Summary Information for Recognized Formal Classes of Artifact Concentration*

Artifact density	Percentage artifacts of chippage and cobbles only	Area designation	Characteristics	Inferred activity
		Primarily ceramic components		
0.53	65.7	E	Moderate freq. of pottery: high limestone counts: lot on chippage	Indirect heating and cooking, food processing
0.91	66.1	C	Very high on pottery and grinding stones	Boiling and food preparation
0.78	69.7	H	High on chipping debris; low on crystalline rock, high limestone, and moderate pottery	Compound work area of boiling and indirect heating food processing
		Ceramic and nonceramic components compounded		
0.66	76.5	L	High daub, limestone, and Mississippian pottery	Food processing and Mississippian localization
0.61	80.3	D,F,K	Moderate freq. of pottery and other artifacts	Graph appears to be a compound of a ceramic and a nonceramic graph
		Primarily nonceramic components		
0.45	85.5	A	High in duab and chipped artifacts; low in chert debris	Tool use and food processing
0.59	86.0	M,I	High in chippage; low in daub, ground stone, etc.	Tool manufacture
0.52	91.1	B,G,J,N	Low in chippage and most artifacts; high in crystalline cobbles	Food processing

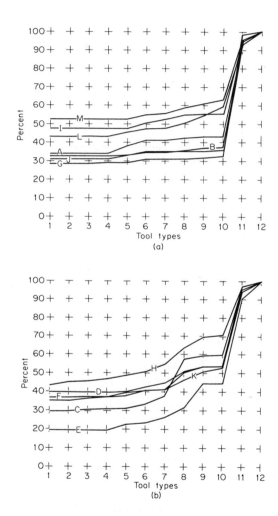

Fig. 3. *(a) Cumulative graph of nonceramic activity loci. (b) Cumulative graph of ceramic activity loci.*

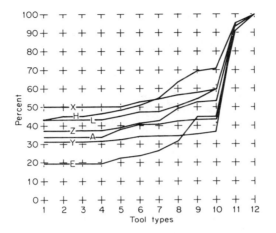

Fig. 4. Summary graph of grouped areas. X refers to grouping D, F, K; Y refers to grouping M, I; and Z refers to grouping B, G, J, N.

Summary

By collecting surface items in a controlled surface collection, it has been possible to discover certain facts about the nature of Hatchery West prior to any excavation of the site. Significant findings follow.

The surface distribution of various gross categories of cultural items are not isomorphic, indicating that the location was occupied at different times, as evidenced by the localizations of artifacts of different known forms, such as Mississippian pottery versus Embarrass series pottery, and cracked rock and chippage in areas outside the limits of the ceramic distribution.

The quantitative variability exhibited between areas of the site demonstrates that different classes of cultural items may vary independently of each other, presumably as a function of the spatial differentiation of activity loci within communities and between different occupants of the site; *this makes the collection of a representative sample of cultural items from any one location on the site impossible.*

Eight generically different types of loci were recognized as representing different and distinct populations of cultural items differentially distributed over the site; each would have to be investigated as independent areas if one would hope to generalize about the site as a whole.

Each type of location was not equally represented on the site; some occurred only once while others were observed to occur at as many as five separate locations; this suggests that certain types of occupation or sequence of cultural events has occurred more often on the site than had others.

Judging from the surface distribution, the most intense and prolonged occupation was centered in area C in the north part of the field, while the second most intense occupation was centered in area H of the south part of the field.

These observations were the basis for our field decisions as to where to place our control hand excavations. A block of eight contiguous 3-m squares was opened up in the center of the artifact concentration in area C. A block of four squares was excavated in the center of the chippage concentration in area H. Once these excavations were completed, the power equipment was used in removing the upper plow-disturbed soil so that the features could be exposed over the entire site and investigated.

Structure of the Site Defined by the Cultural Features and Correlation with the Surface Distribution of Cultural Items

It has previously been argued (Binford, 1964) that because of the differences in the formal properties of cultural items (as distinguished from cultural features) that there are different problems associated with obtaining an adequate and representative sample of both items and features. Excavation and recovery techniques which might be adequate to the recovery of a fair sample of cultural items might not be sufficient for supplying similar information regarding a population of cultural features.

The investigation of Hatchery West was conducted with an eye to this problem, and the methods employed were aimed toward insuring an adequate and representative sample of both cultural items and cultural features. These sampling procedures allowed us to investigate the relationship between these two classes of archaeological data and to assess the degree to which the formal–spatial structure of a population of items is correlated with the formal–spatial structure of a population of features.

Analysis of the surface distribution of cultural items resulted in the recognition of eight distinct kinds of areas; these areas were defined by the spatial clustering of classes of artifacts and the associations within these clusters with other types of cultural items. Fifteen examples of the eight kinds of areas were observed. Within these eight types of locations, there were three broad classes delineated which are believed to represent gross differences in the depositional and cultural history of the site. These three groupings are: (1) mainly ceramic, (2) mixed ceramic and nonceramic, (3) mainly nonceramic. It will be recalled that these three groups exhibited a general centripetal spatial configuration, with 2 generally located peripherally to 1, and 3 peripherally to 2.

Tables V and VI present the summary data on the types of localizations, tabulated by observed frequency of types of cultural features; summary

TABLE V   *Feature Types, by Surface Defined Site Areas*

Class of data	Areas defined by the surface distribution										
	E	C	H	L	D	F	K	A	M	I	B,G,N,J
Stains	o	2	9	1	0	0	3	0	0	0	0
Deep earth ovens	0	0	4	4	0	0	3	0	0	9	0
Shallow ovens	0	0	19	0	0	7	7	0	0	0	0
Compound pits	0	1	24	0	6	2	0	0	0	0	0
Mississippian pits	0	0	2	4	0	0	0	0	0	0	0
Rock hearths	0	0	1	0	0	2	0	0	0	0	0
Burials	0	0	5	0	0	0	0	0	0	0	0
Keyhole houses	0	0	0	1	0	0	2	0	0	1	0
Mississippian houses	0	0	0	1	0	0	0	0	0	0	0
Pole houses	0	1	1	0	1	0	0	0	0	0	0
	0	4	63	11	7	11	15	0	0	10	0

TABLE VI   *Comparative Densities—Cultural Features and Items*

Areas	Density of cultural items (m^{-2})	Density of cultural features—pits (m^{-2})	Averages	
			Items (m^{-2})	Features (m^{-2})
Primarily ceramic components				
Area E	0.53	0.000		
Area C	0.91	0.004	0.74	0.050
Area H	0.78	0.146		
Compounded ceramic and nonceramic components				
Area L	0.66	0.015		
Areas D	0.58	0.018	0.63	0.024
F	0.70	0.019		
K	0.55	0.046		
Primarily nonceramic components				
Area A	0.44	0.000		
Areas M	0.56	0.000	0.52	0.004
I	0.62	0.030		
Areas B	0.58	0.000		
G	0.50	0.000		
J	0.54	0.000		
N	0.40	0.000		

information is also presented on densities of features and items by area and their averages by type of area. Inspection of these tables reveals the following: (1) Those areas whose cultural items suggest mainly ceramic occupations (group 1) are those which exhibit the greatest variability in density of cultural features. (2) Among those areas referable to group 1 there was no direct correlation between density of cultural items and density of features (e.g., Figs. 1b and 1c). (3) Those areas whose items suggest group 2 (both ceramic and nonceramic occupations) exhibit less variation in the observed densities of cultural features. (4) Those areas which represent primarily preceramic occupation (group 3) consistently lack cultural features. In the one case where they do occur, the locus is the area with the highest density of cultural items. (5) If we disregard internal differences between areas assigned to the three groups and consider only the averages of items and features for each group, we can observe a direct correlation between the two classes of archaeological remains.

Although point 5 might seem self-evident, it should be recalled that within a given community areas of items and features may vary independently of each other (see points 2 and 3). The density and distribution figures of group 2 suggest further that features tend to be located peripherally with respect to areas of high density of cultural items.

The major methodological problem toward which excavation and analysis were geared concerned the relationship between the formal–spatial structure of populations of items and features and the degree to which these may be correlated. The summary data cited above suggest the following general conclusions: (1) Within any given community the spatial distribution of items and features may vary independently of each other. Those areas in which the greatest number of cultural items were lost or abandoned do not necessarily coincide with the areas where the construction of features most frequently occurred. (2) In comparing communities, there is no necessary correlation between numbers of cultural items and features. Their numbers are determined by the nature of the activities engaged in by the occupants of the two locations. (3) On sites with complex culture histories there will be a general correlation between the number of items in any given area and the intensity of use of that area by all the different occupants. (4) On sites with complex culture histories the compound effects of points 1–3 above will increase the probability of features coinciding in their distribution with zones of moderate density of items. (5) On sites with simple culture histories the effect of point 1 above will result in the occurrence of a higher density of features in areas peripheral to high density zones of items. (6) In selecting sites for excavation, the mere presence of higher densities of items does not insure a correspondingly high density of features.

We conclude from this analysis and discussion that without a program of stratified sampling and/or a prior knowledge of the culture history of a site that densities of items cannot be used as a guide to excavation. Densities of items by themselves will tell us nothing of the distribution of features on the site, nor of the functional variability represented.

Conclusions

The aims of the research reported here were threefold: (1) to test the utility of certain data-collection techniques; (2) to investigate the nature of the relationship between populations of cultural features and cultural items on a site to provide an empirical basis for the development of independent sampling procedures appropriate to the different populations; and (3) to demonstrate the utility of the suggested data-collection and analytical procedures for providing information amenable to social interpretation. Our conclusions with respect to these aims can be stated as follows.

In cases where archaeological sites occur in modern agricultural areas and lack any above-ground remains of features, it is possible and profitable to conduct a controlled surface collection which will permit the preliminary definition of the site in areal terms. In addition, the variable densities and combinations of occurrences of different forms of cultural items will permit the definition of subareas on the site. These must be treated as internally differentiated areas of the site, possibly reflecting a complex culture history and/or the internal spatial differentiation of activities within the prehistoric community represented. All of this information can then be employed in making decisions as to how to sample the site for cultural features so as to insure an adequate and representative sample.

By using techniques specifically designed to insure the maximum recovery of data relevant to cultural features, we were able to recover *complete* data on features present at Hatchery West. These data proved amenable to formal analysis, which in turn made possible the recognition of functionally differentiated activity areas and houses. In short, we were able to identify the archaeological remains of four distinct communities that had settled on this location.

The comparison of the structure of the site, defined in terms of cultural features and known from the distribution of cultural items, allowed us to demonstrate that the two general classes of archaeological remains were in fact independently distributed. Our analysis allowed us to make the following generalizations.

Between communities there is no necessary direct correlation between numbers of cultural items lost or abandoned and the number of features utilized on the location. The relative numbers are determined by the nature of the activities dominating the actions of the group during the course of the occupation. Within any given community, the spatial distribution of cultural items and features tends to vary independently of one another. Those areas in which activities resulted in the loss or abandonment of the greatest number of items is not *necessarily* the same as the area where the greatest construction of features occurred. On sites with complex culture histories, there will be a gross direct correlation between the number of items occurring in any given area and the intensity of use of that area made by all the separate occupants. On sites with complex culture histories, the compound effects of the situations summarized above will increase the probability of the occurrence of consistent incidences of features located in zones with moderate densities of cultural items. On sites with simple culture histories, the effect of the situation suggested above will result in a greater density of cultural features in areas peripheral to areas of high item densities. In selecting sites for excavation the mere presence of huge densities of items does not insure a corresponding likelihood of high densities of features.

We are therefore able to suggest that data collection prosecuted without a prior knowledge of the culture history of the site or a program of stratified sampling cannot proceed by using densities of cultural items as a guide with any realistic expectation of obtaining an adequate and representative sample of features. In addition, in selecting sites for excavation without a program of stratified sampling, high densities of cultural items cannot be used as a guide to selection without biasing the results.

The demonstration of the utility of the differentiation of data collecting techniques as well as a systemic approach to analysis is hopefully accomplished in the substantive results reported here.

The presence of a number of locations of preceramic occupancy were isolated and were shown to vary among themselves with respect to relative proportions of different artifact classes present. The latter observation was interpreted as reflecting differences in the range and relative frequency of activities carried out on the location. Further study of the tools found will hopefully permit the recognition of different types of sites for the preceramic period.

The investigation and definition of three different La Motte settlements provides us with our first knowledge of the settlements of the Late Woodland period. The recognition of two types of La Motte settlements, winter and summer, implies an annual round involving a complex settlement system in which social units moved seasonally. The association of corporate work areas for the preparation of food suggests that there was a social bond between females of the community. We suggested that this might reflect a matrilocal form of residence pattern, more appropriately sororalocal since each woman would have been housed separately during the winter. The meaning of these two settlement types in terms of the total settlement system cannot at present be assessed. We do, however, know that large sites existed (the Dean site) which would approach the size of small towns. It seems unlikely that these were seasonally abandoned;

therefore, the details of the movement of social segments of these La Motte societies remain a major problem for future research.

In contrast to the La Motte communities, the Mississippian settlement appeared to have been a single household which was part of a larger dispersed community of households along the river terrace. Our data for the Mississippian occupation do not represent a single community as in the case of the La Motte. On the contrary, it is a segment of a very different community type. The specifics of the contrasts between the settlement system and the cycle of the Mississippian and La Motte cultural systems when known should provide many clues to the adaptive changes that resulted in the emergence of the Middle Mississippian in the midwest.

In order to understand these settlement systems a methodology of stratified sampling as previously proposed (Binford, 1964) and justified by the research reported here is a necessity.

References

Binford, Lewis R. (1964). A consideration of archaeological research design. *American Antiquity* **29**, 425–441.

Cole, Fay-Cooper *et al.* (1951). *Kincaid, A Prehistoric Illinois Metropolis.* Univ. of Chicago Press, Chicago.

Hough, Walter. (1926). Fire as an agent in human culture. *U.S. National Museum, Bulletin* **139**.

Maxwell, Moreau S. (1951). The Woodland cultures in southern Illinois. *Logan Museum Publications in Anthropology, Bulletin* **7**.

Struever, Stuart. (1964). The Hopewell interaction sphere in riverine-western Great Lakes culture history. *Illinois State Museum Scientific Papers* **12**, 85–106.

Winters, Howard D. (1963). An archaeological survey of the Wabash Valley in Illinois. *Illinois State Museum, Reports of Investigations* No. 10.

Review of
"A Guide to Field Methods in Archaeology: Approaches to the Anthropology of the Dead" by Robert F. Heizer and John A. Graham [*][†]

This book is a revised edition of the 1949 publication *Guide to Archaeological Field Methods,* edited by Robert F. Heizer. The major differences from the original edition are: (1) the book is printed in larger type, (2) there are more illustrations, and (3) there is an attempt to give the book a more catholic appeal by (a) deleting many provincial references and those sections of the 1949 book that deal only with California Indians, and (b) considerable expansion of the bibliographical references to include some foreign publications. The subjects taken up by the author are essentially the same as those in the 1949 edition, with some updating of reference material. The only new component of the book is a chapter titled "A Review of Techniques for Archaeological Sampling" by Sonia Ragir. This chapter is a useful addition to the literature since it summarizes a number of views on the applicability of sampling methods to different universes of archaeological data. With the exception of Miss Ragir's contribution, this book is substantively the same as the 1949 edition. It approaches archaeological fieldwork from the perspective of excavation procedure with little attention to the problem of scientific data collection as such. It is frequently asserted that certain types of observations are "important," yet there is little discussion of why they might be important or what relevance various types of information may have to the investigation of the past. It is my opinion that this shortcoming stems from the authors' methodological bias that the aims of archaeology are to be accomplished by gaining sufficient remains of human activities to permit empirical generalizations

[*] With a chapter by Sonia Ragir. Palo Alto, California: The National Press, 1967. ix, 274 pp., 4 appendices, bibliography and addendum, 8 data record forms, 33 figures (1 frontispiece, 1 endpaper), index of authors cited, subject index, 4 maps, $7.95 (text), $10.00 (trade). [New, revised ed.; original ed. 1949.]

[†] Originally published in *American Anthropologist* 70, 806–808 (1968).

to be made. After this, one is then free to draw inferences to the conditions in the past that resulted in the patterning and form of the archaeological remains recovered. Once the archaeologist draws his inferences, his job is finished. What is relevant are the self-evident units of observation about which we have made inferences. There is no attention to the scientific problems of confirmation and verification. Data quality control needed in hypothesis testing is never mentioned.

In this reviewer's opinion this is a guide for conducting nonscientific archaeological investigations. Little attention is given to the complex problem of achieving comparability of observations with regard to defined variables when there are a number of field-workers making observations. We are told, "One of the most important functions of the field notebook is to keep a record of artifacts which are not included in the permanent collection from the site" (p. 75). By what criteria are we to decide which artifacts to keep? One would judge from Heizer's discussion that ease of transport is the major criterion.

The authors place particular emphasis on the importance of stratigraphy and artifact analysis for gaining a chronological perspective. Although mention is occasionally made of gaining an understanding of internal variability within occupations, there is no specific discussion of methods to be employed in gaining such understanding beyond the suggestion that horizontal location of artifacts should be noted and "individual judgment must determine which artifacts are not of sufficient importance to warrant a record being made of their exact location" (p. 81).

With regard to the crucial problem of the location of excavation units, we are told "it is, at times, an exceptionally perplexing question and one to which there is no satisfactory answer" (p. 45). Apparently the relevance of Miss Ragir's discussion was not considered by the authors in their discussion of excavation procedure. Despite the authors' pessimism, they go on to suggest two "concepts of approaching" the problem: (1) entire site excavation, and (2) exploratory or test excavations. For the latter we are told that "the best and most generally employed way of obtaining what is literally a representative cross section of the site is by trenching." To those familiar with the internal structure of archaeological sites, it is known that trenching will rarely, if ever, supply an adequate and representative sample of the differential distribution of implements, facilities, and activity areas making up the remnants of human social life at the site. Once again, the sampling problems facing the archaeologist are not discussed, and the authors seem to favor stratigraphic variability without questioning its relevance to problems of culture change.

The authors spend much time defending the recommended procedure of excavating by arbitrary levels; these arguments are justified in terms of the nature of archaeological deposits in California shell heaps. Certainly discontinuous lenses and microstratification in archaeological deposits present a formidable problem to the archaeologist, but if he is interested in investigating the nature of activities conducted at any one time period at a site and the organization of social units performing tasks, he must solve the problem of horizontal variability. Excavation by arbitrary levels hampers the analysis of recovered materials into units of meaning with regard to differential distribution of activities over a site. The authors might have argued that their concern was primarily with changes in inventories of artifacts through time; in this case the demonstration of proportional frequency shifts in artifact categories is some measure of variability, but whether it always measures culture change is certainly debatable.

From the perspective of 1967, this is a very poor book. It is misleading in that it conveys the impression that data collection can be learned by cookbook directives. If one wishes to give amateurs some appreciation for the complexities of archaeological research, then some attention to research design, data quality control, and sampling are necessary. In this volume, archaeology appears to be a series of learned skills: photography, surveying, artifact identification, careful manual work, etc. It has little value as a guide for training contemporary students of archaeology, although Miss Ragir's chapter and the bibliography have some utility. As a book for the amateur, Morris Robbins and Mary R. Irving's *The Amateur Archaeologist's Handbook* (Crowell: Collier, New York, 1966) is more germane.

Part III

THEORY AND ASSUMPTIONS

As outlined briefly in the introduction to Part II, Method of Data Collection, my early notions regarding the understanding of the past consisted of viewing patterned relationships which we might isolate as having reference to the organizational properties of past systems. Attempts at reconstructing the properties of past systems so as to accommodate the observed relationships in a particular set of archaeological data are clearly seen in most of the papers published in this section; these have more to do with theory itself. I quickly learned that publishing and lecturing to my colleagues in archaeology—as I did in many of the papers printed in the other sections of this book—had little direct effect. At most I elicited criticism as to the character of the empirical data used, or my arguments were dismissed as "materialistic" or "evolutionary" or by some other phrase considered derogatory, therefore justifying dismissal. Students, on the other hand, seemed to take to the arguments like ducks to water. Clearly the differences between these responses were more than personality conflicts or professional competition. There was something much more basic. My colleagues for the most part had been educated to accept as valid all the implicit assumptions of a "normative" theory of culture. Culture history was a major aim of archaeology. Inductive strategies were employed, to be sure, but in the context of a series of implicit assumptions about culture and the significance of the archaeological record. They were operating deductively, but they didn't recognize it since all the principles standing behind their interpretations were accepted as valid and functioned in their thoughts as "laws" do in an explicit scientific strategy. It was necessary to explore in very explicit form these assumptions, these "laws," and to demonstrate if possible their nonvalidity, or at least the fact that their validity had not been established.

I tried this approach first in "Archaeological Systematics"; however, it was written in the short polemic form of "Archaeology as Anthropology." It didn't have the effect that I had hoped. I decided on another approach more directly related to a body of recognized subject matter, something that had more content of direct concrete relevance. I worked on the "Mortuary Practices" paper off and on for over four years. I gathered historical data; I searched the literature for every argument I could find dealing with mortuary practices.

I discovered many interesting things which did not get incorporated into my published paper. For instance, I found that by plotting the frequencies of articles published on mortuary subjects by five year intervals a very interesting patterning emerged. The curves for articles of a theoretical nature and those of a descriptive nature showed alternating frequency peaks. Clearly this was a demonstration of the role of theory. Papers appeared first which either challenged some interpretive principles or offered alternative opinions. A burst of descriptive publication followed, generally offering empirical data to support or refute the propositions offered in the earlier papers. Descriptive publication began to decrease in frequency as opinion was solidified. Interpretive principles became secure.

Next appeared a series of theoretical articles either challenging or modifying the secure principles. This was again followed by a burst of descriptive publication. Here was clear historical evidence contrary to the claims of the "inductivists" that they started with the data and generalized from it. Clearly the historical record of anthropological publication itself proved that this was not what happened. I have never worked these data up for publication. Instead I concentrated on the problems of the significance assigned by anthropologists to observed variability in mortuary practices. The results of these endeavors are published here. Since the original publication of this paper and this book will be almost simultaneous, I have no way of evaluating the effect of this paper on traditionalists in the field.

Concurrently with much of the work done on the mortuary research, I started work on another fascinating problem: dealing with the significance of variability in the archaeological record. While I was at the University of Chicago, Sally Schanfield returned from field work in Israel. She had excavated a Mousterian cave. Her research had been encouraged by her thesis director, F. Clark Howell. She returned full of enthusiasm, and during her verbal descriptions of the character of her site she asserted that within a relatively thick deposit the character of the archaeological materials was identical from top to bottom. I flatly asserted that she must be mistaken. In my experience I had never seen two archaeological samples which when submitted to detailed analysis proved to be identical. We had many loud and heated exchanges in Clark Howell's laboratory over this question. Finally I decided to prove her wrong: "You give me the statistical tabulations on your material, and I will show you." She did, and I must have worked at the desk calculator for several days.

Using various statistical tests, I compared frequencies for every combination and permutation of the units in terms of which she had excavated the site. I could demonstrate no real difference except between deposits in the front and rear of the cave! I had at that point analyzed literally hundreds of samples of archaeological materials. I had never encountered a situation like this. I was fascinated; it must signify some different, grossly different, conditions in the past from what I had thus far encountered. All my experience had been with material remains of relatively recent sapiens man. Could this possibly indicate a major difference between the conditions of organized adaptation of recent and ancient man? This possibility fascinated me. If so, then the application of interpretive principles largely derived from observations on the contemporary ethnographic record and intuitive notions of how culture worked might be even more misleading when used to interpret the middle and early Paleolithic materials.

I was quite familiar with the literature of Old World archaeology. My first classes taught at Michigan had been on Old World subjects. I also had taught with Clark Howell and Braidwood at Chicago and had actually spent more study time learning the Old World data than I had on New World materials. After all, I had learned the data of the New World from Griffin, and I knew it. I began to worry myself about the problem of the significance of interassemblage variability. The obvious problem was the alternation of industries documented by François Bordes for the Mousterian. The ideas of Howard Winters regarding the character of expectable interassemblage variability when dealing with a seasonally mobile adaptation was the obvious place to start.

Sally and I were married the following fall, and during the winter I started the analysis of Mousterian assemblages using multivariate techniques and a model of the past which postulated a dynamic, mobile adaptation characterized by a generalized expedient manufacture of tools; that is, tools were manufactured largely at the locations where the stimuli to activity were located, as opposed to the situation more familiar in ethnographic accounts of tools being curated. The latter implies a basic, portable set of tools, regularly maintained and used frequently in multifunctional contexts; Australian technology is a good example. The results of this work were published (Binford and Binford, 1966).

Another problem became articulated as I worked on the Mousterian materials: What is being measured by documented morphological variability among tool assemblages? The whole problem of measurement began to gradually loom larger and larger. Although I had spoken in my methods classes at Michigan of characteristics having multiple explanatory referents, distinguishing between style and function as at least two possible independent dimensions of variability, and had even published these ideas in "Archaeology as Anthropology," the full potential did not really hit me until I began working on the Mousterian. I was dealing with a situation in which a common typology of sixty-two different tool types could accommodate, with some minor exception, the range of variability in actual tools from sites as far distant as China and south central France, from the Near East to north Africa and Spain. Structurally speaking, this was totally different from the character of variability that I was accustomed to in New World materials. Comparative studies of New World materials necessitated changing typologies to accommodate morphologically distinct tool forms from areas not nearly as far apart as China and southern France. Quite clearly the *structure* of variability was in a domain different from the one to which I was accustomed. In addition, when the relative frequencies of the sixty-two tool types were used as the basis of interassemblage comparison, the results were equally surprising. Instead of assemblages with roughly the same composition clustered either spatially or temporally, they varied in a very different manner.

The same general location might exhibit a pattern of assemblage alternation such that forms that were least alike were in temporal juxtaposition, while assemblages that were most alike were separated stratigraphically by many different occupational horizons. The conclusions seemed inevitable: (1) The typologies were measuring very different things, Bordes' typology measuring almost exclusively function, with New World typologies measuring style or a mixture of style and function; and/or (2) the organizational properties of the adaptive systems represented by the Mousterian materials were quite different from those which had served as the basis for traditionalists' interpretive models. My guess was that the two possibilities were related and both were accurate.

It was not until I worked on these materials that I began to consciously distinguish between organizational and distributional variability. I began to think of the structure of variability as opposed to the patterning of variability. The contrasts between the Mousterian situation and the situation to which I was accustomed in New World materials was clearly a difference in the structure of variability itself. Observed differences in patterning might derive from these differences in structure. The key to understanding both was to understand what was actually referred to in the past by typologically measured variability.

Sally had worked for François Bordes, and he had been very kind to her. To Sally, Bordes was one of the most interesting, intelligent, lovable characters she had ever known. As I worked on the Mousterian problem, Sally became more and more concerned. She didn't intuitively believe that Bordes' alternation of industries actually referred to migrations back and forth of different "tribes" of Neanderthal man; yet as my work progressed, she began to worry that I would "attack" Bordes and hurt the man she admired so much. One of my little tricks of analytical thinking is to verbalize arguments with myself, taking an extreme position and developing an argument verbally, exploring all the logical implications of the original position to see where it leads. During the writing of the first manuscript on the Mousterian, I was constantly doing this and to Sally this appeared as a preview of what I would try to do in print or in a face-to-face argument with Bordes. She was as nervous as a cat at the thought of our initial meeting.

I had applied for Departmental funds from the University of Chicago to allow me to travel to France during the 1965 Christmas holidays. From the time of our initial plans to go to France and for me to meet Bordes, Sally became increasingly anxious. I had wanted to mail Bordes a copy of the "Jabrud-Shubbabiq" manuscript beforehand so he would have a chance to read it before we arrived. She was dead set against that, arguing that face-to-face conversation with Bordes before he saw the manuscript was the best way to approach him. In retrospect I think she was right. We did not mail the manuscript.

I don't really recall all the preliminary introductions or the actual events of my first meeting with Bordes. These things were social preliminaries—somewhat phony. I wanted to know this man, the man whose work I admired, the man who had initiated in terms of data collection and beginning analysis many of the things Papworth and I had fought to see established in American archaeology. Every time I tried to start a serious conversation with Bordes, it seemed that Sally changed the subject and introduced some trivial matter about the personalities of the field. She later compared Bordes and me to two male dogs circling and sniffing, trying to find out if the other was really an enemy.

After much circling and sniffing, Bordes and I agreed to discuss the character of variability in the Mousterian and my analysis of it in his laboratory on an appointed day: 28 December, 1965. I arrived early at the lab that morning, surprised to find all of Bordes' advanced students busy as bees, working alone at small desks half-hidden around the lab. Pierre Laurent, Bordes' illustrator and dear friend, was working quietly at his drafting table. Mme. Bordes was working busily in her office. People were not talking; there was an air of suspense, of anticipation. The word was out: Sally's husband was taking on Bordes, the man legendary for his explosive temper and devastating "put-downs" of those who disagreed with him.

I was nervous. Sally was flitting around me like an annoying mosquito. "Don't mention this . . . . Start with that point . . . . If he says . . . . If you say . . .," and on and on. Bordes came in. He greeted everyone present with the traditional handshake. He was whistling, walking around picking up papers, tossing them back down. "Merde . . . . Binford, look here . . . . Binford, can you make stone tools? . . . . Let me show you.." Bordes started chipping flint, whistling, with a big smile on his face. I became somewhat impatient and began shuffling through reams of papers, charts and graphs, which I had prepared to aid in my explanations of the analysis to Bordes. Sally grabbed my arm, shaking her head, whispering "let him call the time." Back in the briefcase went the papers.

I don't recall how long this circling and sniffing went on, but the tension seemed to mount to higher and higher pitch. "Let me see what zis computer of yours has done with zee Mousterian." I started with the explanation of the analytical methods. His eyes flashed, he sometimes anticipated my points, he listened with great interest. I was clearly talking to one of the most intelligent men in archaeology I had ever met. I began to speak of the Mousterian assemblages we had used in the analysis. He immediately questioned the degree that they were "representative"; he began to explain that he had changed his interpretation of some of the variability at the Jabrud site, telling me in great detail what and why were his latest impressions of the differences between typical and Ferrassie Mousterian. This was no dragon, no demon, this was a highly dedicated, extremely intelligent, fascinating man. He really knew his material.

I began to relax, to talk more forcefully, and pushed on into the critical areas of his interpretation of the variability noted as indicative of different "tribes." Both of our arms began to wave. "But François." "But Binford." We must have argued for more than an hour, our voices getting higher and higher, standing up, sitting down, pacing back and forth, leaning over the charts, big clouds of smoke issuing from his pipe, equally big clouds pouring from my cigarettes. The spectators had begun to move in closer; Mme. Bordes was sitting beside Sally, Pierre had stopped drawing, students no longer made any pretense of working. The sniffing and circling had stopped; we were engaged in a counterpoint duel with each thrust teaching one of us something about the other. It was exhilarating; with each *but,* my respect grew.

Bordes' logical strategies became more complicated, more intricate. With each "round" Bordes was finding out about me and I was finding out about him; we both liked what we found. All of a sudden Bordes jumped up and came around face to face. I stood up almost automatically. He put his hand on my shoulder, looked me directly in the eyes, and said, "Binford, you are a heavyweight; so am I." I put my hand on François' shoulder; he turned: "Let's go drink some good wine."

I had the same feeling I had that day Spaulding told me I had gotten an A on his final. How strange I should experience that same feeling after an argument with one of my most powerful opponents. The difference was that Bordes was a colleague, not a "father" as Griffin had been.

The next time I went to the lab, the students knew my name. I was no longer "Sally's husband."

I have been to France several times since then, and Bordes has visited me in the United States; every time, there is some sniffing and circling. Each time, we generally get a chance to be alone and talk; each time my respect has risen. François Bordes is truly one of the most interesting people I have ever known. We laugh and speak of our "war"; we generally announce to one another when we will hit each other with a "heavyweight" punch in the literature. I don't think Bordes will ever agree with me and I don't think I will ever agree with him on the interpretation of variability, but I have learned more from him than from most of the persons I have been associated with in archaeology. I would rather argue with Bordes than any man I know, unless it's Griffin. I can argue with Bordes; things have been too complicated between Griffin and me.

"Models and Paradigms" is a frontal attack on the traditionalists' theory. I have attempted, as I did in the mortuary paper, to outline in explicit fashion the major assumptions and logical strategies of the traditionalists' position. This time, however, I am treating a much more inclusive and concrete subject, the nature of assemblage variability. I try to introduce the notion of comparative analysis of the structure of variability itself. My demonstration that covariant relationships and associational relationships may vary independently of one another, that they may well exhibit different patterns of relationships one to another, is the first concrete suggestion regarding the actual comparative analysis of the structural properties of variation itself of which I am aware. My argument that the particular patterning of these relationships in the Late Acheulian materials determines to a large measure the character of distributional patterning is, to me, a very stimulating idea.

I fear the traditionalists will see these suggestions as destructive. I see them as possibly leading to a far greater understanding of the past. Responding to the published arguments about the Mousterian, my critics (with, I think, the exception of Bordes) have seen my suggestions as destructive, attempting to destroy something with which they feel secure. I have always viewed them as constructive, possibly leading the way through refining debate to getting more and more information from the archaeological record.

As I made explicit in "Models and Paradigms", the recognition of patterning and its interpretation has been the basis of archaeological explication of the past. Quite early—way back in my hand-crank desk-calculator days at Michigan— I realized that patterning comes in many different forms, in very complex and differing forms. I even suggested that the lack of "expected" forms of patterning observed in the archaeological record has behavioral and processual referents. This position was clearly stated in the "Culture Drift" paper. My more recent work on Old World Paleolithic material has led me to consider again the notions of "drift," not only as presented in the paper reprinted here but in its more traditional context of "inevitable" minute directional change through time or across space. When this kind of patterning has been observed among the products of man, it had been called "culture" drift. I think that this may be very misleading. One could argue that such patterning would be expected among any manifestation of learned behavior. No communication system is perfectly efficient. There will inevitably be some inefficiency; some lack of perfect replication in behavior which is learned via communication between individuals is to be expected. Clearly this is true among humans; psychological studies of the transmission of information, rumor studies, clearly demonstrate the inefficiencies of our culturally based system of communication. Ethologists and animal behaviorists have begun to speak of behavioral "traditions" among birds and many other animals whose behavior is largely conditioned by learning. To what extent are the characteristics of culture change, as outlined in the traditionalists' paradigms with their expectations of minute gradual change and differentiation as a function of communication gaps, a feature which is unique to culture? I suspect they are not unique and may be expected within any population of individuals among which learning is a relevant behavioral conditioner. What differences in patterning distinguish culturally based behavioral systems from noncultural behavioral systems in which learning is important? We clearly don't know. We have always assumed that "drift" conceived in this manner is unique to culture. So many problems, fascinating stimulating problems, remain unsolved, each holding out in solution unmeasured potential for understanding the past and present of the human condition.

The "Directionality" paper is still another attempt to argue that all patterning, all distributions, do not necessarily have a "monolithic" significance. I have tried to suggest conditions which may produce the "normal" kind of patterning in the archaeological record and yet have reference to situations totally contrary to the interpretations one would make if he were working within a traditionalist paradigm.

These are all "fighting" papers, attacks on ideas, on beliefs, common among archaeologists, which I am convinced stand in the way of gaining better, more accurate knowledge of the past. The traditionalists' paradigm has provided archaeologists with a series of conventions for interpreting the "significance" to the past of their observations on the archaeological record. I am convinced that these conventions are for the most part invalid, and at best they are limited in their relevance. Our job is to explore the possibilities in terms of both the factors conditioning the accumulation of specific archaeological deposits and the properties of cultural systems themselves which may condition the forms of patterning we observe in the archaeological record. Only by such exploratory modeling and hypothesis formation can we increase our abilities to recover reliable information about the past.

Reference

Binford, Lewis R., and Sally R. Binford. (1966). A preliminary analysis of functional variability in the Mousterian of Levallois facies. *American Anthropologist* **68**, No. 2, 238–295.

Archaeological Systematics
and the Study of Culture Process *†

Abstract

It is argued that the normative theory of culture, widely held among archaeologists, is inadequate for the generation of fruitful explanatory hypotheses of cultural process. One obvious shortcoming of this theoretical position has been the development of archaeological systematics that have obviated any possibility of measuring multivariate phenomena and permit only the measurement of unspecified "cultural differences and similarities," as if these were univariate phenomena. As an alternative to this approach, it is proposed that culture be viewed as a system composed of subsystems, and it is suggested that differences and similarities between different classes of archaeological remains reflect different subsystems and hence may be expected to vary independently of each other in the normal operation of the system or during change in the system. A general discussion of ceramic classification and the classification of differences and similarities between assemblages is presented as an example of the multivariate approach to the study of cultural variability. It is suggested that a multivariate approach in systematics will encourage the study of cultural variability and its causes and thereby enhance the study of culture process.

Willey and Phillips (1958, p. 50) have expressed doubts that current archaeological concepts such as "phase" have consistent meaning in terms of human social units. It is the purpose of this paper to explore some of the reasons for this lack of congruence and to offer a theoretical framework more consistent with social reality.

In any general theoretical framework there are at least two major components: (1) one that deals with criteria for isolating the phenomenon under study and with the underlying assumptions about the nature of the units or partitive occurrences within the recognized generic class of phenomenon, and (2) assumptions concerning the way in which these partitive units are articulated in the operation of a system or during change.

* This paper was presented at the 29th Annual Meeting of the Society for American Archaeology, Chapel Hill, North Carolina, 1964.

† Originally published in *American Antiquity* **31**, 203–210 (1965).

Most of the analytical means and conceptual tools of archaeological systematics have arisen in the context of a body of culture theory which is referred to here as the "normative school." Under this normative view the phenomenon being studied is variously defined, but there is general agreement that culture with a capital C is the subject. In this the normative theorists are in agreement with others. It is in the definition of partitive concepts and the assumptions concerning the processes of between-unit dynamics that normative theorists differ markedly from the position taken here. A typical normative statement is given by Taylor (1948, p. 110):

> By culture as a partitive concept, I mean a historically derived system of culture traits which is a more or less separable and cohesive segment of the whole-that-is-culture and whose separate traits tend to be shared by all or by specially designated individuals of a group or society.

A similar view is expressed by Willey and Phillips (1958, p. 18) when speaking of spatial divisions of cultural phenomena:

> In strictly archaeological terms, the locality is a geographical space small enough to permit the working assumption of complete cultural homogeneity at any given time.

The emphasis in these two quotations and in the writings of other archaeologists (Ford, 1954, p. 47; Rouse, 1939, pp. 15–18; Gifford, 1960, p. 346) is on the shared characteristics of human behavior. Within this frame of thought, culture is defined as an abstraction from human behavior.

> According to the concept of culture being developed here, culture is a mental construct consisting of ideas (Taylor, 1948, p. 101).

Or as Ford (1954, p. 47) has argued:

> First, it must be recalled that these buildings are cultural products—not the culture. These arrangements of wood, bamboo, and grass are of interest to the ethnologists solely because they illustrate the aborigine's ideas as to the proper ways to construct dwellings.

In summary, a normative theorist is one who sees as his field of study the ideational basis for varying ways of human life—culture. Information is obtained by studying cultural products or the objectifications of normative ideas about the proper ways of life executed by now extinct peoples. The archaeologist's task then lies in abstracting from cultural products the normative concepts extant in the minds of men now dead. (For criticism of this general view, see White, 1954, pp. 461–468.)

In examining the problem of how we may observe and study cultural phenomena, a crucial question arises: What types of units can be isolated for the meaningful study of culture? For adherents of the normative school, the assumptions about units or the natural "packages" in which culture occurs are dependent upon assumptions about the dynamics of ideational transmission. Learning is the recognized basis of cultural transmission between generations, and diffusion is the basis of transmission between social units not linked by regular breeding behavior. The corollary of this proposition is that culture is transmitted between generations and across breeding populations in inverse proportion to the degree of social distance maintained between the groups in question. Since culture is viewed as a great "whole" transmitted through time and across space, any attempt to break up this cultural "whole" is considered arbitrary and thought of as a methodological expedient (Ford, 1954, p. 51; Brew, 1946, p. 49). The partitioning of culture is often termed a heuristic device for measuring the degree of social distance between the groups whose cultural products are being observed. (An excellent criticism of this view is found in Spaulding, 1957, pp. 85–87.) Spatial discontinuities in the distribution of similar formal characteristics are perceived as either the result of (1) natural barriers to social intercourse, or (2) the presence of a value system which provides a conservative psychological matrix that inhibits the acceptance of foreign traits, or (3) the migration or intrusion into the area of new peoples who disrupt the previous pattern of social intercourse. Formal changes in the temporal distribution of items are viewed as the result of innovations or the operation of a built-in dynamics sometimes designated as "drift" (Ford, 1954, p. 51; Herskovits, 1948, pp. 581–582). (For criticism of this concept, see Binford, 1963, pp. 89–93.) Both innovation and drift are considered natural to culture, and as Caldwell (1958, p. 1) has said, "other things being equal, changes in material culture through time and space will tend to be regular." Discontinuities in rates of change or in formal continuity through time are viewed as the result of historical events which tends to change the configuration of social units through such mechanisms as extensions of trade, migration, and the diffusions of "core" ideas such as religious cults (Ritchie, 1955).

Cultural differences and similarities are expressed by the normative school in terms of "cultural relationships" which, if treated rigorously, resolve into one general interpretative model. This model is based on the assumption of a "culture center" where, for unspecified reasons, rates of innovation exceed those in surrounding areas. The new culture spreads out from the center and blends with surrounding cultures until it is dissipated at the fringes, leaving marginal cultures. Cultural relationships are viewed as the degree of mutual or unilateral "influence" exerted between culture centers or subcenters.

This interpretative framework implies what I choose to call the aquatic view of culture. Interpretative literature abounds in phrases such as "cultural stream" and in references to the "flowing" of new cultural elements into a region. Culture is viewed as a vast flowing stream with minor variations in ideational norms concerning appropriate ways of making pots, getting married, treating one's mother-in-law, building houses, temples (or not building them, as the case may be), and even dying. These ideational variations are periodically "crystallized" at different points in time and space, resulting in distinctive and sometimes striking cultural climaxes which allow us to break up the continuum of culture into cultural phases.

One of the most elegant and complete criticisms of the normative theorists to appear in recent years is that of David Aberle (1960). He has pointed out that adherents of the normative position are forced to explain cultural differences and similarities in terms of two factors, historical and psychic. He summarizes the normative position as follows:

No culture can be understood solely by reference to its current situation. As a result of the accidents of history, it has had contacts with a variety of other cultures. These other cultures provide the pool of potential cultural material on which cultures can draw. Since there is no general basis for predicting what cultures will have contact with what others, the historical factor has an accidental and fortuitous character. With respect to the psychic factor, there are qualities of men's minds—whether general tendencies to imitate or specific attitudes held by a particular group—which determine whether or not any available cultural item will be borrowed. Although the contacts are unpredictable, the laws of psychology may account for acceptance and rejection. Hence the laws of culture are psychological laws (Aberle, 1960, p. 3).

The normative view leaves the archaeologist in the position of considering himself a culture historian and/or a paleopsychologist (for which most archaeologists are poorly trained). This leaves him competent to pursue the investigation of culture history, a situation which may partially account for failure to develop the explanatory level of archaeological theory noted by Willey and Phillips (1958, p. 5).

It is argued here that a new systematics, one based on a different concept of culture, is needed to deal adequately with the explanation of cultural process. If we define culture as man's extrasomatic means of adaptation (White, 1959, p. 8), in the partitive sense culture is an extrasomatic adaptive system that is employed in the integration of a society with its environment and with other sociocultural systems. Culture in this sense is not necessarily shared; it is participated in by men. In cultural systems, people, things, and places are components in a field that consists of environmental and sociocultural subsystems, and the locus of cultural process is in the dynamic articulations of these subsystems. This complex set of interrelationships is not explicable by reduction to a single component—ideas—any more than the functioning of a motor is explainable in terms of a single component, such as gasoline, a battery, or lubricating oil.

It was stated above that in our definition culture is not necessarily shared; it is participated in. And it is participated in differentially. A basic characteristic of cultural systems is the integration of individuals and social units performing different tasks, frequently at different locations; these individuals and social units are articulated by means of various institutions into broader units that have different levels of corporate inclusiveness. Within any one cultural system, the degree to which the participants share the same ideational basis should vary with the degree of cultural complexity of the system as a whole. In fact, a measure of cultural complexity is generally considered to be the degree of internal structural differentiation and functional specificity of the participating subsystems (White, 1959, pp. 144–145). Within any given cultural system, the degree to which all the participants share common ideational preferences should vary inversely with the complexity of the system as a whole. The sharing of cultural elements by distinct systems will be a function of the nature of the cultural means of articulating distinct groups with each other.

At present our explicitly stated systematics is based on the degree to which cultural traits are shared. The Midwestern taxonomic system (McKern, 1935, pp. 70–82; 1939, pp. 301–313) is a hierarchical arrangement of archaeologically defined culture traits as they appear in spatially or temporally discrete manifestations. Similarly, such units as the phase (Willey and Phillips, 1958, p. 50; Rouse, 1955, pp. 713–714) are groupings of archaeological complexes on the basis of shared traits.

This emphasis on shared traits in our system of classification results in masking differences and in lumping together phenomena which would be discrete under another taxonomic method. Culture is not a univariate phenomenon, nor is its functioning to be understood or measured in terms of a single variable—the spatial–temporal transmission of ideas. On the contrary, culture is multivariate, and its operation is to be understood in terms of many causally relevant variables which may function independently or in varying combinations. It is our task to isolate these causative factors and to seek regular, stable, and predictable relationships between them.

Our taxonomies should be framed with this end in mind. We should partition our observational fields so that we may emphasize the nature of variability in artifact populations and facilitate the isolation of causally relevant factors. Our categories should be justifiable in terms of possessing common structural or functional properties in the normal operation of cultural systems. These categories should then be analyzed in terms of their behavior in various systems and in situations of systematic change.

By such a method we may achieve our aim of expressing the laws of cultural process. Archaeological systematics should be an aid in accomplishing analytical tasks. As an example of the suggested method of partitioning our observational framework, two general problems will be discussed: ceramic classification and the classification of archaeological assemblages.

Formal variation in ceramics occurs because of differences in either the

techniques of manufacture or in the general design of the finished product; both
kinds of variation may occur independently of each other. [This distinction is
analogous to Rouse's (1960, p. 314) distinction between procedural and
conceptual modes.] One example is the production of an abrupt shoulder as
opposed to a gently sloping shoulder while continuing to execute the same basic
set of manufacturing techniques. Such variation is termed *morphological
variation.* In addition to morphological variation, there is *decorative variation* or
modifications that are made as discrete steps in the terminal phases of the
manufacturing process. Painted and incised designs are examples of decorative
variation. We can therefore speak of two major classes of variation or analytic
dimensions, in terms of which ceramic forms can be studied—*technical* and
design dimensions. Morphological and decorative variation may be observed
along either dimension.

With regard to the sociocultural context of formal variability, two broad
classes of variation can be recognized which crosscut the categories mentioned
above. *Primary functional variation* is that which is directly related to the
specific use made of the vessel in question; for example, the difference between
a plate and a storage jar. *Secondary functional variation* is a by-product of the
social context of the manufacturers of the vessel or of the social context of the
intended use of the item, or both. This variation may arise from a traditional
way of doing things within a family or a larger social unit, or it may serve as a
conscious expression of between-group solidarity. Certain design characteristics
may become standardized as symbols appropriate to vessels used in specific
social contexts. At this level of analysis we may recall Linton's (1936, pp.
403–421) statement that any given cultural item may vary with regard to form,
meaning, use, and function in variable cultural contexts. Such distinctions are
particularly important if the social context of manufacture and use are not
isomorphic, as in the case of items circulated widely through exchange systems,
or are used primarily in the context of institutions functioning for intersocietal
articulation.

Formal variation in artifacts need not and, in most cases, probably does not
have a single meaning in the context of the functioning cultural system. The
study of primary functional variation is essential to the understanding of the
sociocultural systems represented by the artifacts, in this case ceramics. The
nature and number of occurrences of functionally differentiated container types
can yield valuable information about the size of social segments performing
different tasks. Even in cases where specific functions cannot be determined for
the recognized types, the spatial configuration of their occurrence tells
something about the spatial structure of differentiated activities within or
between sites.

Variables of primary function may remain stable, change abruptly, or change at rates different from variables of secondary function. The relative rates of change in these two classes of variables can tell us much about the nature of the changes within the systems in question. An example of this can be seen by comparing the Havana tradition of Illinois with the Scioto tradition of Ohio.

Containers of the Havana tradition are predominantly large, open-mouthed cauldrons, but there are occasional flat-bottomed "flowerpot" forms. This suggests that food was prepared in these societies for relatively large groups of people—larger than nuclear families—and that food was stored corporately. This pattern of cooking and storing was common to essentially all the societies participating in the Havana tradition. Secondary functional variation, on the other hand, with respect to both decoration and design exhibits differences through space and time, suggesting that among the participants in the Havana tradition social contacts and generational continuity were changing.

Container forms of the Scioto tradition in Ohio, which is believed to be contemporaneous with the Havana tradition, were smaller vessels with rounded bottoms; the large cauldron is an infrequent form. Nevertheless, there are common design and technical attributes in the ceramics of both traditions. This suggests that, in the Ohio groups, the social units for which food was prepared were smaller and that modes of food storage were correspondingly different.

In the traditional view, the elements in common between the Havana and Scioto traditions would be interpreted as indicating "cultural relationships," and at present the two are grouped into the "Hopewell phase," with each group sharing different traits of the "Hopewell culture." It is suggested here that the sociocultural systems represented in the two traditions may be and probably are totally different and that the common ceramic elements reflect patterns of common regional interaction facilitated through different institutions. This view differs markedly from one which pictures the flowing of "Hopewell culture" out of a "culture center."

The comparative study of secondary functional variation within one class of containers makes it possible to determine the degree of work specialization in discrete social segments as well as the degree of craft specialization in the manufacture of specific container classes. Empirical demonstration of the validity of the assumptions underlying sociological interpretation of variability in craft products is accumulating, and a number of recent studies show that this kind of "meaning" is recoverable from ceramic data. For example, Cronin (1962, p. 109) has demonstrated greater similarity in the conventional use of decorative design elements between pottery types at a single site than between types of the same pottery from different sites. Comparable results are suggested by recent discussions of taxonomic problems encountered by others (Sears, 1960, pp. 327–328; Smith, 1962). I have recently proposed a processual model for this type of phenomenon (Binford, 1963). Several recent studies have utilized the measurement and spatial distributions of stylistic minutiae in the construction of sociological models for prehistoric communities (Deetz, 1960; Longacre, 1963; Freeman and Brown, 1964).

If we expand our analytical perspective to include the problem of formal variability in contemporaneous sociocultural systems and sociocultural systems through time, then our analysis must be even more critical. What is idiosyncratic secondary functional variation in one group may symbolize political ties in another. Primary functional variation in one social system may be partially incorporated as secondary functional variation in another.

The complexities facing the archaeologist who attempts this kind of analysis necessitate the use of multiple taxonomies framed to express multivariate attributes. Such taxonomies should replace the conventional ones, which are either classes based on unspecified kinds of likeness or difference, or are hierarchically arranged traits presumed to reflect generic relationships (Willey and Phillips, 1958, p. 31; Rouse, 1960). We suggest that classification should proceed independently with regard to technical and design attributes and that crosscutting categories should be used to express morphological and decorative variation (Table I).

TABLE I   *Contingency of Formal Variation*

	Morphological variation	Decorative variation
Technical dimension		
Design dimension		

The result of such an analysis would be the recognition of numbers of classes of variables, referable to one or more of the column-and-row contingency spaces in Table I. Analysis would then proceed to the question of the cultural context of the observed classes or variables distinguished in the four categories above. This step is schematically diagrammed in Table II. Each column and row contingency space would contain the formal classes of demonstrable variables derived from the initial classification.

The next step would be the definition of populations of artifacts in terms of recognizable and demonstrably different cultural factors. Discussions of differences and similarities would be based on independent and dependent variables and not on an undifferentiated conglomeration of multivariate phenomena.

The current systematics of archaeological assemblages also stresses the quantity of shared traits. Assemblages are referred to a phase or a focus without due allowances for either seasonal or functional variability. Although it is

TABLE II   *Contingency of Cultural Variation*

	Primary functional variation	Secondary functional variation	
		Context of use	Context of production
Technomorphological			
Morphological design			
Decorative techniques			
Decorative designs			

premature to attempt a final presentation of assemblage systematics since such a presentation should be based on more complete knowledge of the range of classes of variability, we feel that at least three major types of broad cultural alignments can be distinguished which may vary independently of one another.

The first such category is the *tradition,* whose meaning we choose to make somewhat narrower than is conventional in archaeological literature. (For a discussion of the concept as generally used, see Willey and Phillips, 1958, pp. 34–40.) We define tradition as a demonstrable continuity through time in the formal properties of locally manufactured craft items, this continuity being seen in secondary functional variability only. There may or may not be such continuity with respect to primary functional variability. To put it another way, the tradition is seen in continuity in those formal attributes which vary with the social context of manufacture exclusive of the variability related to the use of the item. This is termed *stylistic variability* (Binford, 1962, p. 220), and on a single time horizon such a tradition would be spatially defined as a style zone. Through time we may study the areal extent and stability of style zones and the comparative history of local traditions within the framework of the macrotradition. Historical continuity and social phylogeny are particularly amenable to analysis through the study of stylistic attributes. It should be noted that the concept of tradition as it is used here may refer to either a single class of artifactual materials, such as ceramics, or to several classes of artifacts of a single sociocultural system which exhibit continuity through time. It is assumed that formal variability in secondary function is directly related to the social matrix of production and use. In the case of stability through time in the social matrix of production, we would expect to observe temporal continuity and a regular rate of change. In the case of a changing social matrix of production, we would expect to find discontinuities in rates of change and in the spatial and temporal distribution of formal properties.

A second broad class of sociocultural relationships is reflected in items that are widely exchanged and which occur in a context of social distinctiveness, that is, sociotechnic items (Binford, 1962). Such items would be analyzed in terms of their primary functional variability as inferred through correlation with other archaeological remains which define the context of social relations. Through the study of the spatial distributions of such items on a single time horizon we may define *interaction spheres*—the areal matrices of regular and institutionally maintained intersocietal articulation. This term is adopted from Caldwell (1962). It is my impression that I have seen the term used by other archaeologists, but I have not been able to find it in the literature. Caldwell (1962) has pointed to the essential characteristics of the interaction sphere:

> An interaction sphere is a kind of phenomenon which can be regarded as having properties different from a culture . . . . The various regional traditions were present before there was a Hopewellian situation. The term culture would be better applied to each of these separately than to the overall situation with which they are interacting.

What is essential to the concept of an interaction sphere is that it denotes a situation in which there is a regular cultural means of institutionalizing and maintaining intersocietal interaction. The particular forms of the institutions and the secondary functions which may accrue to them will be found to vary widely in the spectrum of history. Interaction spheres may crosscut both traditions and culture areas. The sharing of symbols and the appearance of similar institutions are less a function of the traditional enculturative milieu of individual societies than of complex articulation of societies of different ethnic backgrounds, levels of cultural complexity, and social types.

The comparative structural and functional analysis of interaction spheres is suggested as an approach which allows us to define, quantify, and explain the observation of Redfield (1941, p. 344) that rates of cultural change may be directly related to rates of social interaction. The distinction between the "shared" culture of a stylistic nature and the "shared" culture of a sociopolitical nature is the basis for distinguishing the tradition from the interaction sphere.

Examples of the interaction sphere come readily to mind. The presence of Mississippian "traits" in local traditions on the Piedmont of the southeastern United States is one. Another is the common "Hopewellian" items in tombs of Illinois (the Havana tradition) and in the charnel houses of Ohio (the Scioto tradition). The nature of the cultural processes responsible for the widespread occurrences of similar cultural items in these two cases cannot be explained by the simplistic reference to sharing of similar ideas concerning the proper ways to manufacture items.

The third category we wish to discuss is that of the adaptive area. An adaptive area is one which exhibits the common occurrence of artifacts used primarily in coping directly with the physical environment. Such spatial distributions would be expected to coincide broadly with culture areas as they are conventionally defined; however, this concept differs from the culture–area concept in that stylistic attributes are excluded from the definition. The adaptive means of coping with changes in physical environment need not coincide with those which are designed to cope with changes in the social environment. Therefore, we need to study traditions (based on styles), interaction spheres (based on intersocietal relations), and adaptive spheres (based on common means of coping with the physical environment), and treat these three isolates as independent variables.

Summary

It has been argued that the normative theory of culture is inadequate for the generation of fruitful explanatory hypotheses of cultural process. An approach is offered in which culture is not reduced to normative ideas about the proper ways of doing things but is viewed as the system of the total extrasomatic means of adaptation. Such a system involves a complex set of relationships among people, places, and things whose matrix may be understood in multivariate terms.

The steps in such an analysis proceed by means of the partitioning of demonstrable variability into a multidimensional framework. Use of such a framework will facilitate isolation of the causes of various kinds of changes and differences and provide the basis for studying comparatively the rates and patterns of change in different classes of cultural phenomena. Such an approach would, it is argued, facilitate and increase our understanding of cultural processes.

Acknowledgments

I would like to acknowledge the intellectual stimulation of many of my colleagues in the formulation of the ideas presented in this paper. Stuart Struever, Joseph Caldwell, Howard Winters, James Brown, Melvin Fowler, and the author have had frequent discussions over the past three years in an attempt to increase our understanding of the prehistory of the Midwest. Although individually all of the participants in our own "interaction sphere" have contributed to the formulation of the arguments presented here, I accept full responsibility for the particular form in which the ideas are presented. In addition, I would like to express my gratitude to Carl-Axel Moberg of the Göteburg Museum, Sweden, who participated in the joint teaching of a class along with Robert J. Braidwood and me. Moberg's arguments and rebuttals have aided appreciably in definition of the ideas presented. My students over the past three years—particularly William Longacre, James Hill, Leslie Freeman, and Robert Whallon—have been a constant source of stimulation and have initiated agonizing reappraisals of my own thinking. Of particular importance is the role played by my wife, Sally Binford. She has been a severe critic of my logic as well as of my syntax, and I gratefully acknowledge her editorship of this manuscript.

References

Aberle, David R. (1960). The influence of linguistics on early culture and personality theory. In *Essays in the Science of Culture: In Honor of Leslie A. White* (G. Dole and R. Carneiro, eds.), pp. 1–49. Crowell: Collier, New York.

Binford, Lewis R. (1962). Archaeology as anthropology. *American Antiquity* 28, 217–225.

Binford, Lewis R. (1963). Red ocher caches from the Michigan area: A possible case of cultural drift. *Southwestern Journal of Anthropology* 19, 89–108.

Brew, John Otis. (1946). Archaeology of Alkali Ridge: Southeastern Utah. *Papers of the Peabody Museum of American Archaeology and Ethnology, Harvard University* 21.

Caldwell, Joseph R. (1958). Trend and tradition in the prehistory of the eastern United States. *Memoirs of the American Anthropological Association* No. 88.

Caldwell, Joseph R. (1962). Interaction spheres in prehistory. Unpublished paper presented at the Annual Meeting of the American Association for the Advancement of Science, Philadelphia, 1962.

Cronin, Constance. (1962). An analysis of pottery design elements indicating possible relationships between three decorated types. *Fieldiana: Anthropology* 53, 105–141.

Deetz, James D. F. (1960). An archaeological approach to Kinship Change in eighteenth century Arikara culture. Unpublished Ph.D. Dissertation, Harvard University.

Ford, James A. (1954). The type concept revisited. *American Anthropologist* 56, 42–57.

Freeman, L. G., Jr., and James A. Brown. (1964). Statistical analysis of Carter Ranch pottery. *Fieldiana: Anthropology* 55, 126–154.

Gifford, James C. (1960). The type-variety method of ceramic classification as an indicator of cultural phenomena. *American Antiquity* 25, 341–347.

Herskovits, Melville J. (1948). *Man and His Works.* Knopf, New York.

Linton, Ralph. (1936). *The Study of Man.* Appleton, New York.

Longacre, William A. (1963). Archaeology as anthropology: A case study. Unpublished Ph.D. Dissertation, University of Chicago.

McKern, W. C. (1935). Certain culture classification problems in Middle Western archaeology. *National Academy of Science–* National Research Council, Circular 17.

McKern, W. C. (1939). The midwestern taxonomic method as an aid to archaeological culture study. *American Antiquity* 4, 301–313.

Redfield, Robert. (1941). *The Folk Culture of Yucatan.* Univ. of Chicago Press, Chicago.

Ritchie, William A. (1955). Recent discoveries suggesting an early woodland burial cult in the northeast. *New York State Museum and Science Service, Circular* No. 40.

Rouse, Irving. (1939). Prehistory in Haiti: A study in method. *Yale University Publications in Anthropology* No. 21.

Rouse, Irving. (1955). On the correlation of phases of culture. *American Anthropologist* 57, 713–722.

Rouse, Irving. (1960). The classification of artifacts in archaeology. *American Antiquity* 25, 313–323.

Sears, William H. (1960). Ceramic systems and eastern archaeology. *American Antiquity* 25, 324–329.

Smith, Watson. (1962). Schools, pots and pottery. *American Anthropologist* 64, 1165–1178.

Spaulding, Albert C. (1957). Review of *Method and Theory in American Archaeology*, by Gordon W. Willey and Philip Phillips. *American Antiquity* 23, 85–87.

Taylor, Walter W. (1948). A study of archeology. *Memoirs of the American Anthropological Association.* No. 69.

White, Leslie A. (1954). Review of *Culture: A Critical Review of Concepts and Definition*, by A. L. Kroeber and Clyde Kluckhohn. *American Anthropologist* 56, 461–468.

White, Leslie A. (1959). *The Evolution of Culture.* McGraw-Hill, New York.
Willey, Gordon R., and Philip Phillips. (1958). *Method and Theory in American Archaeology.* Univ. of Chicago Press, Chicago.

Mortuary Practices: Their Study and Their Potential*

Introduction

Human burials are one of the most frequently encountered classes of cultural feature observed by archaeologists. If this high frequency of encounter were to bring with it greater conceptual elaboration, as postulated in Whorf's "Eskimo and snow principle" (1956, p. 216), then we might expect archaeologists to have developed a complicated paradigm for describing and analyzing human burials. Yet, while there exists a specialized descriptive lexicon (extended, flexed, or semiflexed burials; bundle or flesh burials; cremations or inhumations; etc.) which reveals a concern with the description of observed differences and similarities, there is a surprising lack of literature in which attempts are made to deal with burials as a distinct class of variable phenomena. The majority of both comparative and theoretical efforts have been those of ethnologists, working with data from living groups. Rarely, however, have there been attempts to explain variable burial data as observed at a given location, between locations, or as documented in the general literature.

In approaching the literature on mortuary practices, three general classes of information were sought:

(1) Documentation of the philosophical perspective from which previous workers have approached the problem of explaining various facets of mortuary custom.

(2) An inventory of both the specific arguments and empirical generalizations which have been offered to explain variations in mortuary practice.

(3) From the above, I have sought to document arguments which have been advanced regarding variations in the form of spatial configurations of burials, as well as observable trends, or temporal sequences of formal changes, in mortuary practice.

* To appear in *Social Dimensions of Mortuary Practices,* Memoir No. 25 Society for American Archaeology, *American Antiquity* **36** pp. 6–29 (1971).

Philosophical Perspectives of Past Investigators

The relevance of mortuary practices to the general study of religion served to focus early anthropological interests in this area. Discussion of mortuary customs was normally presented within the context of considerations of "primitive religion."

Tylor (1871) developed the argument that animism, or the belief in spiritual beings, arose in the context of dream and death experience. A body–soul dichotomy was perceived in dream and projected into the death situation in which survival of the ghost–soul after destruction of the body was postulated. Frazer (1886) elaborated on these ideas and argued that all mortuary ritual was motivated by fear of the deceased's ghost–soul and was an attempt on the part of the living to control the actions of the ghosts of the dead. For instance, he states that:

> . . . heavy stones were piled on his grave to keep him down, on the principle of "sit tibi terra gravis." This is the origin of funeral cairns and tombstones (1886, p. 65).
> The nearly universal practice of leaving food on the tomb or of actually passing it into the grave by means of an aperture or tube is too well known to need illustration. Like the habit of dressing the dead in his best clothes, it probably originated in the selfish but not unkindly desire to induce the perturbed spirit to rest in the grave and not come plaguing the living for food and raiment (1886, pp. 74–75).

In the tradition of Tylor–Frazer we can document the rationalist–idealist's argument that ideas or beliefs were the relevant variables to be used in understanding cultural or behavioral differences and similarities. In the same year as Frazer's above-quoted works, the first comparative study of mortuary practices was published in the United States (Yarrow, 1886). Justification for the study was given in the following way:

> The mortuary customs of savage or barbaric people have a deep significance from the fact that in them are revealed much of the philosophy of the people by whom they are practiced (Yarrow, 1886, p. 3).

An early comparative study of mortuary practices as known archaeologically was conducted by the Frenchman Viollier:

> We study burial to gain information on religion and beliefs (Viollier, 1911, p. 123).

Later, the same tradition of anthropological investigation is exemplified by J. M. Tyler:

> The changes in the mode of disposal of the dead are evidently the results of changed views concerning the future life (Tyler, 1921, p. 123).

Those who approached their subject matter from the perspective of the rationalist–idealist normally generated propositions which correlated certain practices with certain postulated or observed forms of belief. Sometimes these proposed or observed correlations are cited as "rational" or "natural" intellectual responses to certain classes of experience.

In defense of this approach it should be pointed out that men like Tylor and Frazer were interested primarily in cultural similarities. They sought to uncover the common basis for diverse practices and to document similarities between the practices of a wide variety of peoples. Seldom was analytical attention given to cultural differences except insofar as they were thought to reflect societies at different levels in a postulated sequence of progressive development.

The argument against an idealist position is, of course, to point out that by a referral of observed differences within one class of phenomena (behavior) to postulated differences within another (ideas), we are forced to seek the explanations for differences in ideas and in the conditions favoring their change. Robertson Smith was one of the early challengers to the idealists' philosophy as exemplified by Tylor and Frazer:

> Our modern habit is to look at religion from the side of belief rather than of practice . . . . So far as myths consist of explanations of ritual, their value is altogether secondary . . . . The conclusion is that in the study of ancient religions we must begin, not with myth, but with ritual and traditional usage (Smith, 1894, pp. 16–18).

This criticism was elaborated and developed by members of the L'Annee Sociologique school of Durkheim. They stressed that rites were related to other institutions of the social system and could be expected to vary in form and structure with the social variables. Hertz was one of the earliest of the Durkheimian thinkers to treat mortuary ritual effectively. He argued that simplistic "explanations" of burial rites as natural human responses of horror to a decaying corpse are untenable since this "natural horror" is mitigated by the social importance of the deceased:

> Within the same society the emotion provoked by death varies wildly in intensity according to the social character of the deceased (Hertz, 1907, p.82).

Hertz goes on to point out that children and aged persons (1907, p. 92) as well as persons suffering violent deaths, death by accident, suicides, death in childbirth, etc., are frequently afforded differential mortuary treatment (1928, p. 95). This is in addition to the differentiations previously mentioned which relate to the social position of the deceased. Hertz develops the argument that death occasions an initiation rite into the afterworld (1928, p. 86), and it is treated by members of society as are other status changes, such as initiation at puberty, birth rites, etc. He argues that differences in mortuary ritual will vary directly with (a) the status of the person within the living community and (b) the perceived relationship of that status to the status of full participant in the "society of souls." Persons who are full participants in the corporal society at the time of their death must be afforded rites which sever their relationship with that society.

A common practice is a second rite which marks the incorporation of the deceased into the "invisible society." For those who are not full societal participants at the time of death, minimal rites of incorporation into the "invisible society" are given. Such is the case with very old men, who have essentially ceased participation, or children, who have not yet become members of the "visible society."

Four years after the publication of Hertz's work, Van Gennep published his famous work *Les Rites de Passage* (1932) (see Van Gennep, 1960) in which there is an expansion of the thesis that rites serve to mark changes of status or condition. There is, however, no specific development of arguments about mortuary practices beyond those of Hertz.

Durkheim, in writing about mortuary rites (1915), treats them in the generic sense as did Van Gennep; there is no development or argument which would offer explanations for differences observed in such rites.

Following the works of the French school was the publication of Radcliffe-Brown's monograph *The Andaman Islanders.* He discusses the problem of the basis for the practice of mortuary rites, stating that

The burial customs of the Andamanese are to be explained, I believe, as a collective reaction against the attack on the collective feeling of solidarity constituted by the death of a member of the social group (1922, p. 286).

Defining the "social personality" of an individual as being the sum of characteristics by which he has an effect upon the social life and therefore on the social sentiments of others, we may say that by death the social personality is not annihilated but undergoes a profound change, so that from being an object of pleasurable states of the social sentiments it becomes an object of painful states (1922, p. 285).

Shortly afterwards, Malinowski (1925) presented his well-known thesis that magic is practiced in the presence of anxiety stemming from inadequate control of the forces of nature.

Death in a primitive society is, therefore, much more than the removal of a member. By setting in motion one part of the deep forces of the instinct of self-preservation, it threatens the very cohesion and solidarity of the group, and upon this depends the organization of that society .... [The] ceremonial of death ... counteracts the centrifugal forces of fear, dismay, demoralization, and provides the most powerful means for reintegration of the group's shaken solidarity (1925, p. 53).

In 1939 Radcliffe-Brown argued strongly against the ideas of Malinowski, setting forth the opposite proposition that

... if it were not for the existence of the rite and the beliefs associated with it the individuals would feel no anxiety, and that the psychological effect of the rite is to create in him a sense of insecurity or danger (Radcliffe-Brown 1952, p. 142).

In this same article, it is quite clear that Radcliffe-Brown was not particularly interested in offering explanations for observed differences. Like his rationalist–idealist predecessors, he was primarily interested in abstracting analogous features from observed situations. These then served as the basis for generalizations about the subject class of phenomena and were in turn cited as "explanations" for the observed behavior.

Ritual values exist in every known society, and show an immense diversity as we pass from one society to another. The problem of a natural science of society is to discover the deeper, not immediately perceptible, uniformities beneath the superficial differences (Radcliffe-Brown, 1952, p. 142).
The basic question is what is the relation of ritual and ritual values to the essential constitution of human society (Radcliffe-Brown, 1952, p. 142).

Although Radcliffe-Brown seems to have shared a basic methodology with his predecessors, he differed in what he considered appropriate features for generalizing. He did not cite generalizations regarding beliefs (as explanation) but rather those regarding sentiments:

The beliefs by which the rites themselves are justified and given some sort of consistency are the rationalizations of symbolic actions and of the sentiments associated with them (Radcliffe-Brown, 1952, p. 152).

These works provide the general intellectual context in terms of which anthropologists have approached the study of mortuary custom. Common to these writers has been the development of arguments regarding the motivational or responsive context in which individuals might be expected to differentially behave, although this differential behavior is always commensurate with the range of behavioral variability known ethnographically.

Little attention was actually given to the study of distributions of variability as documented either within or among sociocultural units. Concern in these works had been with mortuary custom in the abstract or focused on particular categories of mortuary practices: double burial (Hertz, 1907), burial cairns (Frazer, 1886), or the burial practices of a particular society (Radcliffe-Brown, 1922). While there has been some progressive discussion of the most fruitful context in which to perceive customary differences in mortuary practice, differences in belief systems, differences in forms of social organization, or differences in systems of social value, theory has failed to develop to a point where it yields a context in which explanations can be offered for observed differences or similarities.

Anthropologists, particularly archaeologists, working to achieve the reconstruction of culture history have approached the study of mortuary custom much differently. It is to these types of study that I now turn my attention.

HISTORICAL–DISTRIBUTIONAL APPROACHES

The culture historian may begin by plotting the distribution of a given form and then attempt to "explain" it in historical terms or he may present a historical "reconstruction" in terms of which a distributional prediction is advanced. Regardless of the strategy followed, some assumptions or propositions must be put forward regarding the variables which would operate to generate formal variability in mortuary custom and to condition different spatial–temporal configurations.

Further, some assumptions must be made regarding the historical significance of observed differences or similarities and the degree that formal analogies would be accepted as stemming from identical or related historical-event sequences. While not particularly concerned with the specifics of the interpretive principles employed for "reading history" from distributions, I am vitally interested in the methods that have been employed and the assumptions which have been made about the determinant context in which variability might be expected to arise.

The purpose of this discussion is to determine whether or not there is sufficient empirical material extant in the literature to evaluate the accuracy of the assumptions made by culture historians in arriving at historical reconstructions based on mortuary data.

The assumptions commonly governing historical reconstruction can be outlined as follows:

(1) *Culture is a body of custom which arises in the context of the conceptual–intellectual life of peoples; it distributionally varies directly as a function of the patterns of transmission and communication among peoples, and with the differential capacities or opportunities for intellectual experience.* This is, of course, my generalization of the idealist's assumption which has dominated anthropology and is still the most accepted conceptualization of culture (see Kroeber and Kluckhohn, 1952, pp. 180–190).

(2) *The customs of a single sociocultural tradition were originally uniform and formally distinct.* This assumption normally remains implicit in most studies but is easily inferred from one of its corollaries given below. There is an interesting analogy between this assumption and that of the now-discredited assumption of "pure races" which misguided racial studies for many years. The modal or normative assumption is still current in archaeology (see Aberle, 1960; Binford, 1965, for criticism).

Multiple practices observed among sociocultural units results from cultural mixing or hybridization in the past (Perry, 1914; Rivers, 1913; Thomas, 1908; Toulouse, 1944; Davidson, 1948; James, 1928; Stanislawski, 1963; Myers, 1942; etc.).

(3) *For practical purposes, the degree of formal similarity observed among independent sociocultural units is a direct measure of the degree of genetic or affiliational cultural relationship among the units being compared.* It has frequently been argued that this is particularly true with regard to mortuary practices which have been frequently endowed, by observers, with unusual stability (see Rivers, 1913; Perry, 1914; Stanislawski, 1963).

It is recognized that the various schools of historical interpretation differed on many of the qualifications placed on these assumptions. Similarly, they have varied with regard either to the weighting given various culture traits or to the specifics of historical significance attributed to these traits. Nevertheless, these assumptions have been basic to historical reconstruction.

Many regional and continental distributional studies were conducted in the context of the various schools of "historical" anthropology. Both Graebner (1905) and Schmidt (1913) studied mortuary practices as means to historical reconstruction, as did their students (Küsters, 1919). Similarly, the leaders (Perry, 1914) as well as the followers of the "Pan-Egyptian" arguments showed particular interest in mortuary practices, especially mummification (Dawson, 1928) and celestial references in mortuary rites (Rose, 1922). Historical reconstructions based on the comparative study of mortuary rites have also been attempted by American and less extreme British diffusionists (James, 1928; Thomas, 1908; Toulouse, 1944; Davidson, 1948; Stanislawski, 1963).

In 1927 Kroeber published a short paper titled "Disposal of the Dead" in which he questioned the degree that distributionally studied burial practices were as useful for historical inquiries as other features of culture. He observed that the distributions of mortuary traits did not conform to the boundaries of culture areas or subareas as defined by other traits. He reasoned that:

> If the distributions were to be interpreted as is customary, it was evident that methods of corpse disposal have had a history that was less simple and regular, and more fluctuating, than most elements of native Californian Culture (Kroeber, 1927, p. 308).

Kroeber then proceeded to argue that there may be less stability in "affect-laden customs" than in those which are "emotionally low-toned." By the citation of empirical studies documenting great variability in the distributions of mortuary traits he further argues that:

> These variations between adjacent peoples, and the numerous instances of coexistence of several practices within one population, constitute a powerful argument for instability (Kroeber, 1927, p. 313).

From this follows the generalization that intensity of feeling regarding any institution is likely to be a poor criterion, if any, of its permanence. Emotion evidently attaches secondarily to social behavior much as thought does. The completeness and plausibility of a rationalization are no index of the reality of its purported motivation; the immediacy and intensity of emotion concerning a cultural practice are no index of the origin or durability of that practice (Kroeber, 1927, p. 313).

Up until this point Kroeber seems to be directing his argument generally against W. H. R. Rivers, who had argued that because of the affect associated with death rites, mortuary customs would be adhered to with special tenacity. Once Kroeber presents his argument against this position, he states:

More fruitful, perhaps, is a consideration of the type of motivation or historic causality that influences modes of disposal of the dead. Here it appears that a feature which is pretty likely to characterize mortuary practices is their dissociation from certain large blocks of cultural activity, especially those having to do with material and economic life, its subsistence and mechanical aspects. That is, disposal of the dead has little connection with that part of behavior which related to the biological or primary social necessities, with those activities which are a frequent or constant portion of living and therefore tend to become interadapted and dependent one on the other. On the other hand, disposal of the dead also does not lend itself to any great degree of integration with domains of behavior which are susceptible of formalization and codification, like law, much of religion, and social organization. Standing apart, therefore, both from the basic types of activities which mostly regulate themselves unconsciously, and from those which largely involve relations of persons and therefore become socially conscious and systematized, disposal of the dead falls rather into a class with fashions, than with either customs or folkways on the one hand, or institutions on the other. It does not readily enter intrinsically into the inevitable integrations of the bases of life nor into attempts at wider systems (Kroeber, 1927, p. 314).

Kroeber's argument considers the degree that "emotion" plays a role in conditioning the environment for intellectual innovation and transmission of information. In his argument, he is essentially in agreement with Radcliffe-Browne's proposition (1952, pp. 148–149) that the differential intensity of emotional responses to different life experiences would not condition the form and direction of cultural innovation directly. This position, as we have pointed out, was opposed by Malinowski (1925).

Kroeber's argument shifts, however, the emphasis to a consideration of mortuary practices per se, offering the proposition that the apparent "instability" and the documented wide range of formal variability in mortuary practice is evidence of the essential emotional independence of mortuary customs from "core" cultural features. This is a proposition which, if accurate, would be compatible with the apparent failure of mortuary traits to associate with the distributional configurations demonstrated for the "core" cultural features of California aboriginal societies.

Kroeber challenges the implicit assumption that all cultural features, including mortuary practices, were of equal utility for use under the normal assumptions employed in historical reconstruction. This challenge was one of the first serious considerations given to the possibility that all cultural features did not respond mechanistically to the same sets of historical variables. The following materials have been organized to test, with observational data amassed by other investigators, the specific propositions set forth by Kroeber. In addition I hope to use these observations as a basis for judging the validity of the basic assumptions which have guided historical investigations in anthropology.

The two propositions to be tested are:

(1) Mortuary customs exhibit "unstable" histories.

(2) Mortuary customs vary independently of behavior "which relates to the biological or primary social necessities."

In order to test these two propositions, two summaries will be presented: The first will relate directly to Kroeber's initial proposition; the second will synthesize observations that have been made on the sets of variables applicable for understanding variation in mortuary custom. The information synthesized in the latter survey will then be used to test the validity of Kroeber's second proposition and to evaluate the validity of the assumptions used in historical reconstructions.

Erminie Wheeler Voegelin conducted an analysis of the ethnohistorical information available regarding Shawnee burial practices spanning a 114-year period. She concluded that:

> Comparison of the historical material relating to mortuary customs and field accounts of present-day informants has shown the remarkable stability of the Shawnee burial complex. During the period from 1824–1938 the complex remained almost unchanged in its larger features, such as treatment of the corpse, funerary procedure, and construction of graves (Voegelin, 1944, p. 366).

Kroeber pointed out in his original argument:

> There are certainly instances of mortuary habits that have continued for long times with only minor modification: in dynastic Egypt, for instance; in most of Europe during most of the Neolithic, in all but the fringe of Pueblo culture (Kroeber, 1927, p. 314).

These empirical cases to the contrary provide material for argument against Kroeber's generalization that mortuary customs have some intrinsic or "essential" qualities which would tend to insure their exhibiting unstable histories. Rather, there seems to be a wide range of variability in the relative stability of mortuary practices. Some historical sequences exhibit a rather remarkable stability while others change radically and rapidly. Some areas are characterized by vast heterogeneity in practices both regionally and with regard to single sociocultural systems. Explanations for differences and similarities, which are sought by postulating a constant psychological context for the execution of mortuary customs, will never lead to an explanation of observed variability.

The empirical generalization that mortuary customs tend to be inherently less stable and more variable is refuted by numerous empirical cases to the contrary. The attempt to link the postulated instability to the psychological context of "affect-laden customs," where certain behavioral expectations are proposed, collapses with the demonstrated inaccuracy of the initial empirical generalization.

We now consider Kroeber's second proposition: the degree that mortuary customs vary independently of behavior "which relates to the biological or primary social necessities." This can be accomplished by demonstrating that there is an absence of correlation between mortuary customs and social organizational and technological variables. What then of the observations that have been made regarding the correlates of mortuary variability within and among sociocultural units?

Observable Variability in Mortuary Rites

This section offers arguments to account for observable variability in mortuary rites as practiced by members of a single sociocultural unit or among a number of distinct sociocultural units. In the works of previous investigators, three basic arguments are generally offered to account for differences in mortuary practices as conducted among participants of a single society.

(1) The limiting effects of the environment, obtaining at the time of death, on the free exercise of all forms of body disposal

(2) Mutual effects of intersocietal contact in producing amalgamations or replacements of ritual forms

(3) The characteristics recognized as relevant to the relationships either severed or established at death between the deceased and the remaining members of a society

The first argument is one which recognizes a relationship between the form of mortuary rites, particularly the disposition of the body, and the limiting features of the local environment. For instance, Schoolcraft (1855) proposed that the practices of inhumation and scaffold burial as noted for the Winnebago were options to be exercised alternatively, depending on whether the death occurred during the winter, when the ground was frozen, or during the warmer months when inhumation was a realistic alternative.

Although this particular hypothesis has been questioned on empirical grounds (Radin, 1923, p. 140), the proposition that different forms of corpse disposal may relate to the environmental conditions obtaining at the time of death is a reasonable proposition and one which has prompted very little investigation.

Under the second argument fall the diffusionistic interpretations so common in the literature (see Thomas, 1908, p. 388; Perry, 1914, pp. 289–290; James,

1928, p. 229; Griffin, 1930, p. 43; Toulouse, 1944, p. 70; Stanislawski, 1963, pp. 308 and 315). Perry (1914), in considering the results of culture contacts, argues that the demonstrable variety in burial practices among Australian groups is evidence for sustained contact between diverse cultural systems. In a subsequent article he argues that the presence of different forms of grave orientation as practiced by members of a single society is reasonably taken as evidence for the blending of two cultures previously distinct (Perry, 1914, pp. 289–290). Frequently, in regional studies, the citation of mixed practices is offered as evidence for contacts between cultures. It is implied that blending is the expected outcome of contacts between sociocultural systems, each with its own "norm" of mortuary ritual. Diffusionistic interpretations, such as those cited above, are generally given in the context of idealistic arguments where "beliefs" are assumed to be the primary controlling variables in determining the nature of mortuary rites. Contacts are said to foster the exchange of "ideas" which may result in the modification of custom, of which changes in mortuary ritual might be one example.

The following is a list of the most commonly cited propositions as to the relationship between forms of mortuary custom and beliefs.

Propositions Offered in "Explanation" of Formal Variations in the Manner of Treating the Dead Prior to Interment
Propositions regarding the practice of cremation

(1) Cremation is associated with belief in an afterworld in the sky; burning the physical remains releases the soul which is then transported to the celestial afterworld via the ascending smoke (James, 1928, pp. 232–233).

(2) Cremation is associated with extreme fear of the corpse and hence a desire to "be done with it" (Malinowski, 1925, p. 49).

Propositions regarding the practice of mummification

(1) "The aim of mummification both in Egypt and elsewhere was twofold: first, to preserve the body from decay, and secondly to secure the personal survival of the individual" (Dawson, 1928, p. 136; Malinowski, 1925, p. 49).

Propositions Offered in "Explanation" for Formal Variations in the Manner of Arranging the Body in the Grave
Propositions regarding the practice of flexing the body

(1) Flexing of the body was a copy of the position of the foetus in utero which was taken as a symbol of rebirth (Tyler, 1921, p. 124; Wilder and Whipple, 1917, p. 376; Grottanelli, 1947, p. 83; Küsters, 1919, p. 684).

(2) Flexing of the body was the result of binding the legs to the body to prevent the spirit from walking and thus returning to the living (see Tyler, 1921, p. 124; Wilder and Whipple, 1917, p. 376; Grottanelli, 1947, p. 83).

Propositions regarding the orientation of the dead in the grave relative to specific reference points

(1) Orientation of the body in death with respect to cardinal directions "seems to be the working out of the solar analogy, on the one hand is death at sunset . . . new life at sunrise" (Tylor, 1871, p. 508).

(2) Orientation of the body in death with respect to cardinal directions (celestial orientation) is related to a belief in a continued life of the dead man at a celestial land of the dead, orientation being in the direction the deceased must travel in their journey to the land of the dead (Rose, 1922, pp. 132–133).

(3) Orientation of the body with respect to terrestrial reference points is related to a belief in reincarnation since the body is aligned toward the location where the soul must reside before being reborn (Rose, 1922, pp. 129–132).

(4) The direction of orientation of the body at death is toward the original home of the forefathers (Perry, 1914, p. 285; Steele, 1931, p. 81; Grottanelli, 1947, p. 83).

Propositions Offered in "Explanation" for Formal Variations in the Choice of Locations for the Grave

(1) "The dead are buried near, or in, their old homes, because they are wanted back again, in the form of babies born of women of their own clan, tribe or family" (Rose, 1922, p. 129).

(2) The author citing the burial of children under house floors, writes: "It is not impossible that we have here one of the ways in which the fear of the dead may have been gradually dispelled. May we not imagine that one of the first steps was the refusal of the mother to allow her dead child to be banished from the house?" (Tyler, 1921, pp. 125–126).

(3) In contrast is the following suggestion as to the origin of hearth burial: "People did not know yet what death was and therefore tried to warm up the body" (Küsters, 1920, p. 956).

(4) I will cite one final argument analogous to the one given for orientation, namely, that people selected burial sites with reference to the characteristics of their prior habitat. "Tree burial can be explained by the fact that people originally lived in trees" (Küsters, 1920, p. 211).

Change or variability in mortuary practice, as demonstrated, is commonly attributed to change or variability in beliefs. Although we are rarely enlightened as to the causes of change in belief, it would appear from this survey that change in belief is generally assumed to proceed from the cumulative experience of man in coping with his environment. There is also the implication that an increase in knowledge and associated changes in the conceptualizations of experience are vital forces driving culture change. This assumption is normally coupled with the argument of cultural conservatism, which says that new knowledge is rarely obtained and therefore the appearance of similar cultural elements in multiple societies occurs as a by-product of the transmission of acquired knowledge from one unit to another.

The final set of considerations, which have been cited as relevant to understanding observed variability in the practices of a single society, are characteristics of the deceased which might be acknowledged by differentiated mortuary ceremonialism. I have found only three studies which attempted to gather specific data on this subject (Küsters, 1919; Bendann, 1930; Wedgwood, 1927). However, many other authors have offered empirical generalizations relevant to this problem from data which they surveyed. The following quotations are offered as a sample from the literature.

James Yarrow commenting on the study of American Indians, 1880

A complete account of these (burial) customs in any tribe will necessitate the witnessing of many funeral rites, as the customs will differ at the death of different persons, depending upon age, sex, and social standing (Yarrow, 1886, p. 5).

W. Crooke with reference to burial practices in India, 1899

Those tribes which habitually cremate the adult dead bury those who perish by violent or unexpected deaths (Crooke, 1899, p. 279).

Robert Hertz in a general consideration of mortuary practices, 1907

Within the same society the emotion provoked by death varies widely in intensity according to the social character of the deceased (Hertz, 1907, p. 82).

Van Gennep in a general consideration of rites of passage, 1908

Everyone knows that funeral rites vary widely among different peoples and that further variations depend on the sex, age, and social position of the deceased (Van Gennep, 1960, p. 146).

W. D. Wallis in a general consideration of similarities in culture, 1917

The social personality of the deceased does not die with the body but passes beyond the death portal. To the body is shown about the same degree of respect that was shown the deceased while alive. The bodies of women are seldom disposed of like those of men, nor those of children like those of adults. The bodies of chiefs and braves are interred in different manner from those of common people (Wallis, 1917, p. 46).

A. R. Radcliffe-Brown in his consideration of Andamese culture, 1922

Burial customs are not solely due to an instinctive fear of dead bodies . . . customs vary according to the social position of the deceased . . . . There is, then, a close correspondence between the manner of burial and the social value of the person buried (Radcliffe-Brown, 1922, p. 148).

Camilla H. Wedgwood in a comparative study of Melanesian mortuary practices, 1927

We find that in Melanesia the distinctions made by people in life are reflected in those made at death. Of these the simplest are those made between children and adults, and between men and women. But more marked are those which differentiated people who, by virtue of their wealth, their valour, or their magical or secular position, are important to the community from those who lack any claim to public esteem; while those who have alienated themselves from the society or endangered it by bringing upon themselves an abnormal death are frequently cut off from the general communion of the dead (Wedgwood, 1927, p. 395).

Effie Bendann in a general comparative study of mortuary practices from Melanesia, Australia, India, and north-east Siberia, 1930

The investigation shows that the content of the specific features is dependent upon rank, sex, age, social organization, status (Bendann, 1930, p. 280).

James B. Griffin in a general comparative study of mortuary practices of American Indians from north-eastern North America, 1930

We might like to know how these various methods were explained by the Indians . . . those which do give reasons for different practices . . . we see that among some tribes, such as the Potawatomie and the Ottawa, that the division was along clan lines. Of course, within the clan special burials were accorded to those who had been drowned or who had died in battle, but in general the burial an individual received depended on his clan membership . . . . In other writings we find that the various ways burial might take place was occasioned wholly by the manner of death, or the time of year during which the individual died, or the question of absence from the tribal seat would bring about a change in customary procedure . . . . Another reason for different burial is to be found in some cases to correspond to the relative position, social standing and occupation of the deceased, and in some cases the age of the deceased played an important part (Griffin, 1930, pp. 44–45).

Among other investigators offering similar generalizations we may cite Voegelin (1944, p. 376) and Davidson (1948, p. 75), each recognized a direct relationship between the differential treatment at death and variations in the social identity of the deceased.

The following were offered by many investigators as the basic components of the social personality, symbolized through differential burial treatment: age, sex, relative social status within a given social unit, and social affiliation in terms of multiple membership units within the society and/or membership in the society itself. Additionally, it was frequently noted that peculiar circumstances surrounding the death of an individual may be perceived by the remaining members of a society as altering, in a substantial manner, the obligations of the survivors to acknowledge the social personality of the deceased. Such persons are instead treated as "members" of a post-mortem social unit and afforded mortuary ritual appropriate to such a membership group.

Another contingency, which has been noted as relevant to problems of differential treatment afforded members of a single society, was the disposition of deaths spatially and temporally. I need only mention deaths which occurred far from settlements where special treatment, such as cremation, dismemberment, etc., may facilitate easy transport. Deaths occurring simultaneously as a result of epidemics or massacres might be treated corporately, with mass graves, by virtue of their "unusual" coincidence.

These findings and arguments provide information for evaluating Kroeber's second proposition that mortuary practices were largely independent of other "core" components of a cultural system. The empirical generalizations which have been advanced consistently link formal differentiation in mortuary rites to status differences and to differences in the group affiliation of the deceased. This linkage demonstrates a set of mutual dependencies between forms of mortuary rites and social organizational features. We would then expect that other things being equal, the heterogeneity in mortuary practice which is characteristic of a single sociocultural unit would vary directly with the complexity of the status hierarchy, as well as with the complexity of the overall organization of the society with regard to membership units and other forms of sodalities. This expectation is diametrically opposed to Kroeber's proposition regarding the disassociation of mortuary practices from "core" cultural features.

Summary of Findings Regarding the Arguments of Kroeber

It was asserted that three basic assumptions have traditionally guided historical researches. First was the idealist's assumption that cultural variations resulted from either differential intellectual creativity or differential lineal transmission and/or intergroup communication of ideas.

From this, the idealists reasoned that the determinants responsible for temporal or spatial variability of one cultural element would be the same as those responsible for variation in *all* cultural elements; each element was, according to this reasoning, a cultural product responding to identical sets of variables, variables which control creativity and the transmission of ideas.

Kroeber was the first researcher working with mortuary rites to cite empirical materials as a basis for questioning the applicability of some of the fundamental assumptions used in historical interpretation. He observed that many California groups practiced multiple forms of mortuary rite; given the assumptions of historical research, this should have been viewed as evidence for cultural mixing in the past. Kroeber's observations on other distributions of cultural elements did not support such an interpretation. Rather than question the general validity of the normative assumption, Kroeber questioned the categorical appropriateness of mortuary customs as a "proper" cultural element and the degree that the interpretive assumptions used in historical reconstruction could be applied to mortuary data!

Kroeber proposed that there was a continuum along which culture traits might be arranged according to the degree that they were "integrated" with other culture traits. At one end of the continuum were "core" traits which were strongly interdependent and could be expected, as a result, to exhibit strong complementary distributions. Such distributions were appropriate to historical interpretation under traditional assumptions.

At the other end of the continuum were traits which did not "readily enter intrinsically into the inevitable integrations of the bases of life" (Kroeber, 1927, p. 314). Such traits were said to be characterized by (a) detachment from the remainder of culture, (b) a high degree of entry into consciousness, and (c) tendency to strong emotional toning. Mortuary practices and fashions, particularly of dress, luxury, and etiquette, were asserted to be of this type.

With this argument, Kroeber questioned the validity of historical reconstructions based on the analysis of mortuary customs, and indirectly he questioned the assumption that all culture traits were governed by essentially the same sets of determinant variables. Mortuary practices should evidence a pattern of historical instability and free variations, while other cultural elements more "basic" or directly linked to "core" subsistence and integrative practices should exhibit a greater stability and a pattern of determined variability.

From the relatively large body of descriptive material available in the ethnographic literature and the numerous comparative and distributional studies, I obtained data to test the propositions set forth by Kroeber as well as those normally serving as assumptions in historical interpretations.

The result was that Kroeber's first proposition—that properties intrinsic to mortuary practices should result in their general historical instability and free variation—was refuted by the demonstrated lack of any such tendency. Numerous cases of "stability" are known, as well as cases of "instability," demonstrating that such configurations must vary in response to determinants not intrinsic to mortuary practices themselves.

Kroeber's second proposition, that forms of burial are not integrated with more basic cultural features such as subsistence activities and organizational features of the society, is clearly refuted by the numerous observations that forms of burial vary directly with the following characteristics of the deceased: age, sex, relative social status within the social unit, and social affiliation in membership units within a society or in the society itself. These characteristics certainly are fundamental to the internal differentiation serving as the basis for organizational features of a society.

With the refutation of Kroeber's propositions, we are faced with his original problem—the applicability of the assumptions of traditional historical interpretation of mortuary rites. It is argued here that these assumptions are generally invalid; consequently, the historical interpretations which anthropologists have offered in "explanation" of observed differences and similarities in custom are generally suspect and in all probability inaccurate. I will attempt to demonstrate this argument with the development of a frame of reference for comparative study of mortuary rites and provide a test of its usefulness on a body of ethnographic data.

Study of Mortuary Rites: Their Potential

In mortuary ritual we observe a class of phenomena consisting of both technical and ritual acts. (See Radcliffe-Brown, 1952, p. 143, for this distinction.) Technically, burial customs provide for the disposal of the potentially unpleasant body of the deceased. Ritually, mortuary rites consist of the execution of a number of symbolic acts that may vary in two ways: (1) in the form of the symbols employed and (2) in the number and kinds of referents given symbolic recognition.

It will be recalled that the act of symboling is the arbitrary assigning of meaning to form. Therefore, we expect nothing intrinsic in the form of a symbol to limit it to any particular referent. In turn, there is nothing intrinsic in a referent which necessarily determines the form of the symbol to be used in its designation or conceptualization. The forms of symbols may vary independently of their referents and vice versa. In fact, with respect to burial practices, this has been frequently observed. For instance, Kroeber states:

> River burial is sometimes reserved for chiefs, sometimes for the drowned, sometimes is the normal practice of a group. Tree and platform burial is in certain populations restricted respectively to musicians, magicians, and the bewitched, the lightning struck, criminals, and Kings. Cremation is generally reserved for criminals, but also occurs as the usual practice. Exposure is variously in usage, according to tribe, for the corpses of criminals, slaves, children, the common people, or the entire population (Kroeber, 1927, p. 313).

Thus, when considering the degree that symbolic forms are held in common among a number of independent sociocultural units, it becomes a matter of investigating the degree that communication systems are isomorphically distributed among sociocultural systems and/or the degree that there is an identity between the symbol systems and the referent units symbolized. For instance, groups may share the same set of mortuary symbols but employ them antagonistically, e.g., one group cremates its chiefs and the other cremates its criminals. [This pattern is not unknown in Africa (Küsters, 1919). The antagonistic use of symbols probably obtained in the Great Lakes of North America; compare grave goods at the sites reported by Binford (1963) and Ritchie (1949).]

That the form of symbols may vary independently of their referents and that forms may be shared but in a situation of contextual contrasts are features of cultural variability which obviate the normal diffusionists' interpretive frame of reference. The diffusionists would view forms shared among a number of social units as evidence for the "diffusion" of that particular trait among the societies and hence a document of mutual "influences." Similarly, the presence of symbols unique to each sociocultural unit would be viewed as evidence for a lack of mutual cultural influences among the groups compared.

One can readily envision a situation in which independent societies within a region employ a number of symbols of group identity. Some groups might employ symbolic forms which were unique to the group, while others might employ identical forms in antagonistic ways. Given the regional context, each would serve equally well to distinguish among the groups and provide the pervasive symbolic environment which tends to maintain the distinctiveness of the groups.

Nevertheless, the diffusionists would separate those groups employing unique symbols from those who shared similar forms and assert that there was more mutual cultural influence among those sharing identical forms of symbol. The diffusionists' argument would be rooted in the idealists' assumption that knowledge and sharing of ideas are responsible for the formal similarities.

One can readily see that prerequisite to the functioning of the symbols is a common knowledge on the part of all groups. Members of each group would have to know each form and its meaning for the symbols to function as group identifiers. Yet this common knowledge would apply equally to those groups employing distinct symbols and to those employing formally identical symbols. What differential knowledge or shared "ideas" is indicated by the presence of similar symbolic forms among some of the groups? None. Diffusionists' arguments applied to material remains, whether they be related to mortuary practice or not, are universally suspect insofar as symbols are concerned.

We now turn to the problem of structural variability. When we elect to study comparatively some identified formal category of cultural elements, we must seek to determine the degree to which there is isomorphism between members of the formal class studied and the particular roles played by each in the sociocultural systems compared. In the absence of such knowledge, we can expect that different determinants might condition the occurrence and distribution of forms, depending upon the difference in functions performed by the element in diverse systems. This is, of course, one of the basic assumptions of sciences, namely, that the laws governing the occurrence and distribution of an element in any system will differ when integrated into organizationally distinct systems. This is a point which, with regard to mortuary practices, must be explored in some detail.

When a cultural system is altered in its internal organization, new units of organizational relevance are generated for the human participants. The recognition of such referential units by participants in the system may prompt the act of symboling and thereby result in a proliferation of symbols within the sociocultural system. Although all units of organizational relevance may not be recognized or considered sufficiently important to social interaction to be given symbolic recognition, we would expect that, with respect to folk classifications of role-differentiated statuses, there would be a high degree of isomorphism between the functionally differentiated status units and the symbolized social positions. We would therefore expect to discover a near identity between the number of social positions within a social organization and the number of symbols designating such units (see Service, 1962).

Crucial for the considerations of mortuary rites are the number and kinds of referents given symbolic recognition. It is proposed that there are two general components of the social situation to be evaluated when attempting to understand the types of social phenomena symbolized in any given burial situation. First is what we may call, with Goodenough (1965, p. 7) the *social persona* of the deceased. This is a composite of the social identities maintained in life and recognized as appropriate for consideration at death. Second is the composition and size of the social unit recognizing status responsibilities to the deceased. We would expect direct correlations between the relative rank of the social position held by the deceased and the number of persons having duty—status relationships *vis-à-vis* the deceased. This point was made forcefully a number of years ago by Gluckmann:

> A rite in its final form is the summation of the behavior of a large number of persons articulated via the deceased in different ways . . . this analysis may be applied to the variation of death ceremonies with social status. One must note, however, that there is no mean for funeral rites and variation from it, a death creates a different social situation according to the status, manner of death, of the deceased and each funeral involves the participation of different persons behaving in prescribed ways (Gluckmann, 1937, p. 124).

Also, we would expect that the facets of the *social persona* symbolically recognized in the mortuary ritual would shift with the levels of corporate participation in the ritual and hence vary directly with the relative rank of the social position which the deceased occupied in life.

The following contingencies have been offered by many investigators as the primary dimensions of the *social persona* given recognition in differential mortuary treatment: age, sex, relative rank and distinctiveness of the social position occupied by the deceased within the social unit, and the affiliation of the deceased with respect to membership segments of the broader social unit, or in the case of intersocietal symbolism, the form appropriate to the society itself.

Additionally, it was noted that peculiar circumstances surrounding the death of a person may be perceived by the remaining members of a society as substantially altering the obligations of the survivors to acknowledge the *social persona* of the deceased as it was defined in life. Instead, such persons are treated as "members" of a post-mortem membership unit (those killed in war, those struck by lightning, etc.) and afforded mortuary ritual appropriate to such a membership group at the expense of recognition of other components of the social identity.

The utility of any set of propositions is measurable by the degree that they serve as, or provoke, the framing of testable hypotheses and the frequency with which these tested hypotheses are confirmed. As a preliminary test of the utility of the propositions advanced, I have deduced several rather obvious hypotheses and tested them on a body of data drawn from a sample of 40 non-state-organized societies. The sample was drawn from the Human Relations Areas files.

The first two propositions to be discussed relate to what has been termed structural variability in mortuary rites. It was argued that there should be a high degree of isomorphism between (a) the complexity of the status structure in a sociocultural system and (b) the complexity of mortuary ceremonialism as regards differential treatment of persons occupying different status positions.

This proposition could not be directly tested since in *no* case was the ethnographic description adequate either for determining all the forms that mortuary ritual might take in a single society or the correlates for different forms.

Nevertheless, there were generalizations available in the literature regarding the characteristics of the *social persona* differentiated ritually at burial. A number of descriptions of specific burial episodes abound, from which one could determine what characteristics of the deceased served as criteria for differential treatment. For this reason, each society was tabulated, not for the number of different patterns of mortuary treatment practiced, but for the number of dimensional distinctions (age, sex, social position, subgroup affiliation, cause of death, and location of death) recognized in the performance of formally differentiated mortuary practices.

For instance, we might be informed that members of different clans were buried in separate cemeteries. This would allow us to tabulate that subgroup affiliation was one dimension in terms of which mortuary distinctions were made. We might not, however, know how many clans there were or how many formally distinct patterns of mortuary ritual were practiced. In spite of this inadequacy, it was reasoned that there should be a general correlation between the number of dimensional distinctions employed and the complexity of the status structure within the society since the combinations and permutations of multidimensional distinctions are greater than for single or dichotomous dimensional distinctions.

With regard to the other variable in the proposition, complexity of the status structure, the ethnographic literature was completely inadequate. I was unable to obtain adequate information of numbers of status positions or systematic information for any other measure of sociocultural complexity. Rather than devote a great deal of time to the development of such a scale for measurement and attempt to justify its application to a diverse group of social units, I reasoned that a very crude index of complexity might be the forms of subsistence since it is a generally accepted correlation between forms of subsistence production and societal complexity. The sample of societies was grouped into four categories—hunters and gatherers; shifting agriculturalists; settled agriculturalists; and pastoralists. This grouping was accomplished accepting the classifications given in the "World Ethnographic Sample" (Murdock, 1957) for the ethnic groups in the sample.

Information obtained from the sample of societies for these admittedly crude measurements is summarized in Table I.

The results of the cross tabulations for subsistence categories with numbers of dimensional distinctions are given in Table II.

Statistically, there were no differences among hunters and gatherers, shifting agriculturalists, and pastoralists. There is a meaningful difference between these

TABLE I Sample Societies

Name of society	Distinction symbolized						Reference
	Cause of death	Location of death	Age of deceased	Sex of deceased	Social position	Social affiliation	
Abipon						X	Dobrizhoffer (1922, pp. 223, 268, 271, and 273)
Andamans			X			X	Radcliffe-Brown (1922, pp. 106–113); Man (1932, pp. 141–146)
Aleut				X	X		Sartschew (1806, pp. 77–78); Jochelson (1925, pp. 21–25)
Alor				X	X		Dubois (1944, pp. 19, 116, 160, and 511)
Ashanti			X	X		X	Rattray (1927, pp. 48, 70, 104, 144–145, and 159–162)
Barama Caribs				X			Gillen (1936, p. 164)
Bapedi			X		X		Longmore (1952, pp. 36–59)
Bushman-Kau					X		Roos (1931, pp. 81–83)
Bemba					X	X	Richards (1948, pp. 240–241)
Copper Eskimo				X	X		Jenness (1922, pp. 92 and 174–176); Rasmussen (1932, p. 45)
Formosans				X		X	Wiedfeldt (1919, pp. 24 and 37) (H.R.A.F. reference)
Hottentot	X			X			Schapera (1933, pp. 358–363); Schultze (1907, p. 115)
Iban				X	X		Roth (1892, pp. 120–122); Howell (1908, 1910, p. 102)
Iroquois				X		X	Morgan (1901, pp. 116 and 168)
Jivaro						X	Karsten (1935, pp. 456–466)

228

Culture					Reference
Klamath			X		Spier (1930, pp. 71–72)
Mossi	X	X	X	X	Delebson (1932, pp. 94–95, and 134–135); Mangin (1921, pp. 82–84)
Mundurucu	X		X	X	Tocantins (1877, p. 37); Horton (1948, p. 279)
Murngin	X	X	X		Warner (1937, pp. 33, 71, 237, 415, 432–433, and 468–469)
Nahane	X	X	X		Honigmann (1954, pp. 138–139); (1949, pp. 204–245)
Nupe	X	X	X	X	Forde (1955, pp. 39–44)
Nyakyusa	X	X	X	X	G. Wilson (1939, pp. 1–32); M. Wilson (1954, pp. 228–241)
Ostyak			X	X	(H.R.A.F. reference)
Olldea			X		Berndt and Johnston (1942)
Pomo	X	X	X		Stewart (1943, p. 36); Loeb (1926, p. 288); Gifford (1937, p. 376)
Powhatan	X	X	X		Binford (1964)
Samoa	X	X	X		Mead (1930, pp. 98–99)
Samoyed	X	X	X		Islavin (1847, pp. 72–73); Rae (1881, p. 151)
Siriono			X		Holmberg (1950, pp. 21, 66, and 85–87)
Tallensi			X	X	Rattray (1927, pp. 352, 371, and 390–394)
Tanala	X	X		X	Linton (1933, pp. 126 and 170–178)
Tarahumera	X	X	X	X	Bennett and Zingg (1935, pp. 236–239 and 363)
Taureg	X				Lhote (1944, pp. 85 and 157–158)
Tikopia	X	X	X		Firth (1936, p. 180); Rivers (1914, p. 513)
Tiv			X	X	Bohannan and Bohannan (1953, pp. 79, 456–461, and 464)
Tlingit	X	X	X	X	Krause (1956, pp. 156–159); Jones (1914, pp. 151–152)
Trobriands			X	X	Malinowski (1929, pp. 153–154); Silas (1926, pp. 116–118)
Witchita			X		Schmitt (1952)
Yahgan			X		Gusinde (1937, pp. 349 and 1047–1054)
Yurok	X	X	X	X	Heizer and Mills (1952, pp. 34, 41, 118, 152, and 175)

TABLE II   Summary Data

Subsistence category	Average number of dimensional distinctions per category
Hunters and gatherers	1.73
Shifting agriculturists	1.75
Settled agriculturists	3.14
Pastoralists	1.66

three groups and the mean value for settled agriculturalists. The greater number of dimensional distinctions employed by settled agriculturalists is viewed as evidence confirming the general proposition that there should be a direct correlation between the structural complexity of mortuary ritual and status systems within sociocultural systems.

The second proposition which I have attempted to test also relates to the structure of mortuary ritual. It is argued that among societies of minimal complexity, the major dimensions which serve for status differentiation are based on the personal qualities of the individuals involved: age, sex, and differential capacities for performance of cultural tasks (Service, 1962, p. 54). On the other hand, among more complex sociocultural systems, status positions may be defined in terms of more abstract characteristics related to the culturally designated and symbolized means employed for partitioning the socially organized human aggregate (see Service, 1962, p. 155). Given the proposition that distinctions made in mortuary ritual are made in terms of the *social persona,* the composite of the social identities held in life, there should be a strong correspondence between the nature of the dimensional characteristics serving as the basis for differential mortuary treatment and the expected criteria employed for status differentiation among societies arranged on a scale from simple to complex.

In terms employed in this study, hunters and'gatherers should exhibit more egalitarian systems of status grading, while among settled agriculturalists we might expect more incidences of ranked or stratified nonegalitarian systems of status grading. Consequently, we would predict that age and sex should serve more commonly as bases for mortuary distinction among hunter and gatherers; while among agriculturalists, social position, as varying independently of age and sex as well as subgroup affiliation, should more commonly serve as the basis for differential mortuary treatment.

To test this proposition, the information given in Table I was tabulated for the frequency of occurrence of various dimensional distinctions among the four recognized subsistence categories. The results of this tabulation are given in Table III.

This tabulation provides some provocative material. First, there are major

TABLE III *Dimensional Frequencies*

Dimensional distinctions	Hunters–gatherers	Shifting agriculturalists	Settled agriculturalists	Pastoralists
Conditions of death	1	0	6	1
Location of death	1	1	0	0
Age	2	1	7	1
Sex	12	4	10	3
Social position	6	5	11	0
Social affiliation	4	3	10	1
Total cases	15	8	14	3

differences in the features of the *social persona* commonly recognized among the societies (falling into the four subsistence categories). Among hunters and gatherers, 12 of the 15 cases gave some recognition to sex differences, while only six of the cases reported distinctions in social position not reducible to sex or age differences. This observation confirms our expectations regarding the correlation between the basis of status differentiation among hunters and gatherers and the characteristic of the *social persona* given recognition in distinctive mortuary treatment.

Among shifting agriculturalists, however, social position was most commonly recognized, with sex and subgroup affiliation being almost as common.

The same pattern is repeated for settled agriculturalists, although conditions of death were much more frequently recognized. The striking differences noted between agriculturalists and hunters–gatherers are taken as confirmatory evidence for the proposition advanced. Certainly among the agriculturalists, there are more societies that could be classified as tribes and chiefdoms, while among the hunters and gatherers, bands and tribes of minimal complexity are more common.

The "tests," using very crude measures and applied to a sample which cannot be considered representative of the categories employed, are nevertheless viewed as provocative and indicative of the postulated positive relationships between the structure of mortuary ceremonialism and the status structure characteristic of any given sociocultural system. These crude confirmations are viewed as encouraging signs that there are functional determinants which limit the complexity and hence the "freedom" with which multiple forms of mortuary practices may be meaningfully employed by participants in any given social system. The correlations indicated in these preliminary tabulations put the ax to naive assumptions often made in historical interpretations, i.e., that knowledge of, or the transmission of, ideas regarding diverse forms of mortuary practice are sufficient causes for their implementation and for changes in their distributional patterns.

Turning now to a consideration of the forms of mortuary variability, it was argued that there were minimally two components of the social situation to be evaluated when attempting to understand the types of social phenomena symbolized or recorded in a burial situation. The first was the *social persona* of the deceased; the second was the composition and size of the social aggregate recognizing status responsibilities to the deceased. It is argued here that the second component will exert determinant effects on the form which mortuary rites will take. It is argued that the locus of mortuary ritual and the degree that the actual performance of the ritual will interfere with the normal activities of the community should vary directly with the number of duty status relationships obtaining between the deceased and other members of the community (scale of identity). In turn, the social scale of the deceased should vary directly with the relative rank of the social position held by the deceased. Given this argument, it is proposed that in egalitarian societies, very young individuals should have very low rank and, hence, share duty–status relations with a very limited number of people. Older persons can be expected to occupy status positions of higher rank and, consequently, share duty–status relations with a greater number of people. We can therefore predict that age differences may be discriminated in mortuary ritual by differential placement of burial sites within the life space of the community. The choice of placement would vary with status to the degree that the performance of the ritual involves members of the community at large in the ritual activity and thereby disrupts their daily activities.

In order to test this proposition and explore the possibility that there may be other correlations between characteristics of the *social persona* given recognition by differential mortuary treatment and the form of the ritual discrimination, another table was prepared making use of the same societies as tabulated in Table I. To accomplish this, a crude nominal categorization for three variables was generated. The three variables selected were: (1) differential treatment of the body itself, (2) differential preparation of the facility in which the body was placed for disposal, and (3) differential contributions to the burial furniture placed with the body.

For each of these variables, three nominal distinctions were made. For the first variable—treatment of the body—three distinctions were tabulated:

(i) Preparation of the body: distinctions made by differential washing and/or exhibition of the body prior to graveside ritual.

(ii) Treatment of the body: distinctions made by differential mummification, mutilation, cremation.

(iii) Disposition of the body: distinctions made by differential disposition— placed in a grave, on a scaffold, disposed of in the river, etc.

The second variable—differential preparation of the facility in which the body was placed—was also broken down into three categories:

(i) Form of the facility: whether within a single class of facility, such as a subsurface grave, there were differential formal characteristics reserved for individuals of different status, size, architectural details, variations in materials used in construction, etc.

(ii) Orientation of facility: whether the facility was differentially oriented with respect to some established reference point, such as cardinal directions, solstice angles, etc.

(iii) Location of the facility: whether the facility was differentially placed in the life space of the community or in spatially differentiated burial locations.

For the third variable—grave furniture—two independent categories were tabulated, plus a third that included the presence of both of the other two:

(i) Form of the furniture: whether distinctions were made by including different forms of grave goods.

(ii) Quantity of goods: whether distinctions were made solely by the differential inclusion of varying quantities of goods.

(iii) Form and quantity: Whether distinctions were made by a simultaneous differentiation in types of included goods and in quantities of goods.
The results of this investigation are tabulated in Table IV.

A number of interesting, and I might add unsuspected, associations are suggested in the tabulations of Table IV. The first point is the degree that our predictions are verified regarding the types of accommodation expected between the level of corporate involvement characteristic of different funerals, and the location employed for the disposal of the body with respect to the life space of the community. In seven out of twelve cases in which age was the feature of the *social persona* distinguished, differentiation was accomplished by the locations

TABLE IV *Forms of Distinction*

	Condition of death	Location of death	Age	Sex	Social position	Social affiliation
Body						
(1) Preparation	–	–	–	–	2	–
(2) Treatment	2	1	–	–	2	2
(3) Disposition	2	1	3	–	2	1
Grave						
(4) Form	1	–	1	–	3	1
(5) Orientation	–	–	–	3	–	9
(6) Location	3	–	7	–	8	15
Furniture						
(7) Form only	–	–	–	16	5	–
(8) Quantity only	–	–	–	–	9	–
(9) Form and Quantity	–	–	–	–	7	–

of graves of infants and children, as opposed to those of adults. Upon investigation, there appeared to be two general patterns: (1) burial of children under the house floor, with adults buried in a cemetery, or more public location, or (2) burial of children around the periphery of the settlement while adults may be buried at designated locations within the settlement. Both of these distributions, the cellular and the centrifugal, appear as alternative accommodations to the different levels of corporate involvement generated by the death of adults, as opposed to subadults, in certain types of societies. When a child dies within a society in which social position is not inherited, very few duty–status relationships outside of the immediate family are severed. The level of corporate involvement in the mortuary rites is thus largely at the familial level; the rites are performed either within the precincts of the family's "life space" or outside the life space of the wider society, which therefore remains uninvolved in the mortuary rites. Upon the death of adults, their greater participation in the social life of the local group is recognized by rites conducted in a more obtrusive fashion in a location more in keeping with the scale of corporate involvement. Frequently such burials are accompanied by processions through the life space of the wider community.

In the latter case, burial is frequently in corporate facilities or locations, or in areas of the settlement which by virtue of their placement necessarily involve the community at large in the rites. This type of spatial accommodation is noted when rulers are transported to the seats of governmental power for interment or when central repositories for the remains of district leaders are maintained—a situation frequently noted in the cases of internally stratified societies within the sample studied.

An analogous clustering of locational distinctions is noted for differentiations with respect to sodality or subgroup affiliation. Examination of the cases revealed that societies in which various membership groups (clans, kindreds, lineages, etc.) are present, each may maintain a distinct burial location, a cemetery or charnel house, in which members are exclusively buried or their remains stored. Another common form of differentiation noted for membership groups is the orientation of the grave. In many cases in which sodalities maintained separate cemeteries, the graves were differentially oriented with respect to topographic features of solar reference points commonly significant in the sodality origin mythology.

Differentiations related to sex were of a totally different form. Most common were differences in the types of goods disposed of with the body. These differences were related to sex-differentiated clothing, personalities, and tools which symbolized male–female division of labor. Such distinctions frequently cross-cut additional ones made with regard to other dimensions of the *social persona,* such as membership group affiliation, social position, etc.

The differentiations in mortuary treatment related to social position or status of the deceased exhibited the most variability in form. Similarly, they were the most complex, that is, many different forms of distinction were employed. Very high-status persons may be buried in specific locations, after elaborate and unusual preparation of the body, and accompanied with specific material symbols of office and large quantities of contributed goods. Low-status persons in the same society may be differentiated by membership group affiliation and sex only, with no specific treatment related to status. In some cases, status may take precedence over sodality affiliation in mortuary symbolism, in direct proportion to the degree that the roles performed by the deceased were specifically related to the activities of the community at large, as opposed to being subgroup specific.

Regardless of the obvious complexity, the modal tendency was in the direction of differentiation by form and quantity of grave furnishings and the specificity of the location of interment. Status was most commonly symbolized by status-specific "badges" of office and by the quantities of goods contributed to the grave furniture.

Although the number of cases were few, differentiations related to the location at which death occurred (within the village, at a distant place) and the conditions of death (lightning struck, drowning, killed in war, etc.) were most commonly distinguished by differences in the treatment of the body itself and the location of the grave or repository for the remains.

This admittedly limited investigation of variability among a poorly structured sample of societies is nevertheless judged sufficient to demonstrate a number of significant points.

(1) The specific dimensions of the *social persona* commonly given recognition in differentiated mortuary ritual vary significantly with the organizational complexity of the society as measured by different forms of subsistence practice.

(2) The number of dimensions of the *social persona* commonly given recognition in mortuary ritual varies significantly with the organizational complexity of the society, as measured by different forms of subsistence practice.

(3) The forms which differentiations in mortuary ritual take vary significantly with the dimensions of the *social persona* symbolized.

These findings permit the generalization that the form and structure which characterize the mortuary practices of any society are conditioned by the form and complexity of the organizational characteristics of the society itself. Change or variability in either form or structure must take into account the limiting or determining effects exerted on these practices by the nature of the organizational properties of the society. In no way can ideational innovations or communicated knowledge or ideas be cited as a sufficient cause for change, variability, or stability. We must first understand the forces operating on a sociocultural system as a whole, then we may understand the causal nature of changes which we might observe within one of its component parts.

Given these findings, we may now turn to an evaluation of the assumptions which have been basic to traditional historical interpretations of cultural variability.

It was previously suggested that there were three propositions fundamental to a traditional historical interpretative. The first assumption was stated as follows:

1. Culture is a body of custom which arises in the context of the conceptual–intellectual life of peoples and distributionally varies directly as a function of the patterns of transmission and with differential capacities or opportunities for intellectual experience. In contrast I argue that culture is man's extrasomatic means of adaptation. As such, culture is partitioned into numerous systems composed of energy, matter, and information. Cultural systems have both content and organizational properties, form and structure; the structure of a system conditions the nature and variety of its formal content. Information and knowledge of alternative forms is never a sufficient cause for formal change in a cultural system. Other variables must operate to bring about structural–organizational changes. A group of people may be fully aware of numerous alternative ways of disposing of a body, but until the organizational properties of their cultural system are altered, so as to increase the number of socially relevant categories of persons, new behavioral means for symboling differences will not be employed.

Human populations may perceive many features of their environment and have knowledge of great ranges of human behavior, yet while possibly providing certain limits to the necessary conditions for potential change; this knowledge and perceptive insight are in no way the sufficient causes of cultural change. Forces must operate on the cultural system as a whole to alter its organizational properties before this store of knowledge can be drawn upon for developing content elaborations, additions, and changes in the cultural system. The comparative study of forms of cultural content as a measure of variability in flow of information among and within cultural systems is misleading; structural variability alone among cultural systems strongly conditions the degree that information and knowledge will be translated into culturally organized behavior. Traditional historical interpretation ignores this sytemic character of culture.

The second assumption basic to traditional historical interpretation states:

2. The customs of a single sociocultural tradition were originally uniform and formally distinct. This is the normative assumption which is disproven at every juncture when we study the nature of variability observable within a single cultural system. Cultural systems are internally differentiated, partitioned, and segmented into component parts which are organizationally articulated into a functioning system. The degree that customs can be shown to be uniform within a cultural system is a direct measure of the degree that they are unrelated to the organizational characteristics differentiated among the components of the system. The vast majority of human behavior in the context of a cultural system is internally differentiated and nonuniformly distributed among all participants, in direct relation to the organizational complexity of the system. To assume that there should be a single mode of disposal of the dead characteristic of any sociocultural system is to assume that the participants of the system were undifferentiated in roles, and division of labor was absent.

The corollary of this assumption is:

Multiple practices observed among any given set of sociocultural units results from cultural mixing or hybridization in the past. It is argued that multiple practices are to be expected given the varying degree of systemic complexity observed among sociocultural systems. The presence of multiple practices is to be viewed as the by-product of evolutionary processes operating at the systemic level, promoting varying degrees of structural differentiation and functional specialization within the cultural system itself.

Evolutionary processes affecting the internal structure of the sociocultural system may result in more diverse internal differentiations, which are accommodated behaviorally by the participants of the system. The forms these behavioral accommodations may take may well be conditioned by the universe of knowledge possessed by the participants in the system, as to types of accommodations employed by other peoples and by their compatibility with other groups. Nevertheless, the sharing of similar forms of behavior among independent sociocultural systems may be the by-product of their experiencing analogous but independent evolutionary processes in a common environment of intersocietal relations, while the systems share a common store of knowledge.

This same store of knowledge may be shared with societies not undergoing evolutionary change at the structural level. Sharing similar forms could in no way be viewed as cultural "mixing" or "hybridization," because the degree of mutual "cultural influence" might be no greater among those societies undergoing change than that shared with those remaining stable. Sharing forms of cultural content may result from the mutual phasing of evolutionary processes among interacting sociocultural systems as reasonably as it can be viewed as the by-product of their degrees of interaction.

As anthropologists, our job is to explain observed similarities in terms of the operation of cultural–evolutionary processes; it is not to make assumptions as to what similarities mean or to build "conjectural histories" (Radcliffe-Brown, 1958, p. 5) by imposing on our observations unverified interpretive principles or "laws." Traditional historical interpretations are rooted in naive assumptions regarding the processes which operate to promote change and variability in both form and structure among cultural systems.

The final assumption is summarized as follows:

3. For practical purposes, the degree of formal similarity observed among independent sociocultural units is a direct measure of the degree of genetic or affiliational cultural relationship among the units compared. This assumption once again is grounded in the idealists' view of culture, that is, culture is a ramifying reticulate stream of transmitted ideas and knowledge, variously crystallized at different points in space and time. This assumption ignores the possibility that there are processes selectively operating on a body of ideas or knowledge. Selective forces may favor or limit the implementation and incorporation of knowledge as the bases for action in cultural systems experiencing different systematic histories.

This assumption further presupposes that knowledge and ideas are sufficient causes of cultural change and variability. Variability is to be viewed as the by-product of interruptions in the flow of information among human populations, while change may be viewed as the result of additions to accumulated knowledge, either originating through local innovations or arising from changes in patterns of information flow among societies. It is argued here that knowledge and ideas are not sufficient causes of cultural change or variability. Evolutionary processes operating selectively on different segments of human populations result in configurations of variability and change that vary independently of the genetic origins of the populations themselves, as well as the contemporary patterns of communication and transmission of knowledge and ideas. An attempt to view all cultural variability as a measure of patterns of ideational innovation and communication ignores what we, as anthropologists, should be seeking to explain—the processes which result in the differential organization of knowledge and ideas as implemented in independent sociocultural systems.

Implications of our Findings for Contemporary Archaeological Research

This survey of the treatment of mortuary data by anthropologists was undertaken to facilitate an evaluation of the scientific value of many propositions and assumptions around which much of contemporary archaeological conjecture, interpretation, and speculation regarding the past is oriented. It is hoped that I have been successful in pointing out that idealistic assumptions regarding the processes of cultural change and differentiation are inadequate; differences in ideas and knowledge, while possibly relevant as prerequisites to change and differentiations, are never sufficient causes for such changes or differentiations.

Further, variability in behavior or cultural practice are not exclusively explicable by reference to past contacts or influences among peoples; variability must be understood in terms of the organizational properties of the cultural systems themselves.

It is only after we understand the organizational properties of cultural systems that we can meaningfully make comparisons among them in terms of culture content. The contemporary archaeologist's practice of making comparisons among cultural units in terms of inventories of cultural content, while making no attempt to isolate and understand the variables affecting the frequency or distribution of content in the cultural units studied, is a fruitless and, I fear, meaningless pastime. Frequency differences in the incidence of extended burial versus flexed burial, cremation versus inhumation, mound versus cemetery burial, etc., are not measures of "popularity" or degree of intersocietal "influence." Variations among cultural units in frequencies of various forms of mortuary treatment vary in response to (a) the frequency of the character symbolized by the mortuary form in the relevant population and (b) the number and distribution of different characteristics symbolized in mortuary treatment, as a function of the complexity and degree of differentiation characteristic of the relevant society.

This means that we, as archaeologists, must strive to develop methods which will permit us to explain the observations which we make on the archaeological record in terms of causative variables operative in the past. Traditional archaeologists have assumed that they know what these variables were and have proceeded to interpret the archaeological record in terms of assumed laws of cultural change and variability. I propose that we as scientists should be striving to gain sufficient understanding to enable us to formulate the laws of cultural change and evolution.

References

Aberle, David R. (1960). The influence of linguistics on early culture and personality theory. In *Essays in the Science of Culture: In Honor of Leslie A. White* (G. Dole and R. Carneiro, eds.), pp. 1–49. Crowell-Collier, New York.

Bendann, Effie. (1930). *Death Customs: An Analytical Study of Burial Rites.* Kegan Paul, Trench, Trubner & Co., London.

Bennett, W. C., and Robert M. Zingg. (1935). *The Tarahumara an Indian Tribe of Northern Mexico.* Univ. of Chicago Press, Chicago.

Berndt, R. M., and T. H. Johnston. (1942). Death, burial, and associated ritual at Olldea, South Australia. *Oceania* 12, 189–201.

Binford, Lewis R. (1963). An analysis of cremation from three Michigan sites. *Wisconsin Archaeologist* 44, 98–110.

Binford, Lewis R. (1964). Archaeological and ethnohistorical investigations of cultural diversity. Ph.D. Dissertation, Department of Anthropology, University of Michigan (microfilm).

Binford, Lewis R. (1965). Archaeological systematics and the study of culture process. *American Antiquity* **31**, 203–210.

Bohannan, Paul, and Laura Bohannan. (1953). *The Tiv of Central Nigeria,* Ethnographic Survey of Africa, Part VIII. London International African Institute, London.

Crooke, W. (1899). Primitive rites of disposal of the dead, with special reference to India. *Journal of the Royal Anthropological Institute of Great Britain and Ireland* **29**, 271–294.

Davidson, D. S. (1948). Disposal of the dead in Western Australia. *Proceedings of the American Philosophical Society* **92**, 71–97.

Dawson, Warren R. (1928). Mummification in Australia and in America. *Journal of the Royal Anthropological Society of Great Britain and Ireland* **58**, 115–138.

Delebson, A. A. Dim. (1932). *The Empire of the Mogho Naba, Customs of the Mossi of Upper Volta,* Institut de Droit Compare, Etudes de Sociologie et d'Ethnologie Joridiques, Vol. II. Les Editions Domet-Montchiestian, Paris.

Dobrizhoffer, Martin. (1822). *An Account of the Abipons, an Equestrian People of Paraguay,* Vol. 2. John Murray, London.

Dubois, Cora. (1944). *The People of Alor: A Social-Psychological Study of an East Indian Island with Analyses by Abram Kardiner and Emil Oberholzer.* Univ. of Minnesota Press, Minneapolis.

Durkheim, Emile. (1915). *The Elementary Forms of Religious Life* (translated by J. W. Swain), 3rd printing. Allen & Unwin, London, 1954.

Firth, Raymond. (1936). *We, the Tikopia; A Sociological Study of Kinship in Primitive Polynesia.* Allen & Unwin, London.

Forde, Daryll. (1955). The Nupe. In *Peoples of the Niger-Benve Confluence* (D. Forde, ed.), Part 10, pp. 17–52. International African Institute, Ethnographic Survey of Africa, Western African, London.

Frazer, James G. (1886). On certain burial customs as they illustrate the primitive theory of the soul. *Journal of the Royal Anthropological Institute of Great Britain and Ireland* **15**, 64–104.

Gifford, E. W., and A. L. Kroeber. (1937). *Culture Element Distributions IV Pomo.* Univ. of California Press, Berkeley.

Gillen, John P. (1936). The Barama River Caribs of British Guiana. *Papers of the Peabody Museum of American Archaeology and Ethnology* **17**, No. 2.

Gluckmann, Max. (1937). Mortuary customs and the belief in survival after death among the southeastern Bantu. *Bantu Studies* **11**, 117–136.

Goodenough, Ward, H. (1965). Rethinking "status" and "role": Toward a general model of the cultural organization of social relationships. In *The Relevance of Models for Social Anthropology* (M. Banton, ed.), *ASA Monographs 1,* pp. 1–24. Praeger, New York.

Goody, Jack. (1962). *Death, Property and the Ancestors: A Study of the Mortuary Customs of the Lodagaa of West Africa.* Stanford Univ. Press, Stanford, California.

Graebner, Fritz. (1905). Kulturkreise und Kulturschichten in Ozeanien. *Zietschrift für Ethnologie* **34.**

Greenman, Emerson F. (1932). Origin and development of the burial mount. *American Anthropologist* **34**, 286–295.

Griffin, James B. (1930). Aboriginal mortuary customs in the western half of the northeast woodlands area. Masters Thesis, Dept. of Anthropology, University of Chicago.

Grottanelli, Vinigi L. (1947). Burial among the Koma of Western Abyssinia. *Primitive Man* **20**, 71–84.

Gusinde, Martin. (1937). Die Yahgan, vom Legen Und Denken der Wassernomaden am Kap Hoorn, *Die Fruerland-Indianer,* Modling bei Wien.

Heizer, Robert F., and J. E. Mills. (1952). *The Four Ages of Tsurai.* Univ. of California Press, Berkeley.

Hertz, Robert. (1907). *Death and the Right Hand* (translated by R. Needham and C. Needham). 1960 edition, Free Press, Glencoe, Illinois.

Holmberg, Allen R. (1950). Nomads of the Longbow, The Siriono of Eastern Boliva. *Smithsonian Institution, Institute of Social Anthropology Publications* No. 10.

Homans, Goerge C. (1941). Anxiety and ritual: The theories of Malinowski and Radcliffe-Brown. *American Anthropologist* 43, 164–172.

Honigmann, John J. (1954). The Kaska Indians: An ethnographic reconstruction. *Yale University Publications in Anthropology* No. 51.

Horton, Donald. (1948). The Mundurucu. In *Handbook of South American Indians* (J. H. Stewart, ed.), Vol. 3, pp. 217–282. U.S. Govt. Printing Office, Washington, D.C.

Howell, William. (1908–1910). The Sea Dyak. *Sarawak Gazette* **38–40.**

Islavin, Vladimir. (1847). "Samoiedy v domashnem i obshchestuennom bytu." *Ministerstva Gosudarstennykh Imushchesti,* St. Petersburg.

James, Edwin O. (1928). Cremation and the preservation of the dead in North America. *American Anthropologist* 30, 214–242.

Jenness, Diamond. (1922). The life of the Copper Eskimos. *Report of the Canadian Arctic Expedition, 1913–1918* 12.

Jochelson, Waldemar. (1925). *Archaeological Investigations in the Aleutian Islands.* Carnegie Institute of Washington, Washington, D.C.

Jones, Livingston F. (1914). *A Study of the Thlingets of Alaska.* Fleming H. Kimball, Chicago, Illinois.

Karsten, Rafael. (1935). The Head-hunters of Western Amizonos. *Societos Scientianum Fennica: Commentationes Humanarum Litterarum* 8, No. 1.

Krause, Aurel. (1956). *The Tlingit Indians; Results of a Trip to the Northwest Coast of America and the Bering Straits* (translated by E. Gunther). Univ. of Washington, Seattle.

Kroeber, A. L. (1927). Disposal of the Dead. *American Anthropologist* 29, 308–315.

Kroeber, A. L., and Clyde Kluckhohn. (1952). Culture; a critical review of concepts and definitions. *Papers of the Peabody Museum of American Archaeology and Ethnology, Harvard University* 47, No. 1.

Küsters, P. M. (1919). Das Grab der Afrikaner. *Anthropos* **14–15,** 639–728.

Küsters, P. M. (1920). Das Grab der Afrikaner. *Anthropos* **16–17,** 183–229 and 913–959.

Lhote, Henri. (1944). *Les Tourege du Hoggar.* Payot, Paris.

Lhote, Henri. (1947). *Dans les campements touaregs.* Oeuvers Françaises, Paris.

Linton, Ralph. (1933). The Tanala, a hill tribe of Madagascar. *Fieldiana-Anthropology* **22.**

Loeb, Edwin M. (1926). *Pomo Folkways.* Univ. of California Press, Berkeley.

Longmore, L. (1952). Death and burial customs of the Bapedi of Sekukuniland, Johannesburg. *African Studies* 11, 36–59.

Malinowski, Bronislaw. (1925). Magic, Science and Religion; reprinted in *Magic, Science and Religion and Other Essays,* pp. 10–87. Doubleday, Garden City, New York, 1955.

Malinowski, Bronislaw. (1929). *The Sexual Life of Savages in Northwestern Melanesia.* Horace Liveright, New York.

Man, E. H. (1932). On the aboriginal inhabitants of the Andaman Islands. Part II. *Journal of the Anthropological Institute of Great Britain and Ireland* 12, 117–175.

Mangin, Eugene. (1921). *Essay on the Manners and Customs of the Mossie: People in the Western Sudan.* Augustin Challamel, Paris.

Mead, Margaret. (1930). Social organization of Manua. *Bernice P. Bishop Museum, Bulletin* **76.**

Miles, Douglas. (1965). Socio-economic aspects of secondary burial. *Oceania* 35, 161–174.

Morgan, L. H. (1901). *League of the Ho-De-No-Sau-Nee or Iriquois* (edited and annotated by H. M. Lloyd), Vol. 1. Dodd, Mead & Co., New York.

Murdock, George P. (1957). World ethnographic sample. *American Anthropologist* **59**, 664–687.

Myers, J. N. L. (1942). Cremation and inhumation in the Anglo-Saxon cemeteries. *Antiquity* **16**, 330–341.

Perry, W. J. (1914). The orientation of the dead in Indonesia. *Journal of the Anthropological Institute of Great Britain and Ireland* **44**, 281–294.

Radcliffe-Brown, A. R. (1922). *The Andaman Islanders.* Cambridge Univ. Press, London and New York.

Radcliffe-Brown, A. R. (1952). *Structure and Function in Primitive Society.* Free Press, Glencoe, Illinois.

Radcliffe-Brown, A. R. (1958). In *Method in Social Anthropology* (M. N. Srinivas, ed.). Univ. of Chicago Press, Chicago.

Radin, Paul. (1923). The Winnebago Tribe. *37th Report of the Bureau of American Ethnology.*

Rae, Edward. (1881). *The White Sea Peninsula, A Journey in Russian Lapland and Kerelia.* John Murray, London.

Rasmussen, Knud. (1932). Intellectual culture of the Copper Eskimos. *Report of the Fifth Thule Expedition, 1921–24* **9**.

Rattray, Robert S. (1927). *Religion and Art in Ashanti.* Oxford Univ. Press (Clarendon), London and New York.

Richards, Audrey I. (1948). *Hunger and Work in a Savage Tribe.* Free Press, Glencoe, Illinois.

Ritchie, W. A. (1949). An archaeological survey of the Trent waterway in Ontario, Canada. *Researches and Transactions of the New York Archaeological Association* **12**, No. 1.

Rivers, W. H. R. (1913). *The Contact of Peoples, Essays and Studies Presented to William Ridgeway.*

Rivers, W. H. R. (1914). *The History of Melanesian Society.* Cambridge Univ. Press, London and New York.

Roos, Tielman. (1931). Burial customs of the !Kau Bushmen. *Bantu Studies* **5**, 81–83.

Rose, H. J. (1922). Celestial and terrestrial orientation of the dead. *Journal of the Royal Anthropological Institute of Great Britain and Ireland* **52**, 127–140.

Roth, H. Ling. (1892). The natives of Borneo. Edited from the papers of the late Brooke Law, Esq. *Journal of the Anthropological Institute of Great Britain and Ireland* **21**, 110–133.

Sartschew, Gaivrill. (1806). *Account of a Voyage of Discovery to the Northeast of Siberia the Frozen Ocean, and the Northeast Sea,* Vol. II. Richard Phillips, London.

Schapera, Isaac. (1933). *The Early Cape Hottentots,* Publ. 14. Van Riebeeck Society, Capetown.

Schmidt, W. (1913). Kulturkreise und Kulturschichten in Sudamerika. *Zeitschrift für Ethnologie* **45**, 1014–1124.

Schmitt, Karl. (1952). Wichita death customs. *Chronicles of Oklahoma* **30**, 200–206.

Schoolcraft, Henry R. (1855). *Information Respecting the History, Condition, and Prospects of the Indian Tribes of the United States,* Vol. 4. Philadelphia.

Schultze, Leonhard. (1907). *Aus Namaland und Kalahari.* Fischer, Jena.

Sears, William H. (1964). The Southeastern United States. In *Prehistoric Man in the New World,* pp. 259–287. Univ. of Chicago Press, Chicago.

Service, Elmn. (1962). *Primitive Social Organization.* Random House, New York.

Silas, Ellis. (1926). *A Primative Arcadia.* T. Fisher Unwin Ltd., London.

Smith, Robertson. (1894). *The Religion of the Semites.* Meridan Library Edition, New York, 1956.

Spencer, Robert F., and Jesse D. Jennings. (1965). *The Native Americans.* Harper, New York.

Spier, Leslie. (1930). *Klamath Ethnography.* Univ. of California Press, Berkeley.

Stanislawski, Michael B. (1963). Extended burials in the prehistoric southwest. *American Antiquity* **28**, 308–319.

Steele, R. H. (1931). Orientation of the Maori dead. *Journal of the Polynesian Society* **40**, 81–85.

Stewart, Omer C. (1943). *Notes on Pomo Ethnogeography.* Univ. of Califnornia Press, Berkeley.

Thomas, Northcote W. (1908). The disposal of the dead in Australia. *Folklore* **19**, 388–408.

Tocantins, Antonio Manuel. (1877). *Studies on the Mundurucu Tribe,* Quarterly Review of the Historical, Geographical and Ethnographical Institute of Brazil. R. L. Garnier, Rio de Janiero.

Toulouse, Joseph H. (1944). Cremation among the Indians of New Mexico. *American Antiquity* **10**, 65–74.

Tyler, John M. (1921). *The New Stone Age of Northern Europe.* Charles Scribner's Sons, New York.

Tylor, Edward B. (1871). *Primitive Culture.* John Murray, London.

Van Gennep, Arnold. (1960). *The Rites of Passage.* Phoenix Books, Univ. of Chicago Press, Chicago.

Viollier, D. (1911). *Essai sur les rites funéraires en suisse des orgines àla conquete romaine.* Leroux, Paris.

Voegelin, Erminie W. (1944). Mortuary customs of the Shawnee and other eastern tribes. *Indiana Historical Society, Prehistoric Research Series* **2**, 225–444.

Wallis, W. D. (1917). Similarities in culture. *American Anthropologist* **19**, 41–54.

Warner, Lloyd W. (1937). *A Black Civilization.* Harper, New York.

Wedgwood, Camilla H. (1927). Death and social status in Melanesia. *Journal of the Royal Anthropological Institute of Great Britain and Ireland* **57**, 377–397.

White, L. A. (1949). *The Science of Culture.* Grove Press, New York.

White, L. A. (1954). Review of *Culture; A Critical Review of Concepts and Definitions,* by A. L. Kroeber and Clyde Kluckhohn. *American Anthropologist* **56**, 461–468.

Whorf, Benjamin Lee. (1956). Science and linguistics. In *Language Thought and Reality* (J. B. Carr, II, ed.), pp. 207–219. Wiley, New York.

Wilder, H. H., and R. W. Whipple. (1917). The position of the body in aboriginal interments in western Massachusetts. *American Anthropologist* **19**, 372–387.

Willey, Gordon R. (1966). *An Introduction to American Archaeology,* Vol. I. Prentice-Hall, Englewood Cliffs, New Jersey.

Wilson, Godfrey. (1939). Nyakyusa conventions of burial. *Bantu Studies* **13**, 1–32.

Wilson, Monica. (1954). Nyakyusa ritual and symbolism. *American Anthropologist* **56**, 228–241.

Yarrow, H. C. (1886). Introduction to the study of mortuary customs among the North American Indians. *Annual Report of the Bureau of American Ethnology* Vol. I.

Model Building—Paradigms,
and the Current State of Paleolithic Research

In recent years there has been an increasing use of the term *model* in the writings of archaeologists. There have been explicit calls for more model building and these have frequently been coupled with calls for a greater use of scientific method. The purpose of this discussion is to examine the current state of theory and model building in the field of paleolithic archaeology.

The relevant facts of nature do not of their own accord separate themselves from all the others, nor do they come with all their significant characteristics duly labelled for us. Which of the infinite variety of nature's circumstances we would turn to as relevant to or bearing upon any scientific problem depends upon our general ideas as to how that which is sought for can possibly be related to what we already know. Without such guiding ideas or hypotheses as to possible connections we have nothing to look for (Cohen, 1964, p. 77).

We always bring to our observations some expectations in the form of "models" of nature. These are our particular cognitive maps of what nature is like and what we can expect from it. It has been argued that the "desire" for an explanation originates from a reaction of surprise to some experience. This surprise is generated by a conflict between our expectations in a given situation and our actual experience of it (Harvey, 1969, p. 11). One might argue that all persons, whether scientists or not, generally approach nature in this manner. They have a series of "models" of nature, a series of cognitive expectations, and it is when these expectations are not met that an "explanation" is demanded or sought. Kuhn (1962) in his fascinating review of patterning in the history of intellectual activity, has argued convincingly that in science as well as in general intellectual life there are accepted "models" of nature which are shared among a community of scholars. He calls these models a paradigm. The dynamic relations between the paradigm shared among a community of scholars, the activities of the scholars, and the problems selected for solution, are well described by Kuhn (1962, p. 37) as follows:

A scientific community acquires with a paradigm . . . a criterion for choosing problems that, while the paradigm is taken for granted, can be assumed to have solutions. To a great extent these are the only problems that the community will admit as scientific or encourage its members to undertake. Other problems, including many that had previously been standard, are rejected as metaphysical, as the concern of another discipline, or sometimes as just too problematic to be worth the time. A paradigm can, for that matter, even insulate the community from those socially important problems that are not reducible to the puzzle form, because they cannot be stated in terms of the conceptual and instrumental tools the paradigm supplies.

Archaeology appears to me to provide an interesting case of the traditional use of a paradigm, a model of what the archaeological record is like, what we can expect from it, and its significance. Many archaeologists will object, maintaining that they are empiricists, collecting the facts and arranging them according to the order inherent in them. Let's examine the empiricists' argument.

Archaeology is the science concerned with the description and explanation of differences and similarities observed in the archaeological record. The archaeologist may carry out three major kinds of activities in the context of his role. These might be summarized as exploration, explication, and explanation.

Exploration

Much of the work of the past and which continues today is justified on the basis that we simply do not know what the archaeological record is like in a given region or for a given time period. We may engage in exploratory work solely for the purposes of correcting recognized lacks in our observations on the record. During the course of our investigations, whether prompted by exploratory considerations, or by problems posed by the record as it is known, the archaeologist makes discoveries. Most of these are not surprising, and the archaeologist treats them as mundane, referring to them as "data."

Sometimes, however, discoveries are surprising: observations which do not conform to our expectations or our "model" of what the archaeological record is like. Discoveries of the latter class may be of two general types: curiosities and new information regarding the character of the archaeological record. Much of the public appeal of archaeology comes from the announcement of archaeological discoveries which attract attention because of their "surprise" nature. Curiosities may consist of items or extraordinary conditions that we would not expect to be preserved in the archaeological record. Such things as the recently reported frozen body of a man preserved since approximately 20,000 years ago, complete with clothing, or the "ghost" of a body preserved for an even greater length of time in a Spanish deposit, are examples. These surprise us because of our expectations regarding the nature of the archaeological record. We demand explanations as to how they were preserved. Rarely do such curiosities add appreciably to our understanding of the past or our knowledge of the dynamics of cultural processes.

Another type of discovery is one that challenges our expectations about the past itself. Discoveries of this type were the major challenges to the "Biblical" paradigm regarding the history of man, his antiquity and early condition. Every student is familiar with the discoveries of men like Frere and Boucher De Perthes, who discovered materials which should not have existed if the old paradigm was correct. Discoveries of this type are generally falsifying discoveries in Popper's (1959) sense of the term. Their importance derives from the fact that they clearly imply an inadequacy in the prevailing theory, or model, of nature.

There is a third type of discovery which one may make. This is the anticipated surprise—not anticipated in the particular incidence of its discovery, but anticipated by the model of nature which the investigator works within. I will discuss this again under the rubric of "explanation."

It should be clear that even at the exploratory level of investigation we bring certain expectations to our work. These are derived from our paradigm or model of either the archaeological record itself or of the past. Problems are defined and new questions asked as a result of the interaction between our observations and our expectations derived from a paradigm. The empiricists' position seems difficult to defend even at the exploratory level of research.

Explication

Explication generally refers to some systematic description of observations. In this the archaeologist faces the task of breaking down a whole into parts, generally with the aim of elucidating its componential makeup and the interrelationships among its components. Analysis presupposes an aim or goal in research. We may justifiably ask: Analysis for what? Leaving aside for the moment this important question, a discussion of the character of the archaeological record is in order.

The archaeological record exhibits only two kinds of variability: organizational and distributional. Organizational variability refers to all the associations and correlations which in the context of repetition permit the recognition of an entity or the association of entities or characteristics having definable structural properties. Distributional variability refers to the patterning manifest when recognized units or characteristics are plotted spatially or across populations isolated independently of the unit or characteristic being studied. One of the most common procedures is to plot the distribution of recognized components of the archaeological record across populations isolated with respect to the inferred dimension of time. Thus, heuristically, we may speak of the distributional study of variability with respect to the temporal dimension (see Spaulding, 1960).

Taking an empiricist's position the archaeologist may be concerned with assessing something of the character of observed organizational and distributional variability uninformed as to its significance, or meaning, in terms of the past. An empiricist would suggest that this may be accomplished by the development of a taxonomy for classifying observations and materials. A crucial point to be emphasized is that as a scientific tool taxonomies are instruments for measurement. A taxonomy developed in the context of an inductivist philosophy can be said to be an instrument for measuring "recognized" differences and similarities. Classifications of data in terms of such taxonomies cannot be said to inform in any direct way on the significance of the differences or similarities measured. In spite of this limitation there are criteria which will allow us to evaluate the adequacy of a taxonomy. A taxonomy can be judged adequate if all of the "recognized" variability is accommodated and the criteria for inclusion in the various categories are unambiguous. The adequacy of a taxonomy is, however, no measure of its reliability for measuring variability of specified significance. Similarly the inadequacy of a taxonomy in the above terms provides no necessary argument against its reliability for measuring characteristics of specified significance. Significance and adequacy are very different characteristics of taxonomies.

Errors with regard to the above are common in archaeological debate. For instance, it has frequently been asserted that the quantity of differences as measured by some taxonomic evaluation among assemblages is a measure of ethnic affinity between the groups responsible for the archaeological remains. Our ability to measure quantitatively differences and similarities between assemblages and to synthesize our results into such taxonomic units as phases or traditions is in no way a test of the validity of the proposition that measured differences are indicative of degrees of ethnic affinity. This is a point which many archaeologists have failed to recognize.

> I suggest that we are justified in proceeding on the hypothesis that similarity of style and content of assemblages is an indicator of common cultural tradition (Collins, 1969, p. 270).
> If culture tradition theory were entirely wrong, I feel sure that the archaeological data would not pattern as neatly as it does into traditions and stages (Collins, 1969, p. 270).

This fallacy is frequently defended on the basis that an independent body of data is utilized, namely the results of distributional studies. This position is equally indefensible. The most common framework for distributional studies is a time–space matrix. Time is the conventional referent for evaluating the dynamics of transformations occurring within or among organizations. Space is the normal referent for evaluating the disposition of systemic processes and functions. Time and space, however, cannot be considered to be components of a system or variables which act on the system. To argue that time acts causally in activating systemic change or to cite changes in time or space as independent determinants of the phenomena being studied is inconceivable. Time and space are reference dimensions which we use for monitoring the operation of system dynamics. The demonstration of clustering along either of these dimensions only informs us that some systemic processes were at work. Such a demonstration does not inform us of the nature of those processes. The citation of differential distributional patterning as supporting evidence for a particular attribution of significance to the phenomena so patterned is not conclusive. All that such a demonstration insures is that (a) an organizational difference has been isolated and (b) the dynamics of organizational process was existentially independent. It in no way supports directly the validity of the particular characterization of the process proposed by the archaeologist.

Similarly, the argument that the particular method used for giving taxonomic recognition affects the validity of the arguments advanced to account for isolated organizational variability is difficult to defend. For instance David Clarke has recently advocated a rigid inductivist approach to taxonomy following the procedures outlined by Sokal and Sneath (1963) as Numerical Taxonomy. Clarke has criticized other procedures and attempts to solve questions posed by their application in the following way:

> The importance of developing an adequate definiton for the artefact-types and then applying the definition with all possible rigour cannot be overestimated. Many contemporary studies, particularly in the paleolithic field, make great play about variations from artefact assemblage to assemblage of the relative percentages of given artefact-types. . . . However, hardly any of these studies define their unit artefact-types on other than an intuitive and arbitrary basis . . . and one which is certainly not sufficiently comprehensive in application or accurately defined in terms of attributes. The consequent danger is that an alternative or conflicting definition of the artefact-types within such assemblages would radically alter the much discussed relative percentages and correspondingly alter their meaningful interpretation (Clarke, 1968, p. 188).

This appears to be a strange statement, coming from a man who in many ways exhibits a sophistication not shared with many of his colleagues. Surely Clarke knows that this statement would be true regardless of the methods used in establishing the typology, including his numerical methods. A classification system depends upon a selection by the investigator of criteria considered "significant" for use in classifying data. Selection of different criteria may result in a "conflicting definition of the artefacts-types" even if both classifications were being generated by inductive means using numerical taxonomic procedures. If an investigator specifies the criteria to be used and applies them consistently, then differences or similarities noted are "real" and demand explanation. Simply because another investigator selects another set of criteria and generates a different taxonomy by whatever consistent method is no basis for an argument against the "validity" of the first evaluation of differences and similarities. The latter argument can only be claimed if the competing investigators are in disagreement over the relevance of different sets of criteria as adequate measures of a specified variable. This does not appear to enter into Clarke's criticism.

Seeking an explanation for differentiations made by any method is a valid pursuit. The explanations may take the form of recognitions that the taxonomy is not measuring what it is alleged to measure, that the differentiations are spurious because of the methods used, or that the specified organizational properties of the archaeological record are understandable in terms of a developed argument about the past.

At the level of explication there are clearly several problems: (1) the selection of analytical criteria, (2) the selection of analytical techniques, and (3) the ascription of significance to the organizational or distributional patterning made explicit through the analytical procedures. In the absence of a paradigm or set of expectations as to relevance, no selection could be made from the infinity of characteristics potentially, present in the body of empirical material being studied. In the absence of a paradigm, no criteria of judgment could be made explicit for evaluating procedures since they must be offered in terms of specifiable sets of research goals. Similarly it is through the paradigm that arguments of significance are generated for the results of analysis. The empiricist's argument appears hard to defend.

Explanation

As previously mentioned the desire for an explanation originates from a reaction of surprise to some experience. This surprise is generated by a conflict between our expectations in a given situation and our actual experience of it (Harvey, 1969, p. 11). The expectations have been supplied to traditional archaeologists by a minimal set of theoretical propositions, a bridging argument, a model of cultural dynamics, and a set of conventions to be used in "interpreting" surprises. In short the traditionalist's paradigm anticipates surprises and supplies the archaeologist with a set of conventions for bringing his surprise observations back into line with his expectations. It is through the use of these conventions that the archaeologist reconstructs "culture history."

Archaeological theory has been a mentalist theory. The concept of culture is a central theoretical concept, and for archaeologists it has been explicated by reference to other primitive concepts such as ideas, values, mental templates, etc. These are theoretical concepts also and as such are not capable of being directly sensed or observed. How does the archaeologist "operationalize" his theory? The following "operational definition" or bridging argument is traditionally offered:

> Culture is patterned. . . . [Therefore] the patterning which the archaeologist perceives in his material is a reflection of the patterning of the culture which produced it (Deetz, 1967, p. 7).

This bridging argument allows the archaeologist to argue that the organizational characteristics of the archaeological record informs him directly on the character of culture. Such patterning may be recognized at several levels. At the level of the artifact the archaeologist seeks to identify patterning,

> identifying distinct patterns of behavior . . . which can be acquired by one human being from another . . . serve as the tools for the retracing of cultural development and interactions. . . . It is therefore the task of the analysis . . . to recover . . . the mental patterns which lay behind these manifold works (Kreiger, 1944, p. 272).

> Artifacts are man made objects; they are also fossilized ideas. In every clay pot, stone axe, wooden doll, or bone needle, we see preserved what someone once thought pots, axes, dolls or needles should look like. In every culture, there are conventions which dictate the form of artifacts (Deetz, 1967, p. 45).

If the single artifact reflects patterning at the individual level, redundancy observed among numerous cases of artifacts is a measure of the degree that "ideas" are shared among individuals. Artifact typology is the instrument of measurement in this case.

The other basic observational content unit with which the archaeologist works is the assemblage. The totality of materials recovered from an archaeological site believed to represent a restricted segment of the history of the people represented. Redundancy noted between a number of assemblages is taken as a measure of the shared "ideas" among the social units represented. Archaeological systematics generally proceeds as a progressive grouping of assemblages into broader and broader units said to be a measure of different degrees of culture sharing. The differential distribution of such groupings both temporally and spatially is said to reflect the history of culture transmitted among social segments of the human reproductive continuum.

As previously mentioned the archaeological record is capable of yielding two major kinds of information: organizational and distributional. The traditional archaeologist searches the archaeological record for patterning on both organizational (artifact types, assemblage types) and distributional (traditions, phases, etc.) dimensions.

By an operational definition, the archaeologist has "translated" a set of theoretical concepts into observational experience. In so doing he has assigned meaning, or significance, to his observations. He has transformed his taxonomic endeavors from an exploratory function to a measurement function. His classifications of organizational differences and similarities become an instrument for measuring degrees of shared "culture" among the human populations represented. His classifications of different units of observation—since they are generated by the recognition of patterning—become instruments for measuring a single "variable" culture.

The archaeologists' expectations as to the character of patterning to be anticipated in the archaeological record derive from a "model" of the dynamics of culture. This model provides the archaeologists with a frame of reference for the recognition of problems as well as their solution.

Most archaeologists have not given much explicit thought to the model of cultural dynamics which they employ, others have been very explicit. One of the clearest statements has been given by the late James Ford (1962).

> Fortunately the mechanics of change are simple, at least in principle. There are only three ways in which innovations can occur: invention, discovery, and borrowing (1962, p. 7).
>
> Culture change is remarkable in that it is the only perfect example of the democratic process. If individuals do not "vote" for customs, the cultural feature does not drift in that particular direction. The student of cultural processes therefore finds himself faced with the necessity of "tallying". . . . In effect the archaeologist must conduct a prehistoric opinion poll (1962, p. 9).
>
> We have examined some of the facets of evolving cultures, fluid streams of ideas that passed from human brain to human brain. These were ideas regarding the proper and best ways men should adapt themselves to their environment or modify that environment to meet their needs and desires (1962, p. 11).

Although not presented in point by point fashion, I believe that Ford expressed the major components of *the model* of cultural dynamics accepted by most traditional archaeologists.

This model as I understand it may be summarized into several basic statements.

(1) *Culture is localized in individual human beings.* This derives from the fact that only humans are considered to have the biological capacities for cultural cognition.

(2) *Culture is transmitted among human beings.* Through learning, individuals assimilate culture from other persons.

(3) *Culture is shared.* Sharing results from the cumulative effects of common learning experiences, in short the degrees of association or interaction occurring among human beings.

(4) *Culture derives from humans.* It may be generated only by human acts of invention.

(5) *Culture is cumulative.* Inventions once made add to the alternatives among which choices may be made and serve as the basis for recombination into new inventions.

(6) *Culture is a continuum.* It is a continuum because the succession of individuals in generational succession is a continuum. Since culture, e.g., ideas, information, etc., is transmitted across generations, it also is a continuum.

(7) *Culture is continuously changing.* This derives from the fact that culture bearers are continuously being replaced, thereby insuring that the cumulative effects of individual choices at any two points in time vary as the composition of individuals in the population vary. This also derives from the expectation that

individuals are continuously being presented with new alternatives through acts of invention.

(8) *Culture changes gradually.* This is expected because individuals are replaced gradually in human populations, resulting in minute shifts in relative popularity among varying alternatives.

Converting these components of the traditionalist's model into expectations regarding the character of the archaeological record is relatively easy. As an example I will specify some of the traditionalist's expectations for a relatively well investigated region.

(1) We expect a continuous sequence of variability, patterning as gradual directional changes in the relative frequencies of recognized artifact taxa. These expectations are explicated by Deetz (1967, pp. 26–37), Clarke (1968, pp. 187–227), and many others.

(2) A gradual increase in the numbers of artifact taxa recognizable if the isolated part of the archaeological record spans a "sufficient" period of time.

(3) Transformational sequences showing a "development" of artifact forms from antecedent forms (see Clarke, 1968, pp. 131–185).

The archaeologist's model serves to provide him with his expectations as to the character of the patterning in the archaeological record. It provides him with a set of "justified" meanings to be assigned when the expected forms of patterning are observed. In addition it provides him with a set of interpretative principles to be used when his expectations are not met. For instance, since our model assumes that culture changes gradually, we expect to observe gradual replacive patterning in an archaeological sequence. If such is not observed and we are "surprised," then we appeal to our model for an interpretative principle. We find that since culture is localized in individuals and is derived from humans, then breaks in continuity of cultural patterning must derive from breaks in the continuity of human populations in the area. Population replacement (migration) becomes the necessary explanation.

I will examine some of the cases where expectations have not been met and evaluate how archaeologists have dealt with such "surprises." The expectations under review are that contemporary assemblages should be roughly alike and, that interassemblage variability should therefore exhibit some directional patterning temporally. Several good examples of the archaeological record presenting some surprises are well documented.

The Big Surprise—The Nonconformity

A nonconformity is an observed situation where the expectation of gradual change is not met. Instead, abrupt changes and major differences characterize assemblages in contiguous temporal positions.

THE MOUSTERIAN PROBLEM

Early researchers investigating the character of Mousterian remains recognized some interassemblage variability and interpreted it to meet their expectations. One form of assemblage was considered to succeed another in a temporal succession of gradual changes. Early textbooks will show that three "phases" of the Mousterian "tradition" were recognized. Early industries were characterized by the presence of handaxes and a blending of the new with the older traits of the Acheulian. This was called Mousterian of Acheulian tradition. Following this were industries showing less traits in common with the earlier Acheulian and characterized by a wide variety of flake forms of tools; this was called typical Mousterian. Finally there was a kind of Mousterian characterized by many steeply retouched scrapers, frequently found in association with fauna indicative of cold climates; this was called "cold Mousterian" or "Quina Type." This synthesis produced no surprises, and our expectations were met.

Later detailed stratigraphic work (Peyrony, 1930) and an increased sophistication in taxonomic evaluation of assemblage variability, largely accomplished by François Bordes, resulted in the recognition that the older synthesis was inaccurate. Bordes demonstrated that the character of the archaeological record was very surprising, it did not conform to our expectations and therefore demanded explanation. He found that there were at least four major types of assemblage, two of which could be further broken down into subtypes of facies. These were termed Denticulate Mousterian, Typical Mousterian, Mousterian of Acheulian tradition (broken into two facies, A and B) and Charentian Mousterian (broken into two subtypes, Quina and Ferrassie). Comparative stratigraphic studies showed that these various forms did not succeed each other through temporal sequence in any regular manner. On the contrary, an interdigitation of types of assemblage was characteristic in stratigraphic sequences. Comparative stratigraphic studies showed the different forms to frequently be roughly contemporary at locations very close to one another. This situation clearly demands explanation.

Bordes (1961) "explains" these surprises as resulting from the presence of four distinct ethnic groups, "tribes" living in the area of southwestern Europe during the Middle Paleolithic. These distinct groups moved relatively frequently, leaving their distinctive assemblages interstratified at single locations. Once again we see the use of our model: since patterning in the form of archaeological assemblages is a direct measure of cultural patterning in the ideas and values held by people, differences in the composition of assemblages *must* mean differences in the ethnic composition of the groups represented. Having recognized four distinct and parallel cultural traditions, the culture historian now must seek to rearrange his phylogenetic tree of culture history. Seeking the "origins" of these four traditions, Bordes has tentatively related these traditions to variability known during the Rissian times but unfortunately not as systematically studied as the Mousterian (Bordes, 1968, pp. 98–105). This case provides us with two kinds of "surprise": (1) ungraded variability among contemporary assemblages and (2) lack of directional patterning in the observed temporal variability. The latter surprise is accounted for by painting a picture of conservatism and isolation:

> An objection to the existence of these four Mousterian lines has also been raised on the score of a lack of geographical isolation. Contacts, it is said, must have been numerous, and must have led to a blending of cultures. . . . If a woman from the Quina-type Mousterian was carried off by an Acheulean-tradition Mousterian man, she may perhaps have continued to make her tribal type of thick scraper . . . but after her death probably no one went on making them. And finally, it must always be remembered that the Palaeolithic world was an empty world. . . . A man must often have lived and died without meeting anyone of another culture, although he knew "that there are men living beyond the river who make handaxes" (Bordes, 1968, p. 145).

Many examples could be collected; however, I hope that this one is sufficient to demonstrate the strategy of archaeological "reconstructions of history." We have a series of expectations of the archaeological record based on a model of culture, when these expectations are not met, we explain our observations by appealing to the belief which has been stated clearly by Ford:

> Information will always show that these local "nonconformities" result from the replacement of one population by another, with concomitant replacement of cultural baggage (Ford, 1962, p. 8).

I would like to paraphrase this belief into a generalization: Investigation will always show that these local "nonconformities" will be interpreted by traditional archaeologists as the replacement of one population by another, with concomitant replacement of cultural baggage.

"Little Surprises" or "Big Surprises": A Problem?

The previous problem was a situation in which some "break" in continuity, or lack of directional change characterized the archaeological record as a whole. "Little surprises" are cases where there is a demonstrable continuity in many features, but "new" features of the archaeological record exhibit little or no demonstrable "continuity" with the archaeological record as known previously. This is the classic problem of "diffusion" or "independent development."

The Problem of the Oldowan–Acheulian Transition

In 1951 L. S. B. Leakey published the results of his earlier investigations at the impressive site of Olduvai gorge. Based largely on survey data he argued that there was a clear and gradual transition from the crude pebble tools from the lower beds at Olduvai to the more sophisticated "hand-ax" cultures of the upper beds. He argued that the archaeological record at Olduvai conformed to his expectations for a situation of in-place change, invention and "evolution." Based on this argument archaeology texts summarized "culture history" this way:

> It has been found that whereas in the basal or Oldowan stage pebbles were made into cutting instruments by the removal of a few flakes in two directions at one end or along one side, as time went on it became the custom to chip them more extensively. The pebbles were flaked all around the edges first in one direction and then in the other, so that they became two-faced lumps (bifaces), roughly oval or pear-shaped in outline, with a sinuous or zigzag margin formed by the intersection of deep-biting flake-scars. These tools represent the dawn of handax culture, the first stages of which are called Early Chellean, or Abbevillian.
>
> The available evidence suggests that this culture developed in central Africa. . . . It spread over the greater part of the continent, and has extended northwards into western Europe on the one hand, and less certainly into southern Asia on the other (Oakley, 1956, pp. 40–41).

After the war, intensive work was started in Olduvai gorge, and detailed attention was given to chronology, geological stratification etc., resulting in a much more detailed knowledge of the nature of the archaeological record. This knowledge failed to accord with the previous "interpretation"; the archaeological record contained a "surprise." The situation is summarized by Mary Leakey as follows:

> Nine sites have been excavated in the middle and upper Bed II, all of which have proved exceedingly rich in cultural material. They have revealed an unexpected cultural development, more complex and quite unlike the simple succession originally thought to have existed. The occurrence of Oldowan tools in middle and upper Bed II has always been recognized, but there now appears to be no progressive evolution from the Oldowan through the "Chellean" to the Acheulian. On the contrary, the handaxes earliest known represent an early Acheulian stage of development. Some primitive specimens of the "Chellean" type are also present but they are in unquestionable association with more evolved forms. The Acheulian, however, does not occur in all living sites at this level. At other sites, which are broadly contemporaneous, the culture is a developed form of the Oldowan. At a third group of sites, Acheulian handaxes occur in association with the developed Oldowan culture. It would seem therefore that there were two distinct but co-existent cultural elements, during middle and upper Bed II, which at times made some degree of contact with one another (1967, pp. 431–432).

This is a classic example of a "surprise." There is a lack of gradual, minute change resulting in a continuous transformational sequence from pebble tools to handaxes. In addition, roughly contemporary sites do not look alike, some have handaxes, some Oldowan diagnostics, and some have both. How is this situation "explained"?

The argument offered is completely consistent with the operational definition of culture previously discussed, e.g., comparisons between populations of artifacts (assemblages) are considered to be a measure of the amount of shared "culture" or "ideas" between the human populations represented. Therefore, interassemblage variability is interpreted as evidence for the presence and interaction between two distinct ethnic populations. The possibility that these two populations might also represent biologically distinct populations is entertained but left in abeyance due to an absence of associated fossil material with the Acheulian (M. D. Leakey, 1967, pp. 441–442). I think we can look forward to a revision of the "culture history" of early man and much exchange of opinion, for instance in response to Mary Leakey's summary of the data Balout comments:

> Questions of a general nature arise. . . . The problem of the relationship between the Oldowan and the Acheulian; elsewhere, we have reached a different conclusion, that the Acheulian develops out of the "Pebble Culture!" (p. 442).

In reply to this comment Mary Leakey says:

> I do not think that the Oldowan developed into the Lower Acheulian, locally, at Olduvai, though presumably it did somewhere else (p. 442).

These examples of "explanation" should be sufficient to demonstrate the general character of the role of the traditionalist paradigm in archaeological thinking. Most of the controversy occurring among adherents to this paradigm arises over the evaluation of the particular character of a given surprise. That is over which alternative convention is to be used in "explaining" the surprise. I have tried to spell out in detail what these conventions are (L. R. Binford, 1971). Many of these involve the use of distributional information. Let's examine briefly the logical basis for this appeal.

As previously mentioned, time and space are reference dimensions serving as reference frameworks for monitoring systemic processes. Propositions set forth about the disposition of particular cultural referents in time or space can never serve other than descriptive functions. Such facts only become relevant in the context of hypothetical arguments dealing with the dynamics of processual functioning or change. Unfortunately in contemporary archaeology such arguments are rare.

A common form of archaeological argument might be developed as follows:

(1) A sequence of archaeological materials is known from two nearby but noncontiguous regions (area I and area II).
  (a) In both areas up until point A in time, each was distinct.
  (b) At point A in time, a trait previously unique to area I appears in the

archaeological record of area II lacking any evidence of "crude" or experimental beginnings.

(2) This dispositional change is cited as indicative of some alteration in the prior state of the cultural processes documented archaeologically. Several alternative steps are then open to the traditional archaeologist.

  (a) The archaeologist may cite the appearance of the exotic trait in area II as an "influence" from area I. This is, of course, a categorical statement and as such can only be questioned conceptually or in terms of the degree that the term "influence" is accurately used categorically. Empirical testing is out of the question in this case.

  (b) The archaeologist may cite the appearance of the exotic trait in area II as evidence for the operation of a "process" termed *diffusion* (the transmission of cultural content among independent sociocultural units in the absence of population movement or exchange). This too is a categorical statement which can only be tested as to its situational applicability. Nevertheless, many archaeologists might predict that in an area intermediate between the two relevant areas, the trait would be found dating to the period just prior to time A when the trait appeared in area II. If future research in the intermediate area should reveal the presence of the trait at time A–x, to what degree could one argue that an hypothesis has been tested? One could not. The new distributional referent simply betrays the operation of cultural processes, something already known from the initial observation! It in no way adds to the ability of the investigator to justify the observation as covered by the diffusion concept since the new observation in no way eliminates the alternative of population movement or exchange, a necessary criteria for the categorical equation of diffusion with the observations.

Other possibilities are certain to occur in those familiar with archaeological interpretation, the new trait may be cited as evidence for a migration (lots of shared "culture" translated spatially) or a case of "independent invention" (very rare in archaeological interpretation). Regardless of the particular decisions reached by the archaeologist as to the appropriate "concept" to be applied, he has in no way tested a hypothesis. He may make certain predictions which if confirmed would tend to justify his opinion as to the proper concept to be used; such predictions would be about empirical information which would satisfy categorical criteria not previously met. The accuracy of the prediction would then serve to justify the prior opinion as to the appropriateness of the term applied in the absence of complete information. The stating of a proposition about future distributional observations in the context of traditionalists' arguments does nothing more than allow the archaeologist to establish the categorical relevance of a descriptive term applied to his observation.

I have stressed this point because to many archaeologists diffusion, migration, and independent invention are the "processes" of culture history (Trigger, 1968, pp. 26–31). Accurate decisions as to which of these concepts applies in any given empirical situation allows the "accurate" reconstruction of culture history. We know we have accurately applied these terms when our "expectations" are met as to the observed features of distribution and association. Our expectations derive from our paradigm, or model, of the way culture, as a mentalist phenomenon works.

The traditionalist paradigm consists of a few primitive theoretical concepts operationalized empirically by a single bridging argument regarding patterning. An analogous model is built treating the dynamics of culture change. This model provides the archaeologist with his expectations regarding the archaeological record. When "surprises" are met there are a series of "conventions" used to interpret these surprises in historical terms. The degree that each case meets the criteria for categorical inclusion under three major classes—migration, invention, and diffusion—determines the character of the "historical" systematics generated.

Challenges to the Traditionalist Paradigm

The traditionalist's paradigm which sees culture as a mental phenomena manifest in behavior and its conceptual and material expressions is operationalized as we have shown by the bridging argument of patterning. What does the archaeologist do when he observes uncorrelated patterning?

THE LEVALLOIS PROBLEM: A FORESHADOWING OF THINGS TO COME

Early researches, primarily by Breuil (Breuil and Koslowski, 1931), resulted in the recognition of assemblages distinguished by the presence of flakes struck from prepared cores, generally called "tortoise cores." Using the name of the "type site" near Paris, assemblages characterized by the use of the prepared core technique became known as the Levalloisian. This was postulated to represent a separate tradition derived from the "Clactonian" and contemporary with the Acheulian. Careful work by Bordes and Bourgon (1951) and Bordes (1956) has shown that most of the materials discussed by Breuil were later than he had thought, most being contemporary with known Mousterian assemblages of the Würm. Bordes has further argued, quite convincingly, that what was taken as evidence for a separate tradition by Breuil represents only an alternative method of working flint. It may or may not occur in assemblages which in terms of tool frequency composition are otherwise similar (Bordes, 1956).

The presence of the technique prior to the Würm is well established, and assemblages clearly recognizable as Acheulian are known both with and without evidence of Levallois technique (Waechter, 1968). This is a case of patterning in one characteristic which varies independently of patterning in other characteristics. Immediately the archaeologist is presented with the problem of which kind of patterning is informing him about "culture history." Is sharing of culture and hence "ideas" about how to make tools more or less important for charting the "streams" of transmitted "culture" than the ideas or "mental templates" about the forms of the tools manufactured? The tendency has been to give preference to the latter and to consider the former only when it supports the "conclusions" of the latter.

There have been suggestions as to what might be the context conditioning the use of the Levallois technique; the character of the raw material (Bowler-Kelly, 1937, p. 15; Tester, 1958; Collins, 1969, p. 290) is a frequently cited argument. The implications of such a suggestion as well as the validity of the argument have not been followed out by the archaeologists. If an example of patterning, well documented in the archaeological record, can be shown to vary significantly with some contingency variable, such as character of the raw material, then behavior cannot be taken as an adequate and sufficient measure of the "reservoir of ideas" present in the population carrying out the behavior. If this is the case, the patterning in behaviorally manifest "culture" is not a reliable measure of the "culture" present. Measures of similarity and differences among archaeologically recovered materials would at best be a measure of behavioral similarity. The degree that such similarity would exhibit "expected" spatial and temporal patterning should be more a function of the stability and distribution of the conditioning contingencies than a measure of the distribution and stability of the populations possessing the knowledge of the behavior or a "mental template" as to how to behave if those contingencies were present.

The paradigm of archaeologists is essentially an "irrationalist" position in which human behavior was seen as determined by the enculturative milieu of individuals. This has been well stated by Collins (1969, p. 312).

"People X made handaxes (and other Acheulian traits) because their ancestors made them." Man is viewed as uninventive, essentially an automaton, behaving like his ancestors did unless there were interruptions or changes in communicative links between generations or among contemporary populations.

The Levallois case provides a "rationalist" challenge. Man behaved like his ancestors did *in certain situations*. In short, transmitted knowledge and belief are viewed as a reservoir of accumulated knowledge *to be used differentially when appropriate*. Thus, similarities and differences in the archaeological record are no longer sufficient measures of the degree that two population segments share a common culture. They may equally be seen as two population segments sharing or not sharing common situations of appropriateness in the context of a common culture or differing culture! Patterning in the archaeological record results from behavioral patterning; the degree that behavioral patterning is a direct and sufficient measure of shared "ideas" is something that is not quite clear.

The response of most archaeologists was not to view this as a direct challenge to the traditionalists' paradigm. Instead, this case as well as others were seen as the justification for shifting from comparative studies of specific traits as the basis for historical reconstruction to the comparative study of assemblages. It was argued that particular traits may have individual histories and that only by the comparative study of assemblages as populations could accurate reconstructions be made. This shift in emphasis with regard to the units appropriate for comparison was pioneered by Bordes. It has been widely applied to materials from both the earlier and later ranges of time in western Europe and has been adopted as the appropriate strategy by many Africanists. There has been a strong reaction against the use of the "fossil" approaches [see Sackett (1968, pp. 66–69) for a good discussion of this history]. Given a shift in emphasis in the units considered appropriate to the task of reconstructing culture history there has been a general equation of the assemblage as an adequate sample of the shared "culture" present in a community.

> The concept of an assemblage of stone artefacts, rarely stressed 25 years ago, has been increasingly emphasized in recent years. I see it to mean all the available artefacts from a restricted locality, and where levels have been noted, from a specific stratigraphic horizon. . . . These restrictions increase the likelihood that such an aggregate has been left by a single community over a limited time (Collins, 1969, p. 267).

The equation of assemblages with communities and assemblage types with communities sharing a body of culture has greatly modified much of the systematics of Old World archaeology. Effects not nearly as marked have been seen in New World studies where "historical" sequences are still generally based on comparative studies of ceramics, or projectile points, and total assemblages are rarely even summarized, much less used as the basic units for comparison.

The response of most archaeologists to this potential challenge has been to argue strongly for a shift in the units considered appropriate to comparative analysis for purposes of historical reconstruction. The accuracy of the paradigm has gone relatively unchallenged in spite of the behavioral implications. Archaeologists have generally continued in the traditionalists' manner: "Archaeologist X makes culture history the way he does because his intellectual ancestors made it that way."

The Conscious Challenge—The So-Called Functional "Model"

The Hope Fountain–Acheulian Case

In 1929, N. Jones described the materials recovered from a site in the Maramba Quarries near Hope Fountain, Rhodesia. The distinctiveness of the assemblage was recognized, and in traditional fashion this distinctiveness was cited as evidence for a different "tradition." A later summary of the assemblage characteristics was given as follows:

> The culture represents all the attributes of a pure flake and chopper culture. The only primary technique employed is block-on-block. . . . It would appear that the flakes were removed by resting the core on an anvil and striking it with a hammer-stone rather than by striking the core itself against the anvil. The secondary working is almost always of an irregular, resolved nature and is usually very steep. The industry as a whole presents a very crude and primitive appearance (Clark, 1950, p. 83).

L. S. B. Leakey writing about the cultural sequences of Africa states:

> The Hope Fountain Culture in Africa . . . is . . . a very crude culture with certain superficial resemblances to the Clactonian in tool types which occurs both in East Africa and in Northern and Southern Rhodesia.
> At Olorgesailie in Kenya, this culture which is in process of being studied and has not yet been described in detail, occurs in the same geological deposits as Stage 4 of the Acheulean phase of the Chelles-Acheul culture (1960, p. 86).

The conclusions drawn from the later analysis of Olorgesailie by Leakey is summarized by Sonia Cole (1954, p. 142) as follows:

> An industry which may be related to the Hope Fountain Culture of Rhodesia, in which the implements are made by the block-on-block techniques, is found unrolled on land surface 2 and rolled on land surface 6. . . . Possibly the presence of the Hope Fountain industry at Olorgesailie may denote the arrival of a different band of people, who either turned out the former inhabitants for a time or influenced them in making of their implements.

Up until this point the developments are completely predictable, knowing the traditionalists' paradigm. A distinctive assemblage is recognized; it is equated with a distinct cultural "tradition." Later it is found at other locations and its presence is taken as evidence for the movement of people or their "ideas" from one place to another.

In 1953, J. D. Clark published a short note in *Antiquity* in which he questioned the validity of Hope Fountain as representative of a distinct cultural line, pointing out that Hope Fountain forms were demonstrably associated with recognized cultural phases all the way from what we would now call Oldowan through the Sangoan.

In 1959 Clark writes:

> There are also certain unspecialized groups of flake and chopper industries which do not fit into the normal pattern and so have been grouped under the term Hope Fountain . . . though it is now doubtful whether these represent anything more than a special occupational phase of culture (1959a, p. 40).

On the Rhodesian plateau an Acheulian living floor at Broken Hill . . . has demonstrated the intimate association of hand-axes, cleavers, and polyhedral stones with small unspecialized flake tools. Small flake tools of the same type, and the core choppers from which they were made, have sometimes been found unassociated with any other tools and this gave rise to the suggestion that they may represent the work of an entirely separate flake-culture people. Recent work has, however, shown that there is little to support this view and that these assemblages [Hope Fountain industries] most probably represent a special phase of Handaxe Culture such as might have resulted at some "special purposes" camp (1959b, p. 128).

Later Clark remarks that the people of the Late Acheulian "followed a regular seasonal progression over their hunting areas" and "their temporary camping places . . . might . . . be expected to reflect in the stone industry the different occupational activities of its makers" (1959a, p. 221). In this argument Clark is offering a direct and conscious challenge to the traditionalists' paradigm. He is suggesting that variability in the archaeological record arises from behavior contingent on the operation of variables other than "culture." This means that all variability cannot be accepted as a direct measure of the "amount" of shared culture. He seeks to understand the behavioral significance of variability rather than assuming its significance as a measure of cultural "distance". It should be pointed out however, that these "data" do not speak for themselves. A traditionalist would view the cooccurrence of "Hope Fountain" forms with "Acheulian" or some other recognized "culture" as evidence for a "mixed culture," a hybrid resulting from the contact of distinct peoples. Clark's challenge derives from a shift in which he quite clearly views archaeological remains as the by-products of behavior conditioned in its variability by many factors, regardless of the character of the cultural repertoire brought to the life situations by the people.

Subsequent work by Howell and Clark (1963) and Kleindienst (1961a, b) strikingly demonstrates the wide range of variability in tool frequencies characteristic of Acheulian assemblages. More importantly, however, is the demonstration by Kleindienst that variability as measured by tool "type" frequencies varies independently of variability as measured by morphological characteristics within a single class or type of tool. [Compare Land surfaces 8 and 9 from Olorgesailie with J12 from Isimila (Howell and Clark, 1963, pp. 503, 505, and 508).] This demonstration of independent variability is clear evidence that independent sets of determinants are at work. It should be pointed out that it is variability *within* a general class of tools that has served as the common demonstration that the traditionalists' model is accurate.

The demonstration that differences between assemblages in the frequencies of similar tool types varies independently of variability as measured by variant forms of a single class of tools is conclusive evidence that both are not measuring the same phenomena. Continuing work on the problems of variability in the African Acheulian, particularly by Isaac (1968), has led him to summarize the situation as follows:

> Preliminary reports on Olorgesailie, Isimila, and Kalombo Falls strongly suggest that in Africa assumptions of regularity should not lightly be made. . . . It emerges that pene-contemporaneous samples do not behave as normal deviants about a norm either for "type list" percentage composition or for measurable aspects of the morphology of major artefact categories such as bifaces, scrapers, or flakes. For instance, one Olorgesailie set of eight site samples was recovered from a single silt member three feet thick. The percentage of bifaces varied from 0 to 95%; and the mean length of handaxes ranged from 150 mm to 215 mm! Stable longterm trends within the Eastern African Acheulian have proved hard to identify. It is not yet possible to interpret the apparently irregular pattern of variation in detail. Activity differences are probably one contributory factor, but there seem to be other components, including unstable local idiosyncrasy of craft norms. It seems possible that in some areas during the Middle Pleistocene random-walk variation was more conspicuous than stability and regular directional change (Isaac, 1968, p. 306).

These materials seem to me to provide a critical case, a case in which the traditionalists must either ignore one form of variability in assemblages in favor of the other if they insist in the construction of unidimensional "dendrograms" of "culture history." In ignoring one form of variability they must seriously consider the implications of using the same form in other cases where comparable studies of both forms have not been conducted, such as the "Clactonian—Acheulian" problem or the "Mousterian problem." In short, traditionalists can no longer defend their position that measured variability among assemblages is a measure of "shared culture" pure and simple; they must consider the problem of "what they are measuring" and face the problem of "what it means" in terms of the past.

In spite of the critical character of this example and the striking failure of the expectations deriving from the paradigm to be met, the approach to comparison followed by the researchers has been a summarizing approach treating all tools as having additive properties. That is, an assemblage is expressed numerically as a summation of the frequencies of its components generally expressed as percentages. Evaluations are then made as to similarity and difference in the basis of comparisons of percentage graphs or more rarely in terms of some "distance" measure. This results in the recognition of "assemblage types" such as proposed by Kleindienst and summarized by Howell and Clark (1963, pp. 502–507). This procedure pioneered by Bordes on Mousterian assemblages, although a great improvement over earlier methods of assemblage comparisons, assumes a unidimensional set of determinants with a corresponding unidimensional set of manifestations.

The Multidimensional Argument

Under the traditionalists' paradigm the composition of an assemblage is measured by relative frequencies of recognized classes of artifacts. Redundancy is accepted as "patterning" and hence a manifestation of the "culture norms" of behavior transmitted and shared among the people represented. The assemblage is equated with the community. The expectations are that as long as we are dealing with the remains of an identical or related group of people the composition of the assemblage should remain relatively similar since they share a common body of culture.

The behavioral model recognizes that behavior is the dynamics of adaptation. People draw upon a repertoire of cultural background and experience to meet changing or variable conditions in their environment, both social and physical. Our expectations then are for variability in the archaeological record to reflect a variety of different kinds of coping situations. Activities will vary with the particular adaptive situation of the group and the character of tasks being performed. We would therefore expect variability in the archaeological record to reflect these different situations.

Assemblages may therefore be expected to exhibit variability concomitant with the various "structural poses" (Gearing, 1962) of a community through its annual adaptive cycle. In addition, many assemblages may be expected to vary directly with the degree to which the community may be partitioned into specific kinds of task groupings for performing work at different locations. In short, assemblage variability may be expected to reflect a variety of segments of community life and cannot always be expected to exhibit similarities as a direct reflection of the continuities among the persons performing the acts. Similarities may equally reflect continuities in the character of the acts performed. Differences may arise when the organization of activities varies temporally and/or spatially, resulting in a variety of assemblage types characteristic of the life of a given community. Thus far, this is a restatement of the behaviorists' argument which questions the validity of the equation of the assemblage with the community.

Many years ago I began exploring the implications of a multidimensional model of assemblage variability. This model, rather than assuming and treating assemblages as if they were statistical clusterings of examples along a continuous scale of unidimensional variability, as is the case with a color spectrum, asks what if assemblages were compounds of many independent spectra of variability? Clearly such a suggestion can be supported by observations on the character of human behavior. For instance, the major subsistence activities of hunters and gatherers are sets of event sequences generally broken down into a number of different steps. All such steps are rarely performed at the same location. Add to this condition the frequent characteristic of environments, namely that the critical resources in the forms of foods, water, appropriate life space, and raw materials of technological importance are rarely aggregated and clustered in such a way as to make possible the procurement of all of these things in exactly the same spot. This insures that each human adaptation will be characterized by a logistics system in which mobility, optimal positioning so as to reduce the mobility required, and the partitioning of activities into sets, components of which will be conducted at different locations, will in general characterize the adaptive strategy. This is a particularly human strategy based on a culturally partitioned social aggregate, minimally partitioned into reproductive units capable of maintaining themselves as separate self-sustaining units at least for part of a seasonal cycle.

Cross cutting these units are dimensional characteristics, minimally, sex and age, which serve as the basis for the formation of work or task groups performing different types of jobs which contribute to the maintenance of the group as a whole. Since tools are the technical aids used in the performance of work, in the literal sense of the word, we should expect that other things being equal, the composition of tool assemblages would vary directly in accordance with the tasks performed. The differential distribution of assemblages in space should exhibit compositional differences in direct relation to the character of the logistics strategies carried out. Interassemblage variability in composition should increase in direct relation to the degree of mobility characteristic of the adaptive strategy and the degree that mobility was differentially exercised by task group segments of the larger social unit. It should vary inversely with the degree that tools were multifunctional and/or curated in anticipation of future tasks.

Let us further complicate this picture by introducing the expectation that among culturally organized social units many forms would exhibit characteristics unrelated directly to their functional or specific contexts of use. Similarly we can expect different patterns of association to correspond frequently to different forms of organization, both of which might be shown to vary with the ethnic identity or social distinctiveness of the persons responsible.

The analytical task presenting itself to the archaeologist, given these expectations, is far greater than the task facing the traditional archaeologist. For a number of years I experimented with analytical methods which might permit us to analyze assemblages into the components of meaning approaching as near as possible the behavioral contexts which in life contributed to the accumulation of an assemblage (see footnote 1, L. R. Binford and Binford, 1966, p. 293). Some preliminary results of this work have been reported (L. R. Binford and Binford, 1966; S. R. Binford and Binford, 1968).

As a by-product of this research I began to recognize certain variations in the structural properties of variability among populations of assemblages. These observations suggested that falsification of the traditionalists' paradigm was quite possible. I have chosen to argue for such a falsifying demonstration with the following materials.

This demonstration is presented as a basis for the analytic recognition of certain properties of assemblage variability. The traditionalists' expectations regarding variability may be seen as dependent upon several assumptions. A most important expectation is that associations between things, the coincidence of recognized classes of tools at sites, will exhibit directional patterns of gradual replacement and drift in their relative proportions when plotted accurately either temporally or spatially. *For this expectation to be met, all classes of items in the assemblages compared must exhibit some patterns of mutual covariation.* That is, as class a increases, class b decreases; or as classes x and y increase, classes w and v also increase.

Recurrent associations of tool classes at locations is accepted as a form of patterning. Given the traditionalists' expectations, the recognition of patterning in the associations among tool classes permits us to identify assemblage types which, depending upon their degrees of similarity, are accepted as measures of cultural differences between the human populations represented. The expectations that the recognition of different forms of assemblage based on a comparative analysis of associational patterns should result in directional patterning when assemblage types are plotted temporally is dependent upon the implicit assumption that associations also are patterned in a covariant fashion. Things found together should also tend to covary among themselves. When replacive patterning is not observed, a nonconformity is encountered. Nonconformities are recognized by the failure of assemblage types to adequately cluster either temporally or spatially.

Continuity is expected because assemblages are assumed to express in their content a set of integrated norms, values, ideas, etc., common to a culturally distinct social unit. Culture change is assumed to proceed as a gradual shifting of popularity or drift among forms related to one another as "alternatives." We therefore expect in situations of change, a patterned "trajectory" to be expressed in the archaeological record characterized by covariant relationships between forms which are shifting in popularity. For the traditionalist, a nonconformity must therefore indicate cultural replacement rather than change. Migrations, diffusion, etc., are then postulated as an explanation.

I propose to examine the character of relationships among artifact classes in a sample of assemblages. If the assumption that associational relationships are also covariant relationships can be demonstrated as unjustified, then I will have successfully falsified the traditionalists' paradigm by striking down as invalid one of the basic assumptions serving to permit the deduction of expectations about the archaeological record.

THE SAMPLE

The materials used in this analysis represent 32 assemblages from seven locations in East Africa. These are the primary locations which have served as the basis for the behavioral challenge to the traditionalists' paradigm.

Nine assemblages are used from the site of Olorgesailie located some 40 miles south of Nairobi, Kenya. This site was originally excavated by the Leakeys (1951) and later worked by Posnansky (1959). More recently Glynn Isaac (1961, 1966, 1968) has been conducting research at this location. This site is characterized by numerous stratigraphically distinct beds which have been grouped into three major units. Levels 1–5 represent one unit, separated by thick layers of fine sediments from the succeeding levels 6–9. Levels 10–13 are the third group, presenting more problems in their delineation (Isaac, 1966). It is the opinion of several authorities that each land surface yielding artifacts may represent more than one occupation, possibly occupations of short duration repeated numerous times (Isaac, 1966, pp. 141–142).

Nine assemblages were excavated in primary archaeological context from the Isimila location in southern Tanzania. Work was conducted at this site beginning in 1954 by F. C. Howell and continued through 1958 when he was assisted by Glen Cole and Maxine Kleindienst (Howell, 1961; Howell *et al.,* 1961). Further work is currently under way at this location by Keller.

Nine samples are available from the important sites excavated by J. D. Clark at Kalambo Falls, Tanzania. These represent samples reported in 1964 by Clark.

One sample each is taken from Lochard (Howell and Clark, 1963), Kariandusi (Howell and Clark, 1963) and Broken Hill (Kleindienst, 1961a; Clark, 1959b).

These are all Acheulian assemblages provisionally accepted as representing broadly contemporary materials of the "Late" Acheulian period of East African prehistory.

The Variables

The artifact categories developed and applied by Maxine Kleindienst are used as the variables in the analysis. Several modifications have been made, however, in order to eliminate bias as well as obtain comparability between all the assemblages. (1) The category "broken handaxes/cleavers/knives" has been deleted since one of our interests is the degree that these different forms are mutually dependent. This grouped class could add nothing in this regard. (2) Desmond Clark does not report a category of "discoids" from Kalambo Falls. For this reason the average percentage frequency occurring in other sites has been used as the best estimate for the Kalambo data. Percentages were then adjusted for the Kalambo samples. The basic data used in the analysis is presented in Tables I–IV.

TABLE I   Percentages of Implement and Artifact Classes of Late Acheulian
Assemblages at Olorgesailie[a]

Shaped tools	Land surfaces								
	1	2	3	6	7	8	9	10	11
Handaxes (Ha)	1.5	7.5	10.7	23.5	30.0	47.2	34.1	16.2	6.9
Cleavers (Clv)	1.5	1.9	2.4	2.9	29.0	13.6	27.4	10.3	1.7
Knives (Knv)	0.0	0.0	0.0	5.8	7.0	8.8	23.1	7.3	1.7
Flake scrapers (S)	0.0	0.0	0.0	1.5	3.0	4.8	3.3	2.2	0.0
Discoids (D)	0.0	0.0	0.0	1.5	1.0	0.0	0.0	1.5	0.0
Core scrapers (CS)	1.5	4.7	0.0	0.7	1.0	0.0	0.0	2.2	0.0
Picks (P)	0.0	0.0	2.4	0.7	0.0	0.0	0.0	0.0	0.0
Choppers (Ch)	1.5	5.7	3.7	2.9	5.0	4.8	2.2	2.2	3.5
Spheroids (Sph)	0.0	9.4	3.7	5.8	14.0	3.2	3.3	5.9	3.5
Other large tools (O)	0.0	0.9	1.2	0.0	1.0	2.4	0.0	0.0	0.0
Small scrapers (SS)	52.0	44.3	36.9	29.9	5.0	4.8	2.2	19.8	31.0
Other small tools (OST)	42.0	25.5	39.3	24.8	4.0	10.4	4.4	32.4	51.6
Number of tools	69	106	84	137	102	125	91	137	58
Assemblage									
Tools	25.5	35.7	38.5	34.1	59.5	41.3	59.1	32.2	29.9
Shaped	16.4	23.5	18.7	20.3	54.6	30.5	46.1	16.7	13.6
Modified[b]	1.4	2.7	8.6	1.4	–	–	–	–	–
Utilized[c]	7.7	9.5	11.2	12.4	4.9	10.8	13.0	15.2	16.1
Waste	74.5	64.3	61.5	65.9	40.5	58.7	40.9	68.2	70.0
Cores	2.3	11.9	12.0	7.2	14.1	3.7	3.7	7.5	7.1
Large flakes (10 mm)	0.9	0.7	0.0	2.8	6.3	3.6	9.3	3.9	3.5
Small flakes	64.7	50.2	47.5	44.5	17.6	48.3	27.4	54.4	59.0
Chips and chunks	6.5	1.3	1.9	11.5	2.4	3.6	0.5	2.2	0.2
Number of items	428	451	465	740	205	443	215	890	434

[a] Kleindienst (1961a).

[b] The few on land surfaces 7–11 were not segregated from the utilized flakes.

[c] Includes hammerstones (one on land surface 3; two on surface 7; one on surface 9; seven on surface 10; and one on surface 1).

THE DEFINITION OF PATTERNS OF COVARIATION

Covariation refers to the degree to which one variable varies in a related and predictable manner with another variable. Independence between variables is indicated when frequency or value variation in one variable exhibits only random and nondirectional relationships with respect to other variables. When a series of variables are studied we may be interested in the definition of sets of variables which exhibit similar patterns of mutual covariation and independence as a set with regard to other sets on individual variables. In order to explore the

TABLE II   Percentages of Implement and Artifact Classes of Late Acheulian Assemblages at Isimila[a]

	Sandstone 3		Sandstone 2		Isimila occupation areas Sandstone 1b			Sandstone 1a	
Shaped tools	K19	K18 Tr.2	L.H15	J12	K6	L.J6-7	K14	H9-J8	U.J6-7
Handaxes	6.8	6.4	9.8	46.0	63.6	21.6	13.7	41.4	35.1
Cleavers	50.0	9.8	14.6	18.9	11.6	18.2	40.3	27.6	35.1
Knives	5.7	4.3	0.0	18.9	4.0	2.3	1.6	2.3	1.1
Flake scrapers	5.7	0.0	7.3	5.4	5.8	1.1	0.0	3.4	4.3
Discoids	0.0	2.2	0.0	0.0	0.0	1.1	1.6	1.2	0.0
Core scrapers	1.2	5.4	14.6	0.0	4.0	5.7	0.8	2.3	3.2
Picks	0.0	0.0	12.2	2.7	4.6	0.0	1.6	0.0	0.0
Choppers	6.8	14.1	19.5	0.0	0.0	5.7	9.7	9.2	10.5
Spheroids	0.0	0.0	0.0	0.0	1.2	2.3	7.3	4.6	0.0
Other large tools	0.0	2.2	9.8	0.0	2.3	0.0	1.6	2.3	1.1
Small scrapers	17.0	29.0	12.2	5.4	0.0	25.2	13.7	5.7	5.3
Other small tools	6.8	25.9	0.0	2.7	2.9	15.8	8.1	0.0	4.3
Number of tools	88	93	41	37	173	88	124	83	94
Assemblage									
Tools	28.4	15.2	22.6	31.8	63.6	23.9	39.4	58.1	57.3
Shaped	17.0	6.0	12.6	27.0	58.0	9.4	28.8	51.1	40.1
Modified	4.2	5.0	6.1	2.7	0.6	8.8	6.9	4.8	14.1
Utilized[b]	7.2	4.2	3.9	2.0	4.9	5.7	3.7	2.2	2.1
Waste	71.6	84.8	77.4	68.2	36.4	76.1	60.6	41.9	42.7
Cores	0.9	1.3	2.4	2.7	5.2	1.4	4.6	3.2	0.9
Large flakes	0.3	0.1	4.3	6.1	1.1	0.6	1.6	7.0	0.0
Small flakes	30.8	20.6	42.1	36.5	30.0[c]	21.5	20.3	25.8	18.7
Chips and chunks	39.1	62.8	28.6	22.9	–	52.6	34.1	5.9	23.9
Number of items	528	1546	328	148	305	932	434	186	233

[a] Kleindienst (1961b).   [b] Includes anvils (three on K18 Tr.2; three on Lower 815; one on J12; one on Lower J6–J7) and hammerstones (one on K14; two on H9–J8).   [c] Chips and chunks not separated from small waste flakes.

TABLE III   Percentages of Implement and Artifact Classes of Late Acheulian
Assemblages at Kalambo Falls[a]

Shaped tools	Occupation floors							
	A1/56/4	A1/56/V A1/56/Va	A1/56/58	5	6A	6B	7	8
Handaxes	19.1	13.5	17.2	30.0	31.1	20.6	7.8	15.2
Cleavers	11.9	29.8	14.0	18.6	34.5	8.4	31.4	22.2
Knives	0.0	5.8	1.5	4.0	6.9	4.7	3.9	8.1
Flake scrapers	7.1	15.4	4.7	7.0	6.9	4.7	5.8	5.0
Discoids	0.6	0.6	0.6	0.6	0.6	0.6	0.6	0.6
Core scrapers	16.7	8.6	20.4	7.3	3.4	14.9	11.8	11.1
Picks	4.8	0.0	6.3	1.4	1.7	0.0	0.0	0.0
Choppers	9.5	3.8	9.4	4.6	5.2	8.4	5.8	2.0
Spheroids	2.4	1.0	1.5	0.2	0.0	0.9	0.0	0.0
Other large tools	0.0	1.0	0.0	2.0	0.0	0.0	0.0	0.0
Small scrapers	21.4	19.2	20.4	20.5	8.6	33.7	33.4	36.4
Other small tools	7.1	1.9	3.1	4.4	1.7	3.7	0.0	0.0
Number of tools	42	104	64	816	58	107	51	99
Assemblage								
Tools	19.5	32.0	29.6	16.4	42.2	12.4	12.0	8.5
Shaped	12.2	23.6	24.0	12.2	31.0	7.4	7.3	4.3
Modified	nc[b]	nc	nc	nc	nc	nc	nc	nc
Utilized	7.3	8.4	5.6	4.2	11.2	5.0	4.7	4.2
Waste[c]	80.5	68.0	70.4	83.6	57.8	87.6	88.0	91.5
Number of items	343	440	267	6696	187	1456	686	2308

[a] Calculated from Clark (1964).
[b] nc = No count was given.
[c] This category was not broken down in Clark's analysis.

character of covariant relationships among the variables in this study a factor analysis was performed.

Using a factor analytic program (Bio-Med x72) originally developed at the University of California, Los Angeles, a varimax rotation was performed on the matrix of linear correlation coefficients (R) derived from the matrix in which the 12 tool "types" of Kleindienst were the variables and the 32 assemblages were the cases. The data entered in the original matrix were the percentages of tool types within each assemblage as presented in Tables I–IV. A cutoff point for the generation of factors was established by specifying an eigenvalue of 0.95. This was elected because it represented a clear break in the distribution of eigenvalues, the next lower value being 0.72. The program generated a correlation matrix which did not alter the diagonal elements. A five-factor solution was obtained in which 80.32% of the total variance in the matrix was accounted for as common variance. Table V presents the commonalities and

TABLE IV   Percentages of Implement and Artifact Classes of Late Acheulian Assemblages at Lochard, Kariandusi, Broken Hill, and Nsongezi[a]

Shaped tools	Lochard	Kariandusi	Broken Hill	Nsongezi		
				C17 M-N	C13 M-N	C1 M-N
Handaxes	24.1	39.4	1.1	10.9	8.2	5.7
Cleavers	7.1	16.7	8.5	12.7	18.4	3.5
Knives	1.6	13.9	1.1	0.0	0.0	2.3
Flake scrapers	1.1	6.9	1.1	7.3	6.1	2.3
Discoids	6.6	0.9	0.0	0.0	0.0	1.1
Core scrapers	0.5	1.6	1.1	12.7	12.2	17.3
Picks	0.0	2.2	0.0	0.0	2.0	0.0
Choppers	16.9	1.9	4.2	1.8	8.2	16.1
Spheroids	1.6	1.6	26.6	0.0	0.0	0.0
Other large tools	4.3	2.4	0.0	0.0	4.1	9.2
Small scrapers	24.6	5.1	37.2	12.7	4.1	9.2
Other small tools	11.5	7.3	19.1	41.9	36.7	33.3
Number of tools	187	336	93	55	49	87
Assemblage						
Tools	24.3	60.1	64.6	7.4	40.6	21.6
Shaped	14.9	47.3	57.3	2.6	13.2	8.3
Modified	7.2	3.3	3.0	1.7	9.1	5.8
Utilized	2.2	9.5	4.3	3.1[b]	18.3[b]	7.5[b]
Waste	75.7	39.0	35.4	92.6	59.3	78.4
Cores	2.9	3.1	17.7	2.1	8.2	nc[d]
Large flakes	0.0	17.6	0.0	0.9	1.4	nc
Small flakes	52.9	18.8	17.7[c]	55.5	47.0	nc
Chips and chunks	19.9	0.5	—	34.1	2.7	nc
Number of items	1265	717	164	1280	219	615

[a] G. H. Cole (1967), Howell and Clark (1963), and Kleindienst (1961b).

[b] G. H. Cole (1967) classifies these as "trimmed flakes" since he does not agree with Kleindienst that they are artifacts.

[c] Chips and chunks were not separated from small waste flakes.

[d] nc = No count was given.

factor loadings for the solution obtained on these data. Commonalities are the percentage of variance for each variable demonstrated to exhibit variance in common with other variables.

As one can see, about 20% of the variance exhibited by the variables among the 32 samples appears as unique variability, with knives exhibiting the lowest amount of common variance of any of the variables.

This solution provides us with considerable information of some fascination. There are two clear "bipolar" factors, I and IV; two specific factors exhibiting bipolar characteristics, III and V; and one grouped factor. A bipolar factor has

TABLE V   Factor Results

Variable	Factor					Commonality
	I	II	III	IV	V	
1. Handaxes	(−0.884)	0.024	−0.037	−0.183	−0.045	0.818
2. Knives	(−0.701)	0.366	−0.041	−0.183	−0.085	0.669
3. Cleavers	−0.116	0.159	0.040	(−0.882)	−0.028	0.819
4. Flake scrapers	−0.123	−0.098	−0.402	(−0.553)	(−0.519)	0.762
5. Picks	−0.093	(−0.753)	−0.419	−0.059	−0.072	0.759
6. Core scrapers	(−0.462)	(−0.474)	−0.281	−0.133	(−0.505)	0.790
7. Other large tools	−0.098	(−0.859)	0.185	0.136	−0.123	0.815
8. Choppers	0.284	(−0.771)	0.481	−0.127	−0.059	0.926
9. Discoids	−0.002	−0.138	(−0.898)	0.010	−0.018	0.825
10. Spheroids	0.117	0.081	−0.081	0.007	(0.927)	0.886
11. Small scrapers	(0.722)	0.303	0.053	0.355	0.135	0.761
12. Other small tools	0.312	0.154	0.009	(0.828)	0.014	0.807

Proportion of Total Variance = 26.60%, 49.84%, 62.94%, 72.33%, 80.32%.

the property of significant factor loadings occurring as both positive and negative values. Relationships among the variables so represented are of an oppositional type. Harman (1962, p. 110) gives an example: "A bipolar factor ... is one for which several of the variables have significant negative projections. Such variables may be regarded as measuring the negative aspect of the usual type of factor. Thus, if a number of variables identified with 'fear' are represented by the positive projection, variables with negative projections might be interpreted as measuring 'courage.'" These are inversely related phenomena. In our case the best predictor of the low frequency of handaxes is the high frequency of small scrapers. A specific factor is one that is primarily defined by a single variable. Factors III and V are specific factors; however, both exhibit bipolar characteristics in that both have fairly high negative loadings on two variables each. Factor II is a normal group factor. This overall pattern of factor results is unique in my experience with archaeological materials and must express certain unique features of these data.

Factor I

Diagnostic tools in this group are handaxes, with knives as negative projections and small scrapers as an equally strong positive projection. Here we see a clear covariant dichotomy between "heavy duty tools" and "small tools." The significance of this dichotomy may well have been partially isolated by Clark in a most provocative comparative study of locations where fauna were preserved sufficiently for evaluation. He notes that four general types of sites are recognizable on which tool associations occur.

On sites where a single or only a few animals have been butchered, articulated parts are numerous and small tools dominate the assemblage. On sites where many animals are represented, disarticulation is common and bones are broken up, large tools are more common, and the character of the assemblage is more complex. He also notes that large tools may occur on sites where little fauna is represented, and that which occurs is broken and dismembered. He states that "the evidence suggests that paleolithic butchering and meat processing equipment consisted predominantly of small numbers of light duty tools, cutting flakes and small scraping tools with only a few of the large elements" (Clark and Haynes, 1970, p. 409).

The correlations noted by Clark between fauna, evidence of butchering, and small tools (particularly small scrapers and utilized flakes, a class not included in this study) is strongly indicative of their use. Our results demonstrating a dependent but mutually exclusive association between handaxes and large knives on the one hand and small scrapers on the other is completely compatible with Clark's observations of small scrapers in the absence of handaxes with butchered animals and handaxes with few flake tools occurring on sites with little or no fauna. I suggest that handaxes and large knives were used in a context unrelated to the butchering and processing of meat and that the conditions obtaining when they were used were such that the probability of obtaining meat was very remote. The implications of such a suggestion are enormous. If true, the common occurrence of handaxes during the lower Paleolithic may well betray greater dependence upon nonanimal foods than was previously considered.

Collins observes that Acheulian assemblages tend to indicate a "preference for grassland and open terrain, mainly but not always in warm latitudes. . . . Unlike the Acheulian, the distribution of the Clactonian and comparable groups does not yet extend into a zone warmer than the temperate zone, or more especially into the Savannah" (Collins, 1969, p. 289). Quite clearly the further north one goes the greater the dependence upon animal foods that would be expected (Lee, 1968), and according to the results of this analysis, the greater the dominance of assemblages by small flake cutting tools that would be expected. This condition is clearly met in material Collins discusses as the "Clactonian tradition."

Another provocative feature of the European material noted by Bordes is a major change in the character of Acheulian assemblages during the early phases of the Riss glaciation. "It would seem that there is a turning-point in this Acheulian culture, when from this point onwards flake tools become more numerous than the bifacial implements" (Bordes, 1968; p. 58). This turning point may well betray a shift in subsistence strategies in favor of greater dependence upon animal foods.

Factor II

This is a normally grouped factor exhibiting strong factor loadings on three variables: picks, other large tools, and choppers. The most obvious characteristic of this factor is the inclusion of variables frequently considered diagnostic of the Sangoan materials of East Africa. Also loaded on this factor are core scrapers, a variable which exhibits significant loadings on two other factors. indicating a "general purpose" tool being used in a number of contexts or a variable which is inadequately broken down at the typological level of analysis. The recognition in this analysis of a normally grouped factor exhibiting diagnostics of the Sangoan industry is not surprising in light of the recognition of these tools as frequently occurring in the late Acheulian of East Africa.

The Isimila late Acheulian assemblage is of interest in that it contains certain artifact types reminiscent of types common and characteristic of the later Sangoan industrial complexes. These include various forms of picks, push-planes, core-scrapers, chisel-ended tools, discoids and the like. . . . This manifestation appears then to be a general characteristic of the later Acheulian industries in the central and eastern African areas, a fact of considerable importance in understanding the origins of the later Sangoan industrial complexes (Howell *et al.*, 1916, p. 75).

Of interest in this regard is the fact that the tools exhibiting low and opposite (positive) factor loading to this group are handaxes, knives, cleavers, spheroids, small scrapers, and other small tools, all the classes which have been traditionally considered diagnostic of the Acheulian, if we included the small tool variant. The significance of these findings for understanding the "transition" to the Sangoan is left here to the experts in the field.

Factor III

This is a specific factor exhibiting some bipolar characteristics. Part of its weak development may be due to a mistaken assumption made at the time the original data matrix was compiled. In viewing the failure to mention discoids at Kalambo Falls and the problems of equating Clark's and Kleindienst's typological categories, I mistakenly assumed that Clark's failure to mention discoids resulted from differences in the typologist used. I therefore added to the Kalambo frequencies, as the best estimate of occurrence, the average percentage for discoids in the other assemblages. I now know that this was a mistake; discoids were in fact absent at Kalambo Falls (Howell *et al.*, 1961, p. 76). My guess is that if the discoids were deleted from the Kalambo samples, we would have derived a well-defined bipolar factor for III. As it is, discoids are heavily loaded positively, and picks and flake scrapers are moderately loaded negatively. Discoids have been mentioned as a "diagnostic" of Sangoan industries; however, our analysis shows them to vary quite independently of other diagnostics, indicating that the determinants of their frequencies are quite different from the determinants of the frequencies for factor II.

Factor IV

This is a classic bipolar factor with the highest loading shown negatively on cleavers and the next-highest negative loading on flake scrapers; however, this variable is loaded on several factors, demonstrating that it is a "general purpose" tool or that greater typological breakdown may be warranted. The highly dependent but inversely related variable expressed positively is "other small tools." This class included such classes as protoburins, burins, points, and borers of various forms, tools which are frequently considered to be "tools to make tools."

Cleavers are generally cited as tools diagnostic of the Acheulian in Africa. This factor, as in the case of factor I, clearly demonstrates that the "small tools" traditionally considered to be an independent tradition are strongly a part of the Acheulian, exhibiting strong inverse relationships to cleavers. As in the case of factor I, the conditions under which cleavers were used and discarded was such that as their use increased, the probability of conditions favoring the use of other small tools decreased directly.

The recognition that cleavers vary independently of handaxes in Africa makes even more provocative their general absence from Acheulian assemblages over much of Europe. What were the conditions in Africa favoring the use of these tools? Were such conditions absent in the more northern latitudes?

Factor V

This factor exhibits many of the characteristics of factor III in that it is a specific factor with a weakly developed bipolar quality. Spheroids are the variable most definitive of this factor, with flake scrapers and core scrapers showing significantly high negative loadings. These are both variables which do not exhibit any exclusive association with any one factor. They both show fairly high loadings on several factors. It is tempting to see this factor as a "stylistic variant" of factor III which, as we have mentioned, is sometimes seen in its positive manifestation as a diagnostic of the Sangoan. In any event both of these factors III and V have in common a negative projection of flake scrapers.

General Discussion

The above five factors can be seen as definitive of the character of covariant relationships occurring in this sample of Late Acheulian assemblages from East Africa. Each factor isolates tools which, with the exception of flake scrapers, tend to exhibit exclusive patterns of covariation among those diagnostic of each factor and independence between the variables grouped into the five sets. Accepting the traditionalist paradigm we would expect these five sets of variables to represent five traditions since a relationship of independence obtains between them. Further we would expect these bipolar factors to betray some patterned distribution temporally or spatially since inverse relationships should betray "replacive" kinds of variation.

THE CHARACTER OF ASSOCIATIONAL PATTERNING IN THE SAMPLE

Associational patterning has been the form used as the basis for the recognition of assemblage types and hence has served as the basis for comparisons between locations and for temporal studies. Associational patterning simply refers to the recurrent association between two things, although the frequencies of these things may or may not vary in a related fashion. Association says that A tends to cooccur with B, but it does not imply that the frequency of A varies in a related fashion with the frequency of B.

Kleindienst (1961a) conducted a comparative analysis of Late Acheulian assemblages from Olorgesailie, Isimila, and Broken Hill. Her work resulted in the recognition of two major patterns of assemblage variability, with two minor variants. These are as follows:

A. Assemblages with a high percentage of handaxes, cleavers, and knives, low percentages of other large tools, and low percentages of small implements

B. Assemblages with high percentages of small tools and low percentages of handaxes, cleavers, knives, and other types of large tools

A–B, intermediate. Assemblages with approximately equal percentages of handaxes, cleavers, knives, and small implements, with lower percentages of other large tool types

C. Assemblages with a high percentage of core scrapers, picks, and choppers compared to other assemblages, plus some handaxes, cleavers, knives, and small implements

These generalizations summarize something of the character of associational patterning observable among our samples. I will further explore these relationships, making use of a number of kinds of data informed in terms of the results of factor analysis. I will initially discuss variability in terms of percentage frequencies of tool classes discretely isolated as exhibiting covariant relationships. I have chosen to use percentages for the analysis of factors I and IV variables since most readers are familiar with their use and since, as will be shown, when informed by factor analysis, percentages may be quite informative.

In this analysis we will be concerned with two kinds of variability. The first has to do with the degree that particular values for a specified relationship are evenly distributed or alternatively exhibit clusters of redundant values for a number of cases in the sample. The second kind of analysis seeks to discover the degree that there are redundant associations between the measured value of one specified relationship and another independent relationship. The latter is a description of associational patterning between phenomena known not to vary in a covariant fashion.

Since we know that handaxes and knives vary inversely with small scrapers we may ask if the distribution of relative frequencies of these related classes of tools is normally distributed. If not, the distribution will exhibit clustering indicative of repetitive patterning in the content of sites. A value was calculated by summing the percentage values for all three classes of tools and then dividing this sum into the summed frequencies for handaxes and knives. The result is the percentage of factor I diagnostics represented by handaxes and knives. Plotting of the values in Table VI reveals that they are not continuously distributed nor were they normally distributed. Two major clusters and three minor clusters are clearly recognizable. (See Fig. 1.)

Class A. Cases where less than 27% of the diagnostics of factor I are handaxes and knives (seven cases)

Class B. Cases where between 35 and 55% of the diagnostics of factor I are represented by handaxes and knives (14 cases)

Class C. Cases where between 63 and 67% of the diagnostics of factor I are represented by handaxes and knives (two cases)

Class D. Cases where between 81 and 100% of the diagnostics of factor I are represented by handaxes and knives.

TABLE VI Percentage of Summed Total for Handaxes, Knives, and Small Scrapers Represented by Handaxes and Knives

Site	Code	%	Site	Code	%
Isimila	J12	92.3	Olorgesailie	11	22.3
Isimila	K6	100.0	Kalambo	8	39.0
Olorgesailie	9	96.1	Kalambo	A1/56/4	47.1
Karandusi		91.3	Kalambo	A1/56/5B	47.9
Olorgesaile	8	92.1	Kalambo	7	24.6
Isimila	H9-J8	88.4	Broken Hill		5.5
Olorgesailie	7	88.1	Kalambo	6B	42.9
Kalambo	6A	84.9	Kalambo	A1/56/V	50.1
Olorgesailie	6	49.4	Isimila	K19	42.3
Olorgesailie	10	54.4	Isimila	K14	52.8
Nsongezi	C-1	46.5	Isimila	U.J6-7	87.2
Olorgesailie	3	22.5	Lochard		51.1
Isimila	K18	26.9	Kalambo	5	64.2
Nsongezi	C-17	46.1	Isimila	H15	44.5
Olorgesailie	2	14.4	Isimila	L.J6-7	48.6
Olorgesailie	1	2.8	Nsongezi	C-13	66.6

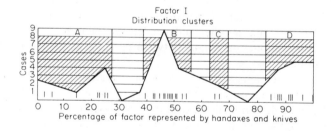

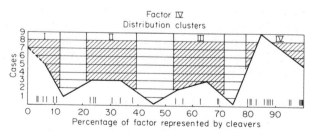

Fig. 1. Distribution of cases on percentage scales for factors I and IV. Actual distribution is shown at base of scale.

Factor IV

Using the same approach we may now ask a similar set of questions with regard to the relative contributions from opposing diagnostics of factor IV. The percentages of cleavers and other small tools were summed and this sum was divided into the percentage of cleavers present. The result is the percent of the diagnostics for factor IV represented by Cleavers. Table VII presents the values obtained.

TABLE VII   *Percentage of Summed Total for Cleavers and Other Small Tools Represented by Cleavers*

Isimila	J12	87.4	Olorgesailie	11	3.2
Isimila	K6	80.0	Kalambo	8	100.0
Olorgesailie	9	86.1	Kalambo	A1/56/4	62.6
Karanduzi		69.5	Kalambo	A1/56/5B	81.3
Olorgesailie	8	56.6	Kalambo	7	100.0
Isimila	H9-J8	100.0	Broken Hill		30.8
Olorgesailie	7	87.9	Kalambo	6B	69.4
Kalambo	6A	95.8	Kalambo	A1/56/V	94.0
Olorgesailie	6	10.6	Isimila	K19	88.0
Olorgesailie	10	24.1	Isimila	K14	83.2
Nsongezi	C-1	9.5	Isimila	U.J6-7	89.0
Olorgesailie	3	5.7	Lochard		38.1
Isimila	K18	24.8	Kalambo	5	80.8
Nsongezi	C-17	23.2	Isimila	H-15	100.0
Olorgesailie	2	6.9	Isimila	L.J6-7	53.5
Olorgesailie	1	3.5	Nsongezi	C-13	33.4

Plotting the values in Table VII demonstrates a very different pattern than was observed for factor I. (See Fig. 1.)

There are clearly four clusters of values indicating sites in which the relationships between the two ends of the bipolar determinant are balanced in a roughly identical fashion.

Class I: Cases where only between 0 and 10% of the diagnostics of factor IV are cleavers

Class II: Cases where between 20 and 40% of the diagnostics of factor IV are cleavers

Class III: Cases where between 50 and 70% of the diagnostics of factor IV are cleavers

Class IV: Cases where between 80 and 100% of the diagnostics of factor IV are cleavers

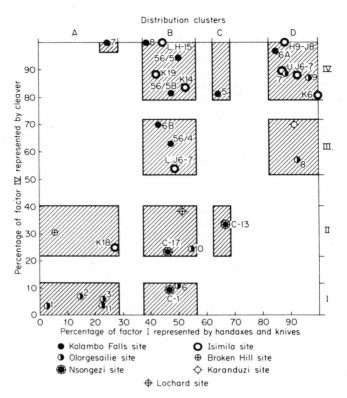

Fig. 2. Distribution clusters.

A comparison of the two distributions shows a very different pattern of clustering (See Fig. 1). Cases tend to cluster at the two ends of the scale for factor IV, that is, where the percentage of cleavers is less than 20% or over 80%. Cases falling near the 50/50 point are fewest. I suspect that if we had a larger sample that included those so-called "Hope Fountain" assemblages, we would obtain a bipolar distribution of values for the proportions of other small tools to cleavers. This means that not only are the tasks represented by the two tool classes inversely related, but they strongly tend to occur at *spatially independent locations.* In contrast the graph for percentage values of handaxes and knives to small scrapers exhibits a clustering at the upper end of the scale, a marked peak in the center indicating approximately half handaxes and knives and half small scrapers, and then a low curve of cases dispersed along the lower half of the scale. As in the discussion above, I suspect that if we had a truly representative sample of late Acheulian materials, we would obtain either a trimodal distribution with the majority of cases falling in the center of the case, or a bimodal distribution with the central cluster exhibiting a marked skew to the left. In any event the curve of cases as known from this sample demonstrates several things: (a) Cases at the high end of the scale tend to be tightly clustered above the 80% level; (b) cases at the low end of the scale are not nearly so tightly clustered, indicating much greater variability in the incidence of handaxes on sites where the percentage is less than 30% than that which we note between sites where the percentage is greater than 70%.

We are now in a position to construct a matrix in terms of which we may observe the degree that there are patterned associations of cases when the distributional clustering characteristic of the two dimensions are considered together. Figure 2 quite clearly shows that there is clustering. All those sites having greater than 50% of the diagnostics for factor IV represented by cleavers cluster in classes C and, D with regard to the handaxe–scraper distribution. Conversely, all those sites where less than 50% of the diagnostics for factor IV are cleavers cluster in classes A and B of the handaxe–scraper distribution. The only overlap is seen in the B class for handaxe–scraper values, that is, where between 35 and 55% of the diagnostics for factor I are handaxes. Three exceptions mar this almost perfect separation: Kalambo 7 and 5 and Nsongezi C-13.

The important point to be made at this juncture is that these materials provide the most graphic demonstration of the structural properties of variability in these archaeological assemblages. First, I have demonstrated that two independent dimensions of covariate relationships dominate the quantitative relationships between four classes of tools in *all the samples*. Small scrapers vary inversely with handaxes and knives; similarly cleavers vary inversely with other small tools. These relationships characterize late Acheulian assemblages regardless of variability in the associations noted between the clustered forms of their expression. Since the assemblages are clustered distributions of artifacts in space (e.g., sites), we observe that there are consistent patterns in the *associations* at sites of patterned expressions of the relationships manifest by the two independent sets of covariant phenomena. These recurrent patterns of association form the basis for the recognition of assemblage types. Based on Fig. 2, we may recognize an assemblage type characterized by over 80% handaxes and knives and less than 20% small scrapers, and over 80% cleavers and less than 20% other small tools (class IV-D in the table and type A of the Kleindienst typology). Similarly, we may recognize another assemblage type characterized by over 70% small scrapers and less than 30% handaxes, and over 70% other small tools and less than 30% cleavers (classes IA, IIA, in Fig. 2 and type B of the Kleindienst typology). Clearly these are very different and represent patterned recurrent associations at different sites. The difference is of such a magnitude that the traditional archaeologist would most certainly recognize these as expressions of different cultures. In fact, in their extreme form this has been done: Acheulian–Hope Fountain; the analogous situation outside of Africa, Acheulian–Clactonian; and a more tenuous analogy for earlier African material, the developed Oldowan–Acheulian dichotomy.

Our analysis has shown, however, that these seemingly different forms are simply reverse images of an identical set of relationships! In both, scrapers will covary with handaxes and knives, and other small tools will covary with cleavers. Each set will vary independently of the others. The assemblage types represent identical behavioral responses to a common set of determinants. The only difference between them is in the expression of dichotomous determinants. This is a highly patterned association between noncovariant forms. We would therefore expect that assemblage types defined on the basis of these associations would not exhibit directional patterning through time or across space. The traditionalist assumption is not met: *Associational patterning is not also covariant patterning.*

The reader will realize that I have not exhausted the information derived from the factor analysis. There were three additional factors isolated. What complications arise when this information is added to that already discussed? In order to explicate these relationships, I must shift to a slightly different approach since the other three factors isolated were all characterized by classes of tools which exhibited multiple high factor loadings on more than one factor. Using the actual percentages of tool classes as I have done above is therefore not possible without involving a great deal of effort. Instead I will use the factor scores as a means of measuring the distribution of the isolated relationships among the assemblages in the sample. Factor scores are a means of expressing the amount of information contributed by each case to the definition of the isolated factors. Table VIII presents the factor scores for all 32 assemblages for all factors.

By using the factor scores we may recognize that factor II, the "Sangoan" factor, is only significantly indicated at Isimila L.H-15. Nsongezi C-1, Kalambo A1/56/4, Kalambo A1/56/5B, and Nsongezi C-13.

Comparison of the factor scores for factors III and V, both specific factors with weakly developed bipolar characteristics, allows us to recognize classes of association between the two sets of determinants in the same way such associations were uncovered by studying the percentages of diagnostics for factors I and IV. Associations of significant factor scores are shown in Table IX.

We may recognize several associations between factors III and V.

Group I. Associations are all those combinations where positive loadings are characteristic, indicating discoids and/or spheroids.

Set A. These are assemblages in which both factors III and V are positively loaded. Discoids and spheroids cooccur (Isimila levels K14 and H9-J8).

Set B. These are assemblages in which factor V is positively loaded with factor III insignificantly represented (Olorgesailie levels 7, 3, and 2).

TABLE VIII   *Factor Scores*

Site	I	II	III	IV	V
			Factors		
Isimila					
K14	0.346	−0.262	1.013	−1.208	1.437
H9-J8	−0.739	−0.341	0.779	−0.819	0.623
U.J6-7	−0.270	−0.049	0.333	−1.076	−0.026
L.J6-7	0.307	0.492	0.478	0.086	0.030
K6	−2.122	−0.644	−1.204	0.459	−0.026
J12	−2.204	0.664	−0.692	0.093	−0.372
H15	0.156	−3.991	−1.163	−0.272	0.066
K18	0.587	−0.164	1.665	0.681	−0.376
K19	0.689	0.886	0.217	−1.819	−0.143
Kalambo					
A1/56/4	0.843	−0.764	−0.881	−0.464	−0.484
A1/56/5	0.650	0.672	−0.556	−1.654	−1.318
A1/56/5B	0.855	−1.012	−0.988	−0.505	−0.464
5	−0.171	0.035	−0.245	−0.332	−0.622
6A	−0.481	0.395	−0.048	−1.168	−0.372
6B	0.803	0.283	−0.048	−0.178	−0.820
7	1.334	0.731	0.047	−1.324	−0.736
8	0.696	0.993	−0.165	−0.653	−0.824
Olorgesailie					
11	0.379	0.766	−0.264	1.976	0.172
10	−0.247	0.750	−0.300	0.874	0.239
9	−1.919	1.016	−0.103	−0.362	0.107
8	−1.667	0.034	−0.171	0.361	0.146
7	−0.649	0.045	0.166	−1.001	1.924
6	−0.301	0.588	0.291	1.089	0.449
3	0.371	0.172	−0.514	1.716	0.516
2	1.068	0.266	−0.355	0.951	1.135
1	1.126	1.144	−0.268	1.827	−0.330
Nsongezi					
C-1	0.298	−1.886	0.863	1.243	−0.973
C-13	0.373	−0.786	−0.558	0.477	−0.872
C-17	0.657	0.606	−0.914	0.709	−1.333
Lochard	−0.207	−0.829	4.144	0.311	−0.171
Broken Hill	1.199	0.094	−0.936	−0.138	3.784
Karanduzi	−1.760	0.096	−0.223	0.119	−0.367

Set C. These are assemblages in which factor III is positively loaded with
factor V insignificantly represented (Lochard and Isimila K18).

Group II. A single case is recorded in which factor III is positively represented
and factor V is negatively represented. This occurred in Nsongezi C-1.

Group III. Associations are all assemblages in which negative loadings on
factors III and V are characteristic.

TABLE IX   Distribution of Cases[a]

Factor V / Factor III	Positive High	Positive Moderate	Positive Insig.	Negative Insig.	Negative Moderate	Negative High
Positive						
High				Lochard		
Moderate		K14 H9-J8		K18	C-1	
Insig.	0–7				Kalambo 7	
Negative						
Insig.		0–3 0–2			6B, Kal 8 A1/56/V	
Moderate			Isimila LH-15	A1/56/4 A1/56/5B K6	C-13 C-17	
High						

[a] Positive = spheroids, Negative = flake sc. and Core sc.

Set A. These are assemblages in which factor III is negatively represented and factor V has insignificant loadings (Isimila L.H-15, Kalambo A1/56/4, Kalambo A1/56/5B, and Isimila K6).

Set B. These are assemblages in which factor V is negatively represented with factor III showing insignificant loadings (Kalambo 7, Kalambo 6B, Kalambo 8, and Kalambo A1/56/V).

Set C. This assemblage has both factors represented by significant negative loadings (Nsongezi C-13, and Nsongezi C-17).

Assemblages exhibiting properties isolated as factors III and V as well as the Sangoan factor II are indicated on Fig. 3. Quite clearly there is a clustering of associations in which both class III associations for factors III and V as well as the Sangoan factor II are clustered with assemblages exhibiting between 35 and 55% handaxes and knives of factor I diagnostics (class B). Conversely, assemblages with significant positive loadings on factors III and V are almost exclusively distributed among those falling either at the low or high ends of the distribution for handaxes and knives versus small scrapers. Discoids, spheroids and to some extent, choppers tend to associate with assemblages exhibiting over 80% handaxes or over 70% small scrapers. Conversely, flake scrapers and/or picks, other large tools, and the majority of choppers associate with sites exhibiting between 35 and 55% handaxes. These associations further complicate the picture since the two classes of assemblages least alike in terms of associations for factors I and IV variables are those with over 80% handaxes, knives, and cleavers versus sites where over 70% are small scrapers, and other

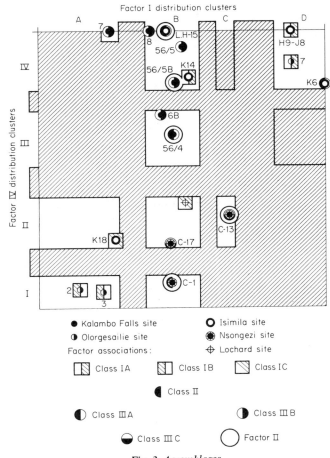

Fig. 3. Assemblages.

small tools share spheroids and/or discoids to the general exclusion of flake scrapers, core scrapers, and picks.

Those assemblages least alike in terms of associations between forms of expression for similar covariant relationships along two independent dimensions (factors I and IV) turn out to be most alike in their associations with respect to two additional independent dimensions of variability (factors III and V)! Clearly associational relationships are not covariant relationships in these assemblages. This demonstrates two independent dimensions of patterning:

(a) mutual patterns of covariation among classes of tools and

(b) patterned associations at locations of classes of tools among which there is no demonstrable mutual covariation.

These findings show a structure of variability among archaeological assemblages which cannot be accommodated by the traditionalists' paradigm. That paradigm assumes that patterns of association are also covariant in character. When an interruption in covariant patterning is observed, it is assumed that an independent organization of patterning measured in terms of associations is intrusive. The intrusive unit is expected to exhibit covariant patterning with other units sharing the same pattern of associations somewhere else.

We have demonstrated that those sets of tools most regularly associated are those among which no covariant relationships obtain. The fact that the two dimensions of patterning—associational and covariant—may vary independently of one another clearly demonstrates the potential complexity of assemblage composition. It further demonstrates a number of points: If covariant patterning is the expected form when assemblage composition is viewed against a temporal or spatial dimension, then patterns of covariation should correlate with associations between tool classes if the assemblage is to be the unit of comparison. That is, if the traditionalists are right and tool forms gradually replace one another in "popularity" through time and across space, then we would expect them to exhibit patterns of mutual covariation. Yet we observed in this case patterns of covariation between classes of tools which are generally not associated with each other in large numbers, e.g., other small tools and cleavers, etc. Clearly this means that transformational patterning will not be demonstrable among assemblages arranged against a temporal dimension or a spatial dimension. This is clearly what we observe in the stratified locations (see Howell and Clark, 1963); an alternation of assemblage types such that those closest in time may be most different in the character of assemblage composition while those separated in time may exhibit greater compositional similarities. It is only when assemblages are exclusively composed of tool classes among which varying degrees of mutual covariation are demonstrable that it is possible for total assemblage composition to exhibit directional patterning when arrayed against a time or space dimension. The greater the degree of covariant independence between associated forms, the less directionality will be demonstrable when assemblages are compared. I have demonstrated that a "nonconformity," as demonstrated by the comparison of assemblage types defined on the basis of associational patterning, does not indicate any lack of continuity in covariant patterning. If a lack of continuity in covariant patterning is the basis for the definition of a nonconformity, why do we view alternations of assemblage types as nonconformities? Because the traditionalists' paradigm assumes an equation between association and covariation!

I submit that the degree to which associational patterning is also characterized by covariant relationships among the associated forms is a variable phenomena. My expectations are that the degree of directionality demonstrable in frequency variations among components of assemblages through time or across space will vary directly with the degree that associated classes of items are also related in a covariant fashion. I further suggest that this relationship will vary inversely with the degree of mobility characteristic of the adaptation represented. It will vary directly with the degree that tools are curated and transported in anticipation of future tasks and will vary directly with the level of behavioral integration achieved within the adaptive system under study.

Clearly within the late Acheulian, the independence between association and covariation is almost complete. As expected, we observe an alternation of assemblage types. This same characteristic is a marked feature of assemblage variability for the Mousterian and, it is suspected, for the earlier ranges of time in general. It is my impression that it is not until the upper Paleolithic that sequences of assemblage types begin to clearly pattern temporally or to exhibit directional change through a time sequence. This contrasts with the growing number of sequences characterized by alternating assemblage types clustering in the earlier time ranges. This has a number of implications for both archaeological theory and for our understanding of the past.

First, it is commensurate with the adoption of the behavioral view of assemblage variability in which similarities are seen as a result of a similar constellation of behavior having been enacted at a given location. We may therefore ask what are the determinants of behavioral similarities. If we accept covariant relationships as a measure of regular and similar behavioral responses, how are we to understand patterned associations between variables not covariantly related. These must be seen as associations deriving from the patterned coincidental occurrences of stimuli which elicit different behavioral responses. The consistent association of high frequencies of small scrapers and other small tools which do not exhibit mutual patterns of covariation must be seen as the result of the common association in the environment of stimuli which independently elicit different behavior manifest by the two classes of tools. In short, assemblages are compounds of independently stimulated behavioral responses. The degree that assemblages exhibit associations which do not also have covariant properties should be a direct measure of the degree of integration in the organization of the behavioral regime expressed.

For instance, in the case of the chimp's manufacture of termiting sticks, it would appear that the numbers of sticks manufactured does not vary with the number of termites consumed; instead it appears to vary directly with the number of distractions experienced by the chimp during his stay at the termite nest. In this case although termite nests and termiting sticks would be expected to be strongly associated, we would not expect a covariant relationship between the numbers of sticks and the size of the termite nests. On the other hand, in a highly integrated behavioral regime we might expect the sticks to be discarded directly as a function of their loss of rigidity resulting from repeated licking. The number of sticks manufactured at any one location would then vary directly with the number of termites present, given some vagaries in the degree of hunger experienced by different animals.

The character of assemblage variability documented for the late Acheulian and implied for the Mousterian by a temporal pattern of assemblage type alternation and suspected for the earlier time periods in general may well be informing us about a very different organization of adaptive behavior than we customarily assume for modern man. The traditionalists' paradigm when applied to these materials distorts the character of the variability and denies to us any chance of gaining knowledge of the behavior of our biological ancestors.

The traditionalists' paradigm is rooted in the main on casual or "obvious" features of the contemporary human experience: "Frenchman have different things than Japanese," etc. Aside from the assumptions previously discussed regarding the covariant character of relationships between associated materials, the paradigm assumes that the human species is partitioned into culturally maintained distinctive populations. The very notion of *ethnic group* implies this assumption.

Although rarely stated, the traditionalist paradigm assumes that this ethnic distinctiveness is "natural" to cultural man and arises in the context of "drift" or minor shifts in the "popularity" of alternative cultural forms. Social groups interacting at the local level but independently distributed geographically should experience different "drift" histories, making it possible for the archaeologist to recognize different "traditions." Given this view, the number of traditions should vary directly with the number of geographically localized subpopulations and inversely with the amount of intergroup interaction. There should be a greater tendency toward convergence as rates of interaction increased and its attendant affect in "diffusing" cultural characteristics among the "traditions." On the other hand the rates of drift or change in the content of traditions should vary directly with the numbers of people participating since the source of variability is believed to be individual variability. We would then expect rates of change and the magnitude of variability to both increase as the numbers of individual participants increased.

If the traditionalists' paradigm is correct, we would expect a number of features to characterize the archaeological record for the early periods of the Pleistocene.

Between the beginning of the Pleistocene and the beginning of the Würm, man radiated over much of the Old World. There must have been a major increase in the number of localized human populations. Nevertheless, we have not documented any major increase in the number of traditions, three being all that most would admit by the end of this vast span of time! Contrast this with the span of time currently said to represent the history of human occupation in the New World (few would admit more than 30,000 years). At the end of this relatively short span of time there must be a thousand or more "traditions" recognized by archaeologists!

The evidence for institutionalized between-group interaction between early Pleistocene populations is meager if even present. Evidence of trade and between-group social ritual is completely lacking. Clearly such evidence is well established for the later periods of human occupation in the New World. This should mean that we would expect a greater convergence between traditions in the New World and greater independence and hence greater numbers of unambiguously defined traditions during the early parts of the Pleistocene. We observe just the reverse!

The lack of variability and almost incredible stability characteristic of the earlier phases of the Pleistocene is even more striking if we adopt the generally accepted notion that human populations were sparse and thinly distributed. These conditions should promote more recognizable and distinct traditions, yet they seem to have had the reverse effect during man's early history!

Another expectation regarding the character of the archaeological record, if the traditionalists' paradigm is correct, has reference to rates of change and within tradition variability. As previously mentioned, the rates of change in the content of traditions should vary directly with the numbers of people participating. Clearly, there is an increase in the rates of culture change during the later phases of the Pleistocene with a parallel increase in human population; nevertheless during the earlier phases of the Pleistocene, defined traditions covered enormous spans of time and tremendous geographical areas. The actual number of participants must have in many cases equalled or possibly surpassed the numbers participating in many later traditions. Why was there so little change and so little variability?

Since the early years of the twentieth century, anthropologists have expended tremendous energy in attempting to evaluate the degree that variations in the biological characteristics of modern geographical races affect the general form and level of complexity of the cultures borne by such diverse forms of men.

The results of these researches have overwhelmingly pointed to the conclusion that variations in culture among modern populations cannot be attributed to biological differences in "capacities for culture." This recognition has led to the assumption as expressed by White (1959) that for purposes of explaining cultural variability we may "consider the organism a constant." I feel the archaeologists, although generally not expressing their views, have tended to think of the archaeological remains of the lower and middle Paleolithic as if they too could "consider the organism a constant." Certainly, the demonstrable anatomical contrasts between the men of the earlier time ranges when compared to modern man is warning of a potential fallacy.

One of the more fascinating and absorbing aspects of prehistoric research is the realization that one may work with the products of man anatomically different from ourselves. On reflection this becomes a major challenge because it becomes incumbent upon the prehistorian to provide what knowledge we may acquire concerning the psychological, social, and cultural capabilities and capacities of our premodern ancestors. The recognition that man of the lower and middle Pleistocene was in all probability a much different kind of creature than is known today has stimulated much of the basic research on the social and psychological capacities of nonhuman primates. Such information is provocative and suggestive, yet the only direct evidence we have concerning the behavior of our ancient forebears rests in their archaeological remains. To what degree is the archaeologist doing his job when he *assumes* he knows the significance of his archaeological observations and *assumes* further that paradigms built from analogous models from modern behavior are directly applicable to the products of early man?

The application of the traditionalist paradigm to the interpretation of the products of early man makes several assumptions. One basic tenant of the traditionalist approach is that man passed a threshold, a "cultural rubricon," before which his behavior was "nonhuman," after which his behavior was "human"—therefore cultural in the sense of modern man. This proposition is no longer acceptable. In a number of recent papers the assumption of a "cultural rubricon" has been strongly questioned (Geertz, 1969; Hallowell, 1959). Did all the aspects of culture as observed in homosapiens come into being together at an early hominid stage? White has pointed out the importance of the capacity to symbol as a criteria for cultural behavior as we know it. Hallowell has expanded and elaborated in psychological terms what is implied by symboling, namely a self-conscious actor. Hallowell suggests that symboling capacity makes possible a creature capable of conceptualizing himself and analyzing his environmental matrix using as a point of reference the self-image.

Anthropologists have generally accepted the presence of manufactured tools, "man the toolmaker," as evidence of such capabilities and hence a marker for the passing of the "cultural rubricon." Recently, new data and new approaches to the study of man cast strong doubt on this rule of thumb. Goodall has demonstrated that chimpanzees in the wild manufacture tools. Hallowell has questioned on other grounds whether tool manufacture does require the cultural and psychological matrix within which modern man exists. I have already mentioned that a basic assumption standing behind the traditionalists' paradigm is that the human species is partitioned into culturally maintained distinctive populations, ethnic groups. I am convinced that much of the variability noted between the material products of distinct sociocultural units known ethnographically results not from unconscious "drift" but from a conscious response to selective advantages accruing to the maintenance and explicit recognition at the cognitive level of group identities and individual identities. I suggest that many of the patterns of variability which are directly referable to groups recognized by other and self-cognizant of their distinctiveness is a product of a particular context of selection and the attendant context of sociocultural development. I suggest that much of the "conservativeness" notable among many ethnic groups, as well as their obvious distinctiveness, may well be a response to the operation of a particular set of selective pressures arising in the context of a relatively complex social geography. Such conditions may not have existed during most of the Pleistocene.

When did man exercise his human prerogative and assign meaning to the various segments into which the species was partitioned geographically? Were local human groups culturally bounded during much of the Pleistocene? Instead of assuming answers to these questions and viewing interassemblage variability as a measure of "cultural" distance or "ethnic" distinctiveness, we might more profitably concern ourselves with establishing when we can demonstrate variability in the archaeological record referable to ethnic differentiations among human groups. My impression is that little if any of the variability thus far demonstrated in the archaeological record prior to the upper Paleolithic is referable to "ethnic" units of hominid populations which were "culturally" bounded.

The Paleolithic archaeologist is faced with a dual problem and a real challenge: (1) Change in the character of the organism may well have modified considerably the capacities of man for engaging in cultural behavior; (2) changes in the ecological adjustments of man to man and man to nature would have modified the selective contexts favoring the exercise of these changing capacities in differing and expanding domains of the hominid experience. As I have argued, the traditionalists' paradigm denies us the chance of studying these problems. In spite of my demonstration that the basic assumptions standing behind traditional interpretation of archaeological remains are not met in the empirical world of Paleolithic remains, I predict that traditionalists will continue to defend the old "secure" paradigm.

Popper (1959) has argued quite convincingly that theories cannot be proven, only by their falsification or inadequacy can we evaluate our lack of understanding of the way the natural world works. He has further argued that during periods in which theories are being doubted, either on the basis of claims of their having been falsified, or on an intuitive "uneasiness" with their efficacy there will appear a defensive strategy on the part of apologists for the traditional paradigm which he has called "conventionalism" (Popper, 1959, p. 78).

According to this conventionalist's point of view, laws of nature are not falsifiable by observation, for they are needed to determine what an observation, and more especially, what a scientific measurement is (p. 80).

This prediction has almost a frightening accuracy when viewed against several recent statements made by traditionalists:

His view that detailed stylistic similarities between assemblages must be due to a community of cultural tradition cannot be challenged. As he clearly points out, the functional approach to accounting for differences is not applicable, since we simply do not possess a single shred of reliable evidence bearing on the possible function(s) of the various categories of tools found in Lower and Middle Paleolithic assemblages. Therefore, the problem of use becomes a sheer game of hypotheses with no established limits, in which everyone's guess has just as much potential validity as the next person's. In the final analysis, the basic assumption of continuity of cultural tradition is abundantly supported by the manner in which patterns emerge when distributions of traditions and stages of common cultural entities are plotted in time and space (Movius, 1969, p. 307).

In contrast to the single-community . . . [view], the hypothesis of continuity of culture tradition is not opposed by an important indication either from archaeological data or from ethnographic analogy. . . . It does not conflict with the view that assemblage-types sometimes represent different activities, for it is in their activities as much as in their culture "traits" that societies are distinguished from one another. A crude example would be the proposition that the culture of France and that of the Australian Aborigines are different only because they indulge in different activities. . . . It is indeed fortunate that the study of culture traditions does not necessarily involve knowing the functions of artefacts, since we can rarely do more than guess at these. I suggest that we are justified in proceeding on the hypothesis that close similarity of style and content in assemblages is an indicator of common cultural tradition. We may also conclude that we have no good evidence for two or more assemblage-types belonging to a single community in Pleistocene Europe (Collins, 1969, pp. 269–270).

I have tried to document that a mentalistic cultural theory, its model, and a single operational definition serve to identify for the traditionalist what relevant observation is and more importantly what it measures.

I have tried to demonstrate that some basic assumptions about the nature of the archaeological record are not met empirically and further that there are serious reasons for doubting those that have not been subjected to empirical testing.

In such times of crisis this conflict over the aims of science will become acute. We and those who share our attitude, will hope to make new discoveries; and we shall hope to be helped in this by a newly erected scientific system. Thus, we shall take the greatest interest in the falsifying experiment. We shall hail it as a success, for it has opened up new vistas into a world of new experience. And we shall hail it even if these new experiences should furnish us with new arguments against our own most recent theories. But the newly rising structure, the boldness of which we admire, is seen by the conventionalist as a monument to the total collapse of science. . . . In the eyes of the conventionalist one principle only can help us to select a system as the chosen one from among all other possible systems; it is the principle of selecting the simplest system—the simplest system of implicit definition; which of course means in practice the "classical" system of the day (Popper, 1959, pp. 80, 81).

References

Binford, Lewis R. (1971). Mortuary practices, their study and their potential. *Memoirs of the Society for American Archaeology* No. 25 pp. 6–29.

Binford, Lewis R., and Sally R. Binford. (1966). A preliminary analysis of functional variability in the Mousterian of Levallois facies. *American Anthropologist* **68**, 238–295.
Binford, Sally R., and Lewis R. Binford. (1968). Stone tools and human behavior. *Scientific American* **220**, 70–84.
Bordes, F. H. (1956). Some observations on the Pleistocene succession in the Somme valley. *Proceedings of the Pre-Historic Society* **22**, 1–5.
Bordes, F. H. (1961). Mousterian cultures in France. *Science* **134**, 803–810.
Bordes, F. H. (1968). *The Old Stone Age*. World University Library, New York and London.
Bordes, F. H., and M. Bourgon. (1951). Le compexe Mousterian. *l'Anthropologie* **55**, 1–23.
Bowler-Kelley, A. (1937). *Lower and Middle Paleolithic Facies in Europe and Africa*. Privately published. Philadelphia, Pennsylvania.
Breuil, H., and L. Koslowski. (1931). Etudes de Stratigraphie Paleolithique dans le Nord de la France. *Anthropologie* **41**, 450–488.
Clark, J. D. (1950). *The Stone Age Cultures of Northern Rhodesia*. Capetown.
Clark, J. D. (1953). New light on early man in Africa. *Antiquity* **108**, 242–243.
Clark, J. D. (1959a). Further excavations at Broken Hill, Northern Rhodesia. *Journal of the Royal Anthropological Institute* **89**, 201–232.
Clark, J. D. (1959b). *The Prehistory of Southern Africa*. Penguin Books, London.
Clark, J. D., and C. V. Haynes. (1970). An elephant butchery site at Mwanganda's Village, Karonga, Malaw, and its relevance for palaeolithic archaeology. *World Archaeology* **1**, 390–411.
Clarke, D. L. (1968). *Analytical Archaeology*. London.
Cohen, M. R. (1964). *Reason and Nature, the Meaning of Scientific Method*. London.
Cole, Glen H. (1967). The later Acheulian and Sangoan of Southern Uganda. In *Background to Evolution in Africa* (W. W. Bishop and J. D. Clark, eds.), pp. 481–528. Univ. of Chicago Press, Chicago, Illinois.
Cole, Sonia. (1954). *The Prehistory of Southern Africa*. Penguin Books, London.
Collins, D. (1969). Culture traditions and environment of early man. *Current Anthropology* **10**, 267–296.
Deetz, J. *Invitation to Archaeology*. Natural History Press, New York.
Ford, James A. (1962). A quantitative method for deriving cultural chronology. *Technical Manual, Pan American Union* No. 1.
Gearing, F. (1962). Priests and warriors. *American Anthropological Association, Memoir* No. 93.
Geertz, C. (1969). The transition to humanity. In *Horizons of Anthropology* (S. Tax, ed.), pp. 37–48. Univ. of Chicago Press, Chicago.
Hallowell, A. I. (1959). Behavioral evolution and the emergence of the self. In *Evolution and Anthropology*, pp. 36–60. Washington, D.C.
Hallowell, A. I. (1960). Self, society, and culture in phylogenetic perspective. In *Evolution After Darwin* (S. Tax, ed.), Vol. II, pp. 309–371. Univ. of Chicago Press, Chicago.
Harman, H. H. (1962). *Modern Factor Analysis*. Univ. of Chicago Press, Chicago, Illinois.
Harvey, D. (1969). *Explanation in Geography*. Arnold, London.
Howell, F. C. (1961). Isimila: A paleolithic site in Africa. *Scientific American* **205**, 118–129.
Howell, F. C., and J. D. Clark. (1963). Acheulian hunter–gatherers of the sub-Saharan Africa. In *African Ecology and Human Evolution* (F. C. Howell and R. Bourliere, eds.), pp. 458–533. Univ. Of Chicago Press, Chicago.
Howell, F. C., Glen H. Cole, and Maxine R. Kleindienst. (1961). Isimila: An Acheulian occupation site in the Iringa Highlands, Southern Highlands Province, Tanganyika. *Acts of the 4th Pan African Congress of Prehistory*, pp. 43–80.

Isaac, Glynn I   (1961). Some experiments in quantitative methods for characterizing assemblages of Acheulian artifacts. *Acts of the 4th Pan African Congress of Prehistory,* pp. 81–97.

Isaac, Glynn L. (1966). New evidence from Olorgesailie relating to the character of Acheulian occupation sites. *Acts of the 5th Pan African Congress of Prehistory,* pp. 135–145.

Isaac, Glynn L. (1968). Traces of Pleistocene hunters: An East African example. In *Man the Hunter* (R. B. Lee and I. DeVore, eds.), pp. 253–261. Aldine Publ. Co., Chicago, Illinois.

Jones, N. (1929). Hope Fountain. *South African Journal of Science* **26**, 631–647.

Kleindienst, Maxine R. (1961a). Components of the East African Acheulian assemblage: An analytic approach. *Acts of the 4th Pan African Congress of Prehistory,* pp. 81–111.

Kleindienst, Maxine R. (1961b). Variability within the late Acheulian assemblage in Eastern Africa. *South African Archaeological Bulletin* **16**, 35–52.

Kreiger, A. D. (1944). The typological concept. *American Antiquity* **9**, 271–288.

Kuhn, T. S. (1962). *The Structure of Scientific Revolutions.* Univ. of Chicago Press, Chicago, Illinois.

Leakey, L. S. B. (1951). The Olorgesailie prehistoric site. *Proceedings of the 1st Pan African Congress of Prehistory,* p. 209.

Leakey, L. S. B. (1960). *Adam's Ancestors.* Harper Torchbooks, New York.

Leakey, Mary D. (1967). Preliminary survey of the cultural material from Beds I and II, Olduvai Gorge, Tanzania. In *Background to Evolution in Africa.* (W. W. Bishop and J. D. Clark, eds.), pp. 417–446. Univ. of Chicago Press, Chicago.

Lee, Richard B. (1968). What hunters do for a living, or, How to make out on scarce resources. *In* "Man the Hunter" (R. B. Lee and I. DeVore, eds.), pp. 30–48. Aldine, Chicago, Illinois.

Movius, H. L. (1969). Comments. *Current Anthropology* **10**, 307–308.

Oakley, K. P. (1956). *Man the Tool-Maker.* British Museum of Natural History, Norwich.

Peyrony, D. (1930). Le Moustier; ses gisements, ses industries. *Revue Anthropologique* Nos. 1–3, pp. 4–6.

Popper, Karl R. (1959). *The Logic of Scientific Discovery.* Harper Torchbooks, New York.

Posnansky, M. (1959). A Hope Fountain site at Olorgesailie, Kenya Colony. *South African Archaeological Bulletin* **14**, 83–89.

Sackett, J. R. (1968). Method and theory of Upper Paleolithic archaeology in Southwestern France. In *New Perspectives in Archaeology* (S. R. Binford and L. R. Binford, eds.), pp. 61–83. Aldine, Chicago.

Sokal, R. R., and P. H. A. Sneath. (1963). *Numerical Taxonomy.* Aldine, Freeman, San Francisco.

Spaulding, A. C. (1960). The dimensions of archaeology. In *The Science of Culture: In Honor of Leslie A. White* pp. 437–456. Crowell, New York.

Tester, P. (1958). The age of the Bakers Hole industry. *Archaeological News Letter* **6**, 123–125.

Trigger, B. G. (1968). *Beyond History: The Methods of Prehistory.* Holt, New York.

Waechter, J. (1968). The evidence of the Levallois technique in the British Acheulian and the question of the Acheulio–Levallois. In *La préhistoire: Problémes et tendances.* (J. Pineteau, ed.), pp. 491–497. Centre National de la Recherche Scientifique, Paris.

White, L. A. (1959). *The Evolution of Culture.* McGraw–Hill, New York.

"Red Ochre" Caches from the Michigan Area: A Possible Case of Cultural Drift *

The Concept of Cultural Drift

In recent years a number of late Archaic sites have been excavated in the Michigan area. This work has been carried out as part of a continuing research program of the Museum of Anthropology at the University of Michigan. As a result of these investigations, a body of data on the late Archaic period is accumulating which has meaning not only for the solution of problems specific to the culture history of the Great Lakes region, but the controlled samples provide a corpus of data which can be utilized to attack more general questions about the operation of prehistoric societies and processes of culture change and differentiation.

It has been demonstrated (Binford, 1963a) that at the Pomranky site, a "Red Ochre" cemetery of the late Archaic period, cache blades of several distinct varieties were included within a single grave. Such diversity, together with the associated information, was used to infer that the several varieties represented goods contributed at the time of interment, possibly by different individuals or group representatives. The first question to be solved in the present analysis is whether or not other "Red Ochre" burials also exhibit the presence of several distinct varieties of cache blades as part of the burial furniture. Secondly, sites will be compared to determine if there is any recurrence of varieties at more than one site, an observation which, if established, would suggest that the various recognized varieties had separate local origins but were being "traded" widely within the region. The final question is whether or not the observable differences between the several populations of cache blades indicate any regional patterns, which might serve as a basis for understanding the processes of cultural change and differentiation operative during the time span of the samples.

While addressing my interests to the latter problem, I began a search for a

* Originally published in *Southwestern Journal of Anthropology* **19**, 89–108 (1963).

general explanatory model which would be applicable to the particular type of detailed observations on differences and similarities resulting from the analysis. Many of the demonstrable differences between samples of cache blades were not of an order that could easily be fitted into an evolutionary model of formal diversification. No obvious selective rationale could be developed for some of the minor and relatively insignificant variations which were demonstrably real between the samples studied. It occurred to me that there was an obvious analogy between the type of variation observable between the populations of cache blades and variations in human populations defined in terms of gene frequencies. In both cases the same range of variation may be present in several populations, but the relative frequencies of specific variant forms differ between the populations. This line of thought led me to explore various genetic models of change, and of course the concept of genetic drift was considered. A review of the anthropological literature revealed that the term drift had been employed by several anthropologists and such a concept might be a profitable and relevant tool.

Three anthropologists have been prominent in their use of the concept of "cultural drift," Edward Sapir (1921), Fred Eggan (1941), and Melville J. Herskovits (1948). Central for all three in their usage of the concept are the characteristics of directionality and cumulation in change. Herskovits and Sapir apply the term to both culture and language to refer to the cumulation of small variations which reputedly can result in long range directional changes. Herskovits (1948, pp. 581–582) states, "The concept of cultural drift follows logically from the idea of culture as the consensus of the variables in the beliefs and modes of behavior of a people. . . . The presence of deviations from norms of concept and conduct, most of them so small as to go largely unrecognized, is important in giving culture an inner dynamic that, in the long run, results in alterations that may be of the most profound character." Random individual variations in the execution of norms are believed to be the "pool" from which inner dynamic "growths" may stem. Eggan uses the term to signify a directional progression of formal differences between the coast and the interior of the Philippines for a number of correlated aspects of social organization, demography, settlement pattern and economy. Eggan's usage combines the idea of small cumulative changes and directionality as characteristics of drift. However, the term remains largely descriptive of these characteristics and does not subsume the "process" explicit in the usage of Herskovits and Sapir.

Aberle (1960, p. 14) has sharply criticized the analogy used by Herskovits and Sapir of the "linguistic model" for the formulation of culture theory in general and the concept of "cultural drift" specifically: "there are three terms . . . to a consideration of linguistic materials: idiolect, language (or dialect), and system of communications. People do not share a system of communication, they participate in it, precisely because they occupy different positions in the communications chain. The organization of a communications system is different in kind from the organization of an idiolect or a dialect: it has no isomorphism with either." The criticism is carried further by pointing out that the cultural "idiolect" is the unique characteristic of individual behavior within a cultural frame of reference, while shared culture is the normative behavior of a society or other social unit. On the other hand, the cultural system is a matter in which individuals participate and is not simply a matter of sharing variations around a norm.

Taking this view, it becomes clear that when cultural process is viewed as rooted in "drift" stemming from variations in the cultural idiolect, there is never any way of understanding the direction which change may take or the structural differences between several cultural systems. The more fruitful view is to recognize that cultural systems are participated in by individuals and articulate individuals into social units. Changes and variations in the cultural system are to be understood in terms of the demographic structure of the human group and the integrative stresses which articulate the group into a society capable of maintaining itself within a given adaptive milieu, defined in terms of both the physical and social environment. Cultural systems change in response to adaptive pressures, not as a result of an autochthonous process where cultural drift leads a cultural system toward a greater consistency largely phrased in psychological or configurational terms (Benedict, 1934, p. 581). As Eggan (1962) has pointed out, "It is clear that random variation about a norm will not change the norm, except by disintegrating it. It is selection of some sort that is responsible for directional changes."

Having determined that the models of "cultural drift" in current usage are not acceptable on theoretical grounds, it remains to examine the areas where the concept may be applicable and to suggest how current usage may be profitably modified so the general idea of drift can be converted to a useful analytical tool.

The concept of genetic drift is applied to the process whereby the gene frequencies of parent and daughter populations can diverge simply as a result of random sampling error. Such an effect is largely restricted to small populations or cases where a small segment of a breeding population is isolated from the parent population. In both cases the relative frequencies of genetic variants in parent and daughter populations may be significantly altered simply as a result of small sample size and accompanying sample error in the continuity between the two breeding populations. For those of us interested in material culture, there would appear to be certain parallels in cultural process which are largely dependent upon the same systematic principles as is the random genetic drift effect. In any given social unit there is a range of variation in the manner of execution of stylistic norms appropriate to the manufacture of particular items or in the use of certain decorative and stylistic modes. This "pool" of variability on the individual level (cultural idiolect) is no doubt as subject to sampling error as is the gene pool in cases of small populations which are either isolated or undergoing demographic change and segmentation. This postulate is based on the assumption that the range and stability of individual variations in the execution of stylistic norms between parent and daughter communities is a function of the generational continuity in learning and enculturation between the populations.

In cases of decreased generational continuity and stability we would expect minor variations to arise in the relative frequencies for different modes of normative execution between parent and daughter communities. Such variation should arise simply as a result of random sampling error in the degree to which individual variants are disproportionally represented between the parent and descendent populations. Changes arising in this manner automatically result in a slightly modified statistical norm in the daughter community. Such a shift may remain a purely statistical phenomena or may, under selection for maximizing the material means of group identification, be objectified and elaborated, thereby serving the functions of enhancing group solidarity. It is then suggested that there could arise real differences between social units in the range and frequency of specific formal characteristics of material items which are simply a function of random sampling error between generations in small and segmenting social units. Vagaries of fluctuations in the proportions of enculturative tasks assumed by any segment of a population because of differential reproductive rates, isolation, etc., may also contribute to such random drift.

It should be pointed out that this suggested process would be operative only within the individual's cultural idiolect or the shared behavioral aspects of culture. Cultural systems as such and the normative structure of the system would not be subject to processes of drift, being modified only through processes of readaptation or evolutionary change. Cultural content alone would be subject to such a process. It has long been recognized that formally different elements of culture content could replace others in a system without affecting any alteration within the structure itself. When such items of culture content can be shown to perform the same function, they are referred to as functional equivalents. It follows that there can be minor changes in the formal properties of functional equivalents which will have no effect on the structure of the system as a whole. Similarly, changes in the frequency of certain formal properties which crosscut functional classes, such as decorative motifs and other stylistic phenomena, may be susceptible to formal differentiation through drift without affecting the structure of the cultural system involved.

In any system there are elements which, for certain tasks, can be considered functionally equivalent but not functionally isomorphic. For instance, horseback riding and bicycle riding in certain situations may be functionally equivalent modes of transportation, both serving to transport a single individual at rates exceeding that of foot travel. On the other hand, they are not functionally isomorphic in that a bicycle cannot be efficiently used to traverse a stream or rugged terrain, whereas a horse may be efficient in such a context. Elements or subsystems may vary in their efficiency and range of task performance. In such cases, change in the relative frequency of nonisomorphic functional equivalents between cultural systems can be explained in evolutionary terms, in which the adaptive milieu is characterized by definable selective pressures favoring one range of task performance at the expense of another and admitting increases in the general efficiency of task performance. In the case of nonisomorphic functional equivalents, drift may continue to operate when selective pressures are slight. However, it seems reasonable to assume that drift would be less operative as the selective situation increases in intensity. Changes or differences in the relative frequency of functional classes is certainly not amenable to interpretation within the model of cultural drift. Such variation must be related to differential task performance and explanation is appropriately sought in an adaptive context.

Radical breaks in the formal continuity between populations of functional equivalents are certainly not to be explained by processes of cultural drift. Such changes should be referable to changes in the regional sociology and evolutionary trends within the structure of intergroup relations for the region as a whole. For instance, the replacement of shell beads by glass beads or ceramic containers by copper kettles during the historic period of North American aboriginal culture history are certainly related to modifications in the component groups and in the underlying structure of interaction between groups.

The term drift, as outlined here, implies a process of formal modification in culture content, particularly within classes of functional equivalents or in the relative frequencies of stylistic attributes which may crosscut functional classes. This process is dependent upon the operation of probability factors in sampling variations between the generations of any given social unit. Two basic models have been constructed as an initial step in exploring the concept of cultural drift as an analytical tool for the elucidation of processes of cultural diversification operative in the past.

The first model refers to the situation in which drift occurs primarily as the result of major demographic increases, with accompanying social segmentation giving rise to the establishment of daughter communities. In such a situation, random sampling error would arise simultaneously with regard to a number of separate attribute classes and behavioral norms. As a result, we would expect a demonstrable pattern of covariation between formal differences characteristic of spatially separated units. Covariation relationships between differences in separate attribute or normative classes should overlap in regular spatial patterns, resulting in radiating or linear distribution patterns. Such complementary spatial distributions, when observed in attribute classes suspected as amenable to the operation of the process of cultural drift, should be investigated as hints to population expansions and migrations. It should be borne in mind that similar distributions could arise as a result of evolutionary process in situations of the presence of dominance differentials in the structure of the regional interaction sphere. In the latter case, complementary distributions should be largely restricted to particular classes of functional items, while different distributional patterns would characterize normative expression in functional classes not relevant to the integration and mutual articulatory mechanism operative within the interaction sphere.

The second model was developed for the case of demographic stability, drift operating largely as a result of discontinuity between generations in learning and enculturative behavior for the region as a whole. Each subregional social segment is characterized by its individual generational continuity, which is subject to sampling vagaries; regional continuity decreases with the social distance between interacting groups as regards the sharing of common learning and enculturative experiences. In such a case we would expect that minor divergences arising through drift would be indirectly correlated with a decrease in the generational continuity of shared learning experiences. Using this model, it is possible to see how subregional styles in the execution of any given mode could arise in the absence of selective pressures favoring differentiation and without major structural change in the sociology or demography of the region as a whole. In such a situation we would expect a reticulate distribution pattern within the region for different modes and attribute differences. Each attribute subject to cultural drift would tend to sort independently of any other attribute, reducing the chances for complementary distributions and resulting in the appearance of numerous "variant centers" corresponding to different attributes. Each separate mode would generally exhibit a variant center with differentiation increasing with the distance from the center. Variant centers for different modes would coincide only as a result of chance occurrence. If such distribution is observable within the range of phenomena susceptible to cultural drift, then we might explore the hypothesis that the demographic and regional sociology is essentially a stable system.

It is recognized that these models need not be independent of each other; both could be simultaneously applicable as well as compounded by the presence of numerous combinations of selective pressures all working in combination. The purpose of separation is in the nature of a trial formulation which may be useful in understanding cultural process. If models such as these could be verified and comparative studies of drift rates were carried out under differing conditions of demographic stability, it might be possible to develop a powerful tool for the investigation of prehistoric demographic processes that does not require the detailed site and burial data currently necessary. For the ranges of time during the Paleolithic where the chances of ever obtaining good site density and distribution data is slight, due to the large-scale destruction and modification of sites resulting from geological events, such a technique based on the study of minor variations in tool form could be of practical utility.

The data presented in this paper are quite limited and do not constitute an adequate sample nor provide the controls necessary to test the drift hypothesis. This material should be considered as part of the documentation for the development of the ideas set forth in the previous sections. In actual fact the analysis of the materials and the recognition of certain configurations of differences and similarities preceded the development of the models presented. The models were developed to fit the data; hence the data and their interpretation are necessarily consistent with the models and in no way constitute a test. For this reason, the models and the inferences drawn from the models and data both constitute a set of hypotheses which must be subjected to further testing. The purpose of this paper can therefore be considered as twofold: (1) to present certain ideas concerning the processes of culture change and differentiation, and (2) to present the body of comparative data which prompted much of the theoretical consideration and, in addition, may be useful to other archaeologists engaged in Great Lakes research.

The data utilized in the study were drawn from material excavated at four sites in the state of Michigan, all believed to be representatives of the period from roughly 1400 to 300 B.C. and generally classifiable as "Red Ochre" sites (Ritzenthaler and Quimby, 1962). The sample consists of 63 cache blades from the Huron Beach site near Alpena, Michigan, heretofore unreported; 516 cache blades from the Pomranky site near Midland, Michigan (Binford, 1963a); 152 of a population of 470 cache blades from the Kimmel site near Niles, Michigan (Papworth, 1958); and 94 cache blades from the Eastport site near Eastport, Michigan (Binford and Papworth, 1963). A total of 825 specimens from four sites constitute the material studied.

The specimens are believed to have been functionally isomorphic. All were elements of burial furniture in association with a similar range of other artifacts; and all are basically of the same form, being of a single projectile point type, the Pomranky point.

Formal Analysis of the Huron Beach Cache

THE SITE

Knowledge of this site is preserved in the well documented collection of Gerald Haltiner of Alpena, Michigan. Included in his collection are 63 Pomranky points (Binford, 1963a), which were excavated by Oscar Sorenson from the Huron Beach site in 1925. Mr. Sorenson found these points, plus four others now lost, in a tight cluster, covered with powdered red ocher and in association with cremated human bone. The locus of this find was the Huron Beach site, located roughly seven miles north of Alpena. The exact spot where the discovery was made could not be identified by Mr. Haltiner, but its general location was known.

At the present time the site is an abandoned orchard, the surface of which exhibits a gently rolling contour characteristic of stabilized sand dunes in the area. The burial with associated grave goods was excavated from a "blowout" in one of these dunes, the heavy concentration of powdered ochre therein exposed and obvious to the casual observer. A search of the surface in the area adjacent to where the burial was excavated failed to yield any evidence of aboriginal occupation. However, included in Mr. Haltiner's collection are several items recovered from the site. Of particular interest is a gouge, a unilaterally barbed bone harpoon and a celt, as well as several notched projectile points. No pottery has been recovered from the area. The lack of chippage, broken rock and organic stains characteristic of the area around the find suggest that the site was used primarily for burial purposes.

RAW MATERIALS

Six types of raw material were represented in the cache of points from the Huron Beach site. Four of the stone types have been recognized and previously described. Of the described stone types, five specimens were manufactured of Eastport chert and six of type S (Binford and Papworth, 1963), three of type G and fourteen of type A (Binford, 1963a). The previously unknown type of raw material is designated as type T. This is a medium to light red-gray opaque chert with a shiny surface. There are numerous fine cavities lined with white opaque chert. Bands are of medium width (5 mm) to very narrow and are generally not concentric. Bands vary from a gunmetal gray to a blue gray and normally exhibit a shinier surface than the mass of the chert. Sources of this material are unknown. However, the banding and color variation resembles materials that are known to come from Ontario. Thirty-one of the specimens in the sample were manufactured of this material.

Observations for discrete attributes were made in the field, and no major variation was observed within the cache as regards the following attribute classes: flaking of the blade, flaking of the base, point of juncture between the basal edge and the lateral edge, haft element, cross section, longitudinal section, or the presence of grinding. All observations for the above classes of attributes were completely within the range of type definition for the Pomranky point (Binford, 1963a). Meaningful variation was observed within the sample for the attribute classes (Binford, 1963b), as shown in Table I.

In order to assess the variation between the points manufactured of different materials, a number of chi-square calculations were carried out to determine the

TABLE I   Frequency of Attributes by Stone Types: Huron Beach Cache

Attributes	A	G	Stone types Eastport	T	S	Total	Percentages
Blade shape							
Contracting ovate	2	–	–	1	–	3	5.17
Ovate	4	–	3	12	3	22	37.94
Excurvate	8	3	2	17	3	33	56.89
Base shape							
Concave	1	–	3	1	–	5	8.47
Subconcave	6	–	2	9	3	20	34.89
Straight	6	1	1	15	2	25	42.37
Subconvex	1	1	–	5	–	7	11.86
Convex	–	1	–	–	1	2	3.38
Basal preparation							
Thinned	7	1	5	22	3	38	65.52
Striking platform	1	–	–	1	–	2	3.45
Skim out	4	1	–	4	2	11	18.96
Transverse scar	2	1	–	3	1	7	12.07
Flake blank orientation							
Distal	6	1	–	7	2	16	27.60
Oblique	–	–	–	1	–	1	0.71
Obscured	8	2	5	22	4	41	71.69

probability that the observed variation, within the attribute classes between specimens of different raw material, arose simply as a result of sampling error. In all cases the observed variation could have arisen as a result of sampling error more than once in 20 cases of samples drawn from a single population. Therefore, there is no justification for asserting that there are real differences between the various specimens manufactured of differing material. However, it must be kept in mind that the samples are very small, therefore not necessarily proving the absence of such differences.

All metrical attributes were recorded in the field and no variation was observed in this sample which was not completely within the range of variation of the Pomranky point. For the attribute class "orientation of the base," this sample fell completely within the range of variation observed at the Pomranky site (Binford, 1963a). Data on the other metrical attribute classes is given in Table II.

Within and between sample analysis of variance was carried out for all possible combinations of the recognized groupings. Results of this analysis are presented in Table III. The results show that specimens manufactured of stone types A, G, and S are indistinguishable from each other, whereas type T and Eastport chert are different from the above grouping and differ among themselves, suggesting that there are three "varieties" represented in the cache.

TABLE II   *Metrical Attributes of the Huron Beach Cache*

| Attribute classes | Stone types | | | | | |
Length	A	G	East	T	S	Summary
Sx	77.8	15.7	27.7	158.7	34.5	314.4
Sx²	436.92	82.25	156.7	816.43	199.44	1691.74
n	14.00	3.00	5.00	31.00	6.00	59.00
x̄	5.56	5.23	5.54	5.12	5.75	5.32
s	0.59	0.30	0.90	0.36	0.75	—
Basal width						
Sx	34.5	6.9	16.50	76.50	15.3	149.70
Sx²	86.51	16.05	55.13	192.81	39.75	390.25
n	14.00	3.00	5.00	31.00	6.00	59.00
x̄	2.46	2.30	3.30	2.47	2.55	2.54
s	0.34	0.95	0.41	0.37	0.38	—
Maximum width						
Sx	37.4	7.5	16.7	80.5	16.1	158.2
Sx²	102.52	18.93	56.35	215.28	39.71	432.79
n	14.00	3.00	5.00	31.00	6.00	60.00
x̄	2.67	2.50	3.34	2.60	2.68	2.68
s	0.35	0.30	0.53	0.46	0.24	—
Thickness						
Sx	9.4	1.9	3.2	19.35	4.25	38.10
Sx²	6.42	1.21	2.16	12.34	3.01	25.14
n	15.00	3.00	5.00	31.00	6.00	59.00
x̄	0.67	0.63	0.64	0.63	0.71	0.64
s	0.09	0.07	0.16	0.09	0.05	—

Formal Analysis of the Kimmel Site Cache

A brief report on the Kimmel site has been published (Papworth, 1958). However, at the time the materials were originally analyzed, the significance of the demonstrable variation between specimens manufactured of different types of stone had not been recognized. For this reason, the formal analysis was undertaken again. Unfortunately, most of the specimens from the Kimmel cache had to be returned to their owners after the initial analysis and only 152 of the original sample of 470 specimens were available for restudy. The degree to which the restudied specimens constitute a random sample of the original population is suspect because, as will be shown (Table V), the mean lengths and widths of the restudied sample do not correspond favorably with the mean values for the entire cache.

Raw Materials

Two types of raw material were utilized in the manufacture of the specimens, both of which (type A and type G) have been previously described (Binford,

TABLE III Results of Variance Analysis: *Huron Beach Cache*
(Percentage entries show the probability levels of drawing the samples from a single population)

Attribute classes	Stone type combinations									
	A & G	A & E	A & T	A & S	G & E	G & T	G & S	E & T	E & S	T & S
Length	Same	Same	1%	Same	Same	Same	Same	Same	Same	1%
Basal width	Same	1%	Same	Same	5%	Same	Same	1%	1%	Same
Max. width	Same	1%	Same	Same	5%	Same	Same	1%	1%	Same
Thickness	Same	Same	Same	Same	Same	Same	Same	Same	Same	5%

1963a). The geographic range and loci of origin for these materials are at present unknown, although it is my opinion that both are obtainable from the middle Cary till of the Valparaiso morainic systems extending south along the Lake Michigan shore from just south of Grand Rapids, Michigan, on around the south end of the lake (Mason, 1958, p. 18).

As was the case with the Huron Beach cache, only the reported attribute classes were observed to vary outside the range of variation of the type definition for Pomranky points. Table IV presents the tabulated frequencies for the listed attribute classes.

TABLE IV   *Frequency of Attributes by Stone Types: Kimmel Cache*

Attributes	Stone types		Total	Percentages
	A	G		
Blade shape				
Contracting ovate	—	—	—	—
Ovate	33	9	42	28.19
Excurvate	86	21	107	71.81
Base shape				
Concave	—	—	—	—
Subconcave	9	7	16	10.81
Straight	82	16	98	66.22
Subconvex	27	7	34	22.97
Convex	—	—	—	—
Basal preparation				
Thinned	87	22	109	73.16
Striking platform	—	—	—	
Skim out	11	8	19	12.75
Transverse scar	21	—	21	14.09
Flake blank orientation				
Distal	31	19	50	33.56
Oblique	6	—	6	4.03
Obscured	82	11	93	62.41

Chi-square calculations were made for the comparison of the tabulated frequency of the discrete attributes of each class between groups segregated by stone type. With the exception of blade shape, the values of chi-square obtained from a comparison of the two samples exceeds the values expected to arise as a result of sampling vagaries less than two times in a hundred cases. On the basis of this analysis, we can assert that there are real differences between Pomranky points manufactured of different materials included in the Kimmel cache.

The metrical attributes are reported in Table V, with the exception of angle of basal orientation, which was observed not to differ from the other samples thus far studied.

TABLE V   *Metrical Attributes of the Kimmel Cache*

	Total sample Length		Length	Basal width	Max. width	Thickness
				Restudied sample		
Variety 1						
Type A stone		Sx	600.15	262.85	289.50	74.10
		Sx²	3,071.74	604.38	712.42	42.62
		(Sx)²	360,180.02	69,090.12	83,810.25	5,490.81
	N = 470	n	119.00	119.00	119.00	119.00
	x̄ = 5.11	x̄	5.04	2.21	2.43	0.62
	s = 0.68	s	0.64	0.44	0.26	0.11
Variety 2						
Type G stone		Sx	159.10	75.45	83.90	19.25
		Sx²	774.4	177.30	216.36	11.97
		(Sx)²	25,312.81	5,692.70	7,039.21	370.56
		n	33.00	33.00	33.00	33.00
		x̄	4.82	2.29	2.54	0.58
		s	0.48	0.39	0.31	0.15

An analysis of within and between sample variance was carried out using the above information, resulting in F ratios which did not exceed the expected values for any metrical class except length. The two samples differed sufficiently between themselves for the latter attributes so that the probability of their having been derived from the same population is less than one in a thousand. Thus we conclude that there are real differences between the points manufactured of different materials. These differences are apparent with respect to length, base shape, basal preparation, and flake blank orientation. Most of these differences could conceivably result from slightly different techniques utilized in the working of raw materials. This is probably not true in the case of base shape, and differences here probably reflect differing stylistic norms.

Summary of Within-Site Comparisons

It has been demonstrated that at the Pomranky site (Binford, 1963a), the Huron Beach site, and the Kimmel site, burials containing caches of Pomranky points exhibit meaningful variation between points manufactured of differing materials. This differentiation within a single burial is interpreted as reflecting contributions to the burial furniture of the interred individual derived from different areas and possibly representing contributions from several individuals.

The specimens recovered from the Eastport site were found to represent a single population, which is commensurate with the hypothesis that the site was a functionally specific quarry location where Pomranky points were initially processed (Binford and Papworth, 1963).

Between-Site Comparisons

We turn now to the problem of the relationships between the sites, as is evidenced by the formal variation in the cache blades. An obvious approach is to consider the problem of whether or not any of the "varieties" found at one site are also represented at others. Carrying this type of comparative analysis a step further, we will consider the problem of whether there is as much or more variation between the varieties represented at a single site than between the samples from separate localities.

Table VI presents the results of comparative statistical analysis for the samples which are manufactured of raw materials found at more than one site. It will be noted that, while at any given site there are real differences between points manufactured of materials common to several sites, there are more similarities between points manufactured of different materials at a given site than there are between points manufactured of the same material at different sites. Certainly the available data does not suggest that Pomranky points were being widely "traded" within the region.

This conclusion points out the fact that "varieties" as originally defined for the Pomranky site (Binford, 1963a) may not be the most efficacious taxonomic approach to the study of variability of the order conducted here. Varieties as conceived in the original publication were regarded as regional variants of a type exhibiting minor proportional differences in the frequency of certain attributes. This study has not been able to establish that any given variety is common to several sites. At this stage of investigating the configurations of variation within the Pomranky point type, it will be more useful to designate the population by the site name and refer to the several variants of each population, as for instance "Kimmel variant 1" and "Kimmel variant 2." Later it may be demonstrated that these variants occur at multiple sites. Only then will it be valid to raise a population variant to the taxonomic position of a "variety."

The pattern of differences and similarities within a single site is not consistent except for the attribute of thickness. On the other hand, sites in which stone types A and Eastport chert occurred were roughly the same as regards flake blank orientation and the pattern of basal flaking. Both of these attributes are believed to reflect primarily patterns of flint knapping, and the observed similarities between sites sharing these two types of raw material may indicate a common source for the points as well as a single group of producers.

TABLE VI Comparison of Samples Within and Between Sites

Attributes	Comparison within a site (Sites)			Comparisons between sites (Stone types)			Totals	
	Pomranky A-G	Huron Beach	Kimmel A-G	Type G Pomranky, Kimmel, Huron B.	Type A Pomranky, Kimmel, Huron B.	Eastport chert	Same	Different
Blade shape	Different[a]	Same	Same	Different	Different	Same	3	3
Base shape	Same	Different	Different	Different	Different	Different	1	5
Flaking	Same	Same	Different	Different	Same	Same	4	2
Orientation	Different	Same	Different	Different	Same	Same	3	3
Length	Different	Same	Different	Different	Different	Different	1	5
Base width	Same	Different	Same	Different	Different	Same	3	3
Thickness	Same	Same	Same	Same	Same	Same	6	0
Total								Total
Same	4 +	5 +	3 = 12	1 +	3 +	5		= 9
Different	3 +	2 +	5 = 10	6 +	4 +	2		= 12

[a] An entry of "same" or "different" means that in chi-square calculations for the discrete attributes and variance analysis for the metrical attributes that the observed differences were or were not greater than would be expected to occur in 1 out of 20 samples drawn from a single population. Maximum width has not been included because comparable observations were not available from the Eastport site.

Tabulations of the number of observed cases of similarity or difference within any given attribute class should be an index of the relative rapidity of change or tendency to vary stylistically. Those attribute classes in which over 50% of the comparisons resulted in real differences are base shape and length; but blade shape, basal preparation, flake blank orientation, thickness, and basal width were found to vary 50% or less. The latter attributes (with the exception of blade shape) are believed to reflect basic flint knapping techniques, while the former attributes are believed to be more closely related to customary stylistic norms. These observations suggest that the greatest variation between the samples of Pomranky points can be attributed to minor variation in the statistical norms of stylistic phenomena for the region. Taking this clue as to the nature of the observed variability, it remains to determine what regularities, if any, characterize the regional configuration of variability. We want to determine if there is any correlation between the degree of variability and spatial separation between the samples, and whether there are any patterns of covariation between several independent attribute classes.

Comparative study was carried out for blade shape and the two attribute classes which were observed to vary the most between the several samples. Means were calculated for the variants of each site for blade length, and percentage frequencies for blade shape and base shape; these were then arranged in terms of systematic variation shown in Table VII.

It will be noted that in almost all cases variants from a single site fall together in the arrangement, suggesting that proximity is correlated with degree of similarity. When the three attribute classes are compared, it will be noted that for length, Kimmel and Eastport fall together with Pomranky and Huron Beach at the two extremes; whereas for blade shape, Huron Beach and Pomranky show the greatest similarities with Eastport and Kimmel at the extremes. On the basis of base shape, Huron Beach and Kimmel fall together with Eastport and Pomranky on the outer ends. This pattern suggests that the traits are sorting independently of one another and are not exhibiting any covariant shifts. Certainly the samples are not numerous enough to prove this suggestion. However, the general configuration which emerges is one in which variation increases with distance between loci for any given attribute, and attributes are sorting independently as regards "variant centers." This pattern is exactly what was postulated for the second model of cultural drift, namely the situation where there is a stable structure to the sociology and demography of the region as a whole. On the basis of these suggestions, we would then hypothesize that for the time-space span of the samples there was a major zone of interaction within which there was little demographic change or displacement of social units. This suggestion is directly counter to the recently postulated migrations and cultural expansions attributable to this region and span of time (Faulkner, 1962).

TABLE VII   *Systematic Variation of Stylistic Norms: Total Length, Blade Shape and Base Shape*

A. Total length (cm)

Site	Pomranky			Kimmel		Eastport	Huron Beach		
Variant No.	1	2	3	1	2		1	2	3
Name	Sag.	Swan Cr.	Mid.						
Total length	4.10	4.23	4.79	4.82	5.04	5.11	5.12	5.54	5.75

B. Blade shape (%)

Site	Eastport	Pomranky			Huron Beach	Kimmel	
Variant No.		1	3	2		1	2
Name		Sag.	Mid.	Swan Cr.			
Cont. ovate	0.00	3.29	0.86	7.25	5.17	0.00	0.00
Ovate	71.97	61.97	51.94	39.13	37.94	28.73	6.67
Excurvate	25.81	34.74	47.19	53.62	56.89	72.27	93.33

C. Base shape (%)

Site	Eastport	Kimmel		Huron Beach	Pomranky		
Variant No.		2	1		2	3	1
Name					Swan Cr.	Mid.	Sag.
Subconvex	8.51	22.88	23.33	14.24	39.13	43.81	55.20
Straight	85.11	69.49	53.33	42.37	27.53	25.97	22.17
Subconcave	6.38	7.62	23.33	43.36	33.33	26.41	22.62

General Summary

It has been shown that there are real differences between Pomranky points occurring as burial goods in single burials at three different sites. This differentiation within a single burial is interpreted as reflecting artifacts deriving from different areas and possibly representing contributions from several individuals. The meaning of the presence of contributed goods in these burials can, at present, not be fully evaluated. Research is currently being conducted at the University of Chicago on a comparative structural analysis of mortuary customs, which will, it is hoped, yield substantial correlations between the structure of burial ceremonialism and total social structure. Once this research has been completed, we will be in a better position to make inferential statements concerning the social significance of the contributed goods as grave furniture.

Study of the patterns of variation between the several sites and their recognized variants shows that demonstrably different variants occurring at a single site are more alike than variants manufactured of the same material or other materials occurring at different sites. In addition, it is suggested that for any given attribute there is a rough correlation between the degree of similarity and the spatial proximity of the samples, suggesting that the Pomranky points were locally manufactured and not widely traded. Analysis of the patterns of variability between separate attribute classes suggests that each attribute is sorting independently of the other, yielding a reticulate pattern of variability for the region as a whole with regard to several distinct attribute classes that are believed to be governed more by normative stylistic criteria than by flint knapping habits. Examination of the concept of cultural drift leads to the postulate that such a configuration of regional variation would be expected if the variation arose from discrepancies in the generational continuity between social units within the region. This lack of continuity would result in the appearance of real differences between populations, stemming from sampling error in the manifestations, between generations, of the range of individual variability in the execution of norms. The observed pattern would be expected to arise only when there was relative demographic and social stability within the zone of interaction between groups. The latter suggestion is contrary to recently published hypotheses which suggest major population movements and cultural intrusions during the period spanned by the material studied.

The concepts presented in this paper must certainly be viewed as hypotheses for testing. However, it is hoped that their presentation will serve as a suggestion of the potential which a well established and refined concept of cultural drift may hold for prehistoric research. Detailed studies of the regional patterns of variation may ultimately allow us to make statements about the processes of interaction and change within a region. They may serve as the basis for the definition of interaction zones and subregional style zones; this is a necessary step if we hope to isolate the archaeological remains of specific sociocultural systems and understand the structure of intergroup relations and the process of change and evolution.

Applications of the concept of cultural drift and postulates which can be derived from it are numerous. For instance, Pomranky points can most certainly be attributed to local manufacture since there is less variability for samples in greater proximity and they are manufactured of local materials. Frequently found in association with Pomranky points are large "knives," generally termed turkey tails (Ritzenhaler and Quimby, 1962), manufactured of material exclusively derived from southern Illinois and Indiana. It would be useful to know whether these items were introduced into the Michigan area as finished articles or whether the raw material alone was introduced. A detailed study of them should clear up the problem. If they were locally fabricated of exotic materials, drift should produce a similar configuration of variability as with the Pomranky points. On the other hand, if they were introduced as finished articles, a much different configuration should be demonstrable. There should be less variability on a regional basis, and similarity need not be a function of site proximity. Similarities would be more closely related to logistics networks than to proximity and hence continuity in shared learning experience. Certainly there are many such problems toward the solution of which the concept of cultural drift may be a useful analytical tool.

References

Aberle, David F. (1960). The influence of linguistics on early culture and personality theory. In *Essays in the Science of Culture: In Honor of Leslie A. White* (G. Dole and R. L. Carneiro, eds.), pp. 1–49. Crowell-Collier, New York.

Benedict, Ruth. (1934). *Patterns of Culture*. Houghton, New York.

Binford, Lewis R. (1963a). *The Pomranky Site: A Late Archaic Burial Station,* Anthropological Papers. Museum of Anthropology, University of Michigan No. 19, pp. 149–192.

Binford, Lewis R. (1963b). *A Proposed Attribute List for the Description and Classification of Projectile Points,* Anthropological Papers. Museum of Anthropology, University of Michigan No. 19, pp. 193–221.

Binford, Lewis R., and Mark Papworth. (1963). *The Eastport Site: Antrim County, Michigan,* Anthropological Papers. Museum of Anthropology, University of Michigan No. 19, pp. 71–123.

Eggan, Fred. (1941). Some aspects of culture change in the northern Philippines. *American Anthropologist* **43,** 11–18.

Eggan, Fred. (1962). Personal communication.

Faulkner, Charles H. (1962). The significance of some red ocher-like artifacts from Lake County, Indiana. *Wisconsin Archaeologist* **43,** 1–8.

Herskovits, Melville J. (1948). *Man and His Works.* Knopf, New York.

Mason, Ronald J. (1958). *Late Pleistocene Geochronology and the Paleo-Indian Penetration into the Lower Michigan Peninsula.* Anthropological Papers, No. 11. Museum of Anthropology, University of Michigan.

Papworth, Mark L. (1958). Artifacts from the Kimmel Site, Berrien Springs, Michigan. *Michigan Archaeologist* **4,** 51–56.

Ritzenthaler, Robert E., and George I. Quimby. (1962). The red ocher culture of the Upper Great Lakes and adjacent areas. *Fieldiana: Anthropology* **36,** 243–275.

Sapir, Edward. (1921). *Language.* Harcourt, New York.

Directionality in Archaeological Sequences [*]

The development of the scientific field of archaeology depends upon continued research into the significance of characteristics observed in the archaeological record to conditions which existed in the past. It is toward the furtherance of this development that this discussion is directed.

Archaeologists frequently encounter changes in the archaeological record which document a temporal sequence of prehistoric occupations at a single location. Commonly the nature of such occupational sequences results in the recognition of trends or sets of directional changes through the sequence. Increasing use of domesticated foods, or increasing or decreasing frequencies in technical or stylistic attributes are cases in point. Multicomponent sites characterized by such directional sequences are commonplace, and observable trends are normally viewed as indicative of changes in the structure or content of the cultural systems represented (see S. R. Binford, 1968). This interpretation is considered particularly secure if the same sequence recurs in a number of sites.

I suggest that this is not necessarily the case, and archaeologists must beware of making such an unqualified assumption. When systematic, directional, or regular changes are observed the archaeologist must seek to explain these observations in terms of the operation of systematic process in the past. However, I submit that there were processes operative in the past which may have influenced the patterning in archaeological deposits, and some of these may be totally or partially independent of the operation of evolutionary processes within cultural systems. Analogous archaeological situations may not always be processually homologous.

DIRECTIONALITY AND SUCCESSION

One such process is termed *succession* after an analogous concept in the field of ecology (Odom, 1953, p. 257). Succession refers to the process whereby the

---

* Not previously published.

characteristics of a location or particular topographic feature are altered by human occupation in such a way as to modify the appropriateness of the location for subsequent utilization in exactly the same fashion as before.

By way of illustration I will take an example drawn from my own excavations of prehistoric remains representing semisedentary horticultural societies once living in the forested areas of what is now southern Illinois. The site in question is Hatchery West (L. R. Binford *et al.,* 1966) located on the banks of the Kaskaskia river near the present town of Carlyle, Illinois. The site was completely excavated using a combination of hand techniques and power equipment. As far as the occupations to be discussed are concerned, an analysis of ceramic stylistic features failed to demonstrate any differences between the samples recovered from features and houses, suggesting that these remains had been constructed by essentially the same group of people over a relatively short period of time. On the other hand, data derived from observations on differential filling and the stratification of features supported the argument that at least three discrete occupations were represented. (For detailed justification of this argument, see L. R. Binford *et al.,* 1966, pp. 125-133.)

The initial settlement (Fig. 1) consisted of two dome shaped houses with extended entryways located on the periphery of a small circular activity area that contained two clusters of deep earth ovens, two clusters of shallow roasting pits, and a central cluster of features interpreted as facilities used in food preparation. The nature of the house construction, the remains of stored nuts, and the high incidence of deer and turkey bones in the roasting pits were viewed as indicative of fall–winter occupancy. With the termination of this occupation a short period elapsed before a second settlement was established of almost identical internal structure (Fig. 2). Two houses of the same type were located on the edges of the central activity area with two clusters of earth ovens, two clusters of shallow roasting pits, and again a central food preparation area. The contents of the features suggested a fall–winter occupation. The major difference between the two settlements was that the more recent one was larger. The latter settlement occupied 1001.8 m² compared to 804.3 m² for the earlier settlement.

After termination of the last settlement a short time elapsed and a settlement of very different form was established (Fig. 3). There were three houses, but this time two of them were constructed with heavy vertical wall posts widely spaced. The third was a small dome-shaped structure. The larger of the houses with vertical post construction exhibited an oval "longhouse" plan enclosing a little over three times the floor space of the earlier dome-shaped houses. Judging from its construction, it was partially open, more on the order of a ramada or sun shade than a tight, heat-retaining house. The areal extent of the settlement was over twice the size of the earliest settlement, 1726.4 m² compared to 804.3 m². This settlement lacked deep earth ovens or storage pits characteristic of the

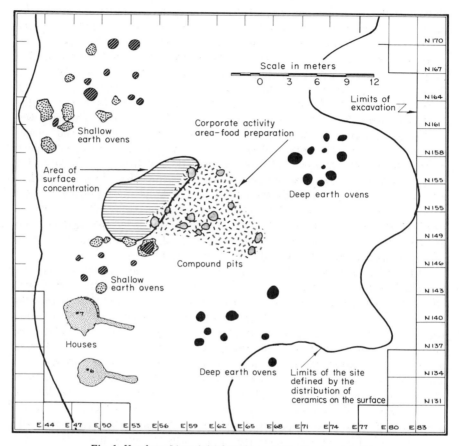

Fig. 1. *Hatchery West, initial settlement. (Author's original.)*

earlier occupations. Shallow roasting pits and cooking features were present, but the contents of the latter were very different from the contents of the features in the earlier settlements. Cooking features contained relatively large quantities of mussel shell, and large mammal bone were infrequent in the roasting pits. In addition there was a higher density of broken ceramics associated with the features and a higher density of miscellaneous post molds and smudge pits (see L. R. Binford, 1967). Further differences were noted in the frequency of spalls broken from flint hoes. These exhibited a clustered surface distribution taken as indicative of the location of a small field or garden in the southern half of the settlement, essentially covering the area of the earlier winter occupations. The overall characteristics of this settlement were judged to be indicative of spring–summer occupation.

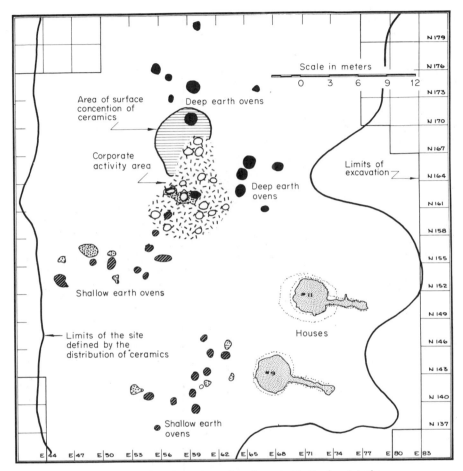

Fig. 2. Hatchery West, second settlement. (Author's original.)

Through this sequence there is a trend toward ever-increasing size of settlement and a major change in the manner in which this particular location was utilized: initial small winter occupations followed by a larger spring–summer occupation where horticultural activities were conducted. These data have served as the basis of an argument for the operation of successional processes.

It was argued that initially a small clearing was enlarged in the forest for the first winter settlement. During the period of occupancy the clearing was enlarged further as a result of collecting wood for construction and for fuel during the cold months. When the second winter settlement was established, the occupants enjoyed a larger clearing and took advantage of this, as seen in the larger size of

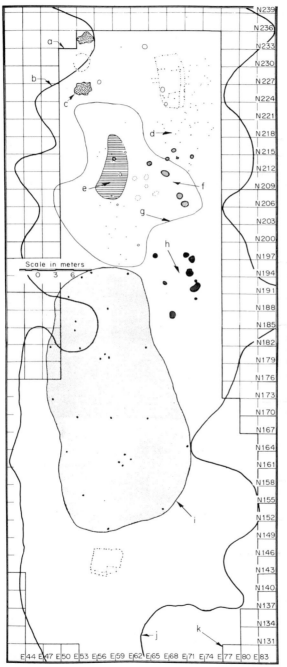

Fig. 3. Hatchery West, last settlement. a, Limits of the excavation; b, Limits of the site defined by the presence of ceramics; c, Shallow stain; d, Concentration of post molds; e, Highest ceramic density >20/sg.; f, Compound pit for food preparation; g, Limits of ceramic concentration; h, Shallow earth ovens; i, Probable location of field based on hoe chip distribution; j, Limits of the site defined by the surface distribution of ceramics; k, Limits of excavation. (Author's original)

the second settlement. During the second term of óccupation, the clearing was enlarged further as a result of normal exploitation of adjacent forest resources. After the abandonment of the second settlement, the clearing was of sufficient size to be attractive for summer occupation where a sizable area of cleared land was available for horitcultural gardens. Given the argument that available cleared land was a major characteristic considered in the selection of locations for summer farming sites, we might expect that the sequence of events recorded at Hatchery West is not a unique case, but could be duplicated at numerous other locations in the region.

Under traditional interpretative frames of reference, the gross differences between the earlier and later settlements at Hatchery West would most certainly be viewed as indicative of culture change, with possibly some speculation regarding the abrupt appearance of a "longhouse"-type of social organization. If parallel sequences were discovered in the region, arguments postulating gross cultural changes or possibly population replacements would most certainly be accepted as secure.

The successional argument given has not been tested; nevertheless, it accounts in an economic fashion for the archaeologically made observations and therefore warrants equal consideration with alternative propositions which argue that the observed sequence characterized by an abrupt change in settlement type is indicative of cultural changes or the replacement of the cultural systems represented by the earlier settlements.

DIRECTIONALITY AND GROWTH

The second process by which phenomena not necessarily related to organizational change in cultural systems might condition archaeological stratification or superpositioning is a growth process. This example is drawn from an argument presented by Maddox (1969) regarding the process of population radiation of Yupic-speaking Eskimos along the upper Kuskukwin river of west central Alaska. Maddox has argued that the Yupic-speaking Eskimos radiated up the river systems from an original coastal habitat in which they had adapted to the exploitation of sea mammals and anadronomous fishes. Settlements were essentially sedentary, characterized by a number of dispersed satellite locations occupied periodically for taking fish (fish camps). As population increased and new permanent settlements were established at points further up river, selection for the location of these villages was in terms of the optimal conditions along the river for taking fish, the same criteria which governed the location of dispersed fish camps prior to the segmentation of a sedentary community. Maddox argued there would be a high probability that permanent villages would be located on the sites of earlier fish camps.

In any archaeological situation of stratification or superpositioning at a permanent village, the lower levels of the site would contain the functionally specific tools and features characteristic of fish camps. The upper levels, in contrast, would contain a diverse tool assemblage of features. A regular superposition of sedentary villages on top of previously occupied fish camps would give the impression of culture change when viewed archaeologically. A "culture" of dispersed fishing peoples was replaced by a more complex sedentary "culture" of different form. If Maddox is correct, viewed archaeologically this particular situation of regular or directional change would not necessarily be indicative of an organizational change in the cultural system represented. The appearance of such would be created by (1) a high degree of isomorphism between the criteria used in selecting sites for fish camps and sedentary villages; (2) at any point in time, the wide dispersion of fish camps with respect to any given sedentary village; (3) population growth and regular segmentation of local villages with daughter communities established further and further upriver; and (4) a high probability that new communities would be established on locations of previously occupied fish camps.

DIRECTIONALITY, SUCCESSION, AND COMPOUNDED PROCESSES

A third example of situations in which directional change in archaeological remains might be unrelated to general cultural change is developed with regard to bounded locations such as caves and rockshelters. In this case environmental change and/or succession are considered.

Caves and rockshelters are natural facilities (see Wagner, 1960, p. 94) which have been occupied for the protected and sheltered life space which they provide. Normally, these locations are characterized by accretional filling resulting from the accumulation of habitational debris as well as filling that might occur as a by-product of the instability of the structure of the cave itself. The process of filling, if uninterrupted, can substantially modify the amount of sheltered life space which the cave or shelter offers at different points in time during its occupational history. A model of a geologically stable rockshelter might be something as follows.

1. Initial occupation begins at some point after stabilization with regard to the processes which were operative to create the shelter.

2. With initial occupation the accumulation of occupational debris begins over what, under normal conditions, would be a maximum area of sheltered floor space.

3. With continued use there is an accretional buildup of occupational debris resulting in the formation of a truncated deposit with an external slope being maintained by erosional processes at an angle of roughly 60°.

4. As the deposit continues to accumulate there is a gradual and regular

decrease in the amount of level, sheltered floor space available for subsequent use.

What are the implications of this type of phenomena as a conditioner for the regular occurrence of different types of occupation during the history of the accumulation of the deposit? Let us consider the situation of a region and time period characterized by human occupants following a hunting and gathering form of subsistence.

Normally hunters and gatherers are characterized by an annual round of seasonal movements during which the size of the group does not remain constant. A common pattern is one in which there is an aggregation of persons in relatively large social units during productive periods of the annual food cycle. The group breaks down into smaller, widely dispersed social units during periods of low productivity. Base camp locations serving as the residential center of operations for social units would be expected to vary seasonally both in location (as a function of group movements during an annual round), size (as a function of variable group sizes during different phases of the annual round), and content (as a function of the performance of different tasks during different phases of the annual round). We would expect that there would be seasonal variations in the mean amount of floor space needed to accommodate different types of social units during an annual cycle, varying directly with the annual variations in group composition. Insofar as different activities characterized the camp life of groups of different sizes during different phases of the annual cycle, we would expect there to be some correlation between group sizes, sheltered floor space requirement, and content of archaeological assemblages. Complications arise when we recognize that in addition to base camps, the adaptive system of any group during any phase of the annual cycle normally includes a wide variety of activities conducted by task-oriented groups such as hunting parties, collecting parties, etc., whose life space requirements while away from the base camp would be highly variable, depending upon the sizes of such groups. The archaeological remains left by task-specific groups at different locations would be expected to vary with the nature of the tasks performed.

Against this generalized model of hunting and gathering adaptations we may reasonably anticipate a set of patterned differences in the content of archaeological assemblages varying directly with the amount of sheltered life space available to accommodate groups of different sizes at bounded locations such as caves or rockshelters. In the context of these expectations it is easy to see how a process which operated to regularly decrease the amount of sheltered space could modify the appropriateness of the location for occupation by groups of variable size. In the case of our idealized history of the accumulation of an archaeological deposit we can expect that initial occupations might be base camps for a society during the season of the year when food was most abundant.

As the deposit accumulates and the amount of available floor space diminishes, the appropriateness of the shelter for continued occupation by a large group will diminish until it gradually will be occupied by groups of smaller and smaller sizes: a family camp, possibly later a hunting camp, and finally, simply a stopping place or transient camp for mobile work groups or moving hunters. The changes in the composition of the archaeological record at the location will vary in accordance with the different tasks performed by social units organized into increasingly smaller units through time. The archaeologist excavating the site will observe a sequence of changes through the deposit, many of which might well be directional in nature and possibly duplicated at other locations. These trends, given the conditions outlined, will occur archaeologically even in the absence of structural changes in the societies. All that is implied in this particular hypothetical case is a redistribution of the sociocultural unit in the habitat.

In practice the archaeologist may rarely encounter a situation in which sufficient time has passed for the necessary modification in a cave to occur in the absence of any culture change. In situations where successional processes are operative at a specific location and evolutionary changes are going on simultaneously in the sociocultural systems represented at the location, the significance of observed variability in the archaeological record to past conditions and events becomes a complicated and difficult problem for the archaeologist to solve.

Other complications arise in areas where cave or shelter morphology is undergoing change during the period of occupancy. A good example of this situation is the French cave of Combe Grenal excavated by François Bordes (1961). In this case the occupational history runs from the Riss glaciation through the termination of the Würm II (in the French chronology) ice advance. The morphology of the cave was modified radically at least three times due to sloughing off the back wall and periodic roof fall. These modifications certainly resulted in periodic increases and decreases in the amount of sheltered life space. The process of cave modification proceeded at different rates in direct response to climatic fluctuations occurring in the context of glacial advances and retreats. There were three periods of radical change in the form of the cave, in each case followed by extended periods when the morphology of the cave remained relatively stable.

One can visualize a situation where occupation began during a period of relative cave stability. Succession begins with the gradual accumulation of deposits and correlated changes in floor space and its effects on the appropriateness of the location for accommodating groups of variable size. With glacially induced environmental changes the geologic processes operating to modify the form of the cave were stepped up so that the rates of attrition of the cave walls resulting from frost action and large rock falls substantially modified the form of the cave and changed considerably the amount of sheltered floor space. This change would act to interrupt the pattern of succession characteristic of the prior period of relative cave stability with the result that the cave may again be appropriate for occupancy by large groups of people. With a slowing down of the geological processes of cave modification the successional sequence may begin again, with a replication of the previous occupation history insofar as it was in response to successional changes. Such a set of conditions could result in an alternation of archaeological assemblages with an apparent absence of directional changes characteristic of the overall occupational sequence. Occupations characterized by one complement of tools might find their closest analogs in subsequent occupations separated by intervening assemblages of different form.

The cave of Combe-Grenal is in fact characterized by a lack of demonstrable directional changes in the sequence of occupations (Bordes, 1961, p. 808) and is a classic example of the alternation of archaeological assemblages which has been demonstrated for a number of middle Paleolithic cave locations in the glaciated sections of western Europe. It has been argued elsewhere that the variations demonstrable among middle Paleolithic assemblages derive primarily from differences in activities that were conducted at the various locations by middle Paleolithic populations (L. R. Binford and Binford, 1966). It is suggested here that the nature of the activities conducted may vary regularly with the size and organizational composition of social units and that a major variable tending to structure the frequency with which certain activities were conducted was the amount of available floor space for accommodating social units of varying sizes. The operation of successional processes at any given location is suggested as a determinant for some of the patterns of variation observed among different sites or between different living surfaces at a single site. No implications for culture change are necessary. I do not wish to argue that these variables are the only ones responsible for the anomalous alternation of industries demonstrable for the middle Paleolithic from western Europe. All that is implied is that they should be seriously considered as potential contributing factors, and until their contributions have been evaluated we are in a poor position to make assertions about the significance of the observed differences between assemblages as measures of population movements, gross changes in cultural systems, or changes in forms of adaptation.

Summary

It has been argued that directional trends and changes observable in sequences of occupations at specific sites may frequently arise as a by-product of the operation of processes not directly related or necessarily relevant to changes in the structure and form of sociocultural systems. Successional processes whereby the characteristics of a specific location or particular topographic feature are gradually altered by human activities in such a way as to modify the appropriateness of the location for continued utilization in a constant fashion have been suggested as one such process. Two examples were offered.

The first described the situation where successive winter occupations increased the amount of cleared land, conditioning the appropriateness of the location for subsequent utilization as a spring–summer farming site. The second example dealt with the situation where the accreational filling of a bounded location such as a cave or rockshelter might well result in a regular decrease, or increase, in the amount of sheltered life space. Such directional changes in turn condition the appropriateness of the location for accommodating social units of differing sizes. Insofar as size of group and organization of activities varied seasonally we might expect to observe directional changes in the artifact composition of archaeological accumulations at such locations.

Systematic growth in the absence of organizational change or evolution was suggested as another process which could result in regular sequences of archaeological assemblages at specific locations. The replacement of functionally specific fish camps by permanent sedentary villages in the context of population radiation was given as an example.

Finally it was suggested that successional processes might work in conjunction with other regular processes such as environmental changes. In this case, caves and rockshelters were discussed in the context of glacial advances and retreats. Such synchronous processes could result in alternations of industries as noted for the middle Paleolithic of western Europe.

These examples of situations in which successional, growth, or local environmental changes may operate serve to point up the need for archaeologists working with remains from the simplest to the most complex sociocultural systems to devise methods for controlling these potentially important variables before assuming that an observed sequence of directional variability actually records processes of systemic change of differentiation among the cultural units represented.

In addition to the passive role which succession might play in generating changes in the archaeological record, it might also operate so as to initiate conditions promoting evolutionary change in cultural systems themselves. For example let us consider a Pleistocene human population establishing itself in a region and taking advantage of the natural facilities (caves and rockshelters) as protected locations for settlement. Gradually, over long periods of time, in areas where the natural processes operating to produce caves and shelters were not active, succession could result in the gradual depletion of these natural facilities as adequate accommodations for human settlement. Under such conditions strong selective pressures might operate favoring an alteration in the group structure or the development of cultural means for providing protected life space in the form of housing. This type of feedback has probably acted in the past. Arguments recently advanced regarding the role played by increasing salination in irrigated fields of the Near East for modifying the basic subsistence patterns of that area (Adams, 1960, p. 290) as well as arguments about overgrazing by domesticated flocks acting to change the effective environments of human groups are additional cases in point. Past and contemporary problems commonly considered under the rubric of "Man's role in changing the face of the Earth" (Thomas, 1956) can frequently be considered in the context of feedback systems initiated as a by-product of the operation of successional processes. Investigation of these contributors to culture change can only realistically be evaluated in the context of knowledge regarding the kinds of conditioning processes which have in fact operated in the past.

I urge archaeologists to consider sequential variability in the archaeological record at specific locations as potentially informative on the operation of a number of distinct processes. The assumption of archaeological interpretation that variability in the content of superpositioned or stratified occupational surfaces is a direct measure of cultural change or differences between independent cultural systems is questioned in the above discussion. The validity of the assumption questioned as well as the exceptional conditions discussed have not been investigated by archaeologists. Until archaeologists accept the challenge of investigating the character of the archaeological record itself, concerning themselves with understanding the conditions in the past which produced the features which we observe today, we will gain little if any accurate knowledge of the past and make little progress in accomplishing the generally accepted aims of archaeological science.

References

Adams, Robert M. (1960). Early civilizations, subsistence, and environment. In *City Invincible* (C. H. Kreeling and R. M. Adams, eds.), pp. 269–295. Univ. of Chicago Press, Chicago.

Binford, Lewis R. (1967). Smudge pits and hide smoking: The use of analogy in archaeological reasoning. *American Antiquity* **32**, 1–12.

Binford, Lewis R., and Sally R. Binford. (1966). A preliminary analysis of functional variability in the Mousterian of Levallois facies. *American Anthropologist* **68**, 238–295.

Binford, Lewis R., Sally R. Binford, Robert C. Whallon, and Margret Hardin. (1966). Archaeology at Hatchery West. *Southern Illinois University Museum Archaeological Salvage Report* No. 25.

Binford, Sally R. (1968). Variability and change in the near eastern Mousterian of Levallois facies. In *New Perspectives in Archeology* (S. R. Binford and L. R. Binford, eds.), pp. 49–60. Univ. of Chicago Press, Chicago.

Bordes, François H. (1961). Mousterian cultures in France. *Science* **134**, 803–810.

Burgess, Ernest W (1925). The growth of the city: An introduction to a research project. In *The City* (R. R. Park, E. W. Burgess, and R. D. McKenzie, eds.), pp. 47–62. Univ. of Chicago Press, Chicago.

Maddox, Darryl M. (1969). The distribution of Kuskowagamiut fishcamps. Unpublished manuscript.

Odum, Eugene P. (1953). *Fundamentals of Ecology,* 2nd ed. Saunders, Philadelphia, Pennsylvania.

Thomas, William L. (1956). *Man's Role in Changing the Face of the Earth.* Univ. of Chicago Press, Chicago.

Wagner, Phillip. (1960). *The Human Use of the Earth.* Free Press, Glencoe, Illinois.

Part IV

ANALYSIS

When I started to emphasize Taylor's point—the need to isolate through analysis relationships between things and characteristics of things—I had a very limited perspective. As I worked on greater numbers of bodies of empirical data, what began as a kind of tentative belief became for me an overwhelming truth. We have no notion of what are the limitations of the archaeological record with regard to the information potentially recoverable. I can recall working seemingly endless hours on projectile points. I had started the analysis armed with Spaulding's article "The Statistical Discovery of Artifact Types" (1953). Things appeared so straightforward in Spaulding's presentation: Artifact types were associated clusters of attributes. All we had to do was use the proper statistical methods, and we should be able to specify in concrete terms the associational clusters.

The complexities I had found appeared as impediments, as stumbling blocks. How could I talk of projectile point types when what I had successfully isolated were haft types, types of flint working, blade types—each of which might have two or more patterned size clusters. Organizational regularity at the level of the entity itself seemed not to exist! I can recall Bordes reporting to me that Hallam Movius had concluded that artifact types didn't exist. Bordes laughed as I did but I suspect that my more gentle laughter was prompted by a very different perspective. I knew that Hallam Movius was trying "attribute analysis" on his materials from the site of Abri Pataud. I had been there; I had once whispered similarly depressing conclusions to Mark Papworth.

Organizational phenomena are quite complex; there are organizations within organizations. I had been working with a selected sample of projectile points, only those that could meet the criteria for inclusion in the type category "Lamoka Point." When I expanded my universe to include points of very different morphology, different types in traditionalist typologies, I found a very different kind of attribute patterning. I could speak of classes of projectile points sharing a common range of attribute variability, clearly distinct from others. I also found that some of the organizational properties isolated while working only within the "Lamoka type" varied independently of my organizationally distinct classes of entities. There were discretely bounded classes; there were patterns of variability distributed as a gradient of variation; there were morphologically distinct classes recognizable to the eye which on analysis demonstrably had no organizational integrity. All the clustered attributes varied independently and were distributed in common with other classes of artifacts. These complexities appeared to me at first as depressing surprises. As I did more work and gradually freed myself from traditionalist expectations, I realized that all these complexities were potential sources of new and different kinds of information about the past. Archaeologists had explored the archaeological record for years by searching for new and previously unknown content. We had just begun to explore the archaeological record for differences and ranges of variability in the structural properties of organizational phenomena themselves. Who knew where such investigations might lead and what new kinds of information and understanding might be forthcoming?

Several kinds of advances might be made in the area of analysis. One clear-cut advance might be the development of better ways of recognizing and expressing relationships between variables. One of my first achievements in this area was in the application of regression analysis to data previously summarized as percentage frequency variations per unit of time. Archaeologists must explore the statistical and mathematical techniques available from other fields in order to increase their abilities in isolating and measuring relationships. This kind of searching is clearly demonstrated in my Kaolin pipe stem paper. Experimenting with statistical techniques has occupied much of my research time, and in some cases the results are clearly evident in my published papers. Much experimenting was done by my students at Chicago, and my current students at New Mexico are again engaged in this form of experimentation. The integration of statistical approaches in archaeology was inevitable, given the availability of computers and the increasing bodies of empirical data with which archaeologists had to cope. This kind of experimentation and the generation of clear advances on this analytical form have been made by many persons not involved in the New Archaeology as I viewed it—an attack on theory and unscientific "conventionalist" strategies of interpretation. I have heard comments from critics: "I am a 'New Archaeologist,' but I don't buy Binford's theory and approaches," meaning that he has used factor analysis, a chi-square, or even possibly read Haggett's book on locational analysis. My feeling always was, "so what: what questions are you asking and what 'interpretations' do you offer for relationships isolated or explicated by your application of modern analytical procedures?" In many cases I could detect no change.

This was essentially my response to David Clarke's *Analytical Archaeology* (1968). He had adopted the statistical procedures of Sokal and Sneath (1963), the sophisticated locational approaches of Peter Haggett (1966), and the "metalanguage" of systems theory, but all of this was integrated into a traditionalist paradigm of "culture." He cited much of my work, he talked of "systems of subsystems," and even entered a few cautions about possible alternative sources of variability in the archaeological record, yet his entire model was in essence what I have outlined in "Models and Paradigms." Assemblage types, artifact types, etc., were to be arranged into a systematics based on measured degrees of similarity as a basis for reconstruction of culture history. Culture is patterned; patterning is cultural. Degrees of similarity in patterning, measured primarily in terms of associations, are a measure of cultural affinity. What progress had been made? I could see very little beyond the hope that as archaeologists did more analysis using statistical procedures, it might dawn on them that their paradigm was outmoded.

Another advance which we may clearly make through analysis is the recognition of organizational properties not previously recognized as components of the archaeological record. This may derive from various kinds of analysis as well as from refined methods of looking, such as the development of better data collection techniques, etc. The "Indian Sites and Chipped Stone Materials" paper is an example of this kind of progress. I had been working on flint materials and the problem of flint working techniques for some time when I had the opportunity of going over collections made by George Quimby from sites in the northern Lake Michigan area. I recognized a kind of artifact which I had not previously noted in my researches in Great Lakes prehistory. I attempted to describe in detail its morphological properties, and we discussed its temporal and spatial distribution as it was then known. I offered some interpretive hypotheses. Surprisingly enough, after these were recognized and pointed out as a feature of the archaeological record to be observed, archaeologists began to identify them in many places and from time periods not previously documented. Some archaeologists pointed out with great glee that Quimby and I were wrong; such little cores were found in association with Paleo-Indian materials! Quimby and I had generalized that they were distributed with Late Woodland materials! our generalizations were accurate, given the data base from which they were made. It was not until others began to look for these items that an accurate generalization about their distribution could be made.

This paper provides us with a case for introducing the more important subject relating to analysis: What significance is ascribed to observations made on the archaeological record? When I analyzed the small "bipolar" cores I argued that their significance was as cores and not necessarily as tools used in processing other raw materials. Other archaeologists were of differing opinion. The most common interpretation in the New World has been that these items were tools used as "wedges." After I had recognized them in the Great Lakes material I began to find that other archaeologists before me had recognized them. In the French literature they had been described quite early by Bardon and Bouyssonie (1906). They had been recognized in Australia by McCarthy (1941). They occur in Africa both north and south of the Sahara (Tixier, 1963, p. 799; Leakey, 1931, p. 174). They occur apparently as early as the assemblages at Choukoutien (Pei, 1939). Suggestions and opinions as to their significance have varied widely: chisels (Malan, 1942, p. 119); adzes (Clark, 1958, p. 149); pressure flakers (Leakey, 1953, p. 63); retouchers or flake-tool fabricators (Leakey, 1931, p. 130); and wedges (Fitting, 1970, p. 43).

Most of these interpretations were based either on analogies with modern tools, the ability to use the tools themselves for certain acts, and opinions reasoned from morphology. At the time no ethnographic analogies were known for these items. J. Peter White during recent research on industrial techniques among peoples of the Western Highlands of New Guinea found that among the Duna speakers near Lake Kopiago these little cores were still being produced.

> The other method of flaking used a bipolar technique, in which the core is held vertically on an anvil and pounded until it shatters. A variant of this involves wrapping a strip of thin bark several times around the core and holding this instead of the stone while flaking. Once the core is shattered (the detaching of one or two flakes is insufficient), the bark is unwrapped and the broken material tipped into the palm of the hand to be picked over. Flakes deemed suitable for tools are kept, small, unsuitable flakes discarded, and the core is re-wrapped for further flaking. The same platforms are usually re-used . . . . The result of flaking broken flint nodules in this way is that thin rather squarish cores with bruising and splintering at both ends are sometimes produced . . . . Among the Duna these cores are not used at all. They are waste material (White, 1968, pp. 660–661).

Examination of White's data and fine photographs and personal discussion with him have convinced me that these are morphologically the same items I reported in the article written with Quimby.

The situation stands as follows: (1) Similar morphological forms have been described from sites covering a wide range, both temporally and spatially. (2) Almost without exception in each provincial area there is a different prevailing opinion as to what these signify in terms of past activities and tool use. (3) A single ethnographic case exists where such forms were actually being produced as part of a flint technology. In this case these forms were the by-products of flint working and not tools themselves. (4) A single subsequent analytical treatment of these has been provided by McPherron (1967 pp. 132–144) in which he points out some differences between his material and the sample described by me. He also notes some attributes which he feels vary in a significant manner, indicative of possible use of these cores as tools. With the exception of White on the Australian materials, no one has attempted to test any of the propositions advanced regarding supposed "function" and only McPherron (1967) has thus far done any detailed morphological comparisons. It is quite likely that the basic bipolar technique is common to these forms wherever they are found. Differences might be expected in the degree that the residual core itself or different kinds of by-products were selected for further modification or use. This is just one of the innumerable cases in the archaeological literature where there are many opinions, much interpersonal backbiting between persons holding differing opinions, but no attempts to answer the questions posed. What were these things used for? Are they all alike? How do we understand differences which might be demonstrable?

The same problem faces the archaeologist whether he is analyzing artifacts, features, or assemblages. The traditionalist paradigm made assumptions about the significance of variability at the level of the assemblage. Traditionalists are generally quite certain they know what variability means at that level of comparison, but few are willing to assert that they know what variability signifies at the artifact level. Most traditionalists recognize that artifacts were tools or must have been used for something, yet they militantly argue that knowledge of their functions is beyond our abilities to understand the past. "The functional approach to accounting for differences is not applicable, since we simply do not possess a single shred of reliable evidence bearing on the possible function(s) of the various categories of tools found in Lower and Middle Palaeolithic assemblages" (Movius, 1969, p. 307). There seems to be the general impression that the farther back in time we go, the less accurate or reliable our knowledge becomes. I think this is nonsense; the only way we gain reliable information about the past is through our ability to confirm or refute the ideas we put forth about the past. I see no reason why the idea that the bipolar cores in use in recent times were "wedges" should be more reliable than the notion that most sidescrapers in Late Acheulian assemblages of Africa were used as knives commonly employed in butchering tasks. In this case the data presented by Clark and Haynes (1970) is more impressive to me than are the opinions advanced by some workers in the Great Lakes area.

This particular case points up another interesting feature of archaeological reasoning. As I pointed out in "Models and Paradigms," the Levallois "problem" offered archaeologists one of the first potential challenges to the traditionalist paradigm. In that case there were few problems in distinguishing cores from tools. Assemblage comparisons are conventionally made on the basis of relative tool frequencies. Cores, chipping debris, etc., if used in comparison, are treated as independent units of comparison, as are the frequencies of technical attributes indicative of the use of the Levallois technique. In the case of the bipolar cores, do we treat them as phenomena independent of the assemblage defined on the bases of tool categories? All we have is opinions. Information is clearly needed in order to make a decision even within the context of traditionalist strategies. It is interesting to me that traditionalists are willing to acknowledge that they are sufficiently knowledgeable of the past to recognize tools from by-products of industrial acts and insist that assemblages be defined in terms of tools, yet for some strange reason they exclude utilized flakes from most comparisons! Most archaeological methods of analysis are rooted in (1) a series of opinions varying widely in their probable validity and (2) a series of conventions which may or may not bear any relationship to the organizational properties of the archaeological record.

Analysis and the recognition of relationships between things, attributes, and the recognition of varying levels and forms of organizational patterning demand that we attempt their explanation.

The archaeological record is a static, contemporary phenomenon. When we investigate it, explore it, and look at it we are making observations on a contemporary phenomenon. The only way such contemporary observations are converted into statements about the past is through our ability to retrodict—to establish on the basis of present evidence what were the conditions in the past which produced the contemporary observations (paraphrased from Hempel, 1965, p. 173). Our ability to do this accurately and defensibly depends on our skills in scientific explanation. "Scientific explanation, prediction, and post-diction (retrodiction) all have the same logical character; they show that the fact under consideration can be inferred from certain other facts by means of specified general laws" (Hempel, 1965, p. 176).

Our ability to engage in postdiction, or retrodiction, if you prefer, depends upon our abilities to devise models of the conditions (facts) obtaining in the past which if true, given the validity of certain "laws," would permit us to deduce with accuracy the character of the observations made at the contemporary time. This means that the archaeologist must be continuously engaged in the development of "models" of the past, specifying the conditions which if true would accommodate our observations in the present. If we observe organized or patterned relationships, referable exclusively to human behavior, between things in our contemporary observations on the archaeological record, they must derive from organized or systemic properties of behavioral systems as they existed in the past. Thus many of our endeavors result in what I will call systems-specific models.

Examples of this type of modeling are seen in the three papers dealing with burials. In addition they represent something of a continuum in the development of models. In "An Analysis of Cremations from Three Michigan Sites," I was primarily concerned with understanding observable differences in the properties of cremated bone itself as a clue to understanding different conditions under which bodies had been cremated in the past. Experimentation was employed which, although minimal in terms of good research design, has been reconfirmed on several occasions since this work was done. I was concerned with establishing the validity of empirical "laws" regarding formal modification in bone under conditions of cremation. In the second paper, "A Cremated Burial from the Riverside Cemetery," I offer certain suggestions as to the possible social significance of comparisons noted between burial features as such. In the third paper, "Analysis of a Mortuary Complex," I further develop sociological models which if true would account for the observations made. Models such as these may serve many functions. First they may be subjected to several kinds of testing. Clearly the testing of the assumptions or statements which function in the logic as "laws" is one obvious approach and one which is badly needed in archaeological science. The other is the testing of the model by predictive statements regarding future observations to be made on the archaeological record. This is seen in ,'Analysis of a Mortuary Complex." I had the rare thrill of confirming some of my predictions after this analysis was completed through subsequent excavation of Mississippian burials at Hatchery West (see L. R. Binford, *et al.,* 1970, pp. 66–69).

Advances in our understanding of the past and the significance which we may justifiably attribute to variations noted in the archaeological record will only be made through the development of sophisticated archaeological theory rooted in confirmed propositions regarding the significance of our contemporary observations to conditions which existed in the past.

Thus far in my writings, I have not offered systems-specific models for assemblage variability. I have offered certain arguments regarding the organization and probable features to be expected in the adaptive systems characteristic of the remote past [see L. R. Binford and Binford (1966) and S. R. Binford and Binford (1969) and the "Models and Paradigms" paper, this volume, pp. 244–294]. From such arguments one can deduce certain expectations regarding the patterning in intersite comparisons and ranges of variability which one might observe as characteristic of such systems, but no specific models for the concrete data have been presented. It is hoped that some will result from my forthcoming analysis of the Combe Grenal Mousterian data so graciously supplied to me by François Bordes.

The last paper in this section is a very different kind of argument. It is a step toward a processual model of evolutionary change. I have written strongly in favor of the development of greater processual understanding and have urged that such understanding should be a major aim. I have even suggested that the accurate reconstruction of culture history is dependent upon the development of such understanding. Some are making only the first feeble steps in this direction. It is not an easy task and not one that can be accomplished by a simple change of perspective. It will require a great deal of work. In the process I look forward to an enormous expansion of our understanding of the past.

For instance, in order to begin to isolate from the archaeological record that variability which is *relevant* as a monitor of systemic process, we must gain a much greater understanding of the significance of variability itself. This will of course contribute to the development of a stronger body of archaeological theory. In addition we must be continually attempting to evaluate the relevance of materials as measures of some postulated determinant dimension so that such things as population growth, etc., may be treated as variables with measured values. This means that a great deal of "model building" at the processual level must be attempted, operationalized, and tested. Modeling is sometimes a deceiving business. I have had the experience of generating what I thought of as a model, only to realize that what I had generated was a cognitive map, a set of descriptive categories in terms of which I could talk about data but which did not have the properties of dimensions that could be operationalized beyond the empirical cases which they subsumed. Any science must, of course, develop a "metalanguage" as it advances in the recognition of relevant phenomena and becomes more sophisticated in the development of models. However, there is a big difference between this and what some persons accept as explanation.

I have often thought that the fields of sociology and, in many ways, anthropology followed a strategy of refining their cognitive maps so as to be able to accommodate greater and greater numbers and kinds of observations to a common cognitive system. If phenomena could be accommodated to such cognitive classes as "status seeking," "diffusion," or "negative feedback," some kind of understanding was produced. Terms such as these are generated in a taxonomy developed for the accommodation of different forms of recognized patterning. These are typological statements for forms that relationships may take when viewed distributionally. They have similarities to such terms as "normal curve," the latter referring to the distribution of values among a series of cases, the former referring to the forms manifest in the distributional patterning of relationships between components of either behavioral episodes or artifact classes of two or more variables viewed against a temporal and/or spatial reference dimension. These are descriptive categories, developed as components of a cognitive map for accommodating different kinds of observations. Systems theorists make use of such a metalanguage for making possible the recognition and understandable communication of common kinds of relational patterning shared among organizational components of natural systems regardless of their particular form. This metalanguage, as well as that developed in the ecological branch of other disciplines, serves the function of communication among persons who may hold very different theoretical positions when it comes to the explanation of the relationships elucidated and distinguished by these common cognitive devices. The development of a new form or adoption of the "metalanguage" of systems theorists by archaeologists engaged in the search for relationships (as opposed to things) is almost inevitable. We have just begun to explore the archaeological record for forms of relationship; many previously unrecognized forms of patterning are almost certainly going to be isolated and recognized, an example of which is explicated in "Models and Paradigms." As this kind of progress is made, it is tempting to feel that some kind of "explanation" has been achieved when such a relationship can be accommodated to a familiar cognitive unit, a term or phrase. Similarly the naming of a recognized form of patterning may frequently be viewed as an "explanation" if one can present a plausible model for the patterning. One point which cannot be overemphasized is that mathematical or cognitive techniques for *describing* recognized forms of patterning and distributional phenomena are just that— *descriptive*. Explanations for observed forms may take very different forms, depending upon the nature of the relationships described or the nature of the variables studied distributionally.

Let me give an example. If one counts the frequency of heads versus tails in a series of coin-flipping episodes and plots these relative frequencies for a large number of cases, one will find that the distribution of variability assumes the form of a normal or "1" curve. There are few episodes where all incidences of coin flipping resulted in 100% heads and similarly there are few cases where all incidences resulted in 100% tails; greater numbers of cases are encountered as one approaches the 50–50 relationship from both sides of the heads-versus-tails end of the curve. On the other hand, if one measures the body height of adult males in a local, breeding population and plots the distribution of these values, they too will take the form of a normal curve: few cases of extremely short and few cases of extremely tall, with more and more cases clustering in the center of the range of variability. Is the explanation for the form of normal or "1" curve distribution in both cases the same? I think not; the first must be understood in the context of probability theory and referable to probabilistic laws treating chance or "unorganized" phenomena. The second case must be viewed in the context of the operation of selection, transmission of genetic material, and numbers of other factors which might result in the differential phenotypic expression of common genetic material.

Similar examples can be offered for any form of relational patterning or distributional clustering. One mistake which anthropologists have made is to implicitly assume that common forms of patterning have common explanations. For instance, the demonstration of a graded temporal–spatial distribution, commonly expressed as a "droop chart" (see Nelson, 1938; Kroeber, 1923; Braidwood, 1963), has generally been accepted as a sufficient demonstration of the operation of a process of diffusion where the idea or the actual traits are said to have originated at a given point in both time and space. Gradually this innovation diffuses out from the point of origin, resulting in a distribution which has the properties of an inverted pyramid: the farther away in space from the point of origin, the later in time the trait will appear. When such distributions have been noted in archaeological materials, they have been accepted as primafacie evidence for the operation of diffusion. In this case the operational definition of diffusion is this form of distribution. It can be easily demonstrated that such a distribution may arise from the operation of numerous *different* kinds of causal processes.

For instance, imagine a situation in which a region is characterized by a graded distribution of population density, the greatest density being exhibited in a limited area near the center of the region with a graded reduction of population density as one moves away from the area offering optimal conditions to population maintenance and growth. When viewing against a temporal dimension, we expect that, other things being equal, rates of population growth will also be distributed in a graded clinal distribution away from the high density center. Imagine a density dependent trait such as the use of fire drives in hunting. One would expect that the efficiency with which fire drives may be employed will vary inversely with population density. Imagine the chaos resulting from the attempt to use such a technique by the Desert Cahuilla Indians in the mountains surrounding the Los Angeles basin today? As population density increased in the center of the region, we might expect fire drives to be gradually abandoned and some new hunting strategy to replace it. This would be the point of origin for a new hunting trait. As time passed and population continued to grow throughout the region, but at different rates, we would expect the new hunting trait to gradually replace fire drives differentially, directly as a function of the differential rates of population growth distributed in a graded fashion out from the high density area in the region. Viewed historically, the result would be a distribution identical to the "droop chart." The explanation for the distribution would not, however, be the gradual diffusion of the "idea" or "knowledge" of the new hunting trait but the differential temporal–spatial distribution of selective pressures favoring the adoption of the new trait, varying solely as a function of a graded distribution of rates of population growth and the resulting graded distribution of population density. These people might well have known about the new technique before it was practiced in any of the areas.

Many other sets of conditions can be envisioned which would yield a "droop chart" form of distribution, each resulting from the operation of different sets of determinants. They would only have in common some form of graded pattern of distribution in the threshold values for the operation of the determinants. Gradient distributions are one of the more common forms known in our experiences; why should they all signify the same "process" when identified archaeologically? They most certainly do not.

As previously mentioned, many terms and phrases which we employ refer to the different forms of relational patterning that we may observe. It is a common error to feel that something has been explained when a particular form of patterning can be subsumed under a general cognitive category. A recent example of this can be seen in the writings of Kent Flannery.

Under conditions of fully-achieved and permanently-maintained equilibrium, prehistoric cultures might never have changed. That they did change was due at least in part to the existence of positive feedback or "deviation-amplifying" processes. These Maruyama (1963, p. 163) describes as "all processes of mutual causal relationships that amplify an insignificant or accidental initial kick, build up deviation and diverge from the initial conditions."

Such "insignificant or accidental initial kicks" were a series of genetic changes which took place in one or two species of Mesoamerican plants which were of use to man. The exploitation of these plants had been a relatively minor procurement system compared with that of maguey, cactus fruits, deer, or tree legumes, but positive feedback following these initial genetic changes caused one minor system to grow all out of proportion to the others, and eventually to change the whole ecosystem of the Southern Mexican Highlands (Flannery, 1968, p. 79).

Flannery then proceeds to describe in very provocative fashion events in the Mesoamerican situation which describe a form of patterning commensurate with the term "deviation amplifying." It should be pointed out that Maruyama clearly recognized the pure descriptive–cognitive function of the phrase deviation amplifying. He says "all processes of mutual causal relationships," clearly indicating that the term refers to a form of relational patterning, the explanation for which must have reference to the character of the "causal relationships."

Flannery concludes his presentation with the statement that "the use of a cybernetics model to explain prehistoric culture change, while terminologically cumbersome, had certain advantages" (Flannery, 1968, p. 85). I submit that Flannery has not explained culture change. He has demonstrated rather convincingly that a "positive-feedback" form of relational patterning is characteristic of the history of culture change in his area. He has explored some of the details of the character of the relationships so distributed, but he has not explained the patterning. Surely genetic changes had occurred in plant species before; why should they have been important at one time in history and not at another? Why should the populations in the area respond to changes which offered greater productive potential? Surely man does not always and inevitably respond to such situations. What were the selective pressures operating on Mesoamerican populations which favored their adoption of more efficient strategies? These problems Flannery does not discuss.

As archaeologists become more concerned with exploring the nature of relational patterning manifest in the organizational properties of the archaeological record, as Flannery is clearly doing, the discovery of new forms of patterning and their description in recognizable terms will become more common. A language will be generated to accommodate these discovered forms of relational patterning. Our ability to refer our observations to a previously described cognitive category is not an explanation for our observations nor does it imply that all similar forms of patterning necessarily have common explanations.

I do not want to give the impression that I am picking on Flannery; his exploratory work dealing with the recognition of previously unrecognized forms of patterning is some of the best in the literature. He is one of the few who has achieved a "processual" model of the past (Flannery, 1969). On this subject I am addressing myself as much as others; this is a very easy mistake to make in a pioneering situation.

The last paper in this section is my only attempt thus far at "processual modeling" or the development of an explanatory argument. The context in terms of which I began this work appears as rather ironic. It is a "fighting paper," as are those in the previous section, but it derives not so much from my battles with ideas but with men. Ideas are involved; these are the weapons in intellectual debate. But my motivations for working on it were not as pure as the recognized intellectual conflicts between my position and that held by others. My initial motives were purely vindictive. Robert Braidwood had hurt me deeply. I wanted to hurt him back. My weapons were ideas. I never really wanted to hurt Griffin; I wanted him to understand. With Bordes, I never cared whether he was convinced by my arguments; it was the stimulation of the problems and Bordes himself which were important to me. With the "Post Pleistocene Adaptations" paper I was out to prove that a man's personal opinions about me as a person, an intellect, an archaeologist, were wrong. I had never been close to Braidwood; I had never seriously fought with him over ideas, although clearly ours were very different. I respected Braidwood for having gone to the field in clearly problem-oriented research. I respected him for his interdisciplinary tactics. I was convinced he was dead wrong in his humanistic, almost romantic, approaches to understanding what he found.

I found him personally annoying. Certainly this is no more a comment on Braidwood than it is on myself. I had been reared in the South. I had been born into a family split between a hills-south, hard-working, coal-mining father's side and a mother's side which lived in the nostalgic world of the antebellum south. As far back as I can remember I was told what a fine family I had come from; yet we lived during the depression in anything but grand style. The society into which I emerged, where I saw my father humiliated by snobbish, socially pretentious men, left its mark. I was frequently embarrassed by my thick accent. I was made to feel that my family and I had to earn any respect we received on a day-to-day basis. Respect was not something to be expected because of a secure social position. Braidwood's manner, his style of living, and his voice all prompted emotions going back to my childhood. These are the social scars we all carry. They frequently come between people for no reason of the moment. I never knew Robert Braidwood. I probably could never have gotten to know him if I had earnestly tried. He pushed too many painful buttons in my past. I have no idea what Braidwood is like. He may well be a fine man. He was one that my past had selected against, regardless of his true character.

As I worked on the literature treating the problem of the origins of agriculture, my motives began to change. I became intrigued with the entire problem of the conditions under which new adaptive strategies would be adopted. I began to put many different observations together with arguments as to the relevance of demographic variables in evolutionary situations. I made connections between sedentism itself and its possible consequences for population growth. A series of processual arguments were eventually presented. Although I had argued that processual understanding was what we should be seeking, I had never before actually accomplished the integration of such an argument in print. There had been processual or explanatory components to my arguments, as in "Anthropology as Archaeology," but it was not until I put together the "Post Pleistocene Adaptations" that I achieved a processual model that was not developed for the explicit accommodation of a specific body of archaeological data. This was a different kind of model; its implications began to reach in the direction of law-like propositions, the goal of science.

I currently have in preparation a sequel to the "Post Pleistocene Adaptations" which I feel will provide some empirical materials supporting many of the speculative hypotheses in that article. In addition, I have developed another processual argument which offers to me some very provocative ideas regarding the conditions under which animals versus plants were domesticated, as well as the conditions under which different forms of domesticants came to be adopted as part of the subsistence strategy of various people. I think I will achieve in this forthcoming presentation a processual explanatory model for the diffusion of agriculture. The paper currently available as well as the forthcoming one will be my first steps toward a processual understanding of man's past, an aim which I had never realized in my other works.

Some may view as ironic and others may view as "historical accident" the events which have conditioned the interests I have pursued in research. I take a very different view. It appears to me that an individual's life shares many features with the conditions under which evolutionary change occurs in cultural systems. My intellectual "culture" came from Leslie White, Albert Spaulding, and Walter Taylor. I am not any of these men; my research interests, my crusades, my writings have largely come as responses, as attempts to cope with my intellectual and personal environment. By knowing the "intellectual culture" one could not have predicted, retrodicted, or understood my work in "Post Pleistocene Adaptations," or for that matter most of my other writings. This is true for understanding cultural evolution as well; culture derives from culture, but the forms and directions that variability takes must be understood in terms of the selective pressures operative. What I have become as an individual and as a spokesman for a particular "Binfordian" position in archaeology derives from my opponents and is the by-product of my attempts to cope with them as persons and with their ideas. What I am that is intellectually distinct from White, Spaulding, and Taylor I owe primarily to Griffin, Bordes, and Braidwood.

References

Bardon, L., and A. Bouyssonie. (1906). Outils escailles par percussion. *Revue Anthropologique* 16, 170–175.

Binford, Lewis R., and Sally R. Binford. (1966). A preliminary analysis of functional variability in the Mousterian of Levallois facies. *American Anthropologist* 68, No. 2, part 2, 238–295.

Binford, Lewis R., Sally R. Binford, Robert Whallon, and Margaret Hardin. (1970). Archaeology at Hatchery West. *Memoirs of the Society for American Archaeology* 35, No. 4 (Whole No.).

Binford, Sally R., and Lewis R. Binford. (1969). Stone tools and human behavior. *Scientific American* **220**, 70–84.

Braidwood, Robert. (1963). *Prehistoric Man,* 6th ed. Chicago Natural History Museum Popular Series, Chicago.

Clark, J. Desmond. (1958). Some stone age woodworking tools from southern Africa. *South African Archaeological Bulletin* **13**, 144–152.

Clark, J. Desmond, and C. V. Haynes, Jr. (1970). An elephant butchery site at Mwanganda's Village, Karonga, Malawi, and its relevance for palaeolithic archaeology. *World Archaeology* **1**, 390–411.

Clarke, David. (1968). *Analytical Archaeology.* Methuen, London.

Fitting, James E. (1970). *The Archaeology of Michigan.* Natural History Press, Garden City, New York.

Flannery, Kent V. (1968). Archaeological systems theory and early Mesoamerica. In *Anthropological Archaeology in the Americas,* pp. 67–87. Anthropological Society of Washington, Washington, D.C.

Flannery, Kent V. (1969). Origins and ecological effects of early domestication in Iran and the Near East. In *The Domestication and Exploitation of Plants and Animals* (P. J. Ucko and G. W. Dimbleby, eds.), pp. 73–100. Aldine Publ. Co., Illinois.

Haggett, Peter. (1966). *Locational Analysis in Human Geography.* St. Martin's Press, New York.

Hempel, Carl G. (1965). *Aspects of Scientific Explanation and other Essays in the Philosophy of Science.* Free Press, New York.

Kroeber, A. L. (1923). *Anthropology.* George G. Harrap & Co., London.

Leakey, L. S. B. (1931). *The Stone Age Cultures of Kenya Colony.* Cambridge Univ. Press, London and New York.

Leakey, L. S. B. (1953). *Adam's Ancestors,* 4th ed. Harper Torchbooks, New York.

McCarthy, F. D. (1941). Chipped stone implements of the aborigines. *Australian Museum Magazine* **7**, 257–263.

McPherron, Alan (1967). The Juntunen site and the late woodland prehistory of the upper Great Lakes area, Anthropological Papers, Museum of Anthropology, University of Michigan, No. 30.

Malan, B. D. (1942). The Middle Stone Age of the Upper Caledon River Valley. The Modderpoort Culture. *Transactions of The Royal Society of South Africa* **29**, 113–128.

Maruyama, Magoroh. (1963). The second cybernetics: Deviation-amplifying mutual causal processes. *American Scientist* **51**, 164–179.

Movius, Hallam L. (1969). Comment on "Culture Traditions and Environments of Early Man," by Desmond Collins. *Current Anthropology* **10**, 307–308.

Nelson, N. C. (1938). Prehistoric archaeology. In *General Anthropology* (F. Boas, ed.), pp. 146–237. Heath, New York.

Pei, W. C. (1939). A preliminary study of a new paleolithic station known as locality 15 within the Cooukoutien region. *Bulletin of The Geological Society of China* **19**, 147–187.

Sokal, Robert R., and P. H. A. Sneath. (1963). *Principles of Numerical Taxonomy.* Freeman, San Francisco, California.

Spaulding, Albert C. (1953). Statistical techniques for the discovery of artifact types. *American Antiquity* **18**, 305–313.

Tixier, Jacques. (1963). Typologie de l'epipaleolithique du Maghreb. *Memoires du Centre de Recherches Anthropologiques, Prehistoriques et Ethnographiques* No. 2.

White, J. Peter. (1968). Fabricators, outils escailles or scalar cores? *Mankind* **6**, 658–666.

A New Method of Calculating Dates from Kaolin Pipe Stem Samples *

In 1954 Harrington published an article on the study of metrical changes in kaolin pipe stem hole diameters through time. He found that there was a general and regular reduction in the hole diameters as you go from 1620 to 1800. In attempting to use this correlation to date Indian occupations in the Virginia–North Carolina area in 1954–1955, I found that Harrington's method of data presentation was rather clumsy when attempting to compare archaeological samples of pipe stems to the control data or basic data on which the correlation was originally determined. Harrington had presented the observed correlation as a series of percentages for the occurrence of various hole diameters by 40-year time periods. Very seldom is an archaeological sample likely to correspond to the 40-year time periods set up by Harrington, so that when comparing observed percentages with the basic chart it was very difficult to arrive at an accurate age estimate. While attempting to eliminate this cumbersome difficulty it became quite obvious that Harrington's observed correlation of a metrical attribute with time was ideal for regression analysis. I computed from Harrington's percentages a straight line regression and arrived at a formula which would allow me to substitute values from any archaeological sample into the formula and determine an absolute date which would be the mean date for the period of sample accumulation. This I was able to do by using Harrington's original percentages and converting them to mean hole diameters for the given time period. This allowed me to calculate a straight line regression formula using years and mean hole diameters. The resulting formula is: $Y = 1931.85 - 38.26X$, Y being the date you are attempting to determine, 1931.85 being the theoretical date, if we project this correlation, at which the stem hole diameters would reach zero, and 38.26 being the slope of the line, that is, the interval of years between a mean of

* Originally published in *Southeastern Archaeological Conference Newsletter* 9, 19–21 (1962).

any one of the various metrical categories 5, 6, 7, 8, or 9/64 of an inch. If you had a sample with a mean of 5/64ths and another with a mean of 6/64ths, there is an interval of 38.26 years between them according to Harrington's correlation. X in the formula is the mean pipe stem diameter for the sample you are attempting to date, and this is determined simply by measuring the hole diameters of the pipe stems in the sample and computing the arithmetic mean for the sample. The formula then gives you the mean date of the pipe stem sample and is the mean date for the period of accumulation.

The first set of data on which I used this particular formula was the historic Nottoway and Meherrin Indian sites in the Virginia area. I had very good data as to the period of occupancy for at least four documented sites, and in all cases (this was the first application of the formula as such) I was amazed. I couldn't believe the results could be so close to the known dates. On one particular site, a Warrasqueoc occupation of 1675–1702, the mean pipe stem date determined by this formula was 1683, and with the other sites I found equally good results. In conversing with Carol Erwin, who is writing up the historic material from the Macon Trading Post, I learned that she had found, in using the formula, that the mean pipe stem dates fall between the known estimated periods of occupation for the site. H. Geiger Omwake, who is one of our better authorities on pipe makers' marks, originally analyzed five fairly well dated historic sites, using Harrington's method in an attempt to demonstrate that the correlation was in fact valid. I have reapplied my formula to his data and was able to make more refined temporal estimates for the sites which were actually closer to the known dates. The other cases of application of the formula are Fort Michilimackinac and Brunswick Town. For the former site we have excellent documentation on the date of abandonment, although its date of establishment is in dispute, being somewhere between 1700 and 1720. In addition to the documented span of the site, we have documented dates for the period of use of various structures, one of which was a soldiers' barracks built in 1769 and torn down in 1781. From the fireplace and a small closet that was adjacent to the fireplace of this structure a large sample of kaolin pipe stems were recovered yielding a mean pipe stem date of 1776, right in the middle of the known period of occupancy. These cases of application have convinced me and others that Harrington's correlation and this method is valid and quite useful for dating historic sites.

There are certain limitations to the method. When I applied the formula in the analysis of a sample from Mackinac Island, occupied from 1780 until the present, I found that the correlation fell to pieces. Known samples of pipe stems derived from hearths dated 1805 yielded pipe stem dates of 1732. In other cases of the application of the technique to late materials the results were equally disturbing. In the way of explanation it is quite obvious that with the influx of pipes manufactured in Montreal and at other seats of American pipe making there is a corresponding reoccurrence of certain "early" styles, in addition to the appearance of a new style of elements. This break in the traditional direction of stylistic change is responsible, I feel quite sure, for the breakdown in the correlation after roughly 1780.

I will mention certain sampling problems which also will affect the validity of any mean date determined by this technique. First, it must be kept in mind that you must have an *adequate sample,* that is, a large enough sample to be representative of the population being dated. The next major caution was brought forcibly to my attention by the material from Fort Michilimackinac. Early in the analysis of the Fort material it was obvious that throughout the span of the fort there had been an increasing logistics efficiency as well as an increase in population. The factors taken together resulted in there being many more pipes in use during the late period as contrasted with the early period. Thus, the increased rates of accumulation for the late period tend to skew the total sample from the site in favor of a later date. This brings us to the point that the accuracy of the date depends upon the possession of a random sample of a population which was stable with regard to rates of deposition through the period of sample accumulation. If either one of these conditions are not met, then you can expect less accuracy in dating.

I might briefly mention that by calculating the standard deviations of the means of samples, you have a rough estimate of the length of time over which the sample was accumulating.

In summary the regression formula presented here allows you to estimate from the variation observed in the hole diameters of kaolin pipes, a mean date for the period of sample accumulation and by using standard deviations estimate the length of time involved in accumulating the sample. The accuracy of the date depends upon (1) derivation of the sample from a population deposited prior to 1780, (2) randomness of the sample, (3) representativeness of the sample, and (4) a constant rate of accumulation throughout the period of sample building. I might mention that these limitations apply whether using Harrington's percentage technique or my regression formula.

Reference

Harrington, J. C. (1954). Dating stem fragments of seventeenth and eighteenth century clay tobacco pipes. *Quarterly Bulletin, Archaeological Society of Virginia* 9, No. 1, pp. 6–8.

Indian Sites and Chipped Stone Materials in the Northern Lake Michigan Area *

LEWIS R. BINFORD and GEORGE I. QUIMBY†

Introduction

Stone materials collected by Quimby from 1959 to 1962 during Chicago Natural History Museum's archaeological survey of the northern Lake Michigan area were recognized in 1962 by Binford as manifesting a particular flint knapping technique, which, insofar as we can determine, has not been reported previously from the New World. This technique is a very distinctive type characterized by the production of small nuclei that have a ridge of percussion produced by the placing of small pebbles on an anvil and directing a blow parallel to the vertical axis of the pebble. It is a crude and poorly controlled method of working stone. Whether or not this bipolar flint knapping technique simply represents a way of utilizing small tabular pebbles within a more diverse and elaborate stone working tradition is not known to us at the present time.

In chipped stone assemblages there are two major categories of artifacts: tools and the by-products of tool production. Since tool production is a process, the techniques and motor habits of which vary stylistically and according to their relative efficiency, it should follow that variations in processes of tool manufacture are as important to our understanding of extinct cultural systems as the variations in the tools themselves. In addition to the patterned or normative factors which may be isolated through the analysis of chipped stone materials, we may discover that some of the steps in the manufacturing process were undertaken at different locations. Understanding of the manner in which manufacturing sequences were broken up and executed by different social units at different places is of prime importance if we are to understand the operation

* Originally published in *Fieldiana-Anthropology* **36,** 277–307 (1963).

† Curator of North American Archaeology and Ethnology, Chicago Natural History Museum.

of extinct cultural systems. For these reasons it is argued that as much analytical attention should be given to the artifacts that are the by-products of tool production as to the tools themselves. Experience has shown that there are certain general steps or phases in the production of chipped stone tools, of which the characteristics for recognition are fairly well known.

Raw material which breaks with a conchoidal fracture normally occurs in two primary forms and a variety of secondary forms. Primary forms are those *in situ* raw materials which can be obtained from the deposits where they were structurally formed. In general, primary sources yield either nodular or vein materials. Secondary forms of raw material are normally either spherical or tabular chunks of eroded and redeposited primary raw material such as cobbles in glacial till and stream-eroded pebbles. The form and size as well as the ease of procurement and abundance of raw materials are important factors for consideration in understanding the techniques and motor habits characteristic of different manufacturing procedures. In the case of primary forms of raw material and certain situations of occurrence of secondary forms, some quarrying may be needed in order to obtain the material. When such is the case there are apt to be sites which exhibit a quality in their flint assemblage resulting from the forms of the raw material and the quarrying techniques used. Such sites may also vary with regard to the number of steps or phases in the manufacturing sequence that were executed there. In cases where the raw material can be easily gathered without quarrying, we would expect all formal characteristics of quarrying activity to be absent; there may be "collecting stations" or places where the raw material was accumulated and then processed through various stages prior to being removed from the locality where it was collected. Flint assemblages which represent quarrying activities will vary with the nature of the raw material but in general will exhibit evidence of very heavy work such as on-anvil or block techniques resulting in flakes with developed bulbs of percussion and striking angles of around $120°$. In addition to the quarry techniques there is normally a large quantity of massive "shatter" (cubical and irregularly shaped chunks that frequently lack any well-defined bulbs of percussion or systematic alignment of cleavage scars on the various faces). It is the result of both heavy percussion techniques and the cleavage of raw material along old fracture planes such as frost cracks and the like. Shatter is particularly frequent in frost areas and in places where the raw material must be "tested" for its fractural qualities before it is selected for further processing.

In the initial phase of processing raw materials there are only two possible procedures: (1) production of tools by the detaching of spalls so as to alter the original form of the raw material or (2) production of *nuclei* from which spalls are detached and then modified into tools. The debris from either process is likely to include large quantities of shatter. However, shatter from this phase of processing is apt to be smaller and show less scarring than shatter from quarry activities. In addition to the shatter there will be trim flakes from the preparation of the nuclei, particularly in the area of the striking platform, and quantities of decortication flakes, that is to say, flakes exhibiting the weathered surface of the original raw material on one or more faces.

Assemblages which are typified by the production of tools from derived elements or spalls detached from nuclei may vary in the types of derived elements selected for further processing into tools as well as with respect to the number of steps in the modification sequence executed at any given location. The elements selected for further modification into tools are termed *blanks.* A *flake blank* is any selected spall which was systematically derived from a nucleus. Chips that were selected for further modification are termed *chip blanks.* Chip blanks are those that have been derived through the modification of a blank of more primary form. A *phase blank* is any artifact which has been processed beyond the point of recognition of the form of the original blank, but is unfinished and was not utilized as a tool. Frequently tools will be "roughed out" at one location and transported to another where further processing is carried out, in which case the end product of the former manufacturing location would be a phase blank. A *tool blank* is an artifact that served as a tool in its original form but has been remodified into another tool type. The debris associated with blank modification is normally composed of large quantities of chips with little or no shatter present. These chips usually exhibit: (1) a tendency to a concavoconvex longitudinal section; (2) a faceted striking platform; (3) a reticulate scar pattern on the external face; (4) a very acute angle formed between the striking platform and the external face; (5) flat or actual negative bulbs of percussion. These attributes arise when chips are removed in the formal modification of blanks ordinarily accomplished by bifacial flaking along the edges. The faceted striking platform is present because in most cases the striking area is the edge of the blank which has already been modified on the opposite face in such a way that the edge is scarred. The reticulate scar pattern is frequent because chips are removed to modify the blank into a desired shape; hence the chips are usually removed at varying angles. The degree of "reticulateness" will be greater when small round objects are produced and less as the length and size increase. This is ordinarily true also for the amount of concavoconvexity that is present.

The degree to which these generalizations hold will normally be a function of the particular phase of processing represented and the degree to which the blank form was modified. Experience in analyzing flint assemblages generally enables one to separate quite reliably chips from spalls derived from other phases of processing. Shatter associated with this phase is normally derived from the breakage of spalls and is frequently found in the form of unattached hinge fractures and small slivers of stone derived from irregular breakage along the cleavage faces.

Ideally the archaeologist analyzing a flint assemblage should be able to determine the type and method of production for the core forms present, identify the flake blank forms selected for the production of various tool types, and be able to identify every scrap of stone debris in relation to the phase of processing during which it was produced. In addition, given a good knowledge of the physics of conchoidal fracture, he should be able to reconstruct the motor habits and general classes of tools utilized in the manufacturing process.

It should be stressed that this report could not have been written unless the by-products of stone tool production as well as the tools themselves had been collected in the field. There were times when Quimby was concerned about the amount of stone "junk" he was bringing back to the museum, but as can be seen subsequently, it was worth the extra effort.

The Archaeological Sites

Point Detour Bay

The stone materials analyzed in this report were collected from four sites in the upper peninsula of Michigan. The first of these sites to be considered here is located in Section 10 (T. 37 N., R. 19 W.), Fairbanks Township in southeastern Delta County. It was discovered by Quimby and James R. Getz in early October of 1962 and named the Point Detour Bay site because it was situated at the head of an unnamed bay just west of Point Detour and about two and a half miles east of the village of Fairport (Fig. 1).

The cultural remains consisted of a layer of flint debris that extended over an area about 3 ft wide and perhaps 5 ft long beneath some 6 in. of wind-blown sand on top of a sand beach. At the southwestern edge of this deposit there were some large patches of charcoal that appeared to manifest a former hearth. The charcoal and flint materials were about 18 ft (measured by hand level) above Lake Michigan. A small trench was dug by trowel across the western edge of the flint deposit and about a thousand fragments of flint were obtained and brought back to Chicago Natural History Museum.

At the time of its discovery this site was somewhat of a puzzle. It possessed all the geographic characteristics of a Late Woodland site—a sandy area back of a sandy landing place. Although the underwater approach to the landing was solidly paved with cobbles in clay there were no large rocks that would interfere with the landing of a canoe. Moreover, this was the only good landing place for a canoe between Fairport and some unknown area northeast of Point Detour. Quimby and Getz dug into the beach fully expecting to find a Late Woodland or Historic Period site. It was somewhat of a disappointment to find only crude flint materials which at first glance didn't even seem to be the product of human activity, yet had to be, because flint cobbles or fragments could not occur

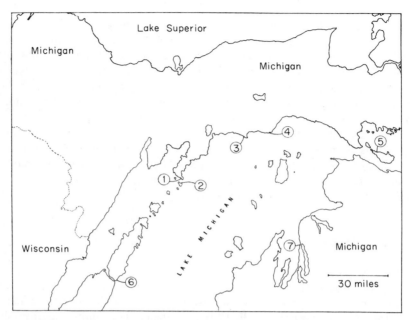

Fig. 1. Map of northern Lake Michigan area, showing locations of sites. ① *Point Detour Bay site;* ② *Summer Island site;* ③ *Seul Choix site;* ④ *Scott Point site;* ⑤ *Juntunen site;* ⑥ *Lighthouse site;* ⑦ *Eastport site.*

naturally in this area in either a sand beach or a foredune ridge of sand. The possibility that the flint materials belonged to a Paleo-Indian stage was considered and then rejected because the elevation of the find was well beneath the levels of the Nipissing and Algoma strand lines in this area and the sand beach upon which they rested was the most recently formed of a series of such beaches that extended inland behind the site. It was therefore concluded that the Point Detour Bay site represented some sort of aberrant flint-working station where some Indian or Indians had landed in birchbark canoe(s), had selected flinty cobbles from the lake shore, had moved back from the water to the top of an old beach, had built a fire there, and had engaged in some flint-working process, the by-products of which were extremely crude. It was this particular collection of flint materials that interested Professor Binford and led ultimately to the preparation of this report.

Summer Island

The Summer Island site (Fig. 1) is slightly more than 3 miles south of the Point Detour Bay site on Summer Island at the northern entrance into Green Bay from Lake Michigan. The site extends over a series of sandy beaches about 21–26 ft (measured by hand level) above the surface of Lake Michigan near the head of an unnamed bay on the northeast side of Summer Island in Delta

County, Michigan. This bay, except for the fairly level sandy area where the site is situated, has a shoreline of angular rocks, cobbles, and stone cliffs.

Through the kindness of Mr. and Mrs. Charles W. Bissell of Grand Rapids, Michigan, who provided transportation on their boat, Quimby was able to examine the Summer Island site in August of 1959. Cultural debris was abundant on the exposed surfaces of the site, which has its lakeward border about 125 ft inland from the best canoe landing area in the entire bay. Suitable surface collections were obtained and test excavations were undertaken. At the southeastern edge of the site, Quimby, assisted by Mrs. Bissell and Mrs. George W. Doolittle, excavated a test trench 3 ft wide, 15 ft long, and 2½ ft deep. This trench was trowelled in 6-in levels and all materials saved by level. In other parts of the site two test pits 3 ft square and 4 ft deep were dug. One of these pits contained a refuse deposit and the other indicated the presence of a grave which we left intact in order to devote the available field time to stratigraphic testing.

The upper foot of the test trench contained cultural materials, particularly pottery sherds, indicative of Late Woodland and Upper Mississippi and the lower 1½ ft contained sherds suggestive of Middle Woodland occupancy. Faunal remains included sturgeon, moose, and beaver among numerous unidentified fish, mammal, and bird bones. The stone materials studied by Binford were from the surface of the site and the upper level of the test trench.

Seul Choix

The Seul Choix site (Fig. 1) is west of Seul Choix Point (Sec. 21, T. 41 N., R. 13 W.) in Mueller Township, Schoolcraft County, Michigan. It was discovered by Quimby and James R. Getz in 1962. At first glance this seems an unlikely area in which to find a coastal site. The shore consists of sloping beds of limestone that have split and eroded into a fantastically fractured rock surface with deep cracks and pits. Near the water the few smooth surfaces are slippery with algae and lichens. With strong southerly or westerly winds, heavy seas crash over the rock shore. In the midst of this coastal mishmash there is a small natural harbor that can be entered from the west through a pass in the offshore limestone reefs. This harbor, not on the maritime charts for northern Lake Michigan, extends less than 200 ft in width and about 200 ft in length. On its landward side there is a gently sloping sand beach ideally suited for a canoe landing. A few hundred feet back of the sand beach is a relatively level sandy area about 20 ft above water level and in this place is the Seul Choix site.

Cultural debris was spread over an extensive area, much of which was wind blown. From this area it was easy to obtain a surface collection of pottery sherds, flints, and fragments of copper artifacts. All of the pottery seems to be Late Woodland. A fragmentary copper blade of "butter knife" form also seems indicative of Late Woodland, judging from context of this type at other sites in Michigan and Ontario. The stone materials collected from the Seul Choix site will be considered subsequently in the analysis by Binford.

Scott Point

The Scott Point site (Fig. 1), sometimes erroneously called Point Paterson site, is located (Sec. 8, T. 41 N., R. 11 W.) in Newton Township, Mackinac County, Michigan. This site was examined on a number of occasions in 1960, 1961, and 1962 by Quimby, assisted at different times by James R. Getz, Helen Z. Quimby, G. Edward Quimby, John E. Quimby, and Robert W. Quimby, all of whom rendered valuable service.

The site is situated some 300–400 ft from Lake Michigan in a small bay just west of Scott Point. Near the middle of this bay the sandy lake bottom is free of boulders all the way into the beach but the points of land at the extremities of the bay and the adjacent lake bottom are covered by boulders of various sizes. West of the site the shore and lake bottom are rocky for at least three and probably more miles and east of the site for a half mile or more. Thus the site itself is located behind the only suitable canoe landing place in the immediate vicinity.

Much of the Scott Point site has been exposed in large sand blows covering an area 200 by 300 ft or more. Numerous clusters of fire-cracked rocks indicate the locations of former dwellings and/or hearths. Pottery sherds, flint materials, and hammerstones lie on the surface in great abundance. Various kinds of flint scrapers and small triangular arrowheads found here were probably made at the site because from time to time the wind blows away the sand, exposing clusters of small chips of the kind that would have been removed from a flake to make a point or from a core to make a scraper.

Bone tools include awls, flat matting needles, and unilaterally barbed harpoons or points for fish spears. Faunal remains include deer, moose, beaver, and considerable quantities of fish, among which are sturgeon. There are large piles of fish remains 2 and 3 ft deep in various parts of the site. These fish bone middens might represent the remains of sturgeon only, for the bony plates of sturgeon are present in all the heaps. Of some thousand or more sherds collected from the Scott Point site, about five are shell-tempered, thin, Upper Mississippi types. The bulk of the pottery is a grit-tempered ware that is Late Woodland in style (judged by rim sherds).

The Late Woodland sites described above and some others not included here but nonetheless situated along the northern shore of Lake Michigan have in common a single principle of locality: A site is found only behind a good landing place for canoes; there is never a site behind a bad or dangerous landing place.

Since drinking water can easily be obtained from Lake Michigan the presence of a spring or stream is not a factor influencing choice of site as it is with interior locations occupied in nonwinter months. Although availability of food such as sturgeon may have been a deciding factor it seems more likely that food was equally available throughout the area and that the deciding factors were distance from one settlement to another and presence of a good beach upon which to land a canoe. It should be noted here that there are more places unsuited for Late Woodland Indian occupancy along the northern Lake Michigan shore than there are suitable locations.

Although there is no direct evidence that Late Woodland Indians had the birchbark canoe, their settlement pattern indicates that they did. Moreover, such would be expected from the widespread use of the birchbark canoe in early historic times. A wooden dugout canoe of the kind known archaeologically in the middle west would have been unsuitable in this context for many reasons.

The Late Woodland Indians with whom we are here concerned occupied the northern Lake Michigan area from about A.D. 1000 to about 1600, and they spent the summer months in settlements along the northern shore of the lake. They traveled by canoe to these villages, which were always located adjacent to a good landing place for canoes. In the manufacture of some or possibly all of their stone tools they used an unusual flint knapping procedure which will be described and analyzed by Binford in the following pages.

Analysis of the Site Samples

The method of presentation has been to describe the classes of items in the inferred sequence of their production. Each described category of material is a distinct formal class definable in terms of a demonstrable clustering of attributes and as such is a valid taxonomic unit regardless of the validity of its inferred meaning in the reconstructed flint knapping procedure. The described formal classes will then be utilized in the comparative quantitative analysis of the site samples.

RAW MATERIAL

The raw material occurs as small tabular and angular eroded and rolled pebbles having their origin in the glacial deposits and beaches of the Great Lakes region. These deposits ordinarily contain a rather wide variety of pebble sizes, yet the raw material selected for use at the four described sites is uniformly of small size, usually not exceeding 5 cm in thickness or 8 cm in length. The material is uniformly a waxy chert of relatively good quality ranging from a gun-metal blue to steel gray or light brown to cream color. It often has small fossil inclusions and usually has the appearance of having formed around and between irregular zones of a tannish sandstone-like material. The latter substance frequently forms the cortex of two or more surfaces, the other surfaces merely being eroded and deteriorated faces of the chert. In my (Binford) experience this waxy chert occurs in the glacial deposits only in small tabular pebbles, while the larger cobbles are normally chert of a lower quality such as Eastport Chert (see

Binford and Papworth, 1963). In view of the latter observation the preference may have been for the waxy chert rather than small pebble size.

REMAINS OF STAGES IN PROCESSING THE RAW MATERIAL

Primary Shatter

Relatively large fragments of shatter exhibiting major cortical surfaces and internal cleavage faces of an unsystematic angular and cubical nature are rather common. The internal cleavage planes frequently follow along inclusions or old "frost cracks," and they lack bulbs of percussion. Specimens lacking major cortical surfaces but exhibiting the angular and irregular cleavage planes are also believed to represent shatter from the initial phase of working the raw material. These specimens more often show cleavage along the lines of inclusions. All material classed as *primary shatter* is believed to have been produced by the initial percussion blows delivered to the raw material, some pebbles breaking up so that further processing would be impossible. In other cases, after the initial shattering, some larger chunks may have been selected for further processing.

Decortication Flakes (Fig. 2)

Flakes of this type have the following attributes: (1) The external face of the flake is the unmodified cortex of the original raw material (Fig. 2C); (2) the internal face shows scarring from heavy percussion (Fig. 2B). Specimens most commonly exhibit strong *negative* bulbs of percussion and extreme concavoconvex longitudinal sections (Fig. 2A). Some specimens, particularly when they represent angular corners of the cortical surface, may have essentially a triangular longitudinal section with the characteristic negative bulbs of percussion. Some few specimens may exhibit strong positive bulbs of percussion, in which case they are invariably derived from the relatively flat sides of a

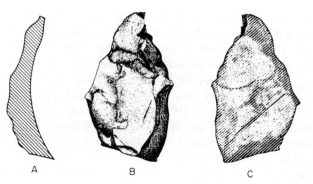

A   B   C

Fig. 2. *Decortication flake: A, longitudinal section; B, internal face; C, external face.*

tabular pebble. Longitudinal sections of the latter flake form tend to be planoconvex.

Both the type of shatter described above and the decortication flakes were apparently produced in a single operation. A tabular pebble was placed on an anvil and struck with a heavy blow so that the axis of percussion was approximately parallel to the vertical axis of the pebble when resting on the anvil (Fig. 3). The point of impact on the upper striking surface was localized,

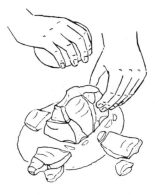

Fig. 3. Reconstruction of "on anvil" work.

thus producing a single cone of percussion, whereas the irregular surface of the pebble base resting on the anvil produced multiple cones from the basal area. However, because of the diffuse nature of the impact zones on the base it sometimes happened that no fractures originated there. Cleavage was of two types: (1) internal shatter, resulting from the presence in the pebble of old fracture planes compounded by the complex stresses associated with the simultaneous production of opposing cones of percussion at the anvil and the upper zone of impact; and (2) external cleavage, resulting from the production of opposing cones of percussion. Flakes fell away from the cones; therefore they exhibit pronounced negative bulbs of percussion. When external cleavage occurred, a roughly fusiform nucleus was produced from the pebble if the points of impact on both anvil and upper striking surface were localized, or a cone-shaped nucleus was produced if the points of impact at the base were diffuse as a result of an irregular surface. The form of the shatter and the form of the decortication flakes do not lend themselves to alternative interpretations. This model is further supported by an examination of the residual nuclei or cores represented in the sample.

Quimby was originally of the opinion that the cores had been utilized as tools. Alan McPherron of the University of Michigan, currently working on a similar assemblage from the Juntunen Site (Fig. 1), has observed that in many cases the flakes drawn from the cores do not show evidence of utilization. McPherron states:

> None shows signs of reworking or use of any kind. It would in fact appear that they were drawn not for primary use as blanks but as wastage in the preparation of cores for use as artifacts. A good proportion of spent cores show a peculiar nibbling or resolved flaking on the flattest or concave surface of flattish cores or core fragments. This causes the core "ridge" to resemble a steel wood-gouge. The resolved flaking is consistently absent from the back of these cores. The nibbling may certainly in many cases have been produced by the bi-polar process; in other cases, it appears to have been achieved through utilization of the core as a tool (McPherron, 1963).

Binford is in agreement with Quimby and McPherron that some cores have been incidentally utilized and they may even represent "core tools" or the end product of the knapping process. At present the solution of this problem is not at hand and we shall treat them simply as cores. However, it should be kept in mind that they may be core tools, in which case we are describing their mode of manufacture.

Cores

Three major forms of percussion surface are exhibited in various combinations on the recognized cores. The most common is a *ridge of percussion,* which is defined by the line of convergence of the two opposite cleavage faces. It is normally straight and considerably bruised with many small short hinge fracture scars on the cleavage faces directly below the ridge. In most cases the flake scars on the opposing cleavage faces exhibit negative bulbs of percussion, suggesting that the ridge is the result of the progressive removal of flakes from both cleavage faces, such flakes having originated at a true striking platform. The ridge is the result of the exhaustion of the striking platform and the production of what amounts to a series of lineally arranged overlapping cones of percussion from which no further flakes could be removed without changing the striking angle. Another common form of remnant striking platform, a *point of persussion,* is formed by the convergence of three or more cleavage faces resulting in a pyramidal form, the apex of which is the point of percussion. This is actually the apex of a cone of percussion from which no further flakes can be derived unless the striking angle is altered. An *area of percussion* is relatively flat, generally the cortical surface of the tabular pebble, from which flakes have been detached along the edges.

All of the cores in this assemblage are bipolar forms of six major varieties. "Bipolar" refers to the fact that on each core there are two opposed striking platforms or zones of percussion. These two zones are directly opposite each other, with the cleavage faces on both sides of the core converging on both zones of percussion. In most cases one zone of percussion can be recognized as the base or the zone resting on the anvil by the following: (1) A large percentage of flake scars originating there end in abrupt hinge fractures and are very short (Fig. 4G); (2) the zone is bruised and irregularly altered by percussion; and (3) the dominating flake scars on the cleavage faces do not originate from the basal zone. The upper zone of percussion, the actual striking platform, exhibits less bruising, the flake scars originating there dominate the face of the core, and the small shatter flakes detached from this area tend to have fewer hinge fractures and are more conchoidal in shape.

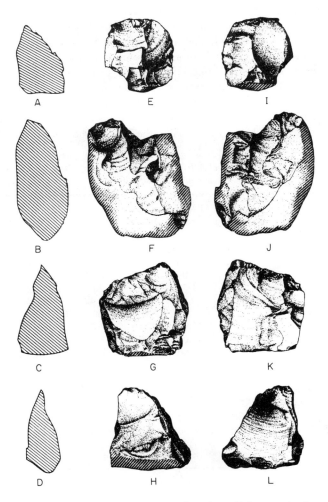

Fig. 4. *Ridge-area cores: A–D, longitudinal sections; E–L, opposite faces.*

The scar pattern on the cleavage faces is of two major types, bipolar cleavage and unipolar cleavage. The former is characterized by a continuous flake scar with bulbs of percussion at both ends of the core. In this case the flake removed would have had a marked concavoconvex longitudinal section and developed bulbs of percussion at both ends. The latter form, unipolar cleavage, is the more normal type with the flake scar exhibiting a single negative bulb of percussion and either terminating at the basal zone or at some point along the cleavage face.

Six varieties of core are represented in the sample, differences between them apparently being the result of minor modification in the production process largely stimulated by the "accidental" factors of breakage and differential cleavage properties of the raw material. The metrical attributes of these varieties of cores are shown in Table I. The most common form of core is one on which the basal zone of percussion is an area of unmodified cortex from the original tabular pebble. The impact zone is a ridge or a series of overlapping cones of percussion (Fig. 4). Scars orginating at the ridge of percussion are dominant on the cleavage faces, whereas scars originating at the basal area tend to be diminutive, irregular, and weak. Another common variety is characterized by a third cleavage face which is essentially the end of the core from which flakes

TABLE I   *Metrical Attributes of Six Varieties of Bipolar Cores*
(Measurements in centimeters)

Length[a]	Ridge area	Point area	Ridge point	Right angle	Opposing ridge	Opposing point
Sx	66.20	29.7	19.30	17.2	12.1	10.8
Sx^2	220.42	104.39	61.53	50.42	38.41	42.32
n	21.00	9.00	6.00	6.00	4.00	3.00
$\bar{x}$	3.15	3.30	3.21	2.87	3.02	3.60
s	0.76	0.88	0.33	0.47	0.77	1.32
Maximum width						
Sx	53.4	24.0	12.10	8.9	8.9	5.8
Sx^2	143.42	66.02	22.71	13.75	20.41	11.40
n	21.00	9.00	6.00	6.00	4.00	3.00
$\bar{x}$	2.54	2.67	2.02	1.48	2.22	1.93
s	0.61	0.50	0.57	0.34	0.44	0.31
Thickness						
Sx	32.20	16.4	7.40	8.4	4.6	4.10
Sx^2	51.62	31.02	9.48	11.96	5.40	5.85
n	21.00	9.00	6.00	6.00	4.00	3.00
$\bar{x}$	1.52	1.82	1.23	1.40	1.15	1.37
s	0.33	0.37	0.26	0.20	0.19	0.34

[a] Sx = sum of all measurements of a given dimension; Sx^2 = sum of all squares of measurements; n = number of specimens measured; $\bar{x}$ = mean dimension; s = standard deviation of mean.

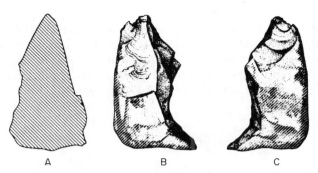

Fig. 5. Point-area core: A, longitudinal section; B and C, opposite faces.

originating at the ridge detach what amounts to a cross section of the core (Fig. 4K). When removal of the latter type of flake has progressed along the length of the ridge, the core is reduced to a point of percussion at the zone of impact while the base still remains an area (Fig. 5).

A third type of core is one on which the basal zone of percussion is a greatly battered and bruised point while the impact zone is a ridge of percussion (Figs. 6, 8A–C). Probably this type was produced as a result of shatter or

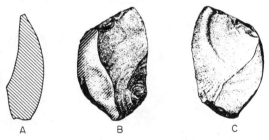

Fig. 6. Ridge-point core: A, long section; B and C, opposite faces.

uncontrolled breakage in the early phases of core manufacture, resulting in the production of a cone of percussion or a point of percussion at the impact zone. When such an event occurred, the core was reversed on the anvil and the point assumed the functions of the base. The area which had previously served as the base was then struck in such a way as to produce a ridge of percussion. Success resulted in a core form with a point of percussion as the base, opposed by a ridge of percussion. Failure in this attempt could result in the production of the fourth variety of core, one with opposing points of percussion, a type also represented in the sample (Fig. 8D–F).

A fifth type of core in our sample is one with opposed ridges of percussion (Fig. 7). With this core form it is impossible to determine which ridge served as the base and which served as the impact zone. Judging from the types of bruising and the frequency with which scars originating at the opposed ridges dominate cleavage faces, it would appear that both ridges variously served as base and zone of impact. This type of core is the result of the reduction of a small area of

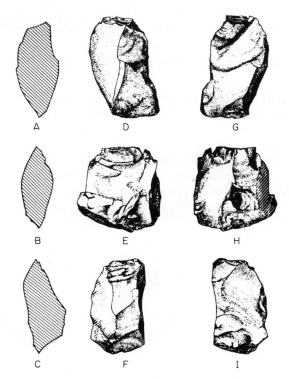

Fig. 7. Opposing ridge cores: A–C, longitudinal sections; D–I, opposite faces.

percussion to a true ridge, therefore obviating the possibility of further flake removal without changing the striking angle. When this occurred the core would be reversed on the anvil, and the base would then be worked until it was also reduced to a ridge, at which time the core would be discarded.

The sixth and last core form represented is also characterized by opposing ridges but they are approximately at right angles to one another (Fig. 8G–L). This form was apparently produced from one originally having a ridge opposite an area. By successive removal of flakes from both ends of the core

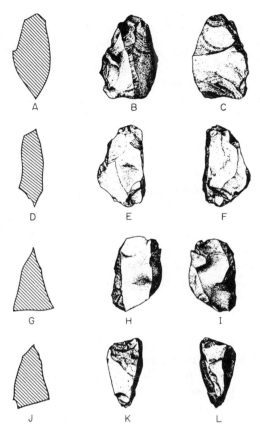

Fig. 8. *A–C, ridge-point cores; D–F, opposing point cores; G–L, right-angled ridged cores.*

(cross-sectional flakes) the terminal flake scars eventually converged, forming a ridge at right angles to the upper ridge of percussion.

In summary then, there are six core forms—ridge and basal area, point and basal area, ridge and basal point, right-angled ridges, opposing ridges, opposing points—all of which can be accounted for in terms of a single flint-working technique, which is bipolar flaking on an anvil. The variations in the form of the cores appear to be the results of minor modifications in the way in which the zones of impact and basal zones were reversed in combination, whether or not flakes were being primarily struck from the lateral faces or ends of the core. In terms of the normative concept of type, we would include all of these variations within a single type of core, the modal form of which is the variety with a ridge of percussion opposite a basal area of percussion.

Flakes

The following presentation is the result of an attempt to determine from which zone of percussion on the core the flakes originated and from which core face they were detached.

Class I. Flakes Originating at the Basal Zone of Percussion. Flakes described under this heading are believed to have been produced incidentally during the removal of flakes having their origin at the impact zone. They were derived through contact of the core with the anvil, the percussion blow having been delivered to the upper striking surface.

Variety A. This form of flake is believed to have been detached from the corner of one of the core forms that had a basal area of percussion. It is characterized by a large triangular area of unmodified cortical surface that forms the base of the flake. The axis of percussion and the longitudinal axis are parallel. The cross section is triangular. The external face exhibits two parallel flake scars converging to form a medial ridge. The internal face exhibits little or no development of a positive bulb of percussion. Some specimens exhibit recognizable negative bulbs of percussion. The overall shape of the flake is triangular, or the lateral edges converge from the base toward the tip of the flake.

Variety B. This form of flake is believed to have been detached from the broad lateral face of a core form having a basal area of percussion. A roughly rectangular area of unmodified cortical surface forms the base. The axis of percussion and the longitudinal axis are parallel. The cross section is roughly rectangular or occasionally triangular. The external face has multiple, parallel, longitudinally oriented flake scars. The internal face exhibits moderately developed positive bulbs of percussion. The shape is triangular or lamellar. The triangular shape would be expected if these flakes originated at the base of a core having an area opposed by a ridge or a point since such a core would be truncated in form. The basal area having the unmodified cortex is identical to those on the recognized core forms.

Class II. Flakes Originating at the Impact Zone of Percussion
Variety C (Fig. 9G–I). This form of flake is believed to have been detached from the lateral face of the core by blows directed at the upper ridge or point of percussion. The zone of impact is very narrow or often only a point exhibiting little or no remnant of the striking platform. The axis of percussion is parallel to the longitudinal axis, and the longitudinal section is generally concavoconvex, although a few specimens exhibit planoconvex longitudinal sections. Cross sections are generally asymmetrically triangular. The external face normally exhibits two parallel flake scars converging to form a ridge; occasionally there may be three parallel scars. Near the base there are generally several small hinge fracture scars extending down the face a short distance. These represent

unsuccessful attempts to detach the flake as well as shatter associated with the flake removal. The internal face has a developed positive bulb of percussion. The shape is either lamellar or excurvate.

Variety D (Fig. 9J–L). This form of flake is believed to have been detached from the lateral face of the core by blows directed at the upper ridge or point of percussion. The basal zone of impact is very narrow or frequently only a point

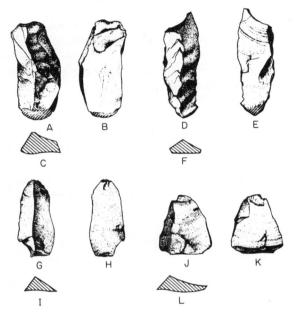

Fig. 9. A–F, end section flakes; G–I, variety C flake; J–L, variety D flake.

exhibiting little or no remnant striking platform. The axis of percussion is parallel to the longitudinal axis, and the longitudinal section is biconvex. The cross section is typically biconvex. The external face is irregularly scarred near the base of the flake, while the distal end may be scarless or only unsystematically scarred. The internal face is almost exclusively a bulb of percussion, sometimes exhibiting what amounts to a half-cone of percussion. Terminal hinge fractures are common forms of the distal ends of the flake. The shape of the flake is generally conchoidal or ovate. This flake form is interpreted as having been incidentally derived from the core in attempts to detach flakes of the form of variety C. The scars on the external faces of the basal end of variety C flakes as well as those along the ridges of ridged cores are believed to be the result of the removal of this type of flake.

Variety E (Fig. 9A–F). This form of flake we believe to have been detached from the end of the core by blows directed at the upper ridge or point of percussion. The basal zone of impact is very narrow and represents a simple segment of the ridge of percussion. The axis of percussion is parallel to the longitudinal axis of the specimen. The longitudinal section with few exceptions is concavoconvex. The cross section is rectangular (65%) or triangular (35%). The external face exhibits a single, longitudinally oriented flake scar, although if the flake was detached from the corner of the core, removing some of the lateral face as well as the end of the core, there may be multiple longitudinally oriented scars. The external face near the base of the flake is scarred with small hinge-terminated flake scars and is generally bruised. The internal face exhibits well-developed positive bulbs of percussion. The flake is either lamellar or expanding in form. In a few instances there are excurvate specimens representing removal from a biridged or bipointed core.

Secondary Shatter

Associated with the removal of flakes from the cores was the production of some shatter which lacks any identifiable morphological characteristics. It is in the form of small slivers of flint, broken or snapped sections of flakes, or broken-off distal ends of flakes. This type of debris is generally more frequent when further modification of flake blanks has occurred at any given location.

Site Comparisons

The samples from the four sites are extremely homogeneous in their range of formal variation. The forms of cores, flakes, and shatter previously described are quite distinctive and easily identified in the collections from all the sites. Formal variation in any given class of items could not be demonstrated between the specimens from the several sites, but the sites do differ considerably in the presence or absence of flint working debris not identifiable as the result of the flint processing procedure outlined in this report, as well as in the presence or absence of pottery and chips. The collection from Summer Island includes relatively massive "expanding flakes" previously identified as being characteristic of forms removed from *block core* (Binford and Papworth, 1963). These types of flakes could not have been derived from the core forms reported here; together with a single specimen of a block core they represent an entirely different flint knapping technology. It seems likely that the presence of this material at Summer Island is further evidence of a multiple occupancy of the location, although the use of two major processing techniques by a single group of occupants cannot be discounted completely.

Another interesting variation is that at all sites except Point Detour Bay, there is pottery of a class generally assignable to the closing phases of the prehistoric period. A comparative tabulation of class frequencies by site is presented in Table II. The Point Detour Bay site is also distinctive in that it lacks

	Point Detour Bay	Scott Point	Seul Choix	Summer Island
TABLE II *Comparative Tabulation of Class Frequencies*				
Initial Phase of Processing				
Primary shatter	113	19	13	8
Decortication flakes	41	20	7	4
Cores				
Complete specimens				
Ridge and basal area	21	21	5	4
Point and basal area	9	2	2	0
Ridge and basal point	6	2	5	0
Right-angled ridges	6	1	0	0
Opposing ridges	4	11	3	5
Opposing points	3	2	0	2
	49	39	15	11
Fragmentary specimens				
Points	12	9	1	2
Ridges	13	10	4	2
Areas	18	13	0	0
	43	32	5	4
Flakes				
Base originating				
Variety A	49	12	12	10
Variety B	33	8	6	7
Impact zone originating				
Variety C	79	64	43	31
Variety D	52	19	25	14
Variety E	58	22	12	2
Secondary shatter	136	93	31	21
Chips	0	23	6	12
Block core flakes	0	0	0	14
Block cores	0	0	0	1
Tools (stone)	0	9	5	6
Pottery	Absent	Present	Present	Present

chips derived from the bifacial modification of tools, as well as the tools themselves. This striking difference will be discussed after consideration of the variation in frequency of occurrence for the various classes of chipping debris associated with the bipolar knapping technology.

If exactly the same flint knapping procedures were used at the several sites in the same relative proportions, there should be no variation among the samples in the frequencies of core, flake, and shatter forms except as a result of sampling error. In order to determine whether or not the flint knapping procedures are in fact differentially executed at the several sites, chi-square calculations were carried out. This is a test of the hypothesis that the observable differences in the relative class frequencies could be accounted for on the basis of sampling error. Table III shows the results of these calculations for the four sites compared with regard to the frequency of decortication flakes, cores, core fragments, basally derived flakes, laterally derived flakes, and end-derived flakes, the basic data for which are presented in Table II.

TABLE III   *Comparison of Flint Knapping Procedures by Site*

| Site combinations | Degrees of freedom | Observed chi-square values | Expected chi-square values calculated at probability levels of | | | Conclusion |
			0.05	0.01	0.001	
Point Detour Bay and Scott Point	5	19.41	11.070	15.086^a	20.517	Different
Seul Choix and Summer Island	5	0.99	11.070	15.086	20.517	Same
Point Detour Bay and combined Seul Choix and Summer Island	5	29.12	11.070	15.086	20.517^a	Different
Scott Point and combined Seul Choix and Summer Island	5	26.82	11.070	15.086	20.517^a	Different

a Observed values exceed expected values at this level of probability.

It will be observed that in all cases when the conclusion is "different" the calculated value of chi-square exceeds the expected value at a level of probability of 0.01 or greater. This means that the observed differences between the compared samples could have been produced only by sampling vagaries of less than one in a hundred cases drawn from a single population. Therefore we may assert with a relatively high degree of confidence that there are real differences between the site combinations marked "different." On the other hand, the comparison between the Summer Island and the Seul Choix sites shows that the two samples could easily have been drawn from a single population. On the basis of these comparisons we can reasonably assert that the flint knapping activities were different at the Point Detour Bay and Scott Point sites and that both of these sites were different in flint knapping activities from the Summer Island and Seul Choix sites, where such activities were the same. It now remains for us to analyze further the qualitative nature of the expressed quantitative differences in an attempt to isolate the possible nature of the differences that we have recognized. Table IV presents the percentage frequencies for the various classes of materials.

TABLE IV   *Percentage Frequencies for Various Classes of Knapping Debris from the Four Sites*

Artifact class	Point Detour Bay (%)	Scott Point (%)	Seul Choix (%)	Summer Island (%)
Decortication flakes	10.15	9.25	5.50	4.44
Cores	12.13	18.05	12.00	12.22
Core fragments	10.64	14.81	4.00	4.44
Basally derived flakes	20.29	9.29	14.41	18.88
Laterally derived flakes	32.42	38.42	54.40	50.00
End derived flakes	14.36	10.18	9.60	10.00

The most striking difference between the classes is the low frequency of broken core fragments at Seul Choix and Summer Island as compared to those at Point Detour Bay and Scott Point. Similarly, the former two sites show a high frequency of laterally derived flakes with a corresponding low frequency for this class at the latter two sites. In addition, there is a consistently lower incidence of decortication flakes at Seul Choix and Summer Island than at the other two sites. These differences seem to form a consistent pattern. The high incidence of decortication flakes and broken core fragments, contrasted with the low incidence of laterally derived flakes, suggests that at Point Detour Bay and Scott Point raw material was being processed through the entire sequence of manufacture. The laterally derived flakes, potential blanks, either were being used up or removed from the sites. For instance, at the Point Detour Bay site 71 cores are represented, while usable flakes detached from the lateral faces of such cores are less than 80. Certainly many more flakes than are represented were struck from the cores, suggesting that such flakes were removed from the location by the flint knappers. It seems quite likely that the removed flakes were intended for use as blanks, and were further processed at some other location. This interpretation is further supported by the fact that laterally derived flakes had been used as blanks for 17 of the 20 tools represented in the samples from the four sites. The low incidence of broken cores at Seul Choix and Summer Island is interpreted to mean that only the workable cores had been introduced at these sites, whereas at the other two sites cores were being produced *in situ* and thus there was a higher incidence of core breakage. This interpretation is further supported by the differential frequencies of core types at the several locations (Table V).

TABLE V   *Comparative Frequency of Core Forms with and without Basal Areas*

	Point Detour Bay		Scott Point		Seul Choix		Summer Island	
	No.	%	No.	%	No.	%	No.	%
Ridge or point opposed by area	30	61.22	23	59.97	7	46.67	4	36.36
Ridge or point opposed by ridge or point	19	38.78	16	40.03	8	53.33	7	63.64
Total	49		39		15		11	

It will be noted that there are more cores with areas opposed by zones of impact at the Point Detour Bay and Scott Point sites than at the other two. The presence of such areas on the cores is indicative of less exhaustion of the core, whereas cores with ridges or points opposing each other have been worked until no further flakes could be derived from them. Cores were being worked to a more advanced stage of exhaustion at the Summer Island and Seul Choix sites, exactly the two sites that on the basis of other evidence are believed to represent locations where the prepared cores or nuclei and possibly laterally derived flakes produced elsewhere were being introduced. The greater exhaustion of the cores at these two sites suggests that the materials were at a greater premium there and may have been largely introduced. However, these differences also could be interpreted as stylistic variations. The samples from Seul Choix and Summer Island may also reflect a prejudice of selection by the collector.

It is difficult to interpret the observable differences in the frequency of the various classes of shatter. By far the greatest amount is present in the sample from Point Detour Bay. Very little is present from the other sites. It should be pointed out that the Point Detour Bay sample was derived from excavation of a flaking station, whereas the other three sites are represented by surface collections from villages. The low frequencies of shatter from the other sites could be the result of selectivity in the gathering of the samples, shatter not being considered worth saving. No attempt will be made here to interpret the observed differences in shatter.

Summary of Site Interpretations

Point Detour Bay Site

The formal composition of the sample from this site is the result of a limited number of processing steps in the tool manufacturing sequence. Raw materials were gathered and collected at the site and initially modified on the spot into nuclei from which were struck flakes for future use as blanks for tool production. The residual nuclei (cores) as well as all the debris associated with the working were left at the site while the flake blanks were removed for future processing into tools. The absence of finished tools, chips, pottery, and other artifacts at this site suggests that any single occupation was of very short duration and that dwelling place activities were not performed there. We interpret this site as a flint knapping station utilized by people practicing a single knapping task, the transformation of raw materials into desirable nuclei and blank forms.

Scott Point Site

The presence of pottery, finished tools, other artifacts, and chips at this site indicates occupancy of this location by people performing multiple tasks, most of which were not directly related to tool manufacture. The presence of chips suggests the processing phases of tool manufacture that were absent from the Point Detour Bay site—modification of blanks by bifacial flaking. The configuration of differences and similarities is similar to that for Point Detour Bay when compared to those for Seul Choix and Summer Island, although the actual frequencies of various classes of items are significantly different. These differences may only represent the difference between a surface-collected sample from a wide area as opposed to an excavated sample from a restricted area, or they may be real differences representing minor variability in the incidence of execution of different manufacturing phases at the two sites.

Seul Choix Site

At this site stone chips, tools, pottery, and other artifacts were present, representing activities other than stone tool manufacture. The relatively high incidence of laterally derived flakes (blanks?), the low incidence of broken cores, and the high incidence of completely exhausted cores and the presence of chips is believed to reflect a concentration on the final phases of tool production as opposed to the earlier phases as those dominating the activities at Point Detour Bay and present to a lesser degree at the Scott Point site. Seul Choix thus is believed to be a site at which activities other than tool manufacture were primary. The production of tools was carried out primarily by expediently utilizing partially processed nuclei and blanks brought into the site from elsewhere, perhaps from a place like Point Detour Bay.

SUMMER ISLAND SITE

This site differs from all of the others in the presence of flint working debris that is not characteristic of the bipolar technique described in this report. The presence of such material is tentatively interpreted to represent another occupation by unrelated populations presumably at an earlier time. This inference can be made alone on the basis of the Late Archaic association of the block core technique in the Great Lakes (Binford and Papworth, 1963). However, as noted earlier, Summer Island is a multiple occupancy site. In other respects Summer Island appears to be identical to the Seul Choix site as far as the technology of flint working is concerned.

Known Distribution of the Bipolar Knapping Technique

The flint knapping technique described here is to our knowledge previously unreported from the New World. It is a very distinctive type characterized by the production of small nuclei having a ridge of percussion produced by the placing of small pebbles on an anvil and directing a percussion blow parallel to the vertical axis of the pebble. Technically it is a crude and poorly controlled method of stone-working. Whether or not it simply represents an adaptive alternative for utilizing small tabular pebbles within a more diverse and elaborate stone-working tradition is unknown. Our knowledge of the temporal–spatial distribution of the technique is limited. The senior author first observed material of this type at the University of Michigan in the excavated sample from the Juntunen site on Bois Blanc Island near the Straits of Mackinac. At the time he examined the latter materials, dated between A.D. 900 and 1300 (Crane and Griffin, 1961, p. 110), he was puzzled by the chipped flint and did not then recognize the assemblage as the result of the reported bipolar technique. Without a doubt many of the Juntunen cores are identical to the forms reported here. The presence of such materials at the Juntunen site extends the distribution of the bipolar technique eastward at least as far as the Straits of Mackinac.

Three other sites from the Lake Michigan basin are known to yield small amounts of materials representative of this technique. These are the Lighthouse site at the Lake Michigan entrance to the Sturgeon Bay Canal in Door County, Wisconsin; a site near the Stony Lake Channel in Oceana County, Michigan; and the Eastport site, located between Grand Traverse Bay and Torch Lake in

Antrim County, Michigan. Late Woodland cultural materials were collected from the first two sites by Quimby. The Eastport site was mainly occupied in the Late Archaic period. However, the variety of projectile point forms from this site suggests multiple occupations. At a previous time, when Binford analyzed a large sample from the Eastport site, he reported one "truncated core" (Binford and Papworth, 1963) which we now know to have been a bipolar core of the type with basal area opposed by a point of percussion. A single specimen of a ridge-point bipolar core was also recently recovered from the site by Quimby. These two finds are not associated definitely with any other materials, so that their temporal and cultural relationships to the well-established Late Archaic occupation of the site are unknown.

The eight currently known sites yielding varying proportions of this material extend along the northwest, north, and northeast shores of Lake Michigan. Late Woodland sites south of this area on both the Wisconsin and Michigan shores have not revealed the presence of this technique, thus suggesting that its distribution on a north–south axis in the Michigan basin may be fairly well defined. Sites from the Huron or Superior basins have not been examined.

Summary

We have defined a new and heretofore unreported bipolar type of flint-working technique and have made the initial steps toward its spatial and temporal isolation. Four sites yielding this material have been analyzed, partly as a demonstration of what can be done with artifacts that are the by-products of tool production. The result was the recognition of a *nonceramic* site, Point Detour Bay, as in all probability being a specific location for the processing of raw material during the initial phases of the tool-manufacturing sequence characteristic of some Late Woodland populations in the Great Lakes. The Scott Point site was identified as being a location where many different activities were carried out, including the initial and later phases of the tool-manufacturing sequence. Seul Choix was identified as a site where activities other than tool manufacture were most important; nevertheless some tool processing was accomplished by utilizing partially modified blanks and nuclei largely produced at other locations. The Summer Island site was identified as probably multicomponent, having perhaps Late Archaic to Middle Woodland occupations as well as the Late Woodland remains that we analyzed. The latter assemblage was functionally identical to that at the Seul Choix site. It is believed that these insights into the activities and occupational histories of the prehistoric sites examined could not have been gained through a conventional approach that was concerned only with tools and other finished artifacts.

Acknowledgments

We wish to thank Mr. James R. Getz of Lake Forest, Illinois, for his assistance, financial and otherwise, in support of Chicago Natural History Museum's archaeological investigations in the upper Great Lakes region. We also thanked the late Mr. Harry W. Getz of Moline, Illinois, for reading the first draft of this report and making many helpful suggestions. We are grateful to the Marian and Adolph Lichtstern Fund of the Department of Anthropology of the University of Chicago for financial assistance in obtaining illustrations of the flint specimens, and we are also grateful to Miss Nancy Engle, who made the drawings of these flint specimens. We are indebted to Chicago Natural History Museum for publishing our report, and last but not least we wish to thank Miss Lillian A. Ross, Associate Editor of Scientific Publications, for her editorial work in our behalf.

References

Binford, Lewis R., and Mark L. Papworth. (1963). *The Eastport Site, Antrim County, Michigan,* Anthropological Papers, No. 19, pp. 71–123. Museum of Anthropology, University of Michigan.

Crane, H. R., and James B. Griffin. (1961). University of Michigan Radiocarbon Dates. VI. *American Journal of Science* 3, 105–125.

McPherron, Alan. (1963). Personal communication.

An Analysis of Cremations from Three Michigan Sites[*]

One characteristic feature of Late Archaic burial customs in the Great Lakes area was the occasional cremation of human remains for, or prior to, interment. Such practices constitute an interesting feature of these sociocultural systems because they may vary in both structural and stylistic features across the area at different times. Several major patterns of variation could be isolated through the study of archaeologically recovered cremated bone: (a) cremation on individual or collective pyres, (b) cremation of complete or dismembered bodies, and (c) cremation of dry, defleshed bones or bodies in the flesh. In addition to variations of this type, further differentiation may be exhibited in the treatment after burning and in the nature of the final distribution and disposal of the cremated remains. Differences may also be recognizable in the age and sex, as well as the associated items differentiating individuals afforded cremation, as opposed to other forms of mortuary treatment.

The investigation of several Late Archaic sites by the staff of the Museum of Anthropology, University of Michigan, has resulted in the recovery of a number of cremations for comparative study. This report is designed to present the results of preliminary investigations into the problem of the formal analysis of cremated bone. In addition, it will provide a limited set of observations concerning the crematory practices of the Late Archaic populations of Michigan represented by eight examples from three separate sites: the Andrews site (unreported), the Pomranky site (Binford, 1963a), and the Hogers site (Binford, 1963b).

* I am deeply indebted to Charles Eyman of the University of Michigan for aid in sorting the cremations, identification of bone elements, and for sexing and aging the fragments amenable to such analysis. Mark L. Papworth, then of the Museum of Anthropology, was of great assistance in sorting and generally carrying out many of the tasks necessary to the analysis.

Originally published in *Wisconsin Archeologist,* **44,** 98–110 (1963).

Unfortunately, the comparisons made between these are not all based on strictly comparable data since the investigations of crematory practices were conducted over a three-year period. Cremations from each site were studied separately, and as our knowledge increased new approaches were added. Unfortunately, the materials analyzed earlier were not reevaluated using more up-to-date methods. Nevertheless, it is worthwhile to make the results available to others as a basis for further comparison and refinement of analytic techniques.

Review of the published literature concerning crematory practices in the eastern United States shows that Krogman (1939), Webb and Snow (1945), and Baby (1954) have conducted the major investigations. These researchers have disagreed on rather basic criteria for distinguishing cremations of dry, defleshed bone from burned bodies. For instance, Webb and Snow report on the work of Krogman as follows:

> It appears that when bones in a dry condition are incinerated, besides being calcined, they show cracking or "checking" . . . like the patina of age on an oil painting. However, if a body should be burned in the flesh, besides possibly showing an incomplete incineration of bone, it is often possible to see under power magnification the remains of incompletely consumed endosteum (Webb and Snow, 1945, p. 189).

Baby's later work on Hopewell cremations indicates that Krogman's observations were not fully correct. According to Baby:

> Krogman states that "the people of the Hopewell culture practiced cremation mainly on defleshed and dried bones, though not to the exclusion of fleshed cremations." This conclusion is based on the examination of a few completely incinerated fragments, which "show burning in the flesh."
>
> The last statement is correct, but the former is incorrect. The characteristic features of the incinerated fragments examined by Krogman are identical with the residue of a recent test burning of a whole fleshed cadaver and of "green bones" from the dissecting room. Burnt dry bones exhibit superficial checking, fine longitudinal fracturing or splintering, and no warping. None of the material examined in this study suggested the burning of dry bones (Baby, 1954, p. 5).

The disagreements between Baby and Krogman can be summed as follows: Krogman suggests that the presence of "checking" is indicative of dry bone cremation, while incompletely burned bone denotes flesh cremation. Baby challenges the hypothesis that "checking" or calcined bone necessarily signifies dry bone cremation.

Baby's experiments revealed that there are distinctive differences between flesh and dry bone cremations. Deep transverse splitting or "checking" is more characteristic of flesh cremations while superficial checking, "like patina of age on an oil painting," and deep longitudinal fractures characterize dry bone cremations. Warping predominates on bone which is cremated while the flesh adheres, but is absent from those bones burned in a dry state.

Before an analysis of the cremated material from the Michigan sites could be made, it was necessary to repeat Baby's experiments in order to confirm or refute them and to provide controlled comparative material obtained when the crematory techniques were known.

A burial approximately 1500 years old, and recently macerated bone obtained from the Anatomy Department, University of Michigan, constituted the dry bone specimens for experimentation. The right humerus, two left fibular, left ischium, left third rib, and ninth thoracic vertebra from each source were cremated under the same condition, a very hot charcoal fire. It was reasoned that the way in which hot bone was cooled might affect its external appearance. Half of the specimens were allowed to cool naturally; the other half were doused with water and thus cooled abruptly. The effects of cremation on the macerated and archaeological bone were the same. The long bones exhibited superficial checking, fine longitudinal striae, deep longitudinal fracturing or splintering with no warping. The soft spongy bone (ischium, vertebrae, etc.) showed almost no checking, but small fractures developed along the "longitudinal" axis of the bone. Water cooling caused the bone to break up, splitting along the heat-produced fractures and longitudinal striae, although there was no increase in the amount of checking. Bone which was allowed to cool naturally remained largely intact. In neither case was there any warping of the bone. The findings completely support Baby's observations.

Experiments with flesh and green bone were more difficult to duplicate. For this phase of the work we employed a partially dissected green monkey cadaver since we could not obtain human specimens. The following anatomical parts of the monkey were cremated as units: the head (severed from the vertebral column at the axis), the left arm (severed from the trunk at the shoulder), and both the right and the left feet (severed from the legs at the ankle).

Like the dry specimens, these units were cremated in a charcoal fire and half were abruptly cooled by dousing with water. The skull of the monkey exhibited differential degrees of calcining. The frontoorbital, maxillary, and mastoparietal regions were completely calcined. The fragile bones inside the orbits and in the nose were calcined so completely that the slightest pressure reduced them to small flakes and minute fragments. The region for the attachment of the internal pterygoid to the mandibles was incompletely calcined; part of this charred muscle adhered to the bone. The basilar and nuchal regions of this skull were incompletely calcined. Warping was marked in all regions, as was warping along cracks which developed in the bone during incineration. The effect of burning was similar on the long bones—deep longitudinal and transverse fracturing, with warping along the edges of the fractures. Transverse fractures tended to be curved and serrated in appearance, as opposed to the straight cracking observed on the cremated dry bones. This was not a presence-or-absence matter, but rather one of relative frequency. No curved cracks were observed on old dry bones, while both angular and curved checking was present on the fresh bone. Checking was superficial on the dry bone, but in most cases extended completely through the green bone. Warping was marked: in some cases the endosteum was identifiable on partially calcined fresh bone fragments. Rapid cooling had the same effect as on the dry bones—breaking along the fire-produced cracks.

It is concluded that the degree of bone calcining is a function of the length of time in the fire, the intensity of the heat, the thickness of the protecting muscle tissue, and the position of the bone in relation to the point of oxidation of the consuming flame. In both experiments the findings support Baby's conclusions. Differences are observable between bone which was dry when burned as opposed to flesh cremation. Dry bone tends to show predominantly longitudinal fractures, an absence of warping, and superficial angular cracking; cremations of green bone or bone with the flesh attached show deep transverse fractures, frequently curved, much warping, and the occasional presence of endosteum.

These experiments provide the basic information necessary for examining the Late Archaic cremations with regard to determining whether dry defleshed bones or bodies were being cremated.

Baby's study of Hopewell cremations provides the model for the analysis of burned bone with an aim of determining whether or not bodies were dismembered prior to cremation. The analysis of anatomical parts as to their degree of burning was the methodology employed. Baby classified the material he examined as follows:

1. Completely incinerated. Fragments range from light to blue-gray to buff and show deep "checking," diagonal transverse fracturing, and warping.

2. Incomplete incineration (smoked). Fragments are blackened through the incomplete combustion of organic material present in the bone. Frequently, bits of charred periosteum are found adhering to the outer surface.

3. Nonincinerated or "normal bone." These fragments were not affected by the heat, but show some smoking along the edges.

Using these attributes, Baby concluded that in Hopewell cremations bodies were dismembered before burning judging from the differential cremation of contiguous anatomical parts. The observed differential firing could not reasonably have been produced had the remains been articulated. Because Baby's study is the only one available as a guide to the analysis of cremated remains (with the question of dismembering discussed), his results will be mentioned here. Aside from the methodological guide, Baby's study also serves as a basis for comparison with the remains from the Michigan Sites.

Baby examined 128 Hopewell cremations. He found the facial region, external cranial vault, mandible, atlas and axis vertebrae, ribs (rarely found), entire arm and hand, iliac blades, distal two thirds of the femur, almost all of the tibia, the fibula, and the feet were consistently calcined. The temporal squamosa were partly burned. The spines and transverse processes of the vertebrae (except the first and second cervicals mentioned above), the greater trochanter, and the posterior part of the tibial promontory were smoked. The upper sacrum, vertebral centra, pubis, ischium, acetabulum, and proximal third of the femur were normal. There is no mention of the sternum, clavicle, scapula, or patella.

Baby opinioned that the variation in burning according to the particular anatomical region was due to partial dismemberment of the body prior to its cremation. He suggested that the head was severed from the neck, the legs severed at the knees, and that possibly the arms were severed at the shoulders. The small bundle which could be produced by such partial disarticulation seems necessary if the body was to be fitted into the small Hopewell crematory basins.

Eight clusters of cremated bone from three Michigan sites constitute the sample studied. Four cremations occurred as part of the "grave furniture" in the single excavated burial at the Pomranky site near Midland, Michigan (Binford, 1963a). One discrete burial of cremated bone from the Andrews site near Saginaw, Michigan (Feature No. 3), as well as two other cremations which occurred as "burial furniture" in Feature No. 4 and the second burial excavated by Rodger Pfeiffer, a local amateur. The final sample was obtained from the single excavated burial at the Hogers site near Saginaw, Michigan (Binford, 1963b).

Table I presents the tabulated data for the Hopewell cremations studied by Baby and the eight cremations studied from the Michigan area, with regard to the degree of burning of the anatomical parts reported by Baby. Examination of this table reveals a striking difference between the cremations from the Michigan sites and the Hopewell sample.

The evidence pointed to by Baby as indicative of dismemberment prior to cremation is absent in the Michigan material. Another important difference between the Michigan cremations and the Hopewell data is the frequency with which incomplete incineration of the elbow region occurs in the cremation from the Pomranky and Andrews sites. The significance of this consistent characteristic is not readily apparent. One would expect the elbow region to be exposed as it is not protected by large muscles; it should, therefore, be calcined. We can only postulate that as part of the preparation of the corpse for cremation the arms were bound in such a way that the elbow region was protected from intense burning—arms across the body and/or thighs flexed with the elbows between the trunk and thighs? The basal region of the skull, which Baby found to be consistently incinerated among Hopewell cremations, occurs incompletely incinerated with the single exception of Pomranky cremation No. 4. This suggests that the head was still attached to the body at the time of the burning of the Michigan bodies. Such an inference is justified in terms of the large nuchal

TABLE I   Degree of Incineration by Anatomical Part.

Anatomical part	Hopewell	Pomranky				Andrews			Hogers
		1	2	3	4	3	4	p 2	
1. Base of skull	C	I	NI	I	C	I	I	NI	NI
2. Upper parts of skull	C	C	C	C	C	C	C	C	C
3. Vertebrae	1st and 2nd cervical, C; other, nonincinerated	C	C	C	C	C	I	S	I
4. Upper extremities	C	C, except elbow	C	C, except elbow	C	C, except elbow	C, except elbow		I
Ribs	C	C	C	C	C	C	C	I	
Pelvic area	Acetabulum and ishium nonincinerated. iliac blades complete	—	—	—	—	C	—	—	S
Femur	Proximal, 1/3 I; distal, 2/3 C	—	—	C	—	C	—	—	S
Tibia, fibula	C	—	—	—	—	C	—	—	S

^a Key to abbreviations: I, incomplete; C, complete; NI, not identified; S, smoked.

muscles which protect the base of the skull. It can be concluded from this comparison that the treatment of the body prior to cremation was strikingly different among the Hopewell societies as opposed to those represented by the Michigan cremations. The Andrews and Pomranky site samples are virtually identical in the degree to which various body regions were differentially burned. Both of these are in rather striking contrast to the Hogers site sample. The latter is admittedly very poorly represented, but nevertheless, it was subjected to much less intense heat and shows a variant pattern of differential burning. Although the entries in Table I do not suggest much variation in the degree of burning intensity among the cremations from the several sites, inspection of the remains shows such variation. Each individual cremation has peculiarities in the degree to which various parts are completely calcined, giving each a slightly different color grade when viewed in mass. This suggests individual treatment for each of the buried units of cremated remains.

In summary, the individuals represented in Baby's sample of Hopewell remains were treated differently at the time of cremation from those at the Pomranky and Andrews sites. The latter two sites differ considerably from the treatment represented at the Hogers site. Regardless of the latter differences the cremations from the Michigan sites represent separate crematory episodes since there is more homogeneity within a single crematory feature in the degree of differential incineration than there is between crematory features. This is viewed as evidence for burning on individual or single crematory pyres. The Michigan data further suggests that the cremations do not represent the burning of multiple elements of dismembered bodies as do the Hopewell samples; instead they indicate the burning of complete bodies or unitary parts thereof. Cremated individuals from the Andrews and Pomranky sites may have been partially flexed at the time of incineration.

As regards the question of whether bodies in the flesh or dry bones were cremated, it can be flatly stated that in all cases, judging from the experiments conducted by Krogman, Baby, and those reported here, the Michigan examples represent the incineration of bodies in the flesh.

Turning now to the interesting question of treatment after burning and the degree to which individuals were afforded differential treatment, a comparison of the contents of the cremation will be made. Table II represents the frequency lists of the various identifiable anatomical parts present in each feature.

Inspection of the table shows that at the Pomranky site, with the exception of cremation No. 3, there is a complete lack of lower limb and pelvic fragments. While the femur is represented in cremation number three there is a general lack of lower limb bones. This sample pattern is duplicated at the Andrews sites for cremations No. 4 and p 2. These observations suggest that the individuals were dismembered prior to burning, the lower limbs not being burned with the torso, or that there was selection in the removal of the cremated bone from the

TABLE II Tabulation of Frequency of Skeletal Part by Cremation as well as Quantity of Bone, Number of Individuals, Sex, and Age

Anatomical part	Pomranky				Andrews			Hogers
	1	2	3	4	3	4	p2	1
Skull	37	26	35	14	x	x	x	7
Teeth	4	–	–	8	x	x	x	–
Vertebrae	1	4	4	3	x	x	x	3
Humerus	38	2	13	6	x	x	–	–
Radius, ulna	4	10	8	11	x	x	–	3
Phalanges	–	1	1	20	x	x	–	1
Ribs	2	5	5	–	x	x	–	6
Pelvis	–	–	–	–	x	–	–	2
Femur	–	–	7	–	x	–	x	1
Patella	–	–	–	–	x	–	–	–
Tibia	–	–	–	–	x	–	–	2
Fibula	–	–	–	–	x	–	–	1
Phalanges	–	–	–	–	x	–	–	–
Weight of Total	36.2 g	109.5 g	93.5 g	46.2 g	?	?	?	334 g
No. of Individuals	1	1	1	1	4	1	1	1
Sex[a]	?	?	?	?	3 female 1?	?	?	?
Age[a]	8–12	12–15	10–13	5–7	3 adult 1 child	child	child	12–17

[a] For recent work on sexing and aging cremations, see Gejvail (1959).

crematory basin prior to deposition in the graves. All of these features have in common their occurrence as associated elements within the grave of a noncremated individual. Unlike the latter, Andrews burial No. 3 was a discrete burial of cremated bone, and did yield fragments representative of the entire skeleton. The Hogers site feature was a cremation *in situ,* buried in the crematory basin, and is also representative of the entire skeleton. On the basis of these limited data there appears to be differential treatment of individuals afforded discrete burial as opposed to those whose remains were incorporated as part of the materials buried with a noncremated person. Inspection of the age and sex data suggests that these differences may be associated with age and sex distinctions ritually recognized among the societies represented. All of the individuals who were incorporated and hence only partially represented were subadults. Cremated adult females were afforded discrete burial at the Andrews sites. As in the case of previous comparisons the Hogers site differs, in this case an adolescent was afforded discrete burial.

Of methodological interest is the observation that there is a generalized regression of weight of cremated bone with age of individual within the samples from the Pomranky site. Certainly this sample is insufficient to establish a reliable correlation; yet the data suggest that such a correlation may exist. If this is so, it could serve as a further aid in aging cremated individuals given certain control on the burning procedures.

We might summarize the findings as follows:

1. Experiments confirmed the findings of Baby; cremations of dry bones can be distinguished from those of green or flesh covered bone. Dry bones exhibit superficial checking of the surface, longitudinal splitting, and a lack of warping. Cremated fresh bones are distinguishable by warping, deep transverse fracturing frequently on curvilinear planes, and longitudinal splitting or a ragged nature. In addition, portions of endosteum are occasionally observed on the surface of cremated fresh bone.

2. Examination of cremations from the Michigan area revealed that they were all burnings of fresh bone and had been incinerated on discrete as opposed to communal pyres.

3. Comparison of the Michigan and Hopewell cremations reveals a much different pattern of treatment of the body prior to incineration. Hopewell practices involved the partial dismemberment of the body prior to its complete cremation. The Michigan samples suggest the cremation of complete or partial bodies but in the latter case disarticulated parts were not burned together. At the Andrews and Pomranky sites, the bodies were probably flexed so that the elbows were protected by the muscle and tissue of the abdomen and thighs. This does not appear to have been the practice at the Hogers site.

4. Comparison of the several cremations from Michigan reveals that those

occurring as inclusions with noncremated individuals invariably were children and young adolescents who had been incinerated at another location. Such cremations were further distinctive in that the body from the pelvis down was not generally represented. In contrast, the burial which occurred at the Andrews site as a discrete interment, as well as the Hogers site burial, represented the complete individual. Discrete burial of cremated remains was restricted to adult women at the Andrews site. The recognition of these distinctions suggest that the practice of cremation was being utilized as an element of social ritual for distinguishing between individuals occupying socially differentiated status positions. Age and sex distinction being most crucial for understanding the crematory practices at the sites studied.

5. The burial practices as elucidated through this study reveal a number of common features in the mortuary ceremonialism represented at the Pomranky and Andrews sites while the Hogers site is singularly distinctive. These findings suggest much closer cultural ties between the societies represented at the former sites than either have with that represented by the latter.

Admittedly these conclusions are based on a very small sample and the pansocial reliability of the age–sex distinctions discussed in the fourth point above are made tenuous on this account. Regardless, the results should be sufficient to point to the necessity for formal and comparative analysis of cremated remains as a profitable approach to the study of differing mortuary practices and to the way various classes of individuals were differentially treated in mortuary rites.

References

Baby, Raymond S. (1954). Hopewell cremation practices. *Papers in Archaeology* No. 1.

Binford, Lewis R. (1963a). *The Pomranky Site; A Late Archaic Burial Station,* Anthropological Papers, No. 19, pp. 149–192. Museum of Anthropology, University of Michigan.

Binford, Lewis R. (1963b). *The Hogers Site: A Late Archaic Burial Station,* Anthropological Papers, No. 19, pp. 124–148. Museum of Anthropology, University of Michigan.

Gejvall, Av N.-G. (1959). *Nagot om Bestamning av Branda Ben och Deras Veterskapliga,* pp. 40–47. Fynd Goteborg, Sweden.

Krogman, Wilton M. (1939). A guide to the identification of human skeletal material. Federal Bureau of Investigation. *Law Enforcement Bulletin* **8.**

Webb, William S., and C. E. Snow. (1945). *The Adena People.* Reports in Anthropology and Archaeology, Vol. VI. Univ. of Kentucky, Lexington.

Analysis of a Cremated Burial from the Riverside Cemetery, Menominee County, Michigan [*]

With the proper approach it should be possible to discover and document a great deal about social systems and the political and religious organizations for most prehistoric [North American] cultures. There must be limits, kinds of information we cannot reconstruct, but until we have tried we shall not know where these limits are (Sears, 1961, p. 225).

At the suggestion of William Hruska of the Oshkosh Public Museum, the analysis was undertaken of a mass of cremated bone from Burial No. 6 at the Riverside cemetery site. Previous work on cremations from Late Archaic–Early Woodland sites in the Great Lakes (Binford, 1963c) has shown that such remains can be analyzed to yield useful information about the mortuary procedure and attendant practices employed by a group. Analysis of the data from Riverside was undertaken in order to determine as much as possible about the crematory practices represented and to obtain information for comparison of crematory data from Riverside Cemetery with other sites of an approximately contemporaneous period.

Analysis of the Remains

The remains from Burial No. 6 consisted of 2946.74 g of cremated bone. The overall color of the mass of bone was grayish; completely white calcined bone fragments were rare in the sample. Almost every fragment had smoked areas which were incompletely incinerated. These characteristics suggest a crematory fire that was (a) not exceedingly hot, (b) not maintained for an extended period of time, or (c) a combination of both these conditions.

[*] Not previously published.

    The bone fragments were uniformly characterized by transverse deep curvilinear fractures, much warping, and the occasional presence of endosteum. All of these features are diagnostic of cremation of individuals in the flesh and not of cremation of dried bone (see Baby, 1954; Binford, 1963c).

    The degree to which different anatomical parts of individuals were differentially calcined provides clues to the position of the body during cremation. Skull fragments, largely from the parietal region, were uniformly blackened rather than being calcined. All individuals exhibited more blackening and less completely calcined fragments of the femoral shafts and the patellae, as well as parts of the tibia. These observations suggest cremation of a body in such a way as to protect the parietal region from exposure to the flames since that region is not protected by heavy muscles. The incomplete incineration of the thighs is understandable because of the heavy protective muscle of that area and the relatively low heat suggested by the general lack of complete calcination of the bone.

    The number of individuals represented, as well as their age and sex, was evaluated.* Bone fragments were sorted into identifiable categories, such as long bone fragments, ribs and vertebrae, pelvic and scapular fragments, hand and foot bones, and the various bones of the skull. By further breaking down the content of each of these categories as to specific bones and parts of bones represented, it was possible to determine the minimal number of individuals that had been included in the burial. This number was determined by the presence of one right and four left mandibular condyles, two right and three left adult patellae and the patella of a child, and temporal parts (petrous portion and post-glenoid process) of four individuals. These data demonstrate the presence of at least four different individuals.

    Analysis of the sex and age characteristics of the bone fragments made possible the identification of the following individuals within the cremation: (1) Adult female, probably slightly more than 30 years of age; (2) One young adult female, between the ages of 18 and 25; (3) One adult of undetermined sex between the ages of 25 and 35 (Although there were no clearcut sexual traits identifiable, it is the opinion of the authors that a female is represented); (4) One child of undetermined sex, between the ages of 5 and 10 years.

    In attempting to assess the relative completeness of the skeletons represented, two general lines of evaluation were used. First, in the segregation of the various categories of bones mentioned above, an attempt was made to evaluate the degree to which the remains represented the four different individuals defined above. It was noted that of all the identifiable anatomical parts, sections of the mandibular body were the least well represented. In fact, there were only five small fragments of mandibular arch, all believed to be from a single individual. It was reasoned that since the mandibular condyles and other portions of the rami

---

* This work was done by Dr. Charles Merbs of the University of Chicago.

of four individuals were present, there had been some conscious deletion of segments of the mandibular body.

A clue to this seemingly baffling situation may be present in the known content of a roughly contemporaneous burial from lower Michigan. At the Pomranky site (Binford, 1963a) a complex burial was studied in which there were five separate clusters of teeth identifiable as segments of mandibles included in the burial, presumably as part of the burial furniture. These mandibular sections had not been cremated. If the removal of mandibular sections as evidenced at the Pomranky site had been a practice of the society represented at the Riverside cemetery, then we would expect to find the remains of individuals lacking major sections of the mandible, presumably removed before major mortuary treatment.

In addition, one individual appeared to be rather poorly represented. Although many fragments appear to be missing, there is no evidence that there was selectivity in the deletion of anatomical parts; all parts of the skeleton appear in the sample. This observation, suggesting loss or deletion of bones prior to interment, is supported by the following comparative data on the gross weight of the bone sample. It has been estimated that the cremated (fully calcined and leached) remains of an adult male would yield approximately 1750 g of cremated bone. Taking this figure as a basis of comparison, we would expect a total of approximately 5260 g of bone for the three adults in the sample and an additional 900 g for the child, assuming that all the bone was burned. We would expect a total of 6160 g of bone. However, the total weight of the recovered bone was only 2946.74 g, indicating a considerable loss of bone, either through the absence of some of the remains of one individual as well as through either mechanical or chemical loss since cremation.

The contents of the cremation were also analyzed to determine (a) if there were any included materials not identifiable as human bone and (b) if there were any attributes of the human bone that would indicate specific treatment either prior to or during the cremation and subsequent burial.

The remains of nonhuman origin mixed with the cremated bone were: (a) one unburned fragment of a large barrel-shaped shell bead; (b) nine fragments of cremated bird bone of unidentified species; (c) seven sizable fragments of wood charcoal tentatively identified as white pine; and (d) two burned and one unburned flint chip.

Inspection of the bone fragments for indications of rodent gnawing, cut marks, or other signs of mutilation yielded negative results. There were, however, a relatively large number of fragments, largely humeri of all the individuals represented, showing some red coloration. Since there was no powdered hematite included in the burial feature at the time of interment, it would appear that the red color was the result of powdered hematite having been sprinkled on the upper part of the body during its cremation.

Reconstruction of the Mortuary Procedure

Burial feature No. 6 represents the remains of four individuals: two adult females, one adult of uncertain sex, and one child. All four of these individuals had been cremated shortly after death under very similar conditions. There is some evidence suggesting that prior to cremation at least three of the individuals had been partially mutilated by the removal of a section from the mandibular arch, presumably for use as a "memento" or heirloom. After this initial post-mortem treatment, each individual had been extended on a crematory pyre with the head protected between log or stone "head rests" which prevented the fire from attacking the parietal regions of the skull. The fire was not of great intensity and does not appear to have been maintained long after the body was visibly consumed; there was no evidence of the bones having been raked around in the fire since adjacent parts of the body evidenced similar conditions of burning. The relatively low intensity of the crematory fire may be explained in part by the use of a soft wood as fuel—white pine. During the period of cremation, powdered hematite was sprinkled over the arms and shoulders of the nearly consume; corpse, resulting an ocherous coloration of the upper-arm fragments. Accompanying one or more of these individuals at the time of cremation were the wings of a freshly killed, relatively large bird.

After cremation, the calcined bone fragments were gathered from the crematory together with small fragments of rock and flint chips that had been in the soil forming the base of the crematory pyre. The remains were presumably stored in some form of container since it is not likely that all four of the individuals died at one time and were cremated simultaneously. Presumably after the lapse of an undetermined period of time, an interment ritual was conducted in which the cremated remains of four individuals were given a common burial in a single pit. Finally the common grave pit was filled with soil from the surrounding area which included flint chips and other debris from the general habitation activities also conducted at the location.

Comparison with Other Sites

These data from the Riverside cemetery document certain interesting points of comparison with approximately contemporaneous sites. This burial, and the cremations previously studied from the Pomranky site and the Andrews site, both in Saginaw County, Michigan, all have in common the following features:

A. There were essentially four recognizable phases to the mortuary rites.

1. Pre-crematory preparation of the body: In both the Pomranky site and

Riverside cemetery, there is positive evidence for the special precremation treatment of sections of the mandibular arch.

2. Cremation: This phase of the mortuary rites was similar at all three sites in the following ways: (a) bodies were cremated in the flesh, (b) certain goods accompanied the body during cremation, including various animal parts as well as limited numbers of items of adornment and/or tools. (See Binford, 1963a and b.)

3. Post-crematory stewardship of bone: After the crematory fire had died down, the remains were removed from the crematory basin (the completeness of removal seems to vary considerably) and placed in containers (skin bags are suggested at the Andrews (Papworth, 1971) and Pomranky sites). These containers were kept by some designated individual or group until an "appropriate" time for the next phase of the mortuary rite. During the time of stewardship, there may have been (a) some division of the cremated remains as suggested at Pomranky or (b) some loss of remains as suggested by the differences in completeness of individuals represented at Riverside.

4. Interment: Interment appears to have been accomplished in two basic ways: (a) Bones of several cremated individuals were placed in a single grave or (b) the bones of one or more cremated individuals were placed in the grave of another individual not afforded crematory rites. In the former case, when goods were contributed as part of the graveside ritual, they were contributed in common to the individuals interred as evidenced at Andrews burial No. 3 and Riverside No. 6. On the other hand, in the latter case the remains of cremated persons appeared to serve as grave goods for the uncremated person. Furthermore, the individual remains in these burials were spatially segregated.

In contrast to the similarities outlined above, differences between the sites examined do occur, they are:

1. At Riverside Burial No. 6 the bodies were extended on the fire with the skull protected, while at Andrews and Pomranky the bodies appear to have been flexed with the elbows against the abdomen and the thighs flexed to the chest.

2. Red maple wood was systematically used in the cremations at both Andrews and Pomranky sites, while white pine was probably used at Riverside cemetery.

3. At Riverside powdered hematite was sprinkled on the burning body, while at Andrews and Pomranky powdered hematite was placed on the calcined bones and contributed during the graveside ritual of interment.

4. At Riverside the remains of a freshly killed bird were cremated with one or more individuals, while at Andrews cremated dry bones of a small mammal were present.

5. At Pomranky, interment did not take place at habitation sites; at both Riverside and Andrews a habitation site was used for interment.

Social Context of Variability in Crematory Practices

Surprisingly, only a few anthropologists have addressed themselves to a consideration of the nature and causes of variation in mortuary activity. Kroeber, considering this problem a number of years ago, observed that the distribution of burial and cremation customs "failed to conform to the distribution of other culture traits" in the California area and "was usually irregular in itself"—that is, specific traits were distributed discontinuously (Kroeber, 1927, p. 312). Comparing this observation with similar distribution studies made in South America and Africa, he noted that analogous situations obtained in both cases. There were numerous cases of the coexistence of several different modes of disposal practiced by the same people and there were characteristically many variations between the practices of adjacent peoples. Generalizing about the African data Kroeber notes:

> Of particular interest are the frequent limitations of a particular method to a particular social class, so that several methods coexist in one tribe, and the same method has different applications in successive tribes (1927, pp. 312–313).

This observation provides a clue to what presently appears to be the best interpretation of the social context of cremation among the societies represented by the burials from the Riverside site as well as those from the Andrews and Pomranky sites. The following facts are pertinent: (1) Discrete burials of cremated remains thus far known are that (a) there are multiple burials of several individuals previously cremated, and (b) in all cases these individuals were adult females and adolescents or children. (2) At both the Andrews and Pomranky sites it was observed that in all known cases where cremated human bone served as grave goods, such remains were of adolescents.

The apparent correlations between mode of corpse disposal and sex and age distinctions lead us to postulate that the social function of cremation among the societies represented in our sample was to afford differential treatment to a recognized category of individuals (a "particular social class" in Kroeber's terms). Affiliation was largely dependent upon the sex and age of the individuals. We further postulate that such social distinctions are probably best understood as arising from the practice of exogamy and the consequent frequent lack of spatial congruence between the location of one's kin based "membership" unit and one's local group (established as a result of a marriage).

With such a perspective we can only look forward to structural analyses of the burial data from a series of cemeteries of this general time period. Such analyses should result in our gaining an understanding of at least some aspects of marriage and residence patterns as well as of "rules of descent" in the societies of the Late Archaic.

References

Baby, Raymond S. (1954). Hopewell cremation practices. *Papers in Archaeology* No. 1.

Binford, Lewis R. (1963a). *The Pomranky Site: A Late Archaic Burial Station,* Anthropological Papers, No. 19, pp. 149–192. Museum of Anthropology, University of Michigan.

Binford, Lewis R. (1963b). *The Hodges Site: A Late Archaic Burial Station,* Anthropological Papers, No. 19, pp. 124–148. Museum of Anthropology, University of Michigan.

Binford, Lewis R. (1963c). An analysis of cremations from three Michigan sites. *Wisconsin Archaeologist* 44, 98–110.

Kroeber, A. L. (1927). Disposal of the dead. *American Anthropologist* 29, 308–315.

Papworth, Mark L. (1971). *The Andrews Site and the Late Archaic of the Saginaw Valley.* Museum of Anthropology, University of Michigan (manuscript to be published).

Sears, William H. (1961). The study of social, and religious systems in North American archaeology. *Current Anthropology* 2, 223–246.

Galley Pond Mound *

General Description

Galley Pond Mound is located on a small spur of land on the east margin of
Wassam Ridge some 250 m south of the Toothsome site (Binford, 1964,
pp. 4–54). The mound exhibits a smooth contour and is approximately 21 m in
diameter, standing at its apex 75 cm above the land surface as prepared prior to
the mound's construction. The mound was heavily forested at the time of
investigation and had been previously disturbed over almost its entire central
area by relic hunters. A dirt road had cut into the west edge of the mound,
resulting in increased erosion in that area.

The soil profile of the mound was complicated by the intensive disturbance
by relic hunters and by rodents on the west side of the mound. In addition to
these complications, the mound had been constructed so that it covered an area
of zonal as well as azonal soil formation. Along the northern boundary of the
mound, there was an undisturbed hardpan base, characteristic of Wassam Ridge.
On the other hand, the southern and eastern margins of the mound had been
built over an azonal erosional surface composed of sands. The mound fill proper
was the loess soil of the normal upper soil zone on Wassam ridge. This made the
problem of distinguishing artificial mound fill from the normal upper zone of
loess soil difficult. Fortunately, in most sections of the mound the fill was
discolored by organic materials and "village debris" from earlier occupations of
the location. Obvious basket loading, so characteristically noted in midwestern
mounds, was not observable in the Galley Pond Mound. The upper undisturbed
sections of the mound exhibited a modern soil profile with the upper zone
composed of modern humus, below which was a discontinuous lens of "gray

* Abstracted from Lewis R. Binford, *Archaeological Investigations on Wassam Ridge,*
with appendices by Melvin L. Fowler and James Schoenwetter. Archaeological Salvage
Report No. 17, Southern Illinois University Museum, Carbondale, 1964.

soil" containing a high concentration of charcoal and ash. This lens was either the result of the kindling of fires on top of the mound prior to its reforestation or to the burning of the structure which had once occupied the location. This alternative will be discussed after the presentation of the structural information. Immediately below the gray soil was the mound fill.

EXCAVATION STRATEGY

The excavations were planned to elucidate a suspected superpositioning of accretional burials since the preliminary investigations had suggested that the mound was of Late Woodland affiliation (Fowler, 1960, p. 15). A trench 3 m wide was opened up through the center of the mound, with the excavation proceeding from north to south. It quickly became apparent that this was not an accretional mound and that the burials were most certainly of Mississippian affiliation. At this time, the presence of a structure was not suspected, and although soil discolorations which later proved to be the archaeological remains of a structure were observed during the early phases of excavation, they were not at that time recognized as elements of a building. The modification of field strategy from a trench approach to that of opening up a large contiguous area was prompted by the recognition that the burials were apparently orientated with respect to the cardinal directions. It was reasoned that a complete ground plan of the burials could yield data relevant to the differential treatment afforded individuals occupying differing status positions within the society represented. For this reason the trenching was not continued beyond the initial central trench, and an area of 36 m^2 was excavated in the northwest quadrant of the mound. Few burials and a great deal of disturbance by relic hunters discouraged the expenditure of more time at this site, and for the next 2 months investigations were conducted at other sites. During this two month period the field notes were reviewed and a number of puzzling features were recognized that prompted me to return to the site during the last 3 days of the field season. During these 3 days, the remaining unexcavated area in the western half of the mound was excavated, with due allowances for the very large trees growing in that area. The additional information obtained in the final 3 days made possible the interpretation of the previously recovered information. We were able to recognize the archaeological traces of a rather large building constructed on the site of the mound prior to the construction of the mound proper. This sequence of events is graphic demonstration that field methods are only appropriate in so far as they are executed within a framework of question asking. When new questions arise, methods must be altered to allow for their solution. In turn, new questions arise only in the context of a running analysis of the data conducted while the work is still in progress.

Galley Pond Mound: Past History

This mound has been known to local collectors as a burial area for over 30 years. The original discoverers of the mound are reported to have been local hunters who noticed human bone in the dirt thrown out by woodchucks. They "investigated and exposed several burials." According to the previous owner, this was done on the west side of the mound. These originally exposed burials are reported to have been *extended articulated burials.* Reportedly in association with these burials was a small human effigy, crudely executed in clay, as well as some "stone arrowpoints." Judging from the reports of local people, these burials were oriented with the heads to the south and lying in a rough north–south orientation. These should correspond to the extended burials located on the east side of the mound. (See burial features Nos. 26 and 27.)

Later a larger area on the west side of the mound was opened up, and bundle burials in small sandstone slab-lined "boxes" were uncovered. No grave goods are reported to have come from these burials. The previous owner reports that he and some friends "mined" large sandstone slabs from the mound in order to build a walk across his yard. They came to the mound with probes and readily located the "big rocks" not more than "20 inches" below the surface. They would dig these up and invariably find small "rock boxes" in which there were fragmentary human bones. A single pottery vessel is reported to have been found during this "mining" of the site. This area is generally the central disturbed area shown on the site plan.

Minor excavations were conducted by both Vernon Carpenter of Centralia, Illinois, and by Gregory Perino of the Gilcrease Foundation. The location of Carpenter's excavations is shown in Fig. 1. Photographs of these items can be obtained from Carpenter. Perino excavated a badly decomposed extended burial on the south edge of the mound. The location of his excavation is shown on Fig. 1, m.

Much digging in the mound was carried on in recent years, but this was largely in areas previously disturbed. When the site was initially visited by the field party in 1962, there were over 17 pits varying from 30 cm to over 1 m in depth, largely clustered in the higher areas of the mound. One local person reports that excavations along the top of the mound slope on the east side revealed "piles of charcoal."

INTERPRETATION

All of these reports are consistent with the interpretation made in this report, namely (1) that this was a burned mortuary structure (reports of charcoal along east edge); (2) that the extended burials were oriented with regard to the

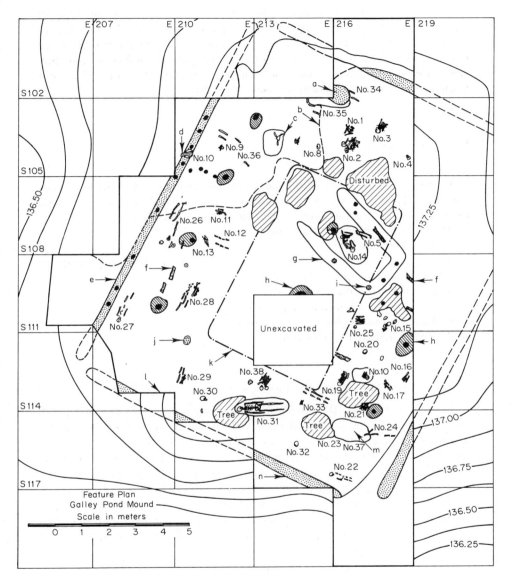

Fig. 1. *Feature plan of Galley Pond Mound. a. Burned area "A;" b. limits of hard clay; c. vessel No. 1; d. burial No. 10 (in doorway); e. wall trench; f. charred log; g. tomb feature; h. post pits; i. vessel No. 4; j. cremation feature; k. limits of central depression; l. limits of excavation; m. Perino's burial; n. edge of hard packed soil.*

structure walls with heads either to the west or south (reports of initial burials uncovered and Perino's excavation); (3) bundles were inside this outer ring of extended burials (Carpenter's excavation); and (4) that in the center of the mound and slightly higher than the other burials were a number of stone box graves (reports of mining operations and the recovery from the fill by pot hunters of numbers of fragments of sandstone slab).

Feature Descriptions

Unlike Toothsome site the excavations reported here deal with a single *complex* cultural feature, an artificial mound and included elements. The major elements of the mound in terms of their temporal juxtaposition are:
   1. Premound occupational surface
   2. Tomb Feature No. 1
   3. Construction of structural Feature No. 1 (mortuary house): (a) included burials, (b) individual burial "mounds"
   4. Burning of mortuary house
   5. Construction of earth mound cover
   6. Intrusive burials placed in the mound
   7. Recent activity of relic hunters.

Evidence for Premound Occupational Zone

In squares E 216-S 102 and S 105 and in squares E 216-S 117 and S 120 excavations into the submound soils yielded abundant evidence of *in situ* distributions of cultural items, consisting largely of cracked crystalline rock, bipitted anvil stones, abraders, projectile points of a generalized "Early Archaic" form (Thebes diagonal notched) and a complete absence of pottery. Concentrations of secondary flint-knapping debris was especially noticable in square E 216-S 117. These items occurred concentrated along a single "level" inclusive within undifferentiated deposits of fluvial sands heavily banded with ferric lenses (Fig. 1). There was a total absence of soil discolorations at the level of concentrated cultural debris. In most of the squares to the west of the central "trench," excavations were not carried down below the point of initial appearance of the ferric-banded clear sands. The presence of this layer of cultural debris as a generalized characteristic of the site is not well established. We can, however, demonstrate that the site had been occupied at a relatively early phase of the Archaic occupancy of the area. The presence of "later" forms of Archaic projectile points in the mound fill are suggestive of additional Archaic occupations.

Tomb Feature No. 1

This feature (see Fig. 1,g) was apparently a tomb which had existed at the site prior to the construction of structural Feature No. 1. Certainly the preparation of the floor and the excavation of the central depression of structure No. 1 intruded into this feature and had obscured most of its details.

Elements of the Feature

1. A rectangular open-ended trench
2. A central oval pit
3. A complete skeleton of a young adult female
4. Four postmolds in the trench.

The three-sided trench, shaped in a rectangular pattern, is 2.40 m wide and 3.60 m long. The trench varies between 45 cm and 65 cm in width. It is flat-bottomed and extended to a depth of 17 cm below the level of the central depression. Postmolds were not obvious in the trench; however, on cleaning the bottom of the trench four postmolds were identifiable (see Fig. 2). This trench surrounded a pit in which burial No. 14 was located (see Burial Description). Due to the fact that much of this feature had been obscured by the subsequent construction of structural Feature No. 1, we can only infer that it represents some type of mortuary "crypt" related to the interment of burial No. 14. The form of this burial (flexed) and the presence of some cultural debris of a Late Woodland type in the fill of the burial pit suggest a Late Woodland cultural affiliation.

The presence in the mound fill and in erosional lens in square E 216-S 120 of numbers of grit-tempered, cord-marked sherds attest to the utilization of this place by Late Woodland occupants. This is supporting evidence for the Late Woodland affiliation of tomb Feature No. 1 and included burial No. 14.

Structural Feature No. 1 (Figs. 1 and 2)

This feature was originally recognized by the presence of an obvious arrangement of burials within the burial area which aligned with a series of very minor soil discolorations suggestive of excavated wall trenches.

Elements of the Feature

1. Four wall trenches filled with loess soil exhibiting only a minor color contrast with the base soil
2. The sporadic occurrence of postmolds in the wall trenches
3. Large internal postmolds (eight)
4. Carbonized fragments of the burned superstructure
5. Doorway
6. Central depression floor
7. Burned areas A and B.

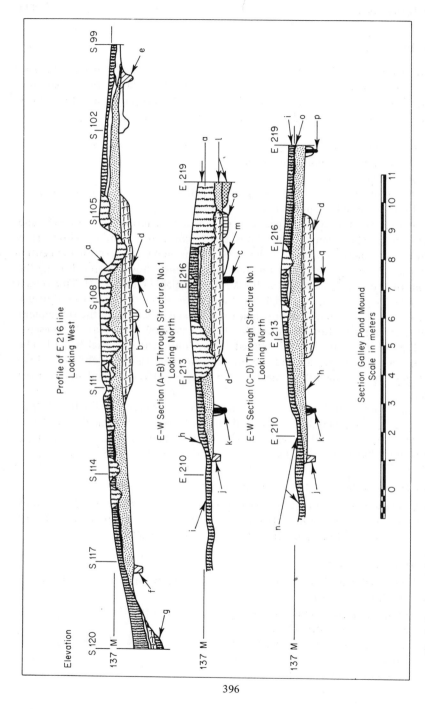

Fig. 2. Section of Galley Pond Mound. *a.* Recent disturbance; *b.* "tomb" trench; *c.* north center post; *d.* central depression; *e.* north wall trench; *f.* south wall; *g.* lens fill, pre-mound; *h.* mound fill; *i.* recent humus; *j.* west wall; *k.* west internal post; *l.* unidentified features; *m.* burial No. 14 pit; *n.* depressions of road; *o.* gray soil; *p.* east internal post; *q.* south center post.

396

Associated Elements
   1. All of the recovered burials and associated grave furniture
   2. Artifacts recovered from floor.

Description of Elements

Wall Trenches. The wall trenches were slightly tapering in cross section, diminishing from a mean width at the top of 45.5 cm for the north and south trenches and a mean of 34.4 cm for the east and west trenches to a mean for all trenches of 30.0 cm. It will be noted that while the south and north trenches were similar in upper width and differed from the east and west trenches, all trenches have a common basal width. The floor of the trench was squared off as if dug with some form of shovel or other implement. The longitudinal section of the trenches exhibited a relatively level and straight profile. The fill of the trenches on all sides except the north and northern part of the west trench was almost indistinguishable from the base soil. In the latter areas the trenches had been dug through the hardpan subsoil and there they were distinguished quite readily.

Postmolds within the Wall Trenches. Postmolds were not easily recognized and were seen only in the west wall. Of these recognized the average diameter was 16.4 cm with a mean spacing of 64.5 cm. The molds did not extend below the bottom of the wall trench, and they appear to have been roughly square at the base. Summary metrical data is given in Table I.

Large Internal Postmolds. Eight large internal posts were recognized; four are aligned parallel to the west wall at a distance of 1.50 m inside the west wall. They have a mean diameter of 23.25 cm, as opposed to the mean diameter of posts in the west wall of 16.44 cm. These posts along the west wall were set in pits which had been dug to a depth of only 14 cm below the floor of the structure, while the postmold extended to a mean depth 58 cm below the floor of the structure. The south and north posts in this line were each 3.25 m inside the south and north walls, respectively, and the mean spacing between the posts was 2.78 m. In the center of the structure were two large internal support posts. These are placed in from the north and south walls a distance of 6.17 m with a distance 2.85 m between them. Unlike the posts along the walls, these posts were set in pit excavations which extended some 61 cm below the floor of the central depression. Located along the east wall was a similar pattern of internal posts as described along the west wall. Summary data is given in Table I.

4. Carbonized Fragments of the Burned Superstructure. These remains occurred at three general locations in the mound: (1) adjacent to the large internal posts, (2) in the upper mound fill along the east edge of the excavations, and (3) on the floor of the central depression. In all cases these remains

TABLE I   Summary Data of Wall Trenches Structure No. 1

Location	Basal width (m)	Upper width (m)	Basal elevation (m)	Floor elevation (m)	Depth below floor (m)	Length (m)
North trench						
West end	–	–	–	–	–	–
Center	0.26	0.46	136.34	136.86	0.52	
East end	–	–	–	–	–	
South trench						10.58
West end	0.29	0.45	135.94	136.57	0.63	
Center	0.31	0.46	135.82	136.39	0.47	
East end	0.28	0.45	135.88	136.27	0.39	
East trench						
North end	–	–	–	–	–	–
Center	–	–	–	–	–	
South end	0.27	0.34	135.90	136.27	0.37	
West trench						14.45
North end	–	–	–	–	–	
Center	0.30	0.35	136.09	136.60	0.51	
South end	0.29	0.35	136.14	136.59	0.45	
Mean	0.29	0.41			0.48	

consisted of (a) large, completely carbonized logs, (b) masses of charcoal, largely disturbed by relic hunters, and (c) carbonized "tops" of postmolds. All identifiable discrete logs appear to have been part of the vertical wall supports; no horizontal members were identified.

Several facts must be noted:

(a) Along the west wall the internal posts burned and collapsed in a northern direction coming to rest almost on the floor of the house. (b) The large posts along the east side of the structure collapsed into the house (eastward) and lie at right angles to the east wall. (c) The latter posts lie on top of soil covering the burial placed on the floor and on the floor of the structure in the central depression. (d) Charcoal concentrations are much heavier along the east wall of the structure.

Given these observations, we may generalize that burials placed on the floor of the structure had small earth "mounds" covering them prior to the burning and collapse of the structure. Floor areas where burials were not located did not have earth coverings. Extended burials along the west wall had much less earth covering than did the bundle burials in that area and along the east wall. Very little can be added to our knowledge of the superstructure from the burned remnants. They all correspond well in size with the few recognizable postmolds. The presence of burned vertical posts along the east wall makes certain that the absence of postmolds reported in the wall trench in that area is due to peculiarities of the fill and soil conditions in that area.

Doorway. A single entryway has been identified, but others may have been present. This doorway was located in the northwest section of the west wall. It was identifiable because of a slightly wider spacing between the posts and the presence of subfloor bundle burial (No. 10) within the wall trench. Over this burial was placed a large limestone slab which was level with the floor of the structure and which served as a threshold. In addition, there was a line of small postmolds running from the south door frame to the large internal support post inside the structure, aligned with the doorway. We may envision an internal partition blocking the view of the majority of the internal features as one approached the entry from he outside. The location of burial No. 10 in the entryway is interpreted as having been related to social ritual conducted at the time of the construction of the building.

Floor. The floor was not specially prepared by the introduction of clay, etc., as a special covering. It was simply a flattened surface prepared on the original soil. It gradually sloped downward from north to south and from west to east; however, the slope was very gradual and probably hardly perceptible to the eye. Several observations suggest that the floor may have been covered with woven mats. Underneath the charred log which fell into the central depression and in burned floor areas, presumably burned in connection with the burning of the building, there were charred fragments of what appeared to be matting. The obvious semisubterranean floor, so characteristic of other Mississipian structures, was not so readily recognizable here. If the floor had been prepared below the original surface, it was only in connection with leveling and cleaning the area, as a deep excavation was certainly lacking.

Central Depression. In the exact center of the structure was a rectangular depression encompassing 33.40 m^2. This depression had been excavated to a uniform depth of 34.0 cm below the level of the floor. The walls of this depression were steeply sloped, and the bottom was quite level. There was an absence of any hearth areas in this depression, and there were no associated features. It is certainly significant that there were no burials located in this area.

Burned Areas A and B. Two minor areas of oxidized soil occurred on the floor of the structure in the north end of the building. Area A is the result of the burning of the structure; however, area B may have been the location of a fire kindled repeatedly directly on the floor of the structure.

Summary Description of Structure No. 1

This building was a rectangular structure covering a total floor area of 176.86 m^2 with a central rectangular depression occupying 33.40 m^2. The house was constructed of vertical posts set in open-ended wall trenches. Larger central supports were arranged in a pattern with four posts parallel to each longitudinal wall and set in from the wall a mean distance of 1.50 m. There were two large central supports in the center of the structure. This arrangement suggests a hip-roof type of construction. The details of wall construction are not specifically known. The floor may have been covered with mats.

The building was evidently constructed to serve as a mortuary house. At the time of construction a burial was made in the north-west doorway, presumably as part of the dedication ritual. After the interments had been placed in the floor, small piles of earth were placed over the burials. Later the structure was burned.

Formal Analysis of Burials

Burials are one type of archaeological feature which offer the archaeologist unusual opportunities for understanding the social relations characteristic of individual interaction in prehistoric communities. Persons differentiated in their social roles, and hence by the status positions which they occupy, are generally differentiated by the form and periodicity of standardized patterns of social intercourse. Differentiated patterns of behavior which surround individuals of differing status positions are one of the basic characteristics of human social life. Persons treated differentially in life are normally surrounded by formally differentiated patterns of social ritual at death. It is offered here that detailed analysis of mortuary practices will allow the archaeologist to isolate and understand the internal structure of social relations in prehistoric communities. This material is offered as an example of such an analysis.

Our methodology is aimed at the isolation of differential treatment afforded individuals at death, as a means toward formulation of hypotheses about the complexity of the status structure in extinct societies. The analytical frame which will structure the analysis is relatively simple. It is designed to isolate the form and sequence of mortuary practices involving differential treatment of individuals. We want to analyze and describe the attributes of excavated burials which will inform about the social ritual afforded individuals (1) after death and and prior to final interment and (2) during the interment procedure. Attributes of the latter class can be further broken down into the following classes: (1) location, orientation, and formal nature of the place of interment; (2) body preparation and positioning within the grave; and (3) form and nature of burial furnishings. Thus far we have discussed only isolation and description of structural variability in the mortuary practices of a single social unit. Once we can accomplish this phase of the analysis, we are faced with the interpretation of the observable differences and similarities in terms of models of social life. These interpretative models are best discussed in the following sections dealing specifically with the interpretative problems posed by this analysis.

EVIDENCE RELATIVE TO THE NATURE OF THE POPULATION REPRESENTED
IN THE SAMPLE

In this phase of the analysis we are concerned with determining whether or not the burials from Galley Pond do, in fact, represent the mortuary practices of a complete community, or whether only a segment of the prehistoric society was interred at this location. We want to know as much as possible about the age and sex composition of the individuals represented and what, if anything, can be said about physical differences which could result from differential treatment during life, such as mutilations and anatomical modifications which may be related to socially regulated or defined differences between classes of individuals. Unfortunately, the only observations which are available regarding the sex and age of individuals at death were made as field notes by the author and are certainly not to be credited with a high degree of reliability. In addition to this type of information, observations were made in the field as to the presence or absence of mutilations and artificial deformations of the skeletons. Summary information is presented in Table II.

A number of generalizations can be offerred from these data:

1. The burials at Galley Pond do not represent a normal human population in that of 36 interments, only one was of a child. The adolescent reported in the tabulation is probably not contemporary with the population defined by the other burials. Children and adolescents were not interred at Galley Pond in proportion to the child–adult deaths which must have occurred in the community. This marks this location as being functionally specific and representative of a differentiated segment of the total population.

2. Of the identified skeletons, roughly half are male and the other half female, suggesting that sex was not a differentiating criterion with regard to burial at this location.

3. The recognition of artificial occipital flattening of the skull of four different males, while no cases were observed among the female population, suggests that *certain* males were differentially treated in their early years of childhood so that their physical appearance was considerably altered. Such treatment, restricted to certain males, suggests the presence within the community of status positions which were ascribed with differential treatment afforded appropriate individuals from birth. That this is associated with only *certain* males supports the suggestion that this type of treatment was linked to socially defined status positions not open to all males.

4. The presence of only three multiple burials is difficult to interpret at this juncture and will be postponed until further analysis.

TABLE II
Burial Inventory

Burial number	No. of individuals	Age at death	Sex	Physical modifications
1	1	Adult	Female	None
2	4	3 Adult	1 Male	Occipital flattening
		1 Child	2 Female	of the male
3	1	Adult	–	None
13	1	Adult	–	None
19	1	Adult	Female	None
21	1	Adult	–	None
38	3	Adults	–	None
17	1	Adult	–	None
5	1	Adult	–	None
16	1	Adult	–	None
11	1	Adult	–	None
18	1	Adult	–	None
25	2	Adults	–	None
4	1	Adult	–	None
8	1	Adult	Male	None
23	1	Adult	Male	Occipital flattening
30	1	Adult	–	None
32	1	Adult	–	None
15	2	Adults	Male	Occipital flattening
20	1	Adult	Male	Occipital flattening
34	1	Adult	–	–
35	1	Adult	–	–
36	1	Adult	–	–
9	1	Adult	–	–
12	1	Adult	–	–
28	1	Adult	–	None
29	1	Adult	Male	None
33	1	Adult	–	None
26	1	Adult	Female	None
27	1	Adult	–	None
31	1	Adult	Male	None
37	1	Adult	Male	–
10	1	Adolescent	–	None
14	1	Adult	Female	None
Totals	41	35 Adult	6 Female	4 With
		1 Child	8 Male	24 Without
		1 Adolescent	22 Unclassified	6 Unknown

EVIDENCE FOR DIFFERENTIAL TREATMENT AFTER DEATH BUT PRIOR TO
INTERMENT

The fact that the majority of burials at Galley Pond are secondary burials, or burials of bones which were delayed until complete or partial decay of the corpse, makes possible some inferences concerning the treatment which the individuals received after death but prior to interment. Summary data relevant to this class of information is given in Table III. Of the 31 burials analyzed, 29 are burials of bones from which the flesh had been allowed to decay at some time prior to interment. There is a definite progression in the burials in the degree of completeness of skeletal parts present in the burial. Table IV shows the rank ordering of skeletal parts represented in the 29 burials of disarticulated bones. This ordering is interpreted as indicating the relative value placed on the different anatomical parts as representative of an individual. The preinterment history of these skeletons has been characterized by either loss or extraction of skeletal parts for use in social ritual. The complete absence of bones of the hand is certainly more than a chance phenomenon and suggests that hand bones may have been removed from the skeleton for use of some form of social or personal ritual. These data suggest that the skeletons had a variable history prior to interment and that loss or neglect of certain skeletal parts characterized their treatment during this period. In order to determine if there had been any major differential treatment afforded "important" skeletal parts, chi-square calculations for the relative distribution in the population of femurs, skulls, and all other bones treated as a unit were made. Table V presents the contingency data. Chi-square calculations reveal that this type of distribution would be expected to occur in a population less than one time in 100 cases if the various anatomical parts were distributed randomly within the burial population. When skulls and femurs occur together they are *always* accompanied by other bones. On the other hand, skulls in the absence of femurs *never* occur together with other bones. Burials of femurs without skulls are associated with other bones in roughly one half of the instances. This suggests that an individual, after death, could be divided up into two parts, one part consisting of the skull, the other part consisting of the body of which the most representative part was considered to be the thighs. The absence of other bones in four cases where femurs are the only bones buried is interpreted as reflecting the general history of care which the partial remains were afforded prior to interment, the other bones having been lost or used. These data make possible the following generalizations.

1. After death an individual may have been divided up, with the skull experiencing a separate history from the body as minimally defined by the bones of the upper leg.

2. Division was never made so that the skull and body parts experienced the same history of care and probably also stewardship.

TABLE III Anatomical Part.

Burial number	1	2	3	13	19	21	5	16	18	11	17	25	4	8	23
Anatomical Part present															
Skull	X	X	X	X	X	X							X	X	X
Mandible	X	X	X	X	X								X	X	X
Teeth	X	X	X	X	X								X	X	X
Vertebrae	X	X		X	X	X									
Ribs	X	X	X	X	X	X									
Humerus	X		X		X	X				X	X	X			
Radius	X	X	X		X	X				X	X				
Ulna	X	X	X	X	X	X				X	X	X			
Hand															
Pelvis		X			X	X				X	X				
Femur	X	X	X	X	X	X	X	X	X	X	X	X			
Tibia	X	X	X	X	X	X		X	X		X	X			
Foot	X	X		X											
Rodent gnawing															
Present	X	X	X	X	X	X	X	X	X	X	X	X			
Absent													X	X	X
Bones modified															
Teeth removed		X			X										
Bones burned						X									

TABLE IV

Frequency of Anatomical Parts in Burial Population

Skeletal part	No. of times present in burial	Percentage
Femur	25	76
Skull	22	69
Tibia	20	58
Teeth	16	48
Ulna	16	48
Mandible	15	45
Humerus	14	41
Radius	13	38
Ribs	11	31
Pelvis	10	27
Vertebrae	10	27
Foot	7	17
Hand	0	0

Represented by Burial

30	32	15	20	34	35	36	9	12	28	29	33	26	27	31	10	14	Total
X	X	X	X				X		X	X	X	X	X	X	X	X	22
X	X											X	X	X	X	X	15
X	X						X					X	X	X	X	X	16
												X	X	X	X	X	10
												X	X	X	X	X	11
									X	X		X	X	X	X	X	14
										X		X	X	X	X	X	13
									X	X		X	X	X	X	X	16
																	0
												X	X	X	X	X	10
				X	X	X	X	X	X	X	X	X	X	X	X	X	25
							X	X	X	X	X	X	X	X	X	X	20
												X	X	X		X	7
				X	X	X	X	X	X	X	X						16
X	X	X	X									X	X	X	X	X	15
		X	X														2
												X			X		4
							X										2

Turning now to the attributes which are believed to inform about the nature of the preinterment history of the skeletal parts, certain explanations must be offered.

1. Bones exhibiting rodent gnawing had been exposed so that rodents had access to the skeleton either during the period of decay of the bone or after the bones had been removed from the location where decay had taken place. None of the gnawing reported here is believed to have occurred after interment.

2. The notation of "teeth removed" refers to the absence of the upper four

TABLE V

	Skulls and femurs together	Skulls with femurs absent	Femurs with skull absent	Totals
Other bones present	15	0	6	21
Other bones absent	0	7	4	11
	15	7	10	32

incisors, removed after death. In no case did the sockets exhibit any bone growth after the removal of the teeth.

3. The notation of "bones burned" refers to the charring of bone which exhibits none of the characteristics of cremations in the flesh (see Binford, 1963). In all cases this is an incidence of cremation of old dry bones.

4. A notation of "bones modified" designates the presence on the bones of incisions or polished surfaces which are attributable to postmortem modification of the bone.

Table VI presents the grouped comparative data for the recognized classes of burials with respect to differentiated preinterment history.

TABLE VI

	Rodent gnawing		Modification			Teeth
	Present	Absent	Present	Absent	Burned	removed
Complete individuals	11	4	0	13	2	3
Body only	10	0	0	9	0	?
Head only	0	7	2	5	0	0

It is quite obvious that as regards treatment of the burials prior to interment, there are two general classes: those burials representing complete individuals and those representing an individual by only the body or the skull. Of the former, all exhibit rodent gnawing, and none exhibit any modification of the bone; all cases of burning and tooth removal occur within this class. On the other hand, the skulls lack rodent gnawing and exhibit the only cases of modifications. We can suggest that care of the divided osseous remains was exercised to prevent rodents from having access to the bones of the skull. On the other hand, the bones of the torso were treated in such a way as to allow rodents access to them. In addition to this difference in treatment, single skulls were sometimes modified by cutting and polishing, something that was never done with the remains interred as complete individuals or with the postcranial parts of "divided" individuals. Two distinct patterns of care and treatment of the skull as opposed to the body is indicated.

Further information concerning the basis for selection of individuals for differential treatment can be obtained by comparison of the recognized classes of individuals treated differently prior to interment and the nature of the population segments represented in the burial population. Table VII presents the relevant data. It is evident that those individuals whose skulls were differentially treated were male, and field estimates invariably show males of advanced age in this class as opposed to other identified males. On the other hand, males and

TABLE VII

	Male	Female	Unknown	Total
Complete individual	3	6	8	17
Body only	0	0	9	9
Skull only	5	0	3	8
	8	6	20	34

females were both represented in the class of burials which were interred as complete individuals.

The removal of teeth is restricted to females and probably is related to the use of teeth of the deceased as personal mementoes of the deceased or in social ritual.

Summary Generalizations

1. At death bodies were allowed to decay at some location other than the place of final interment.

2. After decay of the flesh, the osseous remains were divided so that the skull was afforded treatment which prevented rodents from having access to them, whereas body parts invariably exhibit rodent gnawing.

3. There was an apparent grading of body parts as representative of the individual, the skull and leg bones being considered of major importance. Other body parts may be lost or may otherwise be utilized without destroying the "identity" or "meaning" of the skull and legs as representative of the deceased individual. Bones of the hand may have been consistently selected for *use* in social ritual.

4. Modifications in the form of polish and cutting may be practiced on skulls of males.

5. The upper incisors of females may be removed after death.

INTERMENT PROCEDURE

Under this heading we refer to all those attributes which inform about the activities carried out as part of the rites surrounding the final interment of the individuals represented in the Galley Pond Site. (See, Table VIII.) All the burials, with the exception of No. 31, No. 10, and No. 14, were placed on the floor of Structural Feature No. 1. Number 31 is unique in that it was placed in a subfloor pit which, judging from its form, was excavated while the structural feature was still in use. Therefore, it should be included in the population of burials associated with this structure. Burial Number 10 is unique in that it was placed in a subfloor pit directly in the west entryway to the mortuary structure and was

TABLE VIII

Burial number	Grave type	Articulation[a]	Burial form	Skull locus	Angle of orientation	Grave furnishings
1	Floor	D	Bundle	South	110° 05′	None
2	Floor	D	Bundle	South	33° 00′	None
3	Floor	D	Bundle	South	34° 00′	None
13	Floor	D	Bundle	West	110° 00′	None
19	Floor	D	Bundle	South	34° 00′	None
21	Floor	D	Bundle	South	21° 00′	None
38	Floor	D	Bundle	South	30° 00′	None
5	Floor	D	Bundle	—	112° 00′	None
16	Floor	D	Bundle	—	139° 00′	None
11	Floor	D	Bundle	—	106° 00′	None
18	Floor	D	Bundle	—	128° 00′	1 pot, 1 cu. artifact 8 pins
17	Floor	D	Bundle	—	127° 00′	None
25	Floor	D	Bundle	—	107° 00′	None
4	Floor	R	Element	—	131° 00′	None
8	Floor	R	Element	—	1° 30′	Pot No. 1
23	Floor	R	Element	—	21° 15′	None
30	Floor	R	Element	—	31° 00′	None
32	Floor	R	Element	—	28° 00′	None
15	Floor	N	Element	—	31° 00′	Pots 2 and 3, skull
20	Floor	N	Element	—	31° 00′	
34	Floor	N	Element	—	118° 00′	None
35	Floor	N	Element	—	119° 00′	None
36	Floor	N	Element	—	120° 00′	None
9	Floor	R	Grouped	South	117° 00′	None
12	Floor	R	Grouped	South	110° 00′	Milling stone
28	Floor	R	Grouped	Above	22° 00′	None
29	Floor	R	Grouped	Above	21° 00′	None
33	Floor	R	Grouped	South	119° 00′	None
26	Floor	R	Extended	South	19° 00′	Pot No. 5 and skull
27	Floor	R	Extended	South	23° 00′	Rattle
37	Floor	R	Extended	West	120° 00′	Rattle, knives, flakes, abrader
31	Floor pit	A	Extended	West	90° 00′	None
10	Door pit	D	Bundle	South	31° 00′	None
14	Subfloor pit	A	Flexed	South	310° 00′	None

[a] D, disarticulated; R, rearticulated; N, none.

covered with a limestone slab which apparently functioned as a threshold stone in the doorway. Such a position suggests that it may have been interred as part of the ritual surrounding the construction of the mortuary structure. In other details this burial is identical to other single individual bundle burials placed on the floor of the house. Burial No. 14 was definitely made prior to the construction of the mortuary structure and is certainly not a part of the population of burials associated with the structure. Of the remaining burials, all were placed directly on the floor of Structural Feature No. 1. There appear to have been two basic types of graveside preparation of the bones at time of placement on the floor. Burials designated as bundles all shared the parallel orientation of the bones of the limbs, either arranged around skulls and smaller bones, or placed on the floor in a single pile. All are tightly stacked, and there is frequently evidence in the form of organic staining of the surrounding soil that the bundles of bones had been placed on the floor while wrapped in some form of container. The other method of treatment of the bones was to lay them out on the ground in complete or partial rearticulated position. Completely rearticulated skeletons were found; however, one interesting arrangement termed "grouped" was also noted. In this type of burial the bones of the leg were rearticulated in relative anatomical order, while the skull was placed above or to one side of the rearticulated leg bones. Individual skull burials were relatively common, and when noted there does not appear to have been any type of wrapping or container for the skulls. In all cases, the burials were oriented either on a general north–south or east–west axis. There does not appear to be any correlation between the angle of orientation and the particular location of burial within the mortuary structure. It is therefore inferred that the angle of orientation possibly relates to symbolism associated with a dual social division in the social unit represented by the burials. The presence or absence of burial furniture is highly correlated with the "type" of burial, and it seems quite likely that its presence signifies status differentials among the individuals represented. Other variations were multiple versus single interments. The fact that *all* burials for which the complete anatomy is represented were combinations made presumably at the time of interment of skeletal segments which had experienced different care and treatment during the postmortem preinterment period. Certain general categories can be recognized with regard to differentiated treatment at time of interment. One major category is exemplified by the skull and long bone bundle burials and the rearticulated extended burials. Both forms have in common the undifferentiated treatment at time of interment of the recognized major parts of the body—the skull and the body proper. This does not mean that the two divisions of the body did not experience different histories of stewardship, prior to interment. The presence of mandibular fragments from the same individual in two separate bundle burials (No. 1 and No. 38) suggests that some separation of osseous parts into differentiated custodial hands occurs prior to interment, and that the body parts were reunited at time of interment.

The grouped burials all represent individuals whose skulls and body parts are afforded differential treatment at interment; legs were rearticulated and orientated in one direction, while the skulls were placed to one side and orientated in the opposite direction.

The final major category are· those individuals whose skeletal parts are incompletely represented and whose major parts have not been recombined at the time of interment. These are represented by skull burials and long bone bundle burials.

Table IX presents the summary data for the recognized burial types and direction of longitudinal orientation.

TABLE IX

Orientation	Complete individuals undifferentiated at interment		Complete individuals differentiated at interment	Incomplete individuals	
	Rearticulated extended	Skull and long bone bundles	Rearticulated grouped	Skulls	Long bone bundles
East–West	1	2	3	1	9
North–South	2	7	2	6	0

Orientation is obviously correlated with the various burial forms. Eight of ten burials in the first category are orientated in a north–south direction; this proportional frequency corresponds nicely with that observed for individual skull burials and contrasts markedly with the burials of long bone bundles. This suggests that the skull burials and the interments of complete individuals share some social distinction which is not shared by the grouped burials and the burials of long bones in bundles. The recognition of two forms of orientation differentially associated with a variety of burial modes attests to a dual social distinction which is not the same as the social distinctions determining the particular burial modes.

Turning now to the social significance of the angle of orientation, the following observations may be pertinent: (1) All the houses of Mississippian type investigated on both the Toothsome site and on Sandy Tip had a north–south longitudinal orientation. (2) The mortuary house at Galley Pond has a north–south orientation. (3) All of the burials in the mortuary house accompanied by grave goods or otherwise distinguished in such a manner as to suggest high status exhibited a north–south orientation. (4) A higher frequency of burials in the mortuary house exhibited a north–south orientation.

All this information suggests that north–south orientation is a feature symbolic of the *local community.* Given this interpretation it follows that east–west orientation may be associated with the symbolism of *another* community or with a minor segment of the local community. Since the skull and leg bones of a single individual are observed to be orientated in different directions in the "grouped burial," we must infer that the determinant for orientation of bones at burial is not simply the symbolism associated with the residence group of the dead person. Having recognized that the skulls and bones of the body of interred individuals had experienced different preinterment histories, it seems reasonable to suggest that the two segments of the body had two different custodians during the preinterment period of care of the osseous remains. Such a situation makes understandable the "composite" burials with regard to orientation. Orientation was determined by the group affiliation of the custodians of the bones who could be affiliated with the same or different halves of the two symbolically represented "moieties." If we offer the additional postulate that the interment of individuals in the mortuary structure was a rite exclusive to the *local community,* the entire pattern of variations observed in form of the burials is understandable.

1. Individuals for whom both custodians were locally resident would be completely represented, if only minimally by skull and leg bones.

2. Individuals whose custodians were not both locally resident would be represented by only one body segment, either skull or leg bones.

3. Individuals whose custodians were both locally resident and affiliated with the same "moiety" would be buried as complete individuals with similar orientation for both the body and skull.

4. The remains of individuals whose custodians were both locally resident but affiliated with different halves of the "moiety" would be interred as grouped burials with the body orientated in one direction and the head in another.

This sociological model fits all the observed forms of variation with respect to orientation and completeness of body segments represented. One further postulate makes possible the meaningful interpretation of the demonstrable sex distinctions between completely and incompletely represented individuals (see Table VII). If the determinants for custodial appointment were in terms of (a) affinally related individuals and (b) lineally related individuals for each person, then the following sociological hypotheses can be offered and supported by the available data:

1. Residence was matrilocal or neolocal for women and uxorilocal for men.

2. Descent was matrilineally calculated.

3. The local group was not endogamous, although marriage outside the local group was not equally practiced by all status levels within the local group.

4. The exogamic boundary corresponds to a social segment of more limited inclusiveness than the moiety.

5. The local group was composed of matrimoieties of unequal demographic proportions.

The first hypothesis is supported by the observation that all identified females are represented by complete skeletons, both custodians being locally resident, which would be impossible except under conditions of local endogamy. This condition is demonstrably not the case if the postulate of completeness of skeletal parts as a function of the locality of preinterment custodians is accepted. On the other hand, males are represented by both complete and incomplete skeletons, suggesting that one of the male custodians may or may not be locally resident. These patterns could only arise if it were the male who was mobile with respect to the social groups represented by the custodians, affinally and lineally affiliated groups.

Matrilineal descent is suggested by the fact that females are invariably interred with both body segments treated in similar ways, suggesting that the custodians were both members of the same social group. Males, on the other hand, exhibit differential treatment of the two portions of the body, a condition which could only arise only if the custodians were in some cases members of different groups.

Under the postulated relationship of custodians to the deceased, this pattern is necessarily predicated as matrilineal desent. If ego is a female, lineal descendants in both the ascending and descending generation are members of the same kin group; whereas for males, kin of the ascending generation may not be of the same kin-based group, defined by exogamic bounds, as members of the descending generation. Therefore, on the basis of the differential treatment afforded males versus females in the orientations of their body parts, we suggest matrilineal descent.

Since not all males are represented by complete skeletal remains, we must conclude that both custodians were not locally resident as representatives of either affinally or lineally affiliated groups. This situation could occur only if males were marrying into or out of the local group, giving rise to the presence in other local communities of custodians. That the moieties as symbolized by the two different modes of orientation were not the exogamic boundary is attested to by the presence of males having both body segments orientated in the same direction, symbolizing within-moiety marriage while males exhibiting both patterns of orientation represent moiety exogamy. That the local group was composed of representatives of both moieties is attested to by the grouped burials exhibiting both types of orientation. This necessitates our basic postulates: (a) The custodians were in different moieties; (b) they were both locally resident. This then justifies the generalization that the local communities were composed of representatives of both moieties. The relative proportions of the local population of "north" versus "east" moiety individuals can be calculated as gene frequencies would be calculated since we can work as if the burial pattern is informative of the moiety membership of the individuals (lineally affiliated custodian) and the moiety to which the spouse belonged (affinally affiliated custodian). By counting the burials which are represented by both custodians of a single moiety, custodians of different moieties, and single resident custodians of either moiety, we can determine that 65% of the local population belonged to the moiety symbolized by a north–south orientation, and the remaining 35% belonged to the moiety symbolized by the east–west orientation.

In summary, given the following postulates, we can explain all of the variation observed in the population of burials with respect to orientation, presence or absence of complete skeletal parts, and homogeneous versus heterogeneous patterns of orientation for the separate body parts of a single individual. Postulates: (1) Separation of body parts, each experiencing different preinterment histories, is due to the division of the body between two custodians, one affinally and the other lineally affiliated to the deceased individual. (2) The orientation of the body parts at interment is in terms of the moiety affiliation of the custodian of the particular body part.

It remains for us to explain variations observed in the interment practices with regard to (1) arranging the bones on the floor of the house, as opposed to placing a container of bones on the floor, and (2) presence and nature of associated burial furnishings.

1. Arrangement of bones versus bundles of bones: At present this distinction cannot be directly correlated with any other form of variation and may simply relate to particular family or kin-based differences in the details of care for the bones of the deceased. Such care may be independent of moiety affiliation.

2. Burial furniture: Grave goods consisted of two general classes of goods: (a) technomic items whose primary functional context was apparently coping directly with the physical environment, and (b) sociotechnic items whose primary function was facilitating social intercourse or which served as elements functioning within the social system of the group. Of the technomic items present, tools and facilities are both represented. Tools are those artifacts which serve to enhance or make possible energy transmissions. Facilities are those classes of artifacts which control or prevent movement of solid, liquid or gaseous material as well as animate beings, that is, they restrict or prevent energy

TABLE X

Technomic items		Sociotechnic items	Unclassifiable
Tools	Facilities		
Knives	Ceramic pots	Bone pins	Beaver incisor
Abraiders	Wooden bowls	Copper plate fragments	
Flakes		Rattles	

transmission and exchanges (see Wagner, 1960, p. 97). Table X is a tabular classification of the grave goods occurring at Galley Pond.

Several types of assemblages of grave furniture may be recognized.

1. Interment of personalities or items which are intimately associated with the deceased. Personalities are normally considered as nontransferable goods. In this case the normal pattern is for the goods to experience the same history of treatment as the corporal remains, and frequently they occur as parts of clothing or personal adornment. Personalities may be either sociotechnic or technomic in function.

2. Contributions of "necessary equipment": Items which can be considered "necessary equipment" frequently include a wide range of artifacts which relate to the normal day-to-day performance of individuals within the context of their sociocultural system. These include raw materials for use in the manufacture of "new" artifacts, food, or the normal tool kit appropriate to the person's normal task performance (such as hunting implements for men and household items for women). It is difficult to characterize the "necessary equipment" in specific terms; however, in contrast to personalities, the provisioning of a dead person with necessary equipment for carrying on life in the "afterworld" is carried out by persons participating in the graveside ritual. The items generally do not exhibit the same history of preinterment treatment as do the corporal remains. Goods of this type are contributed, as part of the graveside ritual, although some personalities may make up the total assemblage.

3. Competitively contributed goods: Burial furniture of this type may be far in excess of the quantities that could reasonably be considered "necessary" for carrying on life in the afterworld, regardless of the status of the interred individual. Social ritual accompanying such mortuary contributions is generally more important in validating status and perpetuating status positions of the living members of the community, than as direct difference to the dead person. The classes of items represented do not normally constitute an assemblage of "usable" items in the sense of "necessary goods."

The above are a few of the types of assemblages of grave furniture which are relatively common in the archaeological and ethnographic literature. Cross-cutting all of these types of assemblages are distinctions in the form and content of the assemblage which may relate to status differences among the individuals interred.

In light of the above distinctions, we can recognize at least two types of grave furniture assemblages present at Galley Pond.

Assemblages of Personalities

In burial No. 18 there occurred eight bone pins and a small fragment of a copper plate *lying on top* of a bundle of long bones. These items had obviously been included in the container in which the bones were placed. We can infer from this that their association with the bones had been established at a time prior to the placement of the bone bundle in the final location within the mortuary house. The form of both items is sociotechnic in that neither item was used directly in coping with the physical environment. They both were probably part of the items of personal adornment worn in life by the dead person. They may have been significant of particular status.

Burials No. 27 and No. 37 evidence a totally different assemblage and are probably a combination of personalities supplemented by contributed goods of the "necessary equipment" type. Both share a single type of sociotechnic item, a rattle, but differ in the quantities of tools included in the grave. Raw materials for the manufacture of "new" tools are present in both, suggesting that at least some of the tools are contributed. Both of these burials are extended and both are males, they are distinct from the other burials in (a) the nature of the assemblage of grave goods; (b) they are the only rearticulated extended males; and (c) both are located adjacent to the walls of the mortuary house. These distinctions are interpreted as being meaningful differentiations in the treatment of these individuals when compared to the others buried in the mound. These distinctions are recognized as signifying a particular status position occupied by these individuals.

Assemblages of Contributed Goods

Without exception, contributed goods occur in the form of facilities, pots, and wooden bowls, placed beside the osseous remains. These were placed there as containers for something, and their presence signifies the nature of the contributions, presumably water or food. Examples of this type of assemblage occur with all recognized types of burial except "grouped remains." Such occurrences may be interpreted as signifying esteem, rather than systematic status differentiation. There does in fact seem to be a high correlation between this type of assemblage and advanced age. We might infer that elderly individuals were afforded a certain social difference and that such elderly individuals might have obtained some degree of status elevation simply as a function of their advanced age. This would appear to operate independently of sex differences.

GENERAL CHARACTERISTICS OF THE TOTAL ASSEMBLAGE

This analysis has demonstrated a number of correlations between age, sex, and differential treatment of deceased individuals both prior to and during interment. Thus far our analysis has been concerned with the details of internal variability within the burial complex. By changing our perspective to the character of the complex as a whole, certain generalizations seem justified. Table XI presents the summary data on the assemblage as a whole.

TABLE XI

	Sex			Age	
	M	F	?	Young adult	Old adult
1. Individuals differentiated only on basis of postulated group affiliation	4	5	21	33	2
2. Individuals differentiated on basis of group affiliation and esteem	2	1	1	1	3
3. Individuals differentiated on basis of group affiliation esteem and social status	2	0	0	2	0

All individuals share a common pattern of differentiation believed to be related to group affiliation of the deceased vis-à-vis postmortem custodians. This is the basic and all-pervasive characteristic of the mortuary complex. Secondary to this type of differentiation is the placement of personalities and contributed goods in the forms of facilities (presumably food containers) with certain individuals. This is interpreted as evidence for differential esteem in the local community. It seems significant in this regard that three out of four individuals so treated are adults of advanced age and in the case of males, those exhibiting artificial deformation of the skull. This type of differential treatment would seem motivated by affect and etiquette as opposed to an established set of jural rules governing behavior appropriate to individuals occupying deferred status positions. Finally, we observe two males differentially treated in terms of all previous criteria but in addition having personal ties of a "standardized" type (Burial Nos. 27 and 37), including in both cases sociotechnic items (rattles) which must symbolize some specific social roles, hence, status positions. The absence of competitively contributed goods and elaborate personalities suggests that the particular status was not primarily political nor economic in its role prescription. These men may simply have been curers or ritual functionaries in the local integrative institutions. We may generalize as follows:

1. Mortuary ritual was communal as opposed to individualized in its emphasis.

a. Group affiliation and between group relationships vis-à-vis the deceased took precedence in symbolism over the particular status of the individual as defined by this specific role in the operation of the local social organization. This is evidenced in the orientation patterns and differential handling of body parts common to *all* burials.

b. The common treatment of individuals in terms of placement in a mortuary house and communal activities associated with periodic interment rites during which a number of previously deceased individuals are afforded simultaneous mortuary ritual further attests to our generalization.

2. Status differentiations when observed are limited to individuals esteemed or occupying status positions whose roles are primarily intrasocietal in focus and probably related to curing or performance as ritual functionaries.

These generalizations imply that the burials at Galley Pond represent an even more restricted segment of the local population than is evidenced by the absence of children and young adults. Within the context of Mississippian sociocultural systems as known from such sites as Cahokia and Kincaid, one would expect political and economic roles to be extremely important within the local community, yet there is no evidence for such status differentiation among the individuals interred at Galley Pond. This lack even when seen in the full context of our knowledge of the nature of Mississippian occupations in the central Kaskaskia drainage (e.g., dispersed communities and farmsteads, lacking any known large local "ceremonial centers") does not appear representative of the full scope of local Mississippian social organization.

A possible explanation may lie in the nature of the archaeological investigations of the site. (1) Archaeological investigation was limited to a single recognizable above-ground feature. (2) Other above-ground features are reported in the immediately adjacent area of Wassam Ridge. (3) The immediately surrounding area is heavily forested and systematic surface collection was impossible; nevertheless, unsystematic reconnaissance reveals cultural materials.

We must then view our information from Galley Pond as being partial and in no way "representative" of the total site. Differentiations in mortuary treatment of politically and economically important individuals may well have involved interment in a different location within the site of which the mortuary house reported here was only a single element. We must then limit our interpretative conclusions to the *specific segment* of the local Mississippian community represented, which at present cannot be defined vis-à-vis other segments of the community.

Interpretative Conclusions

The site of the Galley Pond Mound had been utilized as a locus of cultural activity by peoples during the Middle and Late Archaic periods. Subsequently, a single burial had been made on the location during the late Woodland period. Utilization of the spot by Mississippian peoples began with the erection of a mortuary building. The building was constructed with heavy posts set in wall trenches along the external walls. The roof was apparently of the hip-roof form as suggested by eight internal roof supports. The wall covering for the building was apparently thatch, since no evidence of daub was present. The interior of the building had an excavated floor with a rectangular central depression. Around the central depression on the "ledges" were placed the bones of deceased members of the community responsible for the construction of the mortuary house. At the time of construction, a burial had been placed under the entryway, probably as part of the social ritual surrounding the construction of the building. Individuals selected for final interment in the mortuary structure did not represent the total local population; children and young adults were not buried there. It is also quite possible that other socially defined limitations further restricted burial in the structure to particular status positions within the social group. Only comparative data from the adjacent area and other sites will allow us to make more positive statements in this regard.

The particular formal variations among the burials interred within the mortuary house have made possible the reconstruction of certain aspects of the social organization of the social segment represented. At marriage, the male took up residence with his wife in proximity of her natal family. Children born to such a union were considered as members of the mother's kin group but not members of the father's kin group. Marriage was not forbidden to individuals living in the same community nor to members of the same moiety. Incest taboos extended to some social unit of lesser magnitude than either of these social units. The particular community represented was not composed of people belonging to the two "halves" of the community in equal numerical proportions. Approximately 65% of the community belonged to one moiety (symbolized by the orientation of their buildings and their dead in an approximate north–south longitudinal axis); the remaining 35% of the community belonged to a social division symbolized by orientations on an approximate east–west axis.

At death an individual was placed in some location, not the mortuary house, where the flesh was allowed to decay. Later the osseous remains were collected and divided into two parts, the head being placed in the care of a custodian, affinally related to the deceased. The body parts were placed under the care of a custodian representative of a group affiliated with the deceased through lineal kin ties. After an undetermined period of time lapsed, the local community held mortuary ritual. At present, it is not known whether all the interments at Galley Pond were made simultaneously or whether they were periodically deposited in the mortuary over an extended period of time. In any event, at the time of interment in the mortuary house, both custodians, if locally resident, participated in the grave-side ritual. At least one aspect of the grave-side ritual was the proper arrangement of the bones in terms of group or associational affiliation of the custodians of the bones.

The inclusion of grave-side contributions by the participants apparently depended upon the esteem of the deceased in the eyes of the social units responsible for his or her "proper" burial. Advanced age appears to have been important in insuring great esteem. The particular status of the deceased in the internal social organization of his community was also a determinant of the manner of treating his remains. Burial in a rearticulated extended manner, adjacent to the walls of the mortuary house, was one mode of status differentiation. In terms of preinterment ritual, the modification of the bones, presumably as part of commemorative rites, and possibly the artificial flattening of the skull during early childhood, were all status-connected practices. Within the complex of variability associated with status-connected practices, the differentiations between rearticulated males and females seems important. The males were buried with personalities typified by rattles and a number of tools, while the females were buried with contributed goods only. What these differences, believed to be status-connected, actually signify is difficult to envision.

The total pattern of the mortuary practices evidenced at Galley Pond can be summarized as exhibiting a communal as opposed to an individualized emphasis. Individuals were treated primarily in terms of their group affiliations, rather than with regard to their particular status within the community. In addition, when status was symbolized it was with respect to personal esteem or intrasocietal roles of a nonpolitical or economic nature.

These pecularities must be viewed with respect to the lack of information regarding the degree to which Galley Pond is or is not "representative" of the total mortuary complexes of the local Mississippian community. Only more field work in the area adjacent to Galley Pond Mound could provide the necessary information for placing these data in a reliable position with regard to the total mortuary complex.

References

Binford, L. R. (1963). An Analysis of Cremations from Three Michigan Sites. *Wisconsin Archeologist,* Vol. 44, pp. 98–110. Reprinted in this volume, pp. 373–381.

Binford, L. R. (1964). *Archaeological Investigations on Wassom River.* Archaeological Salvage Report No. 17. Southern Illinois University Museum, Carbondale.

Fowler, Melvin L. (1960). *Test Excavations of Selected Archaeological Sites in the Carlyle Reservoir.* Paper on file with the National Park Service, Region 5, Philadelphia, Pennsylvania.

Wagner, Phillip. (1960). *The Human Use of the Earth.* Free Press, Glencoe, Illinois.

Post-Pleistocene Adaptations[*]

This paper will examine some of the major assumptions underlying the current systematics of the archaeological remains of the post-Pleistocene period. The paper falls into three parts: (1) a brief survey of the history of research on the immediately post-Pleistocene period, with particular attention to the conditions affecting research orientation and, consequently, systematics; (2) an assessment of the utility of current concepts, schemes, and arguments which are advanced to explain cultural events of the post-Pleistocene period; and (3) the outlining of a different approach for understanding the nature and extent of cultural changes occurring during the period.

The archaeological remains of the immediately post-Pleistocene period are generally termed *Mesolithic.* They are characterized over wide areas by the appearance of small, highly specialized flint implements; these occur frequently on later sites in the coastal and riverine regions in the context of the systematic exploitation of aquatic resources.

Until 1892, there was widespread agreement among European scholars that there was a break, or "hiatus," in the archaeological record between the Paleolithic and Neolithic epochs (Brown, 1892; G. de Mortillet, 1885, pp. 479–484; Breuil, 1946, p. 25).

It has generally been assumed that a break occurred between the periods during which this country, and in fact the continent of Europe, was inhabited by Palaeolithic Man and his Neolithic successors, and that the race or races of Palaeolithic folk who hunted the elephant, rhinoceros, cave bear, hippopotamus, reindeer, *ursus,* bison, etc., were completely separated as by a chasm from the agricultural people, the herdsmen with their oxen and sheep, and the tillers of the soil of the so-called Neolithic epoch, implying that man in Britain had changed suddenly from the low savage hunter to a half-civilized farmer and drover (Brown, 1892, p. 66).

A. C. Carlyle, who conducted archaeological investigations in the Vindhya Hills of Central India between 1868 and 1888, was the first to use the term

[*] Originally published in *New Perspectives in Archeology* (S. R. Binford and L. R. Binford, eds.), pp. 313–341. Aldine Publ. Co., Chicago, Illinois, 1968.

Mezolithic. Carlyle was also one of the early questioners of the validity of the hiatus between the Paleolithic and Neolithic. Carlyle's excavations yielded typical crescents, trapezoids, and other geometric microliths; it was asserted that these implements were found both with late Paleolithic tools and pettery. This led him to propose that there was no hiatus in India and that the microliths constituted an intermediate industry to which he applied the term *Mezolithic.* These materials were exhibited in England in 1888 at the Royal Albert Hall.

Carlyle's findings served to stimulate John Allen Brown who published an article summarizing Carlyle's work (Brown, 1888). In this article, Brown asked if there had been similar microlithic forms found in the British Isles, pointing out that they were already reported from Tunis, Egypt, Italy, Palestine, France, Portugal, and the Crimea. Brown's main concern was with documenting the widespread occurrences of microliths, and he offered no chronological interpretation. Wilson (1894) reported that in 1892 the U.S. National Museum acquired much of Carlyle's material, and he proposed the acceptance of the Mesolithic as a transitional period between the Paleolithic and Neolithic.

The following year Brown published an extensive paper (Brown, 1892) in which he discussed the problem of the hiatus. He went on to argue in favor of an unbroken continuity between the Paleolithic and Neolithic, setting forth four stages: Eolithic, Paleolithic, Mesolithic, and Neolithic. He based this fourfold division on the transformational sequence of axes, from the crude forms of the "drift" to the well-made polished types of the Neolithic. He documented finds of "intermediate" forms and used a scale of crude–fine as evidence for historical continuity, citing Pitt-Rivers' argument that such a transformational sequence indicated historical continuity (see Pitt-Rivers, 1906, pp. 20–44). Occupation of the same caves by Paleolithic and Neolithic populations is cited as further support for the claim of continuity.

The following year, Dawkins challenged Brown's views:

I shall first of all address myself to the point as to continuity in this country. Is there any evidence that the Palaeolithic shaded off into the Neolithic age in this country without any such break as a I have mentioned above? Next, I shall examine the facts bearing on the point outside of the British Isles, premising that the evolution of the Neolithic from the Palaeolithic stage of culture in some part of the world may be accepted as a high probability, although we may be unable to fix with precision the land where this transition took place (1894, p. 243).

Dawkins went on to question the validity of the reasoning behind the claims for continuity and concluded: "The exploration of caverns has not, I submit, yet resulted in establishing a 'continuity' but simply a sequence" (1894, p. 274).

The English literature of the early 1890's is full of arguments on these issues, and similar questions were also occupying continental scholars. The formal changes in the archaeological record were the subject of controversy, both with regard to the meaning of the observed changes and the reality of a hiatus. Lartet and G. deMortillet claimed as early as 1872 that the apparent break in the archaeological record was in reality simply a gap in knowledge and did not represent a period during which Europe was not occupied (Piette, 1895b, pp. 235–236). Cartailhac, on the other hand, stated that the hiatus constituted a major break in the occupancy of the continent (Breuil, 1921). In 1875 the Congress of Prehistory held a meeting at Nantes, and an argument was presented which attempted to disprove Cartailhac's position by pointing to formal similarities between the flints from Solutré and those of the Neolithic period (Piette, 1895b, p. 238).

Shortly after this, artifacts were found which were dated to the period between the remains of the Magdalenian, or "reindeer," period and that of the Lake Dwellers, the Robenhausian. In 1879 Vielle discovered microliths at Fère-en-Tardenois (1890, p. 961). Almost 10 years later Piette made his discoveries at Mas d'Azil where microliths were found in association with modern fauna. The deposits in question overlay the Magdalenian and lacked the features then considered diagnostic of the Neolithic (Piette, 1895a). These finds were followed by surveys of locations with microliths (A. de Mortillet, 1896), and there was a proliferation of names for these industries which were said to fill the hiatus (see Coutil, 1912). New excavations were also carried out (deLoe, 1908; Hervé, 1899).

In the years following World War I, there was a marked increase of interest in the post-Pleistocene period, and a number of regional syntheses were made (Kozlowski, 1926; J. G. D. Clark, 1932, 1936; Childe, 1931, 1937). Further, there was an extension of European terms to non-European materials which were considered intermediate between the Paleolithic and Neolithic (Garrod, 1932; Garrod and Bate, 1937). Some general works also appeared in which data from various regions were summarized and compared (Obermaier, 1925; Osborn, 1919; deMorgan, 1924; MacCurdy, 1924). Specific syntheses of the Mesolithic period proper have appeared (Burkitt, 1925; Gimbutas, 1956, 1963). In these various summary and interpretive writings, there are several distinct lines of reasoning, leading to a diversity of opinion as to the historical significance of the archaeological record.

One line of argument sought to demonstrate that the Mesolithic represented a way of life, and a subsistence base, intermediate in a developmental sequence between the reindeer hunters of the terminal Pleistocene and the food-producing villagers of the Neolithic. For example, Piette claimed that there was evidence for the domestication of the horse by the Solutreans, reindeer by the Magdalenians, and cattle by the occupants of Mas d'Azil who also, according to Piette, domesticated plants (Piette, 1895b). Less extravagant claims have recently been made for the transitional nature of the Baltic materials (Troels-Smith, 1953) and those from Central Europe (Pittioni, 1962). Few workers, however, have seriously considered the European Mesolithic as a stage transitional to the later food-producing societies.

Other workers were more concerned with the problem of the continuity (or lack of it) between the human groups responsible for the Paleolithic and Mesolithic. Osborn (1919, p. 457) saw in each change in form of archaeological assemblages evidence for the invasion of new "races." Others argued that the presence or absence of discrete traits was diagnostic of population stability or change. For example, J. G. D. Clark (1932, p. 2) and Menghin (1925) based their claims for historical continuity between the Paleolithic and Mesolithic on the continued use of core tools. Obermaier (1925, p. 324), on the other hand, viewed the shift to the exploitation of aquatic resources in Ertebølle and the Auterian as justifying the postulation of movement of new people into Western Europe. DeMorgan (1924, p. 74) saw the adoption of microliths and the loss of graphic arts as "revolutionary" and as proof of a major break in historical continuity. Childe (1925, p. 2), J. G. D. Clark (1932, p. 1), Gimbutas (1956), and Braidwood (1963) are in general agreement that the Mesolithic of Europe is a continuation of the Paleolithic way of life and that the observed archaeological changes can be related directly to the major climatic changes of the post-Pleistocene period. These authors do differ, however, on the degree to which changes in the form of archaeological assemblages can be explained by reference to new populations or to "influences" from other cultures.

We have attempted to show in this brief historical survey that Mesolithic research has been characterized by a series of changing questions and that the answers to any one question have tended to generate new questions. The initial problem was to determine whether or not Europe was occupied between the end of the Paleolithic and the beginning of the Neolithic. The affirmative answer to this problem led to the question of historical continuity. Consideration of this problem necessitated consideration of the criteria for evaluation of formal archaeological variations in terms of their meaning for population change or lack of change. There was considerable diversity of opinion on this question.

Although problems of interpretive theory and method were never solved (see the papers by S. R. Binford and J. Sackett, 1968), they began to occupy scholars less and less as more detailed knowledge of the archaeological record accumulated. Local sequences were worked out, and a more limited geographical perspective led to greater conservatism in interpretive viewpoints. Most recent workers have used a diffusionist model for interpreting geographic variations in archaeological data, with the postulation of actual movement of peoples playing a minor role (see, for example, Waterbolk, 1962). The problem of historical continuity versus population movement has not been so much solved as circumvented. This circumvention has involved two means: first, application of one's own criteria to an extremely detailed sequence in a very limited area, making it almost impossible for other workers to judge interpretations offered;

and second, stressing certain widespread "traits" in macroregional syntheses, traits which are usually so generalized that one might question their relevance to the measurement of detailed changes in culture history.

The work of the past 100 years has resulted in the accumulation of sufficient data to justify some generalizations made by workers in the field of European Mesolithic studies. Some of the generalizations made in distinguishing the Paleolithic from the Mesolithic are:

1. There was a major shift in the centers of population growth in Western Europe.

During the Upper Magdalenian, the density of population was relatively high in France, as evidence by the great number of sites occupied for the first time, and by the richness of the sites . . . . The end of the glacial times was fatal to this striking human expansion. The disappearance of the cold fauna and the replacement of the steppe, rich in game, by forests was followed by the demographic recession and break-up of the Upper Paleolithic cultures resulting in the traditions which are grouped together under the general name of Mesolithic (de Sonneville-Bordes, 1963a, p. 354; see also de Sonneville-Bordes, 1960, 1963b; and Sackett, 1968).

2. There was a major change in the form of stone tools.

Small, geometric flints became very common, and the bow and arrow became wide-spread during the immediately post-Pleistocene period. The changes have occasionally been taken as defining features of the Mesolithic (Childe, 1956, p. 96, see also Gabel, 1958a, p. 658).

3. There is greater geographic variety in cultural remains suggesting more specific responses to local environmental conditions. See deMorgan (1924, p. 74), Garrod and Bate (1937, p. 121), Braidwood and Willey (1962, p. 333), Schwabedissen (1962, p. 260), Pittioni (1962, p. 218), and de Sonneville-Bordes (1960, pp. 497–500, 1963) for specific statements of this generalization.

4. There was a marked increase in the exploitation of aquatic resources and wild fowl. This statement scarcely requires documentation since it is practically a definiens of the Mesolithic (cf. Gabel, 1958a, p. 661; Clark, J. G. D., 1948a, 1948b, 1963).

5. There was a "trend" toward small game hunting. Braidwood (1963, p. 332) notes that this phenomenon has traditionally been explained as a response to the extinction of large mammals at the close of the Pleistocene. He points out, however, that this trend occurs before the end of the Pleistocene and characterizes Africa and India as well as Europe (see also Gimbutas, 1956, p. 14).

6. The Mesolithic represents cultural degeneration when compared with the Upper Paleolithic. This is generally cited in the context of discussions of the Western European materials and the loss of graphic arts (see Osborn, 1919, p. 456; deMorgan, 1924, p. 73; J. G. D. Clark, 1932, p. 1; Sollas, 1924, p. 595;

de Sonneville-Bordes, 1960, p. 498). Reference is also made to the less prestigeful activity of fishing and shellfish collecting, as opposed to reindeer hunting (Osborn, 1919, p. 457).

These generalizations which summarize archaeological observations have been conceived by most European scholars in the following manner (see J. D. Clark, 1962, p. 100):

1. There are major changes in cultural remains which serve to differentiate the cultural systems of the terminal Pleistocene from those of the immediately post-Pleistocene period.

2. This immediately post-Pleistocene period is further characterized by major changes in pollen profiles, fossil beach lines, and the geomorphology of major drainage systems.

3. The demonstrable correlation between the dramatic cultural and environmental changes at this time is evidence for the systematic articulation of cultural and environmental systems.

Therefore:

(a) Archaeological differences observed between the terminal Paleolithic and the Mesolithic can be explained by reference to environmental changes.

(b) Differences not explained by reference to environmental changes are the result of new social contacts; such social contacts were a result of movement of populations in response to local climatic deterioration (for example, the "desiccation" of North Africa cited by J. G. D. Clark, 1936, p. xiv).

This argument is a relatively straightforward mechanistic approach and is completely compatible with a materialistic, systemic approach to the understanding of cultural change. The extent to which this approach might be questioned and the particulars of its application tested depends upon the degree to which (1) equally radical changes in culture can be demonstrated in the absence of analogous environmental changes, and/or (2) major environmental changes can be demonstrated to vary independently of analogous changes in cultural systems.

Such test situations can be found either at a contemporary time period outside the area directly affected by the retreat of glacial ice or in the same regions under similar environmental conditions at a different time period. Researchers concerned with the initial appearance of food production, as well as those workers operating in a variety of non-Western European regions, are the ones to whom we now turn for an evaluation of the explanatory approach commonly used on Western European materials.

The shift from food procurement to food production has been examined by many scholars; Childe termed this change the Neolithic Revolution. In "The Dawn of European Civilization" (1925) Childe suggested that the investigation of the origins of the Neolithic and its spread into Europe would be a major step in the understanding of the post-Mesolithic history of Western Europe. In his "New Light on the Most Ancient East" (1952) Childe offered a model to explain the beginnings of the Neolithic Revolution. Until this point, several other workers had considered the problems of understanding the conditions surrounding the origins of agriculture, and some offered idealistic progressions of conditions under which man would have gained sufficient knowledge of plant and animal biology to permit cultivation (Darwin, 1875, pp. 326–327; Roth, 1887). Others offered mechanistic generalizations about the conditions under which man would have been most likely to have implemented his knowledge (Tylor, 1881, p. 214; deCandolle, 1959). Childe's consideration of the problem was the most influential, since he presented a series of propositions specific enough to be tested through the collection of paleoenvironmental and paleoanthropological data:

> Food production—the deliberate cultivation of food plants, especially cereals, and the taming, breeding and selection of animals . . . was an economic revolution . . . the greatest in human history after the mastery of fire . . . . The conditions of incipient desiccation . . . would provide the stimulus towards the adoption of a food-producing economy. Enforced concentration by the banks of streams and shrinking springs would entail an intensive search for means of nourishment. Animals and men would be herded together in oases that were becoming increasingly isolated by desert tracts. Such enforced juxtaposition might promote that sort of symbiosis between man and beast implied by the word *domestication* (Childe, 1951, pp. 23–25).

If it was Childe who first provided a set of testable propositions as to the conditions under which food-production was achieved, it was Braidwood who actively sought this field data to test Childe's propositions. For a short history of the Iraqi-Jarmo project, the reader is referred to Braidwood and Howe (1960, pp. 1–8); we shall simply summarize the findings of Braidwood and his co-workers with specific reference to the validity of the oasis theory and to the materialistic approach to the understanding of culture change. In discussing the oasis theory Braidwood states:

> So far this theory is pretty much all guess-work, and there are certainly some questions it leaves unanswered. I will tell you quite frankly that there are times when I feel it is plain balderdash (1951a, p. 85).

Braidwood also questioned the relevance of the postulated environmental changes to the origins of food-production:

> There had also been three earlier periods of great glaciers, and long periods of warm weather in between . . . . Thus the forced neighborliness of men, plants and animals in river valleys and oases must also have happened earlier. Why didn't domestication happen earlier too, then? (1951a, p. 86).

Braidwood has made the above point on numerous occasions, but it is in more recent publications (Braidwood and Willey, 1962, p. 342) that the comment is less directly aimed at the oasis theory and more toward questioning the role of environmental change in bringing about food-production.

Braidwood's work in the "hilly flanks" zone of the Fertile Crescent was carried out over a number of years and involved the collaboration of a number of scientists from the fields of zoology, paleontology, geology, palynology, paleobotany, etc. Their investigations had been directed toward the identification of the physical effects of domestication on plants and animals and the documentation of the environmental events of the period between 10,000 B.C. and the appearance of "settled village life." The climatological–Environmental results have allowed Braidwood to generalize:

> It seems most unlikely that there was any really significant difference between then and now in the general land forms and rainfall patterns (1952b, p. 11).
> In southwestern Asia . . . our colleagues in the natural sciences see no evidence for radical change in climate or fauna between the levels of the Zarzian and those of the Jarmo or Hassunha phases (Braidwood and Howe, 1960, p. 181).

Discussing specifically the relationship between environmental change and the beginnings of food-production, Braidwood states:

> We do not believe that the answers will lie within the realm of environmental determinism and in any direct or strict sense . . . we and our natural-science colleagues reviewed the evidence for possible pertinent fluctuations of climate and of plant and animal distributions . . . and convinced ourselves that there is no such evidence available . . . . No evidence exists for such changes in the natural environment . . . as might be of sufficient impact to have predetermined the shift to food production (Braidwood and Howe, 1960, p. 142).

Thus Braidwood argues that: (1) environmental conditions analogous to those at the close of the Pleistocene had occurred previously without having brought about food-production, and (2) there is no evidence to support major climatic changes in the Near East of sufficient magnitude to have "predetermined the shift to food production." These observations are not only directed against the oasis theory but also against the argument that food-production constituted an alternative adaptation to changed environmental conditions at the close of the Pleistocene. Braidwood also argues against the causative role of environmental change in his consideration of the applicability of the term Mesolithic to non-European areas (Braidwood and Willey, 1962, p. 332). Garrod (1932) called the Natufian of Israel a Mesolithic industry, and the appropriateness of this terminology has been questioned by Braidwood:

> The usual conception of the Mesolithic is as a cultural readaptation to post-Pleistocene environments but the conception has become an awkward one, on a world wide scale, since

as we have just seen, there is evidence that the same trends toward readaptation and intensification of collecting activities had begun to manifest themselves in certain area before the conventional date for the end of the Pleistocene. One of us is of the opinion that there was no Mesolithic sensu stricto, in southwestern Asia, at least (Braidwood and Willey, 1962, p. 332).

There is also increasing evidence that there were cultural changes parallel to those occurring in Western Europe in regions where there were no correlated major climatic changes (see, for example, Perrot, 1962, pp. 147 and 151–153).

Braidwood presents a strong case that there was major cultural change in areas where environmental change was minor or absent, as well as in areas such as Western Europe where environmental change was marked. This, together with the fact that earlier interglacial warm periods were not accompanied by drastic cultural changes of analogous form, is sufficient to invalidate the argument that the magnitude of environmental and cultural change can be expected to vary directly in a simple stimulus–response pattern. These data also raise questions about the positive correlations claimed for the form of environmental and cultural changes.

Braidwood, however, is not completely consistent in his application of these findings. He argues *against* the causative role of environmental change in the Near East, yet *for* such. an explanation for the cultural changes observed in Western Europe (Braidwood and Willey, 1962, p. 341). We do not propose here that there is no relationship between environmental and cultural change in Western Europe but rather argue against the direct and simple causative role of environmental change in view of Braidwood's own findings. What we must seek is a set of explanatory variables which will be valid on a worldwide scale at the terminal and post-Pleistocene periods.

If Braidwood rejects environmental change as the principal explanation in the Near East, what does he propose instead? After apologizing for Childe's "materialistic philosophy of history" (Braidwood and Howe, 1960, p. 7), Braidwood offers his "nuclear zone" theory:

In my opinion there is no need to complicate the story with extraneous "causes." The food producing revolution seems to have occurred as the culmination of the ever increasing cultural differentiation and specialization of human communities. Around 8,000 B.C. the inhabitants of the hills around the fertile crescent had come to know their habitat so well that they were beginning to domesticate the plants and animals they had been collecting and hunting . . . . From these "nuclear" zones cultural diffusion spread the new way of life to the rest of the world (1960a, p. 134).

A nuclear zone is defined as follows:

A region with a natural environment which included a variety of wild plants and animals, both possible and ready for domestication (Braidwood, 1963, p. 106).

In his statements Braidwood proposes that cultivation is the expected, natural outcome of a long, directional evolutionary trend, limited only by the presence in the environment of domesticable plants and animals. This is clearly an orthogenetic argument (see Simpson, 1949, pp. 130–159, for a critical discussion of orthogenesis). The vital element responsible for the directional series of events appears to be inherent in human nature; it is expressed by Braidwood in such phrases as "increased experimentation" (1963, p. 106) and "increased receptiveness" (1963, pp. 97–98 and 137–138). Those behavioral traits made it possible for man to "settle into" his environment (Braidwood and Reed, 1957, p. 20), and they serve as the basis for Braidwood's taxonomy of subsistence-settlement types (1960b, pp. 143–151) in which three long-run trends can be seen: (1) increased localization of activity within the territory of a group, (2) more specific exploitation of the habitat, and (3) increased group size. (For a playful treatment of Braidwood's frame of reference, see Binford and Binford, 1966). It is when we have these trends, based on inherent human nature, operating in the context of a "nuclear zone" that things begin to happen:

> Now my hunch goes that when this experimentation and settling down took place within a potential nuclear area . . . where a whole constellation of plants and animals possible of domestication were available . . . the change was easily made (Braidwood, 1963, p. 110).

The explanation for the absence of food production during earlier interglacial periods is that "culture was not ready to achieve it" (Braidwood and Willey, 1962, p. 342).

It is argued here that vitalism, whether expressed in terms of inherent forces orienting the direction of organic evolution or in its more anthropocentric form of emergent human properties which direct cultural evolution, is unacceptable as an explanation. Trends which are observed in cultural evolution require explanation; they are certainly not explained by postulating emergent human traits which are said to account for the trends.

In summary, post-Pleistocene research began with the question of whether or not Western Europe was populated between the close of the Pleistocene and the first appearance of the later Neolithic settlements. When this question was answered affirmatively, emphasis shifted to the question of continuity—were the "intermediate" populations indigenous or were they intruders? In seeking to solve this problem scholars were involved in the methodological question of what archaeological data could be cited as proof or disproof of continuity. As local sequences became better documented, this question was dropped, and there was an increasing tendency to view variability as a direct response to local environments which had radically changed with the retreat of the ice. This stimulus-response reasoning was generalized not only for the European foraging adaptation but was also used to explain the origins of food production (the propinquity or oasis theory). Field investigation in the relevant parts of the Near East showed that dramatic environmental change did not characterize the crucial periods of time. The oasis theory has fallen into disfavor, and Braidwood's nuclear zone theory has tended to replace it. We have sought to demonstrate in our analysis that this theory is based on a kind of vitalism and a postulation of causal factors which are incapable of being tested. We also propose that current explanations for the form and distribution of post-Pleistocene cultures in Europe are implicitly, and often explicitly, based on simple and direct environmental determination which the data from non-European parts of the world tend to refute. What follows is an examination of post-Pleistocene data within a different theoretical framework and the formulation of explanatory hypotheses which, it is hoped, are both more generally applicable and also testable.

If our aim is the explanation of cultural differences and similarities in different places and at different times, we must first isolate the phenomena we designate "cultural." Culture is all those means whose forms are not under direct genetic control [that is, extrasomatic (White, 1959, p. 8)] which serve to adjust individuals and groups within their ecological communities. If we seek understanding of the origins of agriculture or of "the spread of the village-farming community," we must analyze these cultural means as adaptive adjustments in the variety of ecosystems within which human groups were participants.

Adaptation is always a local problem, and selective pressures favoring new cultural forms result from nonequilibrium conditions in the local ecosystem. Our task, then, becomes the isolation of the variables initiating directional change in the internal structuring of ecological systems. Of particular importance is understanding the conditions which favor the rearrangement of energy–matter components and their linked dependencies in a manner which alters the effective environment of the unit under study.

The term "effective environment" (Allee *et al.,* 1949, p. 1) designates those parts of the total environment which are in regular or cyclical articulation with the unit under study. Changes in the effective environment will produce changes not only in the boundaries of the ecological community but also in the internal organization of the community. Both of these changes in turn set up conditions favoring adaptive adjustments among the components of the community. In dealing with sociocultural systems and in trying to understand the conditions under which such systems undergo adaptive change, we are necessarily concerned with the effective environment of a given system.

Cultural systems relate man to habitat, and an equilibrium can be established in this relationship as in others. When an equilibrium has been established culturally between man and habitat, it may be continued indefinitely until it is upset by the intrusion of a new factor (White, 1959, p. 284).

If we hope to understand culture change in general, and the changes of the post-Pleistocene period in particular, we must seek the conditions which have brought new factors into play in the effective environments of the cultural systems at the close of the Pleistocene.

Before undertaking our analysis, one further distinction needs to be made—the distinction between functional and structural differences in ecological niches. *Functional differences* are those which result from differences in the form of the elements of a system and which do not necessarily imply differences in the kind of articulation which exists between a cultural system and the ecological community of which it is a part. *Structural differences* refer to communities made up of nonanalogous components which are integrated in different ways. In citing functional variability between niches, we are referring to differences in the form of the gross environment in which ecological communities occur; in such cases there would be no necessary structural differences in the organization of the ecological communities of the system, but only in the form of their environments. A case in point might be two cultural systems, both of which are solely dependent upon terrestrial resources within their home ranges and neither of which possesses the technological means for food storage or circulation beyond the locus of procurement. If one such system were located in a tropical rain forest and the other in a temperate deciduous forest, we would observe numerous formal differences between the cultural elements in the two systems, yet both can be said to occupy similar ecological niches within their habitats. Despite obvious differences in raw materials, the form of implements, differences in phasing of activities, and even in social organization, all such differences are explicable directly by reference to differences in gross environment. Therefore, we would term these differences functional, not structural.

Structural differences in ecological niches, on the other hand, refer to differences in the modes of integration between cultural and other components within ecological communities. Such differences imply a different set of relationships between the cultural unit and the variables in the gross environment with which the cultural unit is articulated. Cultural systems which occupy different ecological niches would therefore have different effective environments. An example of two cultural systems in the same gross environment but occupying different ecological niches would be the commonly occurring case where horticulturalists and hunter–gatherers live side by side. Each cultural group is in articulation with quite different elements of the gross environment and is integrated with the environment differently. Such cultural systems would be subject to qualitatively different types of selective pressure.

We would argue that understanding the selective pressures favoring the adoption of adaptive means as radical and as new as animal husbandry and cultivation in the post-Pleistocene requires the application of the ecological principles outlined above. A first step would be to determine whether food production constitutes a functional variant of analogous ecological niches in different environments, or whether it is a structurally new adaptive means in an ecological niche not previously occupied by cultural systems.

Braidwood's nuclear zone theory is an argument for the former interpretation; the differences between the post-Pleistocene cultures in the hilly flanks and elsewhere are explicable by reference to formally unique elements in the plant and animal populations of the piedmont regions of the Near East. Childe's position is a statement of the latter interpretation, and he cites changes in the physical environment as the cause for bringing about new structural relationships between plants, animals, and men. Our argument also favors the second interpretation but with demographic, rather than gross environmental, variables responsible for the generation of pressures favoring new ecological niches.

At certain times and places in the course of culture history, the threat of a diminished food supply, coming from an increase of population through immigration, or from a decline in local flora due to climatic or physiographic change, was met by various measures of cultural control over plant life, which collectively, we call agriculture (White, 1959, p. 285).

White's citation of population increase through immigration as a relevant variable in explaining the appearance of agriculture is a radical departure from traditional interpretations.

In the traditional approach, changes and variation in the available food supply have been cited as the major factors which regulate population equilibrium systems (Dumond, 1965, p. 310).

Man must eat to live at all; food is perhaps the one absolute and overriding need for man. In early and primitive societies the quest for food was and is the most absorbing preoccupation for all members of the group. The enlargement of the food-supply was therefore presumably the indispensable condition for human progress (Childe, 1944, p. 12).

The community of food-gatherers had been restricted in size by the food supplies available (Childe, 1951, p. 61).

Similar statements have been made by Braidwood (1963, pp. 121–122), among others.

The inference about population dynamics to be made from these statements is that populations will grow until the food requirements of the group begin to exceed the standing crop in the local habitat. No population could ever achieve a stable adaptation since its members would always be under strong selective pressure to develop new means of getting food. This assumption of the available food supply as the critical variable in population dynamics has prevented consideration of population variables themselves as possible sources of disequilibrium.

Recent studies in demography have argued strongly against the direct control of population density by the availability of food.

> We have the strongest reasons for concluding ... that population density must at all costs be prevented from rising to the level where food shortage begins to take a toll of the numbers—an effect that could not be felt until long after the optimum density had been exceeded. It would be bound to result in chronic over-exploitation and a spiral of diminishing returns (Wynne-Edwards, 1962, p. 11).
>
> Long term population equilibrium ... implies some kind of restraint .... "Food supply" offers a quick answer, but not, I think, the correct one. At any rate, a forest is full of game for an expert mouse-hunter, and a Paleolithic man who stuck to business should have found enough food on two square kilometers instead of 20 or 200. Social forces were probably more powerful than mere starvation in causing men to huddle in small bands (Deevey, 1960, p. 6).

Most demographers agree that functional relationships between the normal birth rate and other requirements (for example, the mobility of the female) favor the *cultural* regulation of fertility through such practices as infanticide, abortion, lactation taboos, etc. These practices have the effect of homeostatically keeping population size below the point at which diminishing returns from the local habitat would come into play (see Carr-Saunders, 1922; Wynne-Edwards, 1962, 1964; Birdsell, 1958, 1968; Deevey, 1960; Hainline, 1965; Dumond, 1965; Halbwachs, 1960).

The arguments of demographers are supported by a number of recent ethnographic studies which document the abundance of food available to even marginal hunters. Some cases of importance are J. D. Clark (1951) on the Barotse, Lee (1965) on the !Kung Bushmen, Woodburn (1968) on the Hadza, and Huntingford (1955) on the Dorobo. Similar conditions of relative abundance have been reported for Australia. For example, life on the Daly River in the Northern Territory led McCarthy (1957, p. 90) to generalize: "For the uncontaminated bush native the food problem hardly exists." Ease in food procurement is also reported for Arnhemland (McCarthy, 1957, p. 90; McCarthy and McArthur, 1960, pp. 145–193). Quimby has described the truly impressive quantities of food obtained in the course of a single year by a Chippewa family in the Lower Peninsula of Michigan in 1763 (Quimby, 1962, pp. 217–239). In a quantitative study of food intake by the Onge hunters of Little Andaman, Bose (1964, p. 306) states: "The region surrounding Tokebuea can supply more food than the requirement of the local people."

These data suggest that while hunting–gathering populations may vary in density between different habitats in direct proportion to the relative size of the standing food crop, nevertheless within any given habitat the population is homeostatically regulated *below* the level of depletion of the local food supply.

There are two corollaries of the assumption that population size is regulated almost exclusively by food supply which we also need to examine. The first corollary is: *Man would be continually seeking means for increasing his food supply.* In other words, there would be ubiquitous and constant selective pressure favoring the development of technological innovations, such as agriculture, which serve to make larger amounts of food available to a group. There is a large body of ethnographic data which suggests that this is not the case.

Carneiro (1957) in his study of the Kuikuru, who are horticulturalists, demonstrated that these people were capable of producing several times the amount of food they did. A small increment in the amount of time devoted to planting and harvesting would have brought about substantial increases in the available food, yet the Kuikuru chose not to do this. Enough food was produced to meet local demands, and it was at that point that production stopped. Equilibrium had been reached, and neither population nor production increased.

In writing about the southeastern United States, Caldwell concerned himself with the question of why no effective early prehistoric agriculture was developed in the region. He concluded:

We have suggested that so many natural foods were available that to place any reliance on cultivation . . . might have seemed risky or irrelevant. The hunting–gathering pattern was developed to a peak of efficiency and jelled, so to speak, in the very heart of eastern cultures (1958, p. 72).

If we recognize that an equilibrium system can be established so that populations are homeostatically regulated below the carrying capacity of the local food supply, it follows that there is no necessary adaptive pressure continually favoring means of increasing the food supply. The question to be asked then is not why agricultural and food-storage techniques were not developed everywhere, but why they were developed at all. Under what set of conditions does increasing the supply of available food have adaptive advantage?

The second corollary to be examined concerns leisure time: *It is only when man is freed from preoccupation with the food quest that he has time to elaborate culture.* A fairly representative statement of this corollary has been made by Childe (1951, p. 61) and is cited above. Also, Braidwood writes:

Proper village life now came into being, and with it a completely new kind of technology. This latter depends on the fact that time now became available for pursuits other than that of simply collecting food (Braidwood and Braidwood, 1950, p. 189).

Braidwood reiterates the same argument in more detail in another place (1963, pp. 121–122). The view of the hunter constantly involved in scrounging a bare subsistence and existing on the brink of starvation has recently received some rather pointed comments by Sahlins:

Almost totally committed to the argument that life was hard in the Paleolithic, our text books compete to convey a sense of impending doom, leaving the student to wonder not only how hunters managed to make a living but whether, after all, this is living. The spectre of starvation stalks the stalker in these pages. His technical incompetence is said to enjoin continuous work just to survive, leaving him without respite from the food quest and without the "leisure time to build culture" (1968).

There is abundant data which suggests not only that hunter–gatherers have adequate supplies of food but also that they enjoy quantities of leisure time, much more in fact than do modern industrial or farm workers, or even professors of archaeology. Lee (1965), Bose (1964), McCarthy and McArthur (1960), and Woodburn (1968) have shown that hunters on a simple level of technology spend a very small percentage of their time obtaining food. On these grounds we can reasonably question the proposition that cultural elaboration is caused by leisure time which is available for the first time to agriculturalists.

In rejecting the assumption that hunter–gatherer populations are primarily regulated by the available supply of food, we put the problem of the development of new types of subsistence in a different light. As long as one could assume that man was continually trying to increase his food supply, understanding the "origins of agriculture" simply involved pinpointing those geographic areas where the potential resources were and postulating that man would inevitably take advantage of them. With the recognition that equilibrium systems regulate population density below the carrying capacity of an environment, we are forced to look for those conditions which might bring about disequilibrium and bring about selective advantage for increased productivity. According to the arguments developed here, there could be only two such sets of conditions:

1. A change in the physical environment of a population which brings about a reduction in the biotic mass of the region would decrease the amounts of available food. The previous balance between population and standing crop is upset, and more efficient extractive means would be favored. This is essentially the basis for Childe's propinquity theory.

2. Change in the demographic structure of a region which brings about the impingement of one group on the territory of another would also upset an established equilibrium system and might serve to increase the population density of a region beyond the carrying capacity of the natural environment. Under these conditions manipulation of the natural environment in order to increase its productivity would be highly advantageous.

The remainder of this paper is devoted to the exploration of this second set of conditions. The first step of our analysis is to build models of different types of population systems under different conditions. One such type of system is termed a *closed population system* (Hyrenius, 1959, p. 476) in which a steady state is maintained by internal mechanisms limiting numbers of offspring at the generational replacement level. Techniques such as abortion, contraception, abstinence, and infanticide serve to lower the birth rate and increase the mortality rate so that a given population would be homeostatically regulated at a given size or density.

The second type of system, the *open population system,* is one in which size and/or density is maintained by either the budding off of new groups or by the emigration of individuals. This would be an *open system of the donor type.* If the size or density of the system is altered through the introduction of immigrants from other population groups, we have an *open system of the recipient type.*

Given these two types of population systems—closed and open, the latter including two subtypes, recipient and donor—we can begin to analyze differences in the ways in which the two system types can be articulated in a given region.

Closed Systems

We can identify the population of a region as a whole as a closed system, yet find that within the region there would be some variability in optimum group size as a response to geographical differences in the regional distribution of resources. Further, each local group within the region may operate periodically as an open system since we would expect some variability in the degree to which local groups have achieved equilibrium. There would therefore be some redistribution of population between groups which would promote a more uniform and steady density equilibrium system over the region as a whole.

We would expect selection favoring cultural means of regulating population to occur in situations where the density equilibrium system for the region as a whole was in fact a closed system and where there were significant imbalances in the losses and recruits for the local subsegments of the regional population. There would be differential selective advantage for cultural regulation of population growth between two closed population systems in different environmental settings if there were discrepancies between the actual birth and death rates on the one hand and the optimal rates for maintaining population size on the other.

Open Systems: Donor Type

We would expect to find this type of population system in areas which are not filled to the point at which density dependent factors are brought into play.

The peopling of a new land mass, such as the New World or Australia, would be an example of such a situation in which there would be positive advantage for this type of system.

The rate of expansion of open donor systems into uninhabited territory has been discussed in the literature, and models for this type of expansion have been built (Bartholomew and Birdsell, 1953; Birdsell, 1957, 1958, 1968; Yengoyan, 1960). Birdsell has made two observations which are particularly relevant here. First, the budding off of new groups occurs *before* optimum local population size has been reached (Birdsell, 1957, p. 54). This observation demonstrates the role of emigration in bringing about and maintaining equilibrium and also shows that the unit on which selection for emigration operates is a subunit of the local population since conditions favoring segmentation appear before the regional population is under pressure from density dependent factors.

Second, the adaptation of any given sociocultural system will determine in part the locus of selection within the social system and the particular selective advantages for different fertility rates. Birdsell writes:

> In a population stabilized at the carrying capacity of its given environment, some limitation on procreative activities naturally filter down to the level of the biological family. These may be examined most profitably in terms of the requirements which affect the spacing of the natal survivors. Generalized hunters with their requirements of high mobility present the most exacting model. Australian data indicate that the inability of a mother to carry more than one child at a time together with her female baggage impose the first insurmountable barrier to a large number of children. Strongly reinforced by an equally limiting incapacity to nurse more than one child simultaneously imposes a minimum of a three-year spacing upon children designed for survival. Since human female reproductive physiology does not reliably prevent conception while still nursing, children are frequently conceived and born which cannot be reared. The result is systematic infanticide (1968).

We have seen that two frequent means of maintaining homeostasis are emigration and cultural regulation of births and deaths. The relative importance to any group of one of these means versus the other will be conditioned by such factors as mobility requirements of the group. Another conditioning factor would be the type of articulation between segments of the population which can directly affect the ease with which budding-off can occur. A third factor would be the degree to which the region as a whole is occupied which would affect the expectations of success in the establishment of daughter communities.

Open Systems: Recipient Type

This type of system could occur under only two sets of conditions; the first would be where there is the expansion of a donor system into an uninhabited region. The frontier of the region would contain a number of population units which could, for a short time, serve as recipient systems. Their change from recipient to donor systems would depend upon the extent to which optimal densities were achieved locally and the frontier continued to advance.

The second set of conditions promoting systems of the recipient type is more relevant to the consideration of early agricultural developments. This is the situation in which two or more different kinds of sociocultural systems occupy adjacent environmental zones. If the adaptation of one sociocultural unit is translatable into the adjacent environmental zone, it may expand into that zone at the expense of resident systems. Cases of this type have been cited by Kaplan (1960) as examples of the Law of Cultural Dominance, and a specific instance referred to by Sahlins (1961) are the Tiv and the Nuer. We would expect expansion of the dominant system until the zone to which the system was adapted was occupied; at this juncture there would be selection for increased efficiency of production and/or for increased regulation of the birth rate.

A different kind of situation would obtain in the case of sociocultural systems occupying adjacent zones if the adaptation of the more rapidly growing group is not translatable into the adjacent zone. Population growth within the area occupied by the parent group might well be so great that daughter communities would frequently be forced to reside in an environment which is incompatible with their particular cultural adaptation. There could be a number of effects under these circumstances.

From the standpoint of the populations already in the recipient zone, the intrusion of immigrant groups would disturb the existing density equilibrium system and might raise the population density to the level at which we would expect diminishing food resources. This situation would serve to increase markedly for the recipient groups the pressures favoring means for increasing productivity. The intrusive group, on the other hand, would be forced to make adaptive adjustments to their new environment (for an example of this situation, see Binford, 1968). There would be strong selective pressures favoring the development of more efficient subsistence techniques by both groups.

It should be pointed out, however, that such advantage does not insure that these developments will inevitably occur. In many cases these problems are met by changes which might be called regressive in that the changes in adaptation which occur may be in the direction of less complex cultural forms. Examples of this sort of change can be seen among the hunter–gatherers of the nonriverine tropical forest zones in South America. Steward and Faron write of the Siriono and Guayaki:

These Indians retreated . . . to inaccessible regions where they largely abandoned horticulture to rely on a predominantly hunting and gathering subsistence. Other enclaves of nomads isolated in the tropical forests and interfluvial regions may also have experienced similar deculturation (1959, p. 378).

Lathrap has offered the possibility that perhaps all of the less sedentary South American groups are "the degraded descendants of peoples who at one time maintained an advanced form of Tropical Forest Culture" (1968).

While in these examples the adaptations along population frontiers were in the direction of less complexity, it is in the context of such situations of stress in environments with plant and animal forms amenable to manipulation that we would expect to find conditions favoring the development of plant and animal domestication. Such situations would be characterized by disequilibrium between population and resources which, in turn, would offer selective advantage to increases in the efficacy of subsistence technology. Rather than seeking the locus for the origins of agriculture in the heart of a "natural habitat zone," we would argue that we must look to those places where a population frontier or adaptive tension zone intersects a "natural habitat zone." This means that archaeological investigations might well concentrate on those areas within the natural habitat zone where there is an archaeologically demonstrated major shift in population density. The presence of such a shift might well indicate a population frontier where rapid evolutionary changes were taking place.

Another archaeological clue to be exploited is the degree to which settlements are characterized by sedentism. The frontier zones would be expected between regions which differed widely in the degree of sedentism practiced by resident groups. In those areas with highly sedentary population, problems of transport of young and belongings would be reduced. Reduced mobility of social units in general and in the daily routines of females in particular would in turn reduce the selected advantages accruing to cultural means of controlling population growth. Therefore, under conditions of increased sedentism we would expect population growth. A consequence of such growth would be the increased relative importance of emigration as a mechanism for maintaining the local group within optimal size and density limits.

Therefore where there is a marked contrast in degree of sedentism between two sociocultural units within a relatively restricted geographical region, there would be a tension zone where emigrant colonies from the more sedentary group would periodically disrupt the density equilibrium balances of the less sedentary group. Under these conditions there would be strong selective pressure favoring the development of more effective means of food production for both groups within this zone of tension. There would also be increasing pressures against immigration, given the failure to develop more effective extractive technologies.

It is proposed here that it was in the selective context outlined above that initial practices of cultivation occurred. Such selective situations would have been the consequence of the increased dependence on aquatic resources during the terminal and immediately post-Pleistocene period. Not all portions of rivers and shorelines favor the harvesting of fish, molluscs, and migratory fowl; it is with the systematic dependence on just these resources that we find archaeological remains indicating a higher degree of sedentism in both the Archaic of the New World and the terminal Paleolithic and Mesolithic of the Old World. This hypothesis is lent strong support by the fact that it is also in the terminal Paleolithic–Mesolithic and Archaic that we find, associated with increased sedentism, evidence for marked population growth and for the development of food-storage techniques, the latter being functionally linked to the highly seasonal nature of migratory fowl and anadromous fish exploited as food crops (for an example of the importance of anadromous fish, see Binford, 1964).

Since the systematic exploitation of these food sources (and of markedly seasonally available terrestrial forms as well—for example, reindeer) characterized adaptations' of this time range in a wide variety of environments, we would expect that tension zones, with their concomitant selective pressures favoring increased subsistence efficiency, would be widely distributed also. This expectation is in accord with the empirical generalizations that: (1) There were a number of independent loci of the development of cultivation techniques—the Near East, Asia, and the New World—and all the developments of these techniques occur within the time range in question; and (2) These loci were distributed across widely different environmental types—root crops in the tropics and cereals in semiaridlands, for example.

The widespread nature of conditions favoring increased subsistence efficiency also accounts for the rapid transmission and integration of contributing innovations from one cultural system to another. Many authors have cited the rapid "diffusion" of cultural elements as characterizing the immediately post-Pleistocene period.

Finally, in the traditional view the "Neolithic Revolution" is characterized by the appearance of a number of traits which are thought to be linked to the shift to food production. The manufacture of ceramics and textiles, relatively permanent houses, and craft specialization are only a few of those frequently cited (cf. Braidwood, 1963, pp. 122–123). These traits constitute part of the definition of the "village farming way of life," and the assumption is that they originated in the "nuclear area" from which they spread as a complex, the spread being achieved by diffusion, stimulus diffusion, and/or migration. As more data have been accumulated, it becomes increasingly clear that these traits are not mutually dependent; indeed, it seems to be quite clear that ceramics, for example, were first used in the Old World in coastal Japan (Griffin, 1961, p. 92), with a cluster of radiocarbon dates averaging *ca.* 7000 B.C. This is about the same time that effective grain agriculture was initially practiced in the Near East (Mellaart, 1961, 1963; Hole, 1966; Young and Smith, 1966), and the occupations in question have yielded no ceramics. Given our model, such traits insofar as they are functionally linked to sedentism and/or food production would be expected to appear in a variety of regions as the result of numerous independent but parallel inventions.

Further utility for the model presented here can be shown by the degree to which it provides explanatory answers for a series of questions posed by Braidwood and Willey—questions which cannot be satisfactorily answered within the traditional framework.

> Why did incipient food production not come earlier? Our only answer at the moment is that culture was not yet ready to achieve it (Braidwood and Willey, 1962, p. 342).

We believe that a more complete answer is possible. The shift to the exploitation of highly seasonal resources such as anadromous fish and migratory fowl did not occur until the close of the Pleistocene. This shift, probably linked to worldwide changes in sea level, with attendant increase in sedentism, established for the first time conditions leading to marked heterogeneity in rates of population growth and structure of the ecological niche of immediately adjacent sociocultural systems. This new set of conditions brought about, in turn, conditions favoring improved subsistence technology. It was not that culture was unready, but rather that the selective conditions favoring such changes had not previously existed.

> What were the . . . cultural conditions favoring incipient cultivation or domestication? Certainly there is nothing in the archeological record to indicate that those few instances of cultural build-up and elaboration, as manifested by the varying art styles of the upper paleolithic from western Europe into Siberia . . . provided a favorable ground for incipient food production. On the contrary, those instances of incipient cultivation or domestication of greatest potential are found in contexts of a much less spectacular character (Braidwood and Willey, 1962, p. 343; see also Willey, 1966, pp. 141–142).

According to our model, we would *expect* to find the selective situation favoring "incipient cultivation" in "contexts of a much less spectacular character"—in those tension zones where less sedentary populations are being moved in on by daughter groups from more sedentary populations. These are the areas where the development of greater productive means is most advantageous.

> The perplexing question of what kinds of natural environmental settings were most propitious for the early development of incipient food production is by no means solved. Nevertheless, the data on hand suggest that generally semi-arid regions . . . with adequate but not overabundant collectible food resources were the hearths of the most important beginnings of cultivation and domestication (Braidwood and Willey, 1962, p. 342).

If we look at the semiarid areas where the crops referred to (wheat and barley in the Old World; maize in the New World) were developed, it turns out that they are adjacent to areas which already supported settled (that is, sedentary) villages whose populations depended in large part upon aquatic resources. The Natufian of the Near East (Kenyon, 1959; Perrot, 1960, 1962) and the coastal settlements of Mexico and Peru (Willey, 1966, p. 144; see also Flannery and Coe, 1968) are cases in point.

The explanation of the distribution noted above of the hearths of domestication of most economically significant crops within semiarid regions lies in the nature of the seeds produced by the plants in such regions. Seeds of xerophytic plants normally have low moisture requirements and can therefore remain viable without being subject to rots which attack many other kinds of seeds. Their economic value also lies in the fact that semiarid regions are areas with low diversity indices (Odum, 1959, p. 281), which means that there will typically be many individuals of a given species within a very limited space.

We would like to note in passing that the post hoc evaluation of some "beginnings of cultivation" as "most important" (because of the ultimate economic significance of the crops produced) and the limitation of question-asking to these instances has served to prevent the recognition of the general conditions under which cultivation may have been initiated.

How did the new elements spread into Europe; how shall we conceptualize the nature of the cultural mechanisms of "diffusion" and the spread of new "influences" through a vast area of already functioning cultural and environmental adaptations? (Braidwood and Willey, 1962, p. 347).

While wheat and barley might have constituted "new influences" in Europe, it has been suggested above that cultivation arose as a response to similar pressures many times and in many places. Given the existence of the selective situation favoring food production and the response to this adaptive situation occurring in a number of places, including Europe, the adoption of easily storable high-yield crops such as wheat and barley becomes readily understandable. However, it is important not to confound the adoption of specific crops with the "spread of the village-farming way of life."

If the model presented here has value above and beyond that of a logical exercise, it must be tested by the formulation of hypotheses and the collection of data. While the outlining of a program of research is beyond the scope of and irrelevant to the aims of this paper, a few predictions follow which, if borne out by field research, would empirically validate some of our assertions.

1. Evidence for the initial domestication of plants and animals in the Near East will come from areas adjacent to those occupied by relatively sedentary forager–fishers. One such area is that adjacent to the Natufian settlements in the Jordan Valley. These settlements have yielded evidence of heavy dependence upon fish and migratory fowl (Perrot, 1960, p. 20) and the architecture suggests

a sedentary way of life. The areas just beyond these villages would have received "excess" population and would therefore have been areas of disequilibrium in which adaptive change would have been favored. Intermontane valleys and foothills which supported migratory hunters far removed from the kind of villages described above will not yield information on the earliest transition to dependence on food production, regardless of the density of wild ancestors of domesticates.

2. Evidence for independent experimentation leading to the development of agriculture as well as animal domestication will be found in European Russia and south-central Europe. We would expect the relevant areas to be adjacent to those where there was effective exploitation of anadromous fish and migratory fowl. Such areas appear to be the rivers flowing into the Black Sea (J. G. D. Clark, 1948b, p. 50).

3. As further research is carried out in Europe, Asia, and the New World, there will be evidence for numerous independent innovations paralleling forms appearing in other areas. Post-Pleistocene adaptations are viewed as the result of the operation of local selective pressures, and the development of food production is one instance of such adaptations. Parallel innovations can be expected where structurally similar ecological niches were occupied, regardless of differences in the general form of the environment.

In conclusion, it is hoped that the theoretical perspective offered here will serve to generate a new series of questions, the answers to which may increase our understanding of the major cultural changes which occurred at the close of the Pleistocene.

References

Allee, W. C., A. E. Emerson, O. Park, T. Park, and Karl P. Schmidt. (1949). *Principles of Animal Ecology*. Saunders, Philadelphia, Pennsylvania.

Bartholomew, George A., Jr., and J. B. Birdsell. (1953). Ecology and the protohominids. *American Anthropologist* 55, 481–498.

Binford, Lewis R. (1964). *Archaeological and Ethnohistorical Investigations of Cultural Diversity*. Ph.D. Dissertation, University of Michigan (microfilm).

Binford, Lewis, R. (1968). An ethnohistory of the Nottoway, Meherrin and Weanock Indians of southwestern Virginia. *Ethnohistory* 14, No. 3–4 (Whole No.).

Binford, Lewis R., and Sally R. Binford. (1966). The predatory revolution: A consideration of the evidence for a new subsistence level. *American Anthropologist* 68, 508–512.

Binford, S. R. (1968). Variability and change in the near eastern Mousterian of Levallois facies. In *New Perspectives in Archeology* (S. R. Binford and L. R. Binford, eds.), pp. 49–60. Aldine Publ. Co., Chicago.

Birdsell, Joseph B. (1957). Some population problems involving Pleistocene man. *Cold Spring Harbor Symposia on Quantitative Biology* 22, 47–69.

Birdsell, Joseph B. (1958). On population structure in generalized hunting and collecting populations. *Evolution* **12,** 189–205.

Birdsell, Joseph B. (1968). Some predictions for the Pleistocene based upon equilibrium systems among recent hunters. In *Man the Hunter* (R. B. Lee and I. DeVore, eds.), pp. 229–240. Aldine Publ. Co., Chicago, Illinois.

Bose, Saradindu. (1964). Economy of the Onge of Little Andaman. *Man in India* **44,** 298–310.

Braidwood, R. J. (1951a). *Prehistoric Men,* 2nd ed., Popular Series, Anthropology No. 37. Chicago Natural History Museum, Chicago, Illinois.

Braidwood, R. J. (1952a). From cave to village. *Scientific American* **187,** 62–66.

Braidwood, R. J. (1952b). *The Near East and the Foundations for Civilization,* Condon Lectures. Oregon State System of Higher Education, Eugene.

Braidwood, R. J. (1960a). The agricultural revolution. *Scientific American* **203,** 130–141.

Braidwood, R. J. (1960b). Levels in prehistory: A model for the consideration of the evidence. In *The Evolution of Man* (S. Tax, ed.), Vol. 2 of *Evolution after Darwin,* pp. 143–151. Univ. of Chicago Press, Chicago.

Braidwood, R. J. (1963). *Prehistoric Men,* 6th ed., Popular Series, Anthropology No. 37. Chicago Natural History Museum, Chicago, Illinois.

Braidwood, R. J., and Linda Braidwood. (1950). Jarmo: A village of early farmers in Iraq. *Antiquity* **24,** 189–195.

Braidwood, R. J., and Bruce Howe. (1960). *Prehistoric Investigations in Iraqi Kurdistan,* Oriental Institute Studies in Ancient Oriental Civilization, No. 31. Univ. of Chicago Press, Chicago.

Braidwood, R. J., and Bruce Howe. (1962). Southwestern Asia beyond the lands of the Mediterranean littoral. In *Courses Toward Urban Life* (R. J. Braidwood and G. R. Willey, eds.), pp. 132–146. Aldine Publ. Co., Chicago, Illinois.

Braidwood, R. J., and Charles A. Reed. (1957). The achievement and early consequences of food production. *Cold Spring Harbor Symposia on Quantitative Biology* **22,** 19–31.

Braidwood, R. J., and Gordon Willey. (1962). Conclusions and afterthoughts. In *Courses Toward Urban Life* (R. J. Braidwood and G. R. Willey, eds.), pp. 330–359. Aldine Publ. Co., Chicago, Illinois.

Breuil, H. (1921). Observations suivantes: M. Cartilhac, La question de l'hiatus entre le Paléolithique et le Néolithique. *Anthropologie* **31,** 349–355.

Breuil, H. (1946). The discovery of the antiquity of man. *Journal of the Royal Anthropological Institute of Great Britain and Ireland* **75,** 21–31.

Brown, John Allen. (1888). On some small highly specialized forms of stone implements, found in Asia, North Africa, and Europe. *Journal of the Royal Anthropological Institute of Great Britain and Ireland* **18,** 134–139.

Brown, John Allen. (1892). On the continuity of the Palaeolithic and Neolithic periods. *Journal of the Royal Anthropological Institute of great Britain and Ireland* **22,** 66–98.

Burkitt, M. C. (1925). The transition between Palaeolithic and Neolithic times, i.e. the Mesolithic period. *Proceedings of the Prehistoric Society of East Anglia* **5,** 16–33.

Caldwell, Joseph R. (1958). Trend and tradition in the prehistory of the eastern United States. Memoir No. 88. *American Anthropological Association* **60,** Part 2.

Carneiro, Robert. (1957). Subsistence and social structure: an ecological study of the Kuikuru Indians. Ph.D. Dissertation, University of Michigan (mimeographed).

Carr-Saunders, A. M. (1922). *The Population Problem: A Study in Human Evolution.* Oxford Univ. Press (Clarendon), London and New York.

Childe, V. Gordon. (1925). *The Dawn of European Civilization.* Knopf, New York.

Childe, V. Gordon. (1931). The forest cultures of northern Europe: A study in evolution and diffusion. *Journal of the Royal Anthropological Institute of Great Birtain and Ireland* **61**, 325–348.

Childe, V. Gordon. (1937). Adaptation to the postglacial forest on the north Eurasiatic plain. In *Early Man* (G. G. McCurdy, ed.), pp. 47–91. Lippincott, Philadelphia, Pennsylvania.

Childe, V. Gordon. (1944). *Progress and Archaeology,* Thinkers Library, No. 102. Watts, London.

Childe, V. Gordon. (1951). *Man Makes Himself.* Mentor Books, New American Library, New York.

Childe, V. Gordon. (1952). *New Light on the Most Ancient East,* 4th ed. Routledge & Kegan Paul, London.

Childe, V. Gordon. (1956). The new Stone Age. In *Man, Culture, and Society* (H. L. Shapiro, ed.), pp. 94–110. Oxford Univ. Press, London and New York.

Clark, J. Desmond. (1951). Bushmen hunters of the Barotse forests. *Northern Rhodesia Journal* **1**, 56–65.

Clark, J. Desmond. (1962). Africa south of the Sahara. In *Courses Toward Urban Life* (R. J. Braidwood and G. R. Willey, eds.), pp. 1–33. Aldine Publ. Co., Chicago, Illinois.

Clark, J. G. D. (1932). *The Mesolithic Age in Britain.* Cambridge Univ. Press, London.

Clark, J. G. D. (1936). *The Mesolithic Settlement of Northern Europe: A Study of the Food Gathering Peoples of Northern Europe During the Early Post-glacial Period.* Cambridge Univ. Press, London.

Clark, J. G. D. (1948a). Fowling in prehistoric Europe. *Antiquity* **22**, 116–130.

Clark, J. G. D. (1948b). The development of fishing in prehistoric Europe. *Antiquaries Journal* **28**, 45–85.

Clark, J. G. D. (1963). A survey of the Mesolithic phase in the prehistory of Europe and Southwest Asia. *Atti 6th Congresso Internazionale delle Scienze Preisstoriche e Protostoriche* **1**, 97–111.

Coutil, L. (1912). Tardenoisien, Capsien, Getulien, Ibero-Maurusien Intergetulo-Néolithique, Tellien Loubirien, Geneyenien. *Congrès International d'Anthropologie et d'Archéologie Préhistorique, 14th Session* Vol. 1, pp. 301–336.

Darwin, Charles R. (1875). *The Variation of Animals and Plants Under Domestication,* 2nd ed., Vol. 1. Murray, London.

Dawkins, William Boyd. (1894). On the relation of the Palaeolithic to the Neolithic period. *Journal of the Royal Anthropological Institute of Great Britain and Ireland* **23**, 242–254.

de Candolle, Alphonse L. P. P. (1959). *Origin of Cultivated Plants.* Hafner, New York (reprint of the 2nd ed., 1886).

Deevey, Edward S., Jr. (1960). The human population. *Scientific American* **203**, 194–204.

deLoe, Baron A. (1908). Contribution à l'étude des temps intermédiares entre le Paléolithique et le Néolithique. *XIII Congrès International d'Anthropologie et d.Archéologie préhistorique, 1907* **1**, pp. 422–423.

deMorgan, Jacques Jean Marie. (1924). *Prehistoric Man: A General Outline of Prehistory.* Knopf., New York.

de Mortillet, Adrien. (1896). Les petits silex taillés, à contours géométriques trouvés en Europe, Asie et Afrique. *Revue de l'Ecole d'Anthropologie* **6**, 376–405.

de Mortillet, Gabriel. (1885). *Le préhistorique, antiquité de l'homme,* 2nd ed. Reinwald, Paris.

de Sonneville-Bordes, Denise. (1960). *Le Paléolithique supérieur en Périgord,* 2 vols. Imprimerie Delmas, Bordeaux.

de Sonneville-Bordes, Denise. (1963a). Upper Paleolithic cultures in western Europe. *Science* 142, 347–355.

de Sonneville-Bordes, Denise. (1963b). Le Paléolithique supérieur en Suisse. *Anthropologie* 67, 205–268.

Digby, Adrian. (1949). Technique and the time factor in relation to economic organization. *Man* 49, 16–18.

Dumond, D. E. (1965). Population growth and cultural change. *Southwestern Journal of Anthropology* 21, 302–324.

Durkheim, Emile. (1897–1898). Morphologie sociale. *Année sociologique* 2, 520–521.

Gabel, W. Creighton. (1958a). The Mesolithic continuum in western Europe. *American Anthropologist* 60, 658–667.

Gabel, W. Creighton. (1958b). European secondary Neolithic cultures. *Journal of the Royal Anthropological Institute of Great Britain and Ireland* 88, 97–107.

Gabel, W. Creighton. (1960). Seminar on economic types in pre-urban cultures of temperate woodland, arid, and tropical areas. *Current Anthropology* 1, 437–438.

Garrod, D. A. E. (1932). A new Mesolithic industry: The Natufian of Palestine. *Journal of the Royal Anthropological Institute of Great Britain and Ireland* 62, 257–269.

Garrod, D. A. E., and D. M. A. Bate. (1937). *The Stone Age of Mount Carmel, Excavations at the ·Wadi El-Mughara,* Vol. 1. Oxford Univ. Press (Clarendon), London and New York.

Gimbutas, Marija. (1956). In *The Prehistory of Eastern Europe* (H. Hencken, ed.), Bulletin No. 20. American School of Prehistoric Research, Peabody Museum, Harvard University, Cambridge, Massachusetts.

Gimbutus, Marija. (1963). European prehistory: Neolithic to the Iron Age. In *Biennial Review of Anthropology 1963* (B. J. Siegel, ed.), p. 000. Stanford Univ. Press, Stanford.

Griffin, James B. (1961). Comments in Edmonson: Neolithic diffusion rates. *Current Anthropology* 2, 92–93.

Hainline, Jane. (1965). Culture and biological adaptation. *American Anthropologist* 67, 1174–1197.

Halbwachs, Maurice. (1960). *Population and Society, Introduction to Social Morphology* (translated by O. Duncan and H. W. Pfautz), Free Press, Glencoe, Illinois.

Hervé, Georges. (1899). Populations Mesolithiques et Néolithiques de l'Espagne et du Portugal. *Revue Mensuelle de l'Ecole d'Anthropologie de Paris* 9, Ser. No. 1, 265–280.

Hole, Frank. (1966). Investigating the origins of Mesopotamian civilization. *Science* 153, 605–611.

Huntingford, G. W. B. (1955). The economic life of the Dorobo. *Anthropos* 50, 605–684.

Hyrenius, Hannes. (1959). Population growth and replacement. In *The Study of Population: An Inventory and Appraisal* (P. M. Hauser and O. Duncan, eds.), pp. 472–485. Univ. of Chicago Press, Chicago.

Kaplan, David. (1960). The law of cultural dominance. In *Evolution and Culture* (M. D. Sahlins and E. R. Service, eds.), pp. 69–92. Univ. of Michigan Press, Ann Arbor.

Kenyon, Kathleen M. (1959). Some observations on the beginnings of settlement in the Near East. *Journal of the Royal Anthropological Institute of Great Britain and Ireland* 89, 35–43.

Kozlowski, Leon. (1926). L'époque mésolithique en Pologne. *Anthropologie* 36, 47– 74.

Lathrap, Donald W. (1968). The hunting economies of the tropical Forest Zone of South America; an attempt at historical perspective. In *Man the Hunter* (R. B. Lee and I. DeVore, eds.), pp. 23–29. Aldine Publ. Co., Chicago, Illinois.

Lee, R. B. (1965). *Subsistence Ecology of !Kung Bushmen.* Ph.D. Dissertation, University of California, Berkeley (microfilm).

McCarthy, Frederick D. (1957). Habitat, economy, and equipment of the Australian aborigines. *Australian Journal of Science* **19**, 88–97.

McCarthy, Frederick D., and Margart McArthur. (1960). The food quest and the time factor in aboriginal economic life. *Records of the American Australian Scientific Expedition to Arnhemland* **2**, 145–194.

MacCurdy, George Grant. (1924). *Human Origins: A Manual of Prehistory,* 2 vols. Appleton, New York.

Mellaart, James. (1961). Excavations at Hacilar: 4th preliminary report. *Anatolian Studies* **11**, 39–75.

Mellaart, James. (1963). Excavations at Catal-Hüyük 1962: 2nd preliminary report. *Anatolian Studies* **13**, 43–103.

Obermaier, Hugo. (1925). *Fossil Man in Spain.* Yale Univ. Press, New Haven, Connecticut.

Odum, Eugene P., and H. T. Odum. (1959). *Fundamentals of Ecology,* 2nd ed. Saunders, Philadelphia, Pennsylvania.

Osborn, Henry Fairfield. (1919). *Men of the Old Stone Age, Their Environment, Life and Art,* 3rd ed. Scribner's, New York.

Perrot, Jean. (1960). Excavations at 'Eynan ('Ein Mallaha). Preliminary report on the 1959 season. *Israel Exploration Journal* **10**, 14–22.

Perrot, Jean. (1962). Palestine-Syria-Cilicia. In *Courses Toward Urban Life* (R. J. Braidwood and G. R. Willey, eds.), pp. 147–164. Aldine Publ. Co., Chicago, Illinois.

Piette, Ed. (1895a). Etudes d'ethnographie préhistorique. *Anthropologie* **6**, 276–292.

Piette, Ed. (1895b). Hiatus et lacune vestiges de la période de transition dans la grotte du Mas-d'Azil. *Bulletin de la Société d'Anthropologie de Paris* **6**, Ser. 4, 235–267.

Pittioni, Richard. (1962). Southern middle Europe and southeastern Europe. In *Courses Toward Urban Life* (R. J. Braidwood and G. R. Willey, eds.), pp. 211–226. Aldine Publ. Co., Chicago, Illinois.

Pitt-Rivers, A. Lane-Fox. (1906). In *The Evolution of Culture and Other Essays* (J. L. Myres, ed.). Oxford Univ. press (Clarendon), London and New York.

Quimby, George, I. (1962). A year with a Chippewa family, 1763–1764. *Ethnohistory* **9**, 217–239.

Roth, H. Ling. (1887). On the origin of agriculture. *Journal of the Royal Anthropological Institute of Great Britain and Ireland* **16**, 102–136.

Sackett, James R. (1968). Method and theory of Upper Paleolithic Archeology in southwestern France. In *New Perspectives in Archeology* (S. R. Binford and L. R. Binford, eds.), pp. 61–83. Aldine Publ. Co., Chicago.

Sahlins, Marshall. (1961). The segmentary lineage: An organization of predatory expansion. *American Anthropologist* **63**, 322–345.

Sahlins, Marshall. (1968). Notes on the original affluent society. In *Man the Hunter* (R. B. Lee and I. DeVore, eds.), pp. 85–89. Aldine Publ. Co., Chicago, Illinois.

Schwabedissen, Herman. (1962). Northern continental Europe. In *Courses Toward Urban Life* (R. J. Braidwood and G. R. Willey, eds.), pp. 254–266. Aldine Publ. Co., Chicago. Illinois.

Simpson, George Gaylord. (1949). *The Meaning of Evolution.* Yale Univ. Press, New Haven, Connecticut.

Sollas, W. J. (1924). *Ancient Hunters, and Their Modern Representatives.* Macmillan, New York.

Steward, Julian H., and Louis C. Faron. (1959). *Native Peoples of South America.* McGraw-Hill, New York.

Troels-Smith, Jorgen. (1953). Ertebølle culture-farmer culture, results of the past ten years' excavations in Asmosen Bog, West Zealand. *Aarboger for nordisk Oldkyndighed of Historie* pp. 1–62.

Tylor, E. B. (1881). *Anthropology*. Holt, London.

Vavilov, N. I. (1951). The origin, variation, immunity and breeding of cultivated plants. *Chronica Botanica* **13**, No. 1/6.

Vielle, Edmond. (1890). Pointes de fleches typiques de Fère-en-Tardenois (Aisne). *Bulletin de Société Anthropologique de Paris* **1**, Ser. 6, 959–964.

Waterbolk, H. T. (1962). The lower Rhine Basin. In *Courses Toward Urban Life* (R. J. Braidwood and G. R. Willey, eds.), pp. 227–253. Aldine Publ. Co., Chicago, Illinois.

White, Leslie A. (1959). *The Evolution of Culture*. McGraw-Hill, New York.

Willey, Gordon R. (1966). New World archaeology in 1965. *Proceedings of the American Philosophical Society* **110**, 140–145.

Wilson, Thomas. (1894). *Minute Stone Implements from India,* Report of the National Museum, 1882. US Govt. Printing Office, Washington, D.C.

Woodburn, James. (1968). Background material on the Hadza of Tanzania. In *Man the Hunter* (R. B. Lee and I. DeVore, eds.), p. 000. Aldine Publ. Co., Chicago, Illinois.

Wynne-Edwards, V. C. (1962). *Animal Dispersion in Relation to Social Behaviour*. Oliver & Boyd. Edinburgh.

Wynne-Edwards, V. C. (1964). Population control in animals. *Scientific American* **211**, 68–74.

Yengoyan, Aram A. (1960). Preliminary notes on a model of the initial populating of the Philippines. *Anthropology Tomorrow* **6**, 42–48.

Young, T. C., and P. E. L. Smith. (1966). Research in the prehistory of central western Iran. *Science* **153**, 386–391.

Retrospect and Prospect

Putting together this book has given me the opportunity to review many things: my relationships with people, my shifts in problem interest, and the developments in my own viewpoint regarding the character of archaeology as a scientific field. I have by no means thoroughly covered all of these in my sometimes overpersonalized discussions, and I rationalize this type of presentation on several grounds. First, it is frank and open. I hope I have made the reader aware of a kind of humanistic set of social values which have only matured out of a stormy history of dealing with people. If many of the episodes which I have related about Griffin and Braidwood are unflattering to them, they are equally unflattering to me. I am sure that I failed miserably in my younger days to give Griffin credit for many things. Why did he tolerate Papworth and myself at all? Why did he invest so much in our education and make so many opportunities available to us? Why did Griffin hire some of the best students to graduate from Chicago, where I was attempting to explore new directions in archaeology? Could it be that Griffin—the demon of my mind's eye as a student, the representative of traditionalists' approaches, the symbol of what I was fighting against—was not quite all of these things? Possibly. Only Griffin knows. I like to think that he understood much more than I have previously given him credit for.

Many of the things I laughed about and poked fun at in Braidwood's social image, things which I found pretentious and unappealing, are in some cases strangely inverted today. I live in a country home and invite students for relaxed discussions under my spreading trees. I even have a tweed coat! I know that people whom I respect very much were encouraged, helped, and inspired by Braidwood—for instance, one of my best students, Bob Whallon. I strongly suspect a similar relationship between Braidwood and my friend Clark Howell. Braidwood has made many contributions.

I don't offer these "mellow" reflections as an indication that I will not fight and even have fun at others' expense. I am certain that my days of delivering papers at national meetings, where my behavior has been compared to that of a male baboon, huffing, puffing, and throwing eyelid threats in all directions, is not over. It is in the exploration of competing ideas and approaches that the relative values of such ideas and approaches are tested. It is in the exposure of weakness and inappropriateness of propositions that advances are made and new questions are asked. This is rarely, if ever, accomplished unemotionally and without personal involvement. In fact, as I suggested in the "Models and Paradigms" paper, the development of the self-image and the importance to such development of the identification of a man with his products may be one of the basic features of a cultural mode of human adaptation. Scientists are not exempt from this phenomenon, yet dedicated men can sometimes rise above the basic defensive response. I am sure that Griffin did on many occasions. Bordes and I consciously strive to achieve this. I guess Braidwood and I accomplished it sometimes when teaching together.

The challenge comes in the role of educator. Clearly the job of a good educator is to expose the problems of the field, familiarize the students with the tentative solutions offered to old problems, and introduce the student to the frontiers of the field, the unsolved problems. In so doing he must be willing to let the students rummage through his own products, and the results may be painful. As time has passed, I have tended to encourage my students to fight more and more. What better way to cut your intellectual teeth than in a situation where you are not threatened by damaging retaliation? This, a good teacher must encourage. Could it be that James Griffin was that big as an educator? Only Griffin knows. There are little deceptions with which we all live; I have come to train myself to stop a moment when students' arguments begin to prompt my adrenalin flow and wonder how many times Griffin was called upon to exercise such restraint when Papworth and I were launching the first season of the New Archaeology. Surely it must have happened many times.

On the other side, there is an interesting set of problems associated with the ability of scientists to openly consider intellectual flaws in the products of their mentors. I have frequently avoided citing Walter Taylor in my writings except in a positive way because his work was inspiring to me. Clearly I disagree with many of his arguments, yet in print I have avoided these issues on more than one occasion. Similarly, I have never openly disagreed with Spaulding and have only cited White in disagreement once that I recall. This behavior must be counterproductive if my evaluations of the value of these men's ideas are at all realistic. Surely a clearing of points of disagreement with them might well be more productive to the field than eight fights with men of more traditional persuasion. Most of us avoid such confrontations because of our personal feelings and attachments. I hope that I can encourage my good students to "take me on" when they disagree, and I hope that I can meet such challenges in a personally detached way. Intellectually I demand of myself such behavior. I look back with an uneasiness about some of the events in the past. There is a glimmering suspicion that Griffin actually encouraged some of my rebellion!

Looking ahead I foresee an exciting set of continuing developments in the field of archaeology. When I wrote "Archaeology as Anthropology" I had a static view of the field of anthropology as the field concerned with the variability among nonindustrially based systems of adaptation. During the years of change in the field of archaeology, a number of changes have been taking place in anthroplogy as a whole. The number of preindustrial societies left in the world have diminished greatly. The opportunities for doing "traditional" forms of ethnographic research have diminished to almost zero. Most of the problems unsolved by ethnographic research will remain unsolved insofar as they depend upon gathering new and different kinds of data from living "primitives." There is a burst of activity current in the field; Lee's work with the Bushmen, Gould's work with the Australians, and my own with the Nunamiut Eskimo and with the Navajo. This is certainly being conducted with the recognition that these are opportunities fast vanishing. Archaeology will become anthropology insofar as it seeks explanations for variability documented among preindustrial peoples. The primary data, unhappily, will all be archaeological.

This inevitability has recently been driven home very forcefully in my own department. We were discussing the hiring of a new cultural anthropologist. I was a strong advocate for hiring someone interested in comparative ethnographic research treating preindustrial peoples. The first striking thing was that of more than 70 vitae reviewed, only three represented persons with such interests. The majority were persons engaged in cognitive studies among urban segments of complex societies, peasants, black minority groups, urban Indians, etc. Clearly the directions which research will take among students of contemporary peoples will involve changes occurring among contemporary peoples. The problems of their development prior to the expansion of industrial-based society will become more and more the domain of archaeology. It is quite fortunate that there are a few opportunities left for the archaeologist to study contemporary primitives using both the techniques of ethnographic and archaeological research. These studies will provide future archaeologists with the all-too-few documented cases of correlations between material remains and the behavioral contexts in which they functioned.

Today we are in something of a transitional period in archaeology. We are coping with the methods explosion; the traditionalists' paradigm is being challenged at every turn with provocative suggestions for new directions in archaeological research. For many it may appear that it is happening too fast and that there are too many new things to do. I firmly believe that in spite of the above stimulants to new research, the single most important thing to be accomplished is to inspire the archaeologist to research the few remaining groups of people who provide him with the opportunity to observe the operation of an adaptation in which the systems of production are locally based and not integrated into the world economy. More clues to the significance of variability noted in the archaeological record will be forthcoming from that kind of research than from any other of which I am aware at the present.

As far as the methods revolution is concerned, the continued experimentation with multivariant forms of analysis is certain to lead in the direction of the recognition of new and unsuspected forms of patterning with the attendant demands for explanation. The technique beginning to loom on the research horizon which I believe will have profound effects on archaeological strategies will be computer-based simulation modeling. I have already suggested that this technique may have major effects on our data collection strategies and most certainly will be increasingly linked with greater use of deductively argued research approaches. This should have the effect of greatly expanding the sophistication of archaeological theory since it would permit entrance into the critical area of hypothesis testing the very basic point of data collection itself. I also foresee a greater use of mathematical techniques, in the strict sense of the word. Computer simulation coupled with mathematical modeling will gradually replace the cumbersome "cognitive mapping" of relationships which we currently employ.

What about the subject matter of archaeological investigation, the archaeological record itself, and our understanding of the past? The recognition of new and contrastive forms of patterning and the search for explanation will be the excitement of archaeology for years to come. As examples let me point out some of the kinds of studies which I predict will be forthcoming and some of the results which I anticipate.

Studies of Comparative Patterning Using Comparable Instruments for Measurement

Working from an essentially inductive approach, archaeological studies have expediently taken advantage of what the archaeological record has to offer. The result has been that Paleolithic studies are generally rooted in the comparative study of stone tool assemblages, while materials from later time periods are more commonly studied comparatively by emphasis placed on ceramics, grave contents, settlement plans, architecture, etc. In the New World most preceramic systematics are based on a kind of "type fossil" approach where differences in styles of projectile points are the basis for recognition of varying "cultures" and "traditions." Comparative studies in ceramics have been the major empirical materials cited as a justification for the traditionalists' assumptions regarding culture change. I wonder what would happen if New World researches in both preceramic and postceramic times were to be conducted using only stone tool complexes as the basis for evaluating similarities and differences. My guess is that much of the confusion regarding the significance of variability in relative frequencies of stone tools would be cleared up. I anticipate that many things currently grouped as *different* on the basis of stylistic variability in projectile points would turn out to be alike if total stone tool complexes were compared. Similarly, many things currently identified as *alike* would turn out to be different. In short, we will begin to conduct studies to help us evaluate the significance of variations noted when differing instruments for measurement are employed.

Studies of Comparative Patterning among Different Components of the Archaeological Record

Why is it that end scrapers as a class exhibit relatively little variability either spatially or temporally compared to projectile points or some other class of item? Why should rates of change in certain broad classes of items exceed others? How do we explain such contrasts? Are contrastive rates of relative change demonstrable among artifact classes for the earlier time periods? My impression is that they are not. How do we understand such a contrast if it is empirically upheld?

The follow-up on some of these questions will lead archaeologists into some very interesting areas of research. My present guess is that many of the suspected contrasts will relate to the differential degrees that persons identify with their products as extensions of the self-image. Structural differences which might be demonstrated between these phenomena will, I predict, relate to the degree of development of a differentiated role structure in the social systems. For instance, in societies such as the Nunamiut Eskimo, role differentiation is at a minimum, and the personal history of specific events provides the content for the self-images manifest by the members of the society. A good measure of this is the character of gossip. Among the Eskimos, gossip takes the form of relating specific event sequences about people. By way of contrast, in my experience with settled horticulturists living in a society with a developed and differentiated role structure, gossip takes the form of evaluating the degree that persons are living up to the role prescriptions for the various roles which they occupy. I suspect that in the latter types of societies insofar as crafts are concerned, there is a greater attempt at conformity and less "self-expression" in the manufacture of role specific items. On the other hand, craft specialization in which role identity is directly related to the products produced in the context of role performance may well manifest greater variability. Craft specialists may develop self-images through greater attempts in individualized production. In short, variability in items produced may well vary directly with the character of the role structure in the society and the degree that it provides criteria for evaluating performance as a component in the development of self-images. Other features which may affect differential rates of change and variability may have to do with the duration of utility from items. Some items produced for immediate use and discarded, compared with items produced with long life expectancy, may show correlated differences in rates of change and variation. The degree that differences in rates of change and degrees of variability can be demonstrated to be associated with or to covary with different forms of organization or with situations of organizational change in the social systems represented is an area of research thus far not initiated. I look forward to some very exciting developments from these kinds of studies.

Studies of Comparative Patterning between Different Gross Time Periods or between Systems Representing Demonstrated Differences in Level of Evolutional Development

As I suggested in Models and Paradigms, the evolution to greater degrees of complexity in the organizational properties of cultural systems is also a history of the emergence of culture into different aspects of man's behavioral regimes. I predict that as more work is done on the earlier ranges of the Pleistocene, it will be shown that alternations of industries are the normal condition. Associated items are rarely being related in a covariant fashion. Later I anticipate a pattern in which assemblage types measured in terms of patterns of association tend to cluster temporally but do not exhibit very clear-cut patterns of gradual or directional replacive change in the content of the assemblage when viewed temporally within the cluster (for instance, see Johnson, 1968). When we can actually demonstrate gradual replacive change in assemblage types as measured by content lists is something which is not yet clear. Most of the demonstrations of this type of patterning have been made with materials such as ceramics where comparison is relatively restricted to a gross functional category. Another type of patterning which we might anticipate is graded clustering when viewed temporally. For instance, I suspect that statistically speaking there is a tendency for Mousterian assemblages from the Wurm. I period in south central France to meet the criteria for definition of "typical" Mousterian. This does not mean that all "typical" Mousterian assemblages are Wurm I in age, only that the relative frequencies between types of Mousterian assemblage tend to pattern temporally in statistical terms. This kind of patterning may well derive from covariant relationships between the features of the gross environment and the organization of activities in different environmental contexts. Explanations for this type of patterning will almost certainly be different from that for exclusive temporal clustering of assemblage types, as is probably the case with some of the Upper Paleolithic materials. Failure to appreciate the differences between graded clustering and discrete clustering is most certainly at the bottom of some of the recent suggestions that variability in the Mousterian exhibits temporal trends (Mellars, 1970). Mellars' conclusion that his statistical demonstrations imply a sequence of assemblage types replacing one another is clear nonsense in face of the concrete evidence. He might more profitably search for patterns of covariation between frequencies of occurrence of assemblage types and measureable environmental variables. This, of course, would demand that he abandon some of the cherished notions of the traditionalists' paradigm, something which Mellars does not appear willing to consider.

Studies such as these suggested here and the explanations for different and contrastive forms of patterning must lead archaeologists into many stimulating areas of model building, treating the character of organized human life during earlier time periods. It is model building and testing in the context of comparative studies of patterning and their implied organizational characteristics which will greatly expand our knowledge of the past.

Development of "Content-Free" Instruments for Measurement

One of the characteristics of the analytical strategies of archaeologists has been the inductivist approach of working directly in terms of observational categories or types distinguished in different assemblages. How do we compare assemblages summarized in terms of Gravette points and Clovis points? Many organizational properties of assemblages may be shown to vary somewhat independently of the specific forms of content. Robert Whallon (1968) has already initiated such investigations with the comparative study of "measures of homogeneity" or the degree of measurable variety characteristic among content classes within assemblages. This is certainly a dimension of variability which will exhibit varying contrasts depending upon the particular manner in which the investigator chooses to select categories of content for comparison—e.g., measuring only ceramics, as Whallon did, or measuring total assemblages. Explanatory modeling of measured variability may lead to still further insight into past behavior.

Complexity, specialization, degree of dependence upon plant foods, degree of sedentism, etc., are just a few of the dimensions of variability which may be very important in some forms of explanatory modeling but at present have not been operationalized into measurable variables. Interest in the development of instruments for measurement to be employed on assemblages regardless of the specifics of the content is certainly to become much more important. Archaeology will become much more a science than it has been in the past.

References

Johnson, LeRoy, Jr. (1968). *Item Seriation as an Aid for Elementary Scale and Cluster Analysis,* Bulletin No. 15. Museum of Natural History, University of Oregon, Eugene.
Mellars, Paul. (1970). Some comments on the notion of 'functional variability' in stone-tool assemblage. *World Archaeology* **2**, 74.
Whallon, Robert. (1968). Investigations of late prehistoric social organization in New York state. In *New Perspectives in Archeology* (S. R. Binford and L. R. Binford, eds.), pp. 223–244. Aldine Publ. Co., Chicago, Illinois.

Subject Index

A

Acheulian,
    tools of, 254–256, 262, 267
        associational patterning of, 276–287
        covariation among, 268–276, 282, 285–287
        Levallois technique and, 258–259
"Action archaeology," 62–64
Activity, classification according to, 71–72
Activity areas, defined by surface distribution, 169–170
Adaptation, 137, 236, 431
    cultural drift and, 297, 299
    ecofacts and, 148
    effective environment and, 431–432
    efficiency of, 23, 26–28
    food production and, 439–440, 444
        environmental change and, 427–431
    variability and, 264, 265
Adaptive area, 204–205
Affect, mortuary practices and, 214–215
Age, bone weight and, 381
Agriculturalists, mortuary practices of, 227, 230–231
Agriculture, see Food production
Analogy, use in archaeological argument, 33–37, 46–49, 52–53, 55–57, 60, 69, 70–71, 85–87
Analytical units, 96–98
Andaman Islanders, mortuary practices of, 211, 220
Andrews site, cremations of, 373, 377–382, 386–387, 388
Animism, mortuary practices and, 209
Arapaho Indians, hide smoking among, 43
Archaeological record,
    exploration of, 245–246
    limitations of, 91–96
    patterning in, see Patterning

Archaeological record–*cont.*
    in study of process, 117–119
Archaeology,
    definition of, 143
    prospects for, 452
Archaic, 66
    cremations of, 373–374, 377–382
    sociotechnic artifacts of, 30, 31
Artifact(s), 143, see also Tool(s)
    in burials, 295, 301–313, 413–417
    chipped stone, 168–169
    ideotechnic, 24–25
    observational populations of, 143–148
    patterning and, see Patterning
    sociotechnic, 24, 28–29
        in burials, 413, 414, 415, 416
        copper, 30–31
    spatial structure of, 63
    stylistic characteristics of, 25, 91–93
    technomic, 23–24
        in burials, 413, 414, 415
        copper, 26–28
    as unit of study, 74–76, 93
Art style, see Style
Assemblages,
    redundancy among, 250
    variation in, 202–205
Associations, patterned, 276–287

B

Behavior, see also Ethnographic data
    "cultural rubicon" and, 290
    ideas and, 210
    patterning and, 250, 259–260, 287
Belief, mortuary practices and, 209–210, 218–219
Bias, in sampling, 141, 151–152, 156, 180

B
C
D
E
F
G
H
I
J

6
7
8
9
0
1
2
3
4
5